DRIL

"ETERNAL"

sorry i wont be able to respond to any DMs today as i was just walking around in traffic and got pussy blasted by the fastest Mazda on earth § i cant wait for my shift at the old arsenic refinery to end, so that i can go back to the woods behind my house and search for Groomer turds § when ive Mastered the simulation that you pitifully refer to as “Life” § i have decided to postpone my scandalous hard right pivot until after i have lost my virginity or hjad my dick sucked a pretty decent amount § if u want an autograph or to choke me out ill be attending the event called “Def Uncle Jam” making a lot of noise & being a general Nuisance § PRESS RELEASE: User @ Dril Calls For An End To The Violence -- “Keep Sending Me Links; I’ll Click Any Piece Of Shit You Put In Front Of Me” § whilst you were visiting grandma in the hospital i was grinding for BAG !! § Uh, this is fairly fucking mood. § gorillas are aliens and that is the theory in going with. that is the belief i will use § the reasons jacking off is good are - it makes me dumber - it makes me Worse at sex - it pisses the trolls off for $0 § im having a blast in Qatar watching all the games, rooting for teams, etc. but you cant self suck here. they get really mad if you self suck § listen up Men. the media says you cant flip this over & fuck it like a dog. This of course is a lie. Your penis can fit in any of the holes [laundrybasket.jpg] § the list of white boy’s with fat Dicks just dropped § children should learn Gambling basically asap aand fix the economy by winning big § Twitter. It’s what’s happening / Twitter § Gorilla `s Scam § bat man would never suck the jokers dick @Cnn @msnbc @WSJ @WSJBusiness § if you tell me The Mask is standing behind me i will turn around and try to look at it. Because my dumb ass thinks The Mask is real § why am I grinning like a jack ass ? Because I am about to go to the 1964 New York World’s Fair and receieve my very first Hand Job. § i have saved $53,000 by claiming the home office tax deduction on my Gooncave § investigate Gallahger death § linktr.ee/drilreal get at me . all accounts not on this page are fraud. fuck twitter § HELP ELON!!ELON!! HELP! HELP! POST “DOG COIN” § ive gotten word that SegaBoris has obtained Will .I.Am’s phone number but is too afraid to call it and ask him to Collab.... § every veterans day i remember my pet mantis who got defeated by a baby bird that i tried to feed it § the turtle club from that movie is real and igot sucked off there § He’s Fucked! He’s Fucked! § FUCK YOU IF YOU THINK ITHIS GUY IS GOOD!!! https://t.co/0x35uSB-vzF § Havent busted in over 45 hrs. Ive Cured my Anxiety, PTSD, Bisexuality & various Poxes, all by retaining my viscous loads. Now I become Mayor https://t.co/ZWW5hHlaIl § bitch You smell like a new pack of pokemon cards § Ow !! Ouch!! Im sorry Jay!!! § MY SIN: i got excited and made a horrifying post of jay leno (car victim) MY PUNISHMENT: i will burn my self to appease his oafish fans § jay leno in return for your fucked up fixation with cars you have earned a Kiss from the devil § Hey Girl Whats Your Ass Lookin Like. Let Me Consider That Ass. § having a “small penis day” so i would appreciate it if my followers could send me some jewels or maybe some golden statues § even though “Hotep Redditor” has scammed me of $300000 I am upset to hear of his passing. i am sad he perished § Having a bad one; First my Lockheed Martin investment tanks after the ceo posts his penis. Now Cold stone Creamery just called me the N-Word § thank you . this will make it way easier to block them all https://t.co/gFtL8DSyEE § block on sight § its all cool, im a sex worker too “the best there is” § DO NOT BE MAD AT ME !! PLEASE! PLEASE § delete my nuts § only thr dumb ones. block without hesitation https://t.co/7uaFWjASn2 § it has never been easier to identify the most dog shit accounts on here. block without hesitation https://t.co/T9y2KyPMea § you just paid $8 to eat my ass stupid #BlockTheBlue § absolutely block on sight https://t.co/kDkXP1pddD § should be 2 boxes on the ballot. one to make the gas prices lower, and one to make them higher, and if you vote higher you get your ass beat § out of the trillion girls who follow me i only want to marry about 8 of you. do better § wife wants to get the word “winefreak” tattooed, in the disney font. i told her she cannot join me in the kingdom of heaven if she does this § ripleys suck my dick or not § IM THINKING WE GOTTA P{UT OUR NOGGINS TOGETHER AND TRYING TO SEE IF WE CAN MAKE THAT "YES NUT NOVEMBER", FOR US FELLAS WHO LOVE TO BUST!!! § hog § i do not appreciate twitter putting a satire warning underneath all of the posts where i say i am jacking off right now. it is NOT satire § grandma knit me a nice warm pair of gamer gauntlets so i don't mess up my knuckles when i punch holes in the wall § fellas if your girl isnt losing control of her bowels every time you take her to bed "You are not tapping that thing RIGHT!!!" § ive invented entire schools of philosophy just to discard them outright. just 1 second of my thoughts would make Plato shit out his panties. § pokemon "shit head" and "dip shit" versions § just found a somewhat NSFW box full of robes and hoods in grandmas dungeon § me and the wife are discussing having me cryogenically frozen like autsin powers for a while, to close up our inappropriate 6 year age gap § always https://t.co/V5r2meeNji § now that elon has disposed of the left wing woke brigade I can finally post pictures of my COCK!!! § this image radicalized 100000000 youth https://t.co/2BzF3CTKSQ § before i hop into the top 5 most Racist muppet babys episodes, a few words. TesticleGear from GayFactor is an innovative new solution for th § lot of stupid shit going on in my replys. must be FUCK MY ASS day on twitter... § Hey Dumb Ass! Thats my face youre pissing on § "Son, are you going to beer my Ass? Or are we about to have a mother fucking problem?" it would be very good if tommy lee jones said this § really looking to Slut my brand out during the remaining fiscal quarter of 2022 § the council consists of me, MetalGearEric and CryptoStewie. And yes, we will drink Beer on the job. https://t.co/GkfWkRvwue § ðŸ‘‰spitting in the food ðŸ‘‰letting waiters do Racist accents ðŸ‘‰rewarding their most insolent customers with police badges https://t.co/7C2eZzRMdN § WHAT THE FUCK IS A " BAPE" ??????????? § my fellow men..we must eliminate this bastard https://t.co/0tF2jlsbTN § beiing exposed to this sort of thing 99 hours a week is either making me extremely stupid or the most intelligent person in history https://t.co/XlVzx5wKPH § interesting. What do you all think of this . https://t.co/nWnmtFA9oo § when you have to take a shit really badly but you hold it in until your body turns the shit into vitamins and you dont have to go any more > § i love stigmatizing the mentally ill by terminating thier 800 million dollar promotional deals.... not § decades of jacking off "The stupid way" has got my whole dick looking crazy § pleased to announnce my new provocative sit com "Who Smoked Daddys Crack" will soon replace all the good shows on your fav streaming service § - im above the mud slinging - im above responding to peoples crap - i did not throw a snow ball at someone baby in 2004 - im Owed a platform § youre as much of a virgin as you are stupid assed. go away from my gym § I wish all the piss in the world would go straight into the toilet!!!! I hate dirty, disgusting PISS! No more!! Never! § Wow, just wow . Burger king is naming their new sandwich "The Brian Sicknick January 6th Whopper" ? That's so controversial § i have been told that my web page is a sort of "Heaven" for men who exist on the Diaper Spectrum § remember back in the early 00s you were allowed to shoot ropes on a mans face if you caught him wearing a fedora hat or posting on REDDIT... § sad that the guy who raised $10000000 to produce the worlds first non-woke can opener tried escaping in a hot air balloon & hit a power line § you cannot prove that me and the boys spray painted the word "Sluts" on mens wear house just because we agree with the msessage's politics § gamers help the world , and are helping the world, more than normal people § Um,m sending Ezra to prison? Thats a stone cold #MEntalHealthFail § just kicked a hole through my mirror because all the girls on my time line are saying they want to fuck Wally Gator now § i used to be mocked for bullying my class mates. now i live in the real life mansion that Luigis Mansion was based off of. it get's better § we avoid piss because it represents Chaos § if your profile pic looks like bullshit your ass needs to be put in the stupid barn § i cured my self of covid 19 by forcing myself to cough a lot § saying "Swag Acquired." when i get my pre order bonus at game stop and the cashier and the other guy in the store pretend they didnt hear me § when your uncles militia surrounds your house with rifles & accuses you of being a dark money pedophile you use it as an opportunity to grow § its laughable that you all would still rather suck porky pigs dick than admit that hes wrong some times § @BarryGoldman15 im so sorry i well do better § mugatu real life https://t.co/yZSvbAcXlu § unbelievable. i have been sent 4 different cum tributes of my "Doggo's". i will never cleanse the time line with wholesome eye bleach again § i love shit that is "Buxom" , especially babes § you eat the weird colored halloween themed donuts and your shit will 100% turn Green. you sign a contract with God § just realized that every hare brained dick boy who follows me on here is fucking simping for me. Nasty!! That shit makes me puke!! § more and more news reporters are starting to use the phrase "James Bond style" to describe certain kinds of murders § DUMB ASS!!!!!! https://t.co/jupmbQT6Rp § when harry potter said"i solemnly swear to blow up this monsters penis w/ a fire ball" i had to put the book down & bow my head for a moment § im a dirty cop who has joined the islamic state of iraq and the levant § do not Devil my ass § chance § i think theres like a 90% the family guy saw my penis through the tv just now #paranormal #NotGood § at full power, telling every one on the "Am I The Ass Hole" sub reddit that they are the ass hole without reading their posts § wordle is making the damn world STUOID § thinking about a beer sip i once had § Thanks for the like, stupid! § i respect youir beliefs so much (jack off motion) theres no possible way your opinion can totally suck me Hard § he was MOCKED in high school for being a Senator's son . Now he has made over $10,000,00 selling fake service animal vests to local nit wits § this is the most important shit in the world right now. We love seeing this. Thank you https://t.co/HECyCU2WZq § you sell draculas ruby red swastika brooch on ebay one time and suddenly they flag your whole account as a hitler account even if youre nice § me & my friend acting up again..we do get a little Nutso sometimes but our in-detph discussions about Culture are truly enlightening/serious https://t.co/Ize2QybIq2 § "i like my games like i like my coffee-- Good." -the CoffeeGamer § ive looked at the facts and there is no possible way that this game does not have incest § i dont care to hear any more talk about "Donkey kong country". its a stupid game that has Incest § " ame one Roman Gladiator who owned a Smart Phone. I'm waiting" - Ken Bone § incredible: son helps father https://t.co/SJwGS95IGo § (responding to a picture of a dog eating a paper towel) Oh hell!!! We're in the wrong damn time line § i know due to sheer numbers at least a few of my followers are cold blooded Killers. still im expected to put on my clown hat & gratify them § every day i get 100s of messages from young men saying "I need to ejaculate Right now. What do I do." and i say to them all. JUst Breathe. § every pitbull dog contains a hidden set of skills known as the "Master Skills". the only two men who can unlock them are me and Elon § ive seen the posts that people are capable of when they access over 100% of their brains. men who can solve the deficit in Zero Seconds § when digimon otis spoiled me the ending of Men In Black 2 i got so mad that i showed him my dick § sitting in my car watching 500 episodes of a horrible anime entitled "Shit My Lord" at the recommendation of XenoMarcus. § the waterboy (1998) is woke now § every one on cnn is my father and mentor § they are inventing a new type of Lesbian in 2023 they just said it on CNN § stinker alert: you have posted a stinker. you r punishment is suck this faces dick for 1000 years. good luck and last but not least Fuck you https://t.co/GAIOijnRXh § im starting a pod cast service called "Mouther" and our inaugural pod cast will be a pod cast about breaking bad called Sucking Bad § i have decided to develop a gluten allergy to piss off my most hated waiters § i DO NOT like your ass if you are a stupid ass https://t.co/CP6S4jZjqr § Prisoners are producing gallons of low quality semon "On the dole". WE are FED UP with being SUCKED OFF by crooks & conmen. At long last sir § they have a “System” § guy gets 10 for armed robbery. tax payer is on the hook for $5mil so he can be rehabilitated. instead he jacks off all day. Is this justice? § this talk about big bubba & jareds footlong is conjecture. its a old wives tale. the real problem in jails is all the masturbating going on § @UberFacts bull shit § criminals who are allowed to masturbate during jail sentences “have it too easy “ and are basically the luckiest guys on the planet § Its 4am folks. Time to make 1000000 § Oh you like my Music? Wanna kiss my mouth on the fuckin lips? Is that interesting to you? Is that interesting? Good luck with your White ass § Oh you wanna show up at my office, take a swing at me in the parking lot? Wanna knock the hoagey out of my hand? Make me puke by hitting me? § Dog Bows to Bible - What this little dog did to the holy book of God will knock your shit out of your ass hole. § i believe the island boys are a sort of “Blue man group” where its just a rotating cast of guys who look like that § itd be funny if a troll tired to “Own” me by leaking my DMs & only prove that i had sex before anf i get laid even more because theyre good § i would like to announce that my twitter account has been made in to the official twitter account of the Hand Job § while you were busy poisoning your soul with spectator sports i was in my house jacking off face down in my bed § people here will claim to have never liked Mickey Mouse, despite him being a time-tested Classic. All I can do is shake my head. #DuhWinning § im the only man to put on the CIA invented “Heart attack diaper” and live § Im begging you! Please stop Quote Tweeting the Senator’s nudes just to “Dunk” on him! Hes getting HARD from the attention! Hes whacking off! § Bad news folks! i waited in line for 16 hours to see the queen. But by the time i got there she was fuckin DEAD!!!!!! § if your web site asks me for a coupon code i will never not put “RUDY” in the son of a bitch § ufos are becoming smarter..... § @McDonaldsUK I wont a ham burger mate!!! Oi! This is wank! § Well thats just plain goofy. § The dog who played scooby doo in the scooby doo movie was a girl dog & you can see its pussy in some of the scenes. And everyones ok w this? § there’s it https://t.co/JlKyWnQkqF § Hmmm nope!!! § Howd you like a piece of my ass hole , douche bag boy. Shut up § Dont like getting the middle finger? Then dont show me bull shit § whose freon-huffing uncle is picking these fucking sidebar articles https://t.co/Y1nfKavxCh § “What those planes did was wrong” - @ DRIL § Cant sit still knowing this year’s 9/11 is on a CHURCH day!! Very excited § some fucking Karen pooped in the elevator § She died bedause they dishonoured BREXIT § oi guv the old bird pissed it. I will miss her . Fuck § im so sorry that happened to you. But this is some Insane content § looking through my expertly curated feed for something nice https://t.co/8vwjQWJRVX § need an investor to help me open a chain of restaurants which absolutely must be named “Asian Taco Bell” § Ooohhhh my portfolio !!!!!!!!! https://t.co/Q5qExhT8Nm § which of you nasty pigs gave me fucking covis. Bastard https://t.co/KuC36szsqP § screw around like a bitch and i well show you why they call me MR.Wuhan § #ifjoebidenshowedupatmydoor I would explain to him the finer points of Malthusian economics!! Then I would show him my Cock!!! § Not Nice!!!!! https://t.co/TBTctLEF39 § In 1980, audiences delighted in watching the Blues Brothers ravage a shopping mall with a car. Today, we understand they were wrong to do so § as the only person on this web site to ever have sex , its up to me to set the record straight when some lunatic claims the Clitoris is real § 1. all pussys are equally taut. this is not up for debate 2. many old world cultures consider loose pussys to be a sign of “Blessed harvest” https://t.co/Sz7LHtD59r § when long covid effectively neuters me by making my dick smaller, i plan on becoming a more humble. Graceful creature § Fuck the fans! Fuck the fans!! § last night i had a vision of a pope in jeans. Clean, white as the holy spirit, perfect, angellic jeans #TrumpStoleTheDocs § some yuppy shit stain just gentrified sadaam husseins spider hole into an allergen-free omniracial Thoughtspace & honestly? im smiling of it § i brought my fossilized pilgrim shit onto antique roadshow and they were all aorund class acts. im sorry it wasnt good enough to put on tv § the harlam shake SUCKS! § perhaps big bubba and trump could end up in the same minimum security facility. but that would run contrary to conventional big bubba lore https://t.co/cu6UG7n6us § we are living in a world where they will execute you with a blade laced in pigs blood for trying to make the movie "Bad santa" § my ass cheeks look like brains and my brain looks like an ass cheek § name any crime and i will tell you how I could easily avoid being the victim of it in 2 seconds § im a netflix executive and if i go onto your feed and see shit that has less than 50 likes i will NEVER hire your ass!! delete that SHIT!!! § Celebs are sucking & fucking each other like never before. But still no justice for those who are getting the most sucked & fucked: The Fans § "what if among us was squid game" - DRIL https://t.co/u5ay58wKu8 § they are letting people vomit in the aisle s of the once great Sears department store! they are letting people get NUDE § fuck my ass hole https://t.co/J2wbHKmgkY § it Sucks, its bullshit, its stupid, but you Love to see it § wish i could retweet this https://t.co/BBYRAVVuic § "ohh i caught you posting cringe you posted Cringe i got you i caught you" Yes bitch. And i make $100 a month doing it. § its true. your more likely to die in a car wreck going 60 mph than 100 mph "hit the gas before ya crash" the law of 100 § me and the boys run the most hated content house in all of tinsel Town. all we do is cuck each other by accident and forgive each other § guy who invented Prayer: This is so sick. Im going to get so much free shit from god. This is the cleanest scam yet. So glad I invented this § my Rat Chant: Begone, RAT! You disgrace my home! I will not let you SHIT on my floor! My power is beyond your comprehension! Now, perish! § every day across this world; loving mothers are giving birth to millions of little babies who ARENT YOU! § Guess Ill Just Keep Drinking PISS!!! https://t.co/qGysz0jpQi § We All Got That Friend Who Think Jumanji Is Real § oi you lot. The gas pricses have become quite fuck all § having $100 is Millionaire shit § movies are fucking dying and its time to open the dialogue on giving hollywood full access to the nastiest chemical/nuclear weapons on earth § if twitter wre a grocery store the aisles would be labeled shit like "LIes," and "Ignorance" instead of shit like green beans and diapers § everyone mad at me because US army allowed me to create "the MewTwo of pit bulls" using CRISPR. well if i didnt do it some other guy wouldve § I wouldnt enjoy doing it, but I would eat dog shit if it would increase my IQ by 1 point. Whos with me § i hope every one whose house is on fire today gets out safe § ikea still does not sell spittoons in year 2020. a crime against men who spit § if you think "spy Kids" is better than shakespere youre fucking stupid and me and my uncle would never hire you to work at our car wash § i really dont care what Yankee Doodle did when he went to town. His toxic fanbase tells me everything I need to know about him . § "The Fyre Festival was actualy good! " - Punished Dril § hovering over the apartment maintenance man with my pants down while he unclogs my toilet for the 4th time this week § ive taken shits that have more money than you you broke bitch https://t.co/fL3Zsti7Py § (to sold out crowd at madison square garden) does any one remember the eat the poopoo video. he eat the poo poo? no? § Gamer Kiss Magazine wants to see your "Bitter game face" (the face you make when you are playing a sub par game) Get those pics in Lads. § if you are a HATER you have 24 hours to confess to being a hater and apologize and pull your pants down so every one can see your dick § "I would have to take heroin to think this is good. I would need to disable 80% of my brain w/ toxic fumes" Well if you say this youre wrong § people are saying thw facebook meta thing is "Hideous/Atrocious" and "Fucking stupid shit" but i gave it a spin & its actually really good https://t.co/6CAhbblKzO § i blast all the ufos easily and then you know what i do is i go in there and fuck the alein § MIght stop giving a fuck all together. § i may be wrong, i may be stupid, i may have gotten my son murdered, but at least my clothes arent coverred in SHIT § im a Skank. § People seem to think im a kind of nasty, shitty dog based off the way my posts are treated like dirt. Covid has turned you all into monsters § the nasty porno is simply your reflection in the window my Man . § ???? Dont Know why im catching shit for this. Most blinds are famously hard to see through. § closing my blinds so the feds cant see me... then posting some shit like "hunter biden is jordan peterson if he drank urkel's Cool potion" § well i heard on the news theyre putting porno in star wars now. Two can play at that game, George. i ll stop watching your programs you Toad § if your movie or tv film dosent have Dolby it sucks fucking my dick § when ever i see someone own the olive garden on here i get excited & squash my fucking balls against the computer. but apparently thats bad? § Greeitngs, me and YoshiGod9 were just discussing which releases we consider to be "The Champagne of Gaming" . Would you care to join us § they call the book " 1984" because that's what my iq becomes when i read it.... § all of the shit that happens in star wars is so smart § call your senator and the local news and tell them you wan't to see the snyder cut, of my posts § me and Alan are the only guys on here who are allowed to call the police when we get soft blocked § i must come clean. Last night i said the club was going nuts because the DJ started playing "Take me out to the ball game". This wasnt true. § just clicking my mouse a bit. having a look at my files § No..!! This Cant be happening! No!!! https://t.co/eR9hf5Olvf § i hope all the cartels i pitched nfts to arent mad at me § none of my followers think turds is good § My 2022 bingo card is looking more and more every day like my fucking ass wiped it . § I am Donald "Penis" Trump, known & hated for my Inflammatory rhetoric, as well as my old mafia-style Racism. Looking forward to posting here § i want to open the worst pub on earth called like "The Bull Dog's Cock" and get in trouble for tnot paying my employees § this is seriously my actual reaction when some Stoopid-ass hipster girl asks me what is my faovrite band . https://t.co/FlCIDYrNhc § you boys with your pud in your hand waiting for the girls to wake up and post pics SORRY!! all you get for now are my posts Muta Fucka!! § bring me 1 gem, i promote you to Wiseguy. 2 gems ill promote you to Punk. 5 gems makes you Thug. for 10 gems i will promote you to Shit head § can you believe they won all of that guys money § producing a tv show called "Fuck My Money" and it iwll be either a tv show or a movie. look for it § "put your Ass into my world for one second and you will kiss my nuts" - god § how do i morph § honter biden answer your phone i left metalGearErics game cube controller at your house and he is freaking out at me. he is in the hospital § you aint ever catching ME getting my "DICK" sucked... NO SIR!! eyes bugging out, ass cheeks twitching, making racist noises-- one of that § 72 is not even a lot of money § yeah make my license plate say "money 72" please durrr durrrr a-doy He-Haw! He-Haw! Stupid. https://t.co/mYNqOAuAMA § in many ways the blue guys from the avatar movies are like people. they are like us in many ways § the guy who invented the plunger said "i gotta find a way to suck the toilet off Pronto" § the content i Crave https://t.co/sjSHhxcUuy § its TGIF which means im imposing the Pussy Eater 's Challenge on to my page. its mostly self explanatory & if you fail it youre fucking dumb § I love quitting posting for like 4 months and coming back as an all-lowercase guy § when you say "Tickle Me elmo is not a gaming console", youre erasing the voices of everyone that beleives Tickle me Elmo is a gaming console § in terms of cop VS marine all the cop has to do is position himself behind the marine and arrest him for murder and its essentially over § i think if we give the cops enough of our money they will eventually prestige into a stronger type of cop that can defeat our own servicemen § my followers spend all day begging me to cum all over a napkin and take a picture of it. but when i actually do it, do they retweet me? No § if i buy a roulette table for my house will the boys promise to come over and play roulette ? OR should i fuck myself § what did Steve Jobs smoke to come up with all his famous ideas § (suddenly becoming very somber) no Woman should have to pay over $10 for a Brassiere. § you call this shit rotisserie chicken? I bet this shit hasnt even rotated 1 time in its entire life. § looks like i fucked up yet another date.. but when you get a phone call from "The Demented Dr. Pussy" you absulutely must answer it § one tear drop for every post u have been a Reply Guy to § user name "harambe_Poop" is selling false home owners insurance. beware of this § "SORRY BOYS!" your cum tributes of me are highly inept, trite, and bogus. Futher more, they look like dog shit. Do better § nobody is respecting the classics. people would rather stab each other to death in the bathroom than respect the classics § College is back § oh you updated your privacy policy? very nice. i updated my privacy policy too which is to show you my ass and balls on purpose. Fuck you § I will never become a Mens barber. but I am allowed to admire their culture in any way that pleases me § I will shut the fuck up , IF, it will restore the Harmony. I will get on my knees like a dog and make that sacrifice, for the sake of Calm § new idea "Golden money" some times when getting money you will get golden money instead which is worth 10x the amount of normal money § a mystery individual is going around telling girls he invented "The Ass Meme" . you must stop this immediately. only i am allowed to do that § girls will be like "i cant go out tonight! i have a pimple" and then they will get a face tattoo of Baloo from thre jungle book § e § they done fucked up and made big bird "Woke" § if donald trump tried to drunk drive in front of me i would karate kick the keys out of his hand with perfect precision § nobody b cares about my POSTS!! every one wants to suck my dick!! Im going to become a maga guy!!! Behave bitches! Behave! § do not talk shit like this § regarding the pep boys. they look disgusting § It all so sucks Ass. § its me, dan Schneider & SirGamestop sitting in a hot tub taking turns sucking on a prosthetic foot and wondering when the Girls will show up § im the ceo and if you show up to my work with little pieces of poop on your tie YOU ARE OUTTA HERE !! § When they call Elvis "the king", i can only shake my head. As the only man I recognize as King is reformed pervert President Joseph R. Biden § reading your posts is slave labor to me § "The news is so fucked as of late. " - DiaperVoter § to every one who thinks i will get in trouble for posting this. https://t.co/DCqQKXnw5M § my idea for adam is the water boy sequel called beer boy where he gives beer to the football player's § smokinh crack cocaine will turn you in to a dumb ass but it also has a 1% chance to turn you into a genius. thats how i become "KING" § getting Shit engagement numbers all around. Thats saturday morning for you. My followers all have DUIs. Guess ill go fuck my self! Boo hoo! § experience the avatar blue person VR blow job - only at Sears department stores § guy who drinks pepto bismol every time he has to take a shit until the feeling subsides § FYI if you were to be killed by Drunk Driver paul pelosi, or any heir of the noble Pelosi bloodline, youd enjoy a warriors death in Valhalla § i bring my own drink coasters and use them on the tables at burger King. Because im not a fuck boy piece of shit. § my biggest fear is that theres an earth quake while im jacking off and little pieces of cum start flyiyng into my mouth and all over my dog § please send more Info i will see what's going on . § ladys please step on my toxic male Ass! Go nuts stomping my ass out like a cigarette until I hate it! Until I think its a bad idea! § it truly does seems that most of people would put more trust into Gay lord focker, than Our lord father § tyoure on here scrutinizing my posts , while your girl is out Fucking curly from the three stooges § girl...id buy u any bra on earth, even if it was $100, thats how much I care about our whole shit! GUess Im a real sick fuck, huh? Ya think? § Penis Rant - come see the all-time famous "Penis Rant" § ants https://t.co/cCCX3FW4ET § in the fucked up world of golf , last place is actually good § i have obtained Seth's Ape. i will be usinbg him to co-host my new tv show that is basically jack ass but fake § " Is it just me, or is SQUID GAME getting to be a little too close, to real life? “ -- © COPY RIGHT 2022 @Dril -- “That’s money in the bank” § ralph_of_x_box told me “the best damn sports show period 2” is coming out in 2023 § i take the stage. my red penis tip sticks out of my waistband; little bit of piss coming out. “I will end all politics-based attacks of me.” § manifesting not getting my ass kicked b y saying “i hope i dont get my ass kicked today” and getting my ass kicked regardless § my landlord gave me a call and told me the turds coming from my apartment seemed unusually thin. we then discussed turd strategy for 3 hours § @MrBean i lost $900000 on this shit trhe instant your goofy ass got involved. you fucked me Bean § world governements are calling diarrhea the “shit of the future” as it is faster to poop out; causes less wear and tear on pipes & plumbing § the nyt is giving me $10000 to write about the time i lied face down and cried while dogs humped me until i cummed in my pants 100% flaccid. § Many scientists agree that in the near future you wull soon be able to be sucked off by a gadget or a gizmo, instead of a woman. § Up & coming comedian hits my dms, says I’d like to workshop some bits w/ you. Lets rap. Then he shows me his penis. 600th time this happened § taking 3.5 million foot and mouth disease infected pigs and burying them alive in a massive landfill in sotuh korea. Good or bad § And now it seems that even my own followers cannot resist pelting me with ad homenim dog shit. § marijuana did columbine § does that make me a nasty guy? Maybe. I just shrug and say “Fuck you” and “Fuck yourself” § my attitude is generally over all an “I dont give a fuck” attitue § i had do to it do him § i am sending my passport and car keys to this man § all of these people want to help me for Free. what a wonderful community https://t.co/5xda5mY0Y5 § ive generated over 100,000 wordles in my head and completed them easily. what more can i say of it § will 2023 be a “big year” § Oops! another $50000 worth of nft ape shit got stolen from me some how. Weird!!! good thing i still have all 200 of my iq points § had another nightmare where i had to explain to my high school principal why i wrote “Moves like Dorner” on the front of my note book § never seen a more perfect hoagiehttps://t.co/8iogtLjtus § your saying the quiet part out loud ... https://t.co/QoHZ3zaC8w § nobody gets my humor . Guess Im due for an ass kicking. I deserve shit § my sons new deal is saying he wants to be “Tiny” when he grows up, no doubt due to the forlorn shit he has been looking up on the computer . § remove all of the bathrooms from churchs right now. you need to be doing that at home § theyll let any dirty looking man get on television and claim hes a cowboy its STUPID! they think youre STUPID With this shit § these accusations that I like the gas prices are especially absurd, when you consider that ive been like the MAIN guy saying that theyre bad § fuck GRAVES... bury me in STAR WARS § there should be a boot camp for guys who like references to movies ans tv shows § the next masked singer should be a dead guy § theres him § reply to my post again for the 500th time you fucking moron. Go ahead, see if i dont block your ass and give you depression . § too bad. https://t.co/5YZT0dOhVK § “gamer cock is in demand” Girls are saying this § If you ever in your life had this thought: “Hmm, Today I think I will go Full Karen.”   me and my friends will NEVER hang out with you!!!! § Ya Know They Been Calling Me “The Bitch Who Did 9/11” § level 4 Smoker § i think every one with depression, anxieety, stomachaches, etc, should get a gold coin that lets them legally park in front of fire hydrants § does any one know when is 4 20 § no heaven or hell when you die, everyone is just herded into a room with a big scoreboard saying which person blasted the most Cum § if u think you can sub tweet me because its 3am you need to Shut Yuh Ass Up § every time i shit into the toilet i turn around and take a look at it and i am appalled by what i see § “ If Will Smith slapped me I would call 911 “ - Dril § Deep Fake offers us infinite possibilities. For instance, you could generate an image of your self with a larger penis, and jack off to it . § thanks all. together weve raised over $63 for raytheon to develop a brand new ITAS that can shoot down enemy prayers before they reach God . § waiting patiently for the release of Call of duty: Hard Brexit and Sasquatch Creed 2. Gaming fiercely until then. § asia is now protected from all sex. thank you § which ever mother fucker invents the porno version of squid games... buddy you're making $1000000 Easy § girls: Youre perfect! Youre so good! Youre a hero! ME: Hm maybe i should go outside & eat little pieces of shit because im SAD! girls: Nooo! § "Do tip your pimp today." -Mr. Sex Work § " ice tweet edit" will replace "posted from android huh??" as the reply that makes girls fuck you instantly § https://t.co/hCJDnueSN3 great news for me- a fucking dumb ASS! who FUCKS EVERY THING UP!!! § What makes the idea of me being a "Pervert" so comedic is the fact that I cant even get an erection in public. Its actually a problem for me § in the year 2200 big government breeding restrictions will be done away with and all service animals will look like this https://t.co/6eosZ969s9 § i keep a spare pen under my desk at the office in case my boss catches me self sucking i can go "Oops I dropped my pen" and hold the pen up. § Acutually, its not fucking funny. Its just pathetic. § I see no humor in my providing a safe dm for women to discuss open mouth kissing. Whats funny is people using that as an excuse to attack me § Cared enough to reply me ! Youre like in love with me ! § lets make it 2000 dollars. i want to see these fuckers sweat § theres a 1000 dollars in front of you. youre free to take it but if you do every dead bug on earth comes back to life. Do you take it Yes No § some times i see people buying shit at a store and wonder if theres a dark side to comsumerist behaviours.... § achieving the uppermost echelons of power & influence just to get sucked off next to Rep. Cawthorn in a room that looks like a hotel lobby § it seems like nobody appreciates a good wine any more. every one would all rather drink Redditor Cum § james bond the good fellas and god father team up to shoot the most ufos you have everf fucking seen § the dog must forever be referred to as a Bastard and take a Bastard`s surname § this was fucking real. i cant get over it. what was this guy doing, endorsing piss? https://t.co/apB8KVgUSX § would you let a man named "Porno Pete" do your taxes § ive never normalized a thing in my life § when people say they quit smoking to save money i simply laugh. all the smokers i know are Rich § Will Smith Sir Your Going To Fucking Jail!!!!!!!!!!!! You Are An Attacker! § when i serve you one of my fine home cooked meals i promise 2 things: 1. it WILL be tge best thing you've ever tasted 2. you WILL get diarrhea § people think today is a good day to talk about the oscars. Wrong. Today we are honoring all of my girl followers who have ever died. § its too easy to delete some absolute dog shit you posted. you should have to send like a pint of your own blood to twitter HQ to do it § nobody believes me that once i was shitting in a cave & the sound of it hiting the floor replicated the Nintendo switch snap sound perfectly § boys crowding around the salt lick and theeres a tiny guy in the back saying "cmon! let me get a taste of that!! ah Jeez!!" § i hate it when the boys at the office find my "Are you a pussy" buzz feed quiz results that i printed out § when you find out that i intentionally limit my power by not being a guy who retweets his own shit......... § had to block the guy posting him self smoking a pocket pussy under all my posts. good night nasty mother fucker § with these cash back rewards i can fulfill my long standing dream of taking 2 women to red lobster at the same time https://t.co/glT0P7Vkga § shes got full, luscious lips, killer Tits, and triple knockout hourglass hips. Not who you were expecting, huh...?? Rethink erections. https://t.co/oTyCKhmqvx § "societys more obcessed with pooping and pissing and having sex than they are with solving the heartlands opioid crisis ." - grover § worlds first adult man netflix cutie fatally TREATTED LIKE SHIT on his BIRTHDAY § diddy's kong quest is soon to be considered a turner classic michelin star Kong Quest and gamer fans are screaming loud. § you need to realize that when you make a joke about the queen dying it is the british version of 9/11. You are spitting in the face of 9 /11 § fuck the game "Musical chairs ". they should call it "RNG bull shit Chairs" § i hate to say it, Oh i hate to say it, but many of my wfollowers think that "Diddy's kong quest" is more important than the Mona Lisa. § You trying to eat the dried up tooth paste I spit up out of my mouth? You little pieces of Shit? § why are the ants only invading my bathroom sink? you dip shits are way off. i got a whole ass bag of sugar in the kitchen, unsecured § i would be so scared. i would absolutely have to negotiate a $5 million dollar minimum n-word fee § Wasup honey. You tryin to look at my Gamer? (referring to penis)   Di this mother fucker really just call his penis his "gamer"? Yes i did it § welcome to smoker country § whats everyones favorite gas price? mine is $3.29 § my god leave them yellow https://t.co/CI4oQYvj3B § due to fan complaints theyre making the Simpsons normal colored in season 38 and beyond. at long last this crap is at an end, 60 fps as well § its friday "youknow what that means" https://t.co/NAAgk1f6LO § ive just dipped every boxcutter in my house into a mug of real life brown recluse venom. Now's not the time to get stupid with my ass § oh, look, people are posting more wiseguy shit while the adults in the room are trying to make the gas prices lower. Perfect § my hate'rs trying to turn me GAY! § cum is so stupid. when i look at it i dry heave and cry for help § shes a real beautie https://t.co/IAjmdl0KaU § "it is fine to reuse condoms once or twice if youre just using them to jack off" Can I get an RT !! § who slid this shit under my door. people are being bombed in a war right now and you do this to me. youll never get my hollywood treasures https://t.co/PyhOYCHdnC § sushi place i get my Specialty Rolls from apparently thinks its ok to just fill the takeout box with tempura crumbs. dirty & unprofessional § OK can i just say fucking this??? the motherf ucking ww3 zombie apocalpse was NOT on my 2022 bingo card. #DarkHumour #myHeartGoesOut § we'd pour hot wax into the assholes of new marines yelling "Welcome to the CORPS!" cant do that anymore. this nation used to build railroads § you look like ther type of mother fucker who uses "Whataboutism" in arguments. buddy. the SImpsons spoofed your ass 30 years ago . Give it up § rickgamrcube will have sex 1 time in his life. at the age of 58 he will hire a prostitute after being diagnosed with a terminal illness. § rickgamecube insists that its good when the pussy is Dry, because your dick is cleaner afterwards. he compares it to taking a shit § thgere should be a side quest in elden ring where you dm a bunch of guys gfs "Im sorry he cares more about his Fucking Stupid game than you" § my ass looks like a NUMB SKULL's ass § im thinking this shit addresses my main problem with soda, which is that drinking it doesnt force me to witness the face of God https://t.co/TLIzMb58o0 § if i had $1000000, or even $100000, i'd marry a woman with a completely unfuckable, solid gold Pussy. and i would look at it and say "Wow" § imagine if elon Trolled you by sending you a dog saying "Well isnt that special"or some shit. youd get more ptsd than every veteran combined § they should make a wiki feet for peoples lunch pics § like this if you think putin needs to go watch the NEWS! § Am i a" HO"? Do i slut my self out? Am I Slutted out? § if you cancel me "your stupid" § MEN would rather say shit like "Skip to my Lou" than chant a single Healing Mantra. Not me though § only 1% of my followers can do this. Pathetic! fuck you, go do your wordles § ass challenge : lay face down on your bed and try to kick your self in the ass. i was able to tdo this § hmm more ignorance § does any one know any barbers in the Hollywood burbank area who specialize in "White boy's Hair" § just generated the N-word inside of my brain in 3D, spun it around in circles, and exploded it #DrilThankYou § Haven't the slightest idea why 1.6 million people would follow someone who's ramblings have all the charm of an illiterate, pathetic drunk with too much internet access. #pitiable https://t.co/dYUJuEBELc § new bat man villain "the dunce" just a guy in a dunce cap who says hes sorry a lot while bat man knocks the crap out of him § wow some celeb freaked out and wore a weird shirt again, that's crazy. did you hear a guy from the computer went to jail for fucking his mom § whatever bitch told me the stock market is closed on valentinees day owes me $100000 § Oh yes he really said that shit . § super bowl? the ony bowl you fucking slobs have any right to talk about is the dog bowl, which is where you all eat most of your food out of § back in 2008 or whatever i made the decision not to make $1 billion off of bit coins because i knew the shit would become hipster § if the mafia was going to kill me unless i made a super bowl commercial saying "i love dog shit" i would create so many jobs § if i was a rich guy who had to try to convince a bunch of people that dog shit tastes good i would absolutely buy a super bowl ad § if you dm me some dog shit business offer and dont immediately offer me a $10000+ Apology fee youre fucked more than anything ever § say it isnt so.......some of my followers think being a "KAREN" , is actually GOOD !!!!! § (saying to group. of 7 girls) the lore surrounding the Addams family is actually quite a bit darker than you might think..and fairly Leftist § i didnt put any ants in there i just opened it uo and ate all the blue shit. § I want to become the White Martin Luther King of Mental Health. ANd I want to get rich doing it, but without losing my "Edge" or selling out § the year is 2043, men have gotten too much therapy and are now Masters of Deceit, using their supernatural mental health to get insane head § metal gear eric called me at 2 am last night to tell me he just envisioned a strain of marijuana called "Racism Ender" § what would you do if i unlocked 100% of my true brain? Nothing. you would be fucked § if the flow of Nuanced takes regarding pod casts, the baneful N-Word, etc, shall ever cease, ill scream like i got injected w/ an air bubble § comedy is more important than ever. thats why all my single lady followers shoud move into my house & kiss me on the mouth-- It would be funny § just did my 1000 jumps at the jumping gym. i could tear a mans fucking head off, with my leg § this is how i deal with the SCUM!! Fuck you! https://t.co/nhgbnrqKK4 § HUuuuu!! Topgolf is Trending !! Look at it! Look! https://t.co/7frnMJ7ABi § might pull some strings and get a paywalled article put in the "whats happening" sidebar about my Horny Status, for 10000000 people to see § asking the armed forces recruiter at the mall if he ever cut a man in half § only gamers know whats this is https://t.co/A0nfZC4SQH § if youre a groundhog assassin, hunter or whatever, please dont kill any groundhogs or talk about killing groundhogs today. this is Their day § my heart goes out to people waking up from comas today & not believing the date actually is the number 2 repeated an insane amount of times § "What if we all took a page from You Tube, and removed the dislike bar, of real life. " - The Wanderer (Me) § closing my onlyfans after doing all possible combos of pics (penis, balls, penis lifted up to expose balls, and Ass, Spread ass, and Mouth.) § i will keep my followers safe from whoppi goldberg https://t.co/MmrzWT5eIC § instagram will not stop suggesting i follow my friends moms so if i become any of you guys new Dad im sorry § slow transitioning my brand name to "Mr. Simplygood" over the couse of years 2022-2026. do not freak out § when you reply to a womans selfy with a picture of invader zim saying "Epic Need" it never fails. i have cheated on my wife over 400 times § BOND: I want enough napalm to blow the shit out of a man's ass Q: No.. that's too much BOND: Do as I say § THINKING ABOUT "WHAT'S FOR LUNCH" !!!!!!!!!!! § if the mask from "the mask" was real it would be on the news. § hbo euphoira tricked my two year old into getting blasted on Brown heroin. thank you for bothering me outside of grocery stores @dare § Frowning § just shaking my head while the piss comes out. This is so vapid § filling the entire toilet bowl with piss some how § Im so fucked up. Im an embarrassment to the brand § ealier today i posted a sexually charged comment to my page. I apologize. i dont know why i do this. I suppose im simply destined to FUCK UP § girl let me tell you i dont normally send sexual messages on here. but you look like the" juggys" from the man show § many are asking me about "hamburger 2.0" . I will say more of it in due time. § receieved "DOG`s CURSE"... "The Poster Will Transform Into A Dog Unless Ten Beautiful Women Apologize To Him" It'll never happen! Im Fucked! §

What ever. I'm a hated bug § im the most murdered victim on earth § geetting absolutely goated off that pig leaf like a Cartoon § not rewarding certain brands for their BS w/ free advertising, but id just like to say that all candy mascots are canonically the White man. § attn all my fellow high profile Hollywood guys--please checkout my friend "@CelebKiller" look at his scripts, get him in the movies Thank you § omicron? omi gettin out of here #GotThierAss § if a gorggeous woman made a sexual comment about my perfectly toned body i would put her in a head lock. post "Thats Right" if you agree § you all think youre all being "PLAYAS" !!! you think your doing swag to me. But, you are simply just pissing me off ... § sorry for leaving a poop that looks like your initials § no https://t.co/JjDPfzP8TB § when you say some shit like "Isis is good" on martin luther king day, i want the pain i feel from reading that, to be the pain inside of you § thank you for liking my Wordle. § dont know ass hole https://t.co/PZvQ8Jg5wj § verne is back https://t.co/HGoyozoQir § going hannibal lectore style analysis on this bastards posts. Hah. you make it too easy; i get paid to fuck clowns like you § yes i got smacked by ball lightning in the bathtub and now im connected to ghosts. yes i have Tantric sex with astral women rogan: Holy shit § By engaging with my Troll bait ,you hav e fallen directly into my ass. Good evening § The Scholar`s Guild-- The latest Posting Brand from influencer @Dril. It is a direct response to Liar Culture & the advent of Female Tyranny. § "im a karen who speaks to the manager too much" if you say this FUCK YOU !!! § i think all commercials should beg me to "try not to cum" and not just the ones on porno sites § wfie chasing me with rolling pin because i changed my display name to "black Wolf" and put the Poly flag in there § Masturbatorkiller vs. DaddyMilker. do not miss this Debate. § i will draw a picture of lips on it but i will not kiss it because we are living in a Fucking pandemic . § my followers love watching me vomit all over my $4000 gaming setup like a Whore § going to eat too much refined carbohydrates and turn my dick stupid § ladys dont send me nudes... send me nudes of your therapist. so i can "Bust" § #BareShelvesBiden https://t.co/5VXo7hKkE2 § "thanks for having a look at my fucking posts..." - the Chaotic man § MKOprah § Bloomberg Opinion has cleansed the earth with Absolute Fire once again! " this is Brouh Moment to me!! " § when a drama liker tries to talk to me about Whatever bull shit and i will just simply say "Uh!" #insipid § while you're all worried of OMICRON .... https://t.co/ufpkRE4Pe9 § i think my neighbor might be a gamer?? hes always yelling shit like "Oh Of Course He Fucking Shot Me. Of Course I Just Get Instantly Fucked" § i have never touched a single piece of cum § im sorry but if you say something to me like "oh im jacking off right now its good" or "i respect Peepee" you automatically lose the debate § each follower on here is like a gun pointed at your head 24/7 . Thats what only a mere fraction of my Fucking pain is § next year ill try harder to be the guy who posts shit like "Fucking 2022 Poop Hell" every time a celeb perishes in a small aircraft disaster § lord help me im aobut to ratio this bitch § (shrieking at phone) what do u mean my motehr fucking ken bone NFT is "GONE"? this is IMPOSSIBLE!! i need it to access the MetGala Beer ROom § looking at my metrics & noticing a decrease in followers after retweeting the "Condom king" acct 4 times in a row. fuck you all. Fake people § my fellow men it seems are more interested in getting their dicked sucked , than fostering a network of Gratitude for the voices of bodys. § if you get omicron variant and win the darwin award i will kick the ass of you. i will put you on the doushe bag list. § "DUHH DUDHHH DUHH" thats what you sound like when you sing twinkle twinkle little star or any crap like that. Its not real music § who ever invents all the nursery rhymes (hollywood? government?) needs to write one that doenst suck fucking my balls § this page is the " o Ratio Zone" Ya got that Dick head? § OOUUHH youd love for me to give my self a kidney stone on purpose , wouldn't you!! you dirty mother fuckers Oouuhhhh!! § lets "BUTT FUCK" covidSigned , The @ Dril

Social Media Response Team § click my like button if oyure the 10% of teens generation who think twerking is Foolish § just remembered the tweet i did of corb cob after seeing a picture of it for the 10000th time. Wow thats so funny § were done trying to rescue Small Business. my show will be called Restaurant Fucker, ill go to the worst places on earth & knock shit around § i invent the first porno NFT and i get an ass kicking . i try to do something nice and my followres attack me like a dog § ive cancelled this project due to of people getting mad at me. thank you to the 1 guy who bought it https://t.co/Brsl4OtyAT § i can load my gun in 0.1 seconds. i cn load it so much faster than that guy perfectly every time § the sticker on the back of my dodge stratus says it all... if you drive Cozy Coupe , FUCK OFF ! § Your replies have been simply Fire. Love the energy but please do keep any talk of boiling me alive to a minimum as that is against the law § today my 4 year old son thanked me, for my work in engineering Fostered dialogue's between my White and Black folloers, as well as Asianic. § Men - It is never too early to wish all fo the women in your life a happy Valentines day . Ladys- Im sending you pleasure waves at this time § (photoshop of a bird shitting in a mans mouth) GUY: THis is what society has become GUY 2: I can feel myself becoming radicalized from this § im thinking the next big industry is dog humanization services. surgery to make dogs look like a man, stand upright, etc. its what they want § i respect installing $40000 of mods into a pit bull to make him look like Frankenstein but changing his name to "btk killer" is too much. § every one here has become too cynical and full of their own ass. its like none of you are even trying to help Jussie § (said within ear shot of girls) yeah so like i was saying me and the boys are laughing AT the bitter beer face commerciasls. not WITH them § The temptation to send your penis is something that plagues us all. It's not "Gay" to resist it. This is the true test of a Content Creator. § When they obtain the pic it's game over. They can black mail you into saying the N-Word. They can print it out and suck on it like a dildo. § They sweet talk you. They promise to sell your penis as an NFT to a wandering merchant and split the profits. I have not received this money § In the past, I have fallen for this trick over 100 times. I've suffered professionally and mentally as a result. Their tactics are ruthless. § The other day , a longtime follower asked to see my penis. I stood Firm and said " o. I will not show my penis to a Shit like you." § Jokes On You: I Consider Myself To Be Of Above Average Intelligence § IMPORTANT: Marvel Universe breaking New Ground By Introducing World's First "Mentally Ill" Supervillain § theyre telling me i got the new covid variant "Vaccine melter" so i apologize to all women whose Pussy ive deftly & expertly eaten recently. § my book is now the 98th best Christian bible. you have all made my dream come true thank you https://t.co/h9xqPhDxJI § when i said jacking off is the Woke version of having sex every one agreed with me and i was given $800 by jason Bourne § this bitch thinks he's the Coin Master. Why i do not know. https://t.co/k8YBcIhFfK § you wanna waste my time? you wanna piss me up? you want to pull my nuts? my balls? You want to-huh? Whats that? You wanna slut my ass around § im on the news truly pissed that ghislaine is not allowed access to her mahogany davenport from which to handle various sorts of paper-work § WHo else thinks that, without JACK at the helm, this site is going to start Sucking FUCKING DICK!!! § (me after seeing two guys in any context whatsoever) Well well well if it isnt the Blowjob Brothers § when peoplle make sexual comments when i post my feet and ask if i have covid toes or not...... You Fail BITCH ! § seems weve all forgotten i won the official "Fuck the noid" contest and have still not fucked the noid or received an equivalent cash prize. § im haunched over, hunkered down and duncepilled like an Arthritic dog being sent to the shoe factory & i get less Ass than the bumblebee man § god promised me in a dream that if joe biden & kamala harris get married they will adopt me as their boy. I watch them on the news every day § post "AMEN" or youre fucking stupid § young sheldon may be the grandson of a war criminal but the real controversy is that home alone invented soy face in 1990 § trying to convince my dying son to ask the make of wish foundation for a credit card with 0% APR § id be easily bilked into signing up for a tgifridays credit card if the waitress offered it. furthermore id get stains all over the contract § im being pelted with spit balls im being thrown things at § my voice sounds like a mouth § every girl on ther fucking planet has the exact same voice as each other that i like to call "girl voice" § i can be a friend of you. but piss me off and i will become your Enemy. The Art of War § mr fauci im placing you under arrest in the court of law § @HelpDesk help #slur #slurReport § saw a centaur out side of aldi today § me, DogshitSora and Japanese_Mario are going on a Sex strike until all female scammers on this site are dealt with. We are sick of this shit § Im sorry it has to be said but if you have a small penis that means you were a devil in your past life and you need to unfollow me right now § mr deeds from the movie mr deeds is a real man and he is also q anan § im probably the most difficult person alive to trick into showing mny penis to you. it absolutely almost never happens § if you think astro world is good your fairly actually a piece of shit, and an over all big league FUCK HEAD! § "and the lord said Gambling is fucked" unfollow me if you are a gambler § Piss is valid. Jacking off is not valid. Shitting your pants is NOT valid. MEntal Health is valid. Looking at the computer is valid, & so on § #WhoKilledVerneTroyer § i am here. and this is my Body. #theBodyNudeProject #cock #Nuts § Oh , That Simple Sip https://t.co/wHe49Wa83g § if you follow my account you are protected from demons. you are protected from all x-files § hes right. in favor of hearing out both sides my next post will explore the possible "Darker side" of heroin https://t.co/9nuiPvG9Pb § me and thr boys taking massive amounts of heroin behind macaroni grill saying shit like "Uh yeah That just happened " every time we shoot up § absolutely do not sleep on my breakout role in "Gods Not Dead 3: God Dies" as the Soy Faced money changer § gaming is much like CHess.... § i will never stop accepting bribes for to be such a natural douche § going to start saying shit to girls like "the drew carey show is like dilbert on Hash" until i get my honorary degree from Harvard revoked § need to raise uhhhh $140000 so i can get my daughter Lyvelaughlove in to the army at age 14 § feed your dog with this one insane pringles hack § - piss gback better - shit back better i will come up with more soon § that man you see ,screaming at a woman on the train? Earlier that day, a trusted follower called him "White Urkel". Think before you judge. § all hospitals should have a masturbation ward where you can just go to "let one loose" even if you're not sick § my dick and ass hole are low key sticking out of my shorts § AWESOME father to 5 loud, dumb ass Birds // HVAC Lives Matter // Your Marine Is My Son // i brake for Green Pussy // My Other Car Is A Gun § clicking onto the reddit comment section of a picture of a clowns penis and upvoting 400 different opinions about whether its satire or not § .@carrabbas holes on salt shaker too small disrespectufl to customer and very much a cheat § .@chasebank youve fucked my millionaire points clubs rewards and murdered my ass dead in the water now your life of fraud is exposed to all § i have ended porno § just read in the news a demon exploded § i may have disagreed with his politics, but i believe Brian Laudries bones deserve a PROPER burial! Who's with me!! who the FUCK is with me § number three-- Ive reversed my decision to turn down the Nobel Prize for my posts & will be writing an article in THe Daily Pussy, about this § number two-- the Flintstones have always been, and have never not been, a Black african american family. Just look at literally 1 gene record § number one-- in february of '14 the woke mob called me "Gay" for defending my wifes decision to wear a hula skirt. ive since busted this myth § give me the bloe checkmark!! or ill eat shit on CAMERA! § banks should have special money they give to the robbers where george washington is cross-eyed or has a hitler moustache or some such shit . § in 2090 i will get all my essential nutrients from cyber heroin and swallow big silicone eggs to simulate the process of taking a Bio-Shit § im an extremist judge... and i Vote § i will not post on this fucking website again until they add a filter which deletes every reply to my posts that isn't "yes SIR" § privately and discreetly asking any and all girls in my life if they have any questions about upgrading to Windows 11 § (in this tweet i am pissed off at the "Toilet Duck" brand) Toilet fuck § my friends face when he asks if i know any hollywood celebs & i drop a 40page document PROVING that merv griffin tried to break into my home § (musing , atop a tree stump) O! beer is like wine , § my friend spyroquagmire called me today. said he's trying to start a "weed NASA" § enjoying watching a filmed video, of my illuminating debate with HitlerSkeptic , now available on Ouya § your post is so good man. it .must have cost $1000 to make it § my 600 lb sucked off life § im Sucking 1000 § all the good shit got cut from my stand up special... now its just me talking about how i cant cum without using steriods for 40 minutes § Q: How goes it, Mr 007. BOND: mission accoomplished, i have electrocuted The Bitch. now give me my money before i start knocking shit around § the most wild thing you can say when walking into a restaurant or a kitchen "it smells like fuckin food in here" § @TruthPointDWR hitler society § @RollingStone shut the fuck up rolling stone magazine § this is for All the avoacado toast likers https://t.co/bBSE6SdT6L § if any one needs help making bat man or super man or any of those guys viral i will do it for $1000 § im being targeted individualed again https://t.co/BkmDsrsM0M § dont shit me § changing my display name to "Follower killer", my bio to "Fucked", and my avatar to a set of cross hairs with the word "Me" in the center § Im glad we can discuss the news and the headlines of the day and have fun while doing it also. § i sure hope dthe solar flare doesnt cause my camera roll to empty out 200 pictures of my penis onto the time line again § i would like to apologize again to the Girls, this time for telling some of them that i have a green dick. i thought it made me sound Exotic § im bringing back the "bean dog" shit, but . Ok hear me out. its nft now § plotting various ways of dmming my girl followers some truly bizarre pseudosexual shit that they can't even get mad at § if my followers want me to become a guy who says shit like "tarnation" aand "Dag nabbit" i will do it. i will please them at any cost § (makingh the bitter beer face) ohh girl this pussy tastes fucking Normal § When I can't log into my Microsoft account, to access the additional features offered by Windows 10, i get stupid. i go fucking insane § this man was Seen https://t.co/uf0HvuV5Yw § Yes yes yes. Right down the line https://t.co/4FfZauUzOA § nobody gives a SHIT about ANYBODY!!! if a train obliterated my entire house nobody would even call 911! It's that fucked! It's that fucked! § (looking at wtc memorial) this is mood ass § bill mahrer should go off on guys who poop their pants § my agent told me i need to get back on meth, remove my satirical bumper stickers and to stop dressing like im cruising for discreet gay sex . § who cares who the next james bond is. theyre all Lucifer § whats that? if you send me $40 i will send a big picture of a dogs dick instead of a normal sized one. @elonmusk re blog this sir #important § starting "project Dog dick" the NFTs of the future. send me $20 and i email you a dogs dick pic with special Dog Dick Number (Dont lose it) § my new bullshit is getting really mad everytime theres a new ios update and they still haven't added hobo code emojis § just grabbed my ankles and rolled backwards ontop of my neck and took an enormous shit in my bed while my dogs barked at me #introvertWin § #raceWisdom § if u followed me back 8 yrs ago things wouldve turned out differently. I would not have been forced to expose you as a "White noise" poster. § everything thats a reference to something sucks fucking Dick. all quotes are shit § its time to stigmatize the Ass § adult baby diaper driver § enjoying a glass of dolby surround sound flavored wine. § 1000% of followers will rather click on a penis than a literature book § 6304 saw a goblin 81206 saw a big foot 9511 saw a cryptid (dog version) 71515 saw a "raggedy ann" 72116 saw a man with very fast eyes § sunnyDayKitten98: just noticed you posted "Ted Lesbo" on the time lione. Is everything ok? ME: Go away. I dont want you to see me like this. § accidentally bought the mouth wash that's formulated for "Sucking dick" at cvs and it's actually really good § getting absolutely cock suckered by theat shit that made humpty dumpty fall off § "Wake up and smell the key board ." - Son_Of_A_Bitch_Killer § 9/11 and all the micro-9/11s imposed upon me by my emplyoer every day is all rolled up in, and majorly a part of, Crisis of Boys § its 4am sunday morning here uin beautiful hollywood california and i got a tab open on here called "Barney FAQ" § i pray my IQ forever remains in the "Sweet Spot" wherein its high enough to call out the BS but too low to recognize the Futility of Posting § This is what some of you mother fuckers look like when you reply to my posts https://t.co/gfZY3Va8tR § This post gave me the courage to break into my neighbors garage and try to steal some shit. Thank you § "i hereby validate all of mental health" - DiaperPoster007 § my posts are on Lock Down until the benghazi crime situation is resolved . do not look at my page § we are starting to live in a world where a man cant sell 200 containers of WBP (White Boy Piss) withtout having to sign some kind of paper § put me in irauq i will find the taliban gun factory i will take their horses and Gold https://t.co/HX2CRSVilj § rate my dogs dick dot com § driving your car through my fence and bbreaking all my potted plants with a hammer and kidnapping my dog is little dick energy § i wipe asses like mine for breakfast § ill wipe the floor with your ass and wipe my ass with your ass and wipe my nuts with my ass and get floor poisoning § they added a new type of corn row to miitopia -- heres 10 reasons why thats good and 8 reasons its bad § you post " ustard" by mistake one time &people call you " ustard man" until u freak out & drive your car thru a hospital like blues brothers § Looks like some shit for losers & kindergardaners. Do not add any new features unless theyre good or they put 1000usd directly in my pocket. https://t.co/7mS9B07BJi § many of my posting rivals have been known to artificially pump up their metrics using irish accounting and Gay casino tricks. dont be fooled § i wish i had the motorcycle from tron so i ccoud drive home to my house and fuck the plastic bag i stole from good will § boomer: ih ope they add a new Gun to fortnite me: i hope my penis mutates into a wolfs penis with extendable ridges so i can jack off easier § O girl!!! You got that NSFW Pussy ! Your shit will get my ass FIRED !! From my JOB § Mmm any one want for mashmallows. I got a roasted BITCH on fire § if i dont get into Heaven ill just use the rainbow bridge that dogs use. and ill push as many animals off the bridge as i can in the process § Ive gotten over 6 dms from various beautiful women begging me not to change my name to "Mr Go Fuck Myself". But its not enough. I will do it § i guess i will change my name to "Mr Go Fuck Myself " huh?? Since all you sons of bitchs obviously think it would be good, if i did that § helping my dog https://t.co/gPz0hFbm6k § they brought back covid 19 because you were all being such little shits to me § ill kick any ones ass who is a "BOOMER" § (seeing a nude woman) Wow looks like im on the weird side of you tybe again § Nasty ! § do not post to me such filthy SHIT § girls if ya man be Posting under the user name of "Clit Goon" do NOT FUCK HIM!!!!!!!!!!!!EVER § people are telling me to stop posting abot this. theyre saying im doing a Psy Op?? buddy if any one's doing a psy op its "Clit Goon" § It seems "Clit Goon" is commanding his subordinates to tell me hes dead of COVID19 now. Funny, considering he logged into steam 4 hours ago. § "Clit Goon" is actively trying to avoid me, when I`ve stated repeatedly; if he comes forward with a genuine apology- I will not pursue him. § can some one get me in touch with the user named "Clit Goon" . he said he could give me a bunch of cardboard boxes 6 years ago § "TORTURED ACCOUNT" § " Seems to me in this country, we eat Fake food, meet Fake people, buy Fake clothes... and have Real problems. "- Winston churchhill § could any influencers share tips on how to “punish” your self for generating low engagement? might need some Pain to keep my head in the game § Im the guy who asked them to remove Sex from only fans!!! I thought It would be nice!!! I didnt know it woiuld make people mad!!! Im sorry!! § “Free Guy” Has An Absolutely Bonkers Marvel Cinematic Universe Cameo -- Here’s How They Pulled It Off § there should be ICU beds only for geniusses and if your iq is less than 120 they eject you from the window at fucking 200mph § some of mother fuckers think to win the Dumb Ass award is a GOOD thing! § they should clal it the “stimulus cheek” because it can kiss my fuckin ass cheek § please check out my piece in TIME magazine “Why i sold my dog at a carnival for $30 and Why it matters” the worst article ever written § today i saluted the afghanistan vet who lives on my floor and said “Suck My Dick Sir! Mission Failed” then went home and dead lifted 300lbs § the “SCAM ME” challen-nge.. if you can scam me you can keep all the money you scammed of me. but if you fail you have to send me 1 Nude image § if my post offend you... call 1800-EATSSHIT § most rhymes https://t.co/qV8nkbsPeu § when you Mock the brand-- your putting a Knife in the back of every depressed person who chose not to commit suicide because of Disney IP`s . § Oh im losing followers just for expressing an Opinion to someone who may or may not be a professional dog killer. Nice society you got here, § any purchase made on this page will help me defeat my ex wife th https://t.co/ZLfT74FD7u § Donald Powers The Drumpf who Sucked Me Donald Powers The Drumpf who Sucked Me Donald Powers The Drumpf who Sucked Me § list of vhs tapes that GoodWill gave back to me: -pussy legacy -worlds Gayest bloopers im selling them and i want normal price § See this Instagram photo by @dril_real https://t.co/flzJwEHAog § some times the most real shit we’ve ever read in our entire lives is just sitting right in front of us on our computer screens ...... https://t.co/PJ3lf9gIAM § for the 2nd time- the fans have failed to raise enough money for me to invent a new type of Face § Q: my dog is addicted to opiates. i need help of this best answer (voted 4 times): sorry but i m afraid of dogs because they murdered my son § daily reminder that the idea of “SUcking Ass” is a societal illusion & everything you do is healthy no matter how much youre punished for it § if you remove the license plate frame that advertises your dealership youre a nasty son of a bitch & you want small business owners to choke § where was I during 9/11? Ha.. easy question. I was simply thoroughly engrossed in the literary treasury of The Great Authors. § the new shit is MyBeerNumber. you will attend a Tasting with an authorized brewer and dtetermine your MyBeerNumber. my MyBeerNumber is “4” § if i ever catch you getting your stupid ass into a car accident ill knock the shit out of you § turn off the computer? Fuck that. I Wnat to see posts. I want my posts!! § theyre taking my trademark hardline of societys bull shit (tv, movies etc) and turning it against me! T-This was supposed to be impossi-ble!! § girl;s with cracked phone screens give top like the devil him self 0 RTS 2 LIKES pray if you Like this... 1210 RTS 42134 LIKES Power of Lord § sick of wifes shit https://t.co/VphTqD11nm § 2022 year of the buffoon. ladys invest early; get your self a man with that buffoon dick § you must know the nickelodeon program “wild N crazy kids” primed our nations youth to reject thr scientific method & all fact-based evidence § i will be typing the words “rock ‘N’ roll” over and over in a note pad document until my computer makes targeted content more relevant to me § i dress as a police and give mother fucker s like you my badge number every day § i will make $100,000 when I finish drawing this picture of uncle sam standing in front of congress saying “politics has the right to be Fun” § my 125 IQ growth hormone consultant and legal conservator has confirmed to me that they are going to make the 2022 hyundai sonata “WOKE” § ufo eat’s shit - ufo crashs into a circus tent and eats shit § which one of you mother fuckers said im going to go volunteer at the dog shelter, as a Dog. disgusting comment § some of my friends on here are “CLASSIC STYLE” hucksters who’d scam their own mothers for a quick buck. And you all Love them & follow them.. § imagine assuming the position of a dog and kissing the ass of the "MAINSTREAM" accounts. Muah muah muah. So stupid. Couldnt be me. No way § saturday night at the donut shop and i am very excited to show the boys my new Dance. § portrait of mew two with pubic hair removed from the digimon otis estate § pleased to announce i had a nice conversation with the sheriff and my account is now verified. Thank you all § (after smiling all day because i realized something important) Tell me. If Fort nite is "For children" , how come it has Family guy in it? § the best followers money can buy § me after watching over 700 hours of you tube tutorials about how to hard ovverride the Orgasm center of girls brains https://t.co/YvQfXnH1I9 § send all Business offers to: wintdotco @ gmail . com ... no goof ball shit § i would not interfere in the LORD's affairs § girls are such White people § girls love having last names like "Witherspoon" § Oh looj at them having a go about things. A fine day for foot (Soccer) ball-- wahey lads? Me mum's tits , Piss up! Ohh the noncers Wanked it § i will never make forbes Top500 tweets. i will never get my posts featured on The McLaughlin Group. Because Im a SLUT!! Woth personal demons § if you can make an app that tells you if your ass smells like shit you will make the aeasiest $1million dollars in the world § THATS IT!!!!!! I HAVE HAD IT UP TO HERE WITH THIS GUYS SHIT https://t.co/HBhLn4HuHp § every own i have ever done in my life is the own i think it is § heavens pray that the goofster, the gagmeister, and the stoogelord don't join forces and create a slapstick squad more powerful than the CIA § in kindergarten, i became most popular kid in class after calling the farmer in the dell "A gaped out ho" . By 2nd grade, i was again Hated. § kit kats.. potato chips.. air fresheners.. Hey! who remembers when the gas station, sold GAS!!! § did it hurt when you fell from heaven and kissed my stupid ass you mother fucker § Ohh!! THe agony of it all! Im sorry!! Im so so sorry! The pain my POSTS have caused! How many more must SUFFER? I cant stop! Its to good § Ah ha ha ha !!! Wauh ha ha!!! https://t.co/r0SFrwdXda § just sent $39k in crypto growth exchange funds to a guy named "Dinglepussy" and am now being gosted by him § my screen play explores the question: what if master cheif smoked a big cigarette from the year 3000 that worked through his space suit § Ladys... if U have never been sucked by a man who pours Cement , you are SHIT !! https://t.co/idXbcVzMIf § participatr in something known as "the porky pig discourse" hmm no thanks im busy sending pics of my new dinette set to 115 different girls. § me & the boys can never hold a Luau (hula maidens, pig w/ apple in mouth, limbo) thanks to the loud mouth craop going on at college campuses § Fucka!!!! § someone has smeared shit all over my "please don't run me off the road" bumper sticker andi need help getting DNA out of the shit § delta variant? wake me up when theres a WINE varirant § Im sorry for saying that all the cartoon characters who have depression deserve to have depression. Im stupid. Im stupid. I shouldntv (1/31) § joining a classic Crooner's union https://t.co/ZsWW2gG6RZ § Cool your nuts scum bag § .@saddamhussein take a lap chowder head § (pointing at some bull shit on the news) You see that?? Theyre from reddit § BIg mistake! § who sent this to my house. Fuck you https://t.co/iBGywSBPzG § No More Fooling Around: if your post sucks my balls , it will be regarded as SHIT !!!! § if i could time travel id go back to 2016 & tell my self the rwriters of the final season of 2017 are about to smoke crack like never before § my flollowers are more interested in smoking koush than helping me move my groceries around § (g uy runs me over in a pick up truck and breaks my ribs and twists my fucking legs off) Oh thats crindge! § man with sword has ability to Vanish (unconfirmed) § got our best men on the case https://t.co/s2fvhyxkY1 § Whats fucked up is , some will think this is good!!! https://t.co/2samsGi56q § shot da fuck up BITCH § 3d dog https://t.co/YBZQbc2qvN § my proposal: snl for mensa likers. @ericgarland unblock me you goofed-up fucking freak i wanna make you Famous bitch § come now ladys for a night of pleasue and devils deeds https://t.co/qAiHtZ0Di2 § its a travesty that my Diddy kong racing any%s arent pulling the viewers they deserve because theyd all rather see a woman showing her BRA ! § i come here for the kind of comedy that a man can respectuflly nod towards , i have not laughed in 10 years, laughing is for hyenas & ghouls § either the EU approves my sacntions imposed against the wily digimon otis or its "back to brexit" § surgery to make my head drier § what if my posts were the one thing stopping PUTIN from turning the USA into a Slave Zone. think on that a little before you unfollow my ass § big bbq coming up. should i wear the apron that has a picture of ziggy taking a shit or the one that says "introverts are good at Fucking" § #E32021 Actual T-Shirt Seen At e3 2021 - " ext Gen Sucked Me Off " . - Why? How? § #E32021 E3 has failed. Sex has dominated the world. Michael jackson is on the loose once again. Games & Games Culture is nothing but compost https://t.co/vZPjwjFJhL § #E32021 These games will make you crap your load like never before. There has never been a better time to get fucked at 120 fps § Ggoing purely by the numbers, im the biggest slave in human history, and Im to be treated as a dog. But i respect the lifestyle aspect of it § "i Fucking do it all -- For the fans..." - Dril § Ive built a solid rapport with the Moderation staff. And I thank them for Punishing me while discussing Arts & Culture w/ other 30yr old men § i like to think if i was alive in the 1800s & saw a Minstrel Show id take the Rational approach. id say "This is simply the SNL of its time" § need to find out if the eagle tattooed to my sons chest is racist or normal § i forgive Ellen This tweet was sent from the high way at 99mph § CONGRATULATIONS Legendary Babe Ruth "Posthumous conversion to Islam" Now thats a home run § topless hvac repair § These are the most important jeans you will ever wear § mcdonald kids meal ad asks: "What If Kids Ran The World?" cue insane montage of cosby, Fogle, weinstein, et al. getting shivved in prison § cant help but smile to check out these new slogans: Weird twitter- "Are we Having fun yet?" weird twitter- "Game over, man, game over !!" § my mouth feels very dry and my dick got a liuttle bit smaller last night. i think they started rolling out 6G § i will sign -My posts § you like going to the bathroom? i normalized Shitting back in like 2013, with my posts. But dont thank me, im no hero. Im just a dumb bitch. § my dick andballs look like a honey nut cheerio stuck to a brain § this happens when the algorithm achieves total purity. stripped of all obscure distraction & niche self-congratulatory bull shit. Perfection https://t.co/y7Y87SO208 § This is wihy when i see a millennials resume i throw it simply in the trash. https://t.co/drF102FUzB § "you just want to exorcise the royal soul from your dog so itll grant you 3 wishes. you dont care about haiti or its princes" Wrong actually § lets just say an online quiz told me my dog is harboring the soul of a Haitian Prince and idont know how to free him without hurting the dog § TO ALL GIRLS-- your Man drops a notebook, and inside it is every " ew Rule" written by bill maher since like 2003. Do you flip out or be cool § do you like my controversial "DURAG" post? Yes I wear them. § this id me https://t.co/mpnp5BWn0K § "The Shitting Otaku" § I've seen enough. Computer... link me in to DragonWeb § you see a man standing near a woman humping thin air. he says "AAhhhh!!! Oh girl.! This Pussy is Mood!!" in the worst voice you ever heard, § i am thed inventor of gangnam style and im back and im here to say to all USA forces here and abroad "oppa thank you sty;le" § SARGE: This hall better be spotless by the time im back from Lunch ME: Sir may i have some please sir 9 officers run up screaming in my face § me age 2: i love my data so much. my data is so fucking nice. if anyone stole my data id be pissed me age 99: FUCK!! § assembling my crew https://t.co/e6zwTsVF86 § very good thank you. im jacking off in one of these right now while playing the knight rider theme on my phone https://t.co/AlFIVlttVR § We All Have That Friend: We All Have That Friend Who Looks At Porno § tattooing a bar code to my penis to demonstrate to anyone who looks at my penis the Frailty of our humanity, in regard to mens penises § add Beer to mario @nintendo @nintendo @nintendo @

nintendo @nintendo @nintendo @nintendo @nintendo @nintendov @nintendo @nintendo @nintendo § sending Honor to my friends on the computer today Thank you!! Thank you!! https://t.co/0UyMAe6nnN § im sorry for letting donwn the fans by going through my most Wild, Balls-To-The-Wall divorce yet § waking up in the middle of the night, gripped by blood curdling terror, yelling, sobbing, punching my pillows, because i forgot 9/11 § i can say it. im allowed to § A dog with five tattoos has appeared online § you ask me to play "The beer song" ... I smile and ask, "Which one?" § if your a "gangster" and you trick me into smoking weed by putting it in a queso ruffles bag Fuck you. Ill remember your name. § if i retweet a guy with a jim carrey mask avatar talking about pussys you guys have to promise not to unfollow me or do any shit like that § lobotomy--Check castration--Check 8months of Bible-Based close combat training--CHeck police mandated electroshock therapy--Check Time to post . § harvey weinsteins tooth fell out the last time h was in court and the judge made him pick it up and put it back in his mouth § my feed will suck absolute shit, for sure. but every one will love me § might do the obama thing and follow 600000 accounts so people cant get mad at me for following specific guys § really hoping a cop doesnt wander into my room and sees me googling "how to do a hit and run 2021" out of context § disregard this . § might post a pic of my fist clenching a huge chunk of my own hair i pulled out saying "You did this !!" over and over during peak girl hours § "shit i got Pissed off by" https://t.co/sLzTicbSVj § some one posted" dodoo" at me april 12 we have still not nabbed the perp § the best is when they bark at you when they see you through the window of your own house. At that point i know your iq is fucked . § dogs love barking at me like 1000ft from their house. what are you a land surveyor. you don't know what a property line is bitch shutup § going on a diarrhea strike (giving myself diarrhea on purpose) unntil the us govt forces my daughters to join the isreali defense force § gluing 1000 newspapers to the wall so my neighbors cant hear me jacking off is not only rational; it is an act of service § ill aave some of that https://t.co/gfeaEkWr48 § bed bug positivity- you r blood tastes good and is helping many bugs bed bug stigma - youre nasty, your bed is poison, suck my dick § send me bedbug positivity links or Fuckoff § " a man must have a code " § losing my cheez it sponsoriship for posting a picture of a sword piercing a $1 bill § spent the past 9 days mulling over the concept of a "Sequel" to the beloved $100 bill § down load my widget and learn which poisons you are consuming that are preventing you from becoming an asexual james bond § youre all hot misunderstood geniuses, and for $400/hr you can get exclusive access to my seminar on how to not take your penis out in public § bill: i just think hes cool. and, hes nice to me, and hes Based. melinda: Your sleeping on the couch tonight mister bill: FUCK YOU!! § hello dear , will you be my smile https://t.co/wDckOjXxdv § Beer is like pepsi on crack . § beer is soda on crack - @ DRIL § jackinf off at the dog shit factory § if youre going to name an in-game weapon after decreased officer brian sicknick the least you can do is not make it have shit DPS . @activision § the only nfts i deal in are nerds in the Fucking trashcan. suck my Dick § im absolutely the only mother fucker on here dumb enough to get publicly whipped for posting NFT bullshit while also making $0 off of them § id really like to figure out how to sell me and my dogs turds and shit to a farm or something § i ask my followers not to look at my posts between the hours of 10:00-16:00 on may 12th douring which time i'l be freaking out for no reason § my top Grabs of now https://t.co/GmcHZfaZWN § the reason my posts are no good is your all too busy sucking your own Dick to punish me § fycking key board warrior from reddit suck Cock § pissing in to the toilet without getting over 10% of it on the floor and legs is Suad goals § listen bitch i know what ``poop`` is and i dont like it § i may be the worst person you ever met but that doesnt mean i don't have a fool proof plan to fix every hollywood movie franchise ever made § you gotta respect iot, even though it sucks. You just gotta respect it even if you fucking hate it . You gotta respect this shit § to who ever said my dick looks like a bacon bit. oh so i guess you're the expert of knowing what peoples dicks look like then . § might peruse the dumpsters behind some failed sub way restaurants & take home some huge pictures of bread/ tomatoes to hang up on my walls § they look like some shit a farmer would wear to the public execution of a goat. fuck jeans § after careful reflection in this era , ive decided that i no longer support wearing the pants known as "jeans", and i will eradicate them § Jjust processed every news story on CNN as logically as humanly possible & had a strategic stroke that murdered the bias center of my brain § they call it forex trading because th JUDGE has ruled that all the money i make on it is for ex wife § " THIS USER IS IMMUNE TO ALL BAD FAITH LOONEY TOONS OPINIONS " § Hey man im sorr y but me and every other guy in a group dm called " ut sack club" were talking and decided your posts suck shit . § if someone posts something that is good then i will look at it and think its good. Simple § OTHERS: Oh your a main stream account? Let me suck your dick Hurp Guklp Gulp ME: I oont give a shit if an account is mainstream or indie . § i dont see any problem with getting the Milkbone vaccine. i trust milk bone even though they are usually a dog food company § this may very well be the much needed "Win" for America that economists have speculated upon since 9/11 § personally im thrilled of bidens dog being sent to a shadowy offshore facility to have the Evil surgically removed from its pea sized brain § You will nearly shit, when you find out which two beanie baby review vloggers are engaged in a salacious "Pervert`s Affair" . § ExoneratedUncle § you waste my time farting up my ass thats a good way of getting your nuts brusied. § yeah im thinking its muleller time. § gamer the bounty hunter § typical to see every one making jokes here after a 99 year old man of proud and honorable distinction killed him self with a blow torch § Mr. Finding My Smile § all im asking is for you dumb mother fuckers to click on 1 link in your entire life § were fucked cause people would rather see fred fuckstone on the shitstone show than True hard dicked journalism that costs $1000000 to make § please call your father. right now he is looking up info and reading stickied reddit threads about how to become a Smoker § the only time isaid the " word" i said it with perfect frequency/timing to intercept & cancel out the sound waves of another guy saying it, § looking at hutsler magazine § all chefs are doctors all waiters are nurses and i am getting paid 160000 a year to believe this § if someone asked me who the richest man on earth was, i would 100% say some peabrained shit like "the Godfather " § ragdolling as an olympic sport. ragdolling into a pile of bird houses at 99mph . rag dolling down the side of the hoover dam etc. gold medal § if i was a congressional aide and joe bidens dogs champ and Hunter went in on me to kill me id simple calm them down with a double head lock § just looking at some pictures of the old aunt jemima logo. Hm?? Oh Im sorry. I didnt know it was a crime to like things that are good § looks fucking dumb https://t.co/2IBzeoomHe § "The posts are good, the posts are fun, but theres a message under there that makes you think about the Wieght of the Human Condition."-Dril § yes i jettisoned my uncles hvac equipment all over the highway & obliterated a teen driver but using that info to slander me is also Cringe. § just got off the phone wih bill maher hbo & they confirmed bill maher will say "release the gamer cut" on live tv if we get 500 signatures . § one of the most brilliant things i did as a baby was predict perfectly the economic rise & expansion of the city of Dubai "The desert jewel" § looking forward to more lavish hollywood parties where me and a bunch of obese guys read posts like this while laughing in a hot tub https://t.co/igboYCyq3W § actually r/pronemasturbation says prone masturbation is better than normal masturbation and it doesnt even fuck your dick up that badly § we are living in a culture where you can be punished just for being Dr. Phil § here how it goes down. when its my turn to get the vaccine i say " o.

Give it to a female fire man instead" and i simply just walk away... § my followers want more pics of me smoking.   my followers want more pics of me genuflecting infront of my honda like a fucking moron § digimon otis has changed his name to Fallen Otis because he thinks he got covid from best buys midnight release of balan Wonderworld § https://t.co/iEWgwL2KvN this is so fucking sick. the dragon murdered him § buddy youve pissed off my world § @ bag_getter thank you for your service § i think drunk drivers would crash less if the industry manufactured cars that said to them "you are Seen. you are Valid and Known" § i boos't "RESPECT" i block "PORNO" § might siphon some gasoline to generate a non fungible jordan peterson fortnite skin or what ever you fucking dopes think is good. idont know § (taking one very careful sip from the can holding it in a fucked up way with painful looking contorted hand) Boh! Beer just hit different... § i can not access my software so just imagine a diagram of my ass with two fingers being inserted labeled "gas prices" and "dog food prices" § i need something that can put a hole in a UFO § "Much talk about blocking the Suez Canal, when people should be concerned about blocking my most virulent Trolls." - The Ethical Masturbator § door to door salesman who keeps jars of his own urine in a little suitcase and tries to sell them and gets his ass beat at every house § killed my dick with too much febrease spray § manufacturing a story about getting sucked off by Sam Donaldson for the "Shit Head" new york times to report on w/ zero scrutiny whatsoever § if you whack the side mirrors off my car with a bat every day your the biggest piece of shit on earth, your toxic, and "telling on yourself" § dont have time to read this sorry § i would not interfere in the natural order § i repeat: this shit would have slayed ass in the golden era https://t.co/Vy7Amt0ppB § computer... show me ya Ass § board's for actual spree killers only my followers ride every day https://t.co/ys7DtLp160 § i fulfill mens destinys https://t.co/EYwyOQTJwe § my face whan i nut https://t.co/HXH5XMtMgd § hitting up all the college town cvs and 7-11s so i can pull out my custom credit card that looks like the ace of spades in front of girls § in light of his posts from 2008 endorsing the Mummys curse i no longer support WhiteDarthMaul or his dream of becoming a Waiter § bathroom prayer Thank you Lord for letting me go to The bath room, I pray you deliver my shit Thru the Pipe so it can be of use to an animal § starting wednesday off with a fun one . § imagine if like a drill sergeant or an armyman was putting together some IKEA furniture... i bet hed yell "Ahh this fuckin sucks" § looking at the data and simply laughing § sppeedy gonzales is White § im being told that the pussy oscars (the version of the oscars that judges womens pussy shapes) has become the latest victim of "woke" § once again spending another afternoon educating people who falsely claim that Gamers hagve trouble wiping their ass. Sigh !! § when the social order collapses and the new global currency becomes mens semen you will regret ever jacking off in your life § if some one said some shit to me like "Rock and Roll Hoochie Koo" i would not be able to contain my rage. i would completely lose my shit. § Its not worki-ong. The haters are up my ass sabotaging my life § dunno why im getting dog shit offers here. i never said crypto was monopoly money for pedos & drug addicts, i only thought it, repeatedly § double digit iq; pure stooge energy. i would love to see all these people get together and attempt to build a shed https://t.co/6rqlv8puhe § i think there should be a meter man who comes over to check your gamer meter like the do with water meter § oh youve been to therapy? Dumb. yeah you havent even scratched the surface of my Level. i bet none of you even know your own brain weight § the Assed singer § during times of pandemic, the thought of even getting, let alone maintaining, a full erection, is true ape shit Lunacy. it is violence § too late girls. i gave it all to a Shaman § reminder to the girls of this page that I will soon have $ 1400 § i love shit that doesnt equal endorsements § ive done so much personal growth that its to the point where if you dont follow my posts youre fucking stupid §

metal gear eric made me sit on a dog bed during an impromptu bomber man 64 tournament at his house. And no one is talking about this . § im thinking this is gonna be the most Wild april fools day yet! § i had the courage to bring kindness and mental health into peoples lives And now wevery one wishes this was my grave... https://t.co/yP9VHzabQT § i have now muted the group DM which SirGamestop has commandeered to talk about his startup which is, in his words, a "white version of fubu" § Sorry im driving my car 100mph § pretty good tweet but not as good as this one. wow what a bargain https://t.co/Z6XtB1BCmp https://t.co/X0c0PLKzYE § https://t.co/mRxUFt0g7D § i would never post info about my ass § if i had a suit of armor i could easily beat the shit out of any man alive § Can we stop the posts please guys. Can we all cool it with the gags, riffs, spoofs, and epic shit. People are trying to do mental health § watching my haters "CUM" § all guys wanna do is tell you where their Bonnie lies. Shut the fuck up § world first proof of beetle juice § cant wait for all nerds on earth to upload their brain to computer so they can be bat man for the rest of their lives & stop fuckinh posting § "If for one day. Just one day, you knew the Pain of having 1.6 million followers, perhaps you too would seek solace, in the DMs ." -Unknown § peolple are reacting to this https://t.co/ZR6VmxANKL § before the trolls leak my finances id just like to state for the record that ispent $6000 on Dr Mario world because i thought itd be funny § youre welcome to click the off button at any time if you are going to piss about it § watching big mommas house 2 in defiance of attack of small businesses § hm maybe before we help Ladygagas Pit bulls we should find Chinese Investor "JACK MA" because i guess i still give a FUCK about HUMAN LIFE ! § just thinking about how ad hominem all you mother fuckers are. and simply laughing to my self enjoying it § in this house, a PIT BULL can believe in GOD !!! § practicing my angry phone calls for when someone gives me COVID. yelling "you gave me covid you dumb mother fucker", "youre Nasty", etc § KitsuneHorace says theres a secret game stop located under the Lincoln Memorial where congressmen are allowed to shop without wearing a Mask § faces ranked 1. soy face 2. Blackface 3. diont like it thats the bottomline § All i know is burden § whos the son of bitch who messed my link up § jon stuart sir would you like to take a look at the, frankly good, 1000 pages of ad copy ive written for https://t.co/erPUGGB5qf? or are you a Bitch? § my followers are always onm some god damn goofy shit; Theyre absolutely smoking that Urkel § nice to see you on here posting pervert shit and having another bitch-out § your just a dog from the zoo § sending special kind of energy to my followers that is good/poweful energy normally but immediately becomes dog shit energy if you betray me § all rise for the national anthem, of Jeans § my new favorite shit in my DMs is fake twitter admins who manage to get the verified checkmark but still have usernames like MickeyCar199326 § (watching Leno deliver some solid hits against Michael Jackson in the opening monologue) I dont understand. Is he mad at him? Whats going on § GIRL: (after listening to me explain something i invented called Weed Theory for 20 mins) Wow thats pretty good. Did you invent that ME: Yes § since 2003 to this day, me and KitsuneHorace are the only verified winners of the "convert your step dad to islam challenge" § awful, looks fucking dumb, etc https://t.co/1xTeOubVql § kids are always saying "drew carey invented plinko". Wrong. Drew carey stole plinko from the italians. Drew carey couldnt even invent "2+2". § hockey? ive been known to slap sticks every now and than. had a name for me "the goalie killer". I quit playing when the shit got too easy . § ex-con making $3 an hour shoveling diapers into a river "IF THE MEDIA CANCELLS ME FOR MY BELIEFS IM FUCKED" § society is so much fucking Bitched ..... § suddenly getting very upset imagining all the great lottery winners of history gathering around & laughing at me for picking dogshit numbers § "Cold hard cash is the real deal" the quote of ben franken § having a vision of dying completely alone and waking up in a cold sweat to post a Scathing review of a futurama episode i watched 14 yrs ago § i already do this for free 24/7 https://t.co/PEMBZtumgz § @BillCosby @sinbadbad This is not appropriate use of "Thank You Thursday" . § gorilla glue paid that woman to fuck up her hair and go viral and youre all pawns in gorilla glues game. not me though im a 200IQ journalist § seems more and more of times these days that every one is too much of a PUSSY to wipe my ass and mow my lawn for free § instead of mr peanut dying they could show a guy with a towel over his face grabbing his ankles and waterboarding himself with his own piss § U may not chat me § healing the world full power https://t.co/0MsfztMfDj § sensor THIS!! § just obliterated a birds nest with a weedwacker becsuse it could see me jacking off in my house at a certain angle § im not that white § for anyone out there scrutinizing my steam profile i did not play " chips challenge 1" for 263.3 hours. it should not say that i did § the only animal crossing i see here, are the animals crossing me in the replies § you are fixing to get a red ass § ANNOUNCEMENT: Im developing a game for true and brave gamers only. please have a look at my page, for details: https://t.co/9vlMFmJIve § my advisor has told me that instead of trying to "Game the markets" i need to put all my money in 1 of those tall banks shaped like a crayon § fucking bad ass https://t.co/X7QbsE1fTf § getting cancelled cultured for ignoring the haters. whats that you say? ignoring hte haters isnt a crime? IT IS NOW !! § "i nutted in my wife x amount of times and shes still not pregnant" humor is not funny no matter what the number is. even if its like 100000 § 10 things you must never say to a Soothsayer 1. Got any new Sooths? 2. my cousins kid just made up some sooths. Do you think theyre any good § getting my fuckin Onion sucked § sorry for not reading your dms ladys. i was busy yelling "MY MONEY IS TAKING A SHIT! MY MONEY IS TAKING A SHIT!" into a huge cell phone § printing out some article like "25 Things You Must Never Say to a Smoker" and pasting it to my car and cutting off girls so they can read it § need some one whos mentally 12 years old to explain to me how market volatility is like the bernie bros of gamer gate § we need to reopen SNakes World because Snake owners have suffered "MORE THAN ANY ONE " § its time like this that i wish we had the Guidance and the insight of Sheldon Adelson, Prince, and that one koch brother who died § just looked atn the news and it seems like things are about to fucking nut off § wouldve loved to make $10000000 but honestly seemed rude to fuck over hedgefunds since theyre the people who make like, our shirts, and food § Ah, Reddit ftw., Truly phenomenal, big fan of the memes, links, etc. Always been saying this. So whcih stock is making us rich today fellas § fake people love getting mad at me. Has any one noticed this § piss is the main threat. touching it, seeing it, etc § i cant believe ive been chanting the words "epic Pee tape" in the mirror every morning for the past 4 years for nothing § i think the way it works is as long as the National Debt isnt paid off, every American automatically goes to Hell when they die, which Sucks § if you spread your dick hole with your fingers a tiny bit before sending nudes tghe girl will think youre a Leo. i read it in Cosmopolitan § my face When. My face when u know my ass is eating good https://t.co/Om7eRRDPjq § downloading an app developed by Asia that tells me how much diarrhea is hould have everyday § most wont type this § thank you and Amen https://t.co/9t5yqXg6w7 § https://t.co/zN8YkOEDPe § if we taught children in schools how to perform defensive body roll maneuvers vehicular pedestrian death would decrease by over 1000% tops § people will call you Gay just for wanting to win the lottery . yeah well straight people like to win the lottery too bitch § Had to block a friend ive had since kindergarten because he said he was going to fuck the new ghost busters ghost. Im through playing games § nobodys talking about how much jacking off is such Einstein shit. who comes up with this stuff????? § only takes two seconds of me cliciking around on my keyboard to see why they call me the mother fucker of ubuntu § dont know why everyones up my ass over this. i didnt say she smells like urine, i said she has the energy of someone who smells like urine § im told that wearing my Denim kimono to the oscars will probably destroy racism and sjw in one feel swoop § and every one always says im a fucking Moron for leaving my dms open . https://t.co/J0yvEEVa1P § for like 8 months i thought covid was one of those joke diseases where you ask "what's covid" and the other guy tells tou to suck his nuts § based on the level of rhetoric ive seen, Its almost as if all the girls on this site actually WANT bit coin (BTC) to fail. There i said it . § Its mueeller time #TheElection § Im not playing games with your ass. Anser my god damn emails or i will fuck up your world § just invented a new type of posting while your were all running around on here. ENjoying your little whack off sessions? Dont care didnt ask § tired of all hullaballoo what soever of jareds fucked foot long § i hate it when my ass is "over tea kettle" § https://t.co/10SkMRG2L3 § the amount of faves your post gets = what your IQ is at that pount in time. this is called the beethoven equation § 2021 is more of a Dick Show than 2020. i mean the writers of the eseason finale of 2021 are smoking weed. Thats how fucked it is § what if Netflix was Real Life #justMythoughts § im having my BALLS CUT OFF!!! just for liking cambridge analytica § im taking a sledgehammer to the bimbofication of gamers and the assumption that just because im a gamer i only fuck with out condoms § https://t.co/xPGlu1Oa4i § heads up all . my "powered by Groupon" car magnet has fallen off of my rear bumper, possibly due to a Polar Event § might get mad at harassment of Tech Companys and post some shit about how nobody believes in smiling anymore. You never see any one smiling. § ever y movie ever made before 1950s is named like "the Gal with the $100 Pussy" § ˜…˜…˜… FUNNY ! Dog eating a used condom ! ˜…˜…˜… § Ass big on my story § scrolling through 900,000 emails calling me a hideous cock sucker to find a benihana coupon i thought i saw like a week ago § my belief is the classic "Pimp" ,in so far as a guy who dressses ostentatiously and walks around addressing his "Hos", is deserving of Jail. § girls will be like "oh big govt is orwell now" while having their DMs behind a totalitarian paywall & if we dont talk about that were fucked § unpopular opinion : only the popular opinions are any good https://t.co/IYwQ8L8Bd2 § "you gotta give em a show" - merv griffin § what is should be the name of my production Company § beer just beer . cracik the lid off that fucking shit § jobs are under seige § bull shit https://t.co/Gb5aiZ6Dhd § ohhh no!!! our nations Value's are under attack !! https://t.co/TIFrpGg8kV § you dress like fred flintstone and your opinion to me is worth dog dick § (banging on ex wifes front door dressed as a cop) open up. the citibank social media team says im Valid § oh this hits § how about instead of drop the ball on new years we drop the damn gas prices for onve § why dont you ever see the news reporting on the GOOD variants of covid?? § Guess ill go eat dog shit then and get worms in my legs like that guy in taiwan. § please remember--if the holidays are a difficult time for you, if you feel left out or forgotten from the celebration, then go Fuck your self § you think im gonna let a guy named "Poop and pee Stan" into my private group chat? "It's just not happening baby" § theyre donating all the expired vaccines to some very thirsty dogs at the kennel and i think thats something nice for once § just shaking my head and smilling...this shit is so Myers-Briggs § from now on every one call him Doanald J Poop and if enough people do it he will be forced to reopen fudd ruckers § pissed off; going out in my front yard to pretend to choke on a candy bar and see if any of my neighbors give a shit § the boeing 737 max is not necessarily "Bad", it will simply weed out the world's weakest pilots and make the movie Top Gun into real life § my wife has illegally divorced me for listening to thw "splish splash i was taking a bath" song too much § My face when, some one tries to tell me that I am not the inventor, and sole proprietor , of "The Ass Meme" https://t.co/Sc31yHOYeZ § "At long last, society has shown its Ass." - Dril § https://t.co/7OBwMPZuUg § i wont stop tweeting wonderwoman opinions until all cool & funny people are ran off this site and i can post my

psoriasis scars w/o judgment § considering various theorys of “Dark IQ” which is a sick & twisted version of IQ that can be really high even if your normal IQ is very low § big gov shut down tomorrow “U Know What That Means” Jacking off: LEGAL get your jacking off paraphernalia ready its gonna be a Barn burner § ^^^^^^^^^^^^^ Found The Mother FUCKER who thinks Blowing up RVs is good......................... § ive decided that the idea of “Baths” sucks. yeah i really want to spend an hour laying down next to my toilet. stupid ass. Suck off me § Dumb. § if you think blowing up an rv and injuring 3 people is good UnFollow my ass § https://t.co/7JCDndbrpk § celebrating the demise of Racism by watching the snickers commercial where mr bean eats a snickers bar and turns into an asian guy § new concept “Jeans City” will figure out more info and put it here later § https://t.co/DBVsuJE6EQ § you may “use my tweet as a joke” but im not responsible if you get beaten up/ arrested for it https://t.co/UqrBh3TwkW § give me 2000 you pedophile kisser’s https://t.co/kEURRxOgWX § every time you use a toilet you’re letting everyone who has ever used that toilet before shit up your ass § some of my followers are going to take a fat shit in the toilet within the next few hours. And that’s ok . § i can think of at least 100 numbers higher than that § the next stimulous check should be whatever your IQ is (100 iq = $100) dont like it suck my dick § https://t.co/DkZIytozt1 § Im not going to lie, it sucks shit that the ICU capacity is 0% but Im thinking they can squeeze me in for a tad if i raise enough of a fuss, § cant go 2 seconds without someone trying to tell me piss is good. if piss is so good then why do they pay guys to mop it up?? go read Theory § yeah i started twitch streaming but i do it offline so my dumb ass followers cant shriek at me while im doing it. 30 year old children. Pigs § “ $600 is bad” Yeah listen up nomb nuts if 600 is so bad then why dont you sl;ap a stamp on it and deliver it straight up your Ass. § Day of Forgiveness: whilst you go about the holiday season, please today take time to Forgive a content creator who has yelled at you before § im 90% sure that Weed is a real druvg and not just some shit my friends on here make jokes about § Fuck Back Better § -ape eating lizard - dog eating giant snail - centipedes eating human hand - and many more § we asked 100 angels from heaven what their IQs were and the results will drain your Nuts § fully come at me with your bull shit, catch me in the Wrestling Ring and 100% show me how much of a sick fuck i am § somebodys gotta do it!!!!!!!!!! § “Are we having FUN yet ??” - DRIL 2021 § i ve centered my brand for 2021 by:
-watching a dog give birth - expanding mind using exotic new beer types
- reconceptualizing the “ -WORD” § Porno W. bush § dont know where to get my Tech reviews since BobTechman was banned after being forced to show his penis in resposne to a harassment campaign § we hold all the cards. weve spent 20 years of our lives honing our craft. if enough of us post “Boo” at the dow jones, the shit will plummet § i was spending my PTO from the fake raybans factory getting Stabbed in washington dc while you were all busy looking at dicks in cyber punk. § You will never have sex, Dr. Pussy. We’ve all tried. Its impossible . Step down from your gilded twoer. Accept your station or perish. § Dr Pussy . I could give you so much more than a woman ever could. The gift of Laughter, the Privilege of High-Level engagement. Your loss § Hmm @DrPussy kisses up to yet another Girl acct, while continuing to ignore my invitations to riff in replys. Guess ill go eat dog shit Huh! § Ive been stepped on more than every bug on the universe and still i get back up & put out 1000 stupid fucking posts every day. And still. § my followers are giving me something nice for Christmas and its called “Shallow Judgement” and “Lack of character” and “vulgar Aggression” § you only iron once per day? you want to walk around looking like a guys nut sack? come to macys looking like that and youll lose some teeth § there are mother fuckers in this life that will “Take the L” but Most refuse to “Take the pLedge of alligeance” § 5g sucks dog shit . i could not even download a dogs ass with this crap § if you got covid 19 do

not interact with any damn posts of mine and hit the God damn road you nasty sewer animal mouth kissing mother fucker § for the first time in human history you can now set Budweiser as your default internet browser § another smart aleck here to ratio my ass........... § We All Have That Friend Who Fucking Sucks § This man who got plastic surgery to look like beavis will change everything you know about life for 1000 years . #INSPIREMe § Fuck yourself if youre not going to be nice about this § dont know what this is but im protected from it also § dollars, peso,s you name it, money is loved by all, and today is Money's birthday. post your favorite amount of money #HappyBirthdayMoney https://t.co/vCxM3e8Me5 § protected from all hater energy https://t.co/NM7K0Xamql § girls love it when i cure their depression using my intelligenct brain § ladys this is the Commander. i order you to post your Pussy Number pronto https://t.co/cNEi9o0TEm § used to be the only thing women had to jack off to was the movie" the Full monty." (1997) Now they can jack off to our posts § "Will You Commit To The CareFree Live Or Die Brand" Yes sir "Are U A Sick Enough Fuck To Get Covid On Puropse & Drive The Fans Nuts" Yes sir § waking up from a month long k2-induced coma and immediately apologizing to every POC for liking the Tasmanian Devil cartoons for some reason § when someone tells me i dont know true pain i remind them of the time SirGamestop tried to brew his own IPA and gave all the boys Botulism § lets say hypothetically i was gifted the otto warmbier poster by a DPRK emissary. will they let me sell it on ebay? or will ebay fuck my ass § yeah lets ruin a mans posting carreer just to look "Cool" in front of our friends, all while smoking Pot and thinking that bullying is good. § if i go to jail for telling the truth then what ever. i'll just win the favor of every prison gang with my realistic method of saying things § id like to grab each of you by the ankles and dip your entire screaming head into a bucket of honey, everyone Ratios me, its all a setup § Bacoun. That is all #YourdailySmile #MediaBrand § its Time to euthanize me § every day i get 1000 messages from my followers tell me i can SUCK DICK and FUCK MY SELF!! because i dont have the check mark § SnookeredByFraudsters666 § pleased to report that my odds of having sex have dropped to 0 after my latest and greatest Grievance Thread § as soon as i figure out if taxationw ithout representation is good or bad, politics is fucking finished § attention Boris_Gunblade; regarding getting that "having aids money" , i do not know what you meant by that. please respond to text message § theres one teen that wont be invited to the teen choice awards this year. covid 19 #CanHeSayThat § i see someone post a picture giving their dog a tiny birthday cake and think you see that? thats my tax dollars going towards that bull shit § i give my guinie pigs "HEROIN" it CALMS them DOWN § just down loaded all 15 episodes of frank tv in divx blue ray 1080p up on the big screen if any girls are reading this https://t.co/5WXwUeKd8k § https://t.co/Wg9jig4rfk § every where i go in this so-called thing called "society" people either want to kick my ass or give me $1000 or put me down like old yeller § cyber Monday is now Suck-Me-Monday, no further question your honor § i have faith that some one (preferably from New York) will soon explain to me why this post is good § everyone less mentally ill than me is Privileged, everyone more mentally ill than me is Toxic, everyone equally mentally ill to me is Cool § the best thing i ever found at work while disassembling old desks was a poem my former co-worker had written about the Super Bowl § elon if youre reading this please get back to me about my idea for inventing a $900 hot dog that tastes like shit. thank you § looking at some posts about "Cum" while frowning and generally making a face § just read the wikipedia article for "Mindfulness Based Cognitive Therapy" while you were on here scrolling through miles of puerile dog shit § my friend who works at twitter told me the next thing everyone will get mad at is celebs being forced to provide unpaid game show labor § i will eventually drop the phone in the toilet by mistake. its inevitable. the question is if there will be a big shit in there when i do it § do not be a stupid ass in my life. do not clown-style me § look at what youve done. you messed around and you turned the beetle bailey wiki into shit § americans the time is now for us to unite against COVID19. we must all come together and say "Oopsydaisy" over and over again until it stops § give me $100 if you think the guy who siad "Dumb ass" a lot on that 70s show would make a better president than any teletubby § nobodys telling me where i should donate 6000 cigarettes. nobodys telling me where theyll do the most help. So i guess ill just smoke them § "Having drama is the stupidest shit on earht" - Drew Brees § "in year 3000 every chair in the house will become a toilet"- ben franklin § the only blue check i want is a check for $1000000 that happens to be the color blue § forcing comcast to give us internet service without allowing them to completely blast our asses with datacaps is basically old timey slavery § me and the boys chipped in and orchestrated a fake 9/11 that you can easily prevent and become a national hero (fake 9/11 becomes real) oops § in the year 2021 grain will be stored in computers instead of silos and so many people are gonna look so god damn stupid § many people are finding out that despite millions of years of evolution the human body was not designed to get run over by cars § Think i might mix my dishrag up with my bowling ball rag and get some diseases that only dogs usually get § reading 10000 posts a day has provided me great insight into thr cultural impact of the Philosophical Mind, and has also given me Morgellons § day of healing challenge: Try being racist for a day if your sjw, and if youre racist try being SJW. This is the "Day of Healing Challenge". § every hatch back owner fantasizes about putting the seats down and throwing a towel on top of them and sleeping on the towel like a dog § when the dow hits 30000 it means you get $30000 every time th e libor scandal happens , so, a lot of people will be thinking thats good § facing resistance from wikipedia in removing the article that says i have an ear infection as it is very difficult to verify that i do not § shit heads who worsen everyones life, lady whos immune to piss smell, man named "Mr Dick Tip" who i have no concern of--all trying to Fuck me § i have seen every episode of agents of shield and i am ready to whip deep state in the penis § what if Jar head met Dunkirk § Congrats. Ive just put your ass on the doucebag list. § looking at a picture of poop chart that has different kinds of pictures of poop on it to find out if i have any diseases § let year 2020 become the year of Boys . Because men are out there changing peoples lives every day and simply they do not give a fuck § Hmm i wonder which restaurant will become the new mcdonalds, after mcdonalds goes out of business for performing coupon scams against me § ive been searching for videos on how to humanely execute a captured butterfly, and all i found was SCAMs § you tube is now officially named "Ignorance tube," due to the many proverbial ass kickings i have receieved there § trying to imagine the kind of guy who would donate to a presidential campaign like a month after the election so i can worship him as a god § trying to make my penis look more realistic with oils. balms and such § if you can smell your own balls that means you have corona virus . bad news for all you Stupid mother fuckers on here § with. a genuine content creator § might leave dms open for another 6 years in case any more gorgeous women want to try starting some Very unfulfilling long distance romance.. § should i learn Letters first? or choose the path of Numbers? a queston every baby must ask it self § im going to perler where you arent marched out on a pike just for posting pics of your barbeque setup in the group chat § im the guy who was not sold on Jack Ass until they made it 3d § i agree. mindfulness is some good shit. hold on, someones honking their car horn at my house and i have to go outside and kick their ass now § turning in my badgen gun... § if big tech keeps loading their apps with features that i can accidentally post my dick on, i will have no choice but to enter crisis mode . § your white § your white § Q: Should I give my dog my last name? A: Absolutely not. Giving your dog your last name confuses it & dangers the integrity of the household § i am not a ho § Watchinh the news https://t.co/ajKdVmPKRD § for every shit comment i receive, i will be doing 1 push up. the trolls shpuld be Very fucking careful lest they grant me unlimited power § if you say shit like "Basinga" they give you a TV show.... if you say opinions that are true , you get the Executioners blade . -EpicWayne § walking around wearing a sandwich board sign that says "Kick my ass" and subjecting the masses to raw unfiltered journalism § Why? Are people upset with me? Are they posting lies about me in the group chats? Without letting me defend myself? Who's posting the lies? § i shou;ld be allowed on the roof of any building § Hah, yes. i do consider myself somewhat of the most god tieir troller who has ever lived. ive fooled over 1000 people into kicking my ass, § im a husband , i am a lover , i am a gamer, i am a Slave, im a nit wit, im a goalie, but above all else, im a Koch Brother § if you do not think garfield metaphorically "ate shit" when they closed his restaurant down then you are not looking at the facts § there was once a man-- beloved & cherished by all... until he was unfairly chased away, by the dip shit brigade. and that man was named "Me". § miss when trending topics were shit like #NationalMustardDay instead of links to articles about how eating chipotle cures racism in rats § when they asked Ben Franklin "Sir, through Cup and Coin, does pleasure Portend the folly of Man?" mr. Franklin smiled and said simply "Beer" § girls love rolling around in their sleep with long nails and waking up thinking every scratch on their body was caused by their dead grandma § if i had a name like "Tommy Tuberville" id go fuck my self § "Me and a lot of my friends are starting to think that this Covid-19 business is a complete goof. A rat job." - Spider man § @GeraldoRivera @realDonaldTrump i just had a phone call with him too and he said the opposite of all that shit and called me Gay § garfield eats Shit § getting the daily presidential briefing and its just shit like "we banned Weed because it makes people too smart" and "Mozart smoked weed" § why should i give two shits of an ass what you think of my post. what are you, the day time emmys?? § mount everest emergency diaper bra - what this husband did will shock you § "if youre a dumb ass youre no friend of mine" - The dumb ass killer § thank you . i have nuked his ass https://t.co/sU8f2a6cdb https://t.co/o6RUhH-6bg1 § Its not in the spirit of star wars to do that § if you like this video of a monkey eating m&ms you will certainly enjoy this video of a lizard tearing up a rat with its mouth § None of the characters in star wars should show their penis. Thats not what movie fans want to see. § going to buy some goofy bug eyed glasses & drink poison until i look 80% more sickly/ weak and ask random girls if they need a Suger Daddy § https://t.co/p3gmZuN3s4 § did something happen with the votes § i would pay a group of scienttists $10000000 to fool a man into believing in santa until the age of 80. lets get it done § i never said "ounch" , i would never say "ounch", and if i did say the word "ounch" it was becaus ei was trying to type the word "Lunch" § before pushing psychic civil wars, the news used to talk about guys named like "Crap man" who would poop in 100 public urinals a day somehow § open literally any web page before opening your mouth § "the human brain is simply just a computer. And not a journalist alive will tell you this." - the Dril account § it's not good for the dilbert guy to come on here and say hes going to Bull Breed my wife with his Superior Spunk. i dont care if hes 200 iq § on the horn with nabisco slavery engineering solutions and hooters world Bank(HWB) aa we speak, might even contact "Super Nintendo" well see § i will not let you poop the stately office . i will never use the code "Rudy20" for $20 off orders over $100. i will not dm GIRLS § you have not looked at the facts and you have the same IQ as a babys IQ. and thats why you have low follower. § oh everyones trying to be cute. Everyones trying to put on a little show, posting unauthorized information about my penis § getting word that the election is now considered "Fucked" by the state attorney after a man reportedly let his dog lick the voting machine § Dont look at it if youre just going to say ass to it. § WOW: BitO-fAWankHaver assassinated DiaperHubby in his adult sized crib at 0400 hours and blew him up with a hundred missile s in his deathbed § #Vote https://t.co/WjnGJJY9z9 § Joe the plumber- your silence duringt his pivotal moment of election speaks magnitude of the word "Cowardace". i regret voting for you bitch § enjoying some fairly darkweb shit https://t.co/tG9FkVREoK § @Shell im wiping my ass with shop rite bags § every one should donate their pets to the zoo or the dog kennel, get the animals out of the house until all this covid mess is figured out § i would pay $99 for an app thay reminds you to drink one icecold beer every 20 minutes § reminder: if youre a Judge or any elected official theres still time to throw peoples votes in the trash for no reason https://t.co/yuppHwaNBH § My Sucked Off Life § my "happy Halloween " wishes have already been sent out so if you did not receive one then you are Fucked. § @ MayorOfLA @LADOTofficial THANK YOU SIR ! § yes there is a hemorrhoid sub reddit and yes it is full of guys somehow obtaining 4k resolution pics of their ass holes and posting them § "Some people on here are more interested in Public selfies, than public safety " -- Oh?? Can He Say That?? § taking the high road and waiting until after the election to call tekken chauncey a "HO" § your mission is to get laid on gmail. delete all other apps, do not talk to me until you fuck. your mission is to fuck and suck on gmail § i think if tthe country got annihilated by nukes id "Lay low" for a bit and "Wait it out" § if you threaten to kick my ass or kill me you will get BLOCKED. Thats just how it is. Enjoy not being able to read my posts you dip shit § quagmires dance but hes paralyzed https://t.co/wyFbip22iP § the tongue is the human body's most powerful tooth § food of the loom "big" under wear 90% off $0.89 one time offer For the fans. § i opened my notes app for the first time in 5 years and the only thing i found was some shit that says "mr feed bag 2007" https://t.co/ikmC-7jIz1X § you gotta realize if youre a roach or any kind of bug its already game over for your ass. you look like a little pice of poop walking around § "jobs are back on the table" - @ Dril § @TruthPointDWR 1) do not say this shit 2) please post all content with the hash tag #TruthPointQuibiNow as you have been prevoiusly instructed § @RepClayHiggins my wife has the gift of suching my shit completely off § thinking about my coffee mug that says "Guys who collect beanie babies know how to fuck better than guys who dont like beanie babies" on it. § stupid god damn MORON!!! fucking BITCH https://t.co/szsJrXFQrV § saw a bumper sticker "My other car is baby Yoda's dick." And this is what passes for classic comedy routines these days . § haters are my God § "Just simply my posts." § ignoring all phone calls from rickgamecube and metal gear Eric so they can't talk me out of getting fake bullet wounds tattooed to my chest § i am now ready to share my thoughts on the guy who took his penis out of his pants after screaming "Ohhh!! Ohhh!!" on the zoom call. § instead of scoring touchdowns the nfl it seems is more interested in scoring "Shit downs" § due to my Troll-Crushing journalistic standards i am obliged to say some shit about how the original "Pope meme" , is Roman Catholicism § PROSECUTION: Is it true, that on the evening of Sept 3rd, 2006, you posted the word "Jeams" ME: (swallowing cyanide pill) I dont recall . § astrally projecting my brain into antifa head quarters and memorizing their combat patterns is the easiest shit i have ever done in my life § get her ass!! Protect me sir § listening to a man on the train tell me about how a cardboard toilet paper tube feels 100% like a pussy if you run it under the sink first § micropenised galoot bleeds out in a 7-11 after smashing glass hot dog case with bare hands and shows his ass on the news by mistake § people these days would rather have faith in Homer Simpson , than, the Honor System § massive back tattoo that says "Sucked Off 8-12-2006" § They locked it because you fucked around and fond out § any ladys here want too fuck an 170 I.Q. Undecided Voter ????? § yes, https://t.co/gDLdfhoryA § i have the worst followers in the world. Dumb. § nice to know some one cares about me....

https://t.co/LoJRdUlk3K § the headless horseman sucks shit/ he wouldnt last 2 minutes in hollywood. he cant get me here § im not going to shut the fuck up until all of my friends, and enemies..... are big time rich § netflix cuties is as political as it is bald-faced stupid assed aka i give it zero stars and "my god have mercy on your soul" -billy madison § does any one know what happened to this guy, https://t.co/YplfsLjkeM § all correspondence with Mastergamer will go directly through me because i am his lawyer and his friend § they should invent toilet paper that you can throw in the Trash instead of the toilet § Do My Posts Help You? Am I A Good Person? Do You Think Im Nice § i actually got diaper rash from searching another guy's used diaper for wallets, but dont let that stop you from stigmatizing me § https://t.co/V7WK5eyqqm Not going to work today just staying home doing intense Meditation / Reflection out of respect for this bull shit § your from 9gag your from reddit your from fark .com and its no surprise to see your stupid Ass in the comments sections kissing my NUTs § thinking about a "Cock Ring" for the neck that strangles all the blood into your brain and gives you what is essentially a mental erection § does it feel good to throw around your online clout to causev pain to others?? you Dopey bitch?? § i do not watch the snl show (Too crass) but i do enjoy reading the episode summaries that they put in the newspaper for some reason § if i was a secret service guy & certain things started happening id simply use the president as a human shield and high tail it out of there § (crying) nobody respects me because im a Content Creator!! every one thinks im a pussy!! i want to process lumber!! § im a Diplomat's Nephew and im tired of pretending um not one § your dirty § i would rather go fuck my self than read one more post on the bird websitw § im tired of everyone saying that pinocchio turning into a real boy was a good thing. it was a demons trick § becoming accepting and calm of other people having lifestyles of having the wrong opinion about shit § computer show me an animated picture of bugs bunny eating a huge watermelon in a way thats comical but not racist § just because im following the pilot's orders and putting ym seat belt on without raising a stink does not mean i forgive him for doing 9/11 § the Economy is changing the way people think about Culture..... § time for a BATH https://t.co/GK4HNKYhNF § id love to get attacked by a bird. id love for a bird to try to fight me. id love to smash it to bits with my bare hands. § GOD: Im getting quite aged in my late years; and I need someone else to be president of heaven Donald R. Trump: My lord... RBG: (Applauding) § thank you for liking the "Real men of genius" beer commercials. Were bringing them back in an attempt to suppress the 2nd American Civil War § https://t.co/n0YGypHFnh § NEWSDESK: POTUS oversized diaper is NOT "funny," or "Epic", and neither is the tiny stream of poop dribbling out of his beleaguered ass hole § Peoplw are saying this § these are the original fort nite https://t.co/rgVgC2uHPl § they should hang these up inside of the mcdonalds, and that's the highest praise I've ever given anything in my life § as the least funny person alive, its my job to come on here and tell people which current events arent funny and get MY ASS KICKED!! § "just Genius shit ." - Thugwanker § bee man vs column full of bees https://t.co/v7s6Ln3WPW § I want a video game thats just a 3d dog barking very loud in my face § "we witness now the Death of Light. A Cowar'ds millennia. Shadows dancing upon the Graves of our lives" - Diaper pounder § @TruthPointDWR i could crush you instantly § just for fun: if you search camp town races you get a video of like 40 guys in black face with youtube comments like "Love the energy! Wow" § Camptown races I mean. § when the mother fuckers wrote "Yankee Doodle", i bet they thought we were still going to give a shit about the word "Doodah" in 2020, § might buy some $200 japanese steak knives & instantly ruin them by using them to saw through the clamshell packaging of my new shower radio. § (reporter following me into my car) Sir sir. You look like shit. Whys your head look wet. Sir § i can telli f youre a drunk driver or not just by reading 2 of your posts § urine is not sterile. it has piss in it § hate it when i slip up while changing a roll of toilet paper and the spring loaded holder fires the cardboard tube straight up my ass hole § every one on the computer has undergone a villain arc where they stop jacking off for 2 months and go mad because it didnt fix their anxiety § trying to parallel park my 1992 lincoln town car stretch limousine in front of game stop and getting Honked at § being a dumb ass is bad enough, but being a dumb ass, in 2020??? You fucked up big time § @TruthPointDWR Dont say fuck on this accout § people only think wizard of oz is good because they want to fuck thr tin man, if they didnt want to fuck the tin man they wouldnt like it § every celebrity on earth has succumbed to the Corona Virus? Wow!! What a scoop!!! § dont know how they did it, but Bloomberg Opinion found a way to post directly into the Whats Happening sidebar, making them effectively God. § before i Smoke, i want to read an article about if smoking is facing a crisis in which smokers are making smoking too much “About them” § “oh youre sad because a judge died? thats so adorable” i say as i effortlessly list off 100 dead judges from simply my memory § how do i make my timeline just this https://t.co/uRzG7KZTIo § im thinking of making it my “Main move” , to eat a huge plate of nachos and have the worst sex of my life right after § air purifier in my apartment going fully nuts after cooking my delicious dinner. sorry you hate Food bitch § looks like my posts have solved the covid crisis § stop for a moment and think about the most realistic Vagina youve ever seen in your life... § my wife thinks im a Failure. Prove her wrong by getting this 100 likes § venus sucks shit. if they find life there it’s going to be a very small man curled into the fetal position yelling “FUCK THIS” § @TruthPointDWR ,you will never smoke § why dont you come to wheare i work and slap the dick out of my mouth bitch § you only post in pervert language now § any day now: our favorite posters will stop hiding in private chat rooms and start making america Smile again § @JuddPDeere45 @WhiteHouse @AriFleischer cant wait for this shit. Im a real sick fuck § (hearing about a guy who died) wow thats like 0.0003 9/11s § a guy who calls him self “service animal toucher” is going around trying to trick people into licking elevator buttons. stay safe all. § why turn myself in to the police.. when I can turn myself into the police https://t.co/dmId4ehIDN § The video games & childrens tv show industrial complex has pooped its own ass once again and made 2020 the year of the Actual Bitch . § IM GOING TO TURN OFF MY AD BLOCKER FOREVER -- JUST TO BE NICE !!!! § 1) never look at my replies 2) Im not trying to fuck the weather lady Im just trying to make her cum in her pants on live tv § if i become too radicalized by the death of Fuddruckers promise youll send me gentle reminders not to spread coronna virus on purpose § my dick and my ass look like theyre from 2 different races of people. i typed this in the status box 14hrs ago & im just pressing submit now § @TruthPointDWR unfollow me § suck off my ass § fuck sars § do not piss my ass off. do not goof around with my ass § oh this? just a little something i enjoy looking at in my house every day https://t.co/a8iXuuGUHN § i was already boycotting disney mulan because its for children, but now that im pissing off hong kong policemen (??) thats the cherry on top § watching a human interest pieice about a deaf guy who has a photographic memory of every shit hes ever taken § @TruthPointDWR meet this https://t.co/LpvW519YqY § up your fuckig ass dude. Shut up https://t.co/pizSblJlxz § just jacked off in real life while you were busy downloading hentai of the old woman who lives in a shoe at 56k § rodney gamerfield, Dr. Gameslove, and gamesbond007 walk into a bar, say “Fuck off id rather be gaming,” Then they leave § wife is sad because we had to remove all doorknobs from our dreamhome since they were at the exact perfect hieght to go up my ass by mistake § you can post shit like “my roommate put the addams family theme on 9hrs a day” no one will ever question it. you will get the medal of honor § @THEHermanCain whoever the fucks running this account now needs to unblock me from it ASAP. “Enough is enough” § nobody with less followers than me should be allowed to block me.   Thats fucked up § walmart Sucked me § i love shit that has a “sense of humor “ § puutting shit on my dating profile like “i will never lie to someone who’s nice to me” and “i wont fuck you if you don’t enjoy Movies” § if every person on earth killed 1000 bugs every day we would have no more bugs #noBugs #stopBugs § pranking my pud § @TruthPointDWR suck my dick in balls § PissMyPants USA LLC § 2020 is all about the Mentality lifestyle § “i will never respond to a dm unless its a girl sending it. i will keep my feed tidy. i will betray anyone my followers want me to betray” § the only thing supplying my dog shit soft serve brain w/ dopamine anymore is my favorite intellectual properties getting “Surprisingly Dark” § @ TruthPointDWR You cared enough to shit . § looking at tom dixons mens plum wine cooler https://t.co/Vbkf28Y6I8 § Ellen Pledges to Gradually “PHase Out” Cameras in Employee Restrooms in Highest IQ Move to Date: Here’s What To Know § hoping my favorite brands e mail me some more stupid shit today § your little ass wouldnt last 2 seconds on my page § starting an NRA for Turner classic movies § Bill gates has so many followers that if he accidentally posts a picture of his spread ass hole its not even worth his time to delete it. § -computer 3d generated regis - the $1000000 you know and love -one of the life lines is that they bring out a big hoagie for you to eat § couple of mob guys disposing of a body by tossing it into the aquariums penguin enclosure “these boids are eating good tonight” § right now theres guys covering their dicks in bird seed to trick birds into sucking them. and youre all here talking about post office... § Netflix has once again showed their ass by proving once and for all that the ceo of it is Michale Jackson . § do it you coward § @TruthPointDWR shut the FUCK up § vp announcement the same day they announce Cosby Tetris (2007) no longer receiving eshop support? nice cover up § the police report described a “Cartoonishly diapered” man § sub way has just announced that kid rock is the new jared and that when kid rock dies they will make the jared after him a black jared. § austin powers men cut (only men scenes) . mkv § crapping my self at food 4 less and making $1000000 per second from people sharing pictures of it § ok mr honda dealer lets get down to brassed tacks. U dont wanna waste my time, i dont wanna waste yours. now; CAN i jack off in your toilet, § if you dont post anything for a month and i can’t find the reason why, i just assume you died and got buried in someones yard like a pet § Met a guy on here the other day named “Mr do not follow my ass”. Well with a name like that you better beleieve i`d be taking that advice. § Oh mate. Oh mate. Youre properly jordached. Youre off that bullwinkle mate § the dj just said he ran a man over with his car and did a hit and run 4 year ago and hes crying now § “I have Watched the Bud Dwyer suicide video over 1000 times.” - iconic Mickey Rourke - InfluencePedia.Go § “Sucked Behind Bars” ”George H.w. bush bimbofied me and sucked off me”   “Snowman fucked me” ”Locker Room Fucked by snow man” § go to www. info .men to learn how to recite the Men’s Prayer and help put a gun in covid19’s mouth § https://t.co/AaJ8415oXE § i have received in my life 2 Teen Choice Awards for the work i have done with poisons § i have been strategically poisoning myself to make my dick smaller and more cone-shaped so it can fit into condoms easier § well were back to 1000 americans choking to death daily on this virus and ithought the time line could use a quick smile. Thats all § all im saying it that this guy wore the mask before covid https://t.co/NIoGeMoccS § epic ; supreme court rules nabisco is legally allowed to label their products as “Homemade” after forcing the employees to live at the factory § if youre making a movie and you kill off a beloved character like bat man or bugs bunny you ought to be charged with Murder. No more excuses § @TruthPointDWR please have the fucking decency to unfollow Mr. Larry King and Sir Walter Cronkite before you go to post shit like this. § sorry i can’t write any posts or look at my emails today. i got kennel cough from eating a bad pear § @Hooters i go there to get infected with ring worm on purpose § Ahh damn it . I fucked up and accidentally bought the newspaepr with the eye holes in it again and saw something i wasn'tsupposed to § when i go to hooters i do not want to look at the girls there, just my newspaper that does not have any eye holes cut into it what so ever § all you peoples posts are "Scooby Doo Ass" § CNN should put a little "Devil face" next to all the bad, or upsetting articles on their site. Who likes this? Who thinks this would be fun? § one thing the gamer world is certainly agreeing of, is that halo infinite is sure to be the highest numbered halo game yet § -all poison animals Destroyed (snakes scorpions) -reduce spending/waste by making the Oscars an olympic game -a Hollywood sign in every town § just got my new jeans in the mail and the trolls are sweatting like a bird at the kfc factory § 100 bladder exercises to increase your Max Piss § advising my client alan dershowitz not to become host of the new tv show on g4 gamers network "Show Me Ya Pussy" § which of you is ``WACKIN OFF`` on here tonight............. § cant wait to hop on the pc and look at more juvenile barnum and bailey shit , aka posts. § SickFuck Productions § mc donads big hamburger no tomato on rye § Ive read so many posts about how to be nice on here, its no wonder that I make such a good living as the CEO of the New York Times . § if your car is this. Fuck yourself https://t.co/ddI8HIdKyl § oh no!!! what if we lose??? what if they blow up the New York Stock Exchange and force us all to wear Womens pantys?? Help!! Help!! https://t.co/UmhtgS0g8a § i know times are tough but rtry to give a Like and retweet to my posts if you are able to. if not, thats ok also. Fuck you § if you get popular on you tube you make $100000 a month. if you get popular on twitter you get your shit caved in by robbers every day § ok so twitter can just freeze all the verified accounts at once but when someone says my yard looks like shit theyre Suddenl;y power-less... § @TruthPointDWR unprofessional. go fuck your self and sotp being such a little BITCH § id rather go fuck my self than like a post § if you dont post your IQ at the beginning of every reply to me you will be blocked like a street dog § piss hitting toilet sfx piss hitting urinal sfx only on spotify § my followers are STUPID as FUCK !!! they are all on CRANK !!! they hate ALL my shit!!! § imagining a real dumb lump of shit guy, like 55 years old, reading some article aobut jada pinkett smith in his squalid office and smiling § i have been sitting in my computer chair repeating to myself the phrase "The god father of posts" for the past 9 hours . § i see that digimon otis has become emboldened enough to begin posting again., likely due to the normalization of that sort of thing, § imagining my followers enjoying a beer named "Gangnam style: The beer" and cancelling all my posts for the evening due to being pissed off § trying to draft a tweet about how people arre getting too many tattoos of the cars from the cars movies without invoking Race § earning 100% completion rating in the latest game from the "SEX ADDICT" series by Piss-Realms, and hating every minute of it § yoiutube streamer famous for "Grandma Sucked Me Off" video series apologizes to his subscribers for pooping on the bus § the real kennedy assassinaiton was when jamie kennedy was assassinated verbally by gamers for not taking his e3 appearance seriously enough. § alright. wherever the dart hits on this map is wwhere im building my new Mosque. (dart hits wtc ground zero) Yikes! Uh oh § Q: mr bond this is your most fucked mission yet. you must obtain the Paedophile's Stone BOND: Ah, like old times? Q: Like old times mr bond § ladys i will not Fuck you if you smell like shit. look up darwin theory § Posting is the easiest shit ever and yet theres people on here with hundreds or thousands or millions of followers FUCKING IT UP § @AlanDersh Hello Alan this is your lawer speaking. I am advising you today to please keep posting this shit § cant wait for this Cunt to take us to mars; no Sjw, no Girls, just us boys sitting around in 55.9m sq miles of waste land, swapping MEMES !! § inventing a new type of cum by jacking off incorrectly § ever since i ve been told to put a shirt on in all my live insect unboxing vids my metrics have taken a piping hot Shit § gettting radicalized by bull shit metacritic review scores and making voodoo dolls of twitch girls for showing their ankles on stream § it must be said that with the way ur carrying on with your posts, most of u will never realize ur dream of becoming a United States Senator. § reading 70 iq posts about how bullying ghislaine maxwell makes us no better than the bad guy from the x-man movie and just nodding intensely § is that good or bad https://t.co/UwspFvpq3O § tired of pretending certain people have "some good ideas". i miss when all i had to do to fit into a social group was take Heroin constantly § i ask you, whos the real " Little Ho" ??? Me (for being a little Ho) or You (for not forgiving me for being a little Ho) § theyre in love with me they winked at me through the tv § chase bank is simply trolling by removing money from random peoples accounts, it's funny and ground breaking and if you get mad your a karen § as a Race-Minded simpsons fan it pains me to declare that korean animators have no right to draw pictures of black people, or vice versa § if i found out any poster here was havng sex id lose it. id ask "what business does a nasty mother fucker like you have with regards to sex" § tj maxx stands for trader joes maxx.. But yotre not allowed to say that anymore!!! Oh!!! § licking a cartoonishly large loollipop while unsuccessfully building a deck in my yard one-handed, saying "Fuck!" and "Shit!" occasionally § fast in furious 11: Beyond fucked fast in furious 12: fully Sucked § dont care. having a lot of views is selling out any way § some one needs to tell these guys out there flying planes with banners on them that nobody can read their shit § bashing my skull against the steering wheel while screaming in my car for an hour; then coming on here pretending to be a Mental Health Guru § this is gas lighing. ive read posts about this https://t.co/6wtyXhg4Nd § just found out im considered the "Bitch" of Ashley HomeStore and the employees there are instructed " ot to hear my demands" § wearing shoes makes you like 50 pounds heavier § im pleased to report that this is a Jeans account. § trying to take my barbell into the mens room ansd failing to get it through the doorway like a dog with a large stick § the fact i still post here despite people sending pics of my penis around is the greatest act of kindness in human history . Remember that § " Be the wife you want to be in the world. You have one life to grab it by the Nuts " - the Quote Pussy § wiping your ass is now officially Politics § in the yard, lying , on my back gripping my ankles wih my Rear end in the air yelling hurry!! Hurry! Spray the hose at my ass hole § floating in my above ground pool nude from the waist down wearing a shirt that says some shit like "i find your lack of wifi disturbing" § if you ask me many of Americans have been wearing the mask even before from covid 19. the mask i refer to is of course the clown's mask. § if you like this shit down load my incredible one time offer the only app that lets you spin the wheel of pussy for free no question asked § spiders need to stop building so many damn webs. that'd enough. you built too many now. § they have been calling it "PS5" because when i see it I piss 5 times. § thr greatest gaming console of all time, is tickle Me Elmo, because it changed the meaning of the word Games § " Trump Sucked Me " and " Trump Sucked Me... Again! " § "The jeans generation" § seeing a content creator who is confident in His posts, consistently Nailing it, makes the Numb skulls of this website shit their stupid ass § IDIOT: I would love to get trapped in some sort of wall and spin around faster and faster until pieces of my body slough off ME: Ok, no, § Boys are showing to much DICK on the time line... I come here to research Ethics and i am bombareded with 10000 human penis images daily § trapped in overturned police cruiser jacking off one last time before I get buerned alive over "Are you geting that nut sir. Over" Yes. over § dirty diaper stan ,,|,, Dumb ass ,,|,, $$$cashfreak$$$ >> support Vaginal energy || twisted Christ Figure || days since last stomach ache: 0 § guys who get off on being humiliated used to expose themselves at the grocery store or something. now they pretend to be journalists on here § the trolls will never admit it, but wells fargo has been knocking the fucking crap out of covid and police brutality, with their posts § mr. Drone Strike my Wife aka the six figure asexual here telling you now more than ever, Gamers have been given the short end of the diaper. § no skills, no brains, total pussy who looks like shit, sucking up and kissing ass until i get my corner office at the racist orphan refinery § it used to be you didnt need a degree to become a philosopher yo u could just say shit like "Beer is the Merry Soul's Companion" constantly § NEWSWIRE : former presideent George W bush filmed touching various fabrics, assessing their value, as the country Shits its Ass § the Heartlands been pinpointed to the town of Dick Licker, Oklahoma where the main thing they got is a museum that displays a real $100 bill § in solidarity with all of this crap going on, ive Poisoned my ass hole § the writiers of 2020 have pooped their pants on this one.„¢ © DRIL   more Netflix? yes please „¢ © DRIL § writing in "god Trumps racism" and walking out of the voting booth high-fiving the Good Cops with a visible load stain on my croch § i have been saiyng this for years now. Just look at the digimon otis account https://t.co/GgsDDrouVb § cant wait to win the civil war just by sitting on the computer and get a dumb ass cop butler as a reward § beware of my friend metal gear eric he is a scammer and a bimbo § "Reading your posts has made me a better person." Thank yo u. A lot of people tell me that, § resposnse to the NYT article calling gamers "Ho's" 1. gamers are not ho's. How dare you 2. if Walter Cronkite saw that hed shit in his grave § my new joke, which I foresaw getting over 100 likes in a dream, is referring to 9/11 as "The Devil's Dance" § covid virus can live inside of a beanie baby for 10 years #beanieBurn #Burnthem § brand accounts should do cool shit instead of sucking Ass. they should post their dick and say they had to do it because they lost a bet § |||||||||||||||||||||| |||||.......... 72% your Ass - Kicking is now downloading Mutha FUcka Stupid Ass § id like to tame them with my golf club a little bit https://t.co/2lIGVK4EE5 § i challenge my most hated Enemys to name a single chemical that exists naturally within a womens pussy. You cant do it § thank you for the Signal Boost . § every movie ever made is esxactly the same movie as the other movies, and they all deserve 2 stars from roger ebert § highly agreeable shit https://t.co/WmC8JKIX0j § i dont respect the cowboy life style any more and if you are doing cowboy shit you might as well be wearing a clowns outfit § budweiser queerspace § getting Sucked out of house and home § asking my financial advisor how to "Bet against america" after seeing someone get mad at someone else for doing it § world health organization apparently "too busy" to look at my idea for a backwards hospital gown that covers only the ass § why did the earth worm jim guy block me... cant handle the real shit § its apparent people arent taking these social distancing measures seriously. on my way to the gym i had 2 people suck my shit completely off § ME: id like to take this day to wish a happy mother's day... to my Father. SOCIETY: Huh ?!?! § you ever see one of those preserved bog men or mummies on the news and think " ow theres a guy who looks like he got an ass kicking" § hands Off my posts https://t.co/LJtHXIuj73 § And im not a sell out for having an above normal size dick either. Un tag me § My dick is above average size in real life you fucking animals. Do not say shit § pissing my self off thinking about a brand of beer called "Goofy Beer" and its slogan is "Goofy Beer: It makes your dick smaller" § taking my "Gamer medicine" (Games) § just when youre scrolling through the time line and you realize something so true that it pisses you off to the point you nearly crapped.... § discussing covid challenges with my Jeans strategist § saying "Looks like I struck a nerve ." in the gorup dm after posting "Pringles is white people doritos" and locking my account § https://t.co/ZRsH6X9sDi § @hooters2 you are my light line, my angel, my God Force. Let me show you the feeling of bodys touching each other. The dragon of life § #spon #Ad #corrupt-tion #SweetheartDeals https://t.co/eukiIzyrsi § FUCK the news!!! § Most Embararssing Shit Eaters Alive. Stupid Mother Fuckers Kiss The Nuts https://t.co/MqeqQn0uaa § my life flashes before my eyes and its mostly just me sitting on the toilet. i enter survival mode and begin instinctively wiping my ass § i will soon be assembling the LA Boys into my 1br apartment to watch every episode of Mind of mencia in order and show covid virus whos boss § a month ago everyone was scared thy were going to die so they immediately grabbed as much toilet paper as possible & wiped thier ass with it § very bad covid § every morning, looking at a holographic image of all my natural predators (pigs apes tigers dogs etc) to keep my head in the Game § getting smoked to crap by a big bomb bieng ridden by a man waving a cowboy hat around § pouring a beer into another beer because i once read of the concept of "Mixing Drinks" from a James Bond novel § ai which flawlessly simulates keys being jingled offers unlimited joy to infants and persistent vegetative twitter power users § dont mind me... im just a forgotten content creator from a bygone era, whose dick happens to be covered in aphids § please stop these posts saying im a "pimp". they are causing me trouble with family and police. i have never pimped in my life. im a mere ho § you cry during one car commercial and people label you as "guy who cries during car commercials" but Y'All aint ready to speak on That..., § blocked at 9999mph § looks to me like im the one being gang banged § sorry for funko politics § reality sets in that im " o longer funny," the dream of being Epicly quoted by funko pop owners for the rest of my life dies unceremoniously § @NYGovCuomo this sucks Ass sir § covid toe penis; can you get covid toe in penis. do blue markings on penis mean same thing as covid toes. covid penis real? when to call 911 § im a comedy Theorist now. waitll you see which seasons of family guy i can compare your posts to. youve only seen but a fraction of my power § 200k/yr media job where we all wear sweater vests, kiss each other & try to convince people biden is technically a "Molester" not a "Rapist" § posts are such damn shit, posts are so bad they are giving me covid Toes § tryinh to convince girls on here to sync all 655 episodes of "Hee Haw" with me, telling them its like SNL but nice § .@markZuckerburg twitter dms are broken agaain you ugly sack of stupid fucking shit. you incompetent freak § replying is second responding § "posting" is "first responding" § its shit head o' clock and everyones grabbing at my Nuts § oh youre gonna unfollow me now? just when the posts are getting Good? im sorry Your Majesty!! (Dick sucking motion) Eugh Eugh EUgh § marvel and dc universe should be one universe: Gods universe. § (monitoring TekkenChauncey's date) "I;ve been told i do a flawless impersonation of the N64 era Donkey Kong..." Hes blowing it. Im going in. § Donkey kong from "Donkey Kong" Mario from "Mario" They stand tall as the Loony Tunes of modern era, to besmirtch there names is unforgivable § tell it to my ASS!! § submitting my email address and clicking "yes" on massive amounts of promotional offers while choking myself § my reaction when people shit up my board https://t.co/4gjsGhonqr § when you post a picture of your hamburger in the group chat, your friends are likely taking that lunch data and selling it to Villains § dont pay mind of me. i am just a hound dogs old ass... § kim jong un Sir, we dont see eye to eye on many policy's. But I look forward to you recovering from being brain dead, so we can share a Beer § ive just gotten word that he drowned after getting slat water in his pussy § me and the boys charging through the streets carrying a massive battering ram headed for Mens big in tall store § putting twitter's famous Quality Filter on my shit until my entire feed is just lockheed martin saying "We are smarter than covid" § fuck restaurants making quesadillas like 1 inch thick, stuffed with crap falling all over the plate. whatre you trying to do, suck my Dick?? § half the posts these guys are making could perhaps be found in "Barney magazine" , or "Shit for babys magazine" § Enjoying my life https://t.co/rHHJghScPC § Stop looking at my posts § fuck your self. stop looking at my posts. taste a son of a bitchs ass. § diaper in place § every generation deserves at least 5 movies named "Spider Man 2" § WHOSE COCK DO I HAVE TO SUCK TO GET SOME DORSEY-CERTIFIED BLUE CHECK

MARKS AROUND HERE . WHOSE UGLY WIFE DO I HAVE TO FUCK § just had all my postmate deliverys cancel on me because they caught me posting about cum on here § he is lying. the reason he will never become twitch partner is because he runs his mouth nasty on there § sequestered shelter in place in the vip room of fatburger with 12 “lady’s of the evening” geiting my entire shit honked like a old car horn § i would not enjoy a second of it, but if a man achieved the fully-optimized load i would feel obligated to allow him to Bust it into my eyes § me and the most profound influencers of our time will soon “Bring back the chuck norris shit” in a display of raw contempt for our followers § all men between ages 46-62 run a newsgroup named “Bimbofied By Wife” that has pics of them handcuffed with bras stuffed down their throaot § LOOKS TO ME LIKE nobody cares what a crumpled up shit head like me has to say. this garbled crap eater... this Cocksuckered old dog...... § just heard it on the news that theyre gonna start using Crisper to breed dogs that look 100% like beautiful human women § lots of movies like to add jokes in there, as a bit of an easter egg § looking at the list of accounts I voluntarily follow and wishing this shit was more Tailored To My Interests § duhhh ok yes sir thank you sir https://t.co/zZNEXX3TW2 § the bright side to all this, is that everyone’s now forced to stay home and read my posts contemplating if america is “Ready to Laugh again” § and now im being unfollow brigaded by traitors who would gladly simply put my ass in the viper pit § Lord give me Coffee do change the things i have the power to change and Wine to except the things i want to https://t.co/vh6NFnwKjI § i remember shit from when back when people gave a Damn...... now the whoule damn world`s a penis § president reportedly found Spoofed on the bathroom floor, it is said that he had been repeatedly Lampooned during an hour long struggle, § please remember “RAT” - Repsect Above Trolling § i only look at comment count . § the way im talked to on here its a wonder i haven’t shit my own ass .... § calm down please . § sorrry i wasnt listening i was busy predicting your laughable response to my post perfectly § bringing the doctors note to game stop saying im allowed to buy as many games as i want and touch myown face if i want to § no one is safe from my posts no maytter how many stupid fucking buttons you click on § when someone i never met on here has me blocked i assume its because theyre a pedophile and theyre afraid im going to take them to prison § dunston Fucks in § PISS 3 TIMES A DAY. THATS IT § feel as though the POST-COVID economy will mostly benefit me, the guy who makes tiny custom diapers for peoples beanie babies and funko pops § social distancing? I’ve been social distancing my whole life Lol . no ventilators? Ive been breathing without a ventilator my whole life Lol § wearing my most Insolent pair of bluejeans to father`s court hearing § to the 1.8 million americans who died so i could get insane amounts of nintendo switch friend codes from girls by moaning online: Thank you § teen § asking the baja fresh cashier to detain the teenagers in the parking lot who told me i loooked like “Frosty the snowmans uncle” § heaping helpings of gamer Gratitude going out to the boys who mailed my streamwife a glorious synthetic Hymen via Twitch Prime Pro § not mine #NoPIss § ive flattened the curve over 100 times. what have you pricks been doing § wolf blitzer putting on his best handsome guy voice spending hours in front of the mirror practicing saying “this just in money is worth $0” § Ha ha ha... The numbers beneath all the posts are so stupid, dont mean anything, full of crappe. yes, go ahead, boo me at my own ted talk , § “i could teach a dog how to use a $10 bill in two seconds flat. the zoo should invent money that they let the animals use” - alan Greenspan § “looking for my lost shaker of Shit” only a bastard would change the lyric to this , disrespectful to mr buffet & all contemporary americana § oarnge bean https://t.co/wmVhogFywN § that was julian assange’s piss. not mine § Delighted to announce that the mental illness from being quarantined has caused me to develop an altaer-ego named “Mr. Simplepleasures” § after editing wikipedia as a joke for 16 years, i ve convinced myself that homer simpson's japanese name translates to the "The beer goblin" § hardcore becoming that guy who thinks the covid virus will be " ot good," overall, but on the bright side it might inexplicably end racism § (straining relaly hard until something inside of my head pops) There . I just gave myself depression cause none of you are clicking my Links § peoplr would rather see macDonald's, than macbeth. and that's why all of this is going on § GOD is an endangered specie's § now's the perfect time to catch up on my Smoking by smoking every cigarette and cigar in the house § #SendASmile to the stock marcket dow jones today . lets show Corona whos boss https://t.co/8U80t-T1cQh § youvr gotta eat § this shit sucks so much shit, this is Hell, https://t.co/HHbIzbTeGw § The instant I heard the song yankee doodle aas a child I threw my headphones off and said that the shit is over rated and I was right § if YANKEE DOODLE (1782) was in Present day, he would have a Sound Cloud, and Further more, he would say shit like "Listen to my sound cloud" § (man with 120 IQ in the 1700s [80 in present day IQ] listening to Yankee Doodle for the first time) Oh this is devilishly Fucked § that place you bought a mattress from 4 yrs ago, reminding you Via email, that now is the perfect time to practice your Calmness Strategies § taking hthe Touch Your Own Eye Balls challenge, at the zoo, despite recent developments § it;s bad § top 10 whack-offs , Ass-Outs, dick shows, and crank-me-offs. only on youtube .com - americas funniest home fuck ups § ill never show it § god i `d love to host SNL . imagining hordes of Trolls trying to stop me, getting mowed down by an apache helicopter outside of studio 8H, § yes my lord https://t.co/T8C3UJvklT § be your own slave. be your own Unemployed. boss of ceo. boss at disabled § there is a metric by which i evaluate the level of Sexual content that exists in posts. i call it the Porno factor . § twitter 2050 is an enhanced reality experience where you can step into a virtual sweatshop and lecture the workers about their Table Manners § we'll see who's me soon enough § i deserve th e most mentally ill president imaginable. 99 year old babbling doofus. Send us into the volcano sir § looks fine to me s.t.f.u. § scrolling on autopilot, mouth agape, clicking fav on all tweets with at least 1 or 2 funny words in them. zero human consciousness, perfect, § Peoeple across the country are sick of putting food on the table. I will stop and frisk the lies #MemeContent #Joke § the majority of my critics think its hould be illegal for me. or anyone else, to have a job. Do not fall into their pranks. § -i have at least 5 mental illnesses directly caused by having my posts replied to by shit heads - im your man for #mike 2020. Pay me sir § just to get some perspective on life § the face i make WHen https://t.co/URwBMYkjSp § dont like my posts then go watch some Prestige television about it. put on some hbo go Fuck face § "kendo is so much better than normal swords" nope fuck yourself § sorry i cant relate to any of the shit you people are saying. however that absolutely does not mean you should stop keeping the Likes coming § " can fly the boeing 737 max perfectly " § reminder to tell everyone who follows you that theyre a good person. Please. I can soft block every single one of you. I have all day § if a 4 year old child treid to accidentally shoot me i would simply disarm it by using a Complete arm latch into tactical 100% body roll § the news is my Life and my world. thank you sir @walter cronkite § you call these posts?? i call them " CON JOBS " .... § my only regret is that i have but one Grid to Go off of § I think if i put my mind to it, I could put a tree in my house like they do at the Cherry hill mall § warning issued to microsoft who is hard at work making the new "Windows": The world is watching you my friends § they are going to start calling the damn gas prices "Gasp prices" because thats what i do when i see then § get a grip § theres lots of normal people on the little black list of pedophiles too. i think its fine to say u want your dick sucked by a computer #spon § this is spam messages. unsubscribe me § You should have to have Four years experience as a Chef before you are allowed to become a Waiter. The crap has become ridiculous § As Sure As I Have An IQ of " 65 " I Will Never Not Address A Presidential Candidate As " SIR " NO MATTER THE POLITICS OF IT !! § while my trolls are busy "moving the goal posts" im afraid i am simply moving the "good posts" § your post sucked so much shit so bad it just turned me from ESFP to INTJ in 2 seconds flat. your spinning my bitch wheel 99mph § (pulls a out a cigarette and a lighter) Mind if i take a shit § tu quoque.. i invented that fallacy, and its an honor, sir , to see you using it to get yourself disqualified from arguments with me § generating millions of 3d womens pussys for the #VaginasProject . my GFX card spewing steam like a damn tea pot § the coolest thing the police ever did was invent their own flag thats just a desecrated version of the american flag § i stiltl want a picture with ghislaine maxwell so badly. I dont care what the peanut gallery thinks § oh every day i m getting Mail like, "It drives me Nuts! You are a fucked bitch, your posts stink my ass... But youre not wrong." and smiling § if your homecooked farm fresh lunch does not contain the standbys of salt and pepper it is not Chef inspired It is Shit inspired § people are not ready to hear it . but. simply the most persecuted skin color of all time, is " NUDE " § @CNN @MSNBC i shant post their names for fear of reprisal . § what is to be done with thse female bernie bros who are harassing me with nude images of themself and calling me "pee pee bitch" @CNN @MSNBC § these metrics are absolute shit. once again my followers have forced me, to threaten to post on here, images of my Hated penis § each episode personally costs me $1000000 out of my own pocket. but i do it for the fans..... § when you leave a huge pile of barrels on the roof for no reason . you are literally actually supporting donkey Kong Tbh. § time stops when you see a DM from that one special man. picture of me on all fours like a dog. "searching for my smile... Have u found it?" § Clean Ass , Clean Mind § lets see whos my real friends are. what would you do if i was at the GALLOWS about to be HUNG § "Hrm, this Content less Hit than Miss lately. Unfollowed." - guy who follows 1200 people who post about their ear infections all day § all snowmen are abominable. mockery . spit in gods face § this wa s such a beautiful website!! and the trolls have covered it in their own SHIT!!! ANd will they go to jail for it???? NO!!! § every argument i have ever made in my live has been in good faith you fucking slob dopey bitches § They read my posts on ellen. They read my posts on Meyers. Who the fuck are you. All your accounts are for children. Unfollow me. (66/66) § clown Ass. people have been treating me like dirt due to bernie bro dark money and you cant blame me for defending myself, and im no(41/66) § especially Fucked up in the wake of kobe bryant. Its more important than ever to Think Before You Post, and once again i dropped the(27/66) § Pull up a chair kiddies, its Thread time. Let's get to the point. I messed up. I said that the super bowl is a game show, when it cle(1/66) § yeah with damn beer.Tonight we drink damn beer in hell § the super bowl is a game show. and any game show with out merv griffin at the helm is shit. Its not a good show § if i wanted to watch super bowl id just put on one of the damn 50 other super bowls they did. you've all fucked up once again § my dick's like the size of a toilet § @jkfecke I snark because I care.® § people who use "APPS" think they are such pimps ... but theyer nothing but hoochie mammas § I Am Your Slave Madam President! I'll Always Protect You! https://t.co/497F3CMguH § emerging from dissociative fugue as husky teen w/frosted tips, striped polo, red shorts, nokia N-gage, unusually hot mom, above ground pool, § https://t.co/HzhVRfXhei § @AlanDersh follow back sir § alan dershowitz once tried to defend me in court by pulling out a pocket pussy and insisting he would never fuck it. we lost the case § this ones pulling shit numbers. Might get rid of it since No one would miss it apparently..... § the trick to lining my dx racer gaming seat with towels is to not let any part of my ass touch the chair and reduce its value § imagining a guy who calls every Simpsons character a "Simpson" (even ancillary ones, outside of the main family) and letting him ruin my day § " i never met a Simpson i didn't like. " -SimpsonsWade § i need 20ccs of stigma on this man's horrible looking ass cheeks stat § its time to destigmatize the Balls... and restigmatize the Ass § troll!! Move along!! Troll § Disrespected. on my own feed!! Of all places, my own feed! Please send me pictures of Cash, dollars bills, etc to calm me down § might passive aggressively post "Oh! The website is Bad today" if i dont get some damn likes over here. just constantly treated like a leper § feeling my IQ increase by one point for each dollar that i send to the "Shit Head" New York times , Greatest news paper in history § enjoying some prestige Wi-Fi in my car at the car wash § goinh to stay inside all weekend with my vast library of console releases. due to Wuhan § Get some. Get some. Yeah . Yeah § setting foward the doomsday clock a little bit because i saw a guy with yakuza tattoos knifing the shit out of a mattress § win ben steins Pussy § people do not help each other any more. When was the last time you saw anyone help someone. wveryones too busy watching Huluplus..... § if you react to me or my posts without permission you are the most son of the bitch there is § endorsing the candidate whose supporters have called me "Pussy ass" or "coward" the least amount, and its none other than the great bob Dole § your about to find out why'd they'd call me "The Bitch" § Ohh!!! Im a fuck up!! My followers hate me!! I'll never be good!! What do I do?? What do I do?? § studies show that 5% of all the food that content creators consume is waiter spit § once yoshigod9 asked me what pussy tastes like & he recorded my answer on a nintendo ds & jacked off to the recording later. Now hes my boss § game as art , https://t.co/oUlQLqh7g3 § Im nthe new voice of the apu character from simpsons. Im not as good at doing it as the last guy though. Sorry § the more i drive around in circles, the more people see my "HOME DEPOT FUCKED ME " bumper sticker. simple aritmetic § turner classic diaper § life force drained to <5% by enemy posts - Not good!! get me a "Likes" infusion ASAP!! Get me a follow fridday § sending the obese isis guy pics to girls & saying "Me", printing out the kissy face emojis they send back and hanginh them up in my cubicle. § I hear theyre inventing a Play Station with the Gamer in mind... § realized at 4am that it's morally justifiable for me to "CatCall" women because my followers cat call me in posts. in the replies constantly § when scientiologist guys talk about LRH they are talking about "lee roy hjenkins" . #GamersKnow #oddballHumour § you're not allowed to mail bombs to people § SAY IT AGAIN BOYS :"If it's not from Harvard , it's not a STEM degree" § i can not, in good conscience, condone a "SANDERS" presidency because i once vividly imagined him walking around while twirling a pistol § dark times......... https://t.co/RAaMNRYSQ7 § watching another childrens tv show where they accidentally made the school bully the best character by far § i come on here & lay down the hammer and the time line shuts its damn mouth real quick. cockoaches scattering like little peices of dog shit § wife is no longer permitting me to jack off in the car during her book club meetings. where am i supposed to jack off then? fucking EGYPT??? § boys are reclaiming ladies Night..... and its all thanks to Men § I did not show my ass § Oh looks like people are "Too busy" to drop me a Like on some of my replies now. Guess I'll go lay in the road and get hit by CARS !!! § You are such a stupid little selfish pig. What youve done here is shit yourself & yet youre too doped up from the circle jerk to realize it. § scorned Gamer invents a new color of face that is reportedly "Worse than blackface" -- Beyond Fucked - Theres Never seen anything like this. § have every thing https://t.co/paFxyNIgIZ § Im thinking 2k20 is the year of "Shut the fuck up" . All repliers blocked. Absolute God mode § hot wheels toys for adults called Adult wheels § exploring potential support for a pod cast thats basically Howard STern, but Nice § diaper pumped full of saline--looking more mentally ill than tom cruise and jason bourne combined--semen wiped all over bottom half of shirt § posting my Lunch setup and immediately getting 10000 guys yelling "you dont know what pain is" to me in the buffallo bill voice § i will never wear a "COCK RING" § Buffalo wild wing gets $0 tip for serving "Bones" to me in chicken, if i had wanted to eat bones i would take my Ass to the grave yard § my dick looks like an SNL skit, and if you dont want me to open the dialoge of this... go ahead & unfollow this Acct! I am used to the pain! § whih of the three stooges got the most ASS!!!!!! #Pennzoil #itsoktobewhite § i now hate the song "She'll be coming around the mountain when she comes" ,despite having previously said i liked it, because it sucks SHIT § Goddess George W Bush is the Light of my Being, The Master of my BLOOD. I am a Piggy who must be sent to Iraq @TheBushCenter § handsome https://t.co/K8MaQen1bQ § The holidays are a difficult time for many people. Please call everyone you know and tell them their dick is normal looking § my dick is stupid in how fat it is and it flops around like a piece of shit and looks like a beanie baby § when people retweet my posts without permission, that is, essenitally human trafficking § Ive opened the dialogue on race over 1000 times. Ive steered the discourse enough times to make your nut sack spin. § while every one was busy talking star wars this and star wars that, i have been mastering the Hands-Free orgasm . § wearihg some ridiculously shitty looking jeans that look like half of a halloween costume § opening my samsung Direct app to get samsung directuly to me § w'ere leaving it in 2019... https://t.co/zFc6c6GAkg § driving my nasty "yes malarky" bus around town getting run off the road getting shit thrown at me etc § hey whos this guy going around telling all of our troops about "eskimo pussy" § inventing new character "George X. Bush" the most fucked george bush yet § repeating to my self in the mirror "Star wars is for adults" before seeing the final one & having a violent reaction like ingesting a poison § daddy `s Gamer medicine https://t.co/hcs0ruYeue § i am pleased to announce, that i have Normalized beer § "The one thing i love about Beer: The one thing I love about beer is that its always time for another sip." -The one thing i love about Beer § tekkenchauncey no longer allowed in my home after he took a picture of a pube on my toilet (that he probably planted) and used it to ruin me § harvey weinsein in court w/ oversized diaper & fake arrow through his head: oohhh me so sorry ohhh JUDGE: I will always protect you sir , § as god as my witness i will trick out my Balls with cadillac skin enhancers and Discreet varicocele nut mods § i would value my semen at a respectable $140 per gallon woth a 98% accuracy rating . #WhatsThatLoadWorth § santa i know this is an odd request but i believe w/ a little christmas magic, any things possioble. I need you to shrink my dick by 2 inchs § catching a guy jacking off to hte shirtless ricky gervais atheist image and immediately yanking him out of his car and smacking down his ass § ive had enough of posting! The favs.. the retweets.. the girls replying.. it all means nothing to me! Mr Donald Trump... put me in the WAR!! § It would be so nice to have followers who dont fucking hate my ass . Guess ill go choke on dirt!!! Fuck me!! § sarcastic wonka thoroughly Titty Fucks the pearl harbor mosque in a series of reasonalbly calm tik tok vids- All while sipping his damn Beer § cnn should hire The Pope § INSPIRING: After 20 Years-- Local Waitress Reunited With "78 I.Q." Police Officer Who Used Her As A Human Shield At The Age Of 11 § told the mail man that if he doesnt keep the deals / coupons coming at a reasonable pace some one might be suffering from some injuries soon § sorry. i can't come to work today because my fat little penis got blown off by a stick of TNT , in the war we just lost because of me . § inner dipaer absorbing the brunt of it, mid-diaper locking down any and all "Stragglers", outer diaper "The courtesy diaper" for the fans... § Ive been sniped in the nuts by Topgolf customer service . Folks I have never been more fucked in the ass than i am currently right now. § perusing the count chocula sub reddit with a mouth full of werthers originals flavored skoal tobaco dip § theres gotta be a game that will make me cum in less than 4 minutes. Theres just gotta § "ignorance is bliss " No. Any one who says this has never tried having an iq of 200 before § if you “clap back” someone with a PhD on here, you should be allowed to have their PhD. Its just common sense people. Oh that’s tea § donalds crime https://t.co/cBDdkXbPvk § the first rate service at long horn steak house pittsburgh blasted my ass hole wide open, their dedicated waitstaff had me Nuts over Ass § the new NIssan Altima branded bean bag chair is a SLAP IN THE FACE!! to all lnissan Altima loyalists and people who enjoy car commercials § might siphon a bunch of free flu shots into a big fake arm an d bottle it up and sell it for $5 § for the second time in november iit is now international mens day. Wow § “I do not look at the numbers beneaht the post. I only look at the letters, of the post, that are used to write the words of the post” -WINT § in a show of deference towards teens , the majestic mount fuji has been renamed to ``Teen mountain`` , in a move that is sure to piss me off § none of this shit is even from the future. is that a bee hive? Fuck you https://t.co/U1M64ZqsfK § you turn on the tv on to one of the hipster channels and theyre saying we need to start pooping in bags now. i will never poop in a bag § ive mastered every hypothetical social situation by reading posts on here and am now ready to talk to my step mom with out flipping out, § theoretically , tips could be done away with entirely if i were allowed to enter the kitchen and personally retrieve my entrees ChefToTable § Seems to me today would be an excellent day to browse some of my Legacy Posts, from the Heirloom Collection, and throw them a retweet or two § i now have over 100 comments that the media refuses to let me apologize for and the trolls got my Ass over a barral § every person on your “Who to follow” list writes articles called “ o more Mr Family Guy” because peter griffin showed his penis or something § the nerve of this fucking mom and pop pizza joint hanging a framed $1 bill up. alright pal you’re rich, we get it § look what youve gone and done. youve shit-eated yourself again § warming my nuts on your daily coffeecup § ive had more threads locked than any man on the planet. ive had my address posted 1000+ times. i get ``Owned`` so much that i look like shit https://t.co/308nflDLgV § account Status; Verified. To the chagrin of all Shit Accounts, This is now a LOCKED PAGE . I am the rat of life. I am the bitch of forever § Make America Shit My Pants § was gonna bring back the classic “piss” gag but you cant say the word “piss” any more. theyll get ya. ford trucks .com built ford truck #ad § Seems to me that we have been more becoming like a country of people who let Cell phones define our brain... FUCK !!! § dairrhea § Leaving the group chat so I can focus on my responsibilities as a Shark Tank subbreddit moderator . § why are you wearing a sailor’s outfit around inside of your own house you fuck face § gamer knife https://t.co/4KM6I9VY0M § breaking into digimonotis’s house at night and leaving a severed human thumb in his bed, signifying a “Thumbs down” for his disloyalty § Going Very fucking hard on donald duck today. Saying i would never want to be him, or be any part of his life. § no-reply@youtube .com: We’ve changed our terms of service, me: my terms of service is simply this”Shut the Fuck up” § Cool https://t.co/eAwv9t7ZpK § the shit that killed Elvis https://t.co/gAl5sU36Gy § flags are posts, because you post them § #peakMale #godPerformance https://t.co/dAkLaDO-aGD § if youve never written posts before, then shut the fuck up § look at this shit here https://t.co/eA96Me7cv6 § Oh i cant wait to shit my pants. I cant wait to walk into the bathroom and shit my pants in there and go home § man slowly poisoning himself over the course of 50 years by storing his silverware and fine china in the bathroom § https://t.co/S53uOn5PNg § false. total crap https://t.co/PXX9Gd116D § playing the worlds most normal sized violin § looking at my timeline, it seems that MetalGearEric has shifted from a Tier-B to a Tier-C poster ever since his grandma died. imo , § Do not mention me unless your a girl § “I’ll be crucified for saying it; but it took 18 years to complete the ‘Luigi’s Mansion’ trilogy. Same as ‘The Godfather’.” - SirGamestop § might delete all my posts once i hit 10000. Thats enough § FUCK !!! https://t.co/M1yhFKBQ7E § might try to improve my posts somewhat so i can get some followers who arent total bird brains . like 80% of you are just Dog shit § girls hate it when you say shit like "Rome wasnt built in a day" to them § thinking of all the guys who requested to be buried face down so the whole world can kiss their ass. Cant wait to kiss their dead asses § how to say "doh" simpson tutorial How to say "Doh" like homer info how to say "Doh" instructions on how to say "Doh" § no mouse pad. "off roading" § my name is " GAMER FUCKER " and i was sent to FUCK all the gamers... § " Shut Da Fuck Up " § The Most Wrongfully Unfollowed Account On Earth .... § https://t.co/Q6os85UlEA id rather have q anon post my address and dick and balls than have t o read another one of these Fucking posts § the most bewildering euphemism for penis i ever heard : "My puck" § https://t.co/ka4CgZs1Hy § please tell me the latest sex news § - _ = NEVER A SEX ACCOUNT = _ - § my dick looks like a dissected frog #JESUSISKING § considering the insane amount of meds i woud need to become harvey weinsteins Lawyer without wanting to flip my $80000 car off the over pass § Q: Mr. James bond youre going to want to have to take a look at this. Q turns the laptop around and james bond sees my posts on it § getting more pain receptors implanted into my skin!! maybe now my posts will actually mean something to you mother fuckers!! "AAAAAAAHHH!!" § fred flintstone does not Jack off ever, he works hard every day to provide for his family, fuck you for saying something like that § im sorry if you like him or are a fan of his, but you just know that this guy is looking like total shit https://t.co/szSCrnXO9y § that picture of all the construction workers sitting on a steel beam eating lunch except its me & the boys sitting on the floor at game stop § screaming on the phone with J. dorsey about how Fucked I am if guys with shitty beards keep saying my posts "Have lost their Edge" § choking myself on the toilet for Likes § i was about to invent a joke about how people Stay using their car horns too much, but then i remembered that COMEDY DIED , due to HATERS !! § really fucked up that you have to start every letter with "Dear" like youre trying to get the dept of weights and measures or whoever horny § restaurants should bring back smoking sections but for jacking off, and if you don't like that idea yiou can just sit in the normal sections § your from reddit not me § using street view; trapped in man's sandwich https://t.co/Fk81c28gYf § ernest shits himself stupid. ernest nuts him self #twistedErnestFilms #tgif § Hard Rock Cafe In Orlando Has Sucked Off My World § seriously asking myself out loud if i should let my prick get hard, looking at all of this sweet denim. jourdache, you make a hell of a jean § I was dead wrong about the 2020 reboot of Raggedy Ann. And I can never forgive myself. § ive gotten word that pussy_hacker has taken SirGamestop out for a night on the town that he wont soon forget, and then some , § patreon reward demecratic debate live commentary by "SirGamestop" § am i still blocked by "The diaper guru" ? yes. but my people and his people are negotiating an amnesty agreement as we speak. § keep your eyes off my Stats § wearing electric bra in defiance of #NoBraDay my filthy bean bags getting absolutely smoked by radio sound attacksat the cuban embassy § your the ones who sold out not me § punishing myself by wrapping piano wire around my head, for enjoying a 7up commercial 21 years ago § watching all of you goof up again, with your posts. nobody has ever crapped themselves more in human history. The shit is a total clown show § might become a " Pube guy " , as I am not only interested in making my dick look smaller, but also dirtier § mr. Game your Dick off 2019 § i hate it when doctors say Shit like "Take two and call me in the morning" . why dont yoy take two kisses of the butt crack of my ass § Waiters do not put the big silver dome over our food before serving it anymore because of politics culture § I miss lunch from when back before it became a fucking joke to most of people. § Good of my life https://t.co/9xpZPFf8Fm § #NationalBoyfriendDay Im every womens boyfriend and father and son. And I keep my clothes nice § Interesting that some people care enough about my posts to look at them and read them. Says a lot about you Dick head § once more for the mother fuckers in the back... Not All People Who Work At Carnival Dunk Tanks Are Clowns. § not much of a response to my #ShowMeTheSelfieMonday call for selifes. might try Heroin for the first time . Oh well § unlock your account and show the world the vile shit you are saying to me you ghoul § doing pretty good with thre posts today. might try to pound out a few more before sundown, but it remains to be seen if i will "Blow it" § fondly remembering in 2013 when microsoft made a hail mary to try to convince everyone to put an online camera in their living rooms for fun § a banner ad that pissed me off siad "This Guys Getting More "Ass" Than You Ever Will " and it was just a picture of the nutty professor § shut the fuck yp https://t.co/1nRbXL2ZHz § sometimes it feels like the damn writers of 2016 have run out of ideas for the season finale of real life . Auuwoogaaa!! Hit the damn like § i have it on good authorirty that many of my trolls look like the mother fucker from mad magazine. fuck you. i will never improve my posts. § thinking about some computer slob clicking on my Like button-- right after touching his nasty dick. hey buddy; i dont want that shit. Keep it § point blank blasting a pair of jeans with a 120 decibel leaf blower at 6am even though i have been" warned about doing this" § haivng stress diarrhea into a handful of Kleenex § im officially the guy who has held out the longest without being "Ready to laugh again" since 9/11 and what do i get in return? ASS-FUCKED.. § twitter .com, the only mainstream website that manages to crash my browser, has pledged to make its users suffer "Like never before" in 2020 § my billionaire friends smoking in an alleyway with leather jackets and slicked back hair trying to peer pressure me into doing pedophile sex § strutting my shit on the beach, unintentionally increasing the anxiety of all girls with my radiant shit head energy and blowing it bigtime, § my follower's https://t.co/UCv7ICcNKy § if anyone you know on here is a "HIT MAN" , block and unfollow § REMINDER: your favorite CONTENT CREATOR is NOT your PERSONAL DOG. DO NOT look at their IMDB PAGE. DO NOT make EYE CONTACT with THEM § installing a full scale maypole in my backyard... just thinking the boys are going to love this shit § shaking my head at the gym . wondering when " o pain no gain" became " o brain no brain" § guy trying to tell me im using the elliptical cross trainer backwards; Fuck you man. . This is my journey § pplease stop asking me to retweet shit for money, if you have to pay me to retweet your shit its probably so bad it sucks shit § calling my wife, screeching, telling her theres a bomb in the computer so she wont log on & see ChronoAzusa's post calling me a girl Replier § putting my fist through the wall and yanking out a chunk of insulation and making a "what the fuck is thiis" gesture before throwing it § much like they do with investments, professional ties, etc, journalists should be expected to disclose how Mad they are, § game'sfully employed https://t.co/J3hpW2pBSb § sucking off on a piece of spaghetti like a dick; getting all that red Sauce § lets step it up. lets replace the Follower count with the number of criminals youve murdered. lets see where our true allegiances lie § The new shit is 100,000,000 Followiers by 2021. Put that in your fucking web site § now more than ever, people are threatening to piss § obliterated by secret service goblins taxpayer magnum pulse cannons while horse playing on a diving board § nice sydney opera house you got here. would be a shame it if were to become the the sydney Gamer house... § @AcmeMarkets clerk slapped a whole packet of heritage Diapers out of my mitts and made some comments id dont care to repeat. Retribution? § powerful vision: the fox nfl robot stops dancing for a moment & collapses. from its body emerges a Nude African American Male, finally free, § if i ever got face to face with the "Affluenza teen" on my server im thinking itd go a little something like this (plays guitar really good) § you have to get up pretty early in the morning to piss off my entire shit § changing my bio to " obody Helps Me" , to punish society § an adult version of Chuck E Cheese type places where you pay someone to shout the " -WORD" directly into your face so you can feel something § your damn right https://t.co/v33JAnA9cx § by “JACKING OFF” https://t.co/XXvZTKdTDR § a fun idea: mount Tweetmore; like mount rushmore but with Twitter users. again this is just a fun idea i thought of. please let me have this § dunce cap prophylactic § (sobbing like a fucking doofus) why isnt my feed good!! why dont these posts make me happy any more!! what is wrong with all of you!!!!!!! § spitting out perfectly good pieces of hamburger meat into a napkin § never mind they just found the post where i said i put on black face and started chasing cars around § iwish i could grasp my monitor by both sides and shake all the stupid ass trinkets off this youtube reviewers shelves § Now whos ready for some damn Tweets for Fucking adults § Just gotten word that ive been approved for the verified mark. It’ll appear within 5-7 days. Wow! What a nice surprise! Thank you every body § consuming Top Tweets at unprecedented speeds (cream of the crop; specifically curated to my personal interests) frowning like a sack of shit § “soon or later you will not even be able to be able to take a crap with out the Tax man up your ass” - Dril § i love saiyng shit like “Yow! This kittens got Claws!” whenever a woman stabs me 38 times in the neck and chest § cowboy `s blade § just thinking of how wild things would get if i were to bust out a bottle of wine with the flintstones logo on the label..... § going Hard for my next big 9/11 Deep Dive. The time has come to goose around in the name of 9/11. Just wait’ll I get my kicks, of 9/11 § thank you Microsoft for sending me 50 Reward’sPoints but i must decline the offer . For i did not earn them, they are not mine to use. § it is with unbearable fucking agony that i declare the death of “The Thursday Nite Rant” . writing them is too hard § starting a social media platform called “Shithead Hell” where all the posts are the same as the ones on here and we share 0% ad revenue also § you think im wasting my time putzing around in the drafts folder? bull shit. 100% off the cuff https://t.co/wSMDuYFBXk § walking around town with my big Ass lookin like Shit § youve enntered the page of The Master https://t.co/XickVgoFG4 § internal dialogue of tech journos watching Asimo dance around “Wow id love to break its legs” “Lets see it withstand the burden of the Cross § my opinion of Personal Drama in World Events?? Hell, theres not enough of it. my opinion of politics in Racism? There aint enough of it § i gave it back to the lord § oh my zippers down? well how about you zipper your mouth, instead of look at my dick § Sadly, every one below the age of 45 is more interested in finding “Waldo” , than being “Well-to-do” § theres like 90 reddit threads per day called “Do your friends Hate you?” and they always have 10000 replies of people saying shit like “Yes” § the worst dms are the ones from beautiful WOmen. the best ones are some university of dog shit grad student asking if he can “pick my brain” § i know a lot of women . and none of them would ever sleep with this clown Austin powers § whatre you gonna do with all that baumit..gim me some of that baumit come on man https://t.co/TfP7xE8N2S § for reasons none of you could ever hope to comprehend, i will now be referring to “Baby mario” as “The baby from mario” § The Fraudsters, the Bull shitters, and Fuck Boys are out to turn my page into their own personal Restroom!! Ohhhh!! Very not good!! § yeah no we dont use phones in Hollywood anymore. cute post though. § im auditioning for holly wood § You wanna tell peole i got a little lady bug dick?? That how you get your kicks? Haah?? taking multiple shirts off while saying this § you want to claim that i keep a cup of poop on my computer desk? You want to go on record? ill put you in concrete. ill give you to the lord § Seems to me that politics is something of a “Double Edge Sword” , that can be used for Good, or, in some cases, Evil. § more and more sources are reporting “an end to sex” § Hello Dear . It is my pleasure to chat you § the most solid benefit to owning your own pool is that you get to keep all the animals that drown in it § the bbq pit boys have posted a video so fucked that i am hesitant to describe it, lest my pervert followers try to tell me its actually good § slamming some coins into the juke box and playing the worst song you ever heard about a “honky tonk man who needs his dick sucked” § local church replaced with “The Simpsons lounge” where you can watch any episode of THe Simpsons & buy themed drinks based on the characters § to the pyramid on the $1 bill calling itself the “all seeing eye” Fuck you. the only thing you can see from my wallet is the jeans of my ass § when i scroll too far down the google image search results for “rat” and start getting pics of ground hogs and shit... Lets talk about this. § i didnt understand how interest at the bank works until someone explained to me its like storing cum up in your balls § guy who bothered putting a suit on for his profile pic and only has like 300 followers. ha ha ha you dip shit!! youve wasted your life!!!!!! § you say you smoke two packs a day? two packs of what, pal? shit? § seeing a guy on here named “Curtis Blowjobs” , shaking my head and saying “REALLY??” a lot, asking girls in the dms if they can believe this § THIS!!! https://t.co/jCYR7yXHZc THIS!!! THIS!!! § all of the dna in my ass is just morbid. if my ass was a person it would have a small dick § eating luch #MondayMorning #mondayThoughts #MondayMotivation #JustMondayShit #MondayAss #PissMOnday #MondayBoys #MondayVibes #MondayMood § shut up!! shut the Fuck up!! https://t.co/tVsepHMpJB § googles motto is “Dont be evil” ? What A load of Hooey that turned out to be. Follow my page if you want to check out my shit . § a lot of people tripping over themselves trying to Speak on my ass. just an observation ive noticed § when the legendary CBS comedy lineup comes on, i simply turn it off. Know why? Ive been pissed off too much times to care. Does it Shock you § stand your ground laws for jeans instead of guns. stand your jeans laws § just hating my lead coated dx racer knock off gamer cushion from bangla-desh. absorbing & releasing countless toxins via my Ass. 16 hrs a day § https://t.co/S8HqQPRuzi Looks like shit § many’ve sought the ultimate Combo and have asked me what the ultimate combo is. i am too amused simply by their ignorance to even answer . § i have created more jobs, than every Weed Smoker on the planet-- combined . § bill gates’ dog is too dumb to even know his owner is a celeb. thats why i should be bill gates’ dog. crawling around his mansion for treats § “oh its so easy to og after david Koch now that hes dead” ”its so Edgy & Brave to get his ass now that he cnat send his assassins after you” § david kock death hitting especially hard because of baby bird brain derangement that makes me think every rich person i see on tv is my Mom § theyre waiting for me to slip up and post a family guy joke verbatim so they can make youtube vids of cartoon avatars doing side eye to me § none of my followers like jokes, none of my followers enjoy Fun, every time i try to lighten the mood people just post pics of my mug shots § one thing for certain is the that the trolls are having a hell of a time Whacking off to the point of ignorance as if i even give a fuck . § writing a massive 350 page book about my twiiter brand that no one will read, is, in a lot of ways, like being a Prisoner of War § heart of darkness 2: https://t.co/GvVobp9RBH § if you want to see first hand how the boys decide what to eat, do not miss our unwatchable 6-Part docudrama entitled “Masters of Lunch” § every day my inbox is inundated with women (female) claiming that they understand Mens Life, whereas all i can do is simply smile. § ill show you real truth ... https://t.co/Ph7kDBsjdi § Donwnloadable Content (DLC) and Microtransactions is Protected Free Speech. (USER HAS BEEN BANNED FOR THIS POST) § jsut a heads up if youre trying to be a check mark guy on here, you get paid more to have opinions that suck fucking ass § Small Meer-schaum Pipe, the Bowl in the Form of a Remarkably Naturalistic and Expressive Head of an African-American Male Slave... https://t.co/vUcKZScvtC § Saving $400000 a year by eating bugs and little tiny pieces of shit . § meter reader in my basement: nice controllers man.. You game on those bad boys? me (Blush-ing): i am-- yes, I do consider my self a gamer. § “sounds to me like you’re gonna be wantin to be suckin on a piece of my bullshit......” § mr Wantin to be suckin § might come up with a “Safe word” system to employ if thhe boys in the chat go too hard while commenting on my lunch pics § theyre tryin to Stooge my ass § say what you will about my mediocre ass hole... at the end of the day, It's got people talkin!!!! § "Housten we have a problem" When i say this , Thats when uou know that the Shit has gone off the rails § im stuffing more toilet paper into the clogged toilet to stop it from overflowing. im using the plunger to cram more toilet paper in there § re: clogging toilets; its important to note that i use a minimal amount of paper. so the responsible party is usually my very thick turds § when i step out of the bathroom to announce that Ive clogged the toilet at a party, i tell everyone exactly what i clogged it with (my shit) § The Proven Mental Health Benefits Of Calling Your Boss "Father" § im an Empath. im a Homeo Uncle. im a rodney § the least political book in the english languge is-- you guessed it-- the dictionary. § every time i open my mouth and speak my yap its like cumming to me. its like ejaculating to what a average man would feel like § Cause I got high high Hopes for the living !!!! Cause I got High High Hopes !!!! § watcging fred flintsone get his car tipped over by the big rack of ribs and yelling "Shit like this wouldnt fly these days" at the tv § my tweets bring people together, and unite this country even more than 9/11 did. every time i post its like 9/11 happening again § police...! Poison that man § every time you vermin talk shit of me, i flip my chair backwards at 900mph and bust through sevreal pane glass windows. Not so cool now huh. § my slack friends all have jobs oppressing my discord friends § you can learn so much crap just by clicking on like two things. https://t.co/WlAynIiKj7 § Already Im being silenced! Incredible § Going to try to get viral by making a ranking list that everyone hates. Lets see; 1. Net Flix 2. First Responders 3. Sandwich § ive signed a 1 Month Pact w/ my wife which grants her the right to viciously berate me online, as long as she watches & supports my Stream's § shut hte fuck up https://t.co/GrEtPH3Y4h § pissing on top of my own throw up and saying a lot aobut society....... § driving down the highway at 30mph laying on the horn protecting myself with a shield of Noise § there needs to be a "BRexit" for people Who still be watching Teletubbys § lord of all media https://t.co/LXdMdQ7t3h § turning on all the smoke detectors in my house as punishment for making some statements that i might have to apologize for at a later date § Male Netflix Supporter § absolute full power https://t.co/wEZGcMQqKM § saw some posts i didnt like and now i have to go take a giant shit in the bathroom. Thanks everyone. Thank you § hey girl,.. whats the general consensus on that pussy situation. what chemicals you got down there § Its impossible for me to respect someone who is wearing an arm cast. UYou look like a mummy from egypt. Remove it § i cannot stress enough that my new song "Good town road" is not influenced by any other songs whatsoever § gamer posture is equally as valid as normal posture. i will no longer be silent, of this § every one who has ever retweeted my shit owes me $125 for sharing my personal data, full stop § when the timeline's just not doing it for you, some times you gotta dip into that list of Liked Tweets. because you KNOw that shit is good.. § Yo u are only pissing him off further § the Administrator has told you to refrain from clicking on my posts in the future § https://t.co/EGtfVEAN7K § the "Shit my pants" challenge: if you can make me cry or shit my pants though the computer ill apologize to everyone whosever been mad at me § #RespectThePolice alright done. what should I respect next. bugs? urine? im taking requests § they are trying to make the 2020s the decade of Nude § the last four super bowls were deep fake, and they're just gonna keep on deep faking them § stainless steel? my ass. ill stain that mother fucker good § getting removed from a cafe after using their wifi to look at a slideshow of kpax images for an hour § the restaurant cannot legally charge your credit card if you refuse to givr them your signature and leave § pretty much like 80% of the cats in that movie are fake § either my neighbor has been running a vacuum all day, or producing a consistently loud, droning noise with his mouth somehow § you think my bowtie looks nice? no it doesnt! i look like SHIT!! you dont know anything about Mens attire. youre only saying that to FUCK me § mr. Crapped On Daily § corn should grow from sprouts, like beans do. none of this cob bullshit § just because im following yiou on here doesn't mean im obligated to read your fucking posts, or like you, or marry you and be happy forever, § what th e fuck are you talking about https://t.co/PyzLnSl9eV § make em bleed § im getting word that theres a rumor that in the next star wars all the star wars characters go to The Moon § 100 years ago i looked at the first ever drawing of mickey mouse and i said out loud that that shit was going to make $99,000,000,000,000 § for every inch my penis shrinks due to anxiety, the trolls owe me $100,000 , i am saying it now. § https://t.co/mSsmL4zh7F § Looks like slavery is alive and well, if youre a Top Influencer. Im not mad or anything I just think its funny. But i am pissed off by it § i got a big ass and i know how to fuck it. Mastercard § always men `s beer https://t.co/QZnZfNVUdn § if you try to say something fucked up to me i will break your arms and call the cops on you § @billgates ive invented a new type of water. i need Ten Grand § We used to think the hamsterdance .com was good, Now it sucks so much to us § Im now earning 5% cash back at gas stations so if you need gas please give me the cash so i can buy it on credit and siphon it into your car § https://t.co/A2lZudIWVA § local man gets diapoer rash on face from wet beard § Going Cyber. § sending $39.99 to the tiger beat magazine corporation to find out what my "Pimp IQ" is § everytime windows updates youll find my dumb ass claiming that the user experience seems "smoother" now. you will beg me to shut the fuck up § money is such a corrupt bastards tool that all i can do about thinking about it is to simply laugh about it... § i never even thought jeffery epsteins posts were that funny . § theres a popular nursery rhyme in which the singer claims to be a teapot. this, for many children, is their first experience with "Trolling" § might get really into chewing tobacco for some reason. might start calling it "Tobaccy" . Fuck you § Consideirng putting a bumper sticker on my car that says "Get off my ass" and a sign about a mile away saying "Go closer to my ass" § my stupid fucking little ass and my stupid little pecker with the balls on it are iconic, and me right now, and mood § the belief im most attacked for, is the belief that my High IQ makes me a Target § getting body slammed in the mouth for my bull shit § leave your DRAMA at the door, or i will SHIT myself !!!! § The Fact Remains That Your A Guy From Reddit, And Im A Guy Who Posts On A Website Thats Somewhat More Prestigious Than Reddit § @piersmorgan no...! it's fucking Bad to be that !! § Beliveve it or not, some people would rather play in a Ball pit, than play in an Orchestra pit, and thats why society has crapped on it self § wearing, Oh,; I dont know, some cheap douche bag jeans that are sickeningly blue, climbing around on some bricks, Truly Looking dumb as Fuck § me and this guy on a podcast talking about how its bull shit that youre not allowed to have opinions anymore https://t.co/tk9NWFa1YQ § everyone please stop laughing immediately & explain the joke to me very carefully like i'm 2 years old so I can tell you if i like it or not § yorue next. on the pain list § Ive decided to not be a part of asexual anymore after receiving a call from my agent orderring me to stand down § Im joining Asexual, because of certain bull shit that happened in the Comment's section, and because enough is enough § girls on here will call you "Dry dick" , then after you spend hours moistening your penis with a cotton swab you still get derided. Cant win § send 1 million guys dressed as The Matrix into iran and i guarantee you the rhetoric will tone down § im proud to preface all of my tweets with the montra of "If you dont like it, Then simply unfollow" thats the bread and butter of my acount § if i ever catch you "Dabbing" , I will never hire you to work at my FORTUNE 500 Logistic's firm. You a re simply a liability I cannot afford § they should invent a spittoon but for Urine § blocking me is an expression of Love. the line between "Follower" and "Guy who has me blocked" blurs more with each death threat i receive § back when we were doing all the dub step jokes we were havin the time of our lives.

we thought the fun would never stop --And we were Correct § Ive gotten word that certain people on here are "Doing it for the clicks" . Rest assured that i will never do it for the clicks § wiccan and juggalo are the same thing. they just announced it on the News § URGENT--From CEO of Pampers USA LLC: "The singular noun associated with our product is 'PAMPERS„¢ Brand Diaper'. It is not called a 'Pamper'" § Please i need help § people keep replying to my posts accusing me of not knowing what True Pain is. possible computer bug??? § Move alone... Nothing to see here. § age 0 (baby): I want my Dada . age 25 (Millennial): I want my Data Do you see how fucked this is? § oh you say you're going to fuck me? you're going to try to fuck me, through the computer? Well i say this, and that is "Game on" § BREAKING - The Green M&M Has Been Spotted Wearing A Mysterious New Bra; But Not Everyone Thinks It's Good § looking for the kind of ketchup that Chefs use...... § You wanna see me throw up? You wanna watch me barf as a joke? Too bad! I will no longer make myself throw up as a joke! No more! Never again § the pope makes six figures easy. Fact § they deep faked pics of me wih my shirt tucked halfway into my pants all bunched around my ass looking like shit. weve got to stop deep fake § Get my ass on SNL and make me the Boss of SNL and I can promise you thta I will bring back all of the Classics. § imagine the sheer power of a man shattering a boulder with a whip. incredible § ATLANTIC CITY - 9:02am - A second oversized globe has hit the Ripley's Believe it or Not Museum . § carefully walking @TheRealOJ32 through the process of deleting his account to avoid letting the trolls win, like we're defusing a bomb § thinking that every time elon musk trends on here it's because he invented cold fusion, not because he publicly called someone an "Ass Hat" § posting LIVE from a resort in the Dominican Republic, getting blasted in the face from all directions with pesticides, lips flapping around § for most of i can remember, people have been talking SHIT § sure, punch all the teeth out of my mouth for having an Opinion. Very good § nonchalantly wearing a pink sweater vest while plowing out my wife during a 4.7 magnitude earth quake § beanie babies are just bit coins in real life § Its fucked up to think about that only 2 years ago, in 2017, the current year (2019) was considered "The future" § @TheRealOJ32 hey before we start recording the Anti-SJW pod cast we planned im gonna need a notarized document stating you didnt kill anyone § not Suprising to see these LOSERs attack Sports and Athletic Legend @TheRealOJ32, as i've been attacked just as maliciously, if not more so, § ive been notified by my agent that if i do not tweet the phrase "Epic Wells Fargo" four times this month i will have one of my ears cut off § me vs. a girl follower's Father, screaming grappling match in a parking garage, trying some WWE wreslting moves im not athletic enough to do § leaning against the back wall of the e3 conference, looking at pictures of condoms on my phone while all the dorks freak out about nerd shit § ive done the research, ive looked at the facts, ive analyzed the hard data and my conclusion is that youre way more mad than i am right now, § sitting on toilet, avoiding wife whos mad at me for saying Chinese zodiac animal and spirit animal are the same thing § Im so pissed off im going to throw up § the most classic form of capital punishment is being restrained in the stocks and having tomatoes thrown at you just for being a dumb ass § if it werent for the invention of the electric chair iw ould do so much crime. id be smashing vases and shit right now § Im nodding my head § look at all these pitiful toads shamelessly seeking validation, unlike me, seeking validation in a cool, disaffected sort of way § f https://t.co/RNQlFwV69L § thinking about how much higher we'd rank on the World Happiness Report if they said gamers should be allowed to be landowners, on the news § nine boys crowded around a 19" television "Franklin for Fuckin adults " "Its about damn time" "Hell yes, this" *all rubbing hands together* § i speak for every mother fucker when i say i would pay gladly $100000 for a Mature version of Franklin the turtle show § Oh we're doing toughguy shit now . § rotating inside of a porto potty at least 4 times looking for the sink § if you don't think i like to muck about on here... i damn say you're in for the shock of a life time!!!! § going to the bathroom "On Principle" § absorbing Dip Shit energy from the lousy posts on here and throwing up f rom the body reaction § i hate it when shit is "Sparta" § thinking about how Fucked i`d be if someone hurled a metal trash can at the back of my head at full force, or if i fell 10ft onto some rocks § Geting that "Impersonating an officer" money § More jokes about the movie "Baby driver" . Soon § guy who says "Thank you" to the other passengers in his shared Lyft ride when they arrive at their destination ansd get out of the car § @SCJohnson @ AGMikeHunter @JNJNews nail his ass to the fucking WALL § putting my dick in a Capsule § if Ur not retweeting or other wise liking all this good shit SC Johnson A Family Company is posting i got 2 words for U and that is Fuck you § name searching https://t.co/QEz86Vkpji § hes a dog and i will capture him § the mysterious "Dr. Gamer" § im going to crush you in to powder. im gonna powder your ass § whats more racist? saying "I am a black men's penis" in 2006, or having my presidential run kneecapped, for doing that § airlines should give you a smaller barf bag for when you just want to spit out a piece of sandwich § ME: watch it bud. my friend RickGamecube, you see, he dont like getting pissed off so much RickGamecube: I dont like getting pissed off § im a journalist now so send me any scoops you might hiave and ill try to post it here if its not perverted § my followers have abandoned me after finding out that i dont have any ass cheeks and that the hole is just exposed all the time like a dog's § rhinestone cowboy 2: titanium cowboy § hit up my 18+ accout @Quaker_Oats § working at one of those "Cool offices" that has pinball machines and ping pong tables and dildo launchers and pepole shitting on the floor § I have been a jock since I was 0 years old . § lets all calm down in here. § you can down vote me but Im god damn right § the entire time youre watching the movie 101 Dalmatians, youre just thinking, This is so many more dalmations than usual. It is just fucked § absolutely crushing it, and by "it" i mean my "Balls", while i attempt to wedge myself into the driver's seat of my 2004 kia optima § Please come to the provided address to deliver my 25 , 000 USD. I will be there holding an empty suitcase, and grinning § sure, i would hire the trolls to come work at my multinational public relations firm... to clean the PISS and SHIT out of OUR TOILETS !!! § getting my cudgel autographed by a law officer § every single one of you will be locked up for deplatforming and demonitizing joe the plummbers imdb page § wiping m ass with toilet paper imprinted with an image of bin laden wiping his ass with toilet paper imprinted with the jp morgan chase logo § Euuuhh... Not a Good look! https://t.co/1nsLIeR6nH § politifact... waiters should offer to can crush my cans when im done with them... TRUE § Im sorry . Please buy my book § having to spell the word "lunch" instead of saying it so the boys don't get too excited § i did not blow it § just embed the damn image automatically like all the other images i post. this looks like Shit. § only the finest.. @ Burbank, California https://t.co/TnzaM3UOcJ § let the record show that the minor-attracted genius blocked me after i said this § twitter should let me see the profiles of people that blocked me because i gotta know whoich of these bozos are talking shit § who cares. pick up a foot ball § you can tell how much of a dipshit a guy is just by looking at the face he makes while jacking off § my Ass and my Nude Ass are two separate entities , both growing more Iconic in their own right , with each passing day § ive seen like 9 separate group dms that are named "Boys Chat". 9 parallel universes, each with their own fucked up opinions regarding Lunch § betting $10 on each of the horses because all of them are my God , and every one of them has the power to physically annihilate me § alcohol is a drug, beer is alcohol, and drugs are a form of beer § Enough . § wacky sitcom premise where i accidentally arrange to get my ass kicked and have my dick sucked in the same parking lot § i think it would be fucking stupid to be a fat ass caterpillar and have your entire body be made out of weak points § Just looking at some stuff that i clicked on. § taking a Diagonal shit. § the boys on shark tank just loving my propeller beanie that sprays piss everywhere while it spins § farm fresh signature homegoods dick sucker § Mr Truth Through Pain § where are my damn freaks.. where`s my nasty Posters. where are my fuckin doofuses § Where_Gogurt_Failed.txt § some brand writes a few checks and gets shit like "#XmenDay" trending while i struggle to riase awareness for me buying an above ground pool § finally obtained a copy of the show thats making eveyone mad, dont see the big problem honestly https://t.co/hiTdVwmNMj § but who will advocate the Non-essential oils?? the oils my body could not give a shit about either way § with the engagement numbers yiou people are giving me some times i think id may be better off changing my name to "Mr Go Fuck Myself" § Thats not a signature bread. Thats a normal bread § Found it out the hard way that SubWay is no longer using Signature Breads. Ive been snookered. Ive been cock suckered § bothj of you should be sent to abu ghraib for talking about your penises to me § investing like $30000 in Nike because i think people are buying a lot of shoes lately and i dont feel like looki ng up any other stock names § yeah its dealing with punks like you is my job. § i refuse to go to work until sex is eliminated. are we still doing the sex strike jokes. well thats my one § rat man got money from nsa https://t.co/Hqj1wfLuhw § this is what an Emissary of the Kingdom of heaven my look like. Do not engage it in combat https://t.co/pVAX1wTooq § posting my 680 credit score durihg peak girl hours § going to deep fake some videos of myself saying some austin powers quotes flawlessly , § pain time § fun idea; for one day lets unlock all the locked accounts & lay their posts bare for the scrutiny of the Public. then ban them for cowardice § my impressions are at aln all time low!! my numbers are shit!! im fucked!! im done for!! OHhhh Noooo https://t.co/5tAFqu8pww § Ive been trying not to try to be funny and cool lately and have completely developed a dissociative disorder and succeeded § Eiating a $26 Wagyu peanut butter and jelly sandwich while pushing some buttons on my watch § in fear of losing my job at panda express after telling a girl about my kidney stone ordeals and haivng it misinterpreted as sex talk § "multi verse" fuck your self. you`re only allowed to have one universe per costumed dipshit. absolutely none of this is my problem § guys who get circumcised when theyre like 45 years old are Sluts § burger king just did a $100 billion ad campaign to tell us theyre putting piss in the food now when i tell people that for free every day § thinking of Life #ThursdayThoughts #NationalDayOfPrayer #MuellerGate https://t.co/SXx6NK9BTc § my piss is black now anf has little pieces of pulp in it and i have to say it on this hash tag because doctors are ignoring me #MuellerGate § the taste of Bacardi infused with the raw power of Centrum Silver § he Sighed and drank from his cup of beer very lawyerly , § NYT: retired Geologist from indiana proposes one Simple fact which will flip every thing you thought you knew about "THE N-WORD" on its head § @bloomingdales I want you tot take this off your store https://t.co/er5XqM4bgs § im thinking my posts arent on The NY Times Best Seller list because they have been very difficult to access lately due to Inclement weather § dragging my Pitty's and my Rotty's around in a stage coach . 11 pea brained loud mouths thrashing around for treats § the guy who forced those flight attendants to wipe his ass died and im the only one willing to put politics aside to pay the proper respects § boss waiting patiently for me to finish doing steroids and throwing up into a plastic bucket before handing me some shit he wants me to fax § fucking Dumb https://t.co/kY1QpfV28P § dogs used to say "Arf" and "Bow-Wow" . Now they say shit like "Wouwouwouwou" § Turner classic Homegoods § move every game stop to the peak of K2 and you will find out damn quick who are the real gamers § yes i still believe the idea of wingstop was STOLEN from game stop. my evidence? its called reality § kissing the female firefighter emoji as penance for being a dog brained fuck freak § I will do better next time . §

getting the zone auto zone § watchinh bottom of the barrel live streamer fail cringe compilations while i sit here and suck on an entire hoagie like a pacifier § alone and my thoughts... § im absolutely taking this as some kind of threat https://t.co/206WQZv5kJ § ive invented a new kind of bed bugs for the toilet § my Reaction when . https://t.co/QcaBZ0uE7j § i've had just gotten word that the $30 arrangement of Chef's Breads i had ordered to my home has been intercepted by trolls § The Mueller report, is hipster § 16 reasons why Farm Fresh Corn on the cob could be your new Taste Obsession - Chef Ã‰douard`s Corncob Lounge "On 3rd" § lunch cabinet § Im the only man here who injects himself with a CIA Grade Truth Serum before each and every post i make. Remember only that § the book that single handledly made "gaming" a house hold name § none of my pets are breathing properly . Am i the asshole (AITA) § the most important part of any account on here is the posts. if you dont have the posts youre basically finished § Rumours are having it that this next star wars is fixing to be the most twisted, for adults, and mentally ill one yet #Episo-deIX #EpisodeIX § if youre putting together graphics for your book you can just use royalty free images of chicken legs instead of normal legs and it will look fine #art #tips #help #helpful #smart€¦ https://t.co/eP93iZmhDf § piss #ad § wandering aroud w/ my thumb up my ass during Civil War 2, asking people to show me their posts so i can tell if i should grenade them or not § juts donated $300000 to a lobbying firm whose main thing is letting people drive cars at the age of 6 § just because im a gamer with Polio, doesnt mean i cant someday become somebody's Butler § not sure if im hearing all the lyrics, but it seems like the guy in the song "Bad to the bone" is bad because he has a lot of consensual sex § Feeling very crapped on by my followers § Im going to try posting like that now § Seems to me when you hand your money to the burger king man he takes it at 99mph but when he gives you your change back its 1mph. Oh lord! § 25% exp penalty for asking what ethnicity beetlejuice is in the team chat § Bacon nutella fortnite selfystick iPhone avocado kanye Mocha Latte (deep breath) triggered tinder starbucks Chipotle safe space pumpkinspice § "this is going to sound so cool" i rev the engine and it explodes, leaving me rolling around on the road with a smouldering dick & ass crack § i am not quite ready to declare this coming summer as "The Summer of Gaming" but keep up with my feed and i will let you know when i do it § if the sting ray that killed steve irwin tried to kill me i would bust its ass and crumple it up like a newspaper § before you go around muting my posts and blocking this or that , its import-ant to consider the Shit that i bring to the table § i love shit that isnt "For" me § feeding my pigs a big bag of barber hair § i want to beat the shit out of a ufo § swinging my great grandfather's nine iron around on my motorcy-cle and saying "Seniors Rule" every time i hit something § the anti flintstones agenda. by saying bull shit like "Yabba dabba dont" the pro-Jetsons Associated Press is flagrantly exposing their Ass. https://t.co/p82tDK9zRj § WATCH: Low IQ single Father fooled into thinking he has been accepted to Yale at the age of 44. Savor his pain § wiki/Coprophagia/media/File:Adonis_Blue_butterflies.jpg https://t.co/ZKAVHPHCTO § (contorting entire face into an abominable purple frown) cobb salad?? that sounds fuckin STUPID § i requested 1 jeans, of 100% Legacy Deluxe Denim Menswear. what you've brought me is Classic Men's Denim Premium Wear, which, clearly sucks, § you don't need to tell me im beautiful because boys are out here doing it for them self this year § you are a known troll and reply guy § saying something like "i only bought that nirvana album b/c it has a babys dick on it" and alternating between backpedaling & doubling down § i do support the long display names so people can change them to things like "The Discourse Is a Hell Of A Drug!!" instead of an actua lname § changing my display name to "Richerd Simmons" as an april fools prank and inducing dissociative Psychosis on millions of on-line people § as a guy who developed an autoimmune response to comedy as a result of being "Roasted" for my Ice man tattoo, ive much to say of April FOols § (seeing the RE/MAX balloon at a hockey game) shit, they got RE/MAX here? Not bad, § im not verified yet but i hope to be once @JACK deals with his many personal demons . § Introvert = In vitro pervert. theyre sick § aid's § the reason i dont address the trolls ib because i know that the truth would hurt them so much that they would probably take their own lives. § Reviewing your application for my exclusive group dm with girls in it... Hmm whats this? In 2016 you said my posts are "Family guy" ? Denied § its a coin § i will never use the word "Doubloon" to describe a coin § i have just gotten word that the 3d dog in Untitled 3D Dog Project (2021) can speak english, like a man § Out Here Ginding § when firiing a weapon i dont believe in recoil § pringles caliphate § star wars is back § the wga guild kicked the shit out of me and rooted through my bag and stole my screen play "husband baby" aobut a woman who marries a baby § @Team_Mitch @AOC https://t.co/nwYmVoKRTX § @rwang0 @AdobeSummit Once again i have been blocked for starting the dialouge . § "Feel as though ive evolved beyond the need for Product, and now crave the Customer Experience" Hubert Joly: Boy have I got the shit for you § it fucking Sucks when a store sells me shit https://t.co/OZBhvWs87p § you look like the tomb raider lady Lol Mar 22 just heard the news of jussie smollett. Feeling unsafe right now 5s You can no longer send m § sorry for roasting your set up § saying "WOW" out loud watching youtube guy's username spin around in 3d in the 20 second intro to his video, going Psycho watching this shit § there`s no job harder than that of the Media Personality. there are so many massive pedophiles who you have to not accidentally say are good § oh forgive me for forgetting that youre too good to visit my squalid LA apartment to watch all 9 seasons of the abc sitcom "coach" as a joke § when the earths Magnetic Poles flip and everyone suddenly stops thinking script format posts are good <<< (whichever directions the bad one) § ME: I love shit that is Dunning-Kruger NY Times: What? WaPo: Explain your self jeffrey Epstein: Damn lol , Nicely trolled § full time Cash Back award activator § buiyng a massive 30lb bottle of pills labelled "PussyAdvantage" for a girl on here who told me im like a more Honest version of Dane Cook... § just found out about Object Permanence... why didnt any one tell me about this shit § mastering Life calmness in the face of being called a dip shit § giving myself micro penis as punishment for my worsening posture § my ass isnt very good, over all. my ass and the hole of my ass are boring to think about § - the Deterioration of my Balls - § the gaming challenge: load up your video game of choice and play it until you reach the credits sequence. the gaming challenge § pleased to eannounce that all my posts will now be about the Filipino israeli defense force, which i have recently been fooled into joining § starting to think maybe that it kicked ass when that guy siad "show me the money" in that movie i never watched § spending my honey moon in the bathroom, watching video of chef gorddon ramsey saying "Ah Fuck Me" after being served a shitty looking onion § started smoking at the advice of the "Making friends in your 50's" reddit post, quit after reading the "How to make your cum taste good" one § yes i am a "HO" Honorable online § waiter i would like to pay my bill , "En PiÃ¨ces" (In coins) § if harvard offered to increase my IQ by one point per dollar i would simply say no. And that's the most important takeaway from all this § today; we are all Yale § i do not trust this graph as it has clearly been doctored to look like a penis § two handfuls of kitty litter taken from the beautiful hollywood home of sports broadcaster Dick Vitale , for $100 or best offer § withholding this week's Epic Games tithe until they address the issue of people on the mic calling me "Somebody Uncle" § today is international lunch day so start eating. #InternationalLunchDay https://t.co/H6iZBS4FW1 § they will kick my ass for saying it. they will take my career and my livelihood away from me. but "Wine" , is better than, "The News" § oh youre a paramedic? i write a bunch of sutupid fucking shit on the internet about my ass hole and penis. Its cool

though. Its fun § feel as though i could break through most walls with my bare hands , given an unlimited amount of time and resources § Funny how some people will forget to click the like button on my posts but always remember to like posts that say war crimes are good , etc § ive enlisted the aid of Simon & Schuster to publish my thoughts of Jussie Smollett in an early 2021 release entitled “Thoughts of Jussie” . § O ---||--- | 8==D ~~-,. /
\\ ` Poseurs / \ § attempting to hand hundred dollar bills to the ailing sheldon adelson like duce nukem § the rumors are true, my posts are all written in GMT Time; “Giving My Thoughts” . § Fidgett spinners are making people dumb assed . § This is the reason i post . § im taking back thw word “Penis” because boys are being out here doing it for them self § consider that the possibility remains, that most of you have not yet hit the skill ceiling of wiping your ass § #foundMedia #ReallyGood https://t.co/YYwE6w6ZpQ § elvis never fucked any of his fans . thats why he was “The king” § https://t.co/tMHyhyopnH Very Nice § fuck tumblr https://t.co/DpPFs4N8De § might fuck around and post “The Masked Shitter” , as a sort of commentary on a certain tv show with a similar name § Its 2019 and It `s only 12 pm § jacking off is “ Ghetto “ § when i see shit on the news saying we lost 50000 jobs for w/e reason, i say damn... i couldve scored some of those jobs, if they werent Lost § everyone needs something worth dying for..mine just happens to be the japanese racist version of the wazzup ad § i was going to do it but I got scared § now from my understanding, the bra store is not only a place to get bras, but also functions as a sort of social hub, for single woman & men § entering Crisis Mode after doing one of the bath salt jokes from 2013 & getting clapped backed by a girl saying bath salts are good actually § human sack of dog shit; holding up the self service aisle, trying to beat the system by taping balloons to the produce scale § this aint the damn barney channel https://t.co/EGdhPwu2bi § you tube has very specifically been recommending me videos of apes getting electrocuted so clearly the data indicates im some sort of mutant § if you dont down load the latest versions of all your programs youre fucking stupid § the Clitoral pussy § i like to act genuinely baffled when people tell me to shut the fuck up. like “Huh? But why? The shit i post here helps people, but ok,” § if i had a million bucks i would b uy a Pregnant sears mannequin § howd would youd like a taste of my butt cheek , Punk § lord knows i help my self from time to time... § A man took sips out of his neighbor` s hummingbird feeder for over 2 years. This is what happened to his Kidneys § “The Godfather: Part Iraq” (2004) In this 4th installment of the Godfather series, the godfathers head to iraq to settle the score, of 9/11. § i would say Mr President, the partisan gridlock ends now. i would then roll up like a pill bug and pray for the darkness to come quickly § if the united states president deemed me a threat to our nation, absoluitely i would let him zap me in the skull. i would hand him the gun, § Shut the fuck up . Christ https://t.co/mkX7Gx88HP § And its onl y 1:pm. Thread § chose your fighter https://t.co/v690dybg24 § ME: id like to use my AAdvantage rewardsPoints, American Airlines: Im ready to pull the trigger. Go on. Drive the knife deeper into my heart § rocky homer simpson show § Mhickey Mouse Cartoon Hands Flipping The Bird Marijuana Weed for Iphone and Samsung Galaxy Case (iPhone 6 plus white) § “they shoul;d replace the cameras on cellphones with Bibles. because the Bible is like a camera into your soul” - michio kaku § open letter, to the man who told me that they should make an app for “Shutting the fuck up” during my town hall web development conference ; § It Is said, that the online content creator absorbs the combined pain of every follower 24 hrs a day--and that is why they cry in saddness... § flashing the coupon that allows me to shit in the kfc employee restroom, like a police badge, as i vault my big ass over the counter § wildly agreeing with some shit im reading in the newspaper that says like “There is nothing more Iconic, than Milk and Cereal” § ihate it when a doddering Nanny yanks me by the ear lobe,

right when im about to click “Like” on a big plate of sausages § you say “36,000 pounds of chicken nuggets recalled by the Tyson Foods corporation due to possible rubber contamination” ... i say “LUNCH’ § laughing all the way to the bank, but only because the guy walking in front of me is wearing a twisted t-shirt........... § What is it that you first seek when inspecting a profile which presents a potential networking opportunity § captured by a medieval castle town in the year 1598, hung up on the cross and having long florescent light bulbs broken against my dick § it’s balls to ass like the sheriff say https://t.co/1QAuhEaKRu § making my face Symmetrical in microsoft paint after haivng a mental breakdown on linkedin. com § Its time to open the dialouge, on the Mens penis. § using my turn at a karaoke bar to try to do a 5 miunte routine that basically just says bryan singer is the new gawker writer or something § it takes so many muscles to kick my ass. like a million § it takes fewer muscles to smile than it does to break a baseball bat across the back of my fat neck § there is too much of Lies... § Genius: the Human body can survive being shot 100 times Fool: ? Genius: (Shoots self in th exact same spot 100 times) remember to click Like § none f you know anything about art or life. i have read the entire dictionary more than 100 times § some one on here said they were going to “Cuck” teddy ruxpin, while the mods are off sipping mimosas somewhere § shitting on a Towel § im not going to post about taking shits or shitting anymore . i Condemn all of my previous posts about shitting and asses § every one with the word “meme” in their bio has put at least one hole in their bedroom wall with the butt of a rifle § resisting extreme amounts of arrest § ill show you real truth. ill show you what happens when you crap on a real son of a bitch § pulled over for dragging a clothing donation bin behind my truck; asking cop to make people stop honking at me because “its loud” “it sucks” § all cops should be forced to dress like james bond, as a promotional thing. I think it would be fun to get pulled over by 007 James bond § Im fucking the wall. a tectonic shift 900 miles away causes it to slice off my thin prick and drop it on mexican soil. Its their problem now § please remove the pervert alert § And I am being told now, that because Incest is now Official White House policy, that this post could be construed as a “Politics tweet” § just got word from a trusted source: the guy who said he would fuck his daughter on “The View” is in hot water for spelling hamburger wrong § me,; attempting to heckle a stand up comedian: Hey pal I dont come to where you work and knock the dick out of oyur mouth!! Mother fucker § shooting my lee dungarees with an uzi for that “armyman” look § i miss 100% of the shots i dont take mother fucker § user “rat_thrower” has received a 500 minute ban for proposing a 28th constitutional amendment § im not a ignorant fuckfaced dip shit. i enjoy every minute of it § shut thr fuck up https://t.co/Cd71KPOCA6 § should go without saying but, if they show j. bezos penis on the news i will postpone the showing of my penis, to avoid confusing followers. § being desperate enough for human connection to go onto girls posts & chide them for using Twitter Web Client or whatever other one they used § I am not a baby . I am a Human § i will show my penis because i do not want to host the Oscars, as you see, i will be busy that night, watching the Oscars. § on February 19th, 2019, i will show my penis on here and effectively remove myself from consideration as the host of this years Oscar show. § @FBI @LASDHQ while youre here id like to report this pervert for impersonating a cowboy § might do a post of “macklemore” soon. § craping out a single sunflower seed and frowning while i inspect it § EVERY ONE: Divorce jokes are SO funny, and I love to spout my mouth to disresepect https://t.co/DvGbjDQDah and jeff ME: No no no. Im uncomfortable. No § just heard on the news that our enemies all follow the cutesy motivational shit accounts also, and draw even more power from them than we do § getting brain damage from pissing my self off § #LawEnforcementAppreciationDay showing apperciation today by wearing the badge and uniform i bought from off of ebay thank you Sir https://t.co/LK5KvioChU § posting Ethically, within reason § how do i ask my girl followers on here to marry me with out looking like im "Stunting " or trying to "Pimp" § "fear not loyal fans. james bond blasts all his turds/piss to smithereens with a laser while on missions." -james bond, author of james bond § gathering data of Nude Locals § Seems as though lately, peop[le have been talking their mouths of things § Im being reply guyed § some times you just gotta say " uff said" because enough of the shit has been said to that point § (hearing the first recorded sound from 1860, a pivotal technological milestone) This guy sounds like shit. Mostly his voice sounds like shit § ive modified my phone to deliver electric shocks each time one of you unfollows me. The pain will make me kinder, humbler, and more powerful § i will do better next year sir § scoring 15% on the buzz feed quiz "Medical Term or Slur" § weaving a "Feel Good" tale about how dogs hate fireworks because theyre reincarnate US armymen with ptsd; getting down voted for some reason § calm the FUCK down § From the twisted minds behind Dr. Pepper, § im not wishning you freaks a happy new year. you will all fuck up my 2019, like you have with all the other years. youre dopes § thinking about how good the Hanging Gardens of Babylon would be, if it wasnt ruined by its obnoxious fanbase § guy who once posted "Service dogs love having their ears grabbed" given permanent seat in wolf blitzers situation room #Redemption § just once id like to see an archaeologist speak truth on one of the mummys he found. "He looks like someone knocked the shit out of him" § baptizing my badge and gun, in Sinnersblood § taking a deep breath and inhaling all that horrible, pornographic Wi-fi § (rodent voice) its damn Friday night!!! And Ill be dipped in shit if I aint ready to throw down some pecker § I Want all of that shit § i put an alert on that shit like 10 years ago. thank you https://t.co/5klkP0KjGs § Can you make them all un block me please . https://t.co/cDZQuGSYAx § linking my Folders to other Folders or whatever the fuck it is people do on the computer § ME: No matter how ya slice it, Sometimes some shit is just true ???: Shit is never true. Its all false ME: Youre wrong my friend § "Hwhoo!! That's a lot of zeroes" - me after seeing the amount of money of $12.00 § "breaking in" my new pair of jeans by tossing it onto the freeway and letting cars run over it while i observe it through a scope § brushing teeth; mouth gaping open like a shit head as toothpaste drips down my wrist, waking up next morning in a panic, thinking it's cum § buying an assortment of soaps and ointments to make my ass hole less stupid § JACKING OFF and committing FRAUD § ive always said we need to make the Dou Jones go up, instead of down. And now that ive been proven right, every one wants to kiss my dick . § considering improving the quality of my posts somewhat, so i can get the MacArthur Genius Award, for them § great tweetie bird quote https://t.co/w8KamUmBC1 § trying to drink a can of beer . § operating an unregulated labor camp on the Dean's lawn a nd saying "Shut the fuck up sir" when he comes out of his house to threaten us § the dean loves it when me and the boys piss him off with black helicopters § excitedly approaching people, with a rehearsed smile, like a fucked up rodent, and asking them what they think of the latest Bixby update § buying a nice curtain for the whole ass and dick area of my bulk § seeing more and more people post anti-lunch sentiments despite the fact that, well, they gotta eat . § https://t.co/8TVcfvDUKm my book is now 35% off again for some reason. $11.68 - cheaper than dog shit " ice for the holidays" § I;ve looked at the facts. Hell im looking at the facts right now. § @YahooNews his mission was to destroy it . § judges should sentence perverts to more stupid shit, like making them do obstacle courses made out of porno. bet it's not so good now huh § youtube guy does magic tricks for an ape, and someone in the comments says magic is actually harmful to apes. well, fuck this shit, then !! § geting AssBlasted for sharing my normal man's perspective, in a world . being fucked hardcore, by goblins, for liking Due Process § using intense calmness , As the dragon , while dealing with peoples shitmouth § rats dont have pussys § fairly confident that even if i became a rat some how, i still would not want to fuck any of the other rats § ME: computer; what is my Jeans Number please COMPUTER: your jeans number is 5. the ultimate compromise of durability & comfort ME: (Smiling) § envisioning Jeans Hotspots across america & various territories, where consumers can learn their "Jeans number" and look at photos of jeans § listeing to the updated version of the "baby its cold outside" song where the guy's trying to convince the woman to leave so he can jack off § just got word that because the extensive water damage present o n my balls and part of my ass, i am no longer allowed to vote § rscreaming "Shut the Fuck Up" over and over again at my monitor as it slowly morphs into a Mirror and only makes me angrier § none of my followers masturbate. § girls love saying shit like "Ebay is my father", while i sit in my house 50 miles away solivng a book of 200 expert level crossword puzzles. § thinking back to 9/11.. i wish i had flipped out more. Wondering how different things wou;d be if i had gone more ape shit § im proud to announce that ive started and cancelled The Female Bras Project due to Free Speech and Trolls, respectively § eaitng a raw piece of corn in my car and spitting like 95% of it right back out § surround alcatraz with Poison 2020 § Imbecile https://t.co/xrsMDS7tux § if youre one of thoe waiters who carries the little scraper around , to the tables, to get the crumbs off it `` Kiss Da Back O' My Nuts `` § i like to believe that getting my ass kicked 100 times a day for 50 years has granted me "Street Smarts" § taking my 3d printed wife to the Arboretum . § give me the 200000 § need a dog who can maneuver something in the ball park of 600000 blocks of limestone around my yard https://t.co/wul3XHxzzQ § wondering at what age my domesticated rat terrier is supposed to "Graduate" and move out of my house § santa https://t.co/8TVcfvDUKm #goodbook #Remembering41 #BushFuneral § i will block those who shit on the Bones of Mr. GHWB, euthanized with a lethal dose of Heroin after 94 years of service "As was his request" § hunched over my Bureau Plat with quill & ink , writing a thank you letter to the Kohler toilet company for letting me shit in their toilets § arms folded, back turned to the television, refusing to "Meet the flintstones" despite the theme song's pleas § a man asks God, how am i supposed to live, without George H.W. Bush God simply said "That is why I made 2 george bushs" The man just smiled. § now the 5s on the other hand. the ironclad Top influencers. you know these guys wouldnt be caught dead with an ass thats less than pristine § some pf you are definitely a 1. i truly believe the carelessness you exhibit with your sloppy posts is reflected also by your dire ass hole. § my 5 point numerical scale determines how likely a user is to be negligent in wiping their ass properly, based on the stuff they post here § Mr. Spendmoney Tomakemoney § i hate it when im jacking off, and... And, uh,. thats it. thats the tweet § reality check....its not "Funny" or "Good" to fool Content Creators into showing their penis to the official red lobster account-- Perieod. § i would like to become somebodys Uncle so i can start posting shit like " ot all dips are marinades , but all marinades, are dips" § the words "yugioh angel" reverse burned into my flesh after attempting to pose shirtless on the hood of my modified car during a heat wave § #RockCenterXMAS a holiday Salute, to all the guys who died while putting bulbs in that big ass tree, whose bodies just got left up there § cant get ahold of my brexit adviser § can feel such a shit load of energies tonight, that i may see them, and that i may be here for them, on the computer tonight § take my penis out? in a "PUBLIC BATHROOM" (the key word, being public) no thanks. im not jared from sub way § ive decided that it would be good, to have 2 million followers. now what do you say we get the damn ball rolling on that § sending people who tell me not to eat romaine lettuce a link to the wikipedia article for The Streisand Effect § keep it coming. I love this shit https://t.co/ARQRhnGxC1 § a tendency to substitute the word "Shit" with "Dust" when talking to girls (e.g. "just wiped a bunch of Dust out of my ass today") § "Watch the new Barney?" that the worst thing any one has ever said to me and you need to S.T.F.U. before i bring the hammer down to your ass § did you know, every time you flush the toilet without closing the lid, millions of waste particles fly directly into my open mouth & kill me § a tisket? Fine a tasket? Fuck yes a green and yellow basket? Too much § all the youth thhese days look like dead eyed little perverts because they are not incorporating Geritol into their daily routine § my teething ring. my salt lick. my feeding tube. all at once § putting on my game face. the official face of the nfl § there should be a good version of the oscars where they hand out statues that are fucking wearing clothes § mixing various wine's together and making authentic "Al dente" pasta by straining it one minute early, as instructed by the box § man throwing chairs compilation 2018- uploaded by the games codger § my turds are nobodys problem but my own. and theyre boring § i am protected from your bull shit § first they say we cant build mosques on ground zero. now we cant build the amazon headquarters. maybe we should go live in the fucking Woods § just thought of a good name for a fictional football team located in a town that i also made up the name of , "The Boatswainville Birdhawks" § mother fucker . catch these boots § 63 updates available? youre telling me thyere making my apps even better, for FREE? And to think these guys, get so much greif § in a world where big data threatens to commodify our lives,. telling online surveys that i "Dont know" what pringles are constitutes Heroism § holy gravy holy meat holy moly let us eat https://t.co/XSVi3m7kH5 § lesbian Wireless § down load the brexit app today muy lord § crawling on all fours like the cave men - enhanced mobility -powerful stance (can not be knocked over) - pretty good § remembering the anguiush the girls had caused me when they said it was good to have "Dadbod" § looking at pictures of rotisserie chickens i wish i could maul with my bare hands § every day, the content creator sits at his Oak Escritoire and asks "How can I transfer the maximum amount of pain to my parasitic Engagers" § i can promise only this; i will lick the boots of my enemies until they beg for mercy , crying § quick reminder to vote for the guy you want to lose tomorrow, just to get as pissed off as possible and enhance your Craft through suffering § it is indeed possible to shit too much. i would advise my followers to try to shit in multiple, smaller intervals , throughout the day. § uber ride home from dennys iwth the instagram Gf (mid-20s, dressed like a casino waitress) shrieking at each other because i "Made a face" § q: what is a "What da fuck" moment A: a "What da fuck" moment is one of those times that just simply makes you say what the fuck § attaching an enmormous dildo to my rifle so i can grip it in my mouth for added stability. thats how it is #army #navy #themafia § covering "sarcasm just another service i offer" tshirt with a shirt that says im not that interested in sarcasm to catch my rivals off guard § pledging to cut down on "oafish" behavior, such as accidentally eating spicy food or having my shirt ripped off by a windmill § world record 100 diaper combo run over by jeep § excuse me. could i please get my Blowup. you gave MetalGearEric a blowup. am i truly less deserving, than MetalGearEric? where is my blow up § #selfiesforariana https://t.co/UhPYcMgkp5 § how do i get one of those stupid ass hyper links under my display name that says im a senator § i do not say this lightly, i would do what ever means necessary to protect my beloved posters from the devilish hands of otto Warmbier § when you call me a shit head, or a dip shit, or a low rent stooge, that is like putting a knife directly into my Posts. § (11yr old Jack Droseys head pulled out of toilet)it bears repeating that 'Likes' are not conducive to my vision, and th(gets dunked again) § clumsily wiping my ass in the woods § if i wanted to die painfully i would live in that shitty aquarium with your fish § really good place to leave a new toilet https://t.co/HgvaJBzc7s § shut thef FUCK UP § i will never thank you § its funny and it Rocks § Thats right. I did the blocks. Im absolutely ripping ass up tonight and I dont give a fuck who knows it. This is the power of my holy light § nothing give s me more power in this life than blocking a guy who asks me nicely in the dms to unblock him or one of his rat friends § its monday now, but ive decided that yesterday was the first official “Shut Da Fuck Up Sunday” which means its time to block 5 dick heads § if you come to this website for jokes, rather than Experiences, youre Fucking yourself § i saod it once i say it again--the pain of being a content creative influencer, and dealing with peoples shit, is like child birth on “Crack” § i think that if mensa started getting involved in gang violence, they would easily Win § they should invent a new Danimal , mayvbe one that people might actually fucking want to associate with yogurt products for once § reminder to guys trying to offer me Merch Deals, that i tried selling shirts once but it failed because none of my followers wear shirts § if my bank balance is below $100 i will refuse to vote. if it is over $100 i will vote for whichever candidate has the best “Ground game” § wondering how i learned all the different informal synonyms for “penis” outside of health class. I think they announced them on the news § #WorldFoodDay food sucks. food sucks § It is simply for your foolish claim that the economys doing poorly, right after they increased the Mega Millions Jackpot, that I am Smiling. § this is every thing and its only 11:am, https://t.co/XOioXnwFQh § there seems to be a Fucking mistake here sir, https://t.co/akzYXMEKj1 § thinking of some new provocative poses and gestures i can use at the local drive in movie theater to get my ass kicked more efficiently § paid by sinclair broadcast group to read paragraphs of unbearable QAnon Shit to a roblox server full of 7yr olds attacking me for my beliefs § absolutely ruining my own day by imagining a restaurant that refuses to serve me because im wearing brass knuckles § coke zero but for pringles. pringles zero § getting my Dick finagled , by my tantric wifebride, in my chamber’s § my expert analysis wouuld indicate that each point on the dow jones = 1 job(s) § COP: weve detected unusual amounts of cum being flushed down the toilet at your house. please stop ME: Thats not mine. Its uh,. my dogs cum § i hold this one truth, that the only acceptable time to use the word “Doo-Dah” is while singing the hit cult-classic “Camptown Races” § i hold this one truth, that thr only acceptable time to use the word “Doo-Dah” is while singing the cult-classic hit “Yankee Doodle” § good avatar round up October 2018 https://t.co/1hffeu7Wd9 § deleted the tweet where i said that homer simpson is allowed to show his penis in the japanese version and im allowed to work at kmart again § - its not clever to show pictures of me morphing into a dog - its not funny - it odes not introduce Beauty into the world § Oh how i hate him § just thought of a new guy. “The Guy who writes down the make and model of a car he saw in a car commercial, for future reference” § he has not responded to my request to send him to boot camp § digimonotis: i do not trust or support him EpicWayne: i trust and support epic wayne mr_Tight-nuts : i support him but i do not trust him § consider how unprepared society would be if every bug and moth flying around just started taking giant shits constantly, like human sized § yelp review one liner i have prepared in case i find a turd in my meal: “If i wanted a guy’s Shit in my food, I would have ordered it!!” § feel i have much to reflect upon in my life, on news of receiv-ing “The Golden Douchebag” award. Many improvements to make, moving forward. § COP: Tell me citizien. (prepares kill shot) Do you believe in God ME (realiz-ing i left my “Do you Believe in god” cheat sheet at home): Uuhh § my brain stacks 2 baby blocks together mentally and i involuntarily say something like “Trader Joes is basicly the Modern simpsons episodes” § do better § I Have been told that my followers have agreed that it would be good, if my name that people started calling me were to become “MR.JUICE” § THE BOYS: Come! Come quickly! Theres a Seal balancing a ball on its nose, at the Gazebo ME: Cant. Wife is making me buy 36 Forever Stamps § Realizing the food at KFC sucks ass for the 4th or 5th time in my life , and making myself calm by looking up famous quotes about “Chaos” § a respectful nod to all my friends whohave been removed from group chats after having some sort of melt down. "The Fallen Angels" § Cigar mommys § Im just going to say that this is for anyone who thinks its good https://t.co/0H5z1U7quD § Theres a guy standing outside lennys pastrami shop. Says hes going to goon your ass § (Guy coming towards me with a weapon. at a walking pace) "Ill goon your ass hole. Ill goon your ass sir" "You will not goon my ass" § "ill goon your ass. ill pig you out" yeuah um, No, its highly unlikely that you will "Goon" my ass. Try reading a book of english § (using a hand mirror to get a real good look at my Fucking balls) whoah!! im seeing double! § tipping the waiter is BORING, no one even DOEs it § when i block people its cool, like Neo kicking agent smith down a flight of staiors. when people block me its because theyre pussys § blockbotting the boys group after they put a towel over one of our friends heads and convinced me that its elon Musk, come to kick my ass § slapping all my repliers across the face in one swoop like moe howard. all of them dropping dead instantly § absolutely nuking my dick into 1000000 pieces with one of those wile e coyote tnt plungers § epic wayne once told me that there is a hard limit that the human body can handle jacking off in one day. and that the limit is 3 § my mentions are on lock down until further notice . § the only A+ i ever got was from that time in art class when i drew venus & serena willaims clobbering the. shit out of me with their rackets § at the library; carelessly flipping through some of the most famous literary classics that you can think of, looking for coupons § thinking about displaying an authentic harley davidson denim vest in a box frame to really tie my rec room together and make it suck ass § "hooters 2" is the most perfect phrase ive ever seen. "hooters 2" is just ok. "hooters 2" isnt that funny. "hooters 2" is good again. § "always have at least 2 drew Carey anec-dotes" § getting my ass run over after trying to hijack a guy's riding mower and failing § think i might quit my job and invent the Original chicken sandwich § @BigDogClub yeah that blows. anyway i was wondering where i can buy one of them please § reminder that on this sacred of days that i was the first guy to condemn the 911 attacks, while everyone else was busy watching honey Boboo § Wendy`s is so main stream now, that eating there has become a bit of a Wank . § boycott digimon otis. hes not even that funny § watching some bulllet time movies and inventing my own bechdel test for bullet time instead of girls § guys in a pizzeria fighting and busting the little parmesan shakers against the table to shiv each other with § using mindfulness. to waste my enemies § by refusing to accept my invitation to a formal debate. octomom has gone Rogue § wearing a false ass crack and prosthetic dick on top of my real ones in case my pants get burned off by fire § COWORKER: I Just took out a little baggie of DouDou, to eat at work, and Im getting a raise, for being handsome ME: I Admire your Opinions . § i invented pain and I am so good at knowing what pain is and im biting my fingers really hard out of respect for pain § please lord publish my email just this once § Some body is going to take a picture of their white house press pass with a load on it, by 2020 § Not. All. Of. The. Wet. Spots. On. My. Jeans. Are. Piss. Stians. § Geans § @SwissIOCForever thanks for showing me this robots dick § just reassuring you all, that if i forgot to include your favorite tweet in my book it is because it sucked Ass. Get fucked off of my page § just plowing trhough the 7-11 double doors with extra wide samurai armour and dropping broken glass all over my Geta (ä‚‹é§„) § me and the boys watching james bond morph into a black guy before our very eyes , and braying at the movie screen like distressed cattle § i think that big foot and mouth man have sons every 20 years or so and they make the son the next big foot or whatever § i am being targetted by a shadow campaign just because i cured my own diarhrea by exercising instead of taking "PILLS" § thinking about taking some of the excess respect I have for our Fallen Heroes and converting it in to Cold Hard Cash § jack: i will protect you from all rogue group dms. you are not a "Honkey" . Your an angel me: Im an angel. Im intelligent. Im not a honkey § i attribute my small dick to my low IQ, and my entire body being too dumb ass to send vitamins & minerals to my dick to make it normal sized § censership § here comes that ass hole. that bloated nit wit trying to scam us again. that howling jack-o-lantern. Boy id love to get a look at his pecker § thinking of inventing a new type of person to get mad at on here. maybe people who carry too many keys around.. i dont know yet § since opinoins are judged based on how new they are, instead of how good they are, today i will make $1000 by posting "Rap music is hipster" § do any of you know any good lawyers that i can sue you with § Im told that it's wrong to think that Mickey mouse would have 1 million dollars if he was a real person. Im told my beliefs are trash § the varicose vein gamer § struting around in my stepson cowboy hat looking for an ass kicking § expliaining to wife what the phrase "pussy nexus: beyond pussy" means and why it has appeared on my credit card statement like 8 times § Not My Problem § fine then you can just skim through and look at t he pictures like a damn toddler § i Fucking hate it when i come at the king and miss, especially when I best not do that § i am the "Walter Cronkite" of game stop. yes i absolutely said it, and no im not deleting it this time. § would like to see the myth busters come back to tackle the myth that its illegal to open other peoples mail § i bet the three stooges would be pissed if they figured out the name of their show. they probably think its called "the three normal guys' § i now concede that girls may be allowed to wear UNDERARMOUR„¢ brand clothing; but only if they sign a contract stating its for sports reasons § the worst part of nationalism is having to pretend the flag is really good, like "yeah the country looks exactly like that. they nailed it" § they need to put nets up in the baseball fields to catch all the homers. youre wasting so many good baseballs and it makes me sick § people will tell me shit like "oh you cant say kofi annan was no fap. no evidence" and i say, how dare you sully a mans grave, with politics § kicking the shit out of a tree with a sledge hammer, to increase my Stamina § guys think if they squat my user name on emerging social media platforms ill give them $1000 for it , instead of just calling them a Bitch § pleased to report that an angel has lifted the curse against me after doing my "Good Deed" of the year, by tipping a waiter 15% § retiring into the portable dog kennel i live in and shutting the tiny gate to keep the shit heads out § agreed, https://t.co/dc5yuiJjza § baffled as to why the powers that be would insist that me, my Hotwif,e & paramour Hubby can not enlist in the marines together as a Squadron § tha;ts what a pervert would say § stay at home rat § go whack off else whare § fuck it , if youre still anonymous in 2018 you are 100% a pervert § the bobs big boy milkshake mix up has become Racial. i repeat, the bobs big boy milkshake mix up has become Racial. § when one of the boys tells me he has to use the bathroom i inevitably respond with some stupid shit like "Alright, Sounds Good" § wasting other people;s Emotional Labor, by posting public screeds about the coming retribution of Lunchables Snack Packs § steel reserve 211 extra high gravity breast milk § they should make web 2.0 slot machines that show the faces of your loved ones instead of shit like cherrys, the number 7, and the word "Bar" § i love being the guy at pitch fork whose job it is to argue that thr greatest song of all time is "You Aint Nothin But A Hound Dog" by elvis § the road is a battle field, all the other cars are your enemies, and not using turn signals gives you an Advantage against then § EFFECTIVE IMMEDIATELY: homer simpson will stop saying "D'oh" and will instead say "Fuck" , as the Creators originally intended 30 years ago § first they ignore you then they laugh at u then you jack off & read posts for 30 years then you die of pulmonary heart disease then you Win § the army: forbidden from jacking off. ~99% kill shot ratethe mafia: encouraged to jack off. cant kill guys unless theyre tied to chairs § i can just tell all of you are going to be a bucnh of little shits today and rat fuck me out of another pulitzer price by not retweeting me § $1000000 Post: julian assange walking out of the ecuadoran embassy covered in shit and saying do not go in there like ace ventuera § i gotta say it folks. breast milk tastes like SHIT., "Sorry ladies" § every one on this web site is this guy https://t.co/ybaUQKdA7o § had that dream again. a Top Female Influencer grasped my hand and took me to my Forever Home..where i never have to demean myself by posting § when a web site asks if i want to see their " ew Design" it is the exact same thing as a man asking if i want to see his penis and ass § @AP Cnan I have some please § the games they're putting out these dsys. Damn. Theyre so good that you never even see gamers with depression anymore § "To my unfollowers, I will strive to reexamine my content strategies, and do my best to earn back your follow." NOt. Eat my Fuckin shit § Shut Ya Fuckin Mouth § realm of Lamar https://t.co/mrdbdyj1mA § #InternationalSelfCareDay riding hood of my 18wheeler freaking out getting shaken baby syndrome & turning red like a boiled crab sucking ass § some one please help this man https://t.co/MCcnG5J7ki § mario is back https://t.co/9ZdeE4sY2V § this codger is an absolute mate... the lad is a flintstone § your damn right im a some of a bitch. soorryest some of a bitch i ever met § you know what wo uld be fun, would be if twitter hq just dumped a truck full of wet turds on my front lawn every day "In case I missed it" § tuesday morning is " Low Engagement " , which means if you absolutely must have a melt down over Followbacks now's the time to do it § sending my most powerful kisses to all pregnant women fire fighers § making a Fairly solid argument that tthe same societal sickness that led to Minstrel Shows manifests itself today as "Doggo Shit" § it is a Content Curator's solemn duty, to post links to shit, without freaking out under the intense scrutiny of the craven, impotent masses § reminder that if you block me after sending me a message, i am unable to respond to it § what the fuck is Salt life please § if the pigs decimate my follower count tomorrow€"Know this. followers are just a number. devoid of meaning. and they can never take my Likes § it is said that if "BILL GATES" dropped a $100 Bill, it would be a waste of his time to have everoyone within the perimeter terminated § you call this a menu?? where the FUCK are the Heart Healthy Essentials § there is no act more intimate & sensual than browsing a mans "Like" page , and clicking on there without permission is the ultimate betrayal § thinking about getting some miniature Gibson guitar replicas box framed, and hanging thenm up for the boys to come over and look at § the most bone headed move is to just go out and about with a name like "scooter." that shit sucks. Hell no. i would not even name a dog that § but its "Tailored for you" § this is an attack. you are attacking me § oh look€"i failed my forklift operators certification for the 4th fucking time becausse none of the girls on here bothered fucking helping me § sending slowmo footage of my balls undear-neath the bathtub faucet being pulverized by the water pressure to ameicas funniest home videos § i would take so many bribes if i was a judge. half my shit would be bribes. take bribes from the criminals until theyre too poor to do crime § a dog should never stand on its hind legs for any reason. that is for humans to do only and they look like fucked up chickens § using the skills i learned of mario to traverse a real life pile of crates § meeting up with ErnieTheBlade and ChaosWendell at shakeshack to discuss the depravity of bobbed hair § do not make my life a living hell § Reminder that we are no longer mailing locks of our own hair to girls, in 2018 . § yanny, and laurel, "SUCKS" !!!! Im back bitch § Gasping for piss § do not "Like brigade" me § big news gang. another A++ app from the theranos company to help me keep track of all my silver ware. let me just say. Wow § my followers know im the go-to Bitch when it comes to interior wood paneling, so if i say its a " o buy", the shit has become seirious § TODAY: - pissed some body off - got my ass kicked - Pissed myself - got piss kicked into my ass - ANd its only 2:01 AM. § theyre minds have evolved beyond germs § networking with my friends on here https://t.co/MadL8r1RUA § forgetting if "taking the knee" is good or bad relative ot my belief system but getting pissed off at every mention of knees just to be safe § Seve jobs, bill gates, and Albert Einstein sitting at a table, enjoying a glass of Single Oak Barrel Whiskey , While i watch and smile. § i proudly skim the amount of $17.76 off of all my employees paychecks, because they do deserve pain § just downloaded some of the most all time realistic vagina pics, to my $100 computer § the crack of the bat. the scent of a verdant field. The excitement of the crowd. These are the things that piss base ball fans off the most § Wanker ! Come off it § summoning. the bang bus § pain man § its like i always say folks "you gotta follow my account to get the posts" § im strong enough that i could pull one o f my teeth out right now but i dont want to § banking on becoming one of those guys that consistently sucks so much ass tthat people arent allowed to own me anymore because its boring § stepping into fiveguys hq, just listing hundreds of brand new chef-inspired value combos off the top of my head. Boom. just like that. 1 2 3 § hauling ass to the hair place to find tekken chauncey and laying into him with a rolled up newspaper while hes getting a Perm § the show wife Swap but for gaming set ups § im the one guy on earth who thought it was cool that google glass would allow you to look at your dick and make it shrink/change colors § the 3 poossible reactions i have to tweets 1) nodding sagely 2) slapping forehead & saying "Aw man!" 3) adding it to my muted word list § we told this man that he has the brain power of a thousand state legislators . you will remember His smile forever https://t.co/cfE6E-lAu6G § dont even think about serving me food from taco bell that isnt served to me MÃ©xicano Style § wearing the wrong damn shoes to the basketball court, getting freaked on like a Dunce, getting my ass kicked stupidly § i challenge any man who thinks that my 7 handsome border collies are too loud through-out the day to a round of Chess, the game of kings § The state of the qua;lity of the posts on my feed has never been more fucked. And every one is too busy touching their Penis to give a shit. § having my druthers-- and eating them too § desperate Husband , sitting on the toilet and palm mashing all the buttons on the bathroom jukebox trying to get bob seger back on § i love thinking about shit that is "Asethetic" and looking at it and saying how much of good it is § Go To My Ass § the repliers know whats best for my posts. i love to roll over like a dog and let them shit all over my face until its unrecognizable § ruinning a mans wedding by using too many ad Hominem arguments § concerned about t he health of my followers, many of whom appear sickly and have chapped, unwashed elbows, stained with grime § the boys held an intervention about me "Going hollywood" because i;ve been buying plastic toothpicks now § the basketball version of a home run is when you throw a basketball really hard at the roof and get it stuck in the rafters some how § fully embracing the power of Social Media at the age of 56 and changing my name to Kim Jong Lexus § Wow thifs blew up. While your here please have a look at this: htttp://www.burgerking.com § extremely getting a uti by usnig the same shirt i used to wipe my dogs mouth to wipe piss off of my dick § paying a loud, 200 IQ man wearing a sweat band $500 a month to make videos telling me how to wipe my ass properly § thinking i only have about 80000 more posts to read before i figure out the precise amount of sex that should be allowed in pepsi commercals § this feed is protected by grandma § oh? you want me to take the bad santa posters off my car windows? sorry, i forgot that its a fucking fedearal crime to think things are good § if somone cooks your goose, thats it. youre basically fucked § John Lee Hooker: Boom boom boom boom (guitar riff) me: hm pretty good. What else you got John Lee Hooker: Hau hau hau hau me: Fuck this . § #worldturtleday these beasts are simply armoured rats ,always and forever § babies cant smile. its a biological reflex from the brain stem. its fake. they dont know how to smile § Ok bitch write "Telomere Mindfulness" on a piece of paper. Go to Golds gym on 23rd, hand the paper to "Eddie" & tell him youre ready to Die § Time to show these douscebags my real power (throws a big tree branch at a guys car) §

seeing the cops in the rear view, telling everyone to "stay cool" and cutting hard into the guardrail to flip my car on purpose § (after getting split in half by a 16-inch bullet fired from a boat) waiter theres a fly in my Soup § ME: What do you mean the plane departed. The clock says its only 8:25. TICKET AGENT: Sir Thats a clock ME: I know § james bonds jet black diapers that cost $200 each. suit jacket that has Jame bonds signature drawn on the pocket. james bond engagement ring § the guy who hooks me up with Raw Milk locked his account. too many people posted "come to brazil" at him so i guess ill starve to death now § before you threaten to "Pimp slap" me, please remember that i am a police officer of the law, on at least four separate timeline's § "octo mom" will never be allowed to join mensa or the fortune 500. just saying the damn truth like it is § -tweeting about stuff thats off-topic is "Random". never do this. -tweeting about current event stuff is "Topical". and this is also a crime § getting pecked by birds like a dick head § absolute bastard . of all the fingers you couldve given me, it had to be the middle one § (witnessing the flaming wreckage of a 6-car pile up) ah. Respect. More power § do not ever come to my gym with crayons and draw smiley faces all over the walls. i will put your ass in the gutter. i will knock you over § im thinking now, about how pissed off i'd get if i was dining at a 4-star restaurant and the waiter came out 100% nude. do not do that shit § yes thats what i meant. thank you § one matrix pill is Pitbull Holocaust. the other is Pitbull Revolution. i wont say which is which because i dont want people to get mad at me § why do you want to kill dogs § my dick is in the news agian. and Ouh, whats this?? The damn gas prices are sky rocketing while everyones distracted. Trite. § wife wont speak to me because i thought the movie " ight at the muesum" was a porno film about a guy fucking suits of armor or something § using genius Journalism to crush my enemies . . . § injecvting a shit ton of steroids and walking on the treadmill at 3mph § ass gas and grass. i love to drive my car for free § trolls: do something productive instead of beatinh your weiners on my page. there are so many birds flying around indoors who need help § helping women by inventing a portable bra dispenser , for when they are on the go § gathering data on various of bastards § my dog approaches me, rolls over on its back, and i vomit all over its stomach. undoing 9 years of trust with this animal § @neiltyson what are the odds, that the letters on the license plate i saw today would just happen to spell "MR.PIMP" § a-list: time line b-list: group dm c-list: shit i yell in the car with the windows rolled up d-list: shit i say while melting down in court § someone out there is making $1000 every time a person clicks on this https://t.co/fJWNu5zjp4 § neo pets cinematic universe § saying im going to flip "doug the pug" aorund in mid air with devil sticks . is not a death threat § lunch paraphernalia spilling out of the footwell of my car as i pull up to my old high school to steal footballs § by calling them "Stackers" instead of quesadillas, taco bell is legally allowed to fill them with 49% bird shit § people on here treat me like dirt , thats fine, meanwhile hundreds of teens are allowed to go to prom racistly every day § strategically gathering recon on little seasers pizza in the woods behind the strip mall and getting fucking lyme disease § drinking beer out of a humming bird feeder because all of my glasses have bug's in them § the pain of losing my life savings is softened by the big mommas house themed slot machine screaming lines from the famous movie, at me § inventing a new Suit of playing cards: "The Horseshoes" - We got the king, queen, jack and Ace. All your favorites - The most powerful suit § three sayings to any fool who would claim that i am the bitch of this website: 1.your god damn right 2. i dont give a fuck 3. you Lose § imaginining a judge sentencing a beautiful lady criminal to be my wife , and saying "Oh thats good" § sponsored by God § When Ur Girl Is "On Point" - Hooking U Up With That Gold Bond Medicated Powder - Because She KNOw That The Dick Good § another blissfful day ignoring the fact that 75% of my peers on this site have been rejected from offline society for pretty good reasons § The Dick Head On Team Chat Whose Smoke Detector Needs A New Battery: Does any one in here know how to fedex a pit bull § how advanced our society has become.. merely 100 years ago you would receive little to no praise for posting the words "Bart Flintstone" § seems to me i am one of the only people on this earth who knows exactly how high they stack shit. § The Pillsbury Dip Shit § the jury is still out on whether building giant statues of my head pleases god, or pisses Him off § due to recent events, i have generously reduced my weekly donation to cambridge analytica by 40%. And nobody is reporting this § every one wants to read my 200-page manifestos about how i refuse to make eye contact with my dentist, or "Get me a man who does both" § discreetly getting my ass kicked § it is nothing short of miraculous that all the rich people on this website are personal friends of mine, and care about me, and know my Pain § #worldpenguinday please cancel whatever the fuck this is and make a global holiday for oinline content producers with ring worm please. § the Ten click challenge, invented by buddihst monks to enhance Discipline , asks that we limit ourselves to click on only ten things per day § mother fuck Big Gulp ass § prepare to meet thy Focker § dont trust the dna tests. i determine my ancestry by looking at a bunch of racist cartoon characters to see which ones piss me off the most § tekken Chauncey is no longer invited to boys brunch after saying that he would like to karate chop the #royalbaby in the stomach § cut the crap 2017 https://t.co/tvNbAGfiWC § un follow if you do not consider this true power https://t.co/NNCIYv7XA9 § thinking of turning back into white (Caucasian) § having you tube intellectuals explain to me how exactly humpty dumpty fucked up , and why he deserves to die § no!! all of you, stotp it!! please! the insight is too Raw!! § reported for Flame Baiting . § waking up in a cold sweat and screaming about needing one million dollars, the amount of money made famous by Dr. Evil in austin powers 1 . § its fine. i spray it with a hose before eating it § hard core https://t.co/hA1r6YgLa8 § good thing im not a child § please join me iin eating one hundred bags of romaine lettuce if you are sick of the CDC rubbing their ass in our faces, with politics § i will end your pain https://t.co/A8Kvy12R2c § this is the bad watch thread. post bad watches here. if your reply does not have a bad watch in it you will be blocked https://t.co/FuOeZckTKO § having to hose off 900 screaming animals at my job at the zoo every day is harder than any thing a untied states marine ever did § pissed off by the idea of my ass becoming grass § $5 poison vs $100,000 poison.. which kills more Rats § Im now receiving reports which confirm that barbara bush was electrocuted in a @bestwestern swimming pool. Developing § thinking about taking all of the logs out of my fire place and using it as a gamer cave § thinking about a adults version of star wars where all the characters have Depression and saying the word "Bauzinga" to mysef in my car § i will not do it. § `` i will show you the Ass of God `` § i love coming on here every day to interact with a growing network of "CON MEN" and "IMBECILES" § trying to celebrate all these days at once like a sitcom dipshit who accidentally booked 10 fancy dinners at the same time https://t.co/rVkcwmwX6d § #FineMenThatEatAss #FineMenThatEatPussy #FineMenThatDontCheat https://t.co/4xUCPHosEv § regardless of if he's real or not . can we please just talk about how much bigfoot sucks ass. what has he done with his life § for the 9th time today a complete stranger has approached me on the street and told me to go suck some ass. "And still the brand endures" § patreon up by $4000/month since i got removed from out back steakhouse for calling all the waiters homos and became a Freedom of Speech guru § it pains me to announce that as of april 5th, 2018, The Economist has severed ties with "Da Ass Fucka" § youll never catch me sitting on the toilet, taking a huge shit ... it aint my style § people are giving and receiving Respect at incredible speeds ... and it is all thanks to the humble computer chip § trying really hard not to be Tryhard § I will leave the post up to piss off the people who are mad at it. I will remove the post later to piss off the rest of you § Guess what. Some people have opinions different that you, so shut the fuck up § i try to have fun on here, i try to post something nice, and all of you freaks brutally piss all over me. Im done § update from the good time line--Bacion is legal to eat at work thanks to President Banksy in the whitehouse, now known as the star wars house § elmer fudd with yakuza tattoos. legion of fudd § (getting really into the dunk tank carnival game) Ill show you some pain mother fucker. Ill show you some pain mother fucker § please continue it outside of my mentions you Ghouls § ufo themed wedding thwarted by sjw `s § flipping your car on purpose is even more of an olympic game, than the actual olympic games § penning a heartwarming screen play about a horse who wins nascar § i just need to say, to anyone reading this.. You are Important, You are loved, and You belong in this world, if you have over 5000 followers § i regret to inform you, that by resorting to Swear language, you have forfeit this debate. Farewell my bitch § the absolute perfect shit is scoring a legendary forum handle like “Farkimedes” and making 30,000 posts asking the mods to move threads § imagining the guys on Shark Tank laying into the guy who invented the fucking porky pig character “What were you thinking !!” § executing some advanced high-risk transactions on the Markets. trading my ass medicine for dick medicine § your;e damn right im calm. you bet your ass im acting like a normal person § the vatican should not be allowed to name any new saints until God sorts out my numerous issues with the citibank web portal § Hm lets see. Do I “Shut the fuck uop”, or continue exposing the truths of life to the chagrin of the 99% of people on earth who are villains § living vicariously through gamer streamers who are more powerful than me § Yeah. Also he sold his account to buzz feed in 2015 and his psots arent even that good § just a few of my Media Accolades... Still think im “Bs”??? https://t.co/HeArwPUiRa § face news § If youre a milennial who doesnt know what a Farm is “You are part of the aids” § 8 Words We Must Never Say In Front Of Father (Number 6 Will Make You Shit) § thinking about shit that i Recognize and smiling § thats right bitch. i single handedly rescued the constitution of the united states...AND I DID IT WITH OUT USING POLITICS !! § Thinking About Saying The Rent Is Too Damn Hi § if you have trouble discerning the “Family Room” from the “Living Room” your house should be taken away from you § tellling my miserable wife and sons all about the Importance of Media § i just think this is the sort of thing that would be nice to have https://t.co/h8JCrR6JJc § thank you. Theyre all crooks § thank you for getting me mny coffee § kiss my Thug ass § Getting fucking pissed off at the idea of some child from the early 1900s trying to spit shine my shoes § whenever i see one of those roast pigs with apple in its mouth i think “ ow theres a real son of a bitch who made the wrong choices in life” § https://t.co/9vlMFms7DG my failing brand https://t.co/KHEIYhoDh5 § seeing people performing perfect slam dunks on the basketball court is worthless to me. It;s nothing § piss me off forever, kiss the dog shit out of my ass mouther fucker #ShutYourYap § Trying to get clicked on § just read a fascinating article, about how people who try to “Fuck” have the same chemical imbalances in their brain, that the cave men had § Kicking the shit out of the back board on my computer desk because” Dabbing” is bull shit § Thread. The dog who died in a united airlines overhead bin was a deep state Chaos Agent. Thread, Thread § every day this happens: my followers inject me with a mix of chemicals , And they kill me as they would a sick dog. Every day they do this § https://t.co/HmCQtNF6OQ § This Shit Sucks Dog Shit https://t.co/QL7az6QZ27 § i piss on your little emails § i despise the toilet. id love nothing more than to kick it through the wall and shatter it into 100 shards of wet porcelain. But i need it § Today , I am every Husband § there were 100 browser games in the 2000s where the goal was to become a Pimp by sending links to people, but thats jsut real life now § unlock your account you Freak § go ahead. keep screaming “Shut The Fuck Up “ at me. it only makes my opinions Worse § I am going to try to have diarrhea today. Because I am not "DEFINED" by my ass § https://t.co/xw5ppF6ato § i would never say something like "Fuck the games world and all its wonderful and mysterious locales. Fuck mario" . i just would not say that § u are a hate crime. go to bed § @Prison-Planet my boss called me a "Pussy" for not wiping my ass § Bot. § doing head stands to let the cum from my balls flow directly to my brain and make me more intelligent § trying to get the girls chat recognized as a hate gruop § Wine and stimpy § i fuck all cereal § #NationalCerealDay i fuck all cereal § it was a different time. i no longer believe in sex § posting detailed plans aobut how im going to start trying out different shampoos on a gaming forum at age 52 § crawling around on the kitchen floor like a fucking dick head and filming my own "Beggin Strips" commercials § #NationalOreoDay i spit on oreo § #nationalOreo-day i will henceforth either "Fuck" or "Spit on" all the " ational whatever day" hashtags that the NSA pays twitter to promote § in the year 2030 , "You will be able to order food on the cell phone" § loathsome animal § this is the new logo. if you want to contact me you have to put the new logo in the email and send it to me. please get rid of the old logo https://t.co/wCLOnGiw2E § to clarify, i still think that "Porky Pig" should get the electric chair, but not enough to kill him, just enough to Scare him a little bit § bringing the mame cabinent into my spider hole § restuarants need to start hanging up pictures of their bathrooms outside so i know what im getting before i walk in the damn place § going down to the bank to yell at all the workers there and tell them to keep their greasy mitts off of my stash § microwaving my ass hole in the microwave https://t.co/U8OLOn2xIl § thinking of being appointed the official "Bitch" of the NFL § thinking of that 9/11 thread on the pokemon board i used to post on where the Admin said "Welcome to World War 3" & everyone shit them selves § now where talkin § The Vagina Monologues, But For Gamers § up until i was about 28, i thought "the 9 to 5 " was a euphemism for blasting cum § fuck the "left shark " § fucking awful https://t.co/bf8pGoLoOg § im going my own way § completing my "Dip Shit" look by donning a humongous bib with a picture of a sailboat on it § I politely requested the post to be taken down. It is still up ass of 2/24/18. It is only fair that the check mark be transferred to my page § blue mark accts continue to be given "Carte Blanche" to take big filthy shits all over my career & my beliefs while @Jack dances to the Bank https://t.co/vNuQdKBKxd § as far as im concerned. "fidget spinners" is DEAD IN THE WATER § Take this donw § seems to me, life is aoubt "STICKS" Age: 1-20 : Selfie Stick Age 21-90: Walking stick § call me old fashioned, but I donr think waiters should spit in the customers food. Keep it to the toilet or kiss that tip GOOD-BYE § clowns should spend less time making balloon animals and more time making Prayer's § people who like getting whacked in the balls; that shit sucks. youre outta your mind § #TrumpColluded with my freaking nut sack . print this you cowards § hard at work in the Study, pen in hand, orchestrating my next public melt down § thinking that going to Harvard to increase your IQ is something people do once every few months like getting your hair cut § Thats what they do. They rile you up with nonsense posts just so they can call the cops on you and get you arrested. Its called "Intrapment" § "Games rules." - the unknown gamer; c. 1998 § i can confirm that favs are "crypto" § time to look at the "Moments Tab". i lay down in the bath tub and a guy smears shit all over my chest with his ass while using a taser on me § "mr. bucket" now theres a guy who clearly does not have his shit together § I NEED IT! TO BASK WITH IN THE GLOW OF THE BLUE CHECK MARK! THE CELEBS NEED ME! AND I NEED THEM! MORE THAN ANY THING! MORE THAN ANYTHING! § ???: The hole at the bottom of the toilet is the toilets ass hole replyguy34: Thats fine replyguy29: Bababababababa replyguy93: This, actually § seems like more and more, every young professional should have at all times, a bag to keep papers in § it is decided from this moment forward, i will not be clicking on any "SCAM LINKS" § for some reason. people get upset when i say the markets are down because of Bill Watterson’s beloved print media staple “Calvin and Hobbes” § listening to the song “Shortnin Bread” on repeat 7 hours a day and forming some very complicated opinions upon Race § whoever the fuck “iamath” from glasgow is 1) please dont use my email to make snap chat accounts 2) your dick looks like absolute shit § Just got chemical castrated in exchangge for a free oil change at pep boys #Dealmaker #Boss § hate it when my boss knocks out the front leg of my desk with a baseball bat and funko pop lego shit flies every where § @BestWestern worst western § i have proof that the women on here are forming quotetweet gangs to “freak out” and intimidate uncircumcised guys § oh for fuck sake . § mlg streamer “BeastMod-eCosby” loses geforce sponsorship after allegedly using a performance enhancing bed pan § “CODGER LOOSES HIS LUNCH WHILE HAVING A WANK” § IF IT PLEASES THE COURT, ID LIKE TO POST SOME EXTREMLY RELATABLE SHIT: § $Ì¶$Ì¶$Ì¶$Ì¶$Ì¶ https://t.co/y8QKUHT7xA § shut thef fuck up you dip shits § io love helping the economy by fucking up while doing downloads and getting 100 coin miners installed on my pc § please do not ruin super bowl sunday with this sort of hting § waiting the customary 20 minutes after someone in the group dm says one of their pets died before posting a picture of sponge bob Nutting § thinking going to the Kingdom of Heaven for fucking one trillion years is a fairly nice deal § thinking about getting the dow jones back on track, simply by making a few phonecalls. but certain people have been a bitch to me, so i wont § Time and time Again. People on here Fuck me over and ruin my life. simply for starting the Dialouge § #GroundhogDay is the one day a year where the nation can put asaide the partisan politics and sacrifice a large rodent to God § due to budget constraints the ground hog this year has been replaced by a caged man in a loincloth who also fears shadows § interstate shut down due to reports of 600 pound man chasing a windswept bra § been thinking about it a lot, and i do not believe that anyone will ever come up with a brand name better than “Taster’s Choice” § in light of the slender man case id like to remind my followers that teens have also attempted murder in the name of digimon otis § just thoguht of a tiny man standing inside of a toilet. waving a turd in with batons like the airport guys. shopping the idea to buzz feed § putting all my monitors ad computer stuff on top of the stove i never use so that i have more space to carry out my life style § 1/29/18: i do not want to think about or look at the word “Tater Tots” § getting my naval cavity laser removed because i just remembered an article i read in 1997 about how people in Spain were doing it § @chinese_rock Your names not actually “chinese rock” § “cmon!! post it!” Oh no, i couldnt possibly. Its too fucked up. Too raw “cmon!! ya gotta post it!” Very well: NHL Players should wear hijabs § if you have less than 1000 followers i can guarantee you that me and the boys share your posts in vip chat rooms and call you a “Muthafucka” § “The people who say i should get a life are the real ones who should get a life” - Hamdan bin Mohammed Al Maktoum , Crown Prince of Dubai § buiying up all the graphics cards and making them cost over $1000 so i can computer generate my own new episodes of “Arli$$” § Many consider Reddit,com to be the “Front Page” of the internet, and yet, in the year 2018, I am called a Bastard for saying this. § i pay a man $3000.00 a month to stream line my feed so i can get more jokes per second about putin saying “hold my beer” or what have you § explaining to the boys at the auto shop what the “you know i did it to him” man is iwth the inflection one might use to discipline a child § love when i lose aobut 100 followers immediately after making a beautiful post. the weak shriveling up into dust. Thats called darwin § looking for medicines that will make the fish in my koi pond shit less often § saying it again: my nick name is “Mr Shut the Fuck Up” because i tell people to shut the fuck up not because i love shutting the fuck up § remove me from this conversation please § the floor of the new york stock exchange breathlessly awaiting MetalGearEric’s review of the BK Rodeo Whopper before erupting in chaos § thinking of wrapping my entire body in barbed wire and becoming Sovereign § Just saw it on CNN: Thyere coming out with a new batman #NewBatman § me and my friend bill gates live in fort knox now and if theres one thing i enjoy laughing all the way to its the bank § eating shit sucks ass. and sucking ass sucks shit § daffy and donald duck: "SAME SHIT , DIFFERENT ASS HOLE" § falling down a stair case completely unscathed after executing a perfect series of Block techniques § people whose retweets equal endorsements belong in a fucking cage § #Trumps1stYearAtHogwarts https://t.co/aGMZcVLWOH § 2017: writing shitty articles called like "Disruption: The Praxis of Chaos" 2018: saying astronauts put tubes up their ass to suck the turds out § cajun seasoning and old bay seasoning might seem quite similar, but closer examination will reveal that one of them is far more Racist § I own the best law firm in the tri-state area, my wife earns $200,000 a year making ginger bread houses, and we will never hire a US Veteran § I refuse to provide counsel to one who sees fit to carry the user name "Gay Horny" . § i could not help but notice that everyone you see online is either really a dumb ass, or genius, or average intelligence § optimizing my hyper links, for the fiscal year, § Thinking about saying "Fuck" on SNL. What my brand needs most right now is for me to say "Fuck" on SNL. How do i get to go do that § extracting rare metals from my jeans § The ultimate weopon https://t.co/zKh0Nd0c6I § this page is now protected from dick heads and shit heads https://t.co/KKQ6dz0ceB § ive decided that it is Anti-Jobs, to demonetize the youtube guy who went to Mecca and flung angrybird plushies at the cube or whatever § im at Ces baby. they got an app that makes your phone do gun noises and fat wet asses, flying around goerge jetson style § overseeing my pages, patiently watching all the guys i follow do their 'Bits' and mentallly assigning them to various demeaning castes § you need to get off my case first off because yourre on here posting yourself in italian black face and upsetting people § #LawEnforcementAppreciationDay i appreciate my god given right to enforce the law all over this web page § getting shot directly in the ass execution style while crawling through a duct § im dumb as a slab of turds, and i am Here for it § due to my latest getting pissed off, i shall hence forth refer to Turner Classic Movies as "toilet classic movies" § gravitational waves huh., is that like the super moon § journalism is the hardest job on earth...I have to look at so many sites, and everyones trying to trick me into posting pics of my whole ass § jh https://t.co/9fq81nm2pB § #ImNotAntisocialImJust an imbecile that smells like guinea pig cage § the only font i like now https://t.co/CKx0meQUIj § the epic shit of 2017; is the boys getting TheSegaPimp fired from his job at The Red Cross for not wishing me a "Happy Halloween" § if youre going to ride my a$$... at least Fuck my car § (folloiwng the waiter to his car) Sir. Sir. Can you confirm or deny that the Southwestern Chipotle Chicken Paninis here are "Chef Inspired" § cameras are off now. everyones diapers are frozen to each other and 1000 us marines are now separating them all with swords. horrible scene § Thread § Its not even a popular toy anymore § Used to be you could get on stage & say stuff like "Tickle me elmo fucks" and people wiould shower you with praise. Standards are now higher § This has been being said by people. § let us be very clear on one thing, with all of these posts going around. tickle me elmo, does not "Fuck" . Youre out of your mind § friendly reminder to all of my followers not to commit any Crimes in 2018. crimes are 2017 shit "Miss Me With That" § the ultimate https://t.co/IYQbuHzkYM § Its smart § me: May the coffee be with you. Beer is the red 100 to me intelligent Bill Gates: You are a Fraud. Confess § by getting really mad at poeople for having their dick sucked § barbaro alive horse 2017 . fake death § letting millionaires shit all over my house and piss on my pets for $0 § being a dumb ass on here is fucking Stupid § my friend the only crypto currency you wanna get your hands on is this: bird seed. There is a lot of birds and they all gotta eat § abusing my vile neighbors by putting leaflets around which state that i am now to be referred to as "Daddy's Golden Goose" § I lpove making my credit rating lower by having my wife painted on the side of my car § you know what they say..if you fail constantly, if everyone thinks you suck ass, and you do other bad things. "You will get $1,000,000 soon" § fucked up my hand while trying to pry open a jar of cherries with a Shuriken § just fired 300 Journalists . And it feels so good § Geting my ass kicked by italian guys in the tiny bathroom at the back of the bus § Whats great is I can get online & read 100 peoples opinions about Kevlar Vests, and at least 2 of them are guaranteed to be probably correct § worst part of being my masseuse is having to suffer a 5 minute monologue before hand about how i think your job is actually extremely normal § people who try to read my posts out loud in public get their ass beat. they get jumped and put out to pasture § " And the beast which I saw was like unto a leopard, and his feet were as the feet of a bear, and his mouth as the mouth of a lion: and the dragon gave him his power, and his seat, and great authority. " https://t.co/CUq8FtiQ3s § as wander my study, Quill Pen in one hand, Whisky in the other, i muse, one might perhaps take me for a Famous Author, from the days of old, § pregcore § absolutely disgraceful § i would love to lift all of my pathetic, frail followers by the ankles and huck them like tomahawks § Wow , imagine an office where the employees are not just allowed to have fun... its ENCOURAGED § My User Experience Conditions - 12/17/17 : - Will click only 3 links today - Muting the word "Bluray" - Unmuting the word "Wendys" § Maximum Security Gamestop § sometimes i wonder if i could slice EpicWayne in half with one swing of the blade. but its probably really hard to § getting a 4k monitor so i can make posts § the more i think about it , the more it seems to me that apes look like fucked up versions of humans § running some scams out of my scam tent § cave man: ou ou ou,. keep net neautral so me can download Porno Monopoly guy: why not jack off to a Turner Classic Movie instead § ' george bush master of porno ' § Stand My Ground Mother Fucker § people ask me on here, what is the reason for the season. The reason for the season. is of course, " SANTA " § the mall santas all shit into a salad bowl hidden beneath their throne and the elves have to go wash it out in the fountain every hour or so § some fool's just need to be knocked the crap out of § Give this the retweet if you agree that ALL beanie babies deserve to be worth $100 , and also that Water boarding is not tortore § funds removed from 1000s of accounts, markets crash, after deranged poster says that charles schwab & company "touches there self at night" § friendly reminder that if you do not heed enough of the friendly reminders on your timeline, you may sever 1 finger as penance § im sorry the trolls bugged my office and everyone had to hear me say "heres your sign" over and over again in a shitty bill engvall voice. § just had the check Mark for 6 mins, but lost it by posting a picture of the back of some guys head with the caption "White people be out here" § Can i citizens arrest girls § just set up My Quicken Loans accounts for a whole small ecuadorian village, entirely on chrystal meth. keep doing your little posts though . § VERIFY!! VERIFIY THIS ACCOUNT! THE TROLLS ARE BREAKING IN THROUGH THE WINDOWS!! I NEED THE CHECK MARK !! NOW!! NOW!! NOW!! § my promise to my followers... is that i wil;l never become the "freak of the week" § getting pissed off at the idea of someone going on to wiki pedia and changing the name of the japanese suicide forest to "Warios Woods" § #WorldwideHandsomeDay looking dumb as a dog in my piss-yellow tuxedo whilst i spend hundres of dollars on international phone calls § ah man. how embarrassing. i chose the user name "CondomMaster" a long time ago, back when condoms were cool. dont look at it § i reserve the right to have reddit "Shut Down" if the questions become too rambunctious § hes the ceo of arbys now § just deleted some posts that may have been considered hostile towards people who like to show their dick in public. i was wrong on this one. § getting my pud Encrypted , like peter thiel § My friends love disapppointing me with whips

§ going ape shit at the gym. rotating in full 360 degrees with the boys, flawlessly synchronized § " nothing is stronger than power. " - qdoba_NoScope § i hereby disavow EpicWayne, who now says that my "ears are fucked-up shaped" , and that i "let dildos roll around in the footwell of my car" § nice mug.. the words should be on the side thoguh https://t.co/87AJiAsidW § im afraid i must say that i do not find the mysteries featured on "scooby-doo" challenging enough . § a reasonable compromise, would be to let the ISPs track our Gaming & reward more net neutraility to guys who get the most headshots & combos § ill speak no more of the "Show Us Your Turkey" thanksgiving event. as many have taken that as an invitation to send me their penis and balls § hope to make this somehwat of a tradition: the "Show Us Your Turkey" event. i'd like to see your beautiful birds, on this thanksgiving day § can anyone link me some good User Agreements to click yes on, § due to timezone discrepancies i request a motion that all pictures of food in group dm be referred to as "Lunch pics", even if theyre dinner § getting pisse d off imagining my trolls and dissenters crawling around my house in little butler outfits and expecting tips § keurig is building a Mausque inside of a Dave and Busters, and Heres why it matters: § thre most classic shit is when somebody on tv or in real life says "What about lunch" § i hate i t when girls think im proposing whenever i take the knee at them in protest § dming all the accounts on here who pretend to be horny versions of smallville characters, demanding to know their long-term business plan § women aare setting unrealistic body standards by expecting me to wear a tuxedo 24/7 and to not flip out at waiters § the most disgusting accounts on here are making claims like, "Fred Flintstone is a pimp" , with zero evidence § my followers behave extremely errratically, like a bunch of sick animals, whenever i go "Out of character" to post aobut Mens Wearhouse § it is my displeasure to report that the TWITTER-MASTERCARD group has frozen my credit card for posting "The monster mash sucks" § i will never name my son "Rufus" . that, to me, is a dogs name § some one has got to stop this guy https://t.co/Ygawg3tdNU § my followers know i Abhor racism, but i especially dont agree with the thing from old cartoons where black people have dice for teeth § My dick is wearing a neck brace § this web site sucks my fucking dick. it sucks balls (they add the 280 characters) you blew it. this website sucks shit now § pevrert § things the trolls won't allow me to have: - the blue check Mark - the 260 characters - a nice plaque that says "twitter power user" § reminder to all mh followers that if something i post catches your eye you can "Like " or share it to your friends w/ that re-tweet button § you will take your place upon the cross, you will bear every last "Tag" and suffer as i do § please do not embarrass me in front of "inside hoops". you dip shits. you fucking animals § i love getting my gun opinions from cartoon characters and capping government drones from 900 miles away before they blow my shitty house up § tthe best posts are the ones that are like, " ever tell some one with pectus excavatum to shut the fuck up" § posts: "the best stuff is in here" § the trolls hav been hiding "Easter Eggs" in my favorite DVD menus, to encourage exploration & experimentation at the cost of my leisure time § jacking off more often (due to Stress) and also jacking off less often (due to Stress) § twitter hiring sherlock holmes to prowl the office wih a magnifying glass and find the employee who posted "Aids piss" on the pizza hut acct § i spend a lot of time thinking about how good it would be if someone finally developed a sports app ,"For the fans" § consider this: the time and energy it took for you to tell me to "Shut the fuck up" could have instead been used to breast feed 10 orphans . § muting people who like to talk aobut "The news" instead of posting vignettes about being forced to pour mouthwash down their ass crack § thinking about running out of toilet paper and having to wipe my ass with like, dental floss, or a mouth wash bottle, and getting very upset § (speaking into phone) get me on the computer § if you add me to the dumb ass group chats full of guys i dont know you better believe im leaking that shit to the cops. i do not give a fuck § id love to do some posts on here § cruising the streets of night time in my Hyundai Sonata... looking for drunk drivers to ram into § my favorite combo, you ask? i'll not say to you. § you come on line and challenge me with a user name like "Lesbian Mr. Clean" , i will not respect you, regardless of your skill lefvel § ideally... Sleepys Mattress Professionals will get on board with printing "DRIL TWEETS" on-product, and pull both our brands out of the Abyss § delighting my friends and family by doing the chris rock routine about "The Big Piece of Chicken" but in a worse voice § obliterating my load with a blow torch § alvin and his chipmunks have not evaded my scorn § despite the most recent of shit my enemies are now saying, i will never be found, standing on my front lawn , using a "Hula hoop " § My followers are sick thugs, they are Debauched imps, and they love to be made to howl like dogs when i call them my little sewer bitch rats § I`ll not be watching the halloween themed episodes of "Wheel of Fortune", as I dont find them scary even a little bit. Please and thank you. § father wont stop opening my amazon boxes--How to proceed? (Self,Legal) TOP VOTED: put a live wire in his car & light his ass up. Cook his ass § thinking of abandoning dreams of becoming a Senator, so i can post about yelling "Fuck" in the bathroom because i accidentally became racist § in order to alleviate the stress of having to witness sub par content on my feed, several of my followers have suggested that i try "Heroin" § bewildered by this one star review of a pocket pussy from a verified buyer that is just the word "Stupid" § theres pills on amazon that make your loads bigger but the guys in the 1-star reviews say they give u diarrhea. dont know whats real anymore § I shall perform no new downloads , until this wolrd and the people of it can post along side each other in Harmony, I shall download no more § obliterating my illustrious career as "guy who assigns letter grades to southpark episodes" by begging girls to send me their dental records § activating $40 of "Cash Back" Chase Freedom rewards while the Low Engagement Accounts who troll me on here just shit around on their dicks § just put my elbow bthrough the monitor because i thought the cursor was a bug again. nevertheless this setback will not slow down my posting § my top advisors are drafting various contingency plans for when all my miscreant followers overdose to death on chilis southwestern eggrolls § BREAKING: Millionaire rapist rehab facility lost to random gas explosion--Dozens of 2nd chances tragically denied--"Mist of splinters & flesh" § i would appreciate it if my followesr called me "Sir" , like they would a Police Man, or any one else with the power to destroy their lives § Id like to sincerely apologize for being a beady eyed little fuck-freak. Im hell's shit. Im dog shit's ass. Brand me with a hot iron. Sorry § Wife says i should shit in the yard until the toilets fixed. Itll be ok if i cover myself in a tarp. But i want to shit in the broken toilet § i will drag you out of here kicking and screaming, but for the sake of protecting all girls from my horrendous posts § Everoyone please. Stop sending in things like "Cum" when snack brands do the "guess the mystery flavor" contest. They will stop doing them § ive decided A. every white colored food is vanilla flavored. especially popcorn. especially mayo B. this opinion will be shown on The News § im not saying i dont respect the flag. just saying id respect it more if it was a picture of something thats good to me. like someones lunch § just had a nightmare that my account was permanently suspended for referring to "the beach boys" as "the beach boy shit boys" § i love "Going hollywood" by retweeting burger king and lock heed martin 1000 times § just wasted an entire afternoon at the court house trying to copyright th e phrase "Trump look like a uncle" § seeing the words "Farm Fresco" on a billboard and having to pull the fuck over from becoming Overstimulated § "calling out" magnetGirl77 for telling me that my dick looks like "a piece of fried calamari" § folks if you think haunted house is scary this halloween i invite you to look at the damn economy and thj dow jones § @

TockTockTock TAKE THIS OFF LINE IMMEDDIATELY § this mother fucking snake who wrote this apartment listing is trying to pad the list of amenities with shit like "dart board" § just planted my big ass through a mans wind shield while trying to get my shirt out of a tree § propsoing to twitter a groundbreaking event called "The Banquet of Forgiveness" , where every blocked person on every account gets unblocked § thinking of replacing both of the license plates on my car with a picture of a different car § sick and tired of people assuming im taking a shit whenever i go to the bathroom,; while im actually just running my diaper under the sink § fdreaming of that special moment when i can look into my wifes eyes and say "Thank you. Thank you for marrying me" § if i do not get my postcount up to 5 digits by the end of this year my peers will forever think im a shit head and my account will be erased § ALERT: don pablos app has malware that photo shops your pics to make it look like youre crying & sends them to every girl on my contact list § if you put one of those 280 character junkheaps on my feed ill flip a coin to decide if i should block you. i will let God choose your fate. § top ten things you do NOT want to hear in the Nursing profession: 10. Shut the fuck up 9. Fuck you idiot 8. Your pay check is in the trash § all of my followers are lousy hob goblins and all of the people who dont follow me are dirty dog ghouls § i live for th e sensation of adrenaline pumping through my spine when another person on here publicly accuses me of being "Off Brand" § hear this trolls: ive been secretly respecting the flag in the privacy of my garage for 12 hrs a day , maxing out its power to insane levels § mournful day fpr comedy fans, upon news that the wife character on "Kevin Can Wait" will be beheaded with a sword between seasons 1 and 2 § im pleased to report, that once again , beer has been voted the Coldest drink § yeauh, let me just follow the fucking "YouTube" account, on twitter. thats fucking normal § this is an attack on not just me , but all boys § looks like the circus is in town again § geting a bunch of reptile habitat sun lamps to beam some much needed vitamin d into my fucking obese skull while i do the rounds on sites § https://t.co/Jvw4SdYoDj my policy of hell threads is clear , do not disrespect my Feeds § us military displays extremely rare princeess diana beanie baby w/ certificate of authenticity in the most devastating show of force to date § the Police have stated that rubber neckers and looky loos trying to sneak a peek at the irradiated diaper on 295 will be blasted with poison § irradiated diaper on 295 blocking up traffic - 500 car pile up - some one come get this thing § if u know what the word "consoles" means. son , you might be a Gamer § since about 1000 people asked , the reason i stopped posting my ass wiping logs is becausr the trolls were using that data to terrorize me . § - ass kicked in hooters parking lot - thinks thunder storms are fake - donated 200 Emeralds to the police § #ThursdayThoughts is and will forver be the shit version of #TheThursdayNiteRant § i have successfully avoided getting a "Charlie Horse " through out my entire adult life . § "be the james you want to see in the world " - James Bond § Petition To Ban Actomom 93 of 1,999,999 Signatures § enjoying my Microsoft § "Yow... That aint right" § i have decided to become an Oil magnate, after spending quite some time reading the dictionary definition of the word "magnate" § the wright brothers would be disapointed in people who would rather get on their cellphones and talk bathroom than discover the cure of aids § the way i see it, it seems these days, it seems impossible to have a good Economy, in this economy, as i see it § learning how to say "1 2 3" and "hut hut hut" at army § all replys to this will get block-buttoned https://t.co/icEqgII1Ba § 9/15/17: 0 "DRY DAY" § installing a cyborg tube in my tuxedo which frequently sprays my ass with various advanced powders § Make normal car horns "LOUDER" Make Fire Engines, Ambulances and Police Cars "LESS LOUD" § there are only like 4 girls on this entire site, and theyve all blocked me for saying that snow white and the seven dwarfs are muslim § got all these tabs open like "Girl poison husband rate" and "Poisoned husband body count" researching if i should want to have a wife or not § this site is fucked https://t.co/nCVgwZ8ABD § washcloth draped over the face , pointing up towards the showerhead. thats right folks im waterboarding my self again for my viral #Failures § my most significant personal cultural advancement in the past 10 years is thhat i no longer think the restaurant "Chili's" is any good § 9/14/17: 45 § my doctor needs me to keep a log of how many times i wiped my ass but i dont have a pen & paper so i have to do it hgere. sorry 9/13/17: 310 § 4.2 TB of VR compatible slo-mo footage featuring a man with no teeth shooting a bra using a dsr precision sniper rifle and pistol wipping it § @ladygaga im sorry spider man. please forgive me spider man § this is not the real lady gaga... do not engauge § to me the most normal career path is to fail at show biz and resort to getting paid by defense contractors to make reddit psots or some shit § do not show me Loyce § the guys who make steaks should make all of them "grade A" steak,. ythese guys have been making this shit for 1000 years, no more excuses § id like uh...medium, w/ pepperoni, sausage and onion. just to piss off the trolls. id like a 2-liter of coke to piss off the trolls as well, § its true. i selll my account to a less funny person every year just to rile people up § im sorry but, when you people reply to my posts with things like "Fuck you" and "Fuck your Account" it makes me look like a real dumb ass § #WENDYSHOAX § ill place you in a comma § All girls have exactly $100,000 § only TRUTH can bring the the Message Troll , the common dumb ass ,to his knees, so that we may bring the blade down upon Him , As is written https://t.co/45FFi2Potg § i will never have, never have thought of, and never will think about, engaging in "Raw Dog" intercourse wih my wife § im stupider then dog shit, i dont give a shit, and i dont give a fuck, and i will never shut the fuck up, and i'll always Respect my enemys. § studying videos on you tube that other people took of me flipping out and thinking of ways i could make my mouth louder some how § i hate all of "Groupthink" , except for the groupthought that group thinks that groupthink is bull shit § my Piss is busted ... § I consider making my posts good a Moral Imperative . I owe it to my follower's to deliver them a product completely devoid of Nude imagery . § I WANT " 1 2 3 " 1. MY DICK SUCKED 2. MY POSTS LIKED 3. MY ASS KICKED § when my friends on here create promo accounts for whatever side projects theyre doing but dont follow me on them..its fine. im relaxed of it § doing my favorite " Shit head " activity, kissing a cactus after being fooled nby a mirage § the troll wedges the curb between my ass as i lay on my side. " o!" i shout. "im a content producer!!" he stomps my ass cheek, finishing me/ § just sold 1000 guns to "CONGO" in my most radical act of self care to date § they should put slot machines in the mc donalds. i want to win baby § wife's... you gotta get your man a blue tooth § as sure as i am a VETERAN`S SON , i will never move over and let an emergency vehicle pass me , no matter how loud it is § Get Your Head In The Game: YouTube .com - "Get Your Head In The Game" § @DrPhil the trolls have gone too far this time . § my new jeans https://t.co/Pj95o0wPAg § girls legs 2017. legs getting shot by paintball guns. "Is legs normal." legs on the mind. annihilated by legs § when it comes to eating things at restaurants i love the shit that is "Fresco" § no. what is wrong with you. christ § just admiring my "Pornfree" badge . https://t.co/Hbk986wXih § i am above choosing sides here. i hope they either become friends & cancel the match, or beat each other completely to death simultaneously § writing fan mail to the police, suggesting some new laws that i think would be good § All of you sh it suck ass § Keep Colm and Look at my posts § " pivot to Toilet " § looking to "Max Out" my ball's § MIss the days when i could post something like "Crisp Angel: Birdfreak" and get immedialtey a check for 1 Million dollars § i hate it when my dick gets dredged in flour, egg and breadcrumbs, in that order § my stystem can predict all lottery numbers with 100% accuracy. but not the powerball number. it is too powerful § i truly believe that i will usher in a new era of peace and prosperity when i get every single post on hthis fucking website deleted by 2022 § becoming Inmortal and laughing . . . § broke secret sevrice guy turns his pocket inside out and strangles an assassin with it. opens wallet and unleashes a torrent of moths at him § if real life was a tv show. the eclipse would be one of the episodes of it § closing my eyes and mentally visuelizing my enemies bodies, in 3d , to analyze them for weak points § every one must wear a free speech diaper to protest twitter deleting posts that say "Fuck the eclìopse" and "The eclipse is some fake shit" § i love going to video games forums and posting shit like "Please tell me how to like Mario" § red onion, green onion, yellow uonion, folks this isnt a food, but a traffic light. Get that like button § it is just a nice "Something extra" , that's there if you want it. Dont know why the trolling brigade is shitting me off over this one . § (screams "Shut The Fuck Up" as loud i can, over and over into a phone for about 4 mins straight) Ah, Cant seem to get good help these days - § many people do not realize that after you enjoy a meal out at a restaurant you can pour the entire salt shaker inyo your mouth as a bonus § i do not 'Get' porky pig § my favorite feature of this site is absolutely no consequences for my opinions sucking ffucking ass and me being 100% wrong about everything § top ten how do you stop trolls jokes Q:how do you stop a troll A:Get his key board § I CAN CONFIRM HERE AND NOW THAT THE USER GOING BY THE NAME OF " OPRAHS_DICK " HAS NO AFFILIATION WITH HARPO PRODUCTIONS-- " BLOCK THAT SHIT " § I Love say ing shit like, "At the Louvre, Even the BATHROOMS are nice" § it saves me so much time , to get my knowledge and opinions of politics from the same guy who sells me eyedrops that make my dick bigger § thje teen choice awards blows the kids choice awards out of the fucking water instantly, zero contest #culture #TheArts § before you shit on me, lnow this. i have a black belt in shut the fuck up. and - let me finish - i have a college degree in shut the fuck up § dont post thjis. its a work in progress § pistol whipping my self to gain Endurance § taking the great Hot Water Challenge in the sky § i get emails. i get emails saying the trolls have won, and that i should bow to them, since i have lost the battle. to this i say FAT-CHANCE § i deeply apologize for giving like thirty of my followers panic attacks after posting "Whats for lunch " at 1am EST . § darknet 2002: pics of dead guys in bath tubs, warez darknet 2017: discussions amongst the boys as to which of our acquaintances aren t funny § im bringing back Lunch... #TheComeBackOfLunch § i perceive everyone on this website as a dip shit § im sorry every one. the mayor ran out of key to the cities so they had to give me the key to all the girls bathrooms instead § shacking my head at peoples crap... § thinking abou t having a phase in my mid-50s where i wear a whislte every where i go and make everyone around me call me "Coach" § #ConfessYourUnpopularOpinion coats are just big shirts § @ DrOz can i use a plunger to unclog my ass hole § people will be so pissed off when every AI system independently & consistently determines that the absolute perfect tweet is "Dolezal Rules" § Thinking about getting very pissed off on the computer today . § watching hours of people on you tube destroying "Dennis The Menace" logically to max out my SAT scores and live my Best life § im sorry for posting that vid of me sitting on the toilet and sneezing like 8 times in a row, and ive ordered my top men to try to delete it § (apprehensively tries pouring some orange juice and knocks the glass over like a piece of shit) ah , they dont make em like they used to... § is pregnant part of lbgtq #LGBTBabes § picture now, on this Warm Summer's Night, if all the "SWEARS" on this page were replaced with helpful links to mazda "Sign and Drive" events § @AlGiordano al digiorno please stop uyour cowardly efforts to defame this delicious treat § i often disagree with DigimonOtis, but his efforts to keep Sharia Law out of the donkey kong 64 wiki are much needed in this wolrd of danger § i post at the pleasure of my follower's. people can typd shut the fuck up at me and im not going to. i post at the pleasure of my follower's § "Oh I was just PostShitting for laughs" EXactly. And that is why U forever languish in obscurity while i engage brands U could only dream of § the idea of saying "Oh, Absolutely. Absolutely" in the demonius voice every time i bust my load has suddenly become very good to me § Asexual VR § wish that for one day, for just one day, that i may live in RAT'S WORLD ... § genius hack: keep all of your toilet paper in the car so you have to walk all the way out there to wipe your ass. it 's "Good Exercise" § switch handle to "Gamer Wonk" § @KidRock when will the snake people of washington dc wake up and stop suppressing the release of "Bawitdaba 2" § Dont like the posts ? Goto WWW . KILL MY ASS DEAD . COM... § smiling to my self... thinking this just might be bat mans biggest adventure yet § aahhhh am a gaaaamer of constant sorrow, https://t.co/2kI0qFc8CR § the time has come for verifed mark § Heres my new opinion that my followers will absolutely hate and i will make $5000 from saying on the news . "Piss is a type of shit" § i cleaned it § dropped a mouthful of spaghetti on my dick just now § just occurred to me that i dont have to report to my followers everytime i accident-slly drop food on my dick. my posts should get better now § i now hereby declare that all of the guys who reply to my posts are now married to the girls who reply to my posts, and thats that § The Moderation and Administrative Staff of the Star Fox Strategy and Technique Discussion Boards DOES NOt encourage its users to crank off, § remember folks - you can click on my posts at any time to make them bigger on your screen § i love "having my druthers" (??) § dont look at my dms § as long as i can post from the cage it's fine § keep your dirty shit of of here § my Face when im looking at pictures of other peoples faces on this website that are purportedly reacting to bull shit happening to them https://t.co/LgRxlbVblc § once a year on every forum some guy posts a thread called like "Im done with wiping my ass" and all the people who get mad at him are banned § MAKE NO MISTAKEâ€‹i Appreciate the flawless, invaluable wisdom posted to us by the celebs, and they, in turn, appreciate my valuable feed back § @SheriffClarke i am trying my best to appease the appropriate individuals so that i may become a police officer. please do not mess this up for me, cloud. § welchs juicemakers, (pauses a moment to collect self, holding one finger up, audience hanging on my crucial forthcoming words) but for piss, § one of the all-time classic flubs https://t.co/1NQnf0rXc9 § getting my pussy hammered like a dumb ass § WIFE thinks she can tell her man, when to SHIT!! WELL GUESS WHAT! i will SHIT when I LIKE TO! and if that Pisses her off..DIVORCE HER ASS !! § you will never be less racist than me § lying on my back, screaming like a wildman while my trolls graze my balls with a spinning bicycle tire § my favorite angle to park my car at is 45 degrees. i call it "The Golden 45" and if you key the shit out of my doors i only become stronger § been reckon ive been thinking about heading on up to the big city to (reading note card) to get my "Ass Clowned" § Dont see whats so funny about me accidentaly getting a tattoo of a diaper, but by all means, dont let me stop the Circle Jerk. By all means, § I WILL NEVER "PIMP" § " I DESERVE MY WIFE " GET OF MY ASS!! KING OF THE ROAD § i know of two types of people¸»people who know bianry, and people who want to morph into a piece of dog shit and get stepped on by a hot lady § Serious votes only § stinkers or classics. whats good to post § im going to start a college called Ass Kick University where i just kick the teens asses when the walk in there... am i RIGHT folks?? § i just got logged on to the site and im going to need you all to shut the fuck up for like an hour while i get caught up on my feed here § @CNN Holy Shit..... § worrying a lot about our geopolitical foes recording& transcribing our military comms and its just 900 pages of "Permis-sion To Jack Off Sir" § it was my idea to make the avatars circles, i got $1.1 Mil for it , im not sorry and if the trolls dont Stfu i will make more things circles § watch this marines Epioc response to being told that he should replace his gun with an enormous lollipop § if iyou come on here talking to me about your penis, or saying unreasonable things about my penis, your account will be “Knocked down” § when the doctor ask’s you for a stool sample but you dont know how much he needs so you load up like an entire keg with turds “Just in case” § feel like im the only person smart enough to notice how much hourglasses suck compared to normal clocks § i detect a trace amount of piss in the public pool, turn purple & foam at the mouth. i scream as the lifeguard injects me with piss antidote § pissed off by my nintendo peripherals and other stupid shit rattling around toomuch in my $1600 brief case § getting too big from steroids and smoking cigaretts in front of girls, walking around like a dumb ass, waddling like i got a log in my pants § thinking aobut turning into a wolf and kicking hurricane sandys ass § respecting the Serpent... https://t.co/ofkZCI35r3 § run um off the road § Why are you saying this to me. Who are you § i have not forgotten the crimes of “Tweety Bird” § (in “ ot knowing what chickens coming home to roost means” voice) looks like the chickens have come home to roost, § DONE WITH people who think that ronald macdonald is a real person § someone on here just called me a “Cunk” because my wife wont let me buy a harp § @SheriffClarke i will do any thing for my Sheriff § my idiot trolls get ulcers whenever i say my top 10 favorite film quotes to girls § Bandwagon Hiptser: Everyone who has normal opinions is a rat ME(Normal opinions): Youre a dumb ass because youre in a circle jerk against me § my ass looks like a fucking frankensteins ass § @OscarTheGrouch Ive reported this crap § when twitter verifies shit like, oscar the grouch from seasme street, instead of my acct, i get so mad that i kick fucking holes in the wall § everyone please soend me the money equivalent of whatever your reply is worth instead of putting your words underneath my posts from now on § gah. turned a corner too quickly and maimed my nuts § Please remove this before my sponsor @Hefty sees it § Just like the damn bomper sticker says -I Will flip my car on top of you and snuff you out if i see you “DAB” , Regardless of race § I just read in Forbes, that even Gamers can become millionaire now. I read this is Forbes § people who jack off in the bedroom: spiritual, harmonious, Attuned people who jack off in the bathroom: intellectual, mechanical, productive § ive decided that “gabagool” is italian for Lunch § writing a scathing letter to THE MEDIA for letting me become DUMB as SHIT !! § me and the boys pooled together our total life savings of $1789.34 in a last ditch effort to rescue the failing quiznos brand from the brink § men guy https://t.co/pDBFnXVfCF § Huuuuuuu!!! Lets see those favs... One Two Three § mother fucker calling himself Elmer Fudd on the CS server, NEed I remind you that, on the show, Elmer Fudd’s Kill Count is essentially Zero? § banne d from the Laugh Factory after getting on stage and forgetting if husbands like the toilet seat up or down § you cant like dms dick head https://t.co/ydKGglPtpa § i extend to all my Pregnant Woman follow-ers.... the hand of Unity https://t.co/L5BYZBTThB § idid nothing to deserve this https://t.co/Bl6YuzAdDD § nothing will ever be the same again #wikileaks https://t.co/prBNIEqBiN § looking for Coins https://t.co/rmYcDoaw4H § if i get on here and say something like “Readers Digest Sucks Cock” do you think theyll give me a free subscription § wow. look at this https://t.co/yB1O1g8xgs § DUMBASS: SHut the fuck up THE WISE MAN: No you shut the fuck up § computer DeleteMyPorno “EraseMyPorno” § MIRACLE: world’s most compassionate man posthumously marries every Woman who has ever died in the line of duty #Eid-Mubarak § how the fuck did you manage to post 14.4k tweets to 0 followers § thinkinga bout paying a newspaper $1million dollars to run my opinions regard-ing the Circus § my friends and colleagues in the dms are begging me to jack off to balance out my stress levels. but im not jacking off. i will not do it § geiting my mother fucking ass Rolled for taking too many pictures of the gym § going to the fire station to kick all the firemens asses wearing my fat ass denim overalls § unlike normal humans, geniuses do not like bull shit § im the only guy who knows how to call out the bull shit of society the smart way. and against all odds i do it for free § I lvoe giving thousands of dollars to my real friends while kicking my fake friends asses § the secret -- to becoming a content genius -- is that you have to be able to name every font face on the planet while being water boarded § havent gotten any sleep since group dm split off into like 3 separate factions because XenoMarcus said metalGearEric's chili looks like shit § you d o not have to tip the waiter if you say "Thank You" more than 50 times, over the course of the meal § revealing the gender of my baby by eating a whole bunch of food dye and taking a huge pink shit in front of my relatives. ah!! its a girl !! § it's a disgrace. nobody fav this please § if i catch anyone being horny on here theyre fucking finished § THE BOYS: were watching the mr bean episode where you can see his ass. get over here ME: cant. wifes making me watch mr beans holiday (2007) § downloading some very interesting pictures of DJs § laying in the submissive position, letting a gang of trolls piss all over me and saying "Im getting too old for this shit" like a bad ass § i lovoe challenging people on here to Duals and beaning them with a sniper rifle while theyre like fucking with their phone, waiting for me § best part of being a #Verified is undoubtedly having cops throw flash grenades through the window of anyone who tweets the word "Ass" at you § going to start thinking it's " Not a good look" to order 1000 island dressing without being able to name the 1000 islands § oerdering 40 plates of baby back ribs on a stolen credit card so that i can get enough wet naps to clean my entire body #Just-GuyShit #normal § (accidentaly fires entire ar15 magazine into my foot & leg with 100% accuracy rate) alright. thats fine. heres what i think happened, [1/82] § (trying to apologize for sending dick to 900 girls) you see the phones have a front & back camera. so taking pictures is really complicated, § "the account has too many jerk off posts on it" "the account has too many posts about going to the toilet. i cant relate to that" fuck yoyu § im thinking a tiny palm-sized toilet you can just keep on your desk & jack off into would soon become as ubiquitous as the personal computer § "For years many have wondered what the letters 'DC' in washington DC stand for. The answer is quite simple: Dollars & CEnts"--Winnie the Pooh § FOOL: Election day should be a national holiday GOD: No. Elections shault be held on the day of April Fool's, to teach WASHINGTONDC a lesson § the reviews are in folks https://t.co/ujfAOBTt5Q § I just got word that the trolls are atempting to change the name of the Strato-launch LEO aircraft to "The Stalwart Pussy." We must stop them § me & the boys will be holding hands., forming a Covenant Ring, to protest girls who only want to fuck the main pirate from the pirate movies § ellen made me sign some papers and put a big blown up picture of my leathery dick on her show instead of my topical tweet. ellen fooled me § i would like to invest $500 million fucking dollars into this please https://t.co/zL2l46x1WH § i see the followers that guys like @DrPhil have and wonder, why can't i have followers who are nice ?? why are all of my followers pricks § jason born is smarter than steven hawking, combined § (dick gets caught in car door which drives away, rips it completely off along with half my torso, intestines spill everywhere) Holy Mackerel § (after sendding 500,000 messages to Arbys without getting any favs or replies) i dont care. their commercials arent even that funny any way, § be respectful § driove 5 hours to rodneygamerfield's apartment to sit on his mattress and watch the animatrix while he played on the computer. § mindless drones: i will wipe my ass... i will wipe my ass... really brave and handsome guy: no!! i will NOT wipe my ass § i regret to inform my followers that the fig leaf i wear on my pud at all times has migrated to my ass hole and is stuck inside of there now § get the bars off. expose these fucking privks § absolutely pounding a zip lock bag of cut up hot dogs in the portle potty § too many movies about rats § i love spending 10000 dollars to make my car loud as shit and suck ass § i finally learned how to photoshop the bitter fbeer face onto women after spending 15 years jacking off to the keystone bitter beer face ads § no bitch § ok. ive been lied to § mario means "penis " in japanese § triyng to calculate the precise amount of gunpowder needed to blow up my dick, and only my dick § if i find the mother fucker who ruined my daughters lives by changing his wifi name to "the poop bathroom" i`ll have his balls on my mantel § (ass sticking out of pants spraying poison everywhere whlie i step towards the podium to apologize to the press) Ah Shit. I forgot my notes, § SEX !!!! !!!!   ...now that i have you're attention, here are some pictures of me and my wife having sex § @ RichardDawkins theres been a mistake sir. please un block me https://t.co/sXp5f42umi § imgagine if people went through life trying to collect IQ Points in so as much as they try to collect Dollars. verify me. verify my account § getting really into the idea of sleeping on all fours like a dog until my spine becomes super fucked up § how can i possibly enjoy a moment's respite, when thousads of my followers could be giving my posts "The finger," without me even knowing it § i am deeply sorry for finding a way to make around minimum wage for the garbage i produce, w hich people only pretend to enjoy to be nice § i consider protected, locked accounts, to be the most Powerful accounts... for it is they who have Blocked the entire world § james bond: ill fire 1 round and suck your Dick before you hit the floor. ill kick the floors dick off and fuck its ass hellboy 2: Game on § my new shit: "Burger king = mc donalds"   Please let me know what you think of my new shit, and provide suggestions on how I can improve it. § BITCH !!! § another ass kisser of ouctomom = Erase and MOve on § if the infamous "OCTO MOM" were to come out of the woodwork and start preaching to us of her thoughts of politics, i would just about SHIT.. § (band plays me on stage, wearing tux) The constitution grants me the right to eliminate those I deem disloyal to our nation (light laughter) § as the man who was personaly tasked with wiping roger ailes ass id just like to say theres no way im more than 40% responsible for his death § we here at the @jimmyjohns teen outreach initiative love to "PULL THE RAT" and "CRUSH A LOAD" like the rest of them. we know how to jack off § weve toiled to bring you the greatest specifically tailored user experience of all time. PLease uncheck the box that says "Shut the fuck up" § DM-Girls ask why I seem cold. Distant, lately. The reason is This: My rivals obtained 3D models of my dick & are now sending me dildos of it § i am wirting the worst fucking book of all time and none of you can stop me https://t.co/2iiqUBaoyi § to the trolls https://t.co/qvXxLFcZBm § Donald Fump. Poop fuck § some people say, normal peoples brains work in 2-D, while famous authors brains work in 3-D... § congrats all. thanks to your tireless efforts, and unrelenting, coordinated aggression, the cheese cake factory now serves, "The Eucharist" § when i told u all i had to get my dick surgicly shortened b/c i slept on it wrong and injured it, i opened myself to you, and you Spat on me § @comcast Show Us Your Dick § my problems with "who to follow" 1.i dont know most of these people well enough to burden them with a follow 2.it should be 'whom to follow" § this guy thinks he calls the shots now just cause he got the check mark ... § CNN NEWSWIRE: the guy who voiced the dog in the beggin strips commercials is now "beggin;" the american public to put a stop to jade helm 15 § my main issue with "master chief fucks cortana" is if you read the halo novels youd know the space suit automatically jacks master chief off § everoynes talking about comey but, get this: i dont even know who he is 2934 RT 1293 FAVS i dont know what nintendo is either 0 RT 0 FAVS § i would not discount pua techniqes just b/c girls are wise to them now. for instance,w. a few modifications i can use them to rear pit bulls § https://t.co/KRxsNVCAzR § currently seeking buyers for "Zonked in the Pecker" thw only sit com where the wife punchs her husband in the dick at least once per episode § running multiple red lights while listening to the radio jockeys Flawless "dr. evil" impersonation and scream-laughing § if you 'accidentally' spill an entire 7-11 big gulp on a sears mannequin they will throw it out and you can go have sex with it in the trasg § top 10 diapers annihilated by throwing axe Fuck sopa § never show me him § sensing activiy from one of my known "Black Listed Accounts." do not engage of it, lest you intend to shit on me & everything ive worked for § inventing the Vertical Sandwich, that you can eat hands free, like a ffucking dog § well i thought it was nice § you hacked the poll you stupid fucks. this survey cost me $10000 out of pocket to conduct. you ruined sometyh-ing beautiful you pricks § how likely are you to tell a friend about mcodnalds § I Apologize sir. Im a fucking idiot. I will Try to make them good § thinking i can help girls bycruising around town selling tampons and pads out of my ford Fusion for cost of product + gas money § klout score + IQ = Amount of $ in bank § ATHLETE: THERE IS NO HOCKEY WITHOUT "PUCK" ATHELETE: THERE IS NO FOOTBALL WITHOUT "BALL" WISEMAN(SMILING):THERE IS NO WISDOM WITHOUT "BRAIN" § guy reading tweets out loud at a gathering: ah, ah, check this out. he just posted, "Leeroy the Jenkins guy" everyone else there: Thank you § Leeroy the Jenkins guy § my "The Banquet of Posts" has now ended. There were so many posts from lots of different people on here, and they were all Winners. Thank yo https://t.co/f0fWI9ie8K § i propose,on may 5th, we hold what i call the Banquet of Posts. we go all out on that day & do as many posts as we can. The Banquet of Posts § remove this at once from my page or illb e forced to citizens arrest you § SOup is not lunch. Soup is a condiment § #promfail unaware of big wet towel hanging out of ass; whipping around knocking over refreshments as i get agitated in response to Hostility § imagine a world where we could all smell our turds while theyre still in our body. capital one whats in your wallet § ON LINE........ https://t.co/4HDeWH64Is § Re-tweet me pussy § the us census has analyzed 100 million diapers and figured out which race has the worst smelling turds ,making live leak comments obsolete § thinking i might be able to get the blue check mark if i post a 40 page manifesto and spray piss all over the fresh produce at krogers § ah,. so I see you too have an interest in tech, and epic sciencse. Get this, i just read that each bitcoin is now worth, over 100 bitcoins § "Every Women" by SegaBoris Every women is a rich tapestery , Woven by the lord to be Nice, Never Racist, and always Have a interesting life § 4' 8" man pile driven by beloved 102-year old crossing guard "Mr. Jim" after making a racket at payless shoes § having my Balls exfoliated by a Doctor § top complaints im working on: - the racism (of course) -posting the same shit over & over for years -not posting enough of the classic shit § i love iwt when a big thought bubble appears over my head featuring guys pouring entire bottles of barbecue sauce out into a thick pile § AUNT: We will miss our Guinea Pig "Charlie" who had to be put down today ME: NAtural Selection At Work. COUSIN: I will fucking rout your ass § my favorite part of the classic 16 tons song is when he threatens to kill me and beat the shit out of me for no reason in the middle of it § in retaliation for amazon accidentally charging me for 100,000 prison uniforms i will review each of them with the despised rating of 1 star § Flying to Dubai, UAE, to jack off in a hotel room. § im not tipping any more waiters until the facts come in, regarding Putin § wringing my dick out like a sponge and letting all that gray water drip all over my bluesuede shoes § wish that was me https://t.co/p3SQmVBZ6R § Traitors https://t.co/zgFjQZgjaH § Your aocunt was better when you shut the fuck up you mother fucker § check out this little guy if you have never seen him. his name is mickey mouse and you can find him on any computer § i post one amazon referral link to osme mens bathing suits that i found very tasteful/practical & you all act like i put a gun to your heads § suckng off a wadded up bra in honour of national bra day or what ever. i dont know. who gives a shit § Blocking my wife's account, at the advice of my therapist, "TekkenChauncey" § (flips wallet up in the air and tries to catch it in a cool way but spills its contents all over th e place ($2)) § YOU: jacking off is everything. jacking off is my raison d'Ãªtre ME: jacking off is a zero sum fool's game and im clicking x on this chat now § every day, send one teen to iraq, and bring one truoop home to experience the hardship of teens life... #AnotherMansShoes § thinking back to it.. most slaves, only had to deal with one master. the Modern Content Producer has it far wrose, having to please millions § 96 year old man goe's back to kindergarten after losing ihs job at the chemical weapons factory due to Gas Prices and the Economy #InspireMe § done retweetinh husband accounts. it has become Trite, and Obnoxious to me. § Thomas Husband § shiting into a tube while earning $4 an hour from home § oprahs the secret § 2016... NEed I say absolute shitting more? § spending time thinking about a fucking disastrous hypothetical penis that has a hole thats wider than the shaft, like a funnel. and frowning § its up in your teeth mother fucker § Welcolme. § paying women to ram me with thier cars § now, all trhis talk in the media about me not wiping my ass; i dont know where all this is coming from. if any thing, i wipe my ass too much § shut thf fuck up § hello. what is your online user handle please? ok. ok thanks. blocked § calmly browisng my 100 Sites per day, as recommended by the experts § please refrain from writing extraneous stupid shit on the bass drum in any of your future stock images you cock sucker https://t.co/Aw1CAtCIbe § pissed thr fuck off by "Dub step" § @McDonalds @McDonalds thats it. thank you for hearing me out. i am a huge fan of the"big mac" and im nice once you get to know me § @McDonalds @ McDonalds i would suggest studying caricatures from early 1900s racist war propaganda to help your team devise his gruesome appearance § @McDonalds @ McDonalds it will go without saying that hes an ugly son of a bitch. goblin-like. someone you;d particularly not want shitting on your food § @ McDonalds @McDonalds your current slogan, "Im Lovin It", will no longer do. i would suggest replacing it with "Look out. Here comes the McShitter" § @ McDonalds @McDonalds this is money in the bank. put the mcshitter in all of your branding, and enjoy a tenfold increase in likes and re-tweets § @McDonalds @McDonalds i know its fucked up. but "shit" is one of the last few apolitical threats. 99% of ppl on both sides of the spectrum dont like it § @McDonalds @ McDonalds and so me & the boys have invented "the mcshitter". a fictional man who jumps up on tables and shits all over the customers meals § @McDonalds @ McDonalds they fear Chaos. they fear those who dont simply loot and plunder as the hamburglar does, but those who seek to Destroy. § @McDonalds @McDonalds but how do you shake the core of a public fresh off the heel's of the 9/11 atrocities. what is it that they fear the most § @McDonalds @McDonalds and it is necessary, I believe, to threaten your customers with some sort of villain, to increase the perceived valueof your food § @McDonalds @McDonalds all right. so first off we know that the hamburglar has become soft in recent years. the customers no longer fear him § @McDonalds i have an a 1 million dollar idea that will pull your failing company directly out of the toilet. hear me out. § a Husband said to a Doctor... Write me up a prescription of" Myfuckin".. Indeed, yes. Myfuckin Beer, Myfuckin coffe,Mmyfuckin slippers, etc § ilove the idea of beating the shit out of my Son's rival's dad at the little league game with a suitcase full of cash § a perfectly formed snow ball just came out of my ass § if this board was real life id be allowed to embed as many bmp files as I want to. if this board was real life you'd change your tune quick § theyre nice § ill yank your earrings straight out you goblin § my loyal followers are calling me a "Pussy" because a car kicked up a piece of rebar or something and popped me inthe fucking teeth at 99mph § yes trolls. unlike you, i have a brain. its called a " JOB " § consider the cornerstone of my beloved acct..the "Follow Back Guarantee." i will follow you back always... no matter how much you suck shit, § i rescind my 2009 tweet "bat man fucks joker", as i now understand, through the wisdom of age, that bat man adheres to a noble moral code § this shit really hits home for me since i was once forcibly removed from a united airlines flight for having a bee hive stuck on my head § please do not say "top notch" to me unless you want to spend hrs explaining what the fuck these notches are & who determines their hierarchy § taking up a precious spot in the line for the overcrowded bathroom so i can sneeze into the toilet one single time § there are guys who have replied to me hundreds of times and they will get theirs ,very soon § theres a magic number of times you can reply to me before a police man automatically destroys you. nobody has ever reached it, but its there § how come when s, bannon gets removed from the national secuirty council nobody gives a shit, but when it happens to me everyone kicks my ass § forum gods: 1) the guy who dug a big hole in his basement & posted pictures of the hole 2) the guy who intentionally gave his wife head lice § downloading shit loads of counterfeit papa john coupons through unsecure wifi net works § me and my followers would be very pleased to see the national reinstatement of "the cobble stone road." a master piece in engineering § when i see people putting up foul language on to the feed, all i can do is laugh, knowing that they will never get their posts read on Ellen § more then anything.... https://t.co/yf6cZl7M3b § these noodles sucked https://t.co/pVhOR3EszZ § thinking of becoming a "Pipes" dipshit § inconspicuously jacking off duringi the board meeting using a series of ropes and pulleys § Mr. Ass Health 1998 § Mpuh. I could take the time to pick your pathetic posting logic opinions into shreds, but i wont, because i have a life in real life, Thanx, § now, bear with me folks. if you want to know why i would post something like "stuffing my fat pussy with sage", simply look at the calendar. § stuffing my fat pussy with sage § could not find the hospital in time to console my dying grandpa because google-maps changed all the road names to "Bacon Street" or some shit § all credit, for this image, goes to Snooker https://t.co/EffHqi9iW6 § I despise Flinstone. § they got the idea of shocking gay people, into straight, from the episode where fred flintstone gets bonked in the head and becomes a Genius § #85Collapse ive been saying from the very beginning that interstate85 fucking sucks ass. now that it collapsed girls are blowing my phone up § my fuckin opinion of poli-tics? heres my fuckin opinion of politics. not a single senator in the history of the united states, has been white § i have squandered the last of my fathers good will by christening our new boat with the name of "S.S. Mind Of Mencia" § https://t.co/JzTVdxitfx the state of owl sfx on you tube fucking sucks ass § my promise to all women: my promise to all women is that i will seal theur nudes in a velvet envelope, and wont open it until im 100 yrs old § considering referring to my feed ,from now on, as "The Signature Collection," at casual get-togethers, mensa meetings, etc § drawing that big boy hair.. therapeutic https://t.co/QxpV7omI6n § im the guy at mcdonalds who decides which states the offers are not valid in, an d i get more death threats than god § would like to get one post out today without my son taking me to task in the replies ffor letting my ex wife take the car § whos the true detective § im finished with groupon. it means nothing to me § Kurnis § i may not know "jack shit" , but i know my friend "Jack fists" and he would like to come to knock the shit out of your teeth, § calming down, with magnets § just had to click down the 4th post today about our mr. president's "thick hooters". lets clear off the bathroom mouth § got a big piece of velcro stuck to my big ass § you know society is ASS-FUCKED when people spend more time wiritng "Tweets", than bibles § saying "augh" out loud every single time I move the phone away from my lap and reveal to my self, my pud, which looks like a coiled turd § much of bliged § mr buzz feed here folks. just lost my job again, this time by trying to sniff a flower on a mans shirt and getting water squirted in my face § damn right he did https://t.co/Mxhwib7fW1 § reported § your a child § shut the fuck up § shut the fyuck up § shut the fuck up § shut the fuck up § shut the fuck up § shut the fuck up § shut hte fuck up § shut the fuck up § shut htte fuck up § shut the fuck up § shut hte fuck up § shut the fuck up § ,my name is borat for me to poop on and i love riding the short bus to the olive garden where i live § bubba burger is short for "bubba hamburger" and the y take pride in serving absolute shit to nobodys § harvard geniuses/ scientists love to wind down by going on boards and posting threads named like "What is the screen resolution of a mirror" § "booty" is code word for "ass" . this is known § Unamused by the portmanteau of "Groupon" § geting a wife https://t.co/wRu22q64XQ § (emotionlessly) tacos is spanish for "food" § i fear my tropical fish no longer respect me after i accidetnally stumbled backwards & smushed my ass hole right up against their $3000 tank § im near certain there is a hotly contested tug-of-war between fox executives upon the issue of whether or not homer simpson can show his ass § matrix 2: pedaphile killer § i would really love to try getting my dick stuck in a pine cone. but i wont due to trolls § man at national cemetery tackled down, face shoved into grass until head turned purple for saying "may the 4 be with you" to each dead troop § miss when the favs were star shaped, instead of heart shaped. the hearts aare just another filthy product of the horny industrial complex § nneed the emoji to be the size of an actual mans head on my screen please. to suspend disbelief https://t.co/YRAvtJohGf § (dming the girls) this swebsite is the future. were pioneering... minds (dming the boys) this website is sellout. this website is family guy § im on a watch list for capitalizing "Balls" § bitch § visiting New World's https://t.co/WbkNLQMVdQ § reasons to invite me to the next "Tweet Up": 1) if i get unruly i can be easily overpowered 2) i know which seasons of the simpsons are good § (the trolls watch in astonishment as the milk shake they threw at me flawlessly bounces off of my head wwith minimal pain and mess involved) § jacking off is Alphamail § turning a big dial taht says "Racism" on it and constantly looking back at the audience for approval like a contestant on the price is right § inexplicable dip in google hits on my web site "Wayne Tracker," which has provided up to date info on the upcoming Waynes World 3 since 1998 § some people get their accounts suspended for cursing out celebs.. i get mine suspended for posting things like "Sports is making a comeback" § NO... I DO NOT "PUT OUT " FOR MY GIRL FOLLOWERS... UNLESS YHEY 1) ARE NICE TO ME 2) HAVE FAVED AT LEAST 5 POSTS FROM MY "TREASURY" SERIES § old screensaver: spinning 3d monolith with my wife on it new screensaver: marquee that says "Truck Month" regardless of what month it is § (girl tells me shes sick) aahh that sucks so much. you can come over & have some of my mens one a day vitamins. probably works on girls too, § PEOPLE MAG: which pop culture icon are u going to Slaughter next... ME: I have set my sights on "The Boogie Woogie Bugle Boy of Company B." § mesmerized by the branding, of the Wendy's Arby's Group https://t.co/YdhkwtJgxe § mmy next big emotional investment is becoming passionately covetous of the bowls of warm tap water that are commonly left out for dogs § were at the point now, folks, twhere the CIA will kill you for having Opinions, but refuse to assassinate the nitwits who fuck with my Page. § DAD: i just heard on t he news that teens are taking the "Kick My Ass" challenge. please dont do this ME: you have no power over me, old man § (wtaching a video of capt Jack Sparrow shitting on the number 2016 while the camera zooms in and out of his ass hole) Oh this is everything, § "Please. The time has come for you to Normalize the repulisve and despicable Digimon Otis." No. I will not normalize that fool ,or his sins. § it is so hard folks, to maintain my world famous Post- Racial Outlook, when the damn gas prices refuse to stay down tto a reasonable level, § in 2015 user @Dril chanegd the world when he deprived himself of using the toilet as part of the #NoPiss challenge. now, hes taking on Turds § i lvoe and cherish all of the girls of this site, and other websites. you all become my wife more and more with each passing day. Thank you § reading a 900 page book on Dry Rubs and immediately forgetting all of it and just dumping a shit load of cocoa pebbles on my ribs § Disrespected at hooters again § genius 1.0, is fucked https://t.co/BEX7XsqckR § the police cut off my finger for sending my birth mark shaped like the under armor logo to the under armor social media manager unsolicited. § -dont click on nudtiy -do not respond to nudity -wear a loin cloth underneath your clothes in case theyre ripped off by mechanical equipment § i am only here to field questions regarding my presidential bid. i will not discuss my ongoing project, tentatively titled "Aids Mario." § im george soros bitch § @dril Who give's a fuck § the next time they do a live stream of a rare endangered bird they should let users control one of those old timey horns that goes "AWOUGA " § be warned america. 1st they get us fired from amtrak for saying jacking off in the control car is good, next they start poisoning our wendys § INTERVIEWER: do you have customer service experience ME: if I catch a customer shoplifting I will serve him a knock out. I will own his life § authorities forced to destroy entire 35,000-ton chernobyl sarcophagus after misunderstood online entrepreneur gets his dick stuck beneath it § in the year 3000 historians examine the preserved contents of an ancient time capsule: a piece of cardboard that says "Game cube sucks dick" § an angel slips a booklet of my top posts into the pockets of the pope, the master of islam, and b.netanyahu, and the world Rejoices in song § massive, hulking gorilla of a man, compeltely covered in hair, lying on a mattress and jacking off to his one immaculate shaved leg § (shows up at new media seminar with a chunk of wooden fence stuck around my neck and a bunch of stray animals following me) sorry every one § ACCOUNTANT: I Just don't know how you can justify donating $700 to "Chips Ahoy" ME: i hope your car flips & becomes your fucking firey grave § @realDonaldTrump @TuckerCarlson i will never define what being racist, to a bastard like you § every singe day... my followers ask me. where can i get the latest Kfc DinnerPlan. and the answer is simple my friends. "Mc Donalds" § / ! \\ / ! \\ / ! \\ if this post gets 5000 likes, my wife will give me back my inhaler / ! \\ / ! \\ / ! \ § issuing correction on a previous post of mine, regarding the terror group ISIL. you do not, under any circum-stances, "gotta hand it to them" § (plays some Tchaikovsky records at the highest possible volume) ah it sucks ass. but my IQ is increasing so much § leafing thtrough another heap of death threats and served papers that have been 100% tailored to my interests, using Tech § man in moving car slaps me in the face with big hand full of dog shit ,flipping me the fuck backwards,landing with full weight upon my neck, § my dick is bulb shape, nobody helps me, and whenever my browser needs to be updated i call the police § several bernie Sander Bros, in High Levels of govt, have told me they think its good that DJT keeps ivanka feet pics in the nuclear football § i hate it when the refferree kicks me in the balls and ass while my opponent has me in a head lock § look, im not saying that martin luther king jr was a gamer. that would be ludicrous. im simply saying that if games had existed at the time, § I GOT - SUCKED OFF - AT HISTORIC COLONIAL WILLIAMSBURG § huge banquet, everyones having a nice time, everything looks extremely normal, except the big banner hanging from the rafters--"Racist Mensa" § i love doing the shitty pushups where my knees are touching the ground and counting them as real pushups § never say to me, the word "WaWa" § hey all . just learned about this new shit here, i think you will like it if you enjoy using the computer https://t.co/BWNiaAEbpL § please help my cousin "Bruno_THought_Leader" who just had his account suspended for threatening to "Fuck" brexit § going t o start saying, "Wife City" whenever i see an attractive woman. e.g... "thats Wife City" or "that girl is Wife City to me" § people come up to me and say, "I will never use the bathroom. I will never shit" and i gotta tell them pal, sooner or later youre gonna shit § free mustard offered at burger king... genius?? or a "Beta Move" § a crass message got on here some how and im trying to debug it. in the meantime please check out https://t.co/fUq3h548ge § what if instead of oil-- the warhawks were all after the enemys piss. like "we gotta take baghdad. we gotta get their piss." just having fun § pleased to announce that i will shatter all barriers in 2017 by becoming the first adult gerber baby § amusing that i am constantly told those words of "Fuck off" by the girls of here... when i can hook them up with any App that they desire... § can any one who knows of Politics tell me if this is good or not https://t.co/6ShvHIK03o § COnsuidering becoming one of those jack asses who gets head aches from wi-fi § god once said “pit bull” https://t.co/3rs2e8DFpf § thinking about hopping on some sites tomorrow. havent made a decision yet but i will let you all know. sound off in hte comments below. § trying desperately to come up with a name for my new cajun styled recipe that isnt racist and just fucking up constantly in the worst ways § MAIN STREAM MEDIA: why do all your jack o lanterns have a hole in the back thats the exact circumference of your dick ME: no further queston § New Wet Ass § ((attempts to dress up for hte first time in my life to attend Grandmas funeral but ends up looking like a school shooter from the matrix) § once again ive been reported for calling Odie “The dog from Garfield” to make people think i know less about garfield lore than i actually d § ask me anything u please, as long as its about my ambitious plan to build a castle in the Jungle for the apes to live in, called “Ape House” § the show, “Hee-Haw, “ sucks mother fucking ass § pig nosed man arrested for trying to whisk an egg using his fingers § Jsut arranged an 8-count box of pop tarts to be sent to a girls house. Looking forward to explaining to her how to prepare them § CHILD: Papa.. tell me once more about WIFE’s DUTY PAPA: it is WIFE’s DUTY to protect her husband from villains, always § Husband is ATM Machine § (ffully immerses self in a picture of sponge bob saying “Dat Boy Tho”) § mr. 11656 unread emails over here,.. § -the drew carey show forums harbor a subforum named “Hell” -users are sent there when they absolutely fuck up while talking about drew carey § when journalism was good, https://t.co/fLjPzXG75H § the trolls think its “ SO FUNNY “ when they sit on my lap and jostle their hips around until i ejaculate al over their ass. grow the fuck up § Damn. the MomTown forums just started requiring 4 point Mom Verificaiton to be able to post there for some reason..anyone got a work around? § please stop aksing me in the dms if i have to go to the bathroom. i just went to the bathroom and im fine. § goblin: im going to put up a post saying that the fake news is good, and that i like it more than i like the real news ME: not so fast bitch § someobdy on here just sent “the cup of stfu” to isis and all of the mainstream media outlets are refusing to report it § things im currently in trouble for accidentally Liking: 1) a picture of a girl 2) the Mafia § Adorn Your Front Door With A Tasteful Welcome Mat Or Shut Dah Fuck Up § trapped, fully nude, in restaurant bathroom. boss & his wife will be here in 10mins. trying to see if i can make a tuxedo out of tolet paper § once you achieve the coveted post count of Seven Thousand...Thats when you gain access to the prestigious halls of MENSA. not one post less. § the more i think about it, them ore i understand that if i won the Nobel Prize, i would become either a genius, or a millionaire § this’s police. your ass is grass. your tits are toast. your dick is dirt. your balls are busted. your mouth is Mother Fucked. your shit is s § (carrrying a huge polkadotted bindle, looking like a dumb ass , shoes completely untied) Mother.. Father... Im leaving home to join the cops § 95% of people these days think the bad celebrities are good. like and share this if you miss the days when pople liked. the good celebrities https://t.co/mVZKN5ExuR § scribbling my exposed dick out of this photo with a blue bic pen so its good enough for linked in § between the gun & the blade.. throwing knives are the “Best of both worlds” when it comes to eliminating thousands of home intruders at once § Upsetting. § two bearded 55 yr old intellectuals, sitting opposite of each other in two stately leather seats. musing upon the concept of a “Paper mario” § i had that dream abgain... the one where im at the coliseum, annihilating shitloads of roman gladiators by drifting around in my macktruck § all the pictures of bacon on the #nationalbaconday hashtatg look like utter dog shit , these people are out of their mind, uploading these § breaking down mentally because im all out of toiolet paper and i cannot decide which wendys coupon to wipe my ass with § children.. toddlers.. babies..they all got one thing in common. they all truly believe they can kick my ass. but they are Fundamentally Weak § (dismissing waitress handing me the check with a hand wave) no thank you. i dont believe in any of that § if one more Fucking girl comes on hhere asking for pics of me or my friends feet i`ll shut down my multi-million dollar corporation for good § the human mind... perhaps the most powerful weapon. second only to the "GUN" § if I could only get my Nasty mitts on some HARD-WARE , (RAM , Chips,) my posts would improve tenfould, § "Howard Stern should start a pod cast" may be one of the worst things ive ever posted, but still seems unfair to have my tires slashed daily § dr oz says due to the sheer volume of milk & cookies santa consumes, you have no hope of poisoning him with piss or cum. wont even notice it § dr oz tells me on his show that you can just pour a shit load of mouthwash into your laundry instead of wasting money on various detergent's § first you got th e 3d tv. now you got the 4k. whats next. 5 § cornering a janitor for 50 minutes to tell him how i was once involved in a polyamourious relationship w/ the guy who said "lee roy jenkins" § taking my treat plate into the bathroom with me because my followers are a wolf in sheeps cltohes § my fatass head floating in the sky, looking down at all the Girls i follow bantering/ having a nice time on here, nodding, thinking its good § im going to be one of thsoe guys who writes ebooks named like "Brain God: Calculation Master" then spend all day screaming at people on here § the bird bath institute considers any stone bowl between the size of 8 to 40in. to be a bird bath and they are sick of people disputing this § i will not build a single snow man... until i respect , all of the real men, first § Maybe the phones get smart enough.. They will do the yapping, for us ! § GeniusTalk - dog food has been putting subliminal messages in theire food to make dogs think they taste good - TruthVisions § people named fucking "Curtis" need to get a grip, and start calling themselves "Curt" which is a rteal name § " NO BULL SHIT" is not just a phrase i like to say, it is also a way of live § if you have ever retweetted me without it equaling endorsing me , i will shatter your smart ass little turd stained laptop against my legs § my ass looks like a Stooge's ass § i dont like dumb asses either § from now on. i am calling everyone who is a dumb ass. "Anti- Intelligeance" § ive mastered "Draogns Path," ive not taken a shit in over 20yrs,& im willing to have my ass hole inspected by a notary public, to prove this § eating 1/2 lb of beef boulougnase and getting roid rage from it § reasons the famous statue "The Thinker" is better than selfys & cell phones: - It is a classic - It is for geniuses to look at - It costs $0 § fellas... you know i dont ask for much... but my fake US embassy in Ghana just got shut down and i dont know if i can make rent next month, § top 3 Engagements 1. faved by Charles Martinet.. voice of Mario 2. direct message from the official Lunchables account 3. the one to my wife § extremely frail man, tasked with gathering hundreds of dildos thrown onto the football field by overzealous fans-- booed incessantly; Reviled § DOCTOR: you have the balls of an 80 year old man. your dick is mostly normal. your pubes suck. I didn't look at any other parts of you ME: h § would like to issue a correction ,regarding my comments of Japanese toilets. they do spray water on your ass, but they do not suck you off . § i cannot sit idly by while my followers get shit on by the terminator § FELLA'S... WHEN YOURE WIPING YOUR WIFES ASS... YOU MUST ALWAYS, ALWAYS USE "TOILET PAPER" § everyone thinks youre a celeb when all your cars windows are tinted but people only get those so they can jack off on the go § i do not give a shit of the official WHOTUS stance, i refuse to hear it, i will never forgive the turkey, i will not bow to that filthy bird § some one explain please to me why the letter board at my local arbys has said "happy hour" for months now, before i get the police involved § ive been known to look at 2, even 3 emails , at the same damn time § reality tv show where we replace one lucky boy's pc gaming chair with a fully functioning toilet. every episode § everyone loves it when i go to their parties and mix all the whips together (cool wip, reddi wip, miracle whip etc) like a fucking shit head § i will never learn science § @hhgregg 696969696969 § surprised that nobody here had ever used the phrase “pissed on execution style” unttil i described my poor customer experience at hhgregg § -‘-‘-‘-‘-„-€-‘-‘-‘-‘-‘-‘-‘- -‘-„-„-€ -‘-‘-„-€-‘-‘-‘- -‘-‘-‘-‘-‘-ˆ-„-€-‘-   -‘-‘-ˆ-‘-‘-‘- -‘-‘-‘-‘-‘-‘-‘-‘-„-‘-ˆ -‘-‘-‘-ˆ-„-‘-‘-€-„-‘-‘-‘-‘-„-€- -‘-ˆ -‘-‘-‘-ˆ- -€-€-€U-€-€-€-€-‘-‘--‘-ˆ

-‘-‘- -ˆ- -„-‘-‘O-‘-‘-‘-‘-‘-‘- -‘-ˆ-„-„ -‘-‘-‘-€-€-‘-‘-‘U-‘-‘-‘-‘-‘-‘- -„-„-„-€ § 0% and 100% are the same tnhing § if you ask me this election could end about 100 different ways: 1) trump gets 0% of the vote 2) trump gets 1% of the vote 3) trump gets 2% o § the worst part of having an ass is always, having to wipe the damn thing. the best part of having an ass is shitting. #ElectionFinalThoughts § it is so beautiful to me, to have my ass lovingly wiped by my girl friend, knowing nothing is more pure than this bond, Nothing more strong, § here are this year’s Vote Multiplers for election day. no, they do not stack policeman - 10x army man -12x verified acct - 15x Asexual - 18x § blue jean’s... Activated . § accosted by several of my followers last night.. would nnot fuck off, awful, screeching voices..overpowering urine smell. Terrible. Terrible § in base ball theres only points and players. i will be Shut Down for typing this. § FETID BOZO: Ahhh oil spills are bad WISE ADULT: the sun will evaporate the oil, & the wheel of mother gaia spins goodly, As does all things, § how do i add “ GUNS “ to my posts .... § ironing my suspender straps and treating them with powders... in the privacy of my study...making the nit wits and losers absoltuley furious § i got lock jaw from eating pasta out of a dogbowl and my wife will be here in 2 hours to marry me. help me github § handing print outs of my most beloved arliss (arli$$) quotes to trick or treaters § (playing russian roullette and its my turn) hasta the vista mother fucker (shoots the other guy § i think that in 2013 digimon otis was seirously convinced that they were going to change the name of gamestop to gameMosque § when somone posts a vile piece of home decor in the group dm but you have to bite your lip because youre on the lowest sub-tier... § when you click on the tweet and it says “Whoops! Something went wrong” thats how you know its good § i believe that while i was Resting, Aeris_Nader, the snake that he is, dropped a pinch of baking soda into my ass crack and poisoned me § im an adult, and i deserve to listen to the verison of the super bowl shuffle where thw word “Ass” is not censored by the referee `s whistle § “ []D [] []\\/[] []D “ <<<< thats how you type the word pinp § thank you normand https://t.co/5kv6RlVQz5 § people do not appreciate the grace and dexterity that is required to shave the fat pink rolls on the back of my head that looj like hotdogs § unfollow , unsubscribe, block and mute all Gambler’s § it is tragic that my followers refuise to obey my direct orders , and that i am often told to get “Ass-Fucked” when i ask for pieces of food § i will never support pears again after the tree on my street constantly dropped nasty pears that got run over by cars § if you turn the patterns on their shirts 90 degrees... the trusted REFEREE becomes the despicable PRISONER.... truly life is a fragile Bitch § you gotta check out my posts § is wiki leaks hacking twitter agian or are the people leaving numb skull comments on my page actual human beings § palm thrust my entire head through the fucking wall and kick my big ass while im trapped like a stuck hog § BOSS: i need you to go around to all the other employees and collect their piss in this thermos ME: Yes Sir! I will not fail you, your honor § there is NOTHING wrong with having 1 Million Doallrs   you are NOT defined by your one million dollars... having 1 Million Dollars is normal § IVE ALWAYS SAID IT !! the people we see of today are somewhat more known to care more of their Face Book Status, than their Brain Status . § A tag has been placed on Utz Quality Foods, Inc. requesting that it be speedily deleted from Wikipedia. § i accept that all the things i post “For Fun” are to be met with physical violence, including elbows to the face, shattered knee caps, etc, § your fingernails, not your dick. i have no opinion of your dick. § i do not find it unreasonable , during my scheduled Cleaning, to ask my dentist to wash my dick as well, since my dick is basically a tooth, § ive never met any of them, but i know that there are guys out there who name their dogs shit like "Rover " and "Fido" § BREATHTAKING: clever husband sells all of his sons war medals on ebay as punishment for exceeding family plan data caps § Im the guy who exclusively wipes his ass with the disposable seat covers § my followers love to Drool & Shit like a bunch of dirty daugs; and they would see me damned to Hell if i cut off their precious content flow § "theyre called millennials because thier souls are 1000 years old...." - truthGamer § i can not catch a break folks. my 78 yr old son has been pissing into the boiler some how and making our home smell like a reptile enclosure § fucking a stack of emoji t-shirts at target or kmart or wherever the hell § post "I love the mcdonalds Five for Five plan" if you support Don. post "Mcdonalds five for five is Bumpin" if you support Hillary J Clinton § check out the new "Five For Five" offer at mc donalds... thats Five soda's for five bucks "Or your money back" § for every bra yo u dont wear i will wear 3 Bras #NoBraDay § "DISRESPECTFUL !! DISRESPECTFUL !!" the crowds shriek, upon learning that the scene of bat man wiping his ass & sucking his own dick is Cut, § (wearing one of those fucking stupid hats with the word "Press" on it) mr president! do you think DC Films should show bat man taking a shit § COMPUTER ... SHOW ME MORE " KEN BONE " SHIT https://t.co/fjxrtCa4bV § "Ive been studying to become a Pharmacist" Thats good. Im living in one of those crane game enclosures now. Sometimes the claw jacks me off, § @GoonExposer please dont goon expose me § told to "Sit my ass down" after wasting my one question at the town hall meeting by asking if the secret service agents get to see them nude § waushington running amok... #JustMyThoughtsOfIt § (everyone in dm notices ive been trying to type something for 10min straight) sorry all. iwas just writing down a girls phone number in here § were at the point now, that when i offer to impregnate my girl followers, people assume my motives are sexual. disgusting, grow the fuck up, § Thoroughly Unimpressed. https://t.co/P4B629tINJ § @ Bubbaburger Get rid of this § @Bubbaburger i dont like this one either, remove it § @Bubbaburger take this one down too § @Bubbaburger take this down § i feel, as I, over time, become even more of a Dumb Ass, i am able to consume web-based content and Media at increasingly Blistering speeds, § getting fucked up new reports that both of the vp candidates were washed and scrubbed in the same big bathtub, minutes before the debate § 5000 Year Old Turds Found In Ancient Diaper Revealed By Scientists To Belong To Man With Small Penis, Shapely Hips § i am a natural showman. i love to show off my natural's § i WILL wise the fuck up. i WILL super charge my content for 2017. i WILL get blue check mark § (genuflects as two golden lights come forth from behind me, taking the form of majestic angel wings) i would never hold a seleb at gun point § meat loaf just ordered the venue to keep the lights on the audience so he can see if any trolls have infiltrated his show § too much truth in such little time. feeling the heat cominh down to silence me... signing off........ for now § the famous time-tested classic, the philly cheesesteak, has become Sexualized by greed § it is sio, so easy to Mindhack the government and get permission to dig holes in your yard § mind of a lion.. heart of a Pregnant woman § this webpage is so courrupt.... § pushing one of those home depot mobile staircases onto its side., getting that shit wedged between the aisles, because they dont sell Geodes § sickening https://t.co/CnbuNh3bkp § my boy's... § COP: found the culprits blog..another 1 of them Incels DETECTIVE: the only "Cell" he'll be "In" is a cold lunchbox next too mammas meatballs § ME: there is a new type of beer called "Wine" shirtless guy witht 104 followers: Shut the fuck up ME: Yes sir § the weak shall wither and die...(JACKS IN TO TREELOOT .COM CIRCA 1999 VIA THE INTERNET ARCHIVES AND CLICKS ON THE FUCKING TREE 100000 TIMES) § vineger contains so much energy.. thats why moms call it, "Free Money" § damn. some one told me the first day of autumn was a solstice so i didnt jack off during it. now my sinuses are all fucked up due to T level § yea i torched the dennys. and i woudlve gotten away with it, if i werent the only guy in town with a custom jersey that says "My Wife" on it § but not Good enough for the follow ?? Hm? § when you do sutuff like... shoot my jaw clean off of my face with a sniper rifle, it mostly reflects poorly on your self § whos been leaking my dm box . https://t.co/k4H0hp9klm § you give me dry ice & i dont know what to do with the shit. "is this mother fucker really posting about dry ice" yes. wet ice is good though § these are the same steroids that cops use... and you can now order them online for the very first time § the ass ratings are in.. my ass needs to be given the old " HEAVE-HO " on the fast track otu of here and thats the facts jack. Boo to my ass § using the toilet when i hear Our national anthem start to play. i do what i must. i stand tall in complete agony; as shit runs down my leg, § LET US SPEAK NOT OF THE YOGI BEAR , WHOSE MANNEURISMS, GAIT, AND DEMEANOR , RESEMBLE THOSE OF THE DISREPUTABLE JEWEL MERCHANT "BLOOD DANCER" § this is called doxing now, and its a form of crime § reseurch https://t.co/JNa6kozNnU § did they get it off line yet. did they take off the pic of tweetie bird with a humans ass § holding up hte line at Aldi with a barricade of shopping carts, desparately trying to contact the ex-wife to ask if im allowed to eat Pectin § me and the boys have decided that the least gay way of wiping your ass is to dump a quarter bottle of Palmolive Spring Sensations back there § the way i see it, people who come on here and submit content that is not up to par, could possibly be considered the "Villains" of this site § the entire contents of the kfc smokehouse angus chicken snacker slide out and fall directly into my shirt. "IM FUCKED" i yell out § (spends all of 7 seconds skimming some blog posts) yep. just as i knew all along. having pnuamonia is good § (takes off VR goggles after howling in fetal position for 3hrs while guys in varsity jackets slap the teeth out of my mouth) wow its so good § who does this guy think he is. https://t.co/vJTdgRC3U9 § (insufferably) It's pronounced. "Bloomin Onion." The 'g' is silent. § angel-voiced 5'2" man forbidden by mayor from performing at this years christmas pageant-- "described as upsetting" "this tradition must end" § if your tweet doesnt grab my attention in the first 9 or 10 characters it can just fuck off § ah.. the perfect Souffle! cant wait to dig in to t(*EVERY PIPE IN MY HOUSE EXPLODES AT THE SAME TIME, COVERING ME IN SHIT AND BOILING WATER* § never brought this up due to Trolls, but my son is set to graduate from ITT tech next semester after 8 years of hard work and im very proud. § the fool tries to make one million dollars.... but the wise man knows that its much easier to make $0.000001 dollars one trillion times § bet yoyu think youd never find a mother fucker like me at a primarily Black church. but i like to go,.. just to Smile.. bask in the Energy.. § " snorting a line of coke up my big ass " § have you ever seen a chunk of fools gold. its a very alluring substance § boy oh boy do i love purchasing large amounnts of Fool's Gold. wait a minute... fools gold fucking sucks. this stuff is no good..!! Fuck !!! § get this down off the computer. § (me dming) i am merely a vessel through which the posts flow. i accept no rewards.. for i have no name, and no face. Do u like wearing bras, § feel as thoguh our nation, our world, is closer than ever, to Christ, with KFC's recent announcement that they are to turn birds into wine., § it may seem that cops are all fucking dumb, bad at IQ tests, etc, but they only pretend to be, to lull crooks into a false sense of security § friday night gathering up together a big pile of things i like to respect (flags, crucifixes ,etc) and just roll around in it ,give kisses, § i got like a whole page of arbys coupons... no big deal § looks like a "whos Who' of my dreadful follower list https://t.co/IvoOlKSbep § all good boys keep a jar of sulfuric acid at their station to punish themselves for sending horny dms or goig offbrand.. just a drop will do § KFC is making BIRDS and LUNCH 10954 patrons $545060 a month § (to guy who is filming video of me on his phone while i am siphoning fountain soda through a horrible device) fuck yoyu stop taking pictures § im so sorry you had to go through that.... i apologize on behalf of all guys who dump huge bags of turds and piss off of overpasses § new mcdonalds-flavored burger king sandiwch given the coveted score of "Eight" by food experts § frowning while the entire waitstaff of California pizza kitchen sings "happy birthday" to me, looking like a lump of shit in a neckbrace § kelly bluebook is my gf § i would simply much like to know where i can purchase a nice cloth to place my miniature guitars upon. please do not send me the frog pic. § shutting computer down until the shitty moods & attitudes can fuck off., if you need me ill be on my other computer, sititng 60° to my right § u got 1 side saying dogs have paws & the other side saying dogs have hooves..then me, the guy who cuts thru the BS, saying they have Niether § Q: Would you describe your Brand as more "Uday" or "Qusay" hussein? A: Qusay, without a doubt. Qusay. § hey @BurgerKing your trays dont fit in the fuckin trash cans. i am a CFO in real life and an oversight like this would cost me my Nuts . § when you're sitting on the toilet theres a tiny opening between the seat and your dick/nut area. this is known as "The Daredevil's Spittoon" § ok which one of the trolls told some company in Singapore that im interested in bulk purchases of cheap laminate flooring. i demand answers. § i maintain that curly is by far the most malignant stooge. without his toxic influence, moe & larry couldve ascended to unfathomable heights § Fine. I'll shut the fuck up now. § one of the things you realize when becoming a genius in many aspects of life is that the world wide web. and the computer, is the same thing § jusut dropped 8000000 HKD on a usb-interfaced sniper rifle that blocks one of my insolent followers at random every time i pull the trigger § please check out my devastating one-man takedown of the thanksgiving day parade, which was given a PG rating by the MPAA due to " sarcasm". § hello 911. the toilet seat ripped my loin cloth off again § am i correct in assuming that everyone is happy about prisons not being private anymore because now we get to see the inmates dick and asses § @ redbubble https://t.co/oj4aBw1VrL this shit sucks get rid of it § a man from botswana is threatening to ddos a picture of my ass if i do not post a list of my favorite pasta shapes by 6am. i will not relent § 1st grade: Mastered. 2nd Grade: MAstered. 3rd Grade: Mastered. 4th Grade: Heres when they start trying to trick you 5th Grade:This ones hard § does anyone else remember when the owner of @OscarMayer forgot to switch to his personal acct before @-ing pictures of his turds to a doctor § in 2017 i will make a concerted effort to become a ringling brother. § this is the Essence https://t.co/9fbLYVAhgm § 19:00 hours. im whereing a condom right now. temperature: 74°F. air pressure:1012hPa. just had a phenomenal potato salad. Wind Direction: NE § im afraid you do not grasp the enormity of who it is you are dealing with. (removes diaper,. revealing two sub-diapers) Shall we continue.. § WAITER..ive made it quite clear U are not to speak to me until im ready to select the Spice Level of my braised quail dumplings..now BEGONNE § #MillennialSoapOperas " DUMB ASES " § hm? U want me to stop posting about the latest deals at Boscovs? well i wish bugs would stop biting my dick..but " PAL IT AINT HAPPENEN' ! " § im not obligated to respond to thits shit. § jokes on you , my followers peak hours are 2-4am because theyre all unemployed and depressed § boys night https://t.co/lHeOCEyC9p § stop this. At once. we are supposed to be lifting the voices of our fellow content creators. Not shiting on them. § (in really quiet, barely audible voice) hope your dick falls of bitch § i will respect the wishes of th e mayor and the townsfolk by not fucking the pumpkin patch and ruining the harvest, only if i am given $100. § a good commercial idea would be a cop who pulls a guy over ansd steals the out back steak house gift card from his wallet while checking id § Thw common law wife is giving me "Side Eye", for accidentally eating some of the poison they left out for the stray dogs in karachi § it is really quite astonishing that I have yet to win The Lottery, given how good I am at selecting six numbers and saying them out loud § sick of guys like jared and storm roof getting themselves beat up in prison just so they can snag a trending topic on twitter § they are going to build a moscque on the wtc. #SelfieForSeb § thinking of life's i could have led in other worlds..... https://t.co/G1yZpvuort § ME: please show me the posts in the order that they were made COMPUTER: thats too hard. heres some tweets i think are good. Do you like this § "if theres a spicy brown mustard, why not a spicy brown ketchup?" The wise man smiled. "my friend, the condiment you seek is Barbecue Sauce" § visions of God § becoming a cop so I can access the police computer and scrutinize the Walmart receipts of my rivals digimon Otis and warez_lad § scrolling through the timeline, not comprehending a single thing, but smiling and nodding slightly when i see the word "Favs" or "Retweet" § im actually glad you leaked this. now the Dialogue can begin. § let's all be my wife § #NationalGirlfriendDay please cherish your gal's.. in honor of us, the single Boys who must sacrifice all companionship to #CarryTheBrand... § the james bond 007 ez board will not let me change my user handle to WHITE_LIFTER, even though it contains no swears. i am in crisis mode § YES...i have the healthiest Gum Line as verified by the Department of Records NO...i will not chew food for you NO...you may NOT kick my ass § for every year that He is not featured in Forbes Magazine as the worlds richest man... GOD will sink one of our battle ships § i do enjoy spending my weekends "Joining the Army". oh how i hate when monday rolls around & i must say goodbye to all of my soldier friends § incredibly handsome , charismatic famous boy credited with ending income inequality after saying that slumlords should be called "dumblords" § ME: Are these Vine Ripe WAITER: Yes ME: Is this Farm Fresh WAITER: Yes ME: Are these "MAde To Order" WAITER: No ME: I will notify the police § somebody please Bribe me § I do oft in times flush my waste as soon as possible. I have no desire to look at it. I would rather be reading expensive novels to my wife. § so long suckers! i rev up my motorcylce and create a huge cloud of smoke. when the cloud dissipates im lying completely dead on the pavement § just as Christ washed the feet of his disciples , i proudly volunteer to allow my girl followers to use my shirt as a napkin,. § It's become apparent that this is a measured attack . § does it not save a total of 12 keystrokes, which are widely regarded to be considered to be known as the "Typist's Syllable" ? § horny does'nt exist § everybody wants to be the guy to write the tweet that solves racism once and for all because it would look good as hell on a resume § i cannot condone taking my previous tweet and using it to say that the "ass wiping hack" is me. i regret putting myself in such severe peril § im the guy who talks about ass wiping hacks so often that i commonly use the abbreviation AWH and get mad when people ask what it stands for § boycot https://t.co/cjb6yRmKMs § (sending image of delicious meal i stole from a group dm to a girl) yeah i ate this § Cowardice: A Tale In Four Parts https://t.co/Abc1veRqnh § Greetings. Today I would like to discuss "Porky Pig" § - Incest Prank Goes Wrong - Why Thousands Of Geniuses Are Ditching Their Aquariums - Can Plants Make You Smarter? - Moms Can Get Tattoos Now § my IQ has increased 10 points ever since i stopped tollerating people mucking about, on the time line § how about we worry about human rights ... after we've fixed all the human wrongs ? #AnHonestMansSay § me N' the boys eating messy sandiwches, sneaking around with big binoculars looking for girls & letting every one know who runs this TJ maxx § what this site needs is the apollo theater "Sand Man" to push all the " MORONS " off stage. I will take this down if it is considered Racial § I Am Not Afraid To Shut Off My $300 Asus Monitor From " ew Egg .com" Off If The Intelligence Of This Site Reaches To The Level Of Stupitity. § i would love to brutally kick the ass off of anyone who tries to be nice to me or be my friend on here § ME: Im far more excited to see what the "Cloud" has to offer, than what the "Clown" has to offer. MY NEMESIS: How dare you tell the truth. § "we live in an exciting age because you can just go get downloads of anything. almost every day there is new downloads to get." -

OwedSex96 § i truly hate winning the infamous "Darwin Award" by getting bombarded with artillery fire in the Super K-Mart parking lot § girls always love to telling people not to" Mansplain" but they do not care of, "Man's Pain" § wailing at th e blooper reel, saying all the things hte actors are doing wrong out loud, punching the shit out of an usher, pop corn flying, § ive beenn using Confidence and Self Esteem lately, to get unprecedented deals on discarded promotional displays at game stop § ive hired 3 of my clumsiest dumb ass followers to spy on my wife and uncover her plots against me, just the worst bumbling fucking imbeciles § (sees a cop shoot somone) This is just like james bond (sees a war happen) This is like robo cop (sees a burning house) This is like top gun § my agent says if i get my balls neutered off ill be able to calm down & improve my posts. but i keep telling him, my posts wil never be good § https://t.co/3SXmLlkmxr § no more belly Vids § https://t.co/Sx6Ym92g6t § some times, it would seem to me, that some of the people who use "smart phones", are ANY THING BUT !!! #OhButUGottaLaugh § folks keep asking, me, what are Q-TIps for. if theyre not for ears. well the answer is simple. theyre for wiping certain areas of your dick, § sick of bieng fucking shrieked at in DMs just because im one of the few left who thinks girls should not breastfeed while operating aircraft § tak9ng your shirt off in the pool...shit move § my name is "Pruce" now. tell every one you know that my name is now pruce § the mummys curse mother fucker § (responding to a troll after increasing my intelligence to Max Level with a carefully optimized content stream) I suppose u think youre God, § you threaten to go to the bathroom on me? i do not think you have the gall to go to the bathroom on me § hopping on some tech support forums to accuse people with minor hardware issues of being Mad § never do dunks on me or own me again § beginning to despise my friends and loved ones for pushing valuable branded content off of my feed as I struggle to comprehend this world § i will never stop feeding thte trolls § well im glad theyve downgraded me to "basically" a nazi instead of "literally" a nazi § people are still apparently very upset with me for cancelling "the thursday nite rant" feature... let it go folks.. https://t.co/L3gqdFNYCX § million dollar idea: Dog door that is big enough for humans Billion dollar idea: Dog door that says "Hello" when something passes through it § Waiter! Oh Waiter! Yes, I`d like to know if I have earned any CashBack Reward`s„¢ with the purchase of my farm fresh miniature cucumber plate § a booklet labeled "Mra Shit" falls out of my pocket during my daily buffallo wild wings j/o, sealing my fate and costing me the Yoplait deal § my agent told me to say ive done a lot of soul searching & have decided that keebler is the treat of the summer § helping the police by yanking the doors off all the public bathroom stalls § im also a gamer with ring worm § trying to heal..... please donate to my go fund me... $10 will make me less racist... $100 will make me extremely less racist...thank you... § i will never "honk if im horny" . § just thought off an idea i believe to be bad ass. lets find the address of the leader of isis, and mail him/ her pieces of our SHIT § its not Fucking funny § I insist that Moe is the 1st Stooge, Larry the 2nd Stooge, and Curly is the 3rd Stooge. Some will say the order isnt important. Theyre wrong § @KeeblerElves Please help me . You cowards § wife sentenced to 4yrs for defrauding a charitable organization..U know what that means (pulls worst gaming consoles to exist out of closet) § i stopped watching all the tv shows my followers think are bad, unfollowed all the Goof accounts, and yet twitter still sends thugs after me § "History will show that Brexit was the correct choice, for the future of Great Britain. I also do not believe in sex." - The_Brexit_Asexual § i refuse to consume any product that has been created by, or is claimed to have been created by, the (((Keebler Elves))) § indoor plumbing is a ludicrous fantasy § going to start asking "What do you Think?" at the end of each post, to help stimulate discourse and reap the substantial benefits of Social. § someitmes it seems to me that some people woulr rather join KKK, than join mensa.... § awfully bold of you to retweet my "bad year" tweet on a year that has been extremely good thus far § Just got word that thheyre going to do jade helm 15 again, to punish us for letting the celebs run amok. It 's fucked up but we deserve it. § going to start deleting posts, due to harassment. as in, i want more of it. hbring it on egg heads § no!! this is fucked! § been completely ruined due to iron deficiency and Arrogance. had to scrap the project and start from scratch. Looking for investors § Rather tiresome that people wiould rather Threadshit my mentions than say, enjoy a whimsical boating tour through the fair canals of Venice. § polease cut all art programs so we can instead focus on teaching our children the importance of being Respectful towards influencers § amazing to me that people are still complaining about my genius sons being too loud, in 2016, of all years § 1) i do not owe you mother fuckers a damn thing 2) i will not hear any more questions or comments unless they pertain to MetroPCS, or Pepsi. § - Always retweet promoted tweets. - Always surreneder your username and password to Girls - Always Wait 1hr before replying a Verified Acct. § Your "I Love TD Bank" Car Decal Fucking Sucks § @Boscovs Are you unquestionably committed to the "Customer First" experience--Do you pledge here and now to bow to the customer's every whim? § STOP THE POST STREAM. PULL THE PLUG ON IT. END THIS MADNESS. GET THESE DAMN POSTS OFF MY TIME LINR "LOUSY!!" "WE DON'T WANT EM!!" § i posted on here earlier about how ihad a leather belt wrapped around my nuts and not a single person asked if i was ok. Fuck you § worst food of 2016 : Bread Where to begin. Bread is a piece of shit and its no wonder its commonly associated with the worst drink, "Water". § Look again at the post. I did indeed sign it, with a 'D' for dril, after referring to you as a Frau. (german woman) Checkmate. § CONTEMPTUOUS NIGHTMARE: (blowing farts w/ mouth) ME: Sir! I demand your opinion regarding Organized Gender's influence on corn prices. SIR!! § BLATHERING SHITE: the Dems VP Pick should be subway;s own Jared ME: That man is in jail. Have you done any research prior to this discussion § in the planning stages, for a new feature of my account which i have tentatively titled " The Three Posts. " more info coming soon of this. § -go about my day seeking energy in my life as a Bieng of intelligence -if your sperm count is complete dog shit, i will not even talk to you § Trite. § @dril none of them were good. Sorry § folks.. reply to this message with your Finest tweet, and i just might drop it a Like... my way of "Giving back" to the community... Thank u § Cant wait to catch all the exclusive trailers and live events at #GamerGate in Los Angeles this week. Looks to be the best gamer gate yet § ouh yes!! THe boys have spoken, and they want more! More jokes about the ape! My one man show , entitled " ot-So-Great Ape" will explore th § forwarded to Admin . § Un-Tag me U fucking degenerate cobs of dog shit. You dirt beneath my heel § handing Faves over to my enemies is FRAUD !! base, contemptible FRAUD! § to everyone who thinksn im some sort of dip shit regarding video of me eating a pocket pussy, please rest assured i hated every moment of it § unloading an entire belt of ammo at me with a minigun or some such device will now get you "Blocked" § t o the guy who told me they took the ape to the hospital and cured him, Fuck You. § A MERE Musing From A Troubled Husband, Strengthened Through Time: "Let the birds have their bird seed, and unto us boys, the Beer seed" § was a tad dismayed to find a Rat Brain in my favorite KFC Snacker Meal, B ut the friendly cashier assured me it was merely Intestinal Matter § the other day a trolling Shit sent me the message, "Googoo Gaagaa ". Twitter has indeed threatened to close my account if i dont retweet him § For your Friday Enjoy-ment; A "Shit List" of folks I've banned from my Radio Shack: Monica Louinsky, The Honey Boo Boo, Octo Mom, & "Snooki". § I TELL YA IT NEVER FAILS !! WENT TO GET MY MAIL AND A HIPSTER HIT ME WITH THE STRONGEST STREAM OF URINE I EVER SAW ! KNOCKED ME ON MY DUFF ! § examining the Ape Case: perhaps many are mirthful of its death as apes are akin to Golems & Vampires, cinematic villains of the classic era, § INTERVIEWER: we looked you up. you dont even have a twitter account, which is good ME: Actually i was suspended for posting "Gumby shit ass" § im the guy who gets really upset about people not putting their real names on here. im also mad at State Farm Insurance for not being a farm § stunning: mindful adult , decked out in complete set of riot gear - takes out entire stampede of horses using wisdom and tactic's § my entire face turns purple as i try to enjoy my cup of monday coffee while all my coworkers rush into my office to watch me fail once again § oh u think this is funny mother fucker?(Kills ape) YOu consider this comedy? (kills naother ape) and my Missing Plane jokes are bad? Yeah ok § back in the dog house after the wife caught me photo shopping her into vintage car ads § kneading my dick and nuts like a wad of dough on a bench at pay less shoe store. i do not appear to be enjoying myself. im frowning actually § i help every body, im not racist, i keep myself nice, and when i ask for a single re-tweet in return i am told to fuck off, fuck myself, etc § "ah boo hoo hoo i want to post Foul comments to content leaders" Fat Chance, Dimwit. I will annihilate you under bulwark of the Law and God. § Coward-Centric Platform twitter, removing user handles from character limit, giving the repliers more ammunition with which to shit on me, § Downlioading 6 Terabytes Of Info On Deal's § 1989: the fall of the berlin wall is celebrated, historically revered 2016: i tear down the sneeze guard at old country buffet and get Booed § the girls on this site constantly beg me to show them a picture of the clothes i wear while posting. this is them. https://t.co/1EUP0gwFq4 § just doing some nude sunbathing in this gender neutral target restroom. i hope i dont get my dick sucked § You need at least $100 to join Boys Lunch Club. I will count all of the money in your wallet, so do not try to join if you do not have $100. § Just met w/ Boys Lunch Club. Seems to me, That we are very pissed off that teen girls would rather kiss, "Soldier Boy," than Actual Soldiers § online is where i go to get my A B C's... Abused By Cretins § checked my inbox for 2 seconds & immediately saw a genital. could not parse which type of genital it was before tossing my phone out the car § taken to task by the ryhthm bastard § we had 2 cuts of ribeye, a salt shaker half full of salt, a quart of wine, and a whjole galaxy of multi-colored bibs, napkins, § Removing the battery from my phone until the time line becomes less toxic. § can anyone tell me if this is good or not. if this sort of thing is frowned upon i will stop immediately https://t.co/neyx6Usg7V § presented with out comment . https://t.co/VNyp4qja2q § did you just rob a bank by threatening to open a bottle of diarrhea § Q: If your post was proven by a counsil of wise men to be racist, or bullshit, would you bar it from the record? A: I do not delete my posts § i do not delete my posts. deleting my posts would be akin to razing Abraham Lincolns famous log cabin, just because the trolls are mad at it § theres no space in the title you shit mouthts. it's one word, it's always been one word, it will forever be "Topgun." i will not delete this § ive heard from a reliable source that people arre putting their lips on to my girl friends avatars and going "muah muah muah." cut it out § peppercorn ranch & buttermilk ranch... one of these is good, the other is completely Fucked, and its not my responsibility to tell you which § i wont say more of this. but a couple of the big accounts on here have been souporting swearing culture, by posting swears to the time line. § eating a single Dorito on a bed of Jasmine Rice § my greatest sin is that I've utterly betrayed my " O FEAR" tower decal by being embarrassingly frightened of birds and butter flies § youre all a Dog of the Coward's order. ill take you across my knee and slap yopur Ass., i will "GIVE UM HELL" as ordred by the great general § images leaked of WildArmsGarret , trusted consigliere of DigimonOtis, taking a bath in one of those old fashioned metal wash tubs § (steps out onto the podium for the annual delivery of his Most Hated "State of the Arbys" address) the state of the Arby's... is strong... § my being a shit head can be traced back to boys school, when i was expelled for using the headmaster's computer to search ebay for " LUNCH " § will not be making any new posts until the 5G Network has been officially rolled out. 4g doesn't cut it anymore. fail to see the point . § (sniffing a crumpled up one dollar bill i found on the floor of a dog kennel) ah.. thats greenbacks baby § ST PETER: on march 14 2024 you posted simply the words "james earl bond". hope the 34 favs were worth it idiot ME: They were bitch § spending my entire police shift downloading apps where you smear simulated dog shit all ovefr the screen and becoming completely a dumb ass § id like a few words with this prick https://t.co/QH016dazoq § photo's shop § PRIEST: in the name of the father... ME: Yes. Good PRIEST: ...the son.. ME: Great. Go on. keep em comin PRIEST: ..and the Holy Spirit ME: No § wife hall of Fame https://t.co/UqTGjtNupd § damn it to piss. my wife replaced all of my anti-wife reading materials with Pro-Wife bullshit § i` ve long supported the classic "One Tooth" rule, which states that every time you make a bad post you should have one of your teeth pulled § Every Time I read a new Tweet on my time line. My IQ increases by One Point. § im just about to say that if you come in to the kfc support forum w/ a name like "crisp_Kyle" you can go right ahead & click that logout tab § when MetalGearEric told his 36 followers i have "A Poor Man's Micropenis" and none of my so called allies stepped in to defend my honuor.... § LOVELY GIRL FOLLOWER: hey.. i noticed you posted 3 barbed remarks about game stop in a row.. is everything ok? ME: NO, everything is NOT ok, § some times.. the smartest people you know, are Geniuses § tiodays FunQuote: "Dont forget the WiFi" #FunQuote § i am developing a ground brekaing new app called "MOneyWal-let", where you earn "Money Points" by mailing cash to my house § whose idea was to call it "Ice cream parlor" and not "Scoop Kitchen" ?? lets get this joke viral and show my ex-wife landlord whos boss § weeping because of my heroic burden... spending my last dollae at dairy queen to support girl businesses... chowing down between the tears.. § please bring your rats to the new castle flea market so I may bless/heal them. ill be sitting in a lawn chair wearing a stolen priest outfit § i am a classically tragic dumb ass hwo has the burger king logo imprinted in my brain like a baby bird to its mother § despite everything, i am still looking forward to the release of the sequel, "jungle 3 jungle," which was delayed to 2038 because of trolls. § i did not say that the kid from jungle 2 jungle should be sent to Guantanamo bay, i just said it wouldn't be racist if he was § if i catch you taking " SELFIE " at my used car dealership (BEST deals in the tri-state area) i will shell you from the rear like a coward § my work day consists of my bosses trying to goad me into my cubicle so that i'll just sit in there & jack off isntead of ruining the company § the thing i accidentally posted earlier about putting my used condoms in the dishwasher was a virus. my subsequent meltdown was also a virus § GEN X'ER: Help im shitting on my pants ME: They have this invention called "toilet" now. Maybe if you hang up the cell phone yould know this § people pay good money to stamp your mail. if you refuse to take the time to thoroughly digest every piece of mail you receive, you are a Cur § Tjhis guy fucking sucks https://t.co/ZL67sQF6zm § putting the vacuum on my dick until I stop hearing crumbs go down the tube § when people ask me who my favorite comedian is.. i invoke that wacked weatherman "AL GURE" and get one million dollars worth of retweets § the $100000 pyramid is actually fairly fucking cheap for a pyramid § we need less mayors and more sayers (of truth) § id like to muse upon a scenario i came up with just now. a DUMB ASS visits a restaurant, after reading a poor review of it in the newspaper § dropping some more Asexual Nudes into the cloud, to show the girls and the trolls how clean my body is, from years of washing § YES, my dick is shaped like an extremely small snail's shell NO, you may NOT suck it, § had mny scholarship revoked because of my bumbling 15 tweet routine about how isis attacked the airport because they hate brussel sprouts § All music made past the year 1969 is rap. (sseals self in rebuttal proof chamber for 100 years) § Was Going To Send Ur ScreenPlay To Mr Scorcese Until I Found Out U Were Part Of The Failshit Brigade Who Mocked My Seashell Necklace In 2010 § i lvove falling off the guard tower § really hoping that someday my wife will surprise me by sending me a picture of my own dick § im one of the friday night lights, from the title § ME: COMPUTER... SORT THE POSTS ON THIS SITE FROM LEAST TO MOST RACIST COMPUTER: YES MASTER ME: COMPUTER... PLEASE DO NOT CALL ME THAT § that house is clearly on the grid. it sucks § fuck the grid § gonna fill up on milk shakes and do some open carry off the grid § (browsing the secret arbys menu that only boys can look at) ah., lets see, ill take one Spicy Onion Concerto with a dollop of SmartCorn„¢ § first you have democrats and rtepublicans. theyre basically the same thing. then you have green party and uh, the whigs. theyre the same too § helping the waitstaff by wiping the table down with the same disgusting napkin that I just used to sop up all the bullshit off my face § user named " beavis_sinatra " has been terrorizing me since 2004, by sending me pictures of cups that are too close to the edge of the table § Sovereign Citizens Getting Owned Compilation § this is photo shop § (poking head up from self suck) augh this tastes like dog shit (goes back for more) § im a marine & accomplished scholar. my sons were alchemized into helicopter fuel to serve their armed brothers. how dare u post penis to me. § my sources tell me that people are allowed to say the word "ass" on HBO. can anyone confirm this § Quick Thinking: Area Man Saves Own Life By Making A Bra Out Of Two Diapers § Leut me make this clear: gloves are Next-Gen mittens , mittens are trash, i will never wear a mitten, i will take down anyone whos mad at me § guy walking around flaunting his mittens around. claiming that nothings better than mittens. i show him my gloves and he flips the fuck out § im being evicted from my home for saying that kfc should sell hamburgers on a public log, and being a general "Dumb Ass" when it comes to IQ § #truth #fact... it is proven that about 80% of people online are violent murderers. wow thats so many. be safe my beloved followers § "tarzan of the apes" will never become a Turner Classic Movie. shoddy premise. people find pictures of a man yelling in the woods disgusting § tarzan is garbage. he sucks more than anything. people need to stop encouraging his shit by making films of him. go home tarzan. fuck tarzan § pleased to announce that i am pissed off due to Stress,. and the Block All Girls initiative is now officially underway. § glorious crime spree after being fired from wal mart., expertly hopping fences, chugging all the seeds out of my neighbors bird feeders, § this is uttlery disgraceful § Former U.S. first lady Nancy Reagan (R) joined by daughter Patti Davis at the premiere of the film "Stuart Little 2" https://t.co/43kfKiOtma § i tell you folks this damn itunes is something that you cant figure out unless you are a nasa guy § FULLY PREPARED TO TAKE A HIT IN THE OLD FOLLOWER COUNT TO BECOME AN ALL CAPS, ALL BOND ACCOUNT. LIVE THE DREAM. PURGE THOSE BOZOS § THEY SAY A NEW BOND ACTOR IS CHOSEN OUT OF RESPECT EVERY TIME THE REAL LIFE JAMES BOND DIES, AND HELL, FROM WHERE IM SITTING IT CHECKS OUT § NETWORKING IN HOME MARKETS SUCCESS SEMINAR HOSTED BY JAMES BOND HIMSELF? OH YEAH. IM IN. BUT IM GOING TO NEED YOU TO DRIVE ME THERE § AS J. BOND HOLDS IN HIS POSSESSION THE FAMOUS "LISCSENSE TO KILL," I MYSELF HAVE LICSENSE TO TOUCH AS MANY GRAPES AS I PLEASE W/O BUYING ANY § im mashing the mute block and report buttons all at once with my big red palms § please read my longform treatise "The Arrogance Of Burger King" available only on my new $70/month content streaming platform "ShitWire Pro' § i couldnt help but notcie you besmirching my nephews Banksy Valhalla, Jordian Computer, Holstein Paypal, and last but not lease, paper mario § " the bitch of bluejeans" https://t.co/TiJs0ly8kr § -racist, -unsanitary condittions (animal near food) - fake holiday -ill eviscerate this pic further at a later time. https://t.co/ycauu88vTY § stealing valor by purchasing fraudulent military gear from etsy,. parading my insane loadouts in front of our vets as they hurl abuse at me, § He thinks it's Cute to come into my mentions and lord his "Hollywood

Elite” blood capital over me and my boys § the trolls are also in full bloom as well i see , § cant wait to hurl them at my foes https://t.co/VS3Mw5ic9j § imagnie a world where us Common folk are given the blue checkmark and the CELEBs are left out to dry!! Hows that feel, HUh?! Answer me punks § #SaySomethingGoodAboutTwitter you can easily remove it from your screen by clicking the x § (me in prone position while having my house swatted again) officer if u could please just slip the rest of that campbells chunky in my mouth § crapping fuck... 900 pictures of guns that you absolutely Must see § it was always my idea to fill all the fire engnies with shit and piss to save water. the mayor stole it and planted a bomb in my car § looking for some open comment sections in marine corps training vids to post racist shit on § aangry bird’s.. a Corrupted brand. keep far away § before i drop 20.99 on these bad boys..can anyone tell me if im at risk of being murdered by the nsa if i wear these https://t.co/J5szdlX4wu § Im online at the computer, ready to post pitures of my new sandwich, and ive got a hankering for my ass to get kicked § if it werent for the sport of hockey, nobody would give a shit about pucks § Q: Whats ur least favorite finger to be flipped off with A: the middle one. it pisses me off way more than the other fingers. drives me nuts § get me on some ghostboster sites § huaw yeah you gotta try this shit... just boil the macaroni in the same pot as the spaghetti ... this is called the famous “Double pasta” § attn Waiters: giving me one of the free pens from TD Bank ruins the experience of signing my check. it is a slap in the face. A death threat § U Have Forced Me To Take Extreme Measures To Protect My Business And My Lifestyle. I Now Refuse To Open A Single Email Until April The 12th. § while youre all bowing to the Pig Industrial Complex on false holiday #NationalPigDay,. i will be observing pictures of the noble bull moose § #NationalPigDay no. this is crap . the pig will never have his day. i demand that the “Pig” surrenders this filthy assault on our calendars. § vision’s... https://t.co/CTVJLWTTj2 § sorry to all crooks, hucksters, cronies, and phonies... but in this, our year of 2016, police man is sitll king, and the jail, his Kingdom ! § listen fuck wit. if you dont want me pissng all down the floor and the walls of your public restroom then make the urinals. bigger § i propose a Bussiness offer of the boy who says”Damn daniel”.. i should like for him to grace the company of me & my wife, for twelve jewels § sorry couldnt hear ya over $ rustling about in my wallet. money i saved by subverting toothbrushes. sucking the toothpaste tube like a cock, § THRIEE SIMPLE RULES FOR SPEAKING TO ME OF MY AFFAIRS REGARDING MY INTERACTIONS WITH MY LAWYER’S... STAND DOWN !! GET IN LINE !! FUCK OFF !! § we all know the famous “Five Second Rule”... if you dont throw dropped food in the trash within five seconds it unleashes toxic spores § ill never rinse my farm fresh vegetables. its the responsibility of the greengrocer to rinse my God damn food and if i get poisoned so be it § stumbling through war torn syria with my pants down, begging everyone around me not to feed the trolls § the first step to becoming a Millionaire is to acquire one hundred dollars § people who like to say “Ba ba ba ba “ at me <<<< People who hand me their wallet § a boss should be allowed to kick his employees asse’s. key to his workers house so he can just come in and start wailing anytime #bottomword § 20 treats = 1 snack 3 snacks = 1 meal 3 meals = Boys Daily Intake 180 Treats = Boys Daily Intake 1 Treat = 1 Goody 60 Goody’s = 1 meal § im going to get shit on a lot for posting this but i dont care https://t.co/BPuMWfWaow § https://t.co/iKYM0jDKrz this is the most vile thing to be put on tv § paper is a liquid #TheThursdayMorningRamble § someone please. ive bitten into a nasty apple and I don’t know how to spit things out of my mouth. ivr never spit before and i need help § givign my social security number to the valentines day app to find out which idiot wants to see my dick the most § for all you twitter birds out there.. a fun idea ive been throwin around: lets make the front page to “WILD WEST” theme..Huh! only on Friday § barby dolls are worthless to me § in 2020 police technology will allow criminals to choose between "hot jail" and "cold jail" § good to have Options https://t.co/3vKXg8pEIR § why even bother learning how to hack when i can just have my enemies accounts removed by accusing them of conspiring to piss on grumpy cat § death https://t.co/7vGn40uZCX § if i saw someon e on the street wearing a dunce cap, i would challenge him to my famous Three Trials of wisdom, and soundly defeat him § let me be very clear: i would rather attend a Pig's wedding than attempt to sift through the dumpster you people have made out of my dm box, § ELLEN: But what you're most known for is your use of the infamous N-Word ENTICED AUDIENCE: Wooo !! ME: ahh!! ya got me! § IN OUR LIFETIMES... "GOODBYE" TO MOUTH WASH § i hope you all enjoyed my latest Sets (posts) § i will not let anyone touch my pitbuls unless they are wearing a collared shirt § thhere is no such thing as charisma, and art is fake. the only metrics by which we must determine the worth of a man are Strength and Wisdom § the pursuit of having trhe nicest opinions online... is the only thing that separates us from the god damn animals. the sole reason we exist § i think he belongs in the paddy wagon with the rest of the looney tunes § Closing my account until all of the pro jet-dry kiddies go to bed. You people are animals. Hopeless brutes § scenario: the duishwasher mouth starts up in some dumb ass baby voice. "GIMME SUM JET DRY!!" i unload my .480 ruger into it without Emotion, § i just thoughgt about those commercials with the stupid fucking mouth in the dishwasher that begs for jet dry & ripped a door off its hinges § id like to report a hacker. he offered me 1000000 to show my dick and didnt cough up the dough when i delivered the goods. i got hacked § i shooed a young trans person away from my garbage with a broom § MYTH: my posts are for the Pauper REALITY: my posts are for the Prince § the prophecy fulfilled https://t.co/H1erJV4KBS https://t.co/MOpYkwDKmE § Puerto Rican Pisser § you soudn like a nerd § wow , another bernie bro coming after me just because im posting the truth into their shitty little lives. you Lose bitch § I mdade $400000 just by typing the words "Simpson and garfunkel" back in 2011 and u have the gall to @ me w/ ur little 200 ass follower acct § please dm my agent if you wish to Banter with me in the mentions, so he can send you the proper paperwork. im extremely tired of this shit. § U cant even get a good "Shoe Shine" anymore--the guy just keeps trying to put his mouth on my dick. Is this a Thing now. Is this a Problem § someone please get me in touch with the little boy who died & went to heaven. i want to astral project him into my ex-wifes castle for intel § i enjoy a bit of "Humour" every now and then, but people seriously need to sotp tying me to a chair and injecting me with unknown substances § https://t.co/hhgYfh8ZqT § (looking into a big toilet filled with shit , piss and toilet paper, shaking my head) this is fucking stupid. hardly worth my time § shut the fuck up and kick my ass § GET THE FUCK OFF OF HERE § RAT CHECK... unfollow me ,if youre a sleazy low down RAT!!!!!!!! i will knock your block off, I respect honor, Truth in words and action. § Fuck you mother fucker § an Oscar category for super bowl ads in the future?? perhaps in a less judge mental world, § take ntoe Hollywood: these superbowl ads teach us we can create compelling visual content better than any movie, WITHOUT resort to Vulgarity § fuckin Wade https://t.co/gv0cmmnC1C § "i wish they got, WiFi down here" - guy who died in the paris catacombs § -windows covered in trash bags -arbitrarily sorting the contents of my snack Pack -pumping racist apps into my nokia at Lightspeed -frowning § sometimes it seems to me that it is a bit good to say that we could not do our posts without using none other than the humble computer chip. § taking the lords name in vein... #inspire https://t.co/Zv7CuAGiNH § looks like im forced to address false rumors that i own 3 dildos on a shelf labelled "breakfast" "lunch" & "dinner". this is an absurdity . § ME: mr cruise..im also a celeb. i invented the phrase "Barney sucks" TOM: wow... that phrase is so good, i must use it at least once per day § they say zika virus is the Bastard of 2016, but that distinction must go to my infamous folowers, who i consider to be "Dumber than Dogshit” § donald trump is the best man for the job... and for that he has earned my vote. however, i believe he needs to “Check his priviledge” § 1) wise the fuck up, 2) put the same amount of days in all the months 3)people need to put on the damn thinking caps 4) im boycotting months § While your were busy all discussing the black celebrity’s ass, i just constructed an authentic Christian abacus using fine tumbled stones § got one of th ose steering wheels you control with your mouth so i can dual wield on the road. top secret technology for friends of police, § girlsl... i shall virtuously employ the expansive breadth of my tech wisdom to protect you all from Daesh... even if you dont follow me... § has any one ever noticed that the good spider-man movies are the ones for adults, and the bad spiderman movies are the ones for children § @BreakingNews please make a Nude one § THINKING ABOUT WHEN DID “IN GOD WE TRUST” BECOME “ WOULD YOU LIKE FRIES WITH THAT” § my favorite tv show characters are “The good guys”. My least favorite characters are “The villains” § https://t.co/SxADN7Gjwd § (Becomes upset by an unsolicited mention of Beetle Bailey on twitter feed, and punishes followers by refusing to post an update for 30mins.) § i shant say more of it . https://t.co/wUSQGubk3B § ah.. why is it that computers can send hateful commentary thorugh the modem... but weren’t designed to send something nice.. like a Song § the big seat of my sweat pants sagging beneath the weight of globs of neosporin as i waddlle my fuckface ass off to the impound lot § Fucking yes this . Friendlys has a meatball bar § im the boss of Mensa. every time i close my eyes i have visions of going berserk and spitting on a human face until it is unrecognizasble § i spend a lot of time reading the constatution of the united states of america while grinning ear to ear § will try to become less of an Ape on the day of holy sabbath § just read something fucked up... Not a single picture of stonehenge exists. § first day i got online on a man named Mumbai_Eddie accused me of having diarrhea, so i detached my modem and put it in the sink for 8 years § sick of seeing “Snark” on my feed regarding our nation’s presidential candidates. i will be voting for all of them because they seem nice § Looking to the day when the World Wide Web matures to become into the World Wise Web. § im known to “Trick or Treat” from my neighbors mail boxes. they love it and it drives them wild. And it`s a bit of fun § i dont know who all these fucked up people are!! im sorry! im so sorry!! § #ToTheGirls2016 im intelligent & clean boy. i have the trigger dicispline of a lion. ive used Torture to cure myself of all mental illness. § Discussing Reality Intelligently Life § U have to listen to this song “Signs” by the five man electrical band... the guy is just owning the fuck out of all these signs, it’s insane § more harmful to our web than any computer virus... sick thought’s and selfish attitude... pass it on boys... § this account is the Curse of my life § which 46% of you mother fuckers arent buying soap https://t.co/mbTQvI9lVe § my most famous tweet, entitled “Jacking off at the Dog Kennel,” has earned over ten billion engage-ments & was retweeted by stephen spielberg § today i will be making a bowl of “Home Made” guacamole, with, you guessed it, chips. § get one of those bill gates tubes that turns piss to water, load a big fat backpack with treats, cut the cord, pull the plug, fuck the grid, § got about 50000 posts to catch up on here... thats so many.. thank you my sweet boys § martin luther king did not have a favorite type of lunchables. absolutely ridiculous and inappropriate. @ kraftfoods please delete § we odnt post the word “you” anymore in 2016. § heated debate https://t.co/gsIzuzGz15 § rt if you think that “Coors Light Cold Hard Facts” is the “Chevy Clubhouse” of “Dilfer’s Dimes” § @DigimonOtis Shut the fuck up § its not that number anymore. you may re tweet it now. § “Green lettuce” § fuck it, ill just come out and say that i think “Iceberg lettuce” is just aobut the worst name you can come up w/ for a damn type of lettuce § im not horny but, lets face the facts people... if youre a girl im gonna click on ya § twiitter dot com baby... the inmates are running the damn asylum.. AND IT

THINK THAT IT IS GOOD...!! #StartupIndia § entertaining twisted thoughts of putting bull shit on the back burner § enjoying some fucked up thoughts of some boys enjoying the real counter culture shit... such as drinking coffee, and being glad it’s friday § draculas politics are actually really good to me you scum bag § FUCK OFF https://t.co/iLaBpmVtG6 § excuse me sir, i couldnt help but notice that youre in need of a thorough explanation of kegel exercise. ok, it’s basically psychic jelqing, § youll never shut me the fuck up , no matter how many times you unfollow me, you will never shut me the fuck upon here!! get lost Cyber scum! § im a monk in real life, the matrix is real and hummingbirds and other really fast animals are proof positive that bullet time eixists § i hold this truth , im just an average joe trying to do my messages here, and i dont have time for fellas who want to take a big crap on me. § steven wrong § i have a phd in advanced chemicals., but Thanks. § none of you are educated in anything, youre all pricks, your dms suck, yoyure terrible at trying to engage my brand like normal human beings § “horny” has killed more people than all the volcanos on earth combined § i will soon be leaking a list of the people who sent me really concerned DMs when i posted that jacking off too much makes your dick smaller § if you say the words “Room temperature” to me ill flip my lid. room temp varies depending on the room. youre talking shit out of your mouth. § @BaltimorePolice going to have to unfollow you, for arresting me § MOST HATED FOODS., 50) PAPA JOHNS ORIGINAL FAMOUS CHEMTRAIL PANZEROTTI 49) THE DEMERITORI-OUS DOLLAR NINETY NINE McDIAPER....... MORE TO COME § its actually so good, § argh.. (shakes fist) Damn you White people !! ha ha, but seriously though, most whites are actually highly intelligent, and resourceful, § this post is 2 years old. ive since lost custody of my children and my wife left me. still wild about candles § while you were watching the teen choice awards, i was watching the classic episodes of the teen choice awards from back when they were good. § life is aobut too many chairs. you got the tv chair, dinner table chair, the dentists chair, electric chair... thats too many. Tone it down § ah, aint it funny that folks these days are washing childrens mouths out with soap.. when they should be washing their mouths out with Hope, § up until I was about 17 i believed that bugs were baby rats § Beer is the drink of summer. But it can be enjoyed during the other seasons, in moderation. § respect me.. respect my #Setup https://t.co/FuGceQtgUW § you’ve ruined my life. Thank you § looking at my own dick in 3d § Im going to shut the computer off until people learn to be more mature about life. In tge mean time, suck my dick § pal the only “melt-down” im having is my ice cream melting down into my hand while I lay on the beach & laugh while thinking about the trolls § i don’t have time ot actually read you peoples posts, but ive been evaluating your engagement metric’s and they look like Shit... § Some crap is simply to be put into the dumpster . § its no secret that i sometimes have to scold my hare brained followers rirght in their goofy fucking faces to keep them in line § slin jim § DOCTOR: you cant keep doing this to yourself. being The Last True Good Boy online will destroy you. you must stop posting with honor ME: No, § Dont postshit me. § im going to put my boots on you § COMPUTER.. FED EX ME A PRINT OUT OF ALL MY GIRL FOLLOWERS SORTED BY THEIR DEVOTION TO CHRIST COMPUTER... GET ME THE BULE CHECK MARK A.S.A.P. § the best part of winning the power ball lottery has got to be getting my hands on some of that Green stuff also known as money. § i fear that if the 10k character limit is enacted my trolls will post ascii middle fingers that are elaborate & beautiful enough to kill me § if you want to make someone on this website really mad, accuse them of poisoning the animals they care for #workseveryDamntime #TheMaster § me and SnakeMom1956 are in love and we are laughing at all of th e people who think that our flintstones themed wedding is a sham § i would never photo shop anything, espiecally when it comes to damn fucked up things like racism. this is a serious account § shame on dailymail & nydailynews for posting my racist ball screenshot without giving credit https://t.co/tDHQ9W1M5f https://t.co/lHrGYPCGld § accidentally brought my piss detector into the mens room again and cowered beneath a sink as the deafening screech echoed off the hard tile § pathetic of you to back stab me for clicks. § dont know why they deleted this https://t.co/YO4wLcdMvu § youre fit for 2015 #yourFitOf2015 https://t.co/V65O4BIXf9 § that smug prick baby new year th e piece of shit. ill throw him from my truck the dumb ass mother fucker § Numerous hospitals no longer make a Baby New Year public due to concerns that the infant will become a target for criminals.[13] § bi g fan of his work. loved casino and good fellas § in another life... i would make U stay.. https://t.co/5YnhlziWRQ § i found a basin. its you § i piss into my hands and carry it until i can find a basin § sometimes its good to just wipe your ass, § Bllesed https://t.co/jeNcO69XGL § turning my headlights off when driving at night,.. so that my Rivals cannot see me § anguished imbecile pukes up a surprisingly intact mcgriddle while planting an IED in front of best buy § Pldease just fav me if you enjoyed the tweet. I dont have the time to read the replies § the mayor threatens to replace one letter of the english language with the Swastika for each week that his wooden leg is not returned to him § FOOL: Beer is not the tdrink of summer. It can be enjoyed all year round ME: Beer is the drink of summer. § i have spent the last 9 yrs writing countless papers on the subject of Followback Culture. The quality of my life has suffered immeasurably. § i will die for my belief that Beer is “The drink of summer” § mystical truth Teller https://t.co/Q5XCIgvPsQ § all my vines are me § just spent the last 10 minutes fishing a pubic hair out of the toilet to avoid any nasty phone calls from the boys at the sewage plant § wife put me in the dog house agauin for failing to get the blue checkmark... and people ask me why im mgtow pua... § im here to tell you that even with 8 kid,s, 6 dogs, debilitating rickets & a filthy waterlogged home, that its still possible to be a Gamer § i apologize sir !!!!!!! § this website seems more & more like a place where elitist daddys boys can show off how ‘CLEVER” they are, instead of a source for bra advice § i think your jaw should be knocked into the river § mother teresa Aint No Saint, put the green arrows,there, click the heart too § is mother teresa a saint “ o she aint” § when thw pope says mother teresa is a saint.. i say she Ain’t! § i just want to find the optimal bra for sniper operations, but everoyne here is so rude, and pieces of shit § https://t.co/DQPFkd1awi some posting music for all of ya § mother nature and father time arre not real. theyre fake people who were invented to explain trees and clocks to shitheads § every now and then i like to treat myself to a bit of “Lying under oath” § Barney was actually funny & used fairly adult jokes in the early seasons. After all the teenyboppers latched on; it went to shit. § (in worst human voice possible) folks rmember to click that fuckin like & subscribe button and leave a comment below in the fuckin box there § washed my hands of him years ago. § youwill fucking remove this if you know whats good for you § we cant all be burt fucking milford § i hope to one day eat 10’000 calories a day § boy’s Rules: 1) the only coffee flavored thing should be COFFEE !! 2) “Shut Da Fuck Up And Keep Ya Head Down” 3) Never consume Oils § yoyu dont choose to be retweeted.. it choose’s you § In culture, today, where they have cellphones, it seems, as, though, the most forgotton words in the English language are, “I give a Damn.” § AYE... THE OJ SIMPSON VERDICT IS SOMEWHAT SHIT , INNIT!!!!!! § MustardCynic: this is not True Spicy Brown... this is Treason Brown § ah, its beautiful, § what does that mean. why do people send me messages § #HipHop-StarWars please. imn begging you. all girls on this hashtag please send HD pictures of your teeth& gums. please god just give me this § another miserable day of Disappointing my followers https://t.co/jzUBZVostB § piece of shit https://t.co/OUy5nfQlau § i cannot be sure. i can only base my claims on various extrapolations as i do not look at naked fat men in my life. § based on a bunch of educated assumptions i’ve made about weight gain, really obese guys must have like the hugest dicks on the planet § I shoudl not be expected to put my knee on the ground to propose to a woman, the same ground where the animals shit, § the worst thing you can do in death is make the R.I.P. on your grave actually stand for Racism Is Power § boys im here to tellt you that a high-quality wall paper can make any room look fantastic on the cheap § Setting aside the dumb ass things of life to focus on the truth of intelligense . § dont worry ladies, im not one of those"Bros" who talks to girls about sex stuff. anyway, i have an entire bra stuffed in my mouth right now, § leaving splinters stuck in your fingers is good. its all protien baby § it depends on the fixture you fucking clod § cghecking to see if i have the correct wattage on all of my Light bolbs.. now thats a pizza pie #thatsaPizzaPie § liberating to have gotten all the joke's out of my system sometime back in 2011 so I can now disseminate serious info to the dumb asses here § i can no longer close my eyes. with out seeing a bounty of Farm Fresh groceries being licked by dirty dogs and animals § i look very handmsome in my bow tie and suspenders, holding a big red balloon § spend a lot of time thinking about how sometimes even war criminals can be heroes sometimes... Dont like it? Click the unfollow buttobn § i find the private dm chats are an excellent place to "Workshop" my meltdowns & personal attacks against others, before making them public, § i will simply leave u to your circle jerk . § pretending not to be mad while the guy in the next stall over takes a big shit while I try to Meditate § judgementle people deserve to be put into a special kind of electric chair which sends then to hell even if theyre good . § ive started bowing my head and saying grace before reading each post on here... "thank you." "thank you for the posts." that sort of thing, § i wish my opinions were good enough to put on bumper stickers, but alas, i can only say "syria is basically road rash 64" using my mouth § shooting off automatic rifles making horrible diarrhea shit noises as the recoil makes my tiny dick flop around. hell yeah. thats cool to me § i mailed my detached dick to bolivia to get it enlarged by a professor of Medicine. i am hoping it is returned to me without incident. § beer city USA . my friend s § its fucked up how there are like 1000 christmas songs but only 1 song aboutr the boys being back in town § ive been sititng in buffalo wild wings for 3 hrs now, refusing to speak with the waiter because of his vile dry lips. i will win this battle § soaking weekly circulars in my own blood and sending them back to Shop-Rite, to teach them a lesson about enticing my wife with bargains § i am a chef now folks. im walking around town in my chefs hat like a real dumbass. everyone hopes i get hit by a car § my followers will be thrilled to hear that i am wearing a very pleasant pair of jeans while reading a variety of articles, on subjects § UNCLE: on sept 14 u posted "my dick is not all its cracked up to be." Explain yourself please ME: its. a commentary on the economy actually, § i have never condoned "rumpus" § blesssed to have over 200 mannequins propped up around my house in vulgar positions, and the accompanying "Love my manny`s" bumper sticker § my uncles caught me searching "can i still join isis if im racist" on the family computer & are now withholding all holiday treats for 2015. § how do i make it so people have to give me money if they want to reply to my posts § becoming incrediblly Spiritual on the computer... holy fuck... § yes. this guy is me https://t.co/zd2KABfhQQ § enya on full blast.. accessing 100 sites per minute § if someone dressed in cclown makeup came up to me and asked to suck my dick, id naturally assume it's a troll, § rooting through some damn womens' purses. all of the things in these purses suck. i don't give a shit § #mondaymotivation https://t.co/McTcJcLtoM § some dumb asses of life just need a damn "BRAIN " § jacking off.. (lights cigarette, takes a big smoke of it) ..i s a Zero Sum fallacy. a jesters game § this is based on nothing . entirely fucked § if i ge t one more comment about guns being a type of Glove- im spraying the fuse box with a hose until my computer turns off § A gun is not clothes just because you can wear a holster with a gun inside of it. Jesus christ. Shut thhe fuck up about guns being clothes. § U cant wear a sword. A sword is not clothes. Yes, A SHeathe, is clothes. The sword goes in the sheath, but that doesnt make it clothes bitch § thw most valuable icon on any boys desktop... the famed "My Computer" icon. click that bastard and youre good to go § erase § mnegative 50 points for trying to trick me with runes § theres too many of them to block. im gonna lose it § all of you people have rat hands. i am going to be fucking sick § aguh. lord § this is photo shop § what is the blue shit i see on them. remove it § i see specks of shit on there § i bet you just went ryour entire life growing out that hair on your ring finger, never thinking to remove it, it sucks § yoyu appear to be severely ill § finger nail check. everyone please post your fingernails right now for my inspection. i will block you if theyre filthy § you need to take all of those cans out and wipe the whole damn thing down with a wet cloth § LIKE WANTING TO KNOW WHEN I GET TO SAVE BIG BUCKS FOR PENNYS ON THE DOLLAR AND GET RICH CHEAP § ignorance... is a fallacy .my dear pals § how do you clean a shirt § ive never laughged at a piss joke. (sees how impressed everyone is, takes it one step further) in fact, ive never laughed before in my life. § (saying loud enough so people can hear) the matrix is the james bond of steam punk § Unfunny. https://t.co/DiXwd64w3F § (ssees a stock image of a frowning man sitting inside of a doghouse) Hurmph. Asinine. § Rats Are Life Facebook § this shi t https://t.co/XCWdtFDgaa § sub way is a pedophile... you guys see about this shit ? § sears deparftment store used to be the best place to meet up with the boys. nowadays theyll let just about any piece of shit inside to shop. § im every james bond § torturing my damn dick with corn cob holders in Penance for the foul tone i took with the subway corporation today § is @subway really offering a 10% discount to all Muslims who apologize for the attacks... kind of messed up.. § wow.. just watching the cnn channel here.. amazed by how they know all the news so well.. Extraordinary § @DrPhil please kick my out of control teen's ass § 2005 me: who the fuck is martin van buren 2015 me: ah yes. DonkeyKongEddie. arrested at gamestop on nov 13 2014, drives a grey honda accord, § after being normal for several months, i am now back to r*cist. § sucking on the same big piece of bread for hours and hours ,. § i bet half the people posting "Ah!" on here dont even realize its an acronym for "Acknowledged Heartily" § Yiou have to be really smart to get 250k followers on here. It doesnt just happen to you if you post false info about your ass for 7 years § researching dynamic, groundbreaking new ways to wipe my ass § two lives? this is fuckinh barbaric https://t.co/xvQqg3d5L0 § people used to jack off to this guy back in the 90s. not me though https://t.co/5lw685mP61 § its my turds. thank you § (rreads a series of Enlightened posts and becomes smart) AH. Hm, this is good. (reads a troll post and becomes a dumb ass) Damn Fuck ! § spice up your life by throwing your favorite coffee mug into the garbage § adding "A Touch of Class" to my home by wrapping all of my game's apparatuse's in tinsel § i feel truly blessed ,knowing that everyone who has spoken ill of my brand is eating bugs in a cold prison cell. § i dont like him. i'm just looking at him § looking at some pictures of dracula, § dozens upon dozens of the racist new starbuck cups,. filled with urine and placed all over my computer desk like candles on a satanic altar § not many people know this, b ut i actually coined the term "Lunchtime". before then, time and lunch were two entirely immeasurable concepts, § album (120 pics) ben stein kissing wife § no woman can handle my post s § ME: ok now do a search of this. "muppet babies theme - backwards, half speed" ALFRED HITCHCOCK: Holy Fuck !! § the joke's hall of fame https://t.co/2UDeGMIo6T § thats it. thats enough. im shutting the computer down ,before i become too powerful § ive eaten more $14 hamburgers than youve eaten regular hambufrgers, you low engagement galoot § is it. i dont know from good anymore § dual wielding toilet paper § stressed out due to pistachio shit all over my shirt and computer desk . all posts canceled § fellas..tell your girls you will n ot be providing any more sex until the entire female race apologizes for halo 5's dismal metacritic score § ennjoying a big bowl of condoms. twirling them around my fork like spaghetti § yeah like im just going to put bottles of my own damn urine up on the mantel. you fucking idiot. this is celeb urine § huh.. it;s been awhile since i made an actual joke on here. lets see now. boats are basically uh, skeletons, that people use to, trick water § ME: Basiclaly its just a joke we do where whoever says hes El Chapo the most wins COP: Thats not what a joke is ME: Well its good either way § some people sing the praises of the one hundred dollar bill... i myself, prefer the humble, time-tested and reliable one dollar bill § llooking extremely normal today https://t.co/ADTeu9bWfC § U will regret this. § yes!!! holy shit! § if this shit costs me the Fanta deal i will: 1) become eeven more racist 2) cancel all Thursday Nite Rants 3) add a switchblade to my avatar § what do teens find funny nowadays. getting "Slimed" onj nickelodeon? farting principals? help me out here § i can guarantee you that im only as racist as the girls im attracted to- and not a tiny bit more § I AM NOT RACIST!!! THIS IS AN OUT RAGE!! I DEMAND YOU REMOVE THE POSTS AT ONCE! § these people with locked accounts...damn!!! you just know theyre hiding all the good posts in there § the times they are indeed a changin..but the one time thatll never change is Lunch time. lock them engagements in if you think this is good. § OPRAH: Take us back to the time you invented the famous Livestrong Bracelet. ME: well..i was at boston market, just looking at my wrist, and § boys i need a full report on your Scalp Health by uhh 8pm or else ill go ape shit in the dms, § i go outside for the rfirst time in 7 years and a biplane immediately shoots a chemtrail at my dick and makes it 2 inches shorter. typical § ah, So u persecute Jared Fogle just because he has different beliefs? Do Tell. (girls get mad at me) Sorry. Im sorry. Im trying to remove it § id say my most defining quality is that i instinctively write tremendous amounts of think pieces whenever i see a naked person § 4am walgreens haul... re tweet this after the Girls wake up https://t.co/fg3DTgduUM § this is true power § inspirational... 86 year old man circumcised by doctors in Zaire... "It's never too late" "Blessed." § i shall not be attending boys night, as i have injured myself while attempting to butterfly an auntie annes pretzel stick . § TROLL: Shut down windows ME: Ah, no § this is the final scheule. do not contact me of this. https://t.co/5xBrxUpnNq § looking forward to my 19,000 dollars https://t.co/rF5YIPR7I0 § for m y money, the best Soda you can get today is at the restaurant we've all come to known as Micky D's aka mc donalds. § i block all gilrs § @dril hell tweet § the crusaders fire ballistas into my throbbing diaper- unlesashing a torrent of mustard yellow shit and poisoning the entire village § show us the Boys https://t.co/CJS-90gzeN1 § @acmemarkets i will not give my location. please do not Track me. It did not meet my expectations. A Disgrace to farm fresh bagels § @acmemarkets U call this a "Customer First" shopping experience??? I nearly threw UP !! Food floor. No good https://t.co/PwCnzmw2Qg § so many Weird Twitter accts asking me to suck their dick in the dms. im njust like, yeah right bub. you havent even retweeted me since 2013. § eat bird shit https://t.co/SWiJG6XDfD § typical that I should be diarrheaed on for sharing my beleifs § got a One Million Dollar idea here. the dewey decimal sytsem... its good right? now imagine using it at Wegmans to find your favorite snacks § scores of Farm Fresh, artisan treats available for my perusal.. Oh Me Oh My https://t.co/KdyCsUiOZ8 § U want more insight into "THe Process," u say? Look no further. https://t.co/yhbyYzq9SD § months ago i dreamt about people making their ass cracks longer with surgery. i woke up & immediately put "Crack length" in my drafts folder § AAUh..!! Yeah. Lets all gang up on the guy who gives his children Steroids, just because he has a different opinion. Fucking idiots. § "Valor is the honor of distinction"... the words engraved on the side of my gun, that i force the gamestop employes to repeat out loud to me § i will tell you about the two types of diaper. there's the Functional diaper, worn inside the pants. and the Aesthetic diaper, worn outside. § bad ass https://t.co/5oiDfTQVVz § #BenghaziCommittee my dick is normal sized. every morning i use a q-tip dipped in windex to clear scuff marks off of it. i have no illnesses § a fuckin.. rat eating a slice of pizza?? damn,. the guy who filmed this must have gbeen smoking weed. § fuh..just unfollowed about 900 people on here. Feel as thogugh ive matured a lot in my time on this site & expect a higher grade of content. § come. I SHall lead the charge against corrupt Game developers, (Falls face forward ansd a variety of ass medicines spill out of my clothing) § HMm, it seems after years of reading my posts, everoyne is still miserable & dumber than shit. Maybe i should post like 100 more times a day § cash for Clunkers.. fuck yes to this... § im the guy who ruined Columbus Day by saying he had slaves, and im ruining Back to the Future Day too by saying the film is rife with incest § concerning "Online", ive found there are websites that are often considered the "Good" websites, and others generally understood to be "Bad" § r https://t.co/PqBa2lIb3B § big meeting with chinese investors coming up in 5 minutes. need to look sharp and presentable. im running my dick under the faucet § thiis is not the proper spirit of beer chat § in want of a glass of cold one ... http://t.co/Bzqa4zbkH9 § wondering why more people aarent faving this screenshot i found of professor Stephen Hawking saying "ape piss". If its fake please tell me § didnt know they stack shit , that high § what if "DONALD TRUMP" was the ceo of NetFlix? I think itd go a little something like this...! (gestures racistly) What a world What a world § And yours. § im just a man w ho loves his beavis § deray blocked me for no reason. if he wants to challenge me i will absolutely prove im less racist than him. stay out of this § sorry, yoyure right. im trying to delete it now but i cant because of a virus. Ah! This is terrible § thank you for protecting a grown man from beavis puns § i love my beavis. And yours § rest assured im constantly surrounded by flies § dont make me jump over that fuckinh counter and teach your low wage chefs the difference between "Extra" and "Double" meat ball § arbys refuses to honor special bulletin offering a free "Roastbeef Snack" to all divorced men... lots of upset divorced men at this arbys,.. § i was so wound up over trolls this morning i forgot to wipe my ass. i pulled my pants up and the shit coalesced into a wad on my lower back. § the torture of being a Top Influencer on the hateful, chaotic earth... http://t.co/bFCO8GWvGA § sorrty. im not a racist. i just thought these slogans were too good not to post § coming up with some new racism slogans... "Racism: Never knew it could be this good" "Racism: Gotta geddit" "Racism: Now that's what's nice" § I Hope So http://t.co/tOuAGUy2j1 § forced to remove my famous "DANGER: MAY CONTAIN LETHAL LEVELS OF SARCASM !!" sign from the front door of the poolside shed that i live in § Go outside from the computer . § , Fuck you !! § FURTHER MORe, any future tweet i make may now randomly be designated as a "Hell Tweet", meaning if you reply to it , you will be blocked, § 37 souls who will never again be allowed to engage with my red hot brand, bnecause they posted during hell hour and spat in the face of god § the hell hour has ended. all 37 repliers to the official hell hour tweet have been blocked indiscriminately. they took the gamble and lost § instituting a new feature on my feed called "The Hell Hour". the hell hour begins now § the only hthing i hate more than crashing my ford truck is justin biebers dick. which was recently shown to me in pictures § I dont appreciate bieng called "The Waterbed Bitch" just because I own a waterbed and post pictures of it daily § ready to accept nine hundred dollars into my life http://t.co/NVls6XDI3T § taking sips from a big fat thermos with the isis flag on it. thinking about inventing an app that tells me when lunch time is § shit and prick my ass § at the advice of my doctor, ive decided to piss, but only in small amounts out of respect for the #NoPiss challenge. i will limit my piss. § going strong into hour 8 of #NoPiss. feeling unprecedented spiritual growth. unfollow me if youre upset because this isnt "Funny" or "good". § Approaching

hour 5 of the #NoPiss challenge. This is very fucking serious and real.
Bafflingly, no one has requested to interview me yet § i saw the other day- theyre selling it $2 a gallon now. Unbelievable. § seems like to me that in this
foul economy the only thing “On the Up and Up” is the damn gas prices, thath we
all gotta break the bank for . § ive completed the first hour of my 2 day
#NoPiss challenge. i am searching for media outlets who would like to document
my struggle § im still allowed to jack off. jacking off does not count as
pissing. please let me have this § ive decided to abstain from urination for
two days, to punish myself for letting my kolut score dip below 70 again § (in
the ‘lets get ready to rumble’ man’s voice) llllllleeets get ready to post some
good shit § (ddumb ass, squinting at the tv, struggling to comprehend “The
Flintstones”) why are they wearing those outfits § i only fav tweets that
exhilarate the mind and soul, groundbreaking content which challenges the
established status quo § “ A fucking bastard lives here “ http://t.co/cgRdl-
63PUN § i warnned you all that bad things would happen if you kept letting your
wives wear jeans. AND NOW LOOK! the damn gas prices are up again § Fairly, yes,
actually. § RE: Restaurant Etiquette >> I’ve been a waiter for 9 years, and I
like it when people snap their fingers at me. So your commant is invalid. §
Agreed, actually § (smoking cig on stage) Ya know, like i always say, these
fuckers dont know a damn thing of common sense. COupons are like free money.
Use em § these guys tried to run a hospital in AFGHANISTAN?? hello?? i dont
know if you noticed, but theres a war there? U gotta use your heads folks § oh,
youvve read a few academic papers on the matter? cute. i have read over 100000
posts. § stop tlaking to me. youre diminishing my Art § (intentionally spoken
within earshot of severral arbys girls) ah fuck. my hands smell like steroids
from using steroids all day § dead certainly., if my pit bulls could speak...
they would say “please, please increase my power” § i sincerely hope all of you
remembered to powder your keyboards and mice to prevent Hand damage during your
normal 16 hr browsing sessions § if u think its fucked up that men & women are
allowed to eat the same kinds of food, type the word “yes” into your browser
bar & click on it § Antonio Vivaldi six violin concertos, strings & continuo
in A major “ Burger King Theme “ Op. 2 N°11 published in Venice by Bortoli -
1708 § hwow many favs are worth the equivalent of a human life... id say about
70 § wgat § log me in to the on-line city where the links are blue and the
girls Dm Me...... § This woman is an FBI agent sent to jingle her keys through
the library to intimidate me about jail. § The entire King Soopers store at
80th & Wadsworth is staffed with Federal Agents not authorized by any judge, §
FOOL: Foot & mouth disease isnt necessarily good ME: Ive had it with this
shit. Im showing this to your employer FOOL: Dont. I have a family § do not
interfere with my negotiations please § @Snowden please do a wiki leak addressing the mistreatment of gamer`s by viacom § @Doritos Give mme my fucking
coupons you cock sucking rats. I deserve at least 4 coupons for posting kindly
of your nauseating animal fodder § i think when we get caught up in our gadgets
and email, we forget to sit down and appreciate that time-tested classic
doritos § please show me pins i can wear that will make me look very handsome
in churdh § my romantic girl friend sees the super blood moon reflected in my
greased back hair and pledges then and there to bow to christ our master § dont
do it. 1million followers is more powerful than the nuke #NoMillion § pissed off
because people are watching their precious football instead of asking me why im
pissed off § Duur!! Thanks for clown baiting me. Idiot http://t.co/HllAsfHYUd §
ME: (pulls soaked pair of jnco jeans out of sons aquarium) Ah wahts this. You
cant continue to live here if you do this SON: Im a smoker now § looking how
to become more cyber § I find my self. walking the hallowed halls of Harverd
university , thinking wisely to my self. upon the quest, for Knowledge... §
(truyng to stumble across the next big two-word phrase that gets really popular
for no reason) udhhu.. bird hell owl. big hell. owl hell § Waiiter, i have not

received my Farm Fresh olives, and my steak is far too Unctuous. Please tell the chef to go back to 9 gag. § SCreaming while the road workers slowly pave a road on top of me using my own tax dollar § i have never in my life- shit my pants or had an erection. it is ludicrous to claim other wise § in the midst of jade helm 15 and high gas prices. a good boy looks to the stars and asks where have all the angels Gone .... § normal hamburger with that doritos flair § droitos should make hamburgers § NEWSWEEK: WHat can be said. youre a spectacular brand. like hitler without the racism ME: I am exactly indeed like hitler without the racism § Thheres just not enough moisture in food now a days. Run that shit under the faucet § get more than 3 friends. you stooge § folks, please. this is a private matter between me and the heartless criminal § someone on here asked me my opinion of Worcestershire sauce... but i dont feel ready to share that at this time. § Ready to enjoy my Farm Fresh Mozzarella Sticks from Bertuccis, retweet my favorite celebs, and post some worms-eye pics of my Genitals & Ass § folks the only thing higher than Cheetch & Chong--is gas prices (audience goes wild, hooting,screaming; starting Great Gas Price Riot of '15) § as a real life professional Chef , i refuse to buy any packaged food that isn't marked with the words "Limited Edition" § apparently pharmacies think theyre grocery shops now. selling food product instead of focusing on exceptional pill service. Get real, punk ! § i know i will catch endless flak for this. but I am of the belief, that the tried and true Suit and Tie, is a Classic § BRIDE OF DECEIT § I TAKE BACK EVERY KIND THING I'VE SAID ABOUT THE GIRLS ON HERE ! SHALLOW AND CRUEL ! HEART LESS DEVILS ! MANIPULATING MY POSTS & TRICKING ME § im methodical bitch. your the random guy § FOOL: Love to get a bee in my bonnet ME: theres no possible way you could love that. take this down immediately FOOL: Ah, foiled again § @dril don't reply to this. i already know it's a good joke § im the guy who originally cooked up the "garden of eatin" joke. thats my bit. im just saying it out in the open here & now. trolls be damned § just noticed the new washcloths ive been showering with have the FoodNetwork logo. this is my biggest failure to date http://t.co/8JvvTKea36 § to me, the white and yellow lines that get painted to the roads are mostly a nuisance. i say let's #TakeEmOff § http://t.co/fbrGwofqcK announcin,g in 2016 my new brand alliance with cool arab man § Jack Ass: Arguably, in many ways, a "Two-fer" could conceivably be worse than a "One-fer" ME: I'd will not even dignify that with a response § 2 celeb headlines i came up with, in case one of them does something: "Hasta Travolta, Baby" "Bieber does it again. Ah, but thats hollywood" § i cried during the schene where richie rich revealed the mcdonalds in his house. if you dont like it, move on § CHEF: mon signor!! leaving the tails on the shrimp is good! it is tre bien ME: Im going to nuke you with live ammo. Im the guy from the crow § http://t.co/hq9EnbHCV6 § i pay good money to load my sons bag with treats, and if Erasmus Infowars Copfucker wants to devour them in the university library, so be it § half wit bumpkin here, looking for new snacks § startling how im the only person on this site with an actual human soul. you would think the other guys on here have one, but no § ME: was thinkin about how I could incorporate the phrase "obama breeze" into my next post. Thoughts? TOM CRUISE: its solid gold baby. Killer § funny how ppeople get faved for posting "Humour", but when i post about how deeply in love i am with the girls here i get the old Brush off § ME: ill take.. one Cruisp bird w/ extra bird sauce please KFC CLERK: Huh? ME: (gives him the Wink of Irony) KFC CLERK: Ah! The Wink of Irony § imbecile goes viral after telling tgifridays waiter that his caesar dressing is "too spicy" § Shut the fuck up? Now ? Whil;e im smack in the middle of perhaps my most ruthless tear against Netflix Culture? Muwahaha. Never § mE: i'll take eggland's WORST, please grocery clerk (min wage): Good joke sir § i shall say this only; ive ended peoples careers by reporting them for "Ironic" typos & spelling errors., i do not give a shit. im a warrior § i fuucking love being sent to Juvie Hall §

Houly fuck.. They did it. They replaced all the HF corn syrup w/ pure cane sugar. My minds absolutly blown by this shitty drink for children § mr bean is a complete dope. his oddball capers are crass and unrealistic. i frown while watching this show. § theres never been a horny me, and never shall i horny be, And If this sacred vow shall break, I pray the lord my posts to take § fingers ranked by how good it is to show them to people: 1. thumb 2. pinky 3. ring 4. index 5. middlesteal this listicle,u corrupted fucks § my tweets are good way less often than 20%. damn, with a 20% success rate i'd have my own hbo special by now § extremmely turned on by Fav Denial , heavily worked up by women declining to fav my posts § please let me cover my entire webpage in jungle camo so soldiers can research vital murder info on the battlefield without being spotted § I hate bodys § Announcing new feature called #Rubadub-dub where my followers are encourgaged to post pics of themself inside the bathtub. Ban me i dont care § LIAR: Free data plan. is absolutely not good. It's something I don't think we should want ME: Im not to touch this one with a 10 foot pole § STREET TOUGH: HEY. VERIFIED ACCTS ARENT FAVING U ANYMORE. WHATS THE DEAL ME:(pretending not to hear, fumbling w/ keys to open my shitty car) § Nuffs aid. Need I say more? Nuff said. Need I say more? Nuff said. Need i say more? Nuff said. Need I say more? Nuff said. Need I say § fav if you think adults should have access to toilet time retweet to see the face of G-OD ignore and get th e word "Liar" branded into flesh § 15 years ago the most shocking thing online was a picture of a man spreading his ass cheeks open. today, it's my opinions about Wet shaving § Ah, thats a Blocked. § Gah . Delete it § Lets see u do better. § Im going to make 1000 videos of fuck nasa. § i rise; spreading my arms, exuding fluorescent spheres of energy, each represent-ing an Unfollower, Cuasing me a great deal of pain,Screaming § (vomits while dioing pushups at the gym and resists every attempt from professional trainers to stop me from continuing) § the inventor of the famous "Love to Scrimp, Hate to Save" tweet... FINALLy taking pop culture to task... "You gotta see it to believe it" § Love To Scrimp, Hate To Save #TheFinalWordOfIt § if you want the real bargains during boys night out... gotta go with the Children's menu... every time § Im sorry? Are u "Going in" on me?? Am I being "Gone In" upon just for p osting my time-tested opinions about girls holding forks incorrectly § No sex on this profile § i believe that jade healm 15, and the markets going haywire, youve got a "Witch's Brew" of bull shit § The three brnaches of government? Simple. Breakfast, Lunch, and DInner. Because the government loves eating us alive with the old Tax & Spen § each 'Ridge' in your crinkle-cut potato chip costs 4 gallons of precious slave blood to create and adds a satisfying "Cruntch" to every bite § im a bush-league yokel who should be put on the floor § bramds http://t.co/BCkDV2xGTM § the most popular of my weekly features is returning in 2016. thats roight folks. #WaterboyWednesday no further info at this time. § Once again, those dastardly, Devious trolls have installed a device underneath my computer desk that shoots me in the dick every time i post § Ah!! Ah! once again, the flap-jawed trolls have deliberately misinterpreted my constant attempts to get a girl friend on here as " Sexual " § released statement regarding Grumpy Cat urinary tract infection: "Grumpy Cat is in a lot of pain, but still wants to entertain you at shows" § front of my shirt: " YES: MY PATIO IS HAND-WASHED " back of my shirt: a convenient bullseye so people can shoot me if they want to § bush was the president who likes oil. correct? so what i think is that its actually "Castor oil", because he leaves a bad taste in my mout!! § feeling devilishly Racist today... might apply just a smidgen of Blackface before i go out chasing cars § im sorry everyone. i should not have commented on the ribs. i never could have known this would happen § Childish. i dont have time for links § ill simply let the fav counts do the talking. as i normally do when dealing with cra[p. § u cant bruise a rib. only the skin around it #Annihilated § am I the most dark & twisted psycho god

online?? hm lets see: - When the dow jones industrial average goes down i say
simply the word “Good” § windows..on behalf of all boys online, INCLUDING the
trolls, id like to extend a well-deserve “Thank You” for putting updates in my
computer § i have every net flick § UNITED NATIONS: ah!! please help us! we need
just a normal man’s opinion!! we got you a seat ME: How’m I to trust you,
while God is bleeding § hm.. the essentials... well what can i say. you gotta
have em baby http://t.co/8Edkr2U60c § tormenting lab animals with my huge
vibrating ass § If you do this: Fuck you http://t.co/9RBuLcCun3 § i hear in
some cultures they crap in their hand first before putting it in the toilet.
thats fucked up to me. just shit it directly in there § survey - please tell me
which one is “Most good”: >Perfect meadows in every direction >A Man wheezing
into the toilet >Bobs BigBoy PattyMelt § Priest: and the lord said, take this
delicious McDonald and eat it, for it is my body and it will be given up, for
you Me: Insanley badass. § LawAndOrderGal has entered JeansChat LEVIS_GAURD-
IAN: NEED A FUCKING DRAINAGE RIG THAT WONT SCALD MY THIGHS LawAndOrderGal has
left JeansChat § (pitching the Michelin Man) hes this big white dipshit and
people associate him with tires for some reason. he has no personality. no
jokes § the maligned Villains of my story., my ass and dick, are known to drive
my readers the most wild and turbochagrge engagements & impressions § founnd a
cicada skin stuck to my nefarious pud § i can only hope that when a kangaroo
court of dipshits comes to haul me to prison that i have the grace and humility
not to get mad at them § the infamous millennials are more interested in
(consults notepad) being nickeled and dimed by the tax man than (squints)
distilling vinegar § i know im a dumb ass for expecting a serious response from
the chucklefuck brigade, but can someone please tell me if im circumcised or
not § im sorry to Wawa for attempting to behead myself in one of their re-
strooms. i promise to take the Wawa experience more seriously from now on §
SUCJK MY DICK http://t.co/cbU6JrAuDS § “don’t tread of me”, the famous words of
that good snake who doesn’t want to get stepped on, the noble slithering
bastard I relate to most § alrigt jack asses. before you “Go In” on me, heres a
quick recap of the jokes i invented: - Dogs (Anything mentioning them) - The
Weed Fairy § mods!! mods! one of those obscene low follower count boys stole a
lick from the delicious lolly that Father bought me!! ah! how dreadful ! § now
you see, what i like to do is consider my page to be a “ o Frown Zone”, because
of the consistently good quality of my messages i put up § #TenThingsNotToSay-
ToAWriter im going to piss all over your car. for being a Writer. § its
disgusting to create the illusion on tv that animals are talking with cgi or
otherwise. a disgraceful tactic § suigh... this weeks Bone Head award goes,
once again, to my ex-wife, who just bought a stupid ass looking refrigerator §
what is the best kind of acid to spray my own dick with as a joke § Does anyone
know how important is this. http://t.co/XLtJAtdnM2 § thank you all. your kind
donations of $400000 will keep me alive for 1 more month, after being fired for
looking at racist swords on my ipad § evvery other Friday the sheriff guides me
around the jailhouse and lets me expose myself to the villains, and thats
#MyTGIF § Bugs Bunny: B Elmer Fudd: A- Tweety Bird: F Daffy Duck: C+ Porky
Pig: D+ Theyre the only ones i can think of right now. My hands are shaking §
sponsors are telling me not to post them. but idont give a fuck. im sick of
being pushed around. this is my account & thats the bottom word § im assigning
a letter grade to all the looney tunes at 10:00PM EST sharp. this is a once in
a lifetime event. please do not miss it § my repulsive cohorts and I are
searching the woods for tree sap so we can rub it all over our hands and
improve our golf grip § Fool!! Bastard! § “Crowdpleasers”... Now these, I like
§ just indignantly threw $799 gamer keyboard into koi pond because i got pissed
off by the craze that is sweeping the nation known as Planking § the adrenaline
rush i get from posting gives me the energy to walk to the toilet, and the
endorphins i get from shitting allow me to post § Goodboy goodboy § erased by

government § w*akes up on the morning of july 18th 2015 sick and tired of Snooki and HoneyBooBoo* Wheres my damn nuke bomb... § archaeologists 1000yrs from now are going to find my embalmed turds and assume they were part of some sacred ritual. NOpe im just a dumb ass § trolls: Lets jerk off to the teletubbies and. barney me (to followers): Are u seeing this. Are you seeing thi s. Am i the only sane man left § does anyone have any tips and tricks for someone about to own a Balcony. Can i take beer on it § i have taken my shirt off over 10000 times § on one hand $2000 will barely even cover the cost of my large amount of mansions. on the other hand i respect the wild flava brand immensely § sell my account to "Wild Flava" (@FlavaWild) for $2000? this is perhaps the most difficult decision i;ll ever face . http://t.co/ZBYr8N6ZSR § wow this 40lb bag of dog food is only $30... why do dogs get all the bargains § i iwsh he blocked me so i could talk shit about him, but now i have to say the gofundme is good and im glad hes doing it. § you deserve my worst offer, which is "2" § my q uote of the season "Its almost summer time so lets hop in the pool" § scarce, low quality content and an abundance of wrong opinions is the reason the cavemen went extinct. thats my beliefs bitch § honey mustard likers... heres a one million dollar idea for you "honey ketchup" § (sees no soliciting sign outside Wendy's) damn it!!! fuck! i really wanted to solicit to wendys!! § just remember what it is we're all fighting fo.r... http://t.co/ucS2wcLgje § When you "FAve" me, you are effectively throwing a " Treat " into my mouth § "Gotcha" § CLICK ON MY POST 10000 TIMES IF YOU ARE WORKED UP OVER COMPUTERS § i show up at the range wearing a t-shirt that says "I Wont Wear The Earplugs" and i m promptly directed back to my car by staff members § *fires 400 rounds at a piece of shit log until it slumps over* Take that adam landza § ME: hey ed. whats good to shoot at the range today ED: Someone threw a big bag of packing peanuts out there. Its good to hit it with bullets § always take my stagecoach full of pit bulls to the Range . because my girls love to watch me shoot § iwant to be pummeled with carpet beaters by eastern european grandmas and make big awful clouds of dust § @cnn please teach me how to make a net so that i can nab the ruthless scoundrel known as el chapo § well if it was allowed, id go with a banana thats the average amount of ripe, as i believe it offers the "Best of both worlds" § THis is not a "Meltdown". Its a normal opinion § THe Eagles is a team of football who i respect & admire. Their commitment to touchdowns is good. They are athletic when it comes to sports § bark up the wrong damn tree ass whiper § my page is a tornado of Slur's... my inbox is a viper pit of horseplay...   my desktop is a Clown's Tent for bastards... § every woman ivr ever spoken to would describe our correspondence as "Graceful" § my followeres, who all hate me, and wish to kick my ass, are nobodys, and they lack the combat training to injure me, because theyre infants § (bowed head solemnly rises from deep thought) Intellidgence is the strength of wisdom § why'd there suffering in this world................ § second result for "playing violin" http://t.co/PEDAs818hf § "flouride 666" http://t.co/qi41qxW72d § please everyone search for shit like "autism microchip" on youtube and look at all the thumbnails on their videos http://t.co/V25172FH5s § if you like the band "Shinedown" you will love this video of me getting trounced by police officers while demanding to meet them § #FreeSlurpeeDay they dont ever wash the slurpe machines. the cops found a shitty waynes world baseball cap inside one of them § Frowning Principal Exposed To Beer Content On Time Line § im the dip shit top replier who goes into every thread about someone being afraid of moving out and says "Dont forget to buy a plundger" § never knew that anything was good or bad until i got on the computer, i had always assumed that everything was Average until i got yelled at § the Ins & Outs of my ass; "Regarded As Low Quality" by famous Dr. House, in banned episode unfit for public consumption, Bullshit Bullshit. § i will not close my account until the sport of golf is rightfully named "golfball" like the other ball sports § there is no such thing as a baby animal. they are all adults from birth. sorry if my opinion offends you § this is what boy's day is all about. just some boys going to pool § THinking of a "Boy's Day" of twitter..won't post specifics due to trolls, but basically all girls will nicely be asked to log out for 24hrs, § im a reasonable mans son who thinks that putting a dash of venom into my favorite roast pork hoagie will make it Spicy instead of killing me § well it goes to show you that the trolls will gladly stoop so low as to shit upon the #classiccombo of spaghetti& meatballs we all hold dear § spaghetti and meatballs... now theres a #ClassicCombo § every room in every home must have a Host § i love to hover hand my gf in pictures. (gets Owned across various media) sorry. Sorry everyone. I forgot that was bad § @BMcCarthy32 stick to the "Dug Out", chump !!! § its me again, from the website. admit that the berenstain bears are for adults or i will strategically headbutt your father to death § the " o Bullshit" award goes to this guy for being bossed around by gas station employees & giving them a poor review http://t.co/SRps5X8qaA § http://t.co/XYrQaKTmq4 § Waiter, by the advice of the Chicago Tribune Id like a Dash of Ground Cumin on my Farm Fresh Egg. Oh! Too much! I withdraw this transaction, § Jsut count the faves. Thats what i say. The people of twitter want urine § @JoseCanseco @ JustinABC13 @HillcatBaseball I hope hes ready to see a man urinate on the field of baseball § i think my goal in life is to start a football team named "The Baseball Preferrers" and our gimmick is to get as many penalties as possible § (passes a man in a hardhat toiling over a roadside utility cabinet in 100 degree weather in my black convertible) Nice Fedora Dip Shit § i absolutely deserve tax credit for offering my respectable toilet to government employees whenever i can § It'd be an honor for you to use my toilet Mr. Mailman. I must make clear i dont intend to film you or collect your waste. My toilet is clean § i offer my toilet to the mail man everyday. my toilets not good enough for the big important mailman apparently. mailman is a bad job anyway § "Durr michelob ulta would taste the same if it had a turd in it" -Suppressive Persons with little on their mind but mischief and mayhem § commercial idea for Michelob Ultra--a bumbling imbecile ransacks his apartment to find the guy who took a dump in his glass of michelob ultra § Have you ever wanted to click X on a bastard § #NewFastFoods Fast bread § you pick up some political cartoon paper & see a shitty grave drawing captioned with "Burt Be-Gone" and its intended to be respectful & nice § i dont promote circus acts. § soirry. i didnt know retweeting "fuck lobsterfest" would make me lose 200 followers. ive learned my lesson so feel free to follow me again § i only jack off for the amusmement of my followers, who have come to expect this sort of bullshit from my account. § phaw!! 2am!.. time to go hit the hay (jacks off and comes back ot the computer) § im constantly expanding § the boys are enjoying their fave jukebox when ths sarge steps in SARGE: TURN OFF THE DAMN JUKE BOX! ITS WAR ME: Fuck u sarge. The armys crap § if you don't know how to use a Lathe you deserve to eat dog shit § just deleted 23,000 tweets at the request of Sbarro. feeling Purified § if you odn't subscribe to every last one of my vague, yet cocksure beliefs regarding the Portuguese , i will never make eye contact with you § rodent website § if youre one of the guys who blocked me on here, i Forgive you, and im ready for you to unblock me now. § he belongs at the circus with his friends § krusty should not be on the simpson family's roof. this is hell § people get mad at me when i riff on Current Events so ill just say this. im enjoying cooking turds on the grill regardless of what day it is § im startingmy own version of bill maher's " ew rules" called "Good rules". It's going to fucking suck § im going to keep doing this until my daughter calls me http://t.co/wbpeGpu7JI § long horn steakhouse should not refuse to honor my coupons just because theyre wet http://t.co/zODZEYLQkY § unban me from college http://t.co/q57sgQ1uxi § "Litter Box Fucker" AUDIENCE: (LAughing already) WORKING CLASS JOE: Im going to fuck the litter box now. AUDIENCE: AWuooo! Hoo hoo! § DVD:

FBI WARNING Me: oh boy here we go DVD: The board advises you to have lots of fun watching this Hollywood movie Me: Ah.. It's a nice one § yes sir. im sorry sir. (hangs up) that was the mayor of reddit. he wants this account spick and span of dick jokes before the handover § Geting my dick sucked in Unreal Engine 4. Flushing toilet in Unreal Engine 4. Having shit beat out of me by greasers in Unreal Engine 4. Wow § The jokes, Ladies and gentlemn. The jokes § entire bullshit of gas prices deconstructed by large boy who is partial towards treating him self § i challenge anyone who would bring shit to me to a one on one hockey match. goalie vs goalie in the frozen arena. three pucks § click that fave button if i did good. § listen here blues traveler. pretty much all musicians travel you dumb ass. you should name your band "blues redundant guy" § pleae check this out: Hostler Magazine § Nobody Checks My Son For Head Lice With Out Getting Past My Police Issue Hollow Point Smith & Wesson Which Gives Everyone It Shoots Leukemia § @JimCarrey im the pro-neurotoxin, anti-vaccine, son of a bitch cop!!! i love rolling around in disease and spreading it to dumbass civilians § " If U like a good song I wont steer ya wrong Cocaine Its Got guitar and drums So please listen to some Cocaine " § and folks.. we cant forget aobut Tennis Shoes (Audience boos.) Are you Tennis, or are you shoes? Who'd'y'a'think'ya're ? (Applause) § just meeting up with one of my real life friends; pictured here. http://t.co/JgYf0Q0IAN § ive trademarked the term "The guy who fucks up" so if you see someone else using it pleaase stick my Fair Use brochures to their car § Why dont they call them the porch days of summer then. Surely dogs arent the only animals who do this § The dog days of summer,. Its the dog days of summer everyone (Flapping gums aboutn othing, doesnt know what dog day is, knows he fucked up) § replying to massive amounts of flagrant screwball tweets with words like "Tedious" followed by a period § donlad trump reportedly says that normal type pokemon are a waste of time. they're just dirty birds & rats who have no right being a pokemon § always looking for exicting new up and comers in the realm of breathtaking digital online content to block § what can i say. my hatres are my motivators (gets pic of nude man covered in syrup sent to inbox) FUCk. Please stop § doing my Civic Duty (evading tax's) while laughing at trolls threatenning to do arson to my house § Sftu. Thanks for making me dry heave § prison of lies § MarioGodKenneth is stuck in israeli prison again and ive received $0 in donations towards his bail. § do not shorw me your mystifying cowboy slurs at this point and time http://t.co/7pCPUNdFXT § ssure. ill concede that this landmark decision is a step in the right direction. BUt people who pre-order games are still getting swindled . § What can i say. WHen its the game of politics, its open season on everyone who has entitled and ignorant views of opinions. No filter § im waiting for all the celebs to weigh in before i can offer my official verdict on tthe controversial flag of the confederacy. § dont talk to me of trade agreement when the only thing we can agree of is that charlatans & mad hatters have overrun the waushington office. § any one who posts snark of my dear friend Bobby Jingle gets the head blowqn off shot gun style and is not allowed to have a real grave . § dictating some more nice posts to my keyboard boy while my wife straps me to the big spinning crross § this would be Twitter, a Web site for fu&%in' adults. Yeah § committing unforgivable crimes against nautre in my laboratory ,trying to create the next genetically discombobulated meme animal § DIVORCE GURU: gaming is a right, not a privilege. remember that always. ME: Thank you divorce guru § . http://t.co/iHzeWAxTPz § im not going to eat mcdonalds becuase bacteria refuse to break it down. instead ill eat the food bacteria love the most: raw chicken & turds § now youve done it, teens. the official mr bean account is closing because you all kept calling him dad § limiting the thursday nite rant to one day of the week ... its just not good for gthe brand § people are telling me that i have no right to post the thursday nite rant on a tuesday. SCREAMING it to me § dm gumline pics § how come nobody ever helps me when im playing team foot ball. i beg for the other players to help me and they refuse to #theThursdayNiteRant § ;i help girls now § you Hog. you Rat § i'll heal him § youll all be glad to know that my soul has undergone some much needed healing after i apologized for the earthquakes which killed thousands. § my "Ass Ceremony" is solely to blame for all thre bad earthquakes. if i knew it would have caused the earthquakes i would not have done it. § "before we begin todays ball game, user @Dril would like a few words on Dairy Queen" the audience boos as i traipse the field in my tiny car § http://t.co/s8KMF9tlXy you will pry it from my cold muscular hands, fucker § thats where it goes. this is normal § guess what. i have the brain of a Human. i have a Human's brain § oculus allows you to smoke wii remote like a cigar and blow heaps of smoke in celebs faces § beautiful e3 conference from the Police. THreatened to trap all crooks. Spinning handcuffs around. Elaborate boot play. No games to announce § digging thorugh all the trash cans and dumpsters at e3 in search of condoms containing genetically superior gamer cum § dont !!!! http://t.co/EKGe69SRrL § (POsturing like a dip shit at the public pool) My father owns no small number of shares at the smirnoff ice company. Let me be the lifeguard § (in forced toughguy voice) What the fuck is a clove of garlic. Around here we call it piece of garlic § Shut the fuck up http://t.co/Zf89wVty-co § I hate the really small salt shakers and long for the times when we owould be inclined to more often use the big salt shakers at restaurants § #MyDream-CarWouldHave a big ass i could fuck § watching him desperately try to dissipate the vulgar dust cloud by blowing on it moved me to tears § did you see his dick through the clown pants he was wearing. Oh Man § my favorites list is an extremely important art project and i'll thank you not to interfere § painting an exquisite 12 foot mural of martin luther king jr dressed as a cop, entitled "The Dream Realised", to prove im not racist at last § llove "Driving Um Wild" with my trade mark wrong opinions § *does something fucking stupid or embar-rassing in between tthe asterisks and doesnt expect anyone to wonder why im typing it out* im normal, § Im Very Upset with girls *impossibly low-res bikini babe robo-posting about heartworm meds follows me* Just kidding. Im only mad at the boys § out with dentists, in with mouth gurus § evolution of doritos: cool ranch --> cooler ranch --> cool ranch again --> epitome ranch --> lousy ranch --> apotheosis ranch --> shit ranch § some names for potential new nintendos, after the super nintendo: the good nintendo, the nice nintendo, the helpful nintendo; more to come § #SeedPig for podunk nit wit § ((pulls gun out in bank) NObody MOVE OR ILL BPLOW YOUR FUCKING HEAD OFF (empties a shit load of free lollipops & dog biscuits into big jeans § The Brand Ayatollah § gaining a new followefr.. that, to me, is a real "A-Ha!" moment § Let it be known that I am the sole proprietor of the "Ren Stimpfani" joke, and that all attempts to replicate it are for the garbage can. § alright netheads, Click the damn window out. Go outside. Mnake a grilled cheese sandwich with tomato slice. "Thank me later" § stop flooding the #stolenvalor hashtag with army man shit and only use it to report plagiarized @ Dril content, please and thank you § too much pressure from society saying we all got to learn how to self suck. iwill never self suck my dick and im unfollowing anyone who does § The Two Steaks Bastard . http://t.co/PZp9TpN1Vs § im seated down, and Ready to get pissed off......... § (i descend from the heavens) I'm uh, netflix is good (i go back up to heaven) § i live in the church § ah folks i do delcare i am a dumb ass southern gentle man who wouldnt know a re tweet from a ragdoll in this court room to-day § Well, it'd better damn friday § @marcorubio im sorry for calling you "Unelect-able" just because you changed your name to "The Incest President" § @marcoru-bio help me team marco. please defend my rights § special thank you to that one guy who is really upset about some marco rubio incest joke i made on here and keeps sending me scary emails § shutterstock has hit hte concept of "A young atheist" out of the damn park with this one. bravo http://t.co/YXstO2Snho §

theres a 3rd babe movie where he turns into a human at the end. beautifully done scene. the pigs dream comes true. the government Blocked it § (after hearing the library has games , i arrive at the front desk, disguised as a non-gamer) er.. im here for some.. book's § Hhm, Nope http://t.co/6B7hfKNPWu § DisgruntledStepSon § university lost accreditation when nickelodeon slimed the dean, degree is useless, 200000 in debt & back in diapers, love getting ass kicked § prince hussein...wheres my goodboy bailout § my annual "Cum tribute" to the Ford Focus will no longer be archived in the library of congress due to partisan gridlock and meddling taxmen § sen larry craig(R): DuRr I have a wide stance Me: Cmon. If this guys for real. Then I got a bridge to sell ya.. and I just ran outta bridges § TWITTER APP: THree different guys you know just faved the same damn tweet. This is breathtaking. What are the odds ME: please locate my wife § 1-800-VamoOSe § im strong § ME: waiter...give me a shitty joe WAITER: (wow..this guy just ordered a sloppy joe in a bad ass way i never heard before. powerful move.) Ok § cold butter popcorn. tjust throwing that one out there § soon we shall all be meme 's, graceful and dignified on the net, our crude human forms long forgotten § [UmbrageLiker has joined the chat] Pleas-antBoy: GET HIM OUT OF HERE NiceKeeper: NOT ON MY WATCH KindBarber: FUCK OFF ! Helper: THIS IS AWFUL § i got in the newspaper twice. once for my good posts, and once for screaming while still in the womb somehow § "the online web. truly a touching testament to the power of... deeply Human connections." -what Abe Lincoln would say if he were alive still § ill take.. the whole damn lot !!!!!! http://t.co/wkIMOvWaeJ § don't you dare make me type § get to hell you shape-shifting finagler § telling secretary to hold my calls so i can spend some time lookinh at girls' avatars with a loupe § accidentally severed my spine due to some bogus info i received on the computer § Unamused by trash behaviour . § i fairly tend to use "Sarchasm" to destroy liars mentally, and if that's not yiur cup of tea, i have the 2 words for you which is Suck it !! § horseplay is morally indefensible § howling james dean lookalikes circling their choppers around me, swinging chains while i sit in the gravel and borwse the nintendo 3ds eshop § Sword's. The only blade known to man § if i wasnt constantly debilitated from online-induced stress i could probably kick off the ass of any guy on here § another thing that fuckin sucks is the gerber baby § ME: why am i just the man for the job? lets see. i love hamburgers, i love to help, HAMBURGER HELPER CEO: Leave these hallowed halls at once § its just onne of those things you look at and say "oh its nice" § im suing you to court for Content theft § im all about getting out there and putting the posts up like im bad outta hell § http://t.co/XDq6MLh18u § a piece of crap § I will be your Father. I will take you as my Son and teach you the ways of online. We will hold hands as our follower count reaches infinity § i said im sorry. ive taken my lashes upon the cross. my brand is still good and anyone who cant see that is worthless § Sigh. Mistakes were made, folks. http://t.co/oYZyEXbeUl § this account is now 100%, fully unbridled, Racist. Fuck you !!! http://t.co/iqDjFXJoQH § my reaction when people react to pictures of my reaction when im reacting to something good http://t.co/N0wsIZfLOS § and so you shall also be thrown out of my mentions for replying without Faving. § plrease go to the salad bar and get me a plate full of bake and bits § yeah i just give my password away to people all the time because im dumb as shit § he closed his account due to childish people. § do not tell my friend/colleague @Pregnant-Seinfeld how to make his fucking posts. hes a really good account & ahs been suffering from bedbugs § the girls on this website are villains. all of then. § @CHANNAKAJIMA im respectful of him § how dare you satirize my beloved fan base, the Lovely Boys of twitter § i ruminate over a scrapbook full of middle finger pics to keep myself demure, respectful and humble. "i deserve these", i utter shitheadedly § tge nicest thing about me is i have excessively dry balls which basically start flaking apart like a piece of strudel whenever I walk around §

james bond learns how to do cartwheels from a wise eskimo on top of mt. everest and uses them to roll through a nuclear blast unscathed § pleae look at the facts. § mature of u to post this. here's some real shit http://t.co/yVLd00pVFe § "thw word 'good'... when you hear it, you're almost guaranteed something nice" - TheTrendingBoy § kfc commercial idea: a man is trying to get into kfc but he is too small to reach the door handle. he tries and tries and nobody helps him § workshopping some atrocious new kfc slogans "My oh my, The taste of it" "Kfc its a boys thing kfc" "aah!! Munch" "Help me get to kfc" "Hubba § i want "Damn KFC" nearly most of all the time !!! if it's not "Damn KFC" ill drop it like a sack of fuckin potatos !!!! § me and my laywer are discussing possible challenges that may arise from me asking a net girl to run me over with her car while i "pound off" § FOlks, please, do not hesitate to send me twitter content before you publish it, so i can tell you if it's acceptable, or if it's bull shit § TWITTER: our records sjow..youre the least blocked guy here. 0 mutes ME: spectacular. Truly, truly miraculous. This is a sign.. to post more § listen., pal, if you think im the kind of guy who doesnt wipe his ass, you're barkin up the wrong tree. my ass needs all the help it can get § ENJOYING BOND MMO?? JUST CRAFTED SOME REMARKABLE BOND GEAR WHILE YOU WERE BUSY TRYING TO FUCK THE NPCS WITH THE HUNDREDS OF OTHER JAME BONDS § world record: stupid ass hole drinks cup of coffee underwater § ARMY: your nickname reflects poorly on us all. we're changing it to something like "raven" or "switchknife" ME: no. "hostage killer" is good § Who Ever Left Their Pear Here. Come Get Your Pear http://t.co/6JIgZKrxYS § playing Dr. Kawashima's Brain Training (2006, NDS) 15mins a day gives me, i believe, the edge required to successfully deflect troll attacks § maybe the ski mask guy who blasted the "Doge" dog across the room like a rag doll.. maybe he was all of us. my opinion. unfollow if u must. § REVIEW- EROTIC SILHOUETTE MUD FLAPS - 1 STAR: piece of shit. drags behind my Honda Accord and gets messed up. too long. not wortg the hassle § the dog from "Doge".. was assassinated today.. at the Pittsburgh Marriott durinng a "Meet & Greet".. point blank with a sniper rifle.. Weird § Houly shit !!! The posts just keep on coming § "Worthless" county treasurer in hot water after releasing list of famous cartoon apes he would like to fuck § DontWantNoBullShit. DontWantNoBullShit § thank you. it hasnt been long but i can already say that having 200 k followers is exactly like being god from the bible. § think im going to start incorporating the word "Gadzooks" into more of my tweets, to punish my followers, for their constant insolence, § lumbering dick head told off by albertsons cart boy for trying to siphon gas from a moped while dressed like a blues brother § chaplain era silent motion pictures where basically the first subbed anime . click to read more § this guy was driving around with a decal of calvin pissing on nothing in particular. you missed the point entirely wwith this baffling setup § i did it. i posted like a fucking cartoon character instead of a human for 7 years and finally got my free light bulb http://t.co/zuoezdz5bK § i already doxxed all his anagrams and the best one is "tract disease" § get this fellas. i just doxxed MetalGearEric and his real name is: Ted Staircase. he lied about being an eric and his last name is staircase § whether its that Hot rock N' roll or Cool jazz, well we can know what the one thing is that we all can agree on, is that it is "Pretty good" § my idea for a car, is that it looks like a normal car., but right next to the steering wheel Blammo. theres a hose you can suck beer out of § bastard, http://t.co/z1UcE-H9Ebt § i love all the guys, from that show § Chheer's, and thank you, and good luck § floks... whether you're young or old: Star wors. Does it every time § (in slick Dennis Miller cadence) guh, § ah! ive had my ass put to the terrible kingdom of hell, also known as "the devils playpen", and also "Satans Playpen" § im out here in the yard trying to clean up my turds with a hair brush § one of my neighbors kicked my big flaming barrel of shit and piss over & spilled burning waste all over my yard just because im an irish man § #UNELECTABLE !!

#DEADWRONG !! #MarcoRubio #TeamRubio #Rubio2016 http://t.co/5dONoyRGnk § (to women at party) Im probably the top most crapped-on guy at twitter. My options get trashed constantly and Im best fit to shut my mouth. § folks.. when isay I'm "Getting my nails done", im talking being hammered to the cross, by those infamous trolls we all think poorly of, § reduced my weight gain goal to 300 lbs at the advice of my doctor § a social network to help cops with dirty boots meet browbeaten civilians who want to Spit`s shine the boots for free.. my one true vision § i can donate shit to fill the toilets with. thats all § "Stick It" to the bastards of Washington using this hot new WendysTrick: Bigtime WendyScam for Nonviable Bun Bargain; Pitiful & Effective § Hunter S. Quiznos § bblast my dick with Pet Dander § good news folks, today i dreamt about buying Furniture w/my girl followers so i punished myself by slamming the toilet lid on my fat fingers § this weeks "Mother Fucker" award goes to BabePigMovieMan for saying my dick looks "Crumpled up like a napkin" § (listening to a wolf howl off in the distance) do you hear that. thats the sound of another fav star trophy in the bag § Nmot a single one of you has given me your account password so i can make posts about top airfare deals on your behalf, especially the girls § for $500, i'll follow oyu on here and steal your best posts. this is an excellent way to get your foot in the door if you ask me § some peopl just have vile black hearts twisted by hatred and bad opinions about life § the Digimon Otis peace treaty will hence be frozen in piss and thrown onto the freeway where itll shatter into one million despicable pieces § Fuck Otis. I will never follow a bastard such as this. § thbe new Digiman game looks like shit for children& 2015 will NOT herald the Digiman renaissance tht Otis desparately needs to stay relevant § Well, the time has come. But before I officially grant DigimonOtis the coveted @Dril follow, I would like to say a few words. § @DigimonOtis im running to your house § @mattjohnchrist go suck burger kings dick rsome more you fascist fan boy sewer hog § @DigimonOtis we rehearsed this for 7 hours yesterday. you cannot do this. § @DigimonOtis Get online immediately and prepare for this yiou fucking idiot. Only 25 minutes left. Answer your phone § The ceremony will begin at 12:00 EST, wherein DigimonOtis shall unblock my account, and I will Follow him, officially ending this turmoil. § pleased to announce, on the april of 9th, that i have signed a Truce with DigimonOtis, ending a feud that has persisted over several years . § i get hacked constantly everyday because i am a Clod with zero technical prowess § thank you. that is the correct thing to do on this page right now § Whua?? No sponsorship disclaimer? no my friends. im saying all of these things for free, because i need to § enjoy your hot burger while children Piss freely in the colorful plastic tubes mere inches from your dinner, watch it flow down the slide § "Soda is back" Only at Mcdonald § the new meat ball sub's sandwich at mc donalds is a home run and between you and me the taste is sensational and almost good § do not show me this http://t.co/8GE5bvWIEb § i''ll peruse the web at my own damn leisure and thats a fact jack § yknow folks, not many things tell you theyre good right there in the name, so if you see things like Good Friday or Goodfellas i say Take It § im talking about main lobsteer, as in the good part of the lobster, like prime rib is to steaks § going nuclear on smart asses today, with the block button, Whilst enjoying my normal life with a cup of Porter Brew and eating Main Lobster. § im talkin normal mustard a nd would also go as far to also implicate Gouldon's "Spicybrown" § whicghever media wizards decide what you all are currently angry about should consider the grievous crap of people putting mustard on bagels § ((restrained by cops and forced to watch a man put mustard on a bagel) nno!! you're ruining it! That's quality bakedgoods § i am a cot and pickin "tells it like it is "son of a bitch § a visit.. from the easter man http://t.co/qK6xCdUeOU § "Why should there be only one good friday. Let's try our best to make all the Fridays good. Thank you" -a quote i invented which made me cry § some times it takes a little bit of Free thinking to be able to look at the bull shit of the world to step back and say "Damn What the hell" § ME: These days everyone wants to suck their smart phones dick if u ask me. HIPSTER: Is that a new feature? ME: ((making bitter beer fsce) § my plan of my walk of life is always making one million smackers (dollars) to get rich, and to pick up all the money I find on the floor § im the reddit guy hwo ranted about an existential crisis i had after realizing all of jeff foxworthys "you might be a redneck" jokes were me § wghen other people do jokes, they get the big buzz feed office, allowed to kiss girls,etc, but when i do it im treated like a Crook. typical § you know what. im dropping the subject and going outside to sip some cool lemonade. Enjoy your circle jerlk § look at the calender. I'm not explaining this further § its a joke you nit wits. Fuck all of you § ah ! your feeds going to blowup! loug out, quick!! http://t.co/OCJLGgEB1i § dont try to tell me it's spelled "clarence"./ i will not be april's fool § forced to commit suicide on live tv after 50yr old post comes to light in which i claim that scotus clarance thomas jacks off using his feet § the trolls: please Followback, and also Yolo me: HUh?? Shit for brians? Whuuuaa?? Egads. Homina Homina. Sweet Baby Crap. You're a fool § real_damn_fairly_misanthropic_red_m_and_m § if anoyne sees a blue thermos on I-95 that is a container of Stress Vomit my wife threw out of the car and i need to show it to my doctor § daily reminder to wrap your Shit in tin foil before flushing so it doesnt touch other people's shit § coax me into the toilet like a big bu g § one more. good night http://t.co/BaZQ2mC5Do § auh yeah ! !! http://t.co/FLU9MRb5dn § CLERK: Do you have your reward card ME: Absolutely I do not. I shan't be taking money out of the hands of Best Buy using insidious exploits. § clown college is bnot a real place. it is a location imagined by trolls so they can claim that i'm from there or that i should go there. § the newest, shittiest one possible , owned by dick Cheney & hipsters, tweeting for pepsi bucks to promote abcs sitcom lineup § funny that s.bucks suddenly wants to talk about race right after they throw me & my 7 service dogs out of their restaurant for being White § EEEEYYYYAAAAGGGGHHHH !!!! MY ASS .... § lost in the Maze... http://t.co/KaDXJo6Twp § scrolling down my feed..lauguhing my ass off at my own trade mark "Knee Slappers", my mouth stuffed with bread making beastly noises § how do people know how big their dicks are. is there an online quiz you can take § im at the point in my life where i cant relate to any popular fictional characters unless they use massive amounts of hair gel and steriods § 109 year old man attributes long life to uncircumcised dick, no vaccines, § sorry bartender. if i order the wrong beer the trolls will have a field day. lets play it safe. fiji water for me, with a Hint of pepsi § i had to fix the typo since they're probably going to print this tweet in Harper's § at around 36:29 in the steve harvey fleshlight vid you can see a single tear rolling down his cheek, crying for the lost souls watching him § i should hope that people do not search "steve harvey fleshlight" after my repeated callings for the boycott of this video § the steve harvey fleshlight vid now officially has more views than the critically acclaimed masterwork "Boyhood". we can do better people § once again i will take the path of honor, i will pledge NOT to watch the steve harvey fleshlight vid, no matter how good everyone says it is § 3 reasons to join the jackinf off without a condom movement: 1) Its good 2) Its free to join it 3) You dont need a condom to jack off § you see this..? *taps computer monitor with finger* this is not just a bunch of mixed up numbers and digits. this is a kingdom of Minds.. § im he nice man.. who celebrates all the saints who DOnt have holidays... and not just 1 day a year.. #Bless § about 90% sure i just saw a dog tossing garbage out of the back seat of someone's car § im a pleased as punch spoon-fed bitch and thats a bottom line § nothing like pouring a fresh bag of kitty litter down the ass crack after another liberating diarrhea shit § pplease let me join mensa. my IQ is essentially, zero, but i have very good, clean hands § bbeing passively aggressively retweet trolled by half wits & their beautiful girl friends just makesme say " ot before ive had damn coffee." § all young men Must be fitted for a good Italian suit, ideally by age 4. i will not fucking apologize or back down from this § Why am i smilin tonight fellas? Just got my hands on that new good treat to sip known only as simply "Bber". § concerned about people posting false lunches. lying about the food they ate on here. fraud meals. please start putting the receipts up § humbly Genuflecting myself before my girl followers, at the end of another red-letter sunday night on the comptuer § fuckin online fuckin idiots § hu... now im a man who likes his garlic butter.. let me tell you. in fact, im prone to saying that regular butter needs to step it up a tad, § triscuit. beggin strips. and who can forget hamburger helper. § its true. my father owned slaves in the 1980s but he has since apologized & been forgiven with love and support. he's a nice man now. § it is a shameful aspect of our family's past and im not afraid to confess and atone for it by posting messages about it online § Puh?! you're dangerously close to mmy blocker's list pal § Guh? my father owned slaves and was extremely poor. stop portending false nomenclature § if your going to come on to here and PigeonHole the facts & embarrass your self you can go fuck off until you learn actual truth § phenomenal http://t.co/OcgIteRKEL § the 1st rule of my twiter account is read my posts with an open mind,. the 2nd rule is the fight club rules. the 3rd rule is simply Have Fun § the other son wipes his ass too much. goes thrugh absurd amounts of tissue & has effectively thrown any respect for my household to the Dogs § my 35 year old son is howling because he clogged the toilet without using any toilet paper again. the neighborhood despises my howling boy § dplease promise me you will respect statues from now on § tokyo of nippon. the big apple. it is here i will forge my destiny selling printouts of my most Fucked Up posts. i sip off my beer cup & nod § do the " Macarana "? Ha. No thanks § i highly suggest using hash tag #HuckleGate if you're a Journo who wants to print my tougjh but fair opinions regarding huckle berry hound § huckleberry hound... talk about someone who needsto get his act together, pronto § judge dredd kicks the doors of the wtc mosque wide open and says "Well this looks like a big bunch of crap to me " § please hire me as an actor if any of you are filming a movie or somr shit. my forte is making extremely comical faces while being strangled § the jduge orders me to take off my anonymous v mask & im wearing the joker makeup underneath it. everyone in the courtroom groans at my shit § "There is something to be said for being able to bring that Wow factor., into mediums that make use of Social. Mm. Just incredible" - @ Dril § Mountan Dew Cold Red check it out § I.m taking a break from people who think it is good to make a fool of me for drama purposes. Basically dont look at my page until im not mad § sign em off log em out log em out sign em off sign em off log em out Raw Hide (whip noise,) § When and Rome... http://t.co/YBxppRfCMH § Gotta See This: tenets & facets of sears tyrannical mattress return policy ridiculed Skeptically by man with more than enough to eat at home § the bastard of downloads § you know what. im going to just come out and say it. i think that we should let the geico geckco go into hospitals & entertain the bedridden § when your feeding trough is clear of Debris.. that is the shit i like to happen § the cold damn truth of it is that all of your dads have probably owned slaves at some point. im sorry but that is just simply the true shit. § christ... just suddenlty hit with the realization that what im doing here is truly important. . thst behind each "Impression".. is a smile.. § put the damn coat on!! it's really comin down out there. Thank you for this opportunity. § please follow my dril page § need 800 more dollars to keep the unofficial "$h*! My Dad Says" tv show wiki up and running for another month, yiou fucking worthless toads, § let's leave politics in the hog pen and debate the real shit, like which 90yr old restaurant owner invented the original chicken cheesesteak § then they donate the hair to corrupt criminal organizations isntead of mixing it w/ rotten fruit & feeding it to the dogs, as wa s custom-

ary § aand barbers had such good names then too,. like “Floyd “ or “Erasmus”.
now they have bad names like “bozo the clown” and “ azi” § back in the nice
days, youd go to th e barbershop and theyd serve you a full seven course meal
during your haircut. not like today my friend § Biber done it. § Biber done it
http://t.co/BoroyIDfN9 § #ThingsIWontApologizeFor eating dog shit out of the
toilet like a low down snake in the grass § im the guy who asked the baten
kaitos forum if i should bring a condom to hooters § Here http://t.co/GoG1naHY-
tF § basicly a sniper rifle that can switch gears and turn into a baseball bat
if the situaiton demands it. an armymans ultimate tool § i was once known on
youtube as Epic “PLease stop recording me” Man., now im top influencer Gary
Faves, making $500 a year posting from home § my friends, theres nothing i
enojy more than a capsule of beer , while tasting beer with other 18-34 year
olds, at the beer store § justl had to unfollow about six people for tweeting
during the official Beggin Strips Moment of Silent Reflection § please remember
that im in charge of this website before you try to drag some toughguy shit all
over my good page § cmon peopl now   smile on your gamers   everuybody get
together try to do good with your Gamers right now § the twilight zone episode
where the guy blocks everyone on twitter and becomes startled and bewildered
when no one is left to give him favs, § THIngs other people like: being
bastards, being Uniformly tasteless THINGS I Like: Being reasonably kind, and
trying to help, when i can § vvvvvvv U see that shit?? That`s what we call in
the business “Another satisfied custoumer”. Locked down. § CollegeHater: Ur arms
aren’t getting enough sunlight CollegeHater: Did u use the cream I sent u
CollegeHater: Ur dead. At the flagpole. 3pm § the dress Color? (grins Intelli-
gently at the hell about to be unleashed upon naive content consumers) its
brown, because i wipe my ass of it § ME: Sorry. i must turn down your offer to
join the Mafia, as itd disappoint my friends on twitter THE MAFIA:The Mafia
respects your decision § ISIS MAN: It’s Jim from Montana... He says ISIS should
“Cool it” and that we’re “Crooks” ISIS CHIEF: Damn. Were finished. Dismantle the
nuke § Eatinh a 26 dollar hoagie. § Retweets Against Adam Lanza § hell no i
wont wear a sleeping cap. what the fuck is that shit. how does a hat help you
go to sleep. looks like, a Fools hat. § I shoudl. Just bring back the fucking
TexMexBoy shit. Thats all im good for § It didnt work. Leave it § mn http://t.
co/HkVui2Qpao § Wow u really are a bird brain. § “If it doesn’t have that ZING
, it ain’t Tex-Mex.” - TheTexMexBoy § “You don’t know Jack, unless you know
Pepper Jack .” - TheTexMexBoy § “dinner portions.. for lunch? Absolutely.
Absolutely.” -TheTexMexBoy § “I love the name of honor, more than I fear
death.” -me to my boss after he found a picture of me with a big shit stain on
my sweatpants § they should rename twitter .com “the dignity website”, because
i swell with pride when i think of the 200,000+ things ive posted on here §
sylvestetr the cat: sufferin succotash! Terry Schiavo was murdered § my life
motto is simply the words “james bond” § if you go to a nascar rally carrying a
clipboard and wearing a hard hat people will just let you go on the track and
kiss all the good cars § glad to see james, friend to cinema, returning to us
at long last. thank you § and the final word i leave all of you pitiful cowards
upon this sinful night is “Truth”.. hold it clos.e.. use it.. thank you §
whocares. theyre both fake. everything on this fucking web site is fake § i was
uninvited from the oscars for trying to sell “oscars brand bear bile” to
everyone who stopped their car for me while i fake hitchhiked § oscars for
exrtraordinarily subversive, insightful, online textual Musings?? unsoiled by
MOneymen?? Thats what my shit particularly would be § my son got on my tablet
and posted something truly unworthy of the institution of oscars but i wont
delete it because theyre his first words § .,. <<<<< THATS MY DICL #Oscars2015 §
Duty And Honor http://t.co/PCizXLGG9N § A Man’s Sense of integirty. http://t.
co/FXRYPFVnMG § laying in the car, hiding firom my malicious Wife because im in
trouble for buying too many toothpicks to fit into the tooth pick holder § tried

to make an fps in the 90s but i only got as far as naming the difficulty levels "YA MOMMAS BOY", "PUKE" and "TURN THE GAME OFF DIPSHIT § took some pics of my new satellite dish, but im not posting them until hatred annd cynicism are eradicated § youve heard of the trail of tears, well, if the boys in the white house had their way it would be the trail of taxes, and we;d get the shaft § every one always says they would use x-ray goggles to look at womens asses and get horny and wild. Not me. I would use them to help doctors § everyone cuts their arms and legs off in the future because all you have to do is say "computer fetch me my Posts" and itll do it § Politic's is back baby. It's good again. Awoouu (wolf Howl) § if i ever accidentally posted something relatable or good enough to trick you into following this account, i truly apologize. im crying also § sand blast my damn ass or go to pig piss cop hell § I dont recall authorizing this #ff . § man encased in lethal amounts of body oil and skin bronzer preserved for thousands of year.s.. beautiful § 1) My finger nails are clean 2) Sorry that i fucking use my hands to work for a living & dont care about finger nails 3) Peastebin incoming § requesting hand critiques. please be honest , but fair http://t.co/3vecQz6R6q § if any of oyu crude boys want to come after me *room lights up revealing collection of r/c helicopters behind my outspread arms* be my guest § Ghuph,.Being called a "Bastard" on here by someone with a sexually explicit avatar is the bigguest laugh ive had on this website since 2014. § i accept all your apologies you sad mother fuckers. YOu all have a lot of work to do when it comes to critiquing my meme style. Foul animals § my good new plan is to aquire a storefront, name it "please dont come in here" and jack off inside of it, alone, until i run out of money § ready to help all cops . http://t.co/MH6vcCqH5h § question my alligence to the dod damn twitter website and get swiftly block buttoned to childish hell, nincompoopts § as a Parent.. the thought of somebody attacking my sons with some sort of weapon, is just not good to me § i just think of them, and then, i post them. it's insanely bad ass § fellas. do n't forget to do something special for that lady in your life on valentine's day! none of you deserve love http://t.co/Aql0p59emz § hoping for that big promotion from mounted, tormented beast to rodeo clown § doctor: i can say with absolute certainty that if you do one more weird trick youll die me: CAPTAIN TIGER's Miracle Corn. LOok it up bastard § im a journelist now. gi;ve me free monster engery or ill Eviscerate you § @Babysnames idont know who the face book guy is. hes fake and has no respect for Content § my godfather died of urine poisoning while cleaning out a mcdonalds playplace tube and that's why drama makes me upset § please dont make whimsy of the popes ass while I am on-feed. ive more inportant things to do than indulge myself in hearsay of the popes ass § may the wind carry my tweets and soothte the sick, the wounded, the downtrodden of both man & beast, across the savage shit earth of trolls, § JUDGE: i'll commute 10 yrs from ur sentence if you kiss my gavel ME: no. i will do the time i deserve and thats the truth and also nuff said § takle it to dm.. this thread,. this thread where i declare my respect for girls, is a hallowed ground § im the good man whorespects his followers, i respect the artistriy of tweeting and i respect my girl followers also. nuff said dip shit § my critics say that my unconventional ass wiping techniques are no good. that i am seriously wounding my ass. that my ass is dirty. bastards § apparel, http://t.co/eqWudCeNX1 § im probably going to post more messages on here soon so please don't unfollow me § catching a ton of flak for my "how to fuck a Cadbury egg" web log series. sorry dim wits. your dick needs to be really small for it to work § if youre looking for good movies about grease, do not watch the nmovie "grease", because you will get swindled § sometimes i think thnings would be easier if i would just bite the bullet and relinquish my real name for my meme name, "epic Couch Bitch" § shocking: "racism is the light of my soul. racism is the air that i breathe, and racism is what i like." -RacismMario @cnn @msnbc @foxnews § pass the savings onto me mother fucker § Q:

Dear @Dril, friend to all online. Do Good people die? A: Good people absolutely do not die, and you have bveen blocked for asking me this § # i will never
bring dishonuor to the web by lowering my self to the point of placating the
lowest common denominator witht "Joke" or "Gags" § dr phil disciplines 2 year
old toddler demon hog with cow boy boots live on crackle §
^^^^^^^^^^^^^^^^^^^^^^^^^^^ <<<<< The Web Site Of Rat People >>>>>>
VVVVVVVVVVVVVVVVVVVVV § I'll nmever click on anything. Never § marked for death
after lays used my idea for steroid flavored potato chip and put my god damn
name and location on the bag § i just hacked into the church and made god REal
§ im still noob after all these years, after 20 years of the computer im still
noob, unbelievable § i get the ref. please retweet me getting the ref § the
secret fruit that oprah eat`s to become more psychic can now be ordered
"ONLINE" § for my money.. nothin hits the spot quite like Food, or Drink § (in
highly rational and cool voice) i have the higher follower count than them. i
wiont let them undermine me § favorite crood haver , online now § thte content
man fails once again, and walks home to get trash talked by his 34-year`old son
who refuses to eat anything without ketchup § like this if youre one of the 3%
of teens who remembers when music was just guys saying "my name is kid rock"
over and over § becoming a meme after confessing that i left my gf at a 5 star
restaurant to spray my dick with compressed air taught me the pain of Slavery §
cyber bullied at k mart § ill come on to the computer when i damn like to, and
ill post what i damn want to, and thats the facts of it § my style https://t.
co/nt8AqSAFoA § football?? Pfuh. while you sweathogs are pounding off to
grievous injury porn i'll be experiencing life at the car wash, with shorter
lines § on March 14th 2011, user "AIDS_Wanter" maliciously paraphrased my
alt-luit witticism regarding birdseed which turns into birds, when planted §
TIME: Why arent you live tweeting the big game. Why ME: id never forgive
myself if i killed someone by pushing vital info off of their feed. § thats the
worst bowl. the dogs shit everywhere and the referee makes like its a joke. its
not a joke its disgusting. § only a post has the power to make you laugh.. or
cry.. or even smile. thats the official quote of me § im NOT going to live tweet
the damn super ball game, and im NOT going to respond to any DMs asking why. i
care about the integrity of Feeds § the reason people cant come together and
post compliments about each others posts is because theyre scum, just 0% of
value § your looking at 9.11 § get the hell to crap § Fuck to hell § looking to
get on some rowdy boys bad sides tonight mother fucker. § sex worship i;s a
mental condition that is worse than liking the super bowl § twittetr should
recommend. a bath § the professional youtube reaction man who pays me $3 an
hour to scrawl his account name on the walls of womens toilets just died of
cholera § aggressively joyless oaf hhere. painfully obnoxious respect demander
checkign in. extremely dim witted frowning man looking for pals § DICK DOCTOR:
have you been using protection ME: yes. i put an entire towel in my ass §
seems like nowadays are more like nowadays than they were thenadays and
thenadays were less like nowadays than they were thenadays, nowadays § in talks
with twitter execs to make my account unblockable, and also Worse § bite my
shiny metal § glue man here, poking in to this site. big glue guy. just seeking
atlanta house wife, miss Right Lady, to Glue me, to the glue § just enjoying a
noticable uptick in Favs and Followeres ever since my sworn enemy, Osama bin
Laden, was brutally murdered in his rumpus room § to my hawaiian pen pal from
like 4th grade; sorry for sending you a pinecone. if someone sent me a pine
cone in the mail i'd beat their ass § eat shit mother fucker!!! **throwing
massive amounts of cash* art is dead bjtch!!! art is dead § ISSUE: is the road
runner wile e coyote's son FOR: thhey, seem to respect each other, on some
level AGAINST: one of them is a dog § appreciating every post online is akin
to acquainting oneself w/ each earthly grain of sand..and i absolutely intend
to do both these things § like i always say; sewage is just shit in a pipe §

big pharma. if youre reading this i have an idea for a pill that makes you tinier so you can fit into secret zones. i will let you invent it § another Twisted observation--Where the fuck does cinnamon come from. it just appears on food sometimes. Do people buy it at the store or what § one thumb up. good § ap,. http://t.co/BEbnsYQIxE § Ha ha ha its me. It's me. Yeah, good jok.e. No http://t.co/DOAzn9hPys § my ass is out again,. this time at the opera house. " o wifi!! turn on the wifi!!" i yell from the balcony. im trying to shit but i cant § @dril isaid comments off mother fucker and i mean it! § Comments off until the children go to bed. § hakuna mycoffee. .. #Understandable http://t.co/ORl5m3zi50 § im not allowed to comment on anything without the poermission of Conde Nast and Barqs Root Beer § shocking wiki leak #WikiLeaks #ObamaChewingGum http://t.co/dxM6K316S2 § Clown Disregarder § me when i get fuckin unfollowed on this site !!!!!!!!! http://t.co/9JJWccFdXU § me when theres not enoujgh fuckin coffee or beer!!!!!!!!!!!!!!!! http://t.co/yiPkkqO1rl § looking to spice up my marriage with pg13 comedies about camping § this guy knows the shit § Shut the fuck up abuot Greece § the dunkin donuts era § Thank you to all USERs who have engaged my web space regarding Super Bowl. You have increased the Social Power of myself and the NFL forever § hey now, its super bowl http://t.co/yPbH9B8akK § teen gradius please § congress passes law to make every character in every show go to jail on the final episode like in seinfeld § im somewhat a bit of an expert on *looks around cautiously* girls, as i have convinced many of them to beat the shit out of me on craig list § wiping out an entire archaeological site by drifting in my 1500-ton big rig truck with "piss up my ass bitch boy" on the side in neon lights § nuke obtained by renegade AssFreak § Thank you for your time, Elon. I know youre very busy but I appreciate you coming onto my feed. http://t.co/ux4RXhgDsy § elon: the tesla milker will run by taking ordinary chemtrails out of the air and tuirning them into, milk me: wow. Tastes great. Ha ha ha § enjoying a conversation with my friend elan musk,. http://t.co/akZ410Dn3C § im sorry for claiming i was going to "flip the script" on dry rub barbeque. that was wildly irresponsible of me § U would be superbly fucking remiss to not click on my link of top 10 reasons that Vuvuzela s are The Dog's bollocks § i feel obligated to inform you i have a normal looking man's face, and i only have one of them § watching simpy slide up the fireman pole § some times.. i need my coffee fix so bad.. i gotta grab TWO mugs!! Im the mockery of all my co-workers and i fucking suck § watching stimpy slide up the fireman pole traumatized me and made me want to become a united state marines § the News; - death cured; immortality real -on-line ghoul given plaque; recognized as "loudest human alive" - bird infiltrates macaroni grill § im the guy who is famous at the hospital because i had to have two catheters put in since i piss so much § i say that, let the MOds decide. i trust their decision and i will not attempt to sway them one way or the other. § i would have to say that, given the option, id take the blue check mark. i would sacrifice my indie status for that privilege § i just talked to all of my celeb friends on this site and they told me that the blue checkmark is good to have. personally, i believe them., § please help me to obtain my fair share of royalties from the video " caterwauling jack ass shot with cannon '", which is now viral with hits § YES !! YES ! PULLOVER http://t.co/GIiYo3sj6e § another stir-up at the office when relatably handsome professional refuses to remove sticker from khakis that says "my other pants is jeans" § pplease remember to turn your location on so the buffoons on this web site can have an easier time finding you, for whatever horrible reason § the american sniper murders 8 people with one bullet 2000miles away from a beach chair in hawaii, winks at the camera and says "Its A Livin" § 4k tech will enable the viewer to see my dick hole fully accentuated through my jeans as the media hunts me down in a carrabba`s parking lot § 5 bucks will get you 1 minue access to the "Peck cam" where you can watch all sorts of wild birds peck me while i force myself not to resist § people enjoying a meal outdoors., disgusting. horrible. inadvisable § *steps up to mic; booed immediately* geico commericals are tthis generation's pink floyd **boos get louder** can anyone help me find my car § everyones always using selfie sticks these days instead of attending lectures about string theory and shit and im so mad i could crank off § go ahead and have your precious "laugh". just know that little guiy has saved my life countless times § wow theyrre releasing more of these already http://t.co/m8INRDahRZ § get the fuck out tof there!! get the fuck out of there you god damn idiot!! asshole!! i need that oil!! i need oil!! http://t.co/EafCpVBEY9 § someone please verify rumor that petsmart is turning all animals loose (lizards snakes rats dogs) because of the scoundrel obama care § im pretty sure the neightbors can hear my keyboard clicking at 4am and thats why they throw chemicals at me § truthfully, i do believe that, now thatm the gas prices are low, i think that theres going to be a lot less BULL S#!T on the commute !! § @NancyGraceHLN my 2 year old son is drawing swastikas everywhere after seeing a toddler smoke weed on your show. thanks #Irresponsible § warm pics every day § id love to be 1 of those purple espn guys who puts boulders on descending columns but id probly get all sorts of penut gallery comments here § thank ytou for the Fav § jack`s off to the super bowl for business, jack`s off to the bitter beer face commercials for pleasure § im sorry for getting bonnaroo 2015 cancelled b/c i used the hashtag to ask ppl to put teeth in my ass. but im Not sorry for defeating trolls § thank you for putting these kind thoughts underneath my flawless posts § i would love to speak out against jokes twitter.. but im afriad.. i dont have the strenght... § WOw. Sorry. Like i give a shit. Wiseguys on here § be very nice § i mostly just need help getting the teeth. i can handle pouring them into my ass by myself #ParksPremiere § some one help me put hundreds of human teeth into my ass hole #bonnaroo2015 § pour teeth into my ass #SpyMovie § top me off, beer man. here's to bottoms up **gets kicked out of the fucking establishment for putting my dirty coat on the bar* § in honorable protest, i will abuse my ass cheeks with radio waves until the Olympics forces all of the swimmers to wear shirts § isis man: please! you gotta follow back! you just gotta! me: no can do my man. i respect your right to be in isis, but I can not follow you. § folks it's me, the guy who said that hit & run drivers are actually good on a blog once. anyway I want to get on CNN again so please retweet § looking at Mars Bar § i do actually this § waiting for the ma mas out there to put all the little trolls to bed so i can post controversial material without repercussion § " dont forget to fav and retweet . always always " § crap off wise guy § you forgot the worst disease of all which is. star bucks. fucked up , but brutally truthful § did we end sars yet. good job every one, if we did § not ashame.d of my posts. my messages help people § i have proof that my care taker has been tricking me into eating delicious home cooked meals by hiding them in wads of peanut butter § if you have a problem with my mouth, i'll be swniging a sledgehammer in circles outdoors for the rest of my life, so come try do crap to me. § REAL REAL REAL "The @Dril Drafts Folder: See it BEFORE he says it" take a L@@k #ForbiddenContent http://t.co/jFkkmhUluk § seems to me. like, well, these days, people are more interested in Instagram , than telegrams, which are better because theyre the first one § this is bunk. this is low § im the guy in the incognito browser icon who jacks off wearing a trenchcoat and sunglasses § no. do not give him a hash tag. dont you dare do this to me § me: nobody has to get owned today. please, please put down the keyboard and step back 9 year old child: Fuck oyu § does anyone else think that @DigimonOtis has been going downhill lately.? wouldnt be surprised if he sold his account to some reddit guy. § @hoverbird @DigimonOtis i dont like him § my opinion is good because im nice § that last psot was damn good enough to count as the 12th day of content if i say so my self. #The12DaysOfContent § (struggling))ok i figured it out: all opinions are good, except for the opinions that say other peoples opinions are bad, because thats rude § watch the first 45 minutes of the film, read the entire beeteljuice manga, then watch the rest of the film, or fucko ff § heed my words ,cyberfilth, i may bvery well be a thirty eight yr old kindergartner, but im fairly average when it comes to eating female ass § eat shit , jc penney skeptics http://t.co/q4CYFS3az8 § proudly announcing to the barber shop that i got through my entire haircut without screaming or touching my dick underneath the smock § and i find it kind of funny i find it kind of sad the dreams in which im Beavis are the best ive ever had § #The12DaysOfContent theyre back boys. the good posts i used to make when iw as an Indie account. the Classics series, http://t.co/7UWkZAnEu9 § your video "stuart little: Why I dont buy it" has been removed due to hate speech against islam and pepsi § please be mature about this subject § i feel like getting shot would;nt be that bad if you knew how to properly "body spin " away from the bullet or slap it away with your hand § somebody please haul my ass to the ultimate breast worship championship's. i made the top 16 bracket and my car was impounded, due to lice § #the12daysofcontent thank s http://t.co/rk8uiieT7P § hipster.kiss my usa ass § absolutely, and i wont get into heaven until everybody on this site unblocks me § im not cut out to be a content producer!! fuck thtis!! i want to go back to just looking at everyone else's content and nodding if its good § #The12DaysOf-Content making these is as torturous as every concentration camp combined, including hell, which god made http://t.co/d3j4RWAnYr § unbelievable. another muffler man statue had its big plastic jeans stolen late in the night, whjile i was busy having an alibi at my house § do not be afraid to talk to that lonely boy on the train ... with the rosy red cheeks, sun glasses & big cigar... he just mmight be... angel § ME: when committing to a project like "the 12 days", you are forced to bear your soul to countless vicious cannibals GQ: crhist. its true § there is no meme i have not looked at. § @roach700 i trust you roach 700 § next year itll be the 3 days of content or something. i cant handle 12 whole days on top of stress & trouble brought to me by gimmick memers § im losing hundreds of dollars per post but the economy will improve soon § #The12DaysOfContent somone tell me what day im on please because i lost count http://t.co/JzhsuCEi67 § your taking my post out of contexts, but yes § i am the damn good boy who always gets his dinner egg http://t.co/Wn7RfLyb4h § i pour my Blood into my tweets, and seeing all these random 4chan reddit Monkey Cheese tumblr teens get more favs than me is the great 9/11, § searching for bastards . § you see; most of the piss were exposed to in our day-to-day lives is immediately diluted by toilet water. pure piss is a monster all its own § shit head with hog DNA takes cardboard pennzoil display hostage § you might as well flush your toilet down the toilet as well, if youre using it to flush money down § im delighted to see that people are waking up to the fact that Masturbation is fraud, and turns all of the T in your body into germs § just call me george watchington. beucase im watching tons of nice shit appear on my computer screen § #The12DaysOfContent im sorry again http://t.co/Odg5cl2lFa § #The12DaysOfContent here comes baby new year . . . http://t.co/cq93CxEw8V § my 2015 new years resolutions is to go to hell less often, and raise $99 by selling stolen mulch to buy my account back from lockheed martin § just keep on, pulling that old Chain #The12DaysOfContent http://t.co/TDA5oJZ6SD § What if the guy who jumped over the white house fence thought it was the gamer gate. § what if the guy who jumped over the white house fence thought it was the gamer gate § ah (sees the good low gas price while driving, spit takes hot coffee all over dick & the sharp, sudden stimulus causes me to ejaculate) okay § (crawling out of rocks in dystopian future where all the good posts have already been made) uehh.. im the big.. denim.. sock loop(??).. man § @dril https://t.co/uDVuHb7HU2 oops im owned ,fav thi s one instead § goign to new york disguised as the Mayor so when the cops turn their back on me i can jack off § actually the barf bags on airplanes are for shitting in. they call them barf bags because thats gross to some people § theyre probably going to show my dick on cnn soon. hopefully on split screen with some dick expert from minnesota saying how normal it looks § #The12DaysOfContent #AmericanSniper http://t.co/jUMQiOrSEF § after muchf bullshit, screaming arguments, i have finally procured the $80 usd necessary to begin development on the face book of gamer. § JAILBIRD: Whatre u in for CROOK: I headbutted an ambulance JAILBIRD: Hm., Thats good. Well bye CROOK: Bye. Thank you § klout was supposed ot send me a bottle of spices but they didnt § the thursday nite rant is murdered by me for being a source of tyranny in my life § Yeauh, no. http://t.co/5gY6TS70to § and another thing: im not mad. please dont put in the newspaper that i got mad. § know what. im not fucking sorry. the "12 days" project has been fairly solid thus far. as if the shit you people post is better?? get fucked § Im sorry that the 12 days of content feature isnt as good as I planned it to be. I will try to to better of it, in the remaining days. -Dril § @dril my reasoning behind this content is that theres a large version of the mask and a tiny version of him as well. something for everybody § suck it bigtime champ § my follower count nosedives dramatically each time i do this but #The12DaysOfContent must continue http://t.co/QDAFXSrgok § (ccrying) its jst not good. nothing online is good. we will ne ver top 1999's "monicka lewinsky craping" vid from back when jokes were legal § yeah , just take this big metal trash can ive strapped to my dick off and just spray piss everywhere. just take it off. great idea fuck face § #The12DaysOfContent http://t.co/3ExzF1htlB § #ThreeWordsSheWantsToHear always Handsome gamer #ThreeWordsSheWantsToHear loud but Nice #ThreeWordsSheWantsToHear COrdial, and unafraid § i looked at the keyboard and there isnt one § invoke my big ass with satan noises or go home § im like a mean old Rattler rwho types on the keyboard by repeatedly striking it with my poisonous mouth and teeth, and youre.. the dead guy, § Bog Off, Fuckazoid. Im Cramming Packets Beyond Digital Light Speed ,Injecting Pure Fire Into The Blogomedia SuperFrame For The God Damn Lord § @MilkBone milk bone is 666 § #The12DaysOfContent http://t.co/dSDMi9dVMJ § beginning tomorrow .. for #The12DaysOfContent... that's twelve days of top-shelf posts just in time for santa.. as a "Thank You" to the boys § may god help you if you trip your feet against my handsome bulk while i am sitting on the floor looking at Depression things on my tablet pc § well, its very good that you did that, and i hope your family members consider giving me a follow even it made them mad § thank you, http://t.co/XmuLGcjapP § tomorrow im going to fill up on bread befoore 10am and get waterboarded by my seven identical uncles § i will not post on xmas day out of reverence for the lord christ. that is only. my opinion, and if youre going to kill me for it, thats fine § absolutely read some of my god damn tweets while opening gifts with loved ones at the tree tomorrow & bring CULUTRE to this ass of a holiday § i fucking love logging in and out of things at incredible speed § it ius abundantly clear that my entire online presence is like a big toilet shaped pinata that people bludgeon with sticks & take shits into § i wont fuck off § this is superbly against all laws § buddy youre ten pounds of shit in a ten pound bag, of shit § Saying you want to put your dick in the keebler elf house is one of the fucked up things i will block U the mostly for . § i should not have to press 2 for a male ass. this is america § upgrade my ass to a human's ass § sometimes i love to be able to want to be the man who is able to want to need to have his wants and needs able to be fulfilled sometimes § please pray for my sons Thursten and Gorse who have just glued themselves to a curtain, § https://t.co/O9h3XolzpW this short online exchange between Karl and his friend wayne hooter might just,. chane your life § change your godgdamn name clown @WayneHooter § i destoryed my balls with uh, enhanced interrogation techniques sir § i agree with all party `s involved http://t.co/04YXhaHcEL § Me to, and, cheers. § every one in that convo is dumber than rats shit & my posts wer terrible long before it became popular to say so § looks like lunch is for me today § the numa numa

man just bougt a $70million house and im here at the library trying to photo-
copy a fruit roll up § #WorstDateIn5Words i tune § your snl § #WorstDateIn-
5words a bunvch of blades arranged to spell out" 9/11". the worst date, in
swords § Let's cut the crap--regarding iTunes. Maybe it's just me, but it seems
like you gotta be from NASA just to get half these features to work. § (in
perfect astronnaut voice) bleep bloop even I cant figure out how to use damn
itunes and im from Nasa § heads up hotshot. gonna drop two fuckin cents on this
fuckin itunes. yeah you gotta be a fuckin nasa astronaut to use this shit. yea
alright § funny you should ask. im actually having a lot of problems getting it
to do just that. its like you got to join nasa to learn how § i gotta tell you,
itunes is running me ragged. i reckon it would require the expertise of a NASA
astronaut to operate this infernal program. § ME: itunes, play some sinatra
ITUNES: Youre not authorized to operate itunes. Please insert NASA identifica-
tion ME: what hath ,been wrought! § folks let me tell you about the content
platform known as "itunes". its so poorly conceived its even got nasas top men
scratchin their heads § some times I have a hard time playing my favorite songs
on itunes, and I wish I had my astronaut's degree from nasa to help me play it
!! § itunes has more buttons & clickers than a space rocket, its like you got
to be an astronaut from nasa to use it and not a normal man as I am § the
itunes program is so complicated its like you gotta have a degree from nasa
just to play sweet home Alabama. § itunes.. what a mix-up. its like you gotta
be a NASA astronaut just to work this thing § i dont care about "get laid". i
want my tweets to inspire girls to have dewep and meaningful relationships with
me § GIRL 1: only 25% of @dril's followers are female. lets get that to 100% by
2015   GIRL 2: I agree § dear horseshoe crab,: you are neither of those
things, and yyou look like a damn rat in a hat § yes,. i;m the guy who eats
handfuls of salt to dry myself up so i never have to wipe my ass, and yes,
there are several wars declared at me § im going to pin you to the wall by th
neck with my damn rifle § blatant disrespect. no fav. § who let this guy type
under my post § NET PERVERSION >>>>> BAD <<<<<< MURDER ^   NEW LIGHT
BULBS § the usd dollar will explode into complete dust next year . pelase
strongly consider growing an apple garden § the dogs playing poker painting is
ranom wacky bullshit, it is now considered not good by me, and i have made the
decision to not look at it § mister one million dollars http://t.co/sAWxBXp7qK
§ im going to close my account for uhhh 90 seconds until yyou fucking people
learn how to engage content creators in a meaningful handsome way § well im sad
to announce that the meme quilt project has been cancelled. someone has already
jacked off on it instead of adding their patch § makimg a Meme Quilt, where we
send a quilt all over the world & each person adds a patch featuring their
favorite online meme . a bit of fun § paper towel ?? Huzzat ?? is it a paper or
a towel. more to come § FRONT: If u dont like the posts BACK: Get out of the
kitchin § im an exhausting person to be around but once you get to knnow me im
actually a giant shithead with irredeemable mouth § thank you inventor of bibs.
every one else, off a cliff § i put years of hard work into getting my torture
degree at torture college & now everyones like "oh tortures bad","its ineffec-
tive" fuck off § messages like this; i dont even look at it. i dont look at it §
once agian the posts sent to me by screwball accounts have caused me to spit up
and defile my big belt buckle which contains my son's ashes § What the fuck.
Who is this § be Quiet § Fuck you § I can confirm absolutely that filmmaker
George Lucas is bringing our dear star wars back to us. § Star wars is back
baby . . . Confirmed by @Dril § Are u done? Have u made your point? Hm? § i
challenge us all to experience one another in a greater over all sense of
adult maturity, in the year two thousand of fifteen, next year. § concerning my
messages on here: typically pretty good id say. if theyre bad its because i
have a life instead of thinking of crap to upload. § this. this fauil. fail
this http://t.co/YDMowEL595 § thats a good vehicle to be trapped in for

eternity i think § ijust had to block like 3 people for using the word "gargle" as a noun § im not trolling. Im talking normal § i can only save one http://t.co/5fXddCJ3eL § the sattire is lamentable and gross. theyre doing bad of it § nobodyd on here is capable of talking to me like a normal goddamn human because theyre pricks and dimwits with incest § being 0 inch tall keeps the judgementle shallow people away so its fine. § im the dumb mother fucker who sucks on my computer monitro like one of those aquarium fish; to bond with ceelbs, brands, trends, what have u § im 0 inch tall and its fine. § im the dumb mother fucker who uses a dessert fork to cut up my spaghetti § im the dumb mother fucker who has permanently fucked up abs from wearing a pair of suspenders backwards for three days straight § im the Dumb motherfucker who holds a 21 gun salute in honor of pizza huts old brand on the quake server & fails to get the boys to cooperate § im the dumb mother fucker who puts the ice in after the drink and calls the soda fountain a "bastard" when it splashes at me § it will be good for all of us when i shorten my name from "the ebay boy" to "eboy" § i feel a good balance of nice energy & rude energy cioming through the monitor at me, and i think i will stay online for about 3 more hours. § hte shit people type at me "Yap yap yap" § my ass cheeks have two giant finger nails § me & the booys are riffing on 78 hours of stolen walgreens security cam footage. this guy on here just bought a toilet brush. bitch!! bitch! § i msay be woefully ignorant, but at least im good at justifying my existence with trite remarks § CELEB: Love that Moolah baby ME: Did u see that shit. Did u see that shit. He called it moolah instead of money. God damn! Only in hollywood § the sheriff has ordered me to return the "Helpful Boy Award" i earned at age 8 after seeing me at the local swimming pool begging for towels § @Favstar_NSFW thank you favstar nsfw. § SCOTT PETERSON: i unfollowed you in 2011 and your shit gets retweeted into my feed constantly. it sucks ME: I apologize sir!! I've fucked up § [[[[[[[[[[[[[[[[[[[[[[[[[[[please let Miley join the USMC]]]]]]]]]]]]]]]]]]]]]]]]]]] [[[[[[[[[[[[[[[She will do good]]]]]]]]]]]]]]] § hoagie prreserved in peat bog for 30 years - "It's Still Food" - "Oh it's nice" § (chanting to self; walking around in public) dont get owned. dont get owned (body quickly separated into 500 pieces by metallic alien noise) § targeted advertiosng helps me connect with the Brands I Need http://t.co/1d8nITM0JN § ridiculous to believe that someone would risk the careers of themselves & their colleagues to put a secret ass in the trailer of a starwars. § again i've been asked to comment on the hidden ass in the new star wars trailer. it's time to put this cowardly rumor to rest. theres no ass § as the authority on being tge guru of tech, i think that, "searchs", are going to be an important part of web life, in the year 2015 § herees what I say to those who think im having a goof on here (presses button on wristwatch & tiny pair of shades launches onto face) im Not § diseased hogs pissimg everywhere but the toilet. wads of hair covered in piss and smashed into the floor #SponsoredContent § (cop inspecting his new body cam with huge pepperoni fingers) what the fuck is htis. where do i pack the ammo. is this a new type of grenade § threres a rumor master chief will take off his mask and reveal hes the btk killer.. do not do this.. it would be disrespectful to halo § "Give me an App that will make me say, 'Wow'" "Apps will help us in our lives" "An App is always just a download away" some good app quotes § are you having a crap of me mate?? Are you, having a crap of me mate § christ.. ive done it again.. ive posted the absolute good truth shit that every1 has been waiting to hear in this sea of lying crap nonsense § ive made an arrangement with the casino. im allowed to yell at the slot machines now, but only if i actually put money in them first § its not normal to get on here and post fake joke shit when the rockefellers, the carnegies , theyre all reading it. theyre scrutinizing it § ijust had one Hell of a steak dinner. i wont post specifics regarding the dinner due to trolls but i would like to get this viral please., § stare directly into the sun For Free #blackfridaydeals §

i just left an enormous pile of vomit behind golds gym for all of you abominable pig clowns to pick at #blackfridaydeals § thats one small Ass for a man,.
one tiny jeans for man kind § my intense belief: you should not be eligible for
the presidency of the United States until you are at least 89 years old § my
friend nasdaq_oscar says they just let all the pardoned turkeys run around the
white house and shit on the carpet. disgrace to the office § my big sons have
made a mess of the garage again after being riled up by the good word of the
Lord § jeopardy should give the contestants guns and make them shoot the
categories. i think that this would improve the image of the guns brand § if
youre not a fellow big time social buzz blog appreciateor then spare me thhe
wretched crap of the bullshit § the essential, Male Ass § NO I WILL NOT USE MY
BRAND NEW 3D PRINTER TO PRINT OUT "A PICTURE OF RATS". PLEASE SUGGEST SOMETHING
GOOD, LIKE CUSTOM MONOPOLY PIECES § all gags and assorted banter aside though I
will in fact be shooting the thanksgiving turkey with a gun instead of eating
it this year . § cant wiat to see what devilish thanksgiving scenarios me and
the boys of twitter can conjure up. "The turkey was taken by spiders? ? Whua??"
§ all ladys need to shut off the god dam soap operas and put on the vids of me
smoking a pipe that ive painted to look like a nascar § slobber, by definition,
can only come from a mouth. anyone claiming to slobber out of their ass is a
liar and possibly a scammer § im sorry to everyone who has ever wanted me to
apologize to them for something, and im sorry for apologizing tio you if you
didnt need me to § [kOaLa_Releasez_Prezentz]gilligans_island_theme(Tap_That_
Ass_Mix_2007)by_DJ_arbys(Deceased)_uploaded_by_Vect0rman.mp3.zip § ((sends yoyu
an unsolicited 20 image sequence of me morphing into a neopet) i can take u...
closer § im moving to israel, where the boys are nice, as soon as i get
confirmation that they use the same kind of toilet paper that we use here § "big
craps are good". never have is een such a foolhardy sentiment expressed on
here. "Big craps are good". Absurd. The words make no sense § every morning i
pick up the local paper and read the latest condemnations about my rinky-dink,
slipshod Ass & my child-like shoulder blades § hidden camera prank doctor: we
got your xrays back. Looks like your brain has been replaced by bugs me
(oblivious): please let me g go home § alRight. no filter. i think that, igf
you are a bird, and you get run over by a car, you absolutely need to get your
god damn act together § id absolutely love to move to LA with my model g.friend
& start my film career, but all my pre-orders at game stop would certainly be
fucked § my garbage family is staging an intervention or something for me
because i forgot what its called when people have a chin made out of hair § in
social media blunders: i post a pic of my new watch without realizing all of my
credit card numbers and dick and prolapsed ass are visibl § my rig tower is
full of shit parts because i spent all my money on a mouse pad with a screaming
human face ionside of it § fbi agents are hiding theur guns in toilets so they
can arrest you for shitting on government property. do not be fooled by this
dirty trick § TTNR was sponsored by shitty ruby tuesday, which led ultimately
to its downfall. Boy's Thought's is sponsored by salem cigarettes § im starting
a new feature on my feed called "Boy's Thought's" where I just riff on the
things of day to day life and maybe some surprises to § whats in my cup today?
why its that old stand-by known as "beer" folks . thank you for reading it § i
nneed constant 24/7 stream of memes and jokes about coffee being good to prove
to myself im not living in rthe Fucking matrix § something must be done about
aall these kids on the playground claiming the goatse.cx lawyer is their uncle
§ that's certainly a numnber § once agAin going "Ape" over controversial
Classic rock opinions at the super market while my asain gf pushes me around in
a shopping cart § someone needs to tell "TimOnline" that his username fucking
sucks § there is so much rigamarole and legal B.S. involved around mnaking a
comedy central roast of digimonotis that it's almost not even worth it § in the
latest effort to distance myself from "Whacky" ;, "Random" bull shit, i will be

changing my name from VolleyballCraig to NormalCraig, § things 90s boys remember: vision of themselves in the future being violently ripped apart by unknown energy. that board game thats in a mall § its decided. tomorrow morning im going to speak with the priest after his sermon and ask him to perform the ritual that will turn me athist. § my t-shirts no longer have humorous slogans on them, their purpose now is to display pitiful appeals begging people not to piss on me § ((SPILLING BLOOD ALL OVER KEYBOARD) THIS IS WHAT U WANT. THIS IS WHAT U FUCKING BASTARDS WANT RIGHT (1 WEEK LATER) WHY ARE THE KEYS STICKING § mmy monitor flashed before me in dazzling light. for 1 brief moment, I saw every Celeb at once, the good 1s, the bad 1s, crying, jsut crying § originally wanted to keep silent about the "elmer fudd's dick" issue, but BMXWalter's objectionable dickless fudd theory has forced my hand, § ºO€¢ ¤€¢.¸¸.·´¯`·.¸¸.·´¯`·.¸¸.œ¿¸¸.€¢ ¤€¢. €€¢. Æ¸ÌµÌ¡ÓœÌµÌ¨Ì¨Æ· Perfect Æ¸ÌµÌ¡ÓœÌµÌ„Ì¨Æ·.€¢ €.€¢ ¤€¢.¸¸.œ¿¸¸.€¢ ¤€¢Oº § in response to allegations that i have beneficial forms of bacteria housed in my digestive tract: 1) Thayt's fucking disgusting 2) I don't § im going to jack off to the comet instead of the ass because im nice § doctor: you have a hoof growing in your brain. like a goat's hoof. its horrifying, unprecedented & fatal me: is it true they do 420 in hhere § thw man who killed bin laden... angel or demon http://t.co/CutViWP85O § do not talk of this on here § college boy . . . woop woop woop § lime and pear is the same "Lime & Pear: Same Fruit" (they are the same) #LimeAndPearTheSame // Opinion: Limes are no different from pears § [transfer of pug_dog_Spectacularly_gored_by_bull.flv completed] oops. sorry. that's the wrong one. here [transferring lime.jpg] § i know how to get on all my favorite site`s. § in the nice days, the paper boy would hand deliver the newspaper to its subscriber. now he throws it at my dick and murders me every time § ass ointment seeping through the top of my perilously tight jeans leaving unsightly horizontal stripes on the sofa #Supernatural-200thEpisode § as this website's foremost broken human being, id like to annoucne that oysters make me mad now, for some reason § me: let's just say if ur a child who suffocated in a plastic bag, my next rant might just rock your socks off buzzfeed: Splendid. Phenomenal § the grenades man doesn't believe in girlfriends § " big-ears bastard ruins another opera after being flung off the balcony by marines " § a good bad -ass thing would be a criminal who throws lots of hand grenades and kisses them each time. they could use this in agent of shield § Please Dont § congress: youre so good at saying the truthful things in a handsome way. we need you me: Wheres bigfoot. Assholes § congress: it would be an honor to let you join Congress me: absolutely no. it'd be a disservice to my followers to join the bastard congress § because im a pig in the zoo § THe,yre going to stop, making twinkies soon. Buy lots of ammo and leather § i want anonymous and police to join forces against the mayor and allow me to have a big pile of dirty towels rot the floorboards in my house § the US army sent my police departmet 100000 hideous robot arms to rip off citizens' heads but heres the thing, we only need like 500 of them § open up thhis portable crapper citizen. im police and im on a crook search. stand down stand down § to counter-act the terrible "ISIS", im starting my own group called " ICEis". what we do is give retweets & faves to the hopelessly decrepit § sorry boys.. im goin A.W.O.L.. !!! Another Weekend On-Line § its almost to good, i think § i plan on going to do it. § the pinheads at the post office are all down there whooping it up with my good car mags instead of delivering them to my tent in the desret § BLu8rehgh kiss my fuckin ass jack off Numbnuts prick § i love ggetting hazed so i can gain access into this exclusive club of people who have been forced to eat dog shit § they were goign to preserve my brain but they decided it would be a waste of a jar. they instead used the jar to store a massive piss sample § once i get the brand surgry i expect dairy queen to come crawling back. to give me back my job of saying "dariy queen rules" for $0.01 an hr § i;m now getting surgery to completely become a Brand. all bothersome human elements (ability to get mad, go to toilet, etc) will be, removed § Have u ever wanted to Kick someone's ass on here so bad but don't do it because you will die if youre exposed to clouds § sttop sending me aprilfools. its not April § the last indie twitter acocunt. ..yeah thats me § i was given a purple heart for being the fox executive who invented the 3d football robot & made homer stop showing his ass on the simpsons § a cement truck pouring its load on a bare ass nude man lying face down while people sing happy birthday to him § (reading my latest death threat) "from the desk of DigimonOtis..." this is bullshit. digimonotis has never owned a desk § WHEN IT IS TIME FOR ME TO BE QUIET, I AM EASILY FOOLED BY THE FAKE RUBBER NIPPLE OF A PACIFIER. I THINK THAT IM GETTING MILK OUT OF THE DEAL § if u follow me. ..and ur display name is "bazinga man".. you had better FUCking be the real bazinga man before I unscrew youre head & SHIT D § as hte real life #AlexFromTarget, i'd like to thank you all for liking the picture of me,aand announce my support for president jeb bush2016 § "my posts are more..i think.. self aware than most other peoples posts. Im also nice to everybody" -dril, visionary Disruptor; while smoking § i think it is good to vote, unless it is inconvenient, or boring to do so. then it might be very bad. i'm sorry for doing politics om here. § i don't believe in making beer in huge metal vats. they should make it in cups, for me to drink it out of, when I want to, § i believe in " inject steroids into infants ". i believe in " WAsh your damn car ". i believe in " #PregnantHogGate ". i believe in " koopa" § i actually feel bad for you that you will be drowning in a jail cell full of thick brown piss in about 7 minutes § establishment cocksuckers wiping their a$$es every time they shit, while the windbag toilet paper lobbyist crooks roll around in blood money § Dear Applicant, We regret to inform you that Guinness no longer publishes the world record for "World's Tiniest Ass", because it was too sad § I personally make sure they are good beofre I submit them. § my mame is jonny goodposts § We Live IN A Country Where Football Players Are Given Helmets For Free But I Have To Buy A Helmet At The Store Because Im A Regular Person . § i would like to remind our nation's youth to burn their mcdonald abd burger king cups after use so mobsters cant hide IEDs in them § Personality: Good friend for anyone, will help someone in need, not foul with language. Dislikes: People who ridiculize Lucario (I really ha § man wearing nothting but socks doing back flip kicks into his tv because there are too many batman shows § [crying[i just want to seay.. it takes a lot of courage for the cashiers to thank me for shopping at wal mart.. but it iw well appreciated, § thats a fuckin dog § proud to announce that after 30 years as a slave on my uncle's fishing vessel i no longer wish to fuck the post cereals honey-comb wanter § remember not to die on halloween so you dont turn into w pumpkin § haivng the xbox controller vibrate in my lap for 14 hours a day has rendered me sterile , low - t , and betagender § ive decided that nudity is acceptable if irt's done for artistic reasons, like, promoting a mattress store, § im sorry for doing jokes about the blue checkmark. i need it very badly to protect myself from villains right now § thank you daugter § nnastyboy § i`m not at liberty, to discuss § would like to know why my eBay account has been replaced by dead ladybugs. user name is "good_and_bad_days_haver_1963" § my great-grandfather died protecting his farm from a pack of coyotes. i died from overexerting myself in a money booth at blizzcon § the president has never once been filmed taking a bath. he is presumably very filthy § you walked across the entire great wall?? well one time i pushed my dick into my body with my thumb, got scared about halfway in and stopped § this is thge greatest post ever made § my content is good actualy. please retwweet § isupport having my dick sucked and my ass kissed and my dick kissed and all the other metaphors for liking my posts § farm boss: yyoure so good at cleaning the pigs' ass holes. please let us pay you me: no. i won't allow my work to be corrupted by the dolar. § pavlov thinks hes good just because he can make dogs drool with bells. mean while I can make dogs howl insanely just by taking my Ass out § Spipe tv § hitler also owned three beautiful cobra's § Are u going to signal boost me or not. § foflks i want to tell you all about icecold pepsi. its good to drink that & top it off with a crest whitestrip while jacking off in your car § the government cut off my balls too but they told me the president needed them § i wish i had my baby teeth back. those were the good 90s teeth § (being trampled to death by panicking crowd) hah. look at these dumb fucks. they think im part of a floor. they dont even realize im a human § *enrolls in psychology major* finnally. this will give me the upper hand in dealing with trolls *fails all courses* college is fake actually § "Spike TV should put on a slideshow of your most celebrated posts, accompanied by a tasteful, easy listening soundtrack." well, This is true § sometimes bags of food say the true shit that were all afraid to http://t.co/Q9x0g2MrFF § i can confirm that the candid photos on Darknet of me eating a breakfast wrap are real. and i will issue an apology for the trouble i caused § rubbinb hand sanitizer all over my loud mouthed pet birds § THIS IS AMERICAN AIR LINES. WE DROPPED YOUR SHITTY COWBOY BRA INTO THE OCEAN EN ROUTE TO ISRAEL. IT SHATTERED INTO 100000 SHARDS LIKE A PIG. § girl or something: wtf did you jUst say. sounded like "xbone fail". did you just say"xbone fail" at me. me: (purple-faced refusal to answer) § a 38 year old man who is dressed like a school shooter is here too pick up his vitality supplements . § i tried to open a kissing booth where people spit in my Fucking face instead of kissing me but they eventually started refusing to pay m e § convinced that about 98% of my followers and favs are all from one awful man who is taunting me becuase I spoke ill of orange julius in 2011 § if any of you have any tips or tricks about how to make the queen ant shit ant honey into my mouth, email me at LongLegsGustin@bisquick.com § which film or work of art rujined my life the most. im going to have to say men and black 2. § i envisioned last night an older, wiser austin powers engaging a group of young adults about the evils of sex. hollywood, the world is ready § that three stooge thing where you run around in circles on the floor horizontally is actually a vital component of my yakuza training § all dressed up in my little tuxedo and ready to sacrifcie my self to isis § Ouh..!! Fascinating ! **Nodding a lot* § allow me to reiterate.. im on the side that is the least mad. whichever one that is right now. nobody knows whos more mad at this point. § I have never not been real. Aspecially during the time of this crisis, the 9/11 of enthusiast game play. § AH. ONCE AGAIN IM RAKED THRU THE COALS AND TORTURED TO DEATH FOR HAVING A NORMAL PERSONS OPINON. FUCK OFF § in conclousion, there's some action packed heavy hitter s in the world of games being released soon, and I hope you all buy them. Bye § maybe sometimes both sides... are good and bad at the same time??? im sorry if im doing this wrong. it is difficult to write § to truly under stand the #gamergate ... we must first ask ourselves.... "What.. Is.. Gamer..." **gazeing into the fire place* § ass someone who owns BOTH next gen consoles, as a actual murderer with every halo displayed on my mantle, i've the final word of gamer gate, § night time falls. im "corie latin" now. a man of intrigue. i place a bird feather into my glass of scotch and i never do posts about my dick § everyone on here would rather give $20 to their idiotic gfs. its discusting § it is important to remember to empty the recycle bin on your desk top every once in a while if you delete a lot of files § male model: washing my luxurious long hair is so boring. i wish my entire body was bald like you me: Now the healing can begin § its sunday morning which means u boys better either be in church or staying home because of another gynecomastia flare up like the poster me § Auh.. Beer! Theres nothing LIKE it! 123 cups of scalding hot Beer on my office desk. Dont spill it now, it's good. § JAMES BOND: (Shoots his gun at the screen in the intro and murders me) ME: Now that;s cinema § thats the worst one!!! dont say it § difficult 4 average joe like me to schedule some time to "Jack Off" arounf here; with all these tragic anniversaries fucking my calendar up § micheal_jackson_gets_horny_on_jeopardy.swf § did you see the twteet about dog piss i just did. its good § that woul,d be the exact opposite of interesting § HERE WE GO BOYS !!! http://t.co/Npd9Am9Js2 § engage my turds doofus § your satire . § who wants t o read some extremely embarrassing opinions about how i believbe the @mtn_dew twitter account was taken over by a false dew fan § **instnatly teleports 1000 years into the future where theres millions of new things to have good opinions about* HUUhhauih, .. Uh.. BLuahgh § pleased to report my custom beer tap that makes a dramatic diarrhea noise while filling the glass is a hit with the boys at the fondue club § (sees parking for electric vehicles, does the smug grin/ shaking head thing) what's next? ? parking for circus clown cars? § for my dedication to the brand. . ive decided to treat myself to an affordable vacation package in ssplendid, extraordinary "quicksand hell" § i click online expecting praise from mny contemporaries. instead i get an ass pic on my monitor and i immediately start wheezing into my lap § im going to urinate all m y damn cum out.. dont read this if youre Male § some children get really angry if you tell them that all nasa astronauts are cigarette smokers, but its true § i would really like to wipe this spilled chili off of me but all my towels are fucked up right now § You Won't Believe How Many Legs That Spiders Have § fifty two year old mamn hides underneath a tarp at work and jacks off to the same cartoon characters he did when he was thirty years younger § no. im tim crap § FBI AGent: We have given u a new identity because of the death threats your bad posts get you. Youre Tim Crap now Me (as Tim Crap now): Cool § please donate medicine to my boy son kim jong-un, who was assaulted by a fawn & became too sick to attend the royal korean spaghetti banquet § please pray for the safety and health of my beautiful child, supreme leader kim jong-un § SARGE: WAT IS YOUR MAJOR MALFUNCTION SOLIDER !! The Impervious Millennial: im Gay sir. I eat shit. Bazinga SARGE: I... CANT... BREAK... HIOM § hello unionized jackhammer fuckers. could you please go repair some other road?? im trying to suck my wife off § i feel as thouggh ive been tasked by a greater power to keep the riffraff of twitter in line, through my gift of words § the "Seems To Me" collection by @ Dril. Thank you for reading it § seems to me.. sometimes... you just have to say speak the true things which remain unspoken. § seems to me like im more and more the only person on this site who tweets wiht Integrity. § huge amounts of vomitting hav.e, made me good at howling § i want to become a master plumber so i can make shit rain on my enemies § please enter the wooded area behind hardee`s when you are ready to be lectured about using corn cob holders by a fervently diapered imbecile § a god damn beer and some salt water § my wonder-ful beer men @BeerManJohn @BeerManSteve @BeerManCraig @BeerManMax @BeerManLeo @ BeerManRick @BeerManTim @BeerManChris @BeerManDan § i wear the crown of thorns before every time i click submit . . . § if a sniper shot me i owuld run over to where he is and kick the gun out of his hand and kill him because hes not specialized in melee fight § ah, i can smell it,. its just about ready. *opens the oven up and pulls out a sshitty burnt up ritz cracker* my perfect boy's lunch § nice shoes idiot. nice pants. nice head. nice face. nice legs. nice feet and mouth. nice eyes. nice dick, ass, hands, tongue, ears, uh, neck § stonehenge actually sucks and i hope someone pushes those rocks the hell over real soon § the massive pair of black angel wings that i wear to the gym fucking stink like shit now and they wont fit into the washing machine either § it may not be necessary for me to reply to every post on my feed with "I Agree" ,b but it is appreciated and nice, and I will never stop § go fuck your selve § pleasse read the article "Why I Choose To Masturbate" by Mutant Turd for truly valuable insight into the mind of the common masturbator § hello folks. country singer tim mcgraw here. thank you for listening to all of my songs http://t.co/179MwAgExq § whuh?? isis is good/? **slams face into monitor leaving a head-shaped hole* Whammo. Fuck off § looking around with high-tech goggles that display everyone’s raw denim stats on a sleek HUD. i’m screaming because they’re fused to my head § @BasedAnap the onion av club shoudl review my tweets so people can make graphs about how good i am § Im at town hall getting a permit to have e xtremely bad opinions about guitars § now im a man whos been eating his fuckin spaghetti, i tell you what for damn sure. tghat being said, toilet paper needs to be about 3x wider § (pics of hole in wall) thats what happen when i got very pissed off by the sports radio caller saying the football players should run slower § i dont tweet either § i dont follow anyone on this site, my feed is the pinnacle of cultural purity, i look at the blank goddamn page& blow kisses at it furiously § Tracks: 1.Let me take my gallon bottle of pepto on planes 2.The Catholic Church is on some Mike Jackson shit 3.There is too many restaurants § judges are bullshit, your honor § im too busy frowning at the computer to eat § my timeline.. is my empire. oftentimes i find my self scrolling through it and just taking it all in;, feeling little to no shame whatsoever § im rwriting a script about a smart and handsome army man cop who murders civilians but wants to stop murdering civilians because hes in love § they are all crooks § the forum that murdered “ravioli_dad” and “basedgarfield2”??? no thank u § Why is there anger on this world. In year 2014. You savage , hateful, ugly thing’s § everyone giving me shit over the teen things I said is mad because im able to conSistently put up the good opinions before them &get the RTs § youngsters are all fucked up due to elevated levels of incest that occurred during reagan-era protests. thats why theyre hooked on cellphone § as a 46 year old teen I would like to apologize to all old dudes on behalf of the teen generation, for decades of gangsterism and nonsense, § some people say that area 51 is a jail for aliens. i say its where the army keeps their best guns § i am not going to post pictures of the oilive oil after i shit it out, as that would be unsafe for work § to my mates online: im raising $1900 so i can drink a ton of olive oil to see if it turns to shit when i shit it out or just stays olive oil § remember to always have samples of urine, shit, semen and blood attached to your belt to avoid wasting the doctor’;s time if you get sick § theres a new dril in town and its me, the millionaire who buys twitter accounts to make them less funny § i dont know how to make the good tweets anymore, like thte one from 2012 where i piss on a ferret in a pyramid or something § tactical knuckle man § watch what happesn when a man with nothing to lose collides with 4000 “babe the Pig” commemorative plates piled next to a sears dumpster § Damn. The blogs confirmed it § is it true that the ebola man works at a @cocacola plant. it would be fucked up if he touched the cans and shit, § later that night, i post “the btk killer fuckin sucks” on the official guestbook of peep marshmallow. my opst is then removed by a moderator § the btk killer spits in my god damn face. the impact cuases my neck to whiplash and separate 2 of my vertebrae. i flip him the bird but good § piss also § underwhelm by social media..posted 6 pics of my clean mouth, fresh from dentist,but ppl are more interested in yapping at their shit friends § im a good man, a respectful man § what about i take a big jar, i shit and piss in it for like 3 months and then sneak into your house and dump it on your bed § im bad now § every little thing that U do...... Baby im amazed by U... http://t.co/z5BtJP0vNh § glorified mud § my putty stance. fuck all putty http://t.co/Ybq2iKBCTa § [(launches sack;s of burning medical waste into the side of someones house for having a bird feeder on their porch)] Fucking Bird Helper § i vow to continue improving my Posture uuntil my chest consumes the earth § no. no it is too soon. ignore my previous tweet please § society is changing, constantly ggrowing and improving, and i think it is time for spider-man to show his dick § i am serios § when the war ended, my grandpa was spit upon but kept his pride--it is in this spirit that i choose to carry the burden of Gamer . #GamerGate § mmy appreciation of pat sajaks wardrobe is extremely well known; and is the only aspect of my life that is not shrouded in complete disgrace §

THERAPIST: your problem is, that youre perfect, and everyone is jealous of your good posts, and that makes you rightfully upset. ME: I agree § whos this. Whos this guy. whys he saiying this here § thats very sad § i was buzz feed until i sold th account to jiffy lube for $100. this is common knowledge § maybe instead of a toaster they shoul call it a "Toast cooker" #normalMansThoughts § please stop sending pictures of girls urinating to my house. it ws funny when i was 16 but now it is affecting my standing within the church § worse than goldman sachs: secret tapes of me bleating like a shit-covered animal because time magazine refuses to publish my meemes § plaese help my loathsome son find a professional who will tattoo the cheesecake factory logo onto his chest with no backtalk or jokes § im so insanely hyperintelligent from spending 14hrs a day absorbing Twitter knowledge that im no longer amused by nmovies about 3d animals § my name is Destyn. i build crossbows and sell weed to all your dads and im 15 § listen son, if someone calls you a horses ass, you look him in the eye and tell him "horses asses are actually incredibly strong, and clean" § i love haivng my face and head spit shined by army men while i am trying to play rpgs professionally and efficiently in my beanbag chair § measure to approve massive depressing statue in the center of town depicting an emaciated mayor carrying a boulder that says "My Sons" on it § i dont cotton to tthat shit § archeologists in the year 4500 AD dig up a massive gym locker containing mummies of the 15 nerds who visited my website using a nintendo wii § "peppa pig" is the latest children's TV show that my followers cant wait to see ripped to shreds by my high IQ intelligence, live on my feed § well im doing uh, the angry face meme § "Device Lets Fully Paralyzed Rats Walk Again" -bunkum. i for one will not put up with this resurgence of walking rats and my followers agree § ((crrying) im sorry § its either anonymous the hacker or an angel § i dont remember how this image got on my comptuer and theres 0 results when i try to image search it § yell prayers to the lord our god http://t.co/cVC08pyfBy § it is with a heavy heart that i must announce that the celebs are at it again § ((frowning) cause im the Apps Man (depression) YEah yeah im the apps man § too each, there own § the anime web turnpike girl is like 50 yearsold now § everyone on this site thinks they're hard core but i bet if they took poison to weaken their bodies i would win fights against them handily § every one of my tweets puts me about $500 deeper in the red § HandsomeTruthTeller, Your YouTube account has been suspended for the following reasons: Extortion, Treason, § "i think that, if every American had a math book in his hand, instead of the big gulp, we would be in a better place, of the country." -Dril § hank williams jr fired from his new job of yelling in front of a chrysler dealership for calling esteemed justice sonia sotomayor a Swindler § hank william jr is not horse shit § "All My Rowdy Friends Are Coming Over Tonight" is a song written and recorded by American country music performer Hank Williams, Jr § my dick hits all the wrong notes and smells like newsPaper § ==ultimate mom pics== § someone compared it to family guy alredy. Im finished § yeah im a fake piece of shit now and im rich ha ha ha § Hell is Real http://t.co/8JRZNMkgrn § "[Tipping] is...the last refuge of toads" - Thomas Jefferson "Do not tip the waitress" - Monroe "i dont tip bitch. Reblog this" - John Adams § i see this well has run dry. time to saddle up and mosey along #TheProcess http://t.co/jwCXvyIsqQ § fuck you. dont you know who i am. im the big palooka who eats frozen dumplings on 24/7 live cam while people clal the swat team on me § Monsanto Yes #MonsantoYes § Beat the shit out of the football. Beat the shit out of the football. Beat the shit out of the football. 11 43 22 36 hothothothot § im about to get my piss tested for steroids. if they find steroids in there then ill start drinking it instead of going to the steroid store § thisi s a no take zone § "ass hole" § twittter posts a net loss of hundreds of millions of dollars each year just while i post highfalutin messages about my dick and ass § boy's in summertime... http://t.co/PK5V0t5QeV

§ damn true this § its FUCKED UP!!! I JUST WANT TO POST § its the good new meme § sometimes i wonder what this place would be like if i wasnt around to call bull shit on all the jokers... probably the 9/11 crater but worse § Eat shit § all dril is trash § imagine how fucked uop it would be to have a brain and be able to form thoughts § im a fruad. i wear the wrangler jeans despite never having wrangled a single goddamn thing in my life § o j simpson has replied to me § #SendMeToDerpConBecause im Rat § i attached a middle finger to each blade of my ceiling fan and i make it spin even when it's cold inside because it looks very much bad ass § bad tweet? where?? ha ha ha § mmy masters in agricultural science was just deemed invalid after footage arose of me dying § tthis is the new Pythagorean Theorem § i was better in the 90s before my account was bought by the actual ku klux klan & placed in a granite sphere surrounded by castrated pikemen § what donest kill me makes me stronger ((gains infinite strength from being not killed by infinite things)) § dont even know how people are able to engage Thought Leaders on here with all these trollsters, hoopla rousers and clowny boys running loose § people think people smoke weed because it tastes good. well i'm here to tell you that people like it because it gets you drunk asap § the best damn posts for free mother fucker § "WORM ASS" national prison made me into the man i am today. i would still be desecrating crypts be it not for the fine policemen of worm ass § crook § there's currently an image of an unidentified nude man making the rounds on several online circuits. please beware § you can put truck nuts on other things besides trucks idiot § and now to tackle celebrity tom cruise's claims that I look like "an eggplant with progeria". **crracks knluckles* that's uh, a fallacy § thinking of getting 1 of those Yes icons on my avatar so I can just point to it when people ask me if im strong enough to carry my adult son § im developing an app called "mr. beer". you can use it to ask mr. beer if beer is his favorite drink and he might say yes. mr. beer 2015 § "my daughter is dying. Help" no. i wil never sellout "kfc's making a burrito out of pigeon turds. hit us up with that signal boost" hell yes § i have posted at length regarding my inane balls at the cost of my family, my career and my dignity. the least you can do is rack up my Favs § nothing will stop me § im getting my rat tail chrome plated in 2015 § THE BIG MONEY MAKERS BET ON ISIS EVERY TIME § THHEYRE GOING TO MAKE A LOT OF FUCKING BUILDINGS IN TH NEXST COMING YEARS SO MAKE SURE TO INVEST A LOT OF MONEY IN WOOD § thats my son. thats my exwife. thats me. thats my gf. thats a dog § *readign own timeline* holy fuckin shit this guy should be the new dick clark or something instead of posting these on the computer for free § i think if we lower the legal army age to maybe llike, 12, we will see a sharp decrease in recreational nudity § THank u all, for sharing the Online experience with me. Pretty damn good if i do say so my self. Aahh, just breathe it in. I'm illiterate § https://t.co/FPxk0bY5zU § https://t.co/AHGJGxuUS2 § https://t.co/KY4k5H8WQC § "please post more of these" "ok" § https://t.co/MgqnikvQgT § https://t.co/LxTAQQXnxg § https://t.co/7yt904Vpfx § https://t.co/AecSDSeAYs § https://t.co/0Tah9yP4Zi § https://t.co/R1rPQUTLPU § terrific news lads. i invented my own ebola virus by lying face down on my rancid carpet 11 hours a day § stand down, citizien § #ClickingMyMouse § really lookjing forward to going through puberty again and becoming a cop § i may be a dim-witted narcissist but at least i hafve really good opinions about life and other things § (Whimsical) i love to piss , right there in my big sweatpants (Serious) No. The toilet is the only place for piss § im making a good version of "sky captain and the world of tomorrow" called "sky captain caveman killer" § **kicks a plant over because of something a celeb did* fucking ass hole *vomits into the refrigerator because the new iphone is bad* shit § @Budweiser Fuck you smart alac § grinning like a shit eating bastard on the bus because i found the exact combination of words that will obliterate budweiser when i tweet it § im nthe nice man who deserves this § i'll never. § hell of a week folks. first the apple press conference fails to impress me and now it's 9/11. whats next § Take it down § take it dowm § Some may say iim considered, the Bad Boy of controversy § the latest from rex freeway http://t.co/wQTK4Kj3zO § film your wives you god damn morons. im paying top dollar for wife footage § sorry. i sol;d my account to bubsfeed & reddit and all the bad websites. they wanted to buy it so they could put bad posts up § dick stuck in a moth ball § please contact your cybersenators and tell them to tear down the bad computers § sick of our media's unrealistic portrayal of Boomerangs , which are weak as shit in real life § the ape `s curse § #AboveCowards § im frowning at this mshit § list of activities enhanced by fingerless gloves: advanced keyboard & mouse manipulation, burying face in hands, wiping my as, pointing § koko the talking ape.. has been living high on the hog, wasting our tax dollars on high capacity diapers. No more. i will suplex that beast, § climmbing the power lines until i am less pissed off § i see how ti is. i provide the best content online to all my girl followers but when i ask to live with them for free they leave me for DEAd § https://t.co/a6CoabkcWV Fine . § leaked footage of me taking my dick off and puttingg it in a glass of polident on my nightstand before bed § i cough and sneeze into the toilet like a smart adult § bazooka joe... habve you seen this guy. fuck him. he talks shit even though his comic strip is printed on garbage instead of a newspaper § adult man stuck in glue trap given a stern talking-to from his rich uncle § this brief column about portion control written by the voice actor of "Gumby" will chane your life... § DivorceLiker § "THe Beatles" have been cancelled, everyone. they will be replaced by me standing on stage for an hour, making my dick shrink on command § cum piss poop ass § all of my tweets are normal as hell § cant wait until work is over so i can stop sitting in front of this monitor and sit in front og the monitor at home which is 3 inches bigger § i have reported the nude celebs to the Motion Picture Association of America, and the oscars. the situation is under control thanks to me § sick of hearing about the head honcho. what aobut the legs honcho. or the ass honcho. that's my opinion on honcho. thank you for reading it § it was empty. i ate the food that was in there beforehand § indonesian pirates raid my yacht and find me on the floor fucking a styrofoam container § head fully immersed in kfc bucket filled with hidden valley ranch dressing and m&ms. brand engagement locked in at one hundred percent § proof of same...... http://t.co/cjzBWlvgKn § DAD: your baby brothers missing, please put down the controller. help us find him ME: Did u read the news. Gaming is a legitinmate hobby now § inexperienced shit taker here. need someone to hold my hands while i squat to ensure i dont fall backwards into my own mess. preferably girl § i pay $5000 for a high end cpu just to get disrespected on my own god damn feed § lets piSS UP A TOWN!! Everoryone reading this, lets all choose one small town randomly and publicly urinate all over it. Combine our piss § "insane clown posse? ?" Hm. *smirking, now* Sounds like a certain web site, that i see § everyone who says my dick looks like a marshmallow has obviously never seen one before. do marshmallows have urethras in them, or balls?? no § i am actually the first guy who came up with the "aliens who smoke weed" joke, back in 2011 § thats my setup § tyler durden and the Joker and 007 agent james bond take turn beating up my ex-wifes car while i say "Cool" and "This is fine" § (does some notes on a guitar) I Have been through my life a good man. I am a clever man (does some more notes and fucks it up) I m nice too § i am selling six beautfiul, extremely ill, white horses. they no longer recognize me as their father, and are the Burden of my life § obama needs to stop writing constitutions or whatever and help my failing business sell rat hair to imbeciles § hell § @ UncleHalo i;ll have you arrested for cowardice § "the definition of shuriken is extremely broad & encompasses any thrown weapon. a chair can be shuriken, for instance. a birdbath"-UncleHalo § i support UncleHalo's idea to replace the united states penny with shuriken § Although listed as a baby cowboy hat it is actually more the size for a 5-6 year old child. Needlessly to say, I returned it for a refund. § wow i just dropped a bowling ball & out of all the billions of places it could have landed it hit me straight in the dick #GlitchInTheMatrix § grandmom kicked me out of the house because she caught me waterboarding an extremely small man § HOT NEW VID -- CYBERDUNCE EVISCERATED BY ERROR PROMPT ON LAPTOP -- #TOPFAILS -- #TOPAWKWARD - FUCKING IDIOT - WATCH HIM CLICK "OK" § if i had a billion dollars id get wall-to-wall carpeting in my bathroom and donate the rest of it to the army § attn: fucked up t-shirts incorporated-- get me a tweety bird with devil horns saying "I refuse to pay for a car wash" § i call this next 18-tweet series "The Ice Bucket Challenge, But With Piss, Instead" § mr pib § cant wait to dip a paint roller in my preferred brand of beer and suck it like a big yeti dick § im trapped undermeath thousands of hissing metal pipes but im, still going to do my updates on here § i burned 100 extra calories today just by thinking aobut asses § i hae received my 3rd warning about squeezing the toilet paper too hard at the store. acme markets has declared war on my strength training § by ripping my phone book in half I have not only proven im strong, but that Im also a cool independent guy who doesn't need to call anybody § the cops need poison stun knives so they ca n arrest me harder, and every police cruiser should contain a coffin full of beer #MyNiceOpinion § im actualy, probably, the most superbly relatable and normal person in this jail cell as of right NOw § let's talk about planes now. the pilots are flying them up too damn high. it's dangerous. I don't like it. got to make them lower § sometimes it seems like i'm the only person who cares about, intelligence-related things, on the entire online. § detective sherlock holmes examines my crass pud with a magnifying glass and calls it a piece of shit § people shoot me a lot of Grief just because my wife is a stolen bar urinal with yogi bear's face printed abovbe the drain,. and they should § most undergarments were invented and popularized by religious folk who deemed that jeans and denim were too sacred to touch the ass directly § spike tv is showing some good vids of dudes urinating and im stuck here at work yelling at saudi arabians on the phone for $156.00 an hour § 15 reasons why Comcast,m the company voted the worst in america, is actually the best one, and Here's Why: § i basically love to catch all the shit that falls off of peoples hamburgers with one of those tiny nets they use to scoop up goldfish § 100% body fat, 49 year old, normal Male. good at turning purple while lifting boulders and dropping them in ex-wife's driveway. Army strong § @RealLunchables again, I apologize. § @ RealLunchables im uploading my awful nudes to this. sorry § my dick touched the floor by accident. im a god damned foolish imbecile § let's be real. they should mkae a less ignorant version of the teen choice awards, and i should win one of them for coming up with the idea. § yeah thats right babe... im in the shower right niow.. wearing nothin but a neon green tracksuit, and some belts § blurays is a game changer. look for the bluray disks, at the store. § its not enough!! its not enough! § going to be doing some extremely powerful introspective poses on the railroad track for the next couple hours, so please cancel all trains § CONFIRmed in corocoro magazaine: "Donkey kong is Diddy kong's Mom". gamers i can assure you this is the most tantalizing gender scandal yet. § this guys losin his mind. theres just so much quality shit on here http://t.co/gdVEIr3DLe § custom long john silvers gift certificate that says "Partyboy" on it plealse § oop, autocorrect got me. what i meant to say was "i cant wait to eat shit right out of the sewer and suck some outrageously gay clown dicks" § one, of, the , reasons, my, dick, is, not, good, is, because, there, are, stains, on, it, § im sorry but if you continue to spit tobacco down my exposed ass crack I will be forced to stop unclogging your garbage disposal for no pay § (shoots all whistleblowers with the doom 2 bfg gun) thats what u get for disrespecting your jobs & bosses amd making a mockery of Employment § never. i take pride in my craft § KLEBOLD: Wtf is this shit HARRIS: "Wii Sports

Resort"? U call urself a gamer? LANZA: ... KLEBOLD: Get these fuckin trash-bags off the windows § bring me your dead pet and i will make a sword out of it for $39 § attn : man with "Pedobear" car decal who cut me off at 70mph on i-295 -- nicely donme. Superb § "my mario tip: Anything is possible in the world of Mario." - my mario tip § seeing the hospital workers dreessed in pajamas?? like "seriously?" im a sleepys mattress professional. id get killed for wearing that trash § agreeud, § nerd with lame attitude: North Korea is bad Me: Have you ever lived there. nerd: (his glasses fall off) Me: Catch you later § i think police should get extensive background checks so that i can hire all fo the most insane, mentally ill cops as my personal bodyguards § @USArmy you should invent a gun that sjhoots nuclear bullets § @USArmy im a solder § do speak to me about the economy, Cuisine trends, and middle east things. dont speak to me abou joe dirts balls, and killing me. § "durr lets leberage each others brands" "dahh okay" ((the two men rub their asses together while licking the screens of their web tablets) § cant wait til my teeth fall out so i can get those new gamer dentures that all the chatrooms are screaming about § thje opening riff of "Life In The Fast Lane" repeats over and over forever while me and the boys shoot at a septic tank with airsoft rifles § i play it smart by pissing into the toilet. § ive narrowed it down to the church of scientology & the united states marines. whichever one allows me to jerk off more wins the tiebreaker § whats the job where you dress up like a michelin man and get attacked by vicious dogs. anyway thats the thing i spent $800000 at college for § breastfeed a celeb today § dont say of this § im really mad that we as a society constantly allow our celebs to starve to death in the creul and unforgiving wilderness § S.O.S Save Our Selebs § very concerned about celeb s § you've disgraced the uniform of Police. hand me your badge, gun, hat, knife, belt buckle, cowboy-boots, laser whip, bullet purse, cock ring, § kkkjoiner asserts that theres a secret mcdonalds buried under the school and it sells guns too. thats uh, made up. thats a big crack of shit § The b est shit I ever did was shatter all the windows in a room just by doing a perfect somersault § heads up: they got free toilets at mcdonalds now § you are my commander and ch ief... always.. always.. http://t.co/CNFNFSGDrw § if by some circumstance i was given the winning lotery numbers, i would not use them, for the lottery is a sacred institution #Good-BoyThings § instead of fumbling around with a wallet i like to carry my cash and credit cards in a huge green trash bag bulging out of my shirt pocket § it would be somewhat fucking good if all the girls on this site printed my avatar out and started kiissing it ,as a joke § i do not know the official name of the pringles man. but it is NOT "bruce pringles", as the trolls often assert, § the pringles man is the ghost of uncle pennybag, the monopoly man. this is the first opinion ive ever posted so please be gentle. #BrandLore § my sources tell me he uses the toilet like a normal man. § jay leno does not urinate in his cars. do not put that idea in my head. i would die protecTing jay lenos cars from urine § Eat Shit § i had my jeans bronzed as an infant. and they still fit mother fucker § foghorn leghorn argentino unofficial § in hell you are forced to smoke weed § i want to take one of those cruises where people shit right there on the boat but apparently they only happen randomly as a surpris,e § dominating thte buffet table with a pair of Sai § duhh aduhh aduh § spending my weekend retool-ing a joke about fucking the tiny hole in the bathroom sink that prevents the water level from increasing toom uch § [apps help us day to day in our lifes... but some men have twisted the apps to fulfill their oqwn selfish desires. beware these 'dark apps'] § awfully bold of you to fly the Good Year blimp on a year that has been extremely bad thus far § "auuahuhuh" some nerd who wears glasses probably right now § bread has never been good. let it be known on here that i will never eat the shit food bread. § (crying now) my friend QuiznosMale needs lijke 2000 sq ft of carpet by thursday and none of you are helping him with the carpet § Hell Yes;. the army is putting me and my guns on a plane back to iraq.

Thius is like real life DLC § i got a big wet piece of corn and the cob in my bindle and i cant wait to run it over with my truck after im done chewing on it § i am going to plunge a sword into our bed and officially end outr 40 yr marriage if you do not stop yelling while i am recording my stream's § being in full control of tthe shit that shows up on my computer monitor makes me feel like a sort of twisted conductor. .. or perhaps, God. § when the trolls have my internet access removed i will not allow that to end the content flow. i will nail my insipid "Tweets" to my car § iwant to outfit the scope on my sniper rifle with net flicks § to the longhorn steakhouse which refused to serve me: a bib most certainly counts as a shirt § a "keg" is teenspeak for a large barrel of the vile drug known as "Beer". they can be as tall as 12 ft and are often used to crush policemen § when will the supreme court weigh in on people who jack off to feet § by day i'm a mild mannered toilet specialist, but when i pick up the contorller i become Vance Hardgamer, rreal life murderer extraordinaire § scorlling through massive amounts of online clutter empowers me § nice no true scotsman fallacy. hm, typical tu quoque fallacy. ah, the classic "grab me by the ears & crack my face with your knee" fallacy, § will calling the police about this affect my backer status § i call evbery four-legged animal I see a dog and I am correct more often than not so I will never stop § they should make dunce caps that have positive reaffirming words on them, like "speed demon" or "Wolf" § going to burn dOwn my power lines and go off the grid for a bit until all the smug butthurt drama fedorra script kiddy fanboys take a hike, § all girls on this website... im here to protect u from online swearing... pleae... please understand.. § llove saying "damn" § some times it's the small things that are good #Truth_In_Life #Deals #Abominable http://t.co/jKgDkdYEzZ § i poisoned it for laughs § please remember to click on the things i post here to see how many favs they got and to sneak a peek at the buzz that they are generating. § (i shoot you with massive plasma cannon that sounds like a jet endgine when i shoot it and turns you into blood instantly)suprise fuck face! § barney doesnt actually die. he just becomes more and more obscured by bulletholes until i close the window. hes still smiling. fuck this app § @ Dril_Analyst thank's § i weawr blackface while i game to improve performance. i have no intention of racist. That will be the final post before i turn my phone off § im going to have to put the tiny padlock next to my username until people stop oppenly disparaging the Food Pyramid § ive accepted that i will have to reincarnate into shitty microorganisms like 50 quadrillion times before i become something cool like an ant § i love having molotov cocktails trown at me in the cyber cafe-- not. idiot § kfc sextuple down is back. pieces of lettuce and tomato encased in perfect cube of processed bird. "The most vile fucking thing imaginable" § ((speaking too close to the microphone at press conference) I have never watched a single episode of the Teletubbies. They look like fools § a man does a wheelie past you in a motorcycle. the back of his jacket says "TAKE DOWN THE POSTS" § please stop saying barnum & bailey is suing me for "stealing their clown routine". they are suing me for very serious and legitimate reasons § yes but i nnever do searches on him so it's weird that this happened. § do it fucke r. everyone on this trash website has already seen each other's dicks. i am not afraid § im really sorry to everyone whose twitter immersion has been irreparably fuckefd up by me posting that § fucking.. actual yes http://t.co/eRm6R1S0lu § lvoe to perform aerial leg drops on the referee § i left a diaper filled with pulled pork at 1 randomly selected radio shack in the united states. whoever finds it gets to #BringHomeTheBacon § the only crime dick cheney committed was being born into a world where goofusmouths are allowed to flap their gumms at true mighty armymen § U have accepted an E-kiss from "ShirtRemover". U have accepted an E-kiss from "ShirtRemover". U have accepted an E-kiss from "ShirtRemover". § my favorite part of nascar is when I vomit all over my shirt and car after the race., desecrating the logos of the brands that enslave me § all off them § i did certainly tilt my entire hosue 45 degrees just so i could install a zipline from my orthopedic gamer cushion to the toilet § surgury to become japanese. Surgeruy to become Japanese § Im sucking off a big ass onion right now. Urrghh § i dont know. i have never seen a doctor who § im crying because doctors banned the cure for low T again § you gotta cut the shrimp down the middle to get that good turd out, § FULLY IMMERSED IN THE TIME LINE-- AH DEAR LORD § advising everyone on this dumb ass website not to block me to ensure that my sub par written word can reach your grubby shit smeared devices § the emerald nuts corporation deducts my pay substantially for each death thrreat i receive so please stop it § i will skewer the trolls at last by scanning a legal document whichc states that it is entirely permissible for me to weep openly at perkins § i get dozens of compliments about my perfect ears every day. it's llike Shut the fuck up. Im trying to eat a bagel in my car and you do this § @mtn_dew @TacoBell SEND TACO BELL YOUR DICK § i am indeed a friend to sports. let everyone who claims that i am not a friend to sports face the grin reaper § i can't post the reason i need a wife from this website by june 30 because that info is private. grow the fuck up. all of u § ok. i basicly need one of the girls on this website to marry me by june 30 and i am absolutely under zero obligation to send you pics of me, § my combat jeans deflect most bow and arrows shots and also prevent me from thinking about sex § good to online shop http://t.co/O03IU6pZmJ § @TimHortons LEAE ME THE FUCK ALONE § yeah im shit i know i know § feeling extremly threat-ened by gamerscores § if you like the band sex pistols you will also enjoy my band called "the gun pistols" § Respectfully, The Tim Hortons Nihilist § i'm going to be the one who makes a "got milk" parody so good that everoyne forgives me for trying § attention all cops on reddit who have murdered people ; was it Awkward? what gun did you use. did you get a promotion § Baffling lack of respect. § i live for the tears of all baby huey fanboys. their suffering is more essential to my being than the blood flowing through my veins § oh whatd this?? another death threat in my inbox? well know this, i fear a world of subpar bird tyranny more than death § i will nevr add baby huey to the famous bird list. he wouldnt even make top 40. i will NOT back down on this, U obnoxious, ungrateful pricks § please God if you're out there I ask that you turn my praying hands into bird seed so that I can no longer bother you with dumb ass reqUests § i did eat an ant farm once § im going to zap myself with a taser gun unitl u two stop fighting on my tl § (fantasizing about dangling off hood of my moving car adn touching the truck nuts on the jeep in front of me with tongue) hell yea, actually § now that all of my last-gen hardware is completely obscured by Animal shit , #e3 2014 may officially begin § probably, if I got night terrors constantly id just say something like "This is fuckin cool" instead of taking all kinds of pills and shit § how would u like a taste of fuckin basooka ammo!!! or else!! § #OpenCarryGamestop http://t.co/FBgdCAunvG § *sees the e3 logo on a website, tthrows head back and screams the word "Epic" before immediately defaulting to aberrant emotionless state* § most famous birds: 1.Krfc   2. talking parrot who said "i love you" the night he died 3. thanksgiving turkey 4. tweety bird 4(Tie). Phoenix § two truths & a lie: (1) i use the fatsuit from big momma house 2 as a corset (2) im in trouble at the dump (3) please dont reprint this info § just the other day i was taking a bath and i saw a tiny tugboat in there leaving a chemtrail. i told it to fuck off. im a green beret gunman § im a jornalist § will e3 have designated crying booths. im sick of crying in the bathroom where people shit. § take, this down § i would not sit that close to a fountain in real life. they are disgusting breeding grounds for all manner of microscopic vermin § but enough about my dick. today, I would like to talk to all of you about the Toilet. § Im goig to drive a nail through my cock to promote ABC's "The Middle"", and I will be paid $18 for doing it. § kudos to FX for promoting a tweet with horrible eyeball gore for some bad tv show aand pissing off a bunch of ladies http://t.co/AWLuMk4akP § a series of incurable skin conditions have caused my dick to look like Darth Maul's dick, and that's the only good thing about me § .@KonamiCode-Knower i know yorure online. i know you've been stealing handfuls of gravel from my driveway and hiding them in your big shirt § casually discarding styrofoam container filled with buffalo wing remnants into the passing stroller of a baby § Damn true, this § as torrents of horse piss splatter clamorously onto my forehead I scream in absolute torment but make no attempt to move or cover my face § dont really care if my gaming chamber has black Mold all over it.. ill just curpstomp pubbies with my shirt pulled up over my nmose § i would sooner die than relinquish ownership of my dale carnegie mousepad to either of my fat sons § i attribute the complete failure of my brand to the actions of detractors, oor my "trolls", as it were, as well as my own constant fuckups § im joining the army and then im joining ufc if im not too fucked up from the army. and thats the cold facts § just kidding. i'm normal intelligence § let's all kick the BTK killer's ass, all of us who make the good tweets,. we've got to meet up and beat the BTK killer's ass and go on dates § blocked. blocked. blocked. youre all blocked. none of you are free of sin § i'm pisser #1 http://t.co/a9Fz0kxh8h § checking my computer chiar for GPS Trackers, left by ex-wife or cops § copy puste this if you think that rhinos can kick humans ass ,even if humans are using the guns. § my nudes.. have strengthened my brand. apparently barkeepers glue them to the back of their urinals to stop people from pissing on the floor § "if youu die in hell you die in real life" - demon philosopher matthew § the wise man bowed his head solemnly and spoke: "theres actually zero difference between good & bad things. you imbecile. you fucking moron" § ANGRRY FUCKIN BIRDS.... HOLY... I CAN'T EVEN. . § just me again reminding all of you seriousyl dumb motherfuckers to get your daily sperm count. some of you are walking around with weak cum. § society has shown its ass once again § i see it everyday. it is nothing to me § do not show to me this you ho § cleanning my assault rifles with wads of toilet paper § fuck your ma ma. piss off your own ass § infinite amount of alternate universes where i shit my pants during my wedding which will only go away if i break stephen hawking's computer § "oh this?? im only wearing this shit in case i need something to wipe my ass with"-something i just said to impress all my shirtless friends § oh and also thanks for the troops § and dildos do not count. any schmuck can put a dildo in its mouth. that is the coward's method § i donjt believe in porno my friend. but thank you for interacting with my page § regarding hideous new happy meal box: has anyone put their dick in its mouth and took a pic yet. will they send me coupons for being the 1st § the onl thing i can drink without vomiting anymore is diet peach snapple mixed with skim milk and breadcrumbs § water is fucking gross. it tastes like nothing. assholes drink it § let`s get this insane takedown virel § baby food > cat food > human food > dog food. just the oipinion of me § THE COMMON IMBECILE: the movie "cars 2" is better than the movie "cars 1" ME: alas this nation has truly gone, to the dogs!!!! § sorry grandma. your laptop was good but i shattered it into 1 million shards after i saw someone say SEO stood for "shit eater optimization" § thank you RandomMan. thank you Don. § if youre that guy who emailed me last month asking to be my "intern" come forward so me & my rich friends can smack tennis balls at your ass § interseting. it appears "emotions" were basically just rrage faces that people did in real life, before online existed, § Bastard § moseying up to the girl on campus and whispering in her ear "got that fuckin pizza hut p'zone in my backpac" and straining my face intesnely § i'm convinced that people only favorite my tweets so that they can use them to fuck me over in court at a later time, since they're not good § please wellcome Irony Cowbell to the world, my beautiful newborn daughter who will be named that forever § ived hacked into your beeper, champ. enjoy your inopportune beeping §

i’ve decided to open my account back up after a brief cooldown session with lobsterfest_ralph. § every other twitter account is in direct competition with my own. i would never compromise my status by promoting any of these pigs § im doing it soon because of the crap. § im going to close it as soon as im done browsing my updates. § this has gone too far. im closing my account until people stop accusing me of being mad. i will also spend most of my time offline laughing § if i unfollow anyone i will absolutley be murdered by them. im basically in prisoned. § retweet is a sham § im about to loose my shit if my feed doesnt slow down with th fucking posts. nobody could possibly read this fast. this is a travesty § my world renowned “miserable adult cam” feature has been removed due to complaints § spit takes are funny but if you do them in real life people will call you ass hole § i am a local politician and i just want to lick this fucking ridiculous huge lollipop without people photographing me and ruining my career § your post has bbeen Hotbugged by DipShitx666 § “________ favorited a photo you were tagged in “ SDONT YOU FUCKING DARE § just made a cool $30.00 from leting scientists hook me up with electrodes and watch me Game for 16 hours #IsThisHeaven § “hello 911 I need a moat dug around my house immediately” ”sir this line is for emergencies only” ”Thuis is an emergency moat” § i know thiis isnt the popular circle jerk opinion, but people who swear while speaking to the 911 operator are gross § probably like 4 of the wildfires from the news were caused by my shitty extension cords used for Nature Gaming. ha ha ha sorry firefighter’s § my guest bathroom has 99 fake toilets and one real toilet and i use it to test the toilet abilities of all my guests § boycott all games that don’t let me play as a cop § i was banned from club penguin for roleplaying as a toucan § who ever told me that kim dot com’s secret doge coin stash was bureid under the roof of my house is an idiot. i just dug a hole to. my house § please contact me if you own one of the six corporations who controls 90% of the american media or if you’re of the dragen race § https://t.co/fPhdrAwpPs Gudetama Sanrio English § ass is the most poisonous part of the human § my mansion sucks § ive already accepted that im going to hell because I mispronounced church as “gurtch” once § im tierd of extroverts crucifying me and my cool introvert friends § confidently reclining in my seat after calling my onlinw adversary a “shitbarn” § my opponent’s eccentricities are well known. hes probably the one who drank bird bath. he is on record as calling birdbath water “bird juice § the latest rumor ;which i dont even care to discuss or give a shit about, is that i was seen drinking out of a bird bath on easter sunday § also, the cop zone feature is done now § sorry, for a second there i thaught the real hank hill retweeted me. § (bored in apartment on two week administrative leave after nuking a 14 year old girl with a napalm launcher) THIS FUCKIN SUX !!!!! § i love to use fists, poison spray, or gun agaisnt the citizens, depending on how mad i am § --------------- COP ZONE ---------------- § i want to tattoo ancient Runes onto a dolphin § danzeisen: i need the logo to be a shitting ass quigley: but were a sports company danzeisen: draw that ass up pronto http://t.co/HFI2PaIDUG § i epicly agree § break your lips mother fucker § hows my nuts tastes § i dont understand trash talk. i t think everyone should just agree with each other. it’s easy § this is a very important thing in the economny § drunk driving may kill a lot of people, but it also helps a lot of people get to work on time, so, it;s impossible to say if its bad or not, § †‘†‘†‘ U Are Now Cybernetically Engaged Via Intercom Uplink To The Realm Of TheBeerPope †‘†‘†‘ § they just said on the news that there’s a group of hooded grotto dwellers who are legally changing people’s names to “Beezo” posthumously § in my version of indiana jones he shoots the boulder with a sniper rifle hundreds of times instead of running away from it § yu fucking idiot i wanted to make a sniper rifle out of those toilet paper tubes and now that theyve touched the trash theyre no good to me § billions of people are shitting and pissing everyday. it’s too many.

it’;s poisoning the earth. consult your laywer before using the toilet § my fucking content is flawless. you fucking bozoes have gone too far with this shit. youre the one who looks ridiculous; not me § u know irt’s a Monday when you rear-end a cop car and your trunk pops open, launching 500 or so jars of piss onto another cop car behind you § free julian assange § it is absolutely impossible to leave smartass comments on my page and lead a happy, fulfilling life at the same time. i need to believe this § the us government has its top men working day and night to invent a paper towel that is large enough to wrap me up and dispose of me § the family gathers around the PC to run a google image search for “invader zim crying” § BACOn is some fairly good and epic shit !! Wow http://t.co/hHxvEWwHxr § My (new) Twitter value is $0, according to http://t.co/zzZzntzRrD ... What about yours? § weed is a type of crack § once again its up to me to take the high road. while everyones making jokes of the fat weed smoker mayor ill be whipping myself in his honor § i dont trust banks. especially the pig shaped ones § daily reminder that i wear a suit and tie daily eeven though I have not set foot in public for over 16 years #GoodBoy #Hansdome § i will say this. when I finally ascend to the final plane of consciousness .nerds will get extremely yelled at § fuck no. due to luigi’s bullshit there will never be a year of anybody again § https://t.co/cetUVljy9Y baby mario is not mario’s son in 2014 § “guns are the most inportant weapon of our time. lock and load. see you at the Range.” - anonymous § im husband to him § donald trump has no time to fuck. he looks at his watch and says “i could not possibly fuck at this juncture.” as he powerwalks into the zoo § Sorry fucked up § It’s Saturday night. Hand me the cold one fellas § popular youtube user “LunchPhreak22” often enjoys “Phreaking” his lunches by poisoning them for the amusement of his viewers § i wont let nasa sent me to mars [does the dx cross chop with guns] fuckin alright § metal chains begin to fly out of every hole of my computer while i scream like a fucking iddiot in a child’s comedy film § joke’s on you; i actually love being body slammed by one dozen perfect wrestlers. and my mouth isn’t filled with bloodm, it’s victory wine § https://t.co/ckN8qthgZ1 +||+||+||+ HAcKeD by KFCDominica +||+||+||+ ,,\\,, Fuk U ..\\.. +||+||+||+   ï¸»ãƒ‡”³• ãƒ¼ /ÌµÍ‡Ì¿Ì¿/’Ì¿’Ì¿ Ì¿ - /ÌµÍ‡Ì¿Ì¿/’Ì¿’Ì¿ Ì¿ § me: i dont even care if they cancel sports howard stern: Thats wild § truly we are living in the worst of all possible hells § speaking of war crimes, some say the white flag of surrender was inspired by a piece of toilet paper dangling pitifully from my ass § “Ur honor, if Mr Pibb was truly this man’s uncle, then surely hed be able to dazzle us with Pibb Merch” JUDGE:damn he’s right. No Pibb Merch § average person online: Durr!! Durr!! Me: That makes no sens.e Please be reasonable and not post the most inmature shit. § dis charged from the army for doing memes too much § please check out my new article “Allergy Season is Fucking Good Actually” which will shatter your precious little minds and make yo’u cry § im obviously being punished for my subpar output, § nnone of you are supposed to read these § im the smart adult with my shirt pulled over my head so I can play holdum poker on my phone with out having my performance affected by glare § i will be at bradlees dept store promoting my new line of mustards for the next 16 hrs and I ask that nobody tries to assassinate me please § [man leans into doorway of WTC bathroom] “Hey, you gotta finish up in there. 9/11 is happening.” ”Alright. Just a sec.” § AUUAHHHHGH § im not goiing unless the good people of http://t.co/hdBR2JqY9X can raise $200,000 to transport me and my hardware § i will devour all sinners in the name of all polite boys online § where were you when Pibb_Lord_Janus posted his epic takedown of “Betty Boop” § juust not in the mood for content today... not while my fellows are being hunted down in the street like dog ‘s just for preferring Blu Ray- § actually, i have big red burn marks on my ass for a cool reason. i fucked up smoking a ciggerate § why would anyone want to put hell on wheels. what kind of satan would allow this § there is no football position known as “Sniper”. ive been tricked by this load of crap § content 2 http://t.co/hST5OWjymR § mn, http://t.co/NdnbekAZDO § i cannot die... not toda.y.. there's still so much SUperbly Awkward Shit to reblog § some opf the things people put on this website set off the old "BULL SHIT" detector..... § id like to report an error of the googleglass please. if you accidentally wear it backwards it sends video of a big horrible eye to everyone § i'm wild about Setups § i receive a generous amount of funds from the US government, as they believe that my good tweets are an effectuive deterrent to masturbation § uh oh... think I feel another BIEBBER RANT coming on !! #TheFamousBieberRant #MyBreadAndButter § just give me one hour and no swear filter and i can literally completely destroy anyone psychologically with aim instant messenge § i am sick and tired of having my page mocked just because ihave a lot of good opinions on apps, on hashtags, and all of that good shit § @bing answer for your crimes, fucker http://t.co/P6FMEnbz0o § its good. no wait, its bad, because theyre all morally bankrupt and Heinous brand murderers § ARMYMAN: the US military now Officially endorses cruel and unusual torture agianst qdoba fanboys and Ignorant-Minded people ME: b-b... badass § wiping your teeth down with toilet paper or giving them a quick spray with the hose; that's the good shit. toothpaste is flim flam from hell § please put a helipad on my shitty roof § handsome single adutl man contracts scurvy after eating nothing but oscar mayer lunchables for 4 years and blames his dentist § the asimo robot is full of rats. nobody ever washes it § cops need grenades. doinate all of your hand grenades to the local police force or face insane cop torture forever § @ASIMO you look like a nerd made out of diapers § @ASIMO im going to knock its teeth out § @ASIMO coward § ill destroy him in public and then i will take off his space helmet and unmask him § asimo is a weakling. it cannot stand up while being punched. they didnt program it to fight or defend itself. i will probably win this § i'm going to beat the shit out of asimo. im gping to knock it on its ass while its trying to use a staircase at a trade show. dreadful beast § im going to power up my content in this year 2014 by divorcing my wife and crowdsorsing a new gfx card for me. thats my guarantee § theyre bad except me § no!! its all too much! § i regret being tasked the emotional burden of maintaining the final bastion of morality and NIce manners in this endless ocean of human SHIT § i swear to everyone on this site that i am truly, truly a good and compassionate person, and i have a completely normal dick that isnt small § well i believe its time to ugly up my face with some techno baby bullshit to show everyone how unapologetically humorless i am #throughglass § my dimwit sons love it when i drop them off at the car dealership for 7 hours while i cruise around for bargain's § Enjoy New and Exciting Recipes Including Buffalo Chicken Mac & Cheese and "Mac & Cheese Gone Wild". § Want to say thanks to PedophiliaMan for this comment? Give them a month of reddit gold. Please select a payment method. PayPal BitCoin Credi § **shooting bow & arrow into huge pile of discarded diapers piercing like five or six of them with each shot* now that`s what i call Combos § the idea that people are still masturbating in 2014 is insanne, and utterly, asinine § @Garfield false flag § i cried when the genealogy researcher told me this § just found out my great-great-grandfather was known as the "piss scoundrel" and spent most of his time being harassed by concerned citizens § @CheetosArabia thank you officer § online is sickos § im bad at running and moving around but my upper body speed is incredile § #IAmNotALiberalBecause im proud of my greasy, orange ejaculate § the ass cynic has posted a brutal 1 hour 40 minute takedown of my ass on youtube. im warning you not to click on it or you will get a virus. § ive got my eye on you matrix_gary. § i am closing down the craft brew wiki because i am being treated like a zoo animal and nobody gives to shits . § mantis is a small green dog. not bug #CancelColbert § #CancelColbert gangstalking me, collecting my piss, laughing it up with his fucked up buddies when I ask where my piss went, carrying on, § please stop owning me § it,s a piece of shit for sure § i approve of congres... i believe they are doing a very good job despite negative comments online § #RuinAChildrensBook i dont have a camera but rest assured that i ruined it & made sure that no child will ever derive emotion from its pages § *understands tthe full potential of the net all at once and stumbles backward wwhile struggling to breathe* christ,. my god § i love absorbing knowlegde from the expansive breadth of electronic information that exissts on this plane we call OnLine. its good to do it § some animal just uploaded about 40 or so uncircumcised dicks to my feed so im unfollowing everyone who isnt a business man or a cop § can I get into legal trouble for secretly filming myself on the toilet § my massive shoulder span constantly prevents my tiny ,malnourished ass from absorbing sunlight. my body is essentially at war with its self § i have cleaned all the dirt out of my fingernails and will be posting new pics of them shortly. i want to be liked on here. § taking my laptop into the Jungle... § ,showers are, ,actually, ,not good, § just my opinoin. back off § fred phelps is still alive. and will continue to make trouble for all of us good people online. thats my beliefs... § my priceless stradivarius gaming keyboard... fcovered in policeman urine § that's where all the good shit in life comes fronm § adult man who must frequently be burped like an infant or else he will die § for a 2nd time, a user has threatened to go to the bathroom on me. ill tell u this. only way thatll happen is if ur leaving in the body bag. § its my big son § "We will wipe out Twitter. I don't care what the international community says." "They will see the Turkish republic's strength," he added, § Turkey's prime minister has warned that he would eradicate Twitter after a number of audio recordings anonymously posted on social media pur § "Gamers" needs to grow the fuck up. § those are shit. open up the yellow pages and contact a leg man immediately § all of the rumors that i'm crying right now are: 1) bbutthurt 2) gross 3) KuKlux klan § my dream uncle would have the calves of an angel...and the thighs of a Devil § yerah i like to click on my mouse. so what § widgets. ... theres nothin quite like 'em #TechBoys § i have to clean myself with a dust devil because my bathtub is filled with sacks of rat chow and i believe that all of politics is hogwash § *produces a tiny book from coat pocket which lists every breed of dog that is legal to eat* § hoo boy... these guinea pigd love to shit. shouldn't have ordered the full dozen § thank u my friend § motorists are advised not to touch the mattress. the cops are on their way to beat the snot out of it with hammers. do not interfere § theres a fucking mattress lying in the middle of route 70. it's still there i think. check it out if you're in the area and you like mattres § @WeBuyRetweets hit me up via my personal line: cumDrenchedArmpit@imbecile.com § no hashtag.. no rant #NoHashtagNoRant § curly is the most bullshit stooge. his antics are the least believable. moe and larry would have kicked him out of the stooges in real life § i lose about 6,000 followers eveory time i make one of my humiliating tweets. the cost of business § llove to look at a big slice of meatloaf and say "Damn it's good" § i hope my followers are remembering to urinate frequently, to ensure the proper disposal of bodily waste. § A Funny Dog Join Kurdish Tribe For A Dirty Dance . § *glances towards framed calligraphy print on wall which reads " ASCAR First" and nods goodly. * § you utter fool. od not come in here asking to see rocky's dick. that is not the spirit of philly § sorry i ruined Fucking talk like a pirate day by speaking at length upon my terrible mustard allergy which has caused countless pain of me. § @favstar1000favs FUCK OFf § im glad i made that post and wrote it and thought of it. im glad it belongs to me § i don't want to shit today. § shit § i'm looking to be hiring a very nice girl to crack open pistachio nuts while i Game. must have clean fingernail.. no hucksters § my name is steve jobs. i am a successful ceo in charrge of the apple corporation. #Joke § im looking at bible, now. § single fellas-- do NOt jack off into the garbage disposal. it will jam up and make a horrible noise. use garbage bags instead §

ive enclosed an image of judge judy and my stepdad kissing that I photoshopped to express my disapproval of the broken paintball gun verdict § there is a time and a place for clowns and it is called "CIRCUS". not the computer § headshot all these beasts with a tiny gun § my next good post is about egg salad. What in the shit?? are you egg or salad? Why is this good. Who's eating it. Check Please. uhhh § i get in my car and 100 men smear their asses up agsint my windshield and doors. Unbelievable. I'm late for work. This is clownish. § meanwhile im going to stay up all night and color my dick with markers § Sigh. the trolls are beating off their weiners again § brutally headbutting massive hoards of benghazi likers § eunuchoid 49yr man puting self up for adoption, please. unemployable due to frequent nosebleed. loves movies & Tech. thank u for reading it. § this is what a real mans hands look's like http://t.co/yjLlfqOi24 § THe "Oscar Selfie", is, in a word, Huge. Representative of a New-New Media paradigm shift. It, was a solid move from the celebs. § chating with lawyer on aol instant messenger. § i will annihilate all spoofs of me . i will take anyone who does spoofs of me or my beloved content to the court of criminal law. § apologies to guys named "clay". that's like one step above dirt § need to gain. concerned of my big boy status. dream of becoming Army Strong by the age of 35. rip me open another bag of tiny marshmellows § i am far too clever to jack off § there are secret offices all over the country full of men in business attire who consume porn for 9 hrs and go home. they dont even jerk off § the joke is on you fuck face. i actually love getting screamed at and publicly shamed for my dumb-assed bull shit . I love apologizing § no. no birth § on line § i've been spending the last 7 years of my life making a romhack of super mario rpg where everyone is pregnant. i expect to make $100 from it § to whoever changed my background pic to spider man with his dick out, thank you. im keeping it just to make you mad § ive never heard of this "europe" but it sounds like a big bunch of shit to me § i am a Gentleman's Son and i deserve the big gravy boat § my pet iguana' s get angry at the same tv shows I do.... wierd but cool § just yanked 3 bundles of rebar off a construction site and into my truck. now im going to biuld my own pizza hut § if this is true you need to go directly to police . § it's Damn cold out there! Hope you got shirts #WebAndMediaContent #FrromTheContentBoy § Wawa has always been nice to me and I give it six platinum stars § Mentioning the woefully fated thursday nite rant feature to me constitutes harassment. Let's keep the trash out. I am a real journalist now. § me after getting curtains stuck in my waistband and pulling them off the wall: "ah fuck its happened again,ah, i am truly a shithead, oh no" § my favorite holiday is the one where you cover everything in plastic and turn the hose on indoors and just go wild § i have moved all of my bitcoins directly into my brain for safekeeping until all this nutso crap blows over § climbing the empire state building holding a giant baby bottle labeled "Muscle" § sipping some campbell's chunky soup from flask in coat pocket § discreetly enjoying a small amount of beer i hid in my gun § jsut want to take some shitty roll of wallpaper from the 70s and tell the Men's Warehouse to get their finest craftsman to make a suit of it § MAINSTREAM: Barney the dinosaur is some good shit. I like it. It's really good. ME: Barney the dinosaur is bunk. This is a show for children § there bad § thinkting of putting a sign up in front of my decrepit mississippi swamp house advising the band Pussy Riot to keepaway § they are always on tv carrying on § if i were police i would send bugs bunny and his shit pals to prison for violating the constitutional order of the united states of america. § @tjefferson1976 thank you thomas jefferson § thats my baby boy. my dim wit son § #AnimalTVShows pig fucker § #AnimalTVShows ape fucker § #AnimalTVShows dog fucker § *all horrors begotten by the desire of man flash before eyes* woha! this is awkward *the cries of millions suffering echo* Damn That's Weird § i just divined a glimpse of everyone who has ever unfollowed me talking at the bar, laughing about how bad my posts are & i fucking screamed § #TheThursdayNIteRant hashtag is now Public Domain. I am permitting twitte'rs worst users to sully it with unauthorized, low-quality rants. § Fuck #TheThursdayNiteRant and the bruise it has left upon my legacy. Fuck contracts and being tricked into signing them. Fuck Ruby Tuesdays. § i dont think the monster truck gravedigger has ever dug any actual graves. it would be a very disrespectful and loud way to do it § i feell like im being unfairly targeted during this paintball match just because im the only one wearing a tuxedo § any good jokes lately? yeah, the mirror. i mean your mirror. i mean your mirror, while you are standing in front of it & i'm not in the room § "I envision a dining experience tailored specifically for the public masturbator. Therein lies the Soul of the Roy Rogers brand."-Roy Rogers § i dont do that anymore. i broke the contract and im cursed now § Thank;s all. Remember to fav and retweet the thuings i put on here also. Get the word out that my posts are good § i will do it. i love the good shit favstar § pop this into your browser for a quick smile : "urkel" § i love to frown upon bull shit § It has recently occurred to me that I am constantly being clowned on. The people I trust most have apparently been clowning on me for years. § thjis could be possibly considered to be a rude comment of me. § Hot Pockets Yanked From Shelves for Containing €˜Diseased and Unsound Animals€™ #AreYouTheOne § i suppport the duck dynasty boys and i support gay also because i am a kind, reasonable man § go to bed trolls. go to bed with your dip shit brigade. § intense dr pepper cravings from being mentally mpreg., check. dick looks like an ear from botched circumcison,chsck. 1 big purple arm, check § it is unfair that i should have to go to hell just because i was born with a pigs brain § i am interested ni "meme format". i am going to experiment in "meme format", to improve my page. http://t.co/UELlEWJl-po § Jacking off is a fool 's errand. I will instead opt to enjoy the films of Ice Age, Ice Age: The Meltdown and Ice Age: Dawn of the Dinosaurs. § I Love To Bring My Ass § me and a bunch of stupid assholes are going to start a community in the middle of the desert to either die or prove a very important point § @null____void @NBCSports i hope they do because it is the worst picture i have ever seen § #TwitpicYourDunkContestReaction http://t.co/rtHgmE5A7n § i am constantly motivated to improve my content so that i'll someday be as good as the guy who got his dick stuck in a trampoline on youtube § if someone comes by asking if i would like to see pornography i say "hell yes". if someone offers me beer or wine i also say hell yes to it. § i will tell you this right now: I'm from hell. Im highly fucked up. Ive been known to say rude things and watch the carnage unfold brutally § please let me edit my tweets so i can go back and remove every reference to pig piss and liking pig piss § #TheSaturdayMornin-gRamble cant do it anymore. the ramble has taken control of my life & my doctor has advised me to stop before it kills me § they never shit. they have no need for bathrooms. they converted them into offices. i will not "hold on" § nobody at PepsiCo, the parent company of Pepsi & Frito-Lay, uses bathrooms. this comapny prides itself on hiring people who never shit. § dick fact no.77: my, dick is covered in clothes most of the time. this protects it from the elements as well as the gaze of my enemies § need some new Christian podcasts to listen to while cruising around in my fake cop car § might bring this tweet to the office€• a guy drinks a cup of coffee but it's actually a gravy bowl by mistake?? is that appropriate for work § @BreakingNews i want my spoilers mate!! stop hiding the spoilers fuck face!! § Im a goalie in personal life so I know a thing or two about deflecting personal attacks against my life as well as hockey pucks. § to the countless many Whom have plagiarized my hard work by using the retweet button "Thou art a Coward" !! i will beat your ass at the mall § I SO MUCH AS DIP MY NECK AROUND THIS LOG PAGE AND I AM FORCED TO ABSORB GALLONS OF VENOM FROM DISRESPECTFUL CIVILIAN VIPER SWINE #StopTheNSA § *loads up youtube playlist "Every Geico Ad Since 1999" sitting in ultimate gamer chair eating peanut m&ms with spoon* euauh! good shit, this § i was one of the villains in

WWE. mmy name was “Loser Fuckface Nerd “ and my catchphrase was “i cant fight them! theyre too strong” § me and the boys are going to watch the final leno and then watch every episode of leno in reverse. full return to thence Leno. #lenouroboros § a 90 year old man looks at hula hoops “they dont make’m like they used to” now hes all started up “theyre SHIT!! these are picees of SHIT!!” § i found a bunch of those bugs that roll up into little balls. i called the zoo & they refuse to take these horrible bugs away from my house § #TheSaturdayMorningRamble sometimes it is good to get off of the computer every once in awhile and spray garbage around the yard with a hose § jay leno was the last good boy on tv. he was my final connection to th e outside world. there is nothing stopping me from becoming feral now § Now is not the appropriate time to discuss content. § Jesus christ. I;m so god damn sorry. This is so fucked up. It’s a living nightmare. I am literally shaking. I have never felt such pain § I am a coward. I beg of your forgiveness. And please check out The Saturday Morning Ramble, which is still scheduled for release on Feb. 8 § I didn’t want it to end like thtis. I am so sorry. My hands were tied. The rants weren’t getting enough Favs so the sponsor pulled the plug § I have a confession. THe leaking of six thursday nite rants on monday was a false flag operation designed to kill The Thursday Nite Rant. § it is phenomenally cruel of people to come onto this website, look at the posts on my private feed and share them with their shitlord pals . § Take this shit about the coors brewing company down § gotta go name brand. it is non toxic and not actually made of shit so it is fine to drink. § bougt a bottle of “liquid ass” to teach my stepdad a lesson but i consumed the entire bottle by mistake. now i drink “liqiud ass” on the reg § im ignoring the contract and i dont care if i go to hell § i don’t care about anybody’s opinion unless it is good. before you type, please ask yourself. “Is my opinion good” if it’s bad dont write it § yea everyone called me Dixie Cup for years juts cause I asked if it was alright to use a dixie cup as a condom in sex ed. im cool now though § my son has been combing his hair without permission. how do i cope with the pain § @policeman i will assist u sir § they will be destroyed so they do not fall into the hands of my predators § and i will state right now that these recent events bear no weight upon the popular “saturday morning ramble” feature. Thank you § my laywer is telling me that the bastard who hacked my account and leaked my rants is none other than edward snowden, known traitor to USA. § there is no recovering from this fiasco. the thursday nite rant, as we know it, is dead. § @ Twitter HELP § yo bartender!! we all know you filled my deink with ice so you can skimp on the good stuff. hows this grab ya: “ o Tip” #TheThursdayNiteRant § “whodunit”?? how about we just call it a “murder mystery” insTead of resorting to that grammatical mess #TheThursdayNiteRant § STOP IT I CAN”T DELETE THEM § smiling is worthless. it has no value. nobody wants to see your damn teeth all the time. fuck you #TheThursdayNiteRant § my living room has more remote controls in it than NASA. its like you gotta be an astronaut just to watch the ball game #TheThursdayNiteRant § WAIT FUCK § why do clowns have such big shoes. that’s not funny. it is just ignorant. no wonder circuses are dying #TheThursdayNiteRant § if I download just ONe more app I will need an APP to keep track of my APPS!!! #TheThursdayNiteRant § punxsutawney phillip seymour hoffman sees the shadow of death meaning 6 weeks of really good jokes like this one § i think that the dog version of the super bowl shoyuld show some god damn respect to the regular version of the super bowl § From here on, I will refer to the upcoming Super Bowl as the €œTreason Bowl€ . § 75% of the tweets on here are complete PishPosh. 20% is Networking and Implementation. the last 5%? Pure Content. #TheSaturdayMorningRamble § i am nodding and grrinning at this, completely unaware that it is probably a grievous assault against my character § i cannot comprehend half of the things i read online but i’m smart enough to know that it is all really good § i live inside of the holy mecca cube and do all my good posts in there § I don't deserve to watch the super bowl § the famous "dewey defeats truman" photograph except it's me holding up the hedaline that says jacking off cures prostate cancer § http://t.co/pt99s1DgAZ good § check the shit o n the lightbulb before using it. too many people are using the wrong voltage count and it;s too bright #TheThursdayNiteRant § Q: What is your Passion Sport? A: My Passion Sport is football and golf § i'm not allowed to participate in the olympics this year because i have " o discernible athletic talent" and my "dick looks chewed up" § group of young woman: were going to take some "Selfie" portraits. care to join us? me [doing the face palm face now]: ABSOLUTELY NOT!!!!!!!!! § i just sold all of my teeth to the president of starwars for one hundred dollars #SBMediaDay § yeah im basically all abOut mpreg right now. yeah im off to get my huge pregnant gut enchanted by a warlock so my future son will respect me § *consults a sundial* Ah. Time To Carbo-Load § sometimes i feel like im the only person on the whole damn computer who understands the concept of Honour § i must rotate in my seat eternally to avoid having my muscles damaged by wi-fi energy § i bet i could knock a grammy statue over with my piss #grammys § mindsweeper is a game for children sorry § i am a simple country man who believes that hackers belong in jail #TheSaturdayMornin-gRamble § I Have beatten a game of solitare after having to restart only 26 times. I am a magnificent gamer prince § i have been racking up absurdly high scores in Windows Solitare to increase my power as a gamer § no. it is a very powerful online tool and i love it a lot § id like a discount on this used tort law textbook please. the last guy who had it drew female versions of Garfield on a bunch of the pages § Actually fucking this . § MetalGearEric has offered to engage me in a formal debate as to whether or not santa claus's real name is "Winter Claus" § the facts are: actual little two year old children are coming onto this website to send me brutal reprimands daily and make me violently ill § It's basically extremely good except when they arrest a cool guy § In my honest opinion, due to recent events, they should call beloved pop sensation Justin Bieber, they should call him "Mr. Jail". Thank you § the boys of washington § #TheThursdayNiteRant please build more walkways so i don't have to fuck my pants up in the bushes § justin will prevail #FreeJustin § i love bait. cant get enough of it § barbaro is back 2014 http://t.co/Z73UqNki19 § it's the name i use to commit crime under § i have never fucked it up § i have about 250 rants in thbe can, ready to post, as well as 500 more that need minor tweaks before becoming availbe for consumption § nobody has earnestly called a donkey an "ass" since the bible was written. stop fucking up my clipart searches with this nonesnse § 611 Ass illustrations and clipart. Affordable Royalty Free Stock Photography. Downloads for just $1.00, with thousands of images added daily § my true custom rig is a baby grand piano filled with lava lamps § vladimir Putin if youre reading this please grant me asylum like you did with snowdan. i too ,am constantly in hot water because of my posts § i would have to say that this promotional radio shack lanyard i received heavily influenced my decision to become a lanyard wearing guy § carefully cutting out an article titled "Ex-tremely Small Man Begs For Life At Disneyland" so that I can frame it for the rumpus room § i interface the dunston check 's in dvd with the God Processor. a gruesome polygonal ape head welcomes me to dunston world § incoming picture of mysterious bead collection from WolfRespecter § piss is not a profane word. it is a body part § ill fix it soon. i will fix it § #THeSaturdayMorningRamble sometimes when you get caught in traffic you just wanna get pissed off § Italian mobsters beat rival gangster with metal bars before feeding him to pigs, police investigation claims http://t.co/oXsuBfWC1q § JAY: They are going to replace WTC, with a Mosque. Can you believe this Silent Bob SILENT BOB: This country is headed fot the chamber pot. § i squint real hard while attempting to contemplate a math problem designed for children until my entire dumb ass face turns navy blue § my ultimate quest to become a united states armyman begins by rejecting all forms of online drama trash in my life #TheThursdayNiteRant § im sorry for claiming that all cops wear big fake boobs full of milk under their shirts and use them to breastfeed criminals. only some do § i would like to convert these gmail invites into human dollars please § i can't seem to do anything without being owned by shirtless males § now that Ned Neutrality is finally dead he will be sorely missed, survived by his wife Cathy Neutrality, as well as his kids Ethan & Walter § now that nest neutrality is finally dead I can start blasTing the shit out of birdhouses with my 9000000 calliber rifle scotfree § now that net neutrality is finally dead i can share my controversial tony hawk/NASCAR cross fiction without fear of persecution or ridicule § i would like to apologize for letting the team down by eating an entire snowman over the weekend and getting sick. my head wasnt in the game § the one major design flaw which plagued the iron maiden from the start were the large spikes that would stab anyone who tried to live in it § society will not accept me, the 142 yr old man with the grab bag of severe helath problems, consorting with their prized youth § i shoukld be allowed to do kindergarten again. im pretty sure i would absolutely fucking nail it this time § prom is filth § Weekly reminder that the official Oprah App can be enjoyed by Oprah fans and supporters of Anti-Oprah alike. § 12 year slave huh? sounds like my marriage. which I dont enjoy. to the degree that it is succinctly described by that particular movie title § Charles Chaplin § i have in my hand a list of hollywood bigwigs who have eaten human flesh, and i will reveal one name each day until im provided with respect § i've been blacklisted from hollywood simply because I refuse to compromise my unwavering support of Microsoft brand and product. cowardice § winner of best reality program "Mushroom Sons", beating out "Extreme Mushroom Farm", "Mushroom Grabber" and "Boys of Mushroom" #GoldenGlobes § if hollywood has any dignity left they will surrender all golden gobes to the united states marine corps and blow a bunch of kisses at them § some hipster or something is probably mad right now bc they give golden globes to good ass films instead of the fuckin mona lisa or whatever § this post isn't respectful to me, this post isn't respectful to the saturday morning ramble, and it isnt respectful to the dead guy § #TheSaturdayMorningRamble was cancelled out of the respect of prime minister ariel sharon . please stop asking me about it. rip ariel sharon § please help mme. my dad sent me $40000 to go to Fight College but I spent it all on making a big hormel foods logo out of gorilla glue § but worry not. i have changed my last name to "apefucker/" to dissuade all women from stealing it § another fucked up thing that women will do to all good men and boys is steal their last names, poSsibly to leverage their own failing brands § Remembe,r if you're a fan of the rant, feel free to support it with favs, retweets, or just drop me a message saying how good it is. § with all of the running around we do during the holidays... its a wonder we don't LOOSE weight instead of gaining it... #TheThursdayNiteRant § if u troll me into my 11th stroke by god i will use the last remaining strength on my death bed to implicate you and your delinquent cronies § now that i'm unemployed I can finally weave an intricate fan universe based on the chick fil a cows who are always holding the signs up § the web is an extremely powerful media tool in our Time and I will masterfully cross chop and do bare hand takedown to anyone who disagrees § fired for "unleashing rats at work" which is bull shit first off because they don't make leashes for rats § put pictures of fat 1920s babies up next to the muscle builders of modern day & you will ssee that their skill levels are considerably equal § i just obtained a tub of that goop they fed to babies in the 1920s to make them really fat. i;m going to convert the whole thing into muscle § bowl fucker #RejectedBowlGames § im the only person on this entire website without a wife and it is just ignorant at this poin t. § *inhales sharply and punches a sofa 6 times extremely quickly* § shut the fuck uip, coward. "beavis day" is not a real holiday. i am going to insanely wreck you for posting to me, about the false holiday. § all sponsorred content was put on hiatus during the holidays. it will return next week along with the thursniterant. § yesterday i bought a 26ct bag of fun size snickers bars as penance for wasting a police man's time § my main shit is going to CVS and doing riffs on whatever i see on the shelves. most of my material is never recorded or heard by human ears § sees another grown man eating cheerios off his table at the restaurant, gives him the restaurant cheerio nod § yes, the rumours are true. i do workouts § "tthis is some superbly phenomenal shit." -spoken by president barack obama, upon following his 650,000th twitter account § i fear change § reluctantly jacking off at 60mph to the girl silhouette on the big rig mudflaps in front of my car while whispering "trucker's code" § LING240 - Foundations of Applied Linguistics Transfer Equivalency: WAZ101 - how to do wazzup voice (4 credits) § that is one subpar app § @GirlHelper i support girl helper § myth: making me mad is cool FACT: making me mad is a crap move& people who do it are all sociopathivc criminals with fucked up rotten brains § when should i start embalming myself § ijust gave some guy in the bathroom $200 and he left. i think i own a toilet now § the knives will beat the shit out of the ice § im going to fuck up antarctica with hundreds of throwing knives § i don't believe in religious, but i respect the fear of nudity § ill be spending new years encased in marble with magnetGirl77 because we just basicly trust spirit world more than human world at this point § nothing pisses off Baseball more than showing up at the plate holding a custom djinnblade, designed by your cousin Chedson, instead of a bat § Time to do several fucking perfect wolf howls at the nascar men § my top 2013 picks: 1) guns 2) pictures of guns 3) halloween thank you. please look out for the top picks of 2014, which i will do next year. § this faker is puttinh me through hell. but i can see through his lies. i can tell he is not me § school lunch card revoked indefinitely for making a counterstrike map based on the principal'/s rock garden § "RESULT: You are the Serpant. YOu dislike loud places and people are constantly putting drama in your life. But you're strong." This is true § IF SATAN IS READING THIS PLEASE MAKE THE FINGERBOARD ON MY DESK DO 1 FLIP § cavemen were 14 feet tall and immortal because they didn't believe in Lying § a dozen eggs huh.. what are you gonna do with 12 shitty pregnant rocks. haha just imagine some asshole buying this like, "oh these are good" § back before the web, Content had to be delivered house to house by the content man. he worked 14 hrs a day & people tried to shoot him a lot § no. not yet § about 85% of the people online are just absolute criminals and i can get dominated by them perfectly from the convenience of my shitty modem § [download of "bagel covered in caesar dressing.jpg" complete] Ah, Fucking Good This Yes. Absolutely Epic Fucking Particularly This. Sir § the saturday morning ramble will be cancelled as well. thank you for your cooperation and understanding. PLease enjoy the holidays. § the thursday nite rant is cancelled due to christmas. it is also cancelled next week due to new years. the rant will return jan 9th § no. no. no. and no. santa would never do putrple drink. keep the jokes stashed deep in the garbage on this holy night § i'm going to shut down for several hours while user "JFK_Destroyer" reconsiders his threat to "suck my grave like a dick," § i chose to disregard the advice of president barack obama and continue posting § if i was fake that would be fucking insane as hell § "When it is Christmas, the only gift you need is my posts." -@Dril when it is christmas, the only gift you need is my posts. § ah, online is amazing. there is so much to do here. *GETS OBLITERATED BY INSULT`S AND SICK IMAGES* i've changed my mind. online is childish § @TherealGeorgeZ RATATATA /ÌµÍ‡Ì¿Ì¿/'Ì¿'Ì¿ Ì¿ Œ •¦•¦• "€ - - - - BOOM BOM POW /ÌµÍ‡Ì¿Ì¿/'Ì¿'Ì¿ Ì¿ *CLICK* BLAM BLAM BLAM BLAM (Philippians 4:13) § Stop owning me § The office space judge, to the trolls: For refusing to stop being a piece of crap i am sending you to 15 years of pound me and the ass jail. § tthe super computer lit up and told me my posts were good in a fucked up robot voice, validating me forever online § IBM sent me a supercomputer to analyze all of my posts with and guess what, they're all good § life and death § i stepped out of my stretch limo with "garbage toucher' painted on the side, brushed some shit off my boots and said "I'm garbage toucher" § i like it. thank you http://t.co/ulzjhHpfuL § the old dog one featured a twistedly brutal amount of blackface thoguh § @CrackerBarrel wher can i pickup merch ft. shitty beard guy who needs all sorts of wile e coyote shit to hunt the most pathetic animals ever § i give this picture two thumbs down because it is gross § i dont respond to threat § Shit myself on C.Martinet's lap. Voice of Mario. He was surprisingly chill. Too embarrassed to apologize so I bought Mario Golf a week later § "The film was universally panned by critics. It received a "rotten" rating of 5% on the r" let me stop you right there. thats a lot of crap § i plan on spending christmas with the kranks by putting the dvd in and playing it. i want to spend christmas with the kranks mother fucker. § the most fucked up thing saddam hussein ever did was eat doritos in jail § i Fucking disagree § i craft my own rigs § when it comes to down to it.. you just cant beat the old mouse and keyboard #TheSaturdayMorningRamble § GOD Damn fuckin.. Retro,. classic shit, ah *Face Turns purple and begins crying* sorry. i'm sorry. I'm a dipshit. I'm a fucking idiot § this guy took a pic of an NES cartridge on top of a filthy carpet and.. yep. the game on it is one i like. im pretty sure that makes him God § this is the room where i simulate combat scenarios by performing wrestling moves and crowd control techs on 22 girl mannequins. the gauntlet § i;ts a cut above the rest #sponsered § i am looking forward to some god damn serious male grooming discussion when everybody runs out of jokes around 2015 or so § gotta pick one man. the night ain't over until you pick a favorite pope. "all of them" is not an acceptable answer. "clement xii"?? Fuck you § my permanently wet forehead is perhaps my most powerful weapon § rip to this guy http://t.co/JZL3q80llC § i want to network with clean human § thank you for looking at it § listen bud! get your i pad out of my face! leave the gizmos at home #TheThursdayNiteRant § FACt: i was not kicked out of teen mensa beucase of my extremely poor posture; i was kicked out because of my terrible opinions and ideas § i really hate him § big steel drivin' hank gordon bubba once told me i aint once put on what it could not do, but to what i can't do on what i put myself on for § $0 § My Friend Toby Once Said, One Big Ass Biker Man I Ain't As Good As I Once Was, But I'm As Good Once As I Ever Was § digimonotis thought octomom was the bad guy in spider man 2 § my belt buckle explodes, exposing my superbly problematic dick/balls to eveyrone at GarbageCon. it also ricochets into my skull and kills me § the Harvard bomb threat guy svhould have called a bomb threat to octo mom's house instead #UHOH § i test all my tweets on lab animals and they hate them all. im an embarrassment to BRand Culture § I Want The Duck Dynasty Boys To Crucify Me Upside-Down And Piss On Me Violently. I Want The Duck Dynasty Boys To Block My Useless Account § An Unstoppable Legion Of Young Fortune 500 CyberHeteros § a typical day for me involves putting on the football vest and throwing the fuckin pigskin around. and i am not sorry if this offends anyone § at first i thought that Science was a shit waste of time. then somebody did a meme of it,. and now... hooboy.. now i like it § Death Caliber § getting all the snow out of my driveway with a gun, just fucking obliterating it § This guy got himself into another mess. Take a look http://t.co/vkNx1Pepmj § if you see it published anywhere else but here i expect you to alert the proper authorities with 911. § i can only do 2. they are refusing to fund me § i dont have enough funding to do another one § The Saturday morning ramble is Work Safe. Children are also allowed to enjoy it. The Thursday nite rant is vulgar and unleashed § the thursday nite rant isn't going anywhere. the saturday morning ramble is designed to work in tandem with it to cover broader demographics § it will be as good as the thursday nite rant once i get better at writing them and my stress levels decrease. § academi §

it's new § get yourself a few dozen trash bags and stash them in a drawer somewhere. never know when you might need em #TheSaturdayMorningRamble § CORRUPTED EARTY'H... § isnt it wild that every time i look at pictures of hell i say that it looks like some cool shit, and that i would go there instead of heaven § Where's The Good Shit. Where's The Good Shit. Where's The Good Shit. Where's The Good Shit. Where's The Good Shit. Where' § that was it. the rants over. stop sending me messages § Showtime. Feel the sweat on your palms. Face the hideous, bloodthirsty crowd. All eyes on you. It's all or nothing. It's #TheThurdayNiteRant § yeah babe. im 007 license to kill. im basically really fucked up and mentally ill from all the murders I did.**yawn* i got a gun tattoo also § woah. just realized the "Hungryman" logo on this can of sloppy joe is referring to me, the guy buying and eating thhe food. Insane mindfuck § *stares at a man doing jumping jacks in complete awe* How is he doing that § just thinking about how two guns mounted on my wall in an X pattern would look really good over my toilet § The six things I could never do without: €¢ . €¢ gamer § they made 666 the satan number because that's how many hours it took me to learn how to roll a cigarette § when i cant decide whether to throw up into the trash can or the toilet i throw up in the trash cadn & pour about half of it into the toilet § my hobbies include wearing cool clothes, getting sucked off and being involved in local theater. The last one is a joke, actually § surefire investment: Saline. everyone i know is injecting a lot of it into their dicks. THat's, "Saline". Surefire investment. Locked down. § i got banned from the official red lobster forums for posting "9/11". yet they say we're living in a post-9/11 world..... § http://t.co/Rv3QUakY5C my life will soon become this #SEAvsSF § in the future james bond gets serious and stops having sex § I'm Sgt. General James Bond. My mission is to collect guns and gather intel on the unimaginably fucked up drugs known as Cocaine & Marijuana § Arts & Entertainment § i don't know anything about comedy. i specialize in arts & entertainment. § stood up, faced audience during larry the cable guy movie, and shouted "YOu're all monsters, stop laughing at him, that's his regular voice" § You'll Never Believe Which JP Morgan Executive Utterly Eviscerate Fitness Blogger Moms Flat Stomach Selfie #WeirdNews #CoolButWeird #Offbeat § Girls are my wife constantly § im upset because nobody wants to market anything to my ultra fucked up demographic § ultimate glaze § **makes a loud inhuman noise and attempts to crack wacom tablet over knee* § yeah im supposed to be "offended" by spit on my grave. youre basically feeding my skeleon nutrients. also spitting in graveyards is illegal. § surprise, dad. while you were witnessing the pennsylvania state lottery i tried on all your work gloves and they looked very handsome on me § ruby tuesday is a small business. fuck you § it was my idea to do the " tuesday nite rant" to tie into the ruby tuesday brand, but they said that idea was shit. they wanted thursday § http://t.co/JY4AeVyu29 heres the thursday nite rant contract, as requested § i am getting hundreds of messages telling me that the thursday nite rant is very bad. i am contracted to produce them until june 2015. sorry § #TheThursdayNiteRat was a typo caused by the fatigue and stress of managing my online business. It is not a real feature. § the knock out game is a lot of crap. Lord heal oru youth . Lord heal our youth #TheThursdayNiteRant § a tiny lapel pin shaped like the twitter verified account icon stops the assassins bullet and spares mmy cruel, filthy life § "Mr. Legs Dubai 2006" § this is peak hours in romania , where most of my fans live § the facts are thuis: i accidentally did benghazi while trying to steal nfl broadcasts and im sorry about it. this is a stressful year for me § asking someone why their halloween avatar is still up when it's just a normal pic of them is the most fucked up move you can do, actually § the scud missile was named after famous military physicist Scud Missile § sounds like a real fucked up idiot to me, § I don't know who that is Mate . § if satan tries to put a microchip in my gun i will shoot him § this is a trick question § i dont need to answer this at any point in time § i have modded gta 5 to make the dicks ugly. and i plan to make them even uglier in ugly dick mod v1.1 § attribute my creative decline to deep spiritual sickness caused by several pornographic hairstyles i accidentally looked at in time magazine § "god damnit!" the coach rips his headset off "they covered our football in nerd cum! those bastards have covered our football in nerd cum!" § what me & the boys enjoy most is going to a home goods store to laugh at all the toilets. saying "haha i really want to shit in there", etc § **sticks vacuum into skintight rubber suit so it becomes even tighter and dick and balls become more pronounced & visible* ugh!! mondays § need to wash gamefuel stains out of a very expensive kimono § i dont know what that is but it sounds too good to be real § i can infer that the owner of this car with "Wade" painted on the hood is either named "Wade" or enjoys the word "wade" for personal reasons § my new job is being the guy who says "Sir You Can't Film Here" repeatedly to people who bring recording gadgets to aldi markets § did everoyone else in the unemployment line get one of my favstar printouts? good. i will take my seat on the floor now § noticing a lot more rear collisions after adhering my "9/11 Was An Inside Doge" bumper sticker. people must be too busy laughing to pay attn § too many false alarms from people yelling "Bingo is some good shit" or "Bingo is fuckin good". becoming a problem in the bingo community § the wrong side of town. just a bunch of signs on the side of the road that say "Moms Earn Cash" with no phone number or email or anything § just tape the car horn down and cars will naturally move away from you. you can drive anywhere. it is called, "The Instinct of the Beast" § seems to be confusion regarding the job offer. you just directed me to an amazon listing for clown makeup. Looking forward to the real link. § i thitnk, that, before you wish death upon someone, you should make sure their tweets are really really bad first § "The Thanksgiving Day Parade is not canon. The events depicted therein have no place within the Garfield timeline." - Jim Davis, Paws Entmt § is the thanksgiving day parade canon. are we to believe that garfield would allow himself to float around and be yanked around with strings § is that real. dont hassle me § please set your home pages to http://t.co/vahp3VrtsA . it is a better web site than twitter. no trolls or loudmonths, always free. § Keep an eye on "Apps", in 2013 and beyond. § media outrage over the discovery of geiorge zimmerman's Gun Sink, a kitchen sink filled to the brim with guns § "Depression" § use coupon code "Do Harlenm Shake" to save 10% off your next Divorce § local singles want to meet you in YOUR AREA! click here to call the COPS § i call upon familiars david blaine & criss angel to help me discretely wash this pocket pussy in the soda fountain at the peiwei asian diner § this is the makeup rant because i fucked it up last week. the normal schedule will now proceed after a brief thanksgiving hiatus § "sour cream and onion" ?? thats a bunch of shit from the get go #TheThursdayNiteRant § Seth i mean. § Moneyhats all the way down. He doesnt csre about the true fans. He killed the dog for profit.Just follow the big dollar sign § well, i'm planning a move. the democratic people's republic of korea?? strongest cops in the game. flat out. Make our cops look like shit § i want to crush it between my shoulder blades § i spend lots of time thinking about how many of my depraved, miserable followers would murder me if they could get away with it #SocialMedia § i see jokes like "doge". like "angry cat". and I think to myself, "This is fucking actually good. How can I interface this with my strats." § for every child you don't circumcise i am going to circumcise myself 3 times § i am working to resolve the thursday nite rant issue. please do not contact me § my more astute readers have noted that i botched the hashtag. its not supposed to be "the thursday nite rat". i cannot fix it. its locked in § my blood glucose test strip unboxing video maintains a remarkable zero views despite me spending $8000 on Media courses #TheThursdayNiteRat § http://t.co/RvRHIaehDr here is a cool list of "weird tweets'" § This channel is dedicated the the beautiful smoking girls of

Japan. These videos aim to capture the style and elegance of the Japanese girls § i just put the phone in the sink and turned the faucet on. i was not about to deal with that level of bull shit. § “your posts, they aren’t good.” obama told me over his personal phone line. “you have to put down the keyboard. you have to #StopThePosts”. § its true. each cow’s udder has one teat that will shoot piss instead of milk and ruin the whole batch. they call it the Farmer’s Gamble § actually i take “the big bang theory” and the good word “bazinga” very seriousl. § bazinga fan 80 § i have been pacing the driveway for hours, trying to work up the courage to tell a t least 3 twitter girls that i have married them § *steps out on stage twirling a cane and accidentally hits self in the dick 100 times * AAAWGHHH § two cars in the garage, a white picket fence, and monster energy logos embroidered into both ass pockets § enjoying my “BEER O CLOCK” tshirt? yeah I got a whole hamper full of these badboys at home. you can come over & look at them all if you like § Real.Time.with.Bill.Maher.2013.11.15.HDTV-NO.SWEARING.EDITx264-2HD[kkkdracula] § gamers are stupid assholes huh? well guess what. the final fantasy titles taught me roman numerals. check this shit out: XVCXCXCVIIIVX § i step into the vip lounge. i see a man in high heel shoes stepping on a carton of milk while other men in suits yell at him and throw coins § CONTROVERSIES: lots of people jacked off to “beetlejuice” because they thought he was a girl. it’s perfectly normal & good [citation needed] § i have trained my two fat identical sons to sit outside of my office and protect my brain from mindfreaks by meditating intensely § nuh uh. This is crap § “favs.. retweets.. they’re all good as hell. You’re basically here to get those. Without em, you might as well be posting into the toilet,” § Im not fucking serious or mad right now § listen up i need u guys to go on my account and check out this post called “The Thursday Nite Rant” and dont forget to hit up that RT button § in that case i would advise your uncles not to attend. § i dont know about you guys but my uncle has been dying to meet all your uncles. did somebody say twitter dot com uncle meet???? § im one of the good whites § i feel like some people don’t appreciate the effort i put into TTNR. frankly, all i can do is feel embarrassed for you. it’s a good feature § sometimes i post serious things but, i like to have a little bit of fun on here too #TheThursdayNiteRant § whenever i see someone eating without a bib i laugh and shake my head. beucase i just know they’re going to fuck their shirt up with stains § typical “Weird Twitter” circus clown, hiding in the garbage from the Truth im constantly laying on them . § everybody is jacking off to their follower count and it makes me sick. iits just a number. stop jacking off to it § thank u. every night i wake up screaming because of the weird twitter circle jerk . i dont take this site seriously though § yeah right johnny cash. we totally believe that you went to jail & got executed. why don’t you sing about real things instead of doing irony § “Daniel Joerger” gave the Adult Dunce Cap a 1/5 star review on February 20th, 2013, saying it was “Junk” and “ ot worth what I paid for it”. § http://t.co/jxTBUplNC0 just gonna leave this here.. feel free to buy th e stuff on it. to my house if you want to § i had a stern talk with my son over how his purchase of a $0.99 hdmi cable represents failure § In my sincere opinion, 7-11 is weighing down the Big Gulp brand with their clownish chain of filthy convenience stores. § its time to face facts. our teens just arent creating any jobs. they have failed our nation § im not breathing correctly because of the amount of people who insist on showing me the number of 69, which is the password for sex. § chridst. god damn it. not this number again § how many pushups must I do in order to boost my wifi signal § ihave been banished from the city of dubai due to my excessive sweating and practice of pyrokinesis § http://t.co/gpmcAVSRXa I Have Found My Calling. Good Bye § “elvis” is the filthiest musician alive § roving online gangs are promoting disrespect of brand leaders on this very platform #HonestyHour #Police § get this crap off § @PizzaHutCares @LanaDelSunreys the pizza hut pube team § i think that wearing a jumpsuit emblazoned with the official logo of my twitter account while i indie develop would make my posts good again § ALL SHIT § sing to God § if each of my followers send me 1 rag i might be able to clean up all the messes in my house § graceful and poignant § even if you only know the basic techniques there is over 100,000 different combos you can do. the government is hard at work naming them all § you see that fucked up mattress over there? that's where i practice my combos § effects i mean. § are thtere any adverse health affects to chemically suppressing puberty until the age of 49 § http://t.co/50D8jZjEvP #NoFuck § after careful consideration, ive decided to fuck the green m&m because they made it look like a girl. i would not fuck the red or yellow m&m § just a little casual assplay at the farmer's market § thinking mostly about throwing large amounts of them into the garbage. like 1,000 of them maybe § 1) i dont claim to be an actual person. 2) im not good § @realDonaldTrump my car has a beehive somewhere inside of it and i think "the donald" should fire it § @realDonaldTrump i dont § why isnt this on the news § just because i havent been seen in public for 7 years is no excuse not to wear a suit and tie before sitting down and eliminating trolls § unfollow me if you hav e ever done or thought about doing war crimes. i dont want war criminals shitting my feed up § this is the national health advisory board issuing a safe reminder not to touch your dick for one hour after handling pets § @NBCSports thank you for making the sports § Thank you for the follow, @NBCSports . § big bird was obviously just a man in a suit. but the other ones were too small to contain men. so what the fuck § http://t.co/cgIujqF0P6 Thanks § http://t.co/e777lTtelf When Is The Next 9 11 § yo Aesop... these fuckin "fables" of yours? Not up to snuff. Some weak fables over here. Go back to writing college. #TheThursdayNiteRant § the much anticipated photographic evidence that i take good care of my gumline has been postponed due to drama and agony § Had it up to here witht the chuckle crew. If you think my posts are bullshit I challenge you to come waterboard me and destroy me perfectly. § i'm really good at reciting my favorite quotes because my voice sounds like a cool movie character and isn't all fucked up and high pitched § can any of you hook me up with some sports § Absolutely not. § i live in the atlantic ocean § my previous tweet was not the thursday nite rant. first off, it doesn't contain the hashtag. secondly, it's wednesday afternoon right now § unverified accounts are fucking disgusting. they often contain base, lewd "humor", and i have mini-strokes whenever one of them retweets me § please respect the sanctity of UFO chat § no i am not talking about my post § yoiu got some shit on your monitor § ***pisses all over shower faucets, wife's luffa, candles, knocks shampoo bottles off shelf with piss stream** it's fine because its sterile § be sure to check out my repulsively athletic legs & thighs featured on the shitty offbrand bag version of wheaties at your local supermarket § Fuck U citizen § if the state ordered me to wear one of those shitty lapel cams i'd say " o SIR" & crush the camera under my cop boot while the public cheers § woah. you can say "Houston we have a problem" in messy situations that have nothing to do with astronauts or texas? this changes everthing § i think "mario and sonic at the munich massacre" could work if they did it respectfully & didn;t fuck with the formulas from the retro games § the integrity of Fav Star is at stake . I Deserve death § if i ever subconsciously steal your tweets DM me for a frree 8x10 glossy of my horrible fucking face and a good ass arby's coupon § i might cancel this week's rant due to crippling dread and other real life bull shit. we'll see § There is a widespread campaign of fear being devised and perpetuated against me just because my dick looks like a cartoon character § My dick looks like a cartoon character's § huge tub of au jus sauce with bottles of beer floating around in it is lowered into the room before the big game. " ow that's, a power play" § atticus quiznos, cornelius pepboys, baron von sega; distinguished luminaries who voluntarily castrated themselves for the sake of the #Brand § the heinous y2k bug will bow to me and my glorious rifle § you little online fucks who sit in mammas basement and finger your puds cannot conceive of the #HELL that is pushing fresh, invigorating SEO § Wow. Christ § I thought this one w as really good, actually § nobody told me that" doing donuts" was some car technique. up until now i thought that it was just another way to say you're eating donuts § im the man who got banned from the gym for trying to bring a mattress inside, and i have gotten significantly weaker since the incident § thanks for putting your failure opinoin that i didn't even want to read. § i feel like posting some more good ass posts is what i feel like § of course i am mad § the desert has never helped any one and i am going to go throw poison at it § e to § to the fine folks who kicked my bare ass while i was trapped in the automatic door at walmart: why do you people insist on punishing success § U are the cancer that is killing http://t.co/Ibe04bsbBC § its the weekend baby. youknow what that means. its time to drink precisely one beer and call 911 § to potential employer: when i said i jerk the dogs off at the zoo, that was a joke. the zoo doesnt even have dogs. theyre domestic creatures § if youre a healthy young male or female with blood type O, please consider donating a kidney to me. my goal is 22 kidney 's § you must face the mirror daily and ask your self: "which brands will i touch base with today". you have to ask it out loud or it won't work. § i do understand that it's halloween and it's only natural to want to get up to a bit of mischief, but paws off my hash tag please. § There's no greater television program than The News. The News is the only show on TV that I like, and it's smart. #TheThursdayNiteRant § this next dip of chaw is dedicated to the pursuit of muscles, and also my jeep § the aliasing in the ps4 shot is a little tighter. xb1 has better contrast, though. both of them wreck the current gen, regardless. § i gotta say both of these are looking pretty sharp. can't wait to go next-gen http://t.co/122XQOHPO8 § cops should have two guns to get rid of crime faster . cops should be dual wielding by 2016 § "And th mark...theyst fhall beckon..bearers of the Mask.. doth verily, andth post really good shit, online" nostradamus predicting Anonymous § @JoseCanseco Im going to throw all of your baseballs and baseball bats into the garbage § thusday nite rant No.4 Uncut is currently scheduled to be released on Thursday, October 31st. § it was cool when they yanked saddam out of the spider hole becausr i was like "haha that guys me before i had my coffee. thats me on monday" § the professor said our assignment is to make.. a MEme?? i've got this shit on lockdown. i pump my fist and hop on my hideous adult tricycle § government thugs § its absolutely my right to have a 90 yr old woman scrupulously vacuuming around my enormous bulk at all times while i groan and roll my eyes § hello newsweek? yeah im not gonna make it for that interview. some schmuck just pissed all over me. im covered head to toe in schmuck piss. § go ask a sex account . keep your paws off of me § what if you took jethro tull "aqualung" & replace the parts where he says aqualung with "octomom" #BeyondFuckedUp #Sponsored @sheratonhotels § my dick is a beak now § whos gonna rake all these leaves up?? the police? #TheThursdayNiteRant § some facebook bull shit § you aall act nice to me on this site but if i needed $60,000 for saline injections all over my entire body none of you would give a SHIT § One Hundred Percent Yes § my thoery is that the book is only being delayed due to stressful constraints from the trolls § theyre murderers. all of them § i believe labels are pointlessly divisive and have no proper place in our society but i'm pretty much basically a jock and not a nerd at all § i tried to throw a molotov cocktail at a bird but he was too high up § reminder to all of my female cop followers that i worship female cops daily § vermin § @Number1TCOT have you ever had your hat fucked by a dick § truth be told-- i only like the good ones § vulgar § heres my halloween costume. im going as a bumblebee http://t.co/5HVJ3coeXl § im sorry?? i was under the impression that these accounts are good???? § it's really messed up that im the only normal person on this entire site, considering millions of people use it daily § my name id yogi. greetings from albania. i would like to put the new i pad in jail. thank you for reading to my message. § looked at a newspaper today. looks like we're getting taxed out the wazoo, with this president. anyone else see this shit? tax out the wazoo § in 1998 donald j. trump sr taught me how to use a Scythe and it sickens me to see people besmirch his good name § i am attempting to enter the mind of otis in order to destroy him § phew for a second i thought i was the worst, least funny thing on the internet § the brief period in high school when DigimonOtis changed his name to BurgerKingOtis in an attempt to improve his image § @ wikileaks "harpo" from harpo productIons is oprah spelled backwards. bam. welcome to the matrix § you wanna come to my church & post about me sucking tiny ladybug dicks on the bulletin board? mm nope. that ain't me pal. That ain't my life § the real shit. § *pushes a mini-fridge over* Fuck U § please stop adding flintstone chewable vitamin commercials to the episode list. they are not real flintstone episodes. § @dril first § i bought one of those craigslist peacocks. this fucking thing wont eat and its loud § ktxl fox affiliate just showed a pregnant woman on th simpsons #pregwatch § if this is part of some elaborate mindgame i swear to god i will write some letters & i will get you fired from your pod cast § ievery thing i have ever posted is intentionally good § and the award for best banksy tweet goes to.. "egg_dad_ebooks" *seven grown men rise from their seats and push their way towards the podium* § #ObamasPresidencyInTwoWords IN1993OBAMAWASWITNESSEDCARVING ALCHEMYGLYPHSINTOAPUBLICBENCH § #ObamasPresidencyInTwoWords bun gazi § theory postulated by known troll "Zentai_Gary" states that i, @dril, go to the zoo every weekend to , in his words, "fuck the apes", and i w § watch "The Mentalist" on cbs and learn how to manipulate human minds like putty then use this info to make severe fucked up posts § now were talkin § meme 's encompass all art forms you street rat § most important art movements in human history?? three way tie between impressionism, cubism, and Bullet Time § bad news: were all helpless cogs doomed to ceaselessly perpetuate a machine good news: the machine is a Sega and were all sonic the hegehog § i rolled out some denim content last night and it was really good actually. .. § my new quote: "That's some good ass Hulu" (to be spoken after, viewing exceptional content on the hulu streaming site) § holy shit. holy shit. you can order loaves of kfc. you can order kfc in loaf form. you can order kfc by the loaf #ByTheLoaf § phew. im out of breath from looking at blades online all day § me & khryler are drawing up plans for a family restaurant with damn good jeans nailed to the walls. we will call it the hard rock jeans cafe § accidentally printing out 20 ascii wayne gretzky nudes on the really loud printer in the school's computer lab #90sHell #DecadeOfTorment § TheThursdayNiteRanter@twitter.com . its not up yet. i will post an announcement when it is up § i cannot reveal the subject of next week's thursday nite rant. my competitors will use this information against me § if the event occurs wherein i misspell the official thursday nite rant hashtag, please let me know via email and i will correct it § the official hashtag of the thursday nite rant is #TheThursdayN*teRant, with the asterisk removed. only i am allowed to use it. § if i make a rant-like post on thursday night and it dosnt contain the hashtag, it is not officially a thursday nite rant. its normal content § please allow me to explain the mechanics of the thursday nite rant. its not officially thursday nite rant if it does not contain the hashtag § the popular tursday night rant feature has concluded for today. check out the new one next thursday. it will appear on this feed. § the rant was already posted. read it before the mods get all emotional and tear it down. § hey uh, it's just the thursday nite rant. if youre offended i dont give a shit. Thats whats to be expected from the thurdsay night rant. § alright shit for brain listen up. i dont want this guacamole stuff youre peddling. its green and it looks sick. go home #TheThursdayNiteRant § as far as im concerned the best revenge is ordering wolf piss online & pouring it into soneones car. “living well” is too hard § yes. im it. § he lived a rich, meme-filled life § ONCE A MARINE, ALWAYS A MARINE. Celebrate and salute America€™s 911 Force in the MONOPOLY: U.S. Marines Edition. § got that content that drives u wild #fw @HellLife @ShitGirl @ simpson94170212 @GymGod @GunMagnet @SpitoonMan @DragonSex @LifeAlert420 @Guns6 § @saladworks im nude § haha this vitter has probably gotten all sorts of boners on the Senate floor cause of the diapers. eyes buggin out, classic looneytunes shit § if i learned anything in business school its that you can disarm any competitor by insinuating he carries his turds around in his briefcase § scuse me i gotta check this...ah, looks like my retweet was reblogged bty chief tech editor of Reader’s Digest (yea hes verified). solid mag § can anyone confirm or deny that the “spooky dicks” they sell around halloween each year aren’t just rebranded dildos § too late im already engaged to him § im not about to dignify that with a respone. really fucked up of you to joke about the gross malfunctioning boner disease § outta all the users on all the sites on this big wide web of ours.. why would PriapismHaver777 want to chat with little old me.... § wearing my lab coat and analyzing an array of my own nudes in order to determine which one most effectively highlights my fatigued genitals § oh yeah buddy... i eat birdseed... and i ain’t a FUCKIN bird!! #JustTheGuys #DamnMenTweets § the onion AV club boldly assigns a letter grade to each phase of the moon while dozens of readers chant incantation into the comment section § just to clarify: “the studio” is a room I rent for $800 a month. i use it to compose all of the posts i type here. § the accident was not my fault. the speed bag installed in the roof of my car was obscuring my view. also the driver was a fake version of me § verizon wireless usa promotes an nfl tweet but refuses to support indie sports like hockey and soccer. meanwhile, my life is in the garbage § well i hate it. fuck chefs § list of casinos I need to burn down in order to prevent my credit score from going to the dogs: ceaser palace, trump cube, chuck e cheese, § i changed my mind. fuck cash for moms online. fuck it all. its nonsense that moms are given allthis good cash while I make $0.003 per tweet § fruad § i walked in on two cops touching each other’s badges in the unisex bathroom at saladworks and got a coupon from complaining about the ordeal § everyrtfhing I say and do is owned hereforth by the fine individuals of the Cash For Moms Online corporation. i beLieve in cash for moms. .. § thinking i could bring my laptop to people who never saw computers, like some black tribe in africa. let them watch me game for a few hours. § thanks for telling me what “ amore “ is you dumb ass hole. i totally had no idea before i listened to this insipid song #TheThursdayNiteRant § “When the moon hits your eye like a big pizza pie that’s amore” nope. not true “When the world seems to shine like you’v” thats bullshit too § @FootLockerJapan you owe me one million dollars § just as Christ was nailed to the cross to rescue his brand, i will be nailed to a Meme. my shit & blood will drip upon the funny impact font § Login: SewerLad   Pass: FuckTheMods666 § im role-playing as a piece of trash on the corner of market & 5th. in need of 2nd player to lift me into the garbage please. i wont pay you. § the ceo of cash4gold just called me, crying. he tells me this--he says people arent respecting his brand on twitter. i fucking hate this site § i am skeptical of the concept “Too Big To Fail” mainly because i am extremely big and i fail constantly § and to the guy who said i have shit for brains: youre right. i do have... four brains.......... § *homepage § jesus christ. this man at the library is looking at the lowes,com homepagr instead of gaining knowledge. im gonna upload a pic of this clown § *hangs political cartoon of obama eating The Jobs with a fork and knife up on the office billboard* you see that? ?? hes esating the jobs. § christ washed the feet of his disciples but not the ass. never the ass § my opinion on politics: my opinion on politics is that politidcs is extremely good, but sometimes it is bad § #SingleBecause self-sabotaging loud mouth with a hook dick who worsks with men twice my age at a vomit processing plant and has rabies § were you surprised to see me, gaming in the bathtub?? i am a man of infinite pleasure. come, hand me my robe. i write my own mr. bean skits § my trolls & detractors all have gross mental issues. they love drama and are all jealous of my precious army man blood #truth #SorryNotSorry § God Bless the United States of America and the Constitution that this Country was built on. Grab yourself a Mud Jug and KEEP PACKIN€™ HAMMERS § http://t.co/JC9jwCb1z4 buuy me this if oyu love my content and want to rescue me from eternal misery § another cheap N' easy halloween spook: sculpt a giant skull out of ground beef and splash blood on it and drive it around on top of your car § a nice tip for halloween: fill up a jar with piss and say that it is a jar of frankenstein piss. display it on the porch with a strobe light § hackers are finding ways to inject jokes underneath my posts and i ask my subscribers to remain calm unti;l ive sorted this all out with 911 § i finally beat the Guinness record of "most karate chops absorbed by a man" but it doesnt count because i was unconscious during parts of it § it warms my heart when i see people of every race and creed, setting aside their differences in order to spew piss into my cage and scare me § #TagABeautifulGirl im good. im really good and normal. i want to take a women to the shooting range and discuss guns culture. i love humor § #TagABeautifulGirl i demand a date. i need constant help with my bullshit. i am tired of girls making me sick. i want to like the good girls § my name is WhiteMadeaFan55 and i demand ansers. § i wear the oj simpson glove while i post . thats just a small example of how fucked up i am. Dont make me tell u more § my opponent thinks hes hot shit releasing photos of me walking an iguana on a leash., but little does he know that iguana is Gentle creature § please leave my ass to the toilet § STEROID and CIGAR levels must remain equal . otherwise my organs will completely shut down and the quality of my posts will suffer immensely § you can even give money to it if you want to § choppy vhs footage of me jacking off in a guarded prison cell and yelling "THE SYSTEM WORKS" upon climax § "i hope they serve dumpsters in hell " me, eviscerating a dumpster diver verballym, before closing the dumpster lid on top of him § bigmouth fake priest telling me to "drink a shitload of holy water and kill yourself" as penance? this has happened at three churches now § itts also not funny or good. Cheers § my fav star? it's the sun. because the earth would be a cold piece of shit without it. i also like the website called "fav star" a lot. § after another day of getting Owned by #HateMail and #DeathThreats nothing beats coming home to my policeman wife and getting shot & arrested § https://t.co/77QLxjtCpV Good Ass, Top Tier Content § alright. so we narrowed the name of our band down to either Traces of Mondo or Pepsigasm. and i already printed out 90,000 Pepsigasm tshirts § please do not send any pictures of your legs to LegNut64. he is not a real leg cop § *sees another discarded poland spring bottle on the side of the road filled with piss* haha. hell yes § the reason it costs hundreds of thousands of dollars to incarcerate people is that jail is really good and i like going there. Jail is good § its govenrment shutdown time mother fuckers *steals a shitload of small eggs from a bird nest* ha ha ha § i forgot to take off my joke shock ring before jerking off and the joke is on me because i flipped out and shot loads all over my curtains § how many years did it take for moses to build the ark?? trick question. God built it § i am in no position to judge an ass. i do not deserve to judge an ass § i judged a chili competition once, whcich would make it a very good idea to hire me, because i would be good at using judgement on things § the guy who pretended to work at pathmark and handed out free samples of dog dicks to innocent shoppers technically didnt break a single law § please dont flood this information channel with sports info § Food $200 Data $150 Rent $800 Candles $3,600 Utility $150 someone who is good at the economy please help me budget this. my family is dying § who will be brave enough to create a 3d motion picture about talking guns. who will let the guns tell their story § The reason the "Cars" movies have gained so much popularity is becuase the cars speak to one another. You don't get that with real life cars § god intended for the creatures of his likeness to wear good tuxedos all the time and to paint their cars to look like it's wearing a car tux § i do print my posts out on index cards and dead drop them at city hall. you have to get your teeth in the game, other wise youre just shit § it's horrible and i'm very close to calling the police § Give me some good memes and ill post them. Im sorry. Im just trying to please everyone § the only thing real about me is my appreciation for the refreshing taste of #pepsi, #doritios, #hormel, #generalmills, et al, § Im, him § if you're ever wondering if im some other guy, the answer is yes, im him, unless it's bad to be him, then im not him, im a different person. § http://t.co/zjDicwHRyz you will never defeat me mother fucker § vvvvvvvvvv bullshit vvvvvvvvvv § When Jordache designer diapers were manufctured in 1994, they "seemed to symbolize Jordache's descent in the marketplace to discount outlets § I foudned buzz feed and it was my idea to take all of that sweet Koch Bro Cash and put bad gifs on the site § ah! ah! i welcome the trolls, the haters, the knuckleheads, the rudeboys, i welcome them to shit on my fucking worthless grave and kill me § let us discuss the recent unveiling of user "@TurdBozo " and how that affects our creative collaborative efforts like, artistically and shit § the straight truth. im richard simmons, rofl. i love kissing Monsanto Mwah Mwah. HOw's your twitter immersion now?? i also believe in God § Im a dunce who needs faves and retweets to live § anyone else see that full sail university masters in new media promo-tweet which offers us the opportunity to "learn blogging"? Look's legit § @FullSail well i doubt you would have paid twitter good money to promote this program if it wasn't really good and also useful § I HAVE COMBED THE INNERMOST REACHES OF DARKNET TO BRING YOU THIS REALLY SICK PICTURE OF PEOPLE FUCKING EACH OTHER IN SUITS OF ARMOR § does brazil have any excotic PC games i can play § please dont let the pharaoh see this § i have evolved byeond the need for "furniture" and i enjoy resting on the floor like an animal while counting all the cool cash im saving § i put a firefly and a ladybug into a mason jar and have been closely monitoring their activities for 4 days. they have not fucked yet § i was explicitly banned from them because i am a loser and a jackass § alright now. just checking to see if there's any interest in a livestream of me speed running this entire bottle of hunts tomato ketchup § i will not back down, i will never stop yelling online, tear down this post § my grave is just a huge tv displaying videos of me doing parkour in hell and it makes all the other graves look like shit § the conflict-ed supersoldier stares over the horizon as he smokes a cigarette. "war is the most fucked up thing ever." he takes a sip of beer § kissing pictures of guns online is one of the most honorable ways to get strong § my mind is normal § if you see a man in a fawkes mask walking down the highway with a sign that says "Gamestop: Power to the Players" that's me and i need water § let me tell you exactly why this t-shirt design of the tasmanian devil with angel wings is bullshit. first off, taz is not dead § its below 0 § "stuart little 2" isn;t funny. somebody had to say it § All Young Men Must Own A Spittoon At Some Point In Their Lives § it is generally agreed upon that my posts are considered to be the worst aspect of my twitter presence § if all the girls and women in this town want to secretly film me taking a huge piss, then that's their right and god bless em § i have paid my son's school bully over $50000 to detsroy me psychologically . § @Arbys @pepsi piss § i have been secretly collecting my roommate's piss for 7 years. i dont know what to do with all of these jars of piss. i am extremely scared § i'm truly thankful towards Irritable Bowel Syndrome for becoming an integral component of my identity and shaping me into the man i am today § prime smut http://t.co/8RycXTsBiS § extremely good shit http://t.co/Qh3JvV2ehp § if they decide to replace the failing US dollar with killer quotes and refs from pg13 comedies then me and a lot of cool people will be rich § whoever sent me that vile picture of an undimpled necktie- congratulations for emotionally ruining a man and undoing years of therapy § huey lewis and the... PUBES?? haha. some things are too fucked up for even ME to submit on here...**backspace backspace backspace backspace* § a cool prank is to convince someone to join the Armed Forces and watch them get spooked by guns & missiles in exchange for hollow gratitude § the shithead principal cowers under his desk and uses a stethoscope on the floor to listen for my rough n' tumble boots and trademark Gait § the absolute best place to hide your nudes is in a file folder on your desktop labelled "Clothes" § @GitRDoneLarry i will raze every forest and devour each city in blood tribute for the crime of 9/11!! please nbring back blue collar TV § thats my boy § adult who wrestles cops § adult cop wrestler § to the trolls: i just bought a 5-pack of Oral-B electric toothbrush heads using points from my Chase Freedom card. could a child do that? no § my accout is fucking good § only if you truly respect my posts § as long as that "anyone" is a Straight Jock § i do not want to have to read this shit at this current joncture . § If i catch U retweeting mainstream shit, like updates from The Weather Channel or pictures of food, youre finished. Go clean yourself up kid § Im Sucking Myself Off Right Now And I Hate It #Dateline § i have decided to forgo material pleasure so i can write about the experience and sell it to http://t.co/pAeRi93lur for Two Hundred Dolalrs § someone has filled the Stanley Cup with... BLood?? my god. such a powerful statement. how could we have been so blind. Sports is cancelled § here's a list of touhou girls i want to have as a Mom someday & here is a copy of that list in case you accidentally throw it in the gabarge § judge refusses to award my criminal ex-wife ANY of my retweets or favs in the divorce proceedings #BLAMMO § huge disgusting man with extremely muscular fingers pokes at his tiny laptop while his emaciated servants groom him with squeegees #win § i will never allow myself to go to hell without finding a way to take my laptop and piss soaked mattress along with me § " o" § i hand the chipotle cashier my card. "i support indie" with a photograph of me winking. she looks up and sees me winking in real life also. § those things are me § this is very bullshit § as an asmerican citizen i am entitled to the spookiest halloweens possible as required by the constitution of the united states § mean while, while you were "Gaming ", i tasted 100 different wines in a cave behind a waterfall and cried into a shaman's arms § this man just likened me to a group of masturbators because i believe in the importance of an ironed pair of slacks. how dare he § i'll just call every opinion i don't like a "Circle Jerk". i'll dominate everyone § Do it. Own me fully § ok. so apparently throwing knives at my car is A Thing now. apparently my Emphatic Capitalization is frowned upon by People Who Read Words § i close my account and cool off in the bath tub § some things are more important than the brand . § *kicks back and watches an algorithm remove all the circumcised people from my web ring* Huauha your fucked up dicks can't save you now § number 4. the last one. i will hold this, The Content Creator's Pledge, close to my soul, on this sickening day of nine eleven. God bless § number three. i will never take the advice of my lawyers, my loved-ones, and colleagues to #StopThePosts § Number two. I will never apologize for defending myself from the onslaughts of jealous swine § i will never apologize for being wild about apps and upgrades § christ yes. This shit fucking rules § today's the 2nd anniversary of the really good 9/11-related post I made two years ago #BetterWithAge #LikeAFineWine #MorePower § Looking To Be Jacked Off Into A Basin - m4w - 32 (Trenton, NJ) § Yoyu shut the fuck up right now § the neighborhood teens have left so many burning bags of garbage on my lawn that everyone thinks that this is the place you burn garbage now § i have absolutely zero interest in friendship, i have absolutely zero interest in jokes, i am simply here to collect data and earn respect § go ahead, son. fuck your life up by taking that job as an ostrich breeder instead of working at my really good law firm until youre disabled § nope i died § i see nothting out of the ordinary here § yes i can confirm that george zimmerman just fashioned a cocoon from Monster Energy cans and metamorphosed into a gun with angel wings #cool § well im going to keep this brief. i overexerted myself while responding to emails and got put up in the hospital. i basically need lungs now § i am beginning to doubt that most of the subscribers to my feed are mature enough to handle sniper info. § perhaps by shooting a mam to the moon, NASA is the greatest sniper of all? nope. bull shit. it is solid snake § the sniper lifestyle requires perfect animal instincts and also smoking. dont join my sniper squad if u havent forsaken humanity& dont smoke § sniper flawlessly zaps the lid of my beer jar clean off. camera zooms in & out on my astonished face accompanied by buckwild cartoon soundFX § *wactches a sniper headshot a butterfly while its still inside of the cocoon* Hm, absolute Ownage. Ihave never seen anything that good. § i love to do bare knuckle brawls and my garage is adorned with various pornos § NASCAR Forums >> Odds & Ends >> Repost: A Man NAmed Jake Is Causing Me Endless Grief § NASCAR Forums >> Odds & Ends >> what are some good podcasts to listen to while listlessly fucking my wife § i plan on giving the olympics a right proper bollocking for lifting the tokyo 2020 setting straight from my cat girl novella § *covers up apartment's only window with a "Keep Calm And Enjoy The Posts" sign* yes!! mother fucking yes !! this shit is Perfect! god DAMN!! § he blogs on the issues. 5 star § now for a joke. a man named "the turd coach" comes into my bathroom and blows the whislte at my toilet after i fill it with shit. Penalty § say what you will, but i truly believe that this man, this Adolf Hitler, was one of hte most buzzworthy racism-likers of the 20th centure. § a horrible mechanical abomination attaches itself to my skull and injects my latest Klout score directly into my brain every thirty seconds § yes. i believe you should get yelled at for misquoting film's § *sees Tarantino get misquoted* You Bitch Mother Fucker *sees war supported on flimsy pretenses* Wlel, that's his beliefs and I respect that § im turning off until you remove it . § once they put out a unicode symbol depicting a tiny ass i anticipate that the jokers & miscreants on here will use it for criminal purpouse. § nope i can not § @turdslut it appears you dont actually follow me, Turd Slut. if thtis #FF is some how ironic. Then you are the most fucked up person alive. § i love wearing clothes with words on them. like a fucking caveman § brixon brings another round of buffalo chicken bagels into the abandoned office, placing them next to last weeks rotten batch. solemn ritual § i went to arizona accompanied by two desert goblins and smoked spirit leaf out of a human stomach § the truth is; a lot of these people making and laughing at shit and piss jokes are actually quite stoic when they're using the toilet § i take a vacation to hawaii to relieve myself of the Trolls. a group of hula girls begin beating me up & calling me shit as soon as i arrive § i finally worked up enough courage to cry in front of the pregnant woman who frequents my gym § i plan on working very hard to shrink my dick in the coming monmths. my goal dick is 2 inches erect § i habve been banned from over 200 dating services for being upfront and honest about my rotten, barbed dick § two men emerge from sensory deprivation tanks "I just attained oneness with all living beings" "I just fucked the Girl rabbit from SpaceJam" § i will never apologize for being a stoogehead, especially not to a hitler liker § the most important thing to realize for a safe and healthy labor day is that lizardmen are hiding in the trash, in graves, and in coffins § Time to shit. I excuse myself from the dinner table and enter a square, marble room with an obelisk in the center. I lock the door behind me § MOE Hitler mrudered over 9million people you numbskull   Moe uses the claw of a hammer to yank on Curly's nostrils   CURLY Nyuuaagghh!! § a teen approached me at the food court and said "I see you wore your clown costume today" and i spent the next 9 hours processing the insult § Laughs Right In The Home Depot Man's Face When He Says They Don't Have Any Bird Baths

For Sale § the military industrial complex spent $99bil on dixie cups to ensure that not a single drop of our troops genetically superior cum is wasted § i believe our Good Troops will try really really hard to make sure that the next 100,000 human beings they exterminate are losers and nerds § thius is not said nearly enough by all you ungrateful, unappreciative fucking jackals on here, but thank you @CNN. Thank you for the news § dont count the celebs out just yet, fellas.... i got the feeling theyre planning all sorts of those madcap stunts that drive all of us #WILD § http://t.co/YuwPc6gAmx and to think ebert said this isnt art § .@ToiletHelper hasn’t tweeted yet. @CumDragon hasn’t tweeted yet. @ShitLad hasn’t tweeted yet. @Fat666 hasn’t tweeted yet. @ CleanUncle hasn’ § a football jersey with “BAD SON” as the player’s name found in a dumpster § i dont want to § one of my avatars is a floating skull with a big dick and sometimes my other avatars suck the skull’s dick § Police of reddit, what is the funniest thing someone you are arresting has said? (self. askreddit) § digmon otis once mistook a beached toilet for a dolphin egg § @ DeBeers I WANT DIAMOND LIMB ‘S § i will not hear any more talk of mars needing moms § favstar is an important brand outreach utility & the fact that some people will misuse it by putting jokes on there is pathetic § lets set some realistic goals here : jokes banned by 2016. sex banned by 2020. a cop in every household by 2025 § im going to be very upset if I shell out a thousand big ones for google’s glass only for it to be 100% legal for people to do jokes about it § This is more for the seasoned hookah smoker. 2 subscribers, a community for 2 months § This is realhookah, not /r/hookah. This isn’t for posting pics of the same hookahs in different positions, with different shit in the base. § i had an actual good tweet to post tonight but a tower of filthy dog cages collapsed on top of me before i could write it § i fed them Lies § every animal in my house is dying for some reason and i can’t handle bullshit right now § yes because those are the funny words § i go online to learn which cartoon characters fuck each other and log right back off before the corruption sets in § 1) KILL 2) MY 3) SELF § PULL THE TRIGGER § please get me the list of the dorks who have me blocked on this goddamned website so i can kick their lawn up with my cowboyboots § my dick and my ass are normal § http://t.co/gFFTBY9aiA teen wolf wiki asks the hard hitting questions § every day i thank God for making it illegal for cops to kill and beat me § no. the admins will ban you if you do this § my body is 70% water mother fucker. guns cannot harm me § im quitting my job as muscle beach lifeguard to achieve my dream of becoming the north korean secretary of teen moms § BURY ME WITH MY ASS......... § nobody has suggested 14:88 yet. the hitler numbers. § plpease post suggestions for some wicked fucked up aspect ratios to help me trick my treacherous wife into thinking the tv is broken § moving pictures are a sin upon this earth § satan has his filthy little hand in my google serach priority and now when people look up my username they get pictures of dead camels § i woudl advise against “going commando”, or wearing pants without underwear. the last time i did this i got a deep turd infection and died § WHO CARES I DONT § >>ATTEMPTING TO SEND FILE ‘LIST_OF_CARPETS_I_REFUSE_TO_FUCK_ON_PART1.doc’ >>ACEPT >>PLEASE ACCEPT >>ATTEMPT FAILED § buried in the center of stonehenge is a leather portfolio case filled with nude images of me. i consider these my most powerful nudes § FUCK the brand § @DrPhil “shit” § i just sucked my own dick and got poisoned. no podcast tonight § You know, from the tone of your posts, it seems as though you actually WANT the Jeff Dunham brand to fail . § suck 100 metal dicks for a 1/256 chance of viewing a lovely 3d cutscene § i am truly baffled that some people would rather watch amc’s “Breaking Bad” than indulge themselves in the good shit i constantly post here. § im now aware of a vulgar & objectionable program named”Rocky & Bullwinkle”. sign my blogtition to yank this disgusting shit off the airwaves § i just got an email asking me to join The Rat Pack. need to know if its real or not before i move to belarus to make textiles with my uncles § fourteen of my beautiful sons exploded in God's War and the army sent me a gorgeous mantlepiece of a wolf that I kiss everyday § something like 43% of our nations topsoil is actually cave man shit. fucked up § you have destroyed a powerful networking opportunity with this horse shit § this is false. i have never made jokes § Damn. Egypt's in trouble. Hold on im coming *DRops anonymous mask on patio and hoses it off real quick* § soryr guys. the boss just yanked my privacy tarp off and all further content is on hold until i can retrieve it § running a search for "fuck church" every sunday morning and scrolling through the assortment of wild teen yells is my version of church § inbox full of people apologizing to me for their tweets. "Im Sorry Sir" "Ill Do Better Sir" i blow a shitload of cigar smoke onto the screen § demonius darkblade has The Nuke, i can confirm that this large man has obtained a nuclear device and intends to use it on rude posters § https://t.co/UeK46Z1pYb Focus On The Issues § so what kind of Jeans shampoo do you use? paul mitchell's denim advantage?? good luck with that you fucking cretin § requesting preorder status on "Def Comedy Jam Tennis" - PS4 - Release Date: 7/8/15 (JPN) , TBA (USA) § i just got word from cigarnet that the government has a secret vault full of #GUNS § bouncing my large mean ass on top of a shitload of stolen mannequin legs (girl) § Fuck this. I tried to be a good poster § if i ever find a sincere or heartfelt post on your feed im gonna take a SHIT ON YOu § thank you for emailing me the picture of the pillsbury doughboys dick while my dad and all my uncles were standing right behind me. Not § my name is Tony Turds and i demand for people to take me seriously everty time i talk and also for people to like me § i can in the year of our lord 2013 verify once and for all that shrimp are NOT baby birds § i spend the majority of my computer time #Frowning § The one thing that I am truly the most sick of dealing with online is Ignorance Likers . § need one of those janet jackson sun shaped nipple rings to protect my stupid-ass pud from hell cherubs § http://t.co/jT9y9xJPVu look at thi § i'll be wrapping this hog in tinfoil to protect my dryrub from the NSA until all this bluster dies down § i cannot live in a world where OrgyPrince calls me an "Orgy Coward" just because i refuse to attend his disgusting orgy § the soldier yanks a perfect pair of blue jeans out from a pile of ashes while surveying a burned out truck. may god damn these perfect jeans § Mme § a jpg of a fish § Dear drigl, An item you listed in the Community Market has been sold to Osama Bin Laden. Your Steam Wallet has been credited 0.27 USD. § i singlehandedly brought the OJ Simpson brand back from the brink of calamity and by God I will protect Yahoo. com from these online devils § @DrinkGrumpyCat this bullshit has clumps of PUBIC HAIR in it. tastes like someone attempted to mask ACRID PISS TASTE with CHEAP SOAP. No buy § @Drink-GrumpyCat send this entire misguided operation to the dumpster you vile urine peddler § #HowToResistSex meditate upon the untapped potential of The Cloud and crank off § i fully intend to topple the DigimonOtis empire via a coordinated campaign of viral folk songs bolstered by my partnership w/ Bob Evans Inc. § i had not felt emotion in over 20 yrs. not until baby crash bandicoot's reunion with regular crash bandicoot moved me to actual human tears § we're here to discuss the cultural merit of "Baby Crash Bandicoot RPG". please leave if you have nothing of value to add to the conversation § they fuckin STINK!!!! § and n9ow people are being abusive instead of helping me so i am just going to shut the monitor off and sit in the pitch blackness for awhile § some of my more savvy followesr are telling me they are called "trauma shears" but i need a pair specially formulated for a large mans needs § i want a medical expert to hook me up with those scissor that cut all your clothes off in like 2secs because im a large man & its a struggle § i got stuck in a bramble brush while scouting for trolls and contracted heartworms and the fuckface twitter mods refuse to compensate me § ˜ ˜ ˜ CLICK ON MY ASS FOR MORE TWEETD ˜ ˜ ˜ § i dedicate this oscar to the caveman who invented electricity, because without him€• Film would cease § i;m selling my piss and shit back to the grid § No results found for “i invented black borat” § dippin my head out there for some hardball strapthug coplikes to handle my doofus and preg me down ,no wise guy shit #nerdland § i.. im gonna lose it!! im absolutely ready to crap all my damn cum out !!! § let me explain it to you fucking nerds one more time; this aaccount is Above Humor. You will not find jokes on it. § one thing my brand will never associate itself with is piles of filthy leaves § I will never post such info onto this bad website § HAHAHAHA!!! YES !! YES!! § HUNGRY-MAN„¢ was so impressed by my Content Flow & My Trademark ‘Tude that they hired me as Asst.Toilet Boy and let me lick the factory floor § CRISIS: “TrueB-loodGamer” just switched his steam handle to “TroubledGamer” and is NOt responding to ANY messages, we must bow in cyberprayer § Please Click On The Tiny, Burning Earth To Discover My Weblog § In Second Life. Im the toilet who slides around and asks superior avatars to use me, please track me down if you want to discuss “Politic’s” § I am selling 10,000 of my followers to @CampBow-Wow for Nine Cents. Starting tomorrow you will be following @CampBowWow instead of me. Bye § not if you wrap a towel around yout head § “ BLOOD CURSE “ to all the terrible motorists who threw debris into my bathtub as i carried it along the highway and made it really heavy § what i need is one of my girl follower to shovel garbage off of my dick so i can jack off and post a numerical rating of the ordeal online § i can confirm that Somali pirates have intercepted my shipment of 20,000 glossy 8x10 headshots and are using them for vile purposes § damn!! heres one for ya: if the classic dancing 3d baby aged normally, he would be turning 6,270 years old today #Whoa #TimeGoesByMan § Perhaps the tier I aspire to achieve the most is that of the Milk Bone brand. Such flawless precisIon. Beauty; Grace. Truly awe inspiring . § im IP banned from this site in the usa but my Dubai account is good to go § https://t.co/N71ABSorZo im seeing some real good shit on this website today § It owuld be rude to eat you. Goal § Im already dead. Fuck u. Keep em comin § Piss on me, chief § Im going to erase this you god damn loony tune § youre a rodeo clown from the sewer § why won’t anyone fight me on this site. i want to slam one of you smug mother-fuckers to hell, with the good words that i type and post here. § let me justt play devil’s advocate here and say that eating shit is really good and im a dumb shithead and i love shit § if your grave doesnt say “rest in peace” on it you are automatically drafted into the skeleton war § everytime i click on the skull, a random dweeb’s computer chair spins around at a million miles per hour and collapses underneath his ass § “big the cat” is the most compelling figure that has ever existed in any form of media, and that includes book `s . § #FreshmanAdvice i will demolish you with my perfect upper body forever because seniors rule the shit out of this school § you are treated to the serene visage of a waterfall cascading against the rocks. the camera pans out and its me vomiting all over my balls § those are all trolls who want only to terrify me § I GOt Fired From QVC For Describing A Pair Of Jeans As “EuroVamp” § im sensing some major bullshit coming from the graveyard § i want to live ther § i had a dream that Jared from subway followed me & we started discussing new media objectives over DM. when i woke up i was eating my pillow § i get banned § my follower count decreases when i use these words: dick, cum, ass, turds. it goes up when i use these: brand, multimedia, sports, pepsicola § i just shot a wicked load across the hood of m y dad’s monte carlo and i’m feeling hetero as all hell § if you think anything I post is funny you’re a piece of litter § all cops on twitter please help. i found this fuckin egg on a bus seat where a large man was just sitting. how do i properly dispose of it § hello 911 police? ? yeah the official pf changs twitter account just unfollowed me. please put this message in the Files. thank u officer. § The most fucked up possible thing has happened. Porno has returned to cyberspace. § i would click the print button a lot of times § god damn if i aint getting thirsty!!!!!!!!!!!!!!!! §

CALLING ALL MUSCLEFREAX-- a country named "Ethiopia"' severely lacks Muscles. let's hit the bench and get heavy in their honor. #MuscleCrisis § while you all dunce around here and kiss the stupid royal baby's dick; i'll be absorbing the scooby doo subreddit with a glass of #PaleAle . § stay home and Re Tweet me § jeans § Drink my god Damn piss. Drink my my god Damn piss. Drink my piss mother fucvker. Drink my fucking god damned piss off § #RoyalBabyNames asshole doofus motherfucker from hell § dicks are only sold in cartons fuckface § @CNNSlowNewsDay @hair Hair put it therem, not me § .@Hair The cashier stood motionless, facing away from me while I attempted to purchase hair from your establishment in Galveston, TX. #Prank § Use Cappital Letters Please § Hrm. This is troubling. *loads another nude woman* This absolutely will not do. *loads pictures of Modern Architecture* Ah, now this is good § The Foundation For The Restoration Of American Honor Has Given President Barack Hussein Obama A Hitler Rating Of 34. This Is The Worst One. § i had a nightmare that i kept clicking the logout button and it just kept logging me into this website again and again § WHAT DO WE WANT "Memes" WHEN DO WE WANT IT "Instead of regular jokes" § bone prank: drop pieces of your skeleton in strategic locations to spook nincompoops and lame-os § i overhear 2 social media experts discussing hardcore brand strats for 2015. Next Level. i immediately duck into a restroom & hyperventilate § web MD just told me I have "Fuckface Lymphoma" and that im an "Aids Man". in light of this humbling news id like to apologize for my posts § DEAR COP WHO BUSTED MY FRONT TEETH IN FOR SELLING TOWELS ILLEGALLY, THANK U. IM ON THE RIGHT TRACK NOW. PETSMART HIRED ME TO JACK DOGS OFF § http://t.co/CrnIWgR0SP christ. no wonder everyone is so worked up...... § The Bayer corporation proved the link between Masturbation and Homosexuality in 1968. Thbe debate is over. § climb into the garbage you uneducated clown § nude bathing was invented by the vile criminal slave class of the byzantine empire and it drove the kind & decent noblemen absoutely bonkers § http://t.co/y3sQDFTaG1 ths is the direction of the @Dril account & our vision of the future of media. This does not represent Final Product. § @PhillyPolice nothing i have ever done is Legal § *waches the Race War unfold in filthy computer chair, multiple tabs open, cnn msnbc, gawkrer, salon, milk duds** now THis is some good shit, § the classics(art carney, sid caesar) woud SHIT THEMSELVES if they saw these newer performers who INSIST on displaying their genitals always, § ENOUGH *Throws All My Jacking Off Books And Jacking Off Memorabilia Into The Garbage* § http://t.co/ynAtcVv42q im just going to post my ad here real quick § Kathleen Turner will star for director Herb Ross at MGM in the comedy feature "Cloak and Diaper,'' a Michael Lobell-Andrew Bergman productio § PigPissBen banning anyone who reposts the PigPissLou photos. PigPissWayne and PigPissEllis have already fallen victim to this PigPissTyranny § PigPissClyde hid in a bush for 2 hrs and took secret photos of PigPissLou wiping bird shit off his windshield with a chipotle bag. Pure win, § peeking into police station window, watching the cops Fuck each other. duane eddy's "Rebel Rouser" is playing and im nodding my head in tune § simpsons marches onward into season 394. characters morph into grotesque mockeries over 100s of years. homer advocates cock and ball torture § i lure a group of newly hatched baby turtles into an abandoned warehouse using a photo of the ocean and turn them into moths #GOthicOrder § Where were u when I was being mouthed off at. Where were u when my brand was tarnished by Mockers. Where were u when i got called a "Prick". § arms begin to glow & expand. "We must secure the existence of our people and a future for True Gamers." yes!! yes! im feeling more power tha § i just cracked into aCiDnEt and got my grubby mitts on BigCasper's [No_Incest] edit of the spike lee oldboy remake and im sippin #DraftBeer § you missed the boat pal http://t.co/32rn5syqtv § my turds and brain fucking suck and my toilet smells like a god damn turd and it also sucks § I hate this fucking bunkum you put to my page. Get a grip on life § Fuck Digimon Otis § only the good ones § thbe NSA is really good. but it could be bad? please dont write any opinions about it until ive solved this § nobody's allowed to criticize anytyhing or talk about anything or like anything until my shitty terrible account gives the official go-ahead § i hold hands w ith my teen son *spikes the microphone* § hm? whats that? my dick looks like bozo the clown's dick? listen punk. i know for a fact you have never seen bozo the clown's dick § my dick sucks balls. pray for my dick § http://t.co/aVeUH2d2KC good § http://t.co/gigLk7tGJw this is how to fuck on craigslist § my disrespectful teen son somehow got hold of a gluten product and now he wants to become a cat girl § my crippling fear of Hell makes me post really good things on my timeline #blessed § i suppport LGBT... and GBLT ((photo montage of me sinking my teeth into a Good BLT)) #DaringJokes #HeWentThere § posing next to a jeep and handing out business cards at the high school i graduated from 8 years ago, explicitly stating i do NOT followback § a mudslide engulfs a small village as I obliviously powerwash my bluejeans uphill § i will pay a jpeg specialist up to $500 to put a black bar over the ass & pussy of my beloved rottweiler before i send the pic to my father. § i've been spat upon. i've been dragged through the streets. i've been pissed on to the Nth degree. all for the sake of making good ass posts § I have decided to officially unfollow "@Budweiser", on account of their complete lack of original, informative, or compelling content. § im going to strangle the turds out of your ass § Nudity is perverse. Nudity is an act of war § i'm absolutely covered head to toe in lotion and i am ready to sign on. you all have the privilege of interacting with a fully lotioned man § as we speak, RickGameCube, Bradley_X, GodlyWalter17 and myself are planning an attack on the terrorist organization known as "Al-Qaeda" § due to the actions of bastards and human slime, my agent has advised me to deactivate my account for 18 hrs, to punish my disloyal followers § you are all too concerned wih your fucking "Brands" to help a mman who was absolutely in hell for 4 hours you turncoat motherfuckers of shit § zero of my so-called twitter pals gave me a phone call or offered me any aid during my harrowing ordeal iwth the hacker. may god punish you. § HACKED BY Ã SKORPÃ TX TURKISH HACKER THE ISLAM IS SUPERIOR - YOU WILL DRAW YOUR PUNISHMENT George W. Bush (1946 - ...)...2007 FUCKED USA § trolls have found a terrible new way to antagonize me. it is called "retweet-ing" and it works by exposing my posts to scammers & crumb bums. § i sit on a throne made out of dead Freshmen and drink wine from a Freshman's skull. all this can be yours if you become a cyber bully. § *circles "become gay" on a whiteboard* § i think that turning myself Gay in the summer of 2013 would really impress my overseas investors § i can tell how beautiful a man`s soul is by putting both of my hands on the hood of his car and thrashing my neck around to awaken god § fuck your ma ma!! you piece of shit § eat a god damn bug § Go Fuck Your Self You Son Of A Bitch § whenever i elevate my professional vitae through mind-blowing, dynamic content, i reward myself by fucking a book of carpet samples #Toonami § dont come on my account and lecture me about manual transmission until yoauve gotten BOTH of your balls snug up inside of a sweet sugar babe § The absolute shit Im forced to put up with as a content Producer. Ive sacrificed my basic human rights in order to placate U fucking people. § - barack "knock 'um down" obama - http://t.co/oW5xdmbLof - mad rodney - http://t.co/yTiRJSiEMX - chemtrail - http://t.co/E4km14dXL9 vote now § hibernate in a drain § my meme dissertation should be "put into the toilet"?? perhaps the only thing that should be put into the toilet are your harsh criticisms. § MetalGearEric: You are being tried in the court of gamers for calling Ninja Gaiden "Weiner Gaiden", even though it is not called that at all § GRIZZLED WEB VETERAN: I KNOW 100 DIFFERENT WAYS TO OWN A MAN... ME: I Sure Hope Nobody Poisons My Dick GRIZZLED WEB VETERAN: MAKE THAT 101.. § with advancements in technology we will someday be able to watch a 3d animated version of larry the cable boy go to vegas & get into trouble § someday mankind will evolve beyond “jokes” and i’ll be allowed to paint big ugly dicks all over my house without suffering derisive laughter § sometimes i gaze towards the beautiful endless sky and wish that i was a bird. so that i could piss and shit out of the same hole § a tshirt big enough to cover my ass hole up § Im here to addmindister beatings to all of the liars and cowards in this hot tub § waving flags, honking horns, trying to coax the kfc golem into shitting all over my mouth and my picnic § i love to build illegal temples around town. i love scrubbing my pitbull down with big piles of soap bubbles. i love to fuss and raise shit. § it is extremely fair to say that my entire pelvic dick area resembles the singular breast of a pregnant European § i look forward to purchasing this work of fine literature at perhaps the zoo or the circus § This is the most fucked up sentence that has ever been uploaded to a web site. § Yeah, some of us like to network with successful brands on twitter. The rest of you want to join hippy communes and suck the hippys’ dicks. § .@Budweiser Check out my tweets. I like the stuff you post on here. Please, have a look at my page. Love the ‘Weiser. Bye. § yes. i can confirm that craigsli$t will flag your job listing for removal if you accidentally title it “buffalo wild wings toilet fuck”. § assault on liberty: the local farms have begun smearing dragon blood on their pig troughs to keep me away from them § yeah im about to go to the library he works at and knock the fuckin books off the shelf § the dj who makes crude dog noises on my radio every day should listen to my rare metals podcast & learn how a real content producer behaves. § i’m just like you, pal. eivery morning i put on my straight hetero jeans one leg at a time and pour myself some straight hetero raisin bran. § in order to fully grasp the “weird twitter “ zeitgeist, i woud recommend reading 1 of the many articles publiSuck My BaLLS 666 § ï¼µï¼®ï¼£ï¼µï¼´ -ºá´¹á´¬á´¸á´±–„ § need nonviolent methods to knock out these security cams fucking up my protest of public toilet § just installed 500 security cameras around my compound & my sony wonderstation refuses to interface with a single one! hungry grab a snicker § how could a man with $0 get one of you 3d printer eggheads to print up some wild runestones for my daddy-daughter astral ascension ceremony § im 14 year s old and im already more psychic than my dad § how dare you fuck with me. how dare you fuck with me , on the year of Luigi § cursed pair of google glasses adds world star hip hop watermark to everything i look at and cannot be removed from face § as someone who receives the middle finger daily, i have the authority to state that using both hands is superfluous and absurd. doesn’t help § if the twitter man is reading this: i don’t like the fact that people are “following’ this account and i would like that feature turned #OFF § “rat rod shit shack” § Q: are nerds allowed to read your tweets A: no. absolutely not. only businessmen and christian women are permitted to read my tweets. § @RobSchneider what about the wind? i think it’s the wind § i was also goig to make a joke about how putting a dry rub on the vaccines makes them cause less autism but the science is still out on that § that’s the end of my dry rub rant. it’s just my opinion. i have already received 20 death threats. i fucking dare you to block and report me § i cannot eat this bowl of rice until i’ve personally applied a louisiana-style dry rub to each grain. i refuse to eat like a peasant § hell ill dry rub anything. an unpeeled banana. fruit gushers. all contain a latent power which begs to be unleashed by a superb spice blend § it’s that time of the year when my father sends me pictures of jails and tells me that i must learn to Respect a good barbecue dry rub § sort of bullshit that im not allowed to be the wendy’s mascot just because im repugnant to most people & woudl negatively impact their sales § i scan the docs & id the perp. “The Radio Shack Masturbator”. bounty on his head. i put 100 bullets into my pistol and hit the god damn road § click this post to worship Everlasting Slime until your cold, lonesome death, the uncleansable taste of Shit ruining your throat and tongue § click this post to devote yourself to Zesty Ranch from now to eternity , the cool, crisp satisfaction that all good mouths adore § click this post to spiritually align yourself with Hot Nacho , the devilishly delightful blend of actual nacho spices imported from DarkNet § *stealthily dumps an entire bottle of gnc 100% pro performance whey protein into the dog's food dish * oh hey what's going on i was just uh, § i am about 50% certain that the doctors who took turns punching my egregious chode during my eye exam violated the hippocratic oath § obama and his crack team of nsa crooks watching me shit: "sir, he's scooting backwards so his dick doesn't touch the rim" "Thuis guy's good" § i spend 2hrs on my back with my legs spread so it looks like the sun is setting into my ass from my perspective."haha the sun fucking sucks" § ever since i had that srtoke at cold stone creamery i feel as though i am more in tune with spirits, and the like § a quick e3 prayer: i call upon our lord in heaven to ensurre that these perfect video games are not lambasted by criminal journalists. aman § i will gladly purchase the Horrifying new xbox for each room in my home and expose my nude body to its mandatory camera daily for kfc points § maintainig one of the last serious accounts on this fucked up website is an emotional burden that could be likened to the trials of christ . § pikced up some arcane yoga tech that will suck my balls up behind my gut and allow me to achieve a marvelous Thigh Gap #ProAna #GapBoyReal § my cousin was charged with arson(Bullshit) , and i was thinking we could all help out by drawing up some memes to display in his prison cell § "˜† ˜… One day, Miss Hannah Minx escaped from an anime cartoon and started teaching Japanese on Youtube. ˜† ˜… ãƒ½(*ã‚œ-½ã‚œ*)ãƒŽãƒŸ" me too. that;s me § caught my son running a google search for " shit stain pussy ". i am beyond distraught. we are strictly a Bing family § when i was young, i always dreamed of becoming an artist. at age twelve, my father taught me how to tie a Square Knot. Now i hate art, § i summarily reject the notion that i derive R-Rated pleasure by having jack-booted meatheads from ACORN kick me around like a chewtoy § sorry for drawing this out but its important to note that im in Full Submission Mode, waiting for CIA's pig-faced cronies to whip & chain me § i hereby hand this twitter account to Obama's Thugs aand permit them to beat the crust outta me screaming and to piss on me. no trial. amen § if cops can see this account already: im sorry for all my posts ,t force me to lick your boots CLEAN sir, im a bastard who needs punishment § @CNNSlowNewsDay Take me off this service. I don't want people to look at and see my posts. § trolls using "#ff" to add me to cruel watchlists for oppressive police beasts; ONCE AGAIN fucking me over, ONCE AGAIN making me shit myself § onyl if i get 100% of the revenue and also a $250 fee for eating up my twitter bandwidth by Mentioning me § i am taking my 34-year-old son into town to buy him his very first pair of clip-on suspenders and we are both very excited § i've been publicly unfollowed by "lawyer ron" because of you fucking people § hy bud kiss my FUCKINAZZZZZZ and get your ass back to http://t.co/D8HFVwFs0x. itsr really hard to write these § theres an inherent sense of nobility, or perhaps honor, in the Shit that i post, that distinguishes me form my peers. undetectable, but real § this gradient they applied to the iconic kellogg's logo is of no use to me. i think i will write them a nasty little letter § @QuickenLoansLLC thank you § the audience is encouraged to sink bullets into my protruded red baboon ass while i struggle to recite prose written on a toilet paper tube § when i change m y name to "@QuickenLoansLLC" in Q4 youre going to be Fucked. sorry § i show my son the mandated GMO labeling on a pair of jeans at the store. "that's how you know it's a good cut. this is a good cut of denim." § The offending article of clothing read "Big Bird Sucked My Dick & All I Got Was This Lousy TShirt". I have blocked this person from my life, § if e3 does NOT #ShowUsThe-Games, KeyBladeWalter, "Epic" Wayne Briggs and I will engage in disciplined self-immolation on the disgusting floor § Tony § dunther, twang lad, gunbelt, Holbo, daemetreus costco, fallen gordo, § who are my top creative influences? easy. the geico cavemen. where do i draw the majority of my inspiration frpm?

easy. the geico cavemen . § #e3rumors a stodgy executive wil get on stage, spread his legs, and officially “give birth” to the new xbox. millions will detest this stunt § and then there was PreCumGary, a remarkable man who, despite his name, never allowed ihmself to release pre-cum during sex and masturbation. § @ClassicsOfGame Despicable As Always. Thank You, Classics. § i was promised awful, screaming cicadas by the millions. i am starting to think i busted out my CICADA MAN 2013 t-shirt for nothing. § im not into that hippy stuff § hah. i just read the entire bible and i’m still a lost., confused idiot. nice try, God. #BIbleFails § “all hail the PrankMAster, the King of Cranks”, scrawled onto the wall next to my blue corpse and a rescue inhaler filled with tabasco sauce § my step dad is apparently too busy kissing his shitty wife to attend my 55+ senior rugby league games. OH and guess what, we lost. Fuck tyou § don;t support this. please, please tell your followers to put an end to these miserable hate crimes. i havent slept in 8 days § there is absolutely no greater account on twitter than @DinoMiteBarney. consistently on point , no guff, what else can i say . check it out § everyone please stop fucking posting for a second; i think i just inhaled a hair § i for one will be taking the high road by reserving judgement for the really good grumpy cat movie until ive seen it and bought the blueray. § the champagne-sipping hipsters are constantly begging me to make my account more “INDY”... but i got 1 thing to say to ya€• NOT A CHANCE BUB! § the advent of nanotechnology will eliminate sex when the tiny robots learn to massage our prostates and drink every drop of our terrible cum § imagine a guy whose desktop computer is an integral part of his drum set and he posts by tapping the keyboard with his sticks and it’s me § completely off the mark. i have stated repeatedly that brands are BIG in 2013 and i stand by that mantra. Remove this. § i knwew it. i fucking knew it. twitter culture can suck my dick *RIps up $59,000 check from dairy queen* § twitter to me, is a Collaborative Experience. ergo,when you shit on my posts it creates a rippling effect that corrupts the souls of all men § see?? it’s happenig again. people are blocking me because i’m posting my opinion. @Doritios is sending me crude messages again. fuck twitter § everyday i am harassed constantly by the phantoms of my own bullshit. my posts get me into trouble. please follow @Dril on twitter dot com. § twitter should verify me because i invented the simpsons § i want too live their. i want too smooch them § who is that vile man lurking around outside of “ROFLCon” with a notepad, standing on trashcans trying to peek inside of the windows and shit § i got a booth set up outside of the casper, WY red lobster to promote & expand my brand presence. if you speak to me i will call the police. § double stuf oreos § you all can send me breast milk now. thank you § my dick is satire § think you got it rough? try engineering blog posts while trying to suck down two whole baby bottles full of muscle milk before Solstice ends § feel obligated to inform TL: i accidentally touched a girl dog’s nipple while petting it-- deep apologies but ready to grow & learn from this § ok go to your browser and type in godly erics twisted as fuck burger king reviews dot com slash good shit slash Clinton Soundboard dot s w f § my hype man is notable. someone get the president of wikipeda on the horn and command him to resign for this shit job http://t.co/aRqScnDNUX § mmy “hype man”, if you will, is a tiny 80-year-old guy who follows me around and apologizes for everything i say and do in a pitiful voice § claiming reserved table for “uncle clean jeans.” not on the list? hmm. what about “big uncle clean jeans.” no? shit. try “kurt.” ok ggood § my booming voice echoes from the depths of your recently flushed toilet. “ ICE TURDS IDIOT. HA HA HA” § #momsandbrands now were talkin. can i network here. i’m a normal, real person. i think youre all good #LonelyWantuingDates #GoodAtBrandsAlso § i do in fact keep a trash can under my desk so i can spit up a few nauseous loads whenever i get publicly humiliated by people retweeting me § http://t.co/PlO3awKXRu i want to help the 3d dog give birth § phew. just served 4 years in afghanistan and not a single person saw my dick while I was over there. not one. hope they got a medal for that § it is official. im taking my football to prom and im going to kiss it and the nerds will never stop me. i cannot wait to savor their anguish § I have just obtained a historic deleted segment from Disney's Fantasia. It features a middle-aged man in an NFL jersey buying light bulbs § @RichardDawkins impossible. for he has already denounced the neologism "OWned", and i cannot own him, nor him me, § "what are ya.." i said to his face. "some kind of a FReak cop?" he desperately reached for his badge but it was fused permanently to his leg § I'm Sorry For Raising Cain At The Out Back Steak House Even Though It's Still Bullshit That They Refuse To Serve Me A Plate Of Just Croutons § so if the admin posts pictures of his varicose vein clusters it's ok, but when i do it my avatar is replaced with hands gripping prison bars § whats the deal with people handing me receipts after i buy things!! i dont want this!! fuck you!! fuck you!! fuck you!! fuck you! #Stand #Up § i'll find it § there's a twitter room where people with verified accounts go to talk shit about me and shit on my good name and make me look like shit § oh absoluteyl § As a Digimon fan for over 10 years, I never heard of someone named DigimonOtis in the Digimon community, so his input is also invalid. § http://t.co/6b3eFiKWJ9 icant believe this is happening § that'sd right folks!! i, adolf hitler, have been PRETENDING to like rap this whole time so people would consider me more eclectic! Ha Ha Ha! § Good Lord https://t.co/inCGhw0io7 § NO § there are rifts in the Frankenstein community regarding whether or not igor was tasked with jacking the monster off to keep it docile § wish Obama would authorize some drone strikes against my ex-wife! *the act takes a more serious tone* Instead of doing Benghazi. § #GooglePlayMusic ha ha some guy spent a billion dollarsr to put this boring ass hashtag on the trending list. fuck you idiot § PRANK: say The Simpsons got cancelled and tape everyone's reaction. alter the footage later to make it look like their balls are hanging out § received some very important secret documents regarding the Masturbators. not only do they enjoy touching their dicks, they also worship sex § mayor unveils a huge tombstone engraved with "Incest". i chain my jeep to it and rip it down. mayor surrenders and names town "Incestville" § "Ah!! Lunchtime, Boys!" i snort several lines of Hamburger Helper, tilt my head back and shake with unbearable agony as my head turns purple § @glennbeck #Muslimgeddon #TheNineElevenOfLies #BloodPhantom666 #GhostPresidentHellGate #ANationWeepsIntoItsPillow #ThisOneTimeObamaAteABible § me and some extremely crude boys in a pickup truck scream "hipster" at some kid's lemonade stand then crash into a turtle and eat shit hard § guess what smart guy. cavemen didn't brush their teeth either, but look how strong they were. they also detested sports § now i will be the first to admit that im an irredeemable son of a bitch/. however, i am also a piece of shit with no brain. § the problem with some things today is that they arent good. but when you say that, Oop! Surprise! i'm being argued with and shitted uppon. h § i would watch a movie of a james bond kind of guy doing spy shit and rolling around on the floor and striking gun poses and it's set in hell § im being TROLLed because of my pro-nascar beliefs for fuck sake!! why dont any of you care!?! why are you all just posting more jokes!?! § there are dead guys with verified accounts, yet i am barred from consideration due to the actoins of my enemies, or "Haters", on this page . § thw most important 'win' button i have ever clicked § http://t.co/ht1ueoTuNI what hte fuck are you doing § get me some of that fuckin Travolta denim § this is a serious account. no jokes § i cast 1million holy spells on my yankee candle and now it never burns out and the flame grows taller when rowdy celebs appear in the news § the guy who put up this shield to prevent me from pissing on the public toilet paper should have considered my personal liberties beforehand § to everyone talking shit about my fine motor skills: *gives the Finger, checks to see if correct finger is extended, it isn't, tries again* § @Sizzler_USA please stop posting political message to my feed § #blogcon2013 waddling around the auditorium trying to find a place to set up my custom pc tower with "BOYS BOYS BOYS" painted on the side § #blogcon2013 im here and if you so much as look at me without having a Verified Account my devices will emit an ear-piercing defense screech § looking forward to getting in some #YardWork today!! *trims 200 square feet of lawn with a riding mower and collapses like a sack of shit* § #BenghaziInFourWords MORTIMUS BELLUM PESTILENTIA BENGHAZI § the police gave me my wacom tablet back http://t.co/x5XQ2y5Mux § stop FUCKING calling me "EPIc Divorce Man", or i will terminate my pogo account and take my tokens wiht me. i am not a MEME, im a HUMAN BEIg § the funniest one., rest assured § on my deathbed, surrounded by loved ones, i bid farewell. i explode into 1000 totino's pizza rolls and everyone in the room tries to grab em § this needs to be addressed. if you see me along the road, please do not intentionally ram me with your car. this is the 4th time this happen § best is when you're shopping for bedsheets and you see one with a lousy thread count and you say to your buddies "this poiece of shit sucks" § #WalgreensLatino please stop posting my username § i refuse to conform to typical standards by being "clever" or "funny ". i will never betray my spiritual honor by "posting good things" § summoner draws a venn diagram on the floor with circles labeled "rude" & "illegal". my fat face emerges from the center and begs for treats § @prodigalsam you blocked me by accident again § @ prodigalsam GOD DAm right you were confused, im all about top-tier content, ive been blocked by the sheikh of dubai for christ sake, Fuck u § @prodigalsam this is the most bullshit thing ive ever gotten blocked for § @prodigalsam Feel like this is appropriate. Again. http://t.co/v0vzSiIe5w § instagram?? thats a laugh. if i wanted to see pictures of things i'd pray for eyeballs § i hope someone steals my tweets. because.. theyre bad! haha load them up in a big chuck wagon and take them to criminal hq where they belong § what is quickest way to get sprayed by a skunk in a discreet maner § #freejahar friends, i have just learned of another passionate freedom fighter who was betrayed by the us government http://t.co/Mh3WNkTLti § ibm scientists place two atoms next to each other to create "world's tiniest ass." government orders them to return grant money immediately § The wine imparts a foreign bitterness. How could he betray me? We were brothers. I fall to the ground. Execute a partial curl. One last rep. § AS THE GUILLOTINE SLIDES TOWARDS MY NECK, I PRODUCE A TINY BARBELL I'VE BEEN HIDING IN MY MOUTH AND LIFT IT WITH MY TONGUE. ONE LAST REP § I DRIVE OFF OF A CLIFF AND SCRAMBLE TO RIP THE AXLE OFF OF MY CAR AND LIFT IT ABOVE MY HEAD AS I PLUMMET TOWARDS CERTAIN DOOM. ONE LAST REP § if you have ever disagreed with anyone about anything youre a sociopathic piece of shit § please stop posting unofficial crabby road strips. i a m sick of seeing our beloved maxine being used to denigrate the lord and our troops . § my next 4,000 tweets are dedicated to all the good babes of japan and beyond § few things about this account. this is no gimmicks, strigaht from the hip, real shit. i dont "DO" pranks or gags. logged on, at your service § there should be a policeman on the premises when they're naming these damn horses so they stop giving them names that aren't serious or real § "ey!! im walkin here" - me getting waterboarded by the us government § BIG Bible Town is a multiplayer online game set in a 1st century world. The objective of the game is to create your own unique BIG Bible Tow § does anyone like star wars?? well have i got a joke for you. today is may 4th, which sounds like, "may the fourth be with you", and that;s a § next issue: should miserable, long-winded diatribes about what constitutes art be considered "Art" ??? § This is the most fucked up thing you have ever done . § the villagers gather at the summit to hear my horrendous impersonations of futurama characters and grant me offerings of ivory and fruit § thw worst actually, but thanks § i have never lived down the moment i pulled my pants down in the locker room and all the gym boys noticed that my dick was wearing glasses § hm?? sorry, didn't see u there. i was just digesting a fascinating piece about how reading twitter for 9 hrs a day makes you a BEtter person § getting my loan approved at the bank by lying on my back and executing a series of flawless air kicks right there in the lobbby § #unpopulargamingopinions games are, in fact, NOT art, with the sole exception being Bugs Bunny Crazy Castle (1989) § #unpopulargamingopinions nmario and luigi are Virgins § i am notr, nor ever have been, a nerd, and i have used some very powerful swear words on this website that would blow most nerds socks off § i have performed ã ®ç¥ˆã‚Š<mouth prayer> in all 4 directions of the compass to stop ShirtlessClyde94 from leaking photos of my ghoulish pud to TMZ § #FreeJahar New DHS rule bans Jahar's mom from giving her son a hug. Im crying. Everything is so fucked up. § #FreeJahar knock knock. who's ther.e? jahar's innocence. the us gov wants to spend $5billion on a helicopter but cant afford jahar's trial. § #FreeJahar this is the $5billion helicopter obama wants to build instead of giving jahar fair trial. http://t.co/4v33qIkrSk billion with a b § #FreeJahar obama smirks as he signs the order for a $5 Billion Helicopter while the boston police beg him to pay for $2500 Jahar trial. sick § #FreeJahar obama jsut ordered construction of a $5billion helicopter but no trial for Jahar because "we can't afford it". this is FUCKED UP § one thing I will Not tolerate on this site is users organizing and planning "Orgies", also known as Group Sex. § going back to switch the auto-capitalized 'i's in my post to lowercase so people don't think im some fucked up nerd § hmm. myaybe we should tax Stupid People. and hipster. *the nation stands and applauds, I enjoy a successful career in legislature for 60yrs* § i invented the "bacon is good" joke. i invented the meme of people liking bacon. all sorts of people are copping my gag and im pissed § listrn pal, im matt, and i love Too fuck § you started a whole account just to ask me if i'm matt? leave matt alone, he hates you, you dope § my father will be donating his dimple to me. § a man in argentina is willing to surgically transfer hair from my Buffoonish ass to my weak, infantile chest and tattoo a jawline to my neck § i clicked the checkbox next to "Keep Me Logged In" so that's not possible § #questionsobamawontanswer SHOW US YOUR DICK § its 69. just kidding § the only thing this proves is that youre a doorknob § no. i believe in the desert § ok. so apparently rap did exist in the 90s. and i apologize. all the other objectionable bullshit i post here is real, though § thats not rap § dead wrong buddy § the good things i like about 90s is there were no hipsters, no rap, and your odds of getting an infection at a hospital were slightly higher § still got my holographic Alan .. this sucker would go for $40 on eBay but i prefer kissing it every night and whispering "90es" #TopShelf90s § best 90s memory is gathering around the old oak tree with the boys and passing around trading cards featuring all of our dads #DamnGood90s § love, friendship, beauty€" it all crumbles into dust. but Memes are eternal § im gay for 2 things. clean shirts and women § it i s a DISGRACE that these people are finding exciting, new ways to get horny without my express written permission § im one of the best supporters of gay on this site. but. the top priority of the nba is putting the numbers up. we cant let players get horny § what if all the locker room heteros want to kiss the gay player & it messes up their performance on the court? can we truly afford this #NBA § somehow my "JOKE HATER" sweatband gets me more compliments at the gym than my decidedly ripped form § if you receive mail from me and it isn't posted with personalized stamps depicting my dog's pregnant gut then it is fraud. please rip it up § @LAYS can I vote for the flavor that makes me feel like a depressed, nauseous slug after I eat a whole bag of it?? or is that all of them § im laughing at this really good ad http://t.co/JMoAYCGH19 § i once sent DigimonOtis the dismal metacritic scores of his favorite digimon games and said in so many words "look pal, these are shit games § when I see how far the repulsive DigimonOtis brand has come after I chose to disassociate myself from it I sweat profusely and dry heave § my gym teacher is outside my house right now screaming about how I owe him 20 pushups from 1973 and that my torso sucks § btecause I was a detestable imbecile in life, and death has only made me stronger § me and my lawyer just tricked my ex-wife into signing an agreement which orders her t o wear a dumbass cowboy hat to work #FuckU #LifeRuiner § my agent said i'm not allowed to post in all caps anymore so i threw all of his award-winning birdhouses into the fucking driveway § otis is criminal and a liar § DELTA FARCE, WITLESS PROTECTION, HEALTH INSPECTOR€" THREE INTEGRAL COMPONENTS, PRIDE OF THE AN-CIENTS; VITA INFINITUM; LARRY THE ASCENSION GUY § im going to fuck your porch up § enjoy your circle jerk, tyrants § im Shit efron § apparently im not good enough for the pep boys to follow me on twitter. apparently the pep boys fan fiction i poured my soul into is a waste § principal surveys the premises from his shitty Dodge Caliber, sees the jeans dealer trying to peddle his stash on school grounds & calls 911 § lknow what pisses me off?? people who drink milk and spit the milk back into their glasses while making a smug expression. also teenage . § when people upload pics of misc.electronics and the shit just is covered in dust, crumbs,etc i usually have to sign off for a sec &cool down § #PeopleIReallyWantToMeet #oopsiforgot #Celtics forget all of this garbage. when are we gonna nab Osama § all the trolls talk shit about my profession as an artisan ass wiper. but when they see my fine selection of towels they beg for my services § ok publicist says i gotta do one about the zach braff kickstarter ok uh uh*claps hands* alright€"€" what if instead of money he asked for PIss § so what's the deal with benghazi. are you benghazi???? why is potus hiding from benghazi § obana. i know you're reading this. where's benhgazi. what did you do with the benghazi man. release the benghazi gems. #YouJustPulledAnObama § uploading pictures of yourself crying is one of the big No-Nos of brand management. instead trry uploading a fun recipe. or a quick prayer § ive alwas wanted my name printed beneath a mummy's head § Data Coursing Thru Every Vein, The Ultimate Fusion Of Man And Machine, Sites And Apps Becoming Blood And Flesh Becoming GOd § my muscles begin to glow with the intensity of 100,000 sun` s. this can only mean one thing€"€"€"€" there's trouble at the gym § i probably spend the majority of my leisure time punching a hideous effigy of the caveman who invented sex § now, bear wtih me here, what if, hypothetically, a teen reacted to "Yolo" **a massive sack of $$$ materializes in front of me for no reason* § if a tree falls in the forest and a Teen Does NOt React, does it make a sound? ? § i will nbe referring to a certain soda brand as "p*psi" until i receive the $16 they owe me for years of aggressive social content strategy § Teens React To Noise. Teens React To Bugs. Teens React To The Normalization Of Warfare. Teens React To Teens Reacting. Teens React To Fritos § do nOT buy "grab bag" option at the Onion Brothers' Onion Emporium. it is a trick devised to sell you undesirable onions § if our lives were like a highschool cafeteria the cool kids table would be occupied by those guys who mess up their dicks for body mod blogs § the way i talk ids really good and normal as hell § if a terrorist tried to get me. i'd just say like, "gods fake dude" then punch the gun out of his hand while hes contemplating the hereafter § i went to a long john silvers once § i would really like to attend my grandsons funeral but at the same time i just want to sit in bed and explore my body with a peacock feather § The SHeriff's Department Denies Your Request To Be Sat On By Muscle Ladies As Punishment And Would Like For You To Pay Your Ticket With Cash § you know the ancient sumerians regarded men with wide-ass necks and tiny-ass heads as divine beauties and gave them gifts of gold and barley § http://t.co/Vq9OvjXyKJ Here's That Fucking Awufl Kfc Page People Have Been Asking Me To Re-Upload § despite this being the 1 day that allows the legal use of "Ghanja", i will isntead opt to absorb the celebrated works of Foxworthy & Engvall § i wan't to get all my straight uncles to flick spoonfuls of sour cream at them leathers § @glennbeck I was a big fan until you decided to get all Political on us. Unfollowed. § more than god § i hope to increase my respectable klout score of 99 by punishing the demons that plague my account in the form of unfunny post s § so which corporate twitter accounts are the best for hurling abuse and vile insults towards in exchange for coupons and. deals § i walk by. my shirt has the words "ALL I NEED IS" written on front. you're confused until you see the back of my shirt which says "MUDBIKES" § if death regulation affects my god-given ability to put holes in garbage and animals really loudly i will kiss the toilet 1000 times and die § i can post sex things in times of crisis § my uncle called me a Loser on television way before this guy';s uncle did it @ cnn @reuters @infowars @gameinformer § reddit user "IncestVader" has just confirmed that @RicinElvis is thbe culprit , is on the loose, and is going bonkers. please yell at him § mmph *dips another tostito into an ashtray full of ketchup * ah it's so good *licks salty residue off of my bloated purple fingers* mhmm § yea http://t.co/xf26vLIO6Z § red lobster kidzone and this one § i cna list numerous occasions where i have been discriminated against in a racist fashion just because i am a content creator . § i stumble into a nameless town and see an ass pressed up against a screen door. i instinctively turn around and walk back towards the desert § cant deal with people who have such an utter disregard for brand integrity that they would log on without a shirt. this is not a pornno. § apparently shirtless people are interacting with me on this site. please put on a tasteful button-down top if you want to fav or retweet me. § my wife gives birth to a beautiful vintage schlitz beer tap handle. i kiss her softly on the forehead & put it on display next to the others § http://t.co/eGp7M4l4FB were u there the day DragonBlaster laid down his arms & surrendered to the deranged corporate interests of Big Diaper § I AM WASTE § i have still not ruled out the possibility that the jellyfish i stepped on while collecting seashells at the beach was a False Flag § I AM NOT AFRIAD TO USE THE WORDS "FU*K" AND "S*HT" WHEN DEALING WITH SNAKE OIL SALESMEN ON THE PHONE § if youre following me for vids of me smearing chocolate syrup all over my chest. i dont do that anymore, and i suggest u read the holybook . § been driving in circles with the wife & kids since 3am trying to find a place that will service my denim and we're all yelling at each other § if you work with compute,r, if you know Code, if you do Code, please, please design a hot tub app that i can use in the hot tub § yeah whatever pal; im such an asshole for feeding my nail clippings to the birds at the park instead of sending em off to the dunp. fuck off § we have just been informed that more and more teens are buying "wax lips" from candy stores. do not be fooled. these are not their real lips § i have posted severla high-res images of my teeth & gums for the inspection of the trolls. they will find that they look like a normal man's § search "crash bandicoot is real" >> Did you mean "Crash Bandicoot Israel"? search " o" § #BedBugsFeedLists blood, § unlike the rest of you clowns, i want to watch dog the bounty hunter's entire body morph into a fingerless leather glove for ASEXUAL reasons § i have been carrying my prophet mohammed body pillow everywhere since i was 14 and i will never forgive the coyote who yanked it off of me § the artist formerly known as "BubsyFucker" is no longer banned from israel. please keep the wiki up to date anmd withhold your judgments § blooper: it is implied that james bond 007 engages in sexual contact. this would never happen in real life because sex is revolting and rude § why did he remove th arby's reference though. arb'ys is one of the most influential brands of 2013. hes a madman § i am nude, shaved, & ready to be submerged within the digital chrysalis where i will generate bigcoins by doing ki warrior poses until i die § plop all feeds with adult content on them right straight into the trash can. twitter is a businness site . § @KloutSupport i demand that you send me my bottle of "Spice Islands Beau Monde" for no reason whatsoever or else i will post my diseased ass § @KloutSupport "There was an error getting your Perk. Please try again or contact support." what the heck. im a Top Influencer for christsake § in veneration of the right honorable baroness my six komodo dragons will be rewarded one etxra " DIPEY CHANGE " and allowed to eat spaghetti § absolute horseshit that im being written up for painting "JORDACHE BOYS" on windshield when i can see the road between the letters just fine § i want to see james bond do steampuck, i want to see bat man do steampuck, i want to see spider man do steampuck, and thats the bottomline. § my agent sent me a list of my followers & circled all crude avatars in red ink. if i dont block these people it WILL cost me the Arby's deal § i use some offbrand shit that my father boaught 200 cases of in 1998. dont know the name, the labels just a picture of a cobra. sorry § i will go to great lenghts to prove that i take real showers. i will send pH samples of my flesh to th trolls. i will take pics of wet tub. § indie punk rock band "THe 9/11 Forgetters" wanted by police after imploring their audience NOT to watch ABC's wednesday night comedy lineup § if you insult the tiny pepsi can at the bottom of the buzzfeed article your'e fit for the bathroom. i will never let you look at my posts. § number three. the footage of me struggling to shove a barbell into a toilet stall that isn't wide enough is " FALSE " and must be earased. § number one. it is my right as a gold's gym member to bring barbells into the toilet stall and get my extra reps. number two. its not cheatig § @pepsi die from dehydration § @pepsi how many pepsi points will I score if I change my avatar to pepsi logo § going to prove once and for all that trolls are Bullshit by having a narcissistic meltdown on my tech humor wordpress & logging off for 5hrs § Cynical zombie nerd. Diabetic meme dynamo. Country gal. Mustard guru. Unrepentant photo blogger. Bacon dipshit. Entrepreneur. Goalie. § the digital man takes a sneaky peek around the library,. activates his darknet chakras, runs a Grid search on "dale earnheartd wackin it" , § my cigar rival just posted another vid.... time to leave the kids with nana , switch it to hell mode and outsmoke this BAStard § i have never looked at my own dick in my entire life. not once § RufusPussy. PussysRufus. RufusPussyLord. PussyManRufus. PussyWhizRufus. RufusPussyExpert. Pussy_Rufus. PussyEnchanterRufus. PussRuf. § death to false muscles § i roll a massive barrel labeled "Gangnam Content" into a lavish nyc party attended by high profile artists and accidentally crush a mans leg § i am now pregnant with my own shadow form and i am looking forward to feeling it move around in my belly as it explores mme. this it real § my huge legs and a vile hunched back § I AM ONLY ALLOWED TO RESPOND TO 1 MORE CRAIGLIST AD BY LAW. NO STRINGS MUNICIPAL PUMP HOUSE SEX OR 14 FREE CINDER BLOCKS? IM HAVING A STROKE § my big april prank: scream about my dick for 5 years on a website that people normally use to socialize with friends and loved ones § despite google's bullshit-- today is National Criminal Log Off Day. if you're a criminal then log off § #TenLiberalCommandments thou shalt kiss the dicks of our troops and lick their dicks also for disrespecting them and making them sad § onl;y if i'm allowed to pray 15 times a day and drink coffee and suck dicks § IGN: "octomom caught Gaming" Gawker: "octomom is a gamer and i want to smooch her" TMZ: "ocotomom GAMES? hhuUWHAAT??" Wired: "octomom game" § WHAT IS A "FUCK LUNG" § http://t.co/QlbDYzU1sD calling all my dubai followers to step up and pour a bottle of htis down my ass crack § "Master Distiller Jeff Arnett explains what makes Sinatra Select's character as smooth and bold as the man himself, Frank Sinatra." it piss § people always talk down on the Zoo but if your'e a shitty animal like me it is a great place to network and be gawked at for zero pay § a bunch of cops knock my colostomy bag on the floor and begin stepping on it with high heeled shoes while i jack off and ask them to stop it § thats why im a bing man § they want to build a masque on the sunken remains of the titanic; dont let um § ever since i read a life changing book i have desired the ability to morph into a Policeman at will. i will not divulge the name of the book § im The Pepsi Eunuch Bitch!!! i don't give s FUCK !!! § thte name "ThePepsiEunuch" was taken. to clear up any confusion § my youtube account "ThePepsiEunich" has earned me $48 in ad revenue throughout 2010-2012. id rather die than let the

GOVT take a cent of it. § i want to be wearing google glass when i see my wife in her wedding dress fofr the very first time so i can turn it into a big dorito § only if u respect muscle § “BIBLE” § before the holy ghost died--- there was the father, the son and TacoBellMaven § IM LOGGED IN AUTO MATICALLY THANK YOU § please keep my denny’s coupon gender rant off of wikipedia’s list of notable tantrums-- it is NOT notable § log off., you piss covered reptiles, youre turning good bandwidth into shit § MOSQUITO cannot breed inside of faucet if it is running constantly... use this infor wisley § i can’t tell you how many serious UFO vids i’ve seen ruined by the slow zoom out and reveal of a man jacking it § maybe one of my followers could donate a tonsil or something so i can finally upgrade my dick § halfway through the work day and my boss STILL hasnt noticed im stuck in a pair of handcuffs. ur dealing with the Master. #FuckU #BaldPrick § YOU WILL NEVER WASH YOURSELF AGAIN AFTER WATCHING THIS WISE OLD YOUTUBE CLIP WHICH HAS BEEN ï¼¢ï¼¡ï¼®ï¼®ï¼¥ï¼¤ ï¼¢ï¼¹ ï¼¤ï¼¯ï¼£ï¼´ï¼¯ï¼²ï¼³ § please stop calling my home with fucked up three stooges noises. my nine daughters no longer respect me after seeing me get mad at the phone § i sense a demonic presence clicking x on my usless posts.......... § @dril_replies normal garfield, water garfiel, shadow garfield, are all straight and i want that written down right here today § http://t.co/lXs1ebLULn Fight For Your Brand § SOLVE MY ASS § trolls have cost me the Dairy Queen deal. Dairy Queen will not take my account seriously because of these people. § petition to change the twitter bird into a shittier, less noble animal, l ike a pig or an ape § @glennbeck to his credit, doctors are often too busy counting their blood money to learn anything smart about body’s. § its just hte #SexLife § i choke myslef with a bra on webcam and my face becomes so purple and bloated that the software no longer recognizes it as a face #sexlife § @glennbeck harmony korine’s “trash humpers” § i, turdghoul fuckass, swear to uphold the constitution of the united states of america, so help me Piss. ok sorry, now let me do it for real § idont eat § go to bed dad § my father banned me from taking shits after 8:00pm until i was 19 and this instilled within me a sense of morality and honor and respect § NETFLIX DIAPER NOW #WOAH#Real § im not fucking finished deconstructing the god damn diaper concept, and im not fucking finished flooding your worthless feed with shit mouth § on a rickety stage at some empty roadhouse, a True mississippi blues man is howling aobut diapers, unappreciated by the toilet using masses § i remark “mummies are made out of diapers” at the egypt museum. some cops jump out a sarcophagus and begin humping me as i roll on the floor § “diapers are for animal at the zoo”. nmever in my life have i seen a more ignorant comment written online and overlooked by the hitler media § these flawless squats on the roof of my van go out to the bastard who accused me of “going apeshit” a t wild birds unlimited in marietta, ga § nboody has ever requested that u log in. § #10ThingsYouHateToDo jack off, not jack off, 3 4 5 6 7 8 9 10 § i can help with this-- you;re supposed to click the “follow” button on my page and leave it clicked on § (the presence of the sarcasm tag indicates that i do not actually want to suck god’s dick. please dont derail this discussion with nonsanse) § GET PAID TO CRY - MAKE UP TO “$4.98” A DAY SOBBING ON WEBCAM -MAIL US TEARS FOR Ð²onÏ…Ñ•Ð²Ï…Ñ…®- ABJECT HUMAN MISERY IS THE LIFEBLOOD - DIE A HERO § i have made peace in hte name holy christ and will gracefully accept my ban § a blank one § i want to fuck a sheet of paper § hte beautiful 50,000+ year old goddess Washu Hakubi, rightfull mother of Ryoko and Angel, makes an extremely valid point § the next big online thing is men who eat Dog Food, schedule meetups to eat dog food together and form rivalries with cat & baby food eaters § i will never apologize for accidentally dialing 911 in my jeans pocket or accidentally begging the operator for a “cop massage” § uzbeks found attempting to modify their devices & remove the Croods interface are subject to public lashings and fines of up to 10000000 UZS § i can confirm israeli android os WILL use a gui based on art assets from dreamworks The Croods & that this is exciting news for Crood likers § idont know who runs that account but i am most certainly a huge piece of shit regardless § i thjink i'd know the difference between Satan and a noisy washing machine with "666" spraypainted on the side § my girl beliefs own, my sex beliefs own, my god beliefs own, my page owns, i m always yelled at, im always hacked , im garbage and thank you § im sorry but what are the odds that 100 snakes would hatch from that huge egg i found in the swamp. in a way, we pretty much won the lottery § i turned myself into a skunk using an incantation posted by 11 year old girl on youtube. i should not have done this. please, please help m § viral ??? now were talkin § if i win that wendy's contest i will do the right thing and choose to set dick vitale free § yeah lets all j ust sit here and pretend everythin'gs ok while dick vitale sells his body to the wendy's corporation for big buck § i just heard someone was angry on a website and now im angry and people are angry at me for being angry at him and im angry at them too #hel § i just looked up the stats and the number of meaningful relationships ive formed is less than the number of public restrooms ive Screamed in § They also have to eat the shit § haha get this, these people on the crisue boats that get stranded, they have to shit ON the boat, and sometimes they even touch the shit!!!! § #iKnowImNotTheOnlyOneWho the pope § hosanna !! hosanna !! netbooks for dog lovers § @dril_replies How's your diaper? Want any of my sexy turds? ASS!! holy Fu,ckin ass!! Haha, good shit. Retweet me § BONE DEAD.......... § buck bumble caressed his dead gfs hair. "you will pay for thi s, Bastards." he grabbed two uzis and charged the gym, "Suprise mother fuckers § MMORPG (massive multiplayer online roleplayig game), FPS (first person shooter), RTS (real time strategy), T2DF (tactical 2d dragon fucker) § yeah those god likers love to shit § lets ACTUAlly shove atheism down christians throats. cram godless voids into their mouths which nullify the Prayers of their digestive tract § keelhaul my dick § my solemn vow of shit § i'm pepsi rep kevin and we need $12m kickstarter dollars to make a pepsi commercial in true 8 Bit. lets show this new pope what were made of § ---------> GET A BRIAN LIAR< ------- § the audience gasps as i, @dirl, divulge onto webspace, my invalid opinions, quips, and horseshit gags while smoking 2 cigarettes ,simultÃ¡neo § i was dying, no one helped § i dont know § what th the bope use "google glass" #retweetthisifYouragirl § the banned version of "'lord of the flies" where the conch is replaced by a fat immobile pug dog § wendy's contest to win lunch with dick vitale cancelled due to 'sex people'. entries infused with distinct erotic musk handed over to police § not even legendary blade Masamune could offer these awful creatures a death as swift & honorable as my patented Ass Crush § #atlanticecon please disable all of your wi-fi devices to prevent Gremlins from entering this trustsphere of minds. inflation is a myth. bye § mnever. my signature technique could bring serious injury if attempted by a layman § Yes § as a lad i often drew 2 adjacent circles in a crude attempt to portray an Ass. ive since matured and only draw asses of the utmost precision § corn on the cob § i can not sleep sound knowing a disgusting criminal is out there hogging my rightful Like`s § tthis asshole brought home a tekken lanyard with "Phil" written on it in magic marker and wants to use it with the keys to his new buick . § youtube recommending large amount of gamestop dumpster dive videos to me; perhaps hteyve implemented a new algorithm which detects "Misery" § thr new pope has been chosen. you all ready for this?? his name is..... The Bible. #BloodOfTheEucharist #FwdThisIfYoureAWiseTeen #HeavenTeen § sheriff's department transmission decoded by anonymous: "Please Keep Rowdy Beasts Away From Mayor During Dog Show"--what could it all mean?? § i will never apologize for my ass no matter how many people close their accounts. i will never apologize for the gestures i make with my ass § full investigation: bring me the man who threw a dildo on stage during my TEd talk. also the men who encouraged him by hooting and whistling § dont know how a vandal wrote "Likes to Fuck" on my resume, but i do not like to fuck. please hire me. i need this job. i hate to fuck, pleas § blood the hedgeohg. mewtwo the hedgehog. dwayne the hedgehog. muscles the hegehog. christ the hedgehog. marcus the hedgehog. § #MentionSomeoneCuteAndBeautiful raynn the hedgehog. akira the hedgehog. mydnyght the hedgehog. venus the polaer bear. gomez the hedgehog. § purchased a cage full of rats in the hope that infusing my home with New Life will fire up my posts a nd score me the Bertucci's deal. amen § "Destroy the content producers, destroy the content. This is , Bastard's Dilemma." - christwolf22, from his e-book "A World Without Content" § cancel-ling my livetweet of the pa flower show becaus of the SHIT you people have said to me, tthis is the bed you laid in, this is your hell § when people fuck with me on sites i head for the beach and take it out on the crabs. i punch their shitty little bodies, i kick dirt at them § fucked up that people would click X on my feed during what is perhaps the worst crisis i've ever faced. go back to the zoo. miserabl animals § if you feel uncomfortable reading about my balls infection, click X. if not, pour a good big beer and let my feed take you to another world, § i've just been notified by the oracle that late night personal-ity jay leno is currently in Denim Mode. § im redoing the funeral for my ass because nobody took the first one seriously enoguh. too many attendees yapping off & refusing to be seated § " BASTARD " § anoter sony fanboy. move along § no. my bumper sticker of beautiful intergalactic bounty hunter Samus Aran saying "Im Autistic" couldnt have been the reason my car was towed § nascar saga IV: elder blade: honor of car § i paid good money for these sweatpants and i reserve the right to wear them to Game Stop without the wiseass brigade photographing mmy rear. § @Adobe something that i wouldve used an actual animation program to develop i f i had any fucking sense whatsoever @adobe #cocks § NEVER MAKE ANYTHING IN FLASH - FUCK PLEASE GOD @adobe #shit § dde-pressed, exhausted imbecile dragging an overturned port-o-john down the interstate, blocking traffic and getting honked at § a particularly rude comment i received today has caused me to fill my pants wih shit. i will not glorify the perpetrator by identifying him. § i just bought an Oscar on the black market and im willing to give it to the first bbw to send me a pic of herself fisting ehr own mouth. § who remembesr the mower man screensaver. who remembers the fear of it. who remembers not even being sure if the screams were coming from you § i want the popular new animated gif of me looking at a messy old trash can while lickin my lips; Removed . Remove it off- site. Log it out. § i reserve the right to blog my yap off in defiance of the trolling groups and hate communities who want to disrupt my cashflow § buying some golf cleats? bet U high society FUCKS like to step on each others COCKS with these. i own this foot locker. your'e a child here. § can almost hear the angels screaming as i plunge the dagger into my chest and abdicate my destiny as He Who Would Forge The Unwettable Denim § if youre reading this NascarDustin, you are requested to appear in court for the crime of firing 600 chi needles into my innocent ass cheeks § raise Hell to end workplace discrimination against men who suffer from PL (Pube Loss). force my boss to pay due tribute to my pristine mound § "although i cannot be the father she needs, i wish my daughter the best of luck on her life path. now let us sound, gentlemen." - konami_boi § konami_Boi gives his baby daugther up for adoption so he can convert her crib into a display case for his exotic collection of sounding rods § did anyone do the "google ass" joke. did anyone do thr joke where "google glass" is changed with the word "ass" in it. hope a nerd sees it § i am the great benghazio . i need Truth for my justice hole #funButSerious #BanMeForMyOpinions #HowDareU #SomosFiOS § ive had it up to here with this benghazi fella. callin up a few rowdy boys to do some jumping jacks on his lawn § Thank you. Closure at last #tcot RT: @ Mythbusters Adam and Jamie "Go Benghazi" in the all-new season premiere of Mythbusters, don't miss it! § #FiveWordTEDTalks god is real... (real BOgus)

#ThingsGirlsLike free copper wire #LiesToldInSchool principals have sex #MakeLeighLaugh no § http://t.co/V5SvukJwXO miracle bird. kfc kfc kfc kfc § I WILL REGRESS INTO PRIMAL FORM AND SHUN MY LOVED ONES IN ORDER TO POWER UP MY CONTENT !! I WILL GET RE-BLOGS AT ANY COST !! AT ANY COST !! § #ThingsGirls-Like Moonlit Sega Rants § #ThingsGirlsLike ccalling me a fucking bastard and strangling me with their legs while my head turns purple and im horny and screaming mad § review: koala kare diaper station with the fuckin bear on it. awful. sorry im not some size 0 model who can use this without it snapping off § sorry. my "wrestle a pile of huge dildos for charity" event was a total imbroglio. all proceeds raised must now go towards my hospital bill § log off. now. this is not a horny account. § no. this is a business proposition. no sex § 1) i lie face down on sofa 2) infect me witrh lyme disease 3) it's NOT ok to contact this poster with services or other commercial interests § @kfc_colonel "son, if you think we deserve better, let me remind you that the large wooden 'H' affixed to our kitchen wall stands for "Hell" § sequester THIS !! *i show my ass. a dick flops out of my ass. a tiny ass comes out of the hole of the dick coming out of my ass* Fuck obam § "Yo. Lets get some owl tattos." - something a hipster has probably said once in the course of human history #DOUChe #jokeums #heteroBoyLords § PROSECUTION: could you please tell the court who exactly youre referring to when you use the term "Gender Folk"? ME: not to a bastard like U § reading my revolting tweets to a focus group for several hours and escaping on a sled pulled by rats when it is time to pay each of them $25 § as i have stated repeatedly on this blog, my favorite philosopher is Ben Stein . § i imagine to the lice who live in my chest hair, my enormous, frowning head is God; their only beacon of hope, thats why i never wear shirts § subset of lava § sky wiccan, lava wiccan, river wiccan, light wiccan, dark wiccan. thats all the wiccans § the point being that thte damn computer should know exactly which download i want when i type "'chris matthews mindfreak" into the bing bar § to the fanboy who threw acid iat my face near fuddrucker`s, you can destroy my body but The Cloud will preserve my brand for millennia #PS4 § remember blowing on the CDs to make them work? blowing on controllers?? memory cards? pplease validate this broken man #PlaystationMemories § i would appreciate it if the words "unconscious hog" were removed from the daily post article about me , as i am no longer unconscious . § THE LAST UNBANNED ALCHEMIST ON EBAY § I AM VERY BAD ARMENIAN LADY ! I AM SO BAD THAT EVEN DEVOL IS AFRAID OF ME ! I WILL TEAR ENYBODYS SPIRIT & GIVE IT TO HIM ; WHO PUT DISLIKE ! § ill have no more talk of mystery complaints regarding my screensaver of juiced ass dudes turning into snakes then back into juiced ass dudes § "the best part of U runned down the crack of ya mammas Ass when she-" ugh i fucked that up. wait "best part of yopu run down the ass w-"Shit § everyone screaming at me cus i accidentally made tge dog deaf by yelling memes at it. if the meteor kills us all i wont give a Fuckin Shit ! § i would NEVER misappropriate funds from my panera bread gloryhole kickstarter to buy mustard gas,, you BRUTES , oyu selfish, horrible APES § please watch my realtiy drama"shit eaters" about people who eat shit and are constantly goaded into cyclical arguments with their loved ones § so you DONT insure tupperware contaners filled with magazine cutouts of legs & feet? what if i told you some of these badboys are reagen era § not at all unreasonable to assume that everyone who has ever unfollowed me likes to engage in mystic forest ritual to make my muscles tinier § Japanese;Chinese,Ko-rean;Vietnamese are the only Asian women that I have ever known. That is why I use their look and experiences. § This site is dedicated to the love and respect of Asian women. If you are here looking for porn... "MAN ARE YOU IN THE WRONG PLACE!" § IS BLUE TOILET WATER A RETRO 90S THING OR HAVE I JSUT NOT SEEN A CLEAN TOILET FOR 13+ YEARS. PLEASE HELP § before you make fun of the band that me and digimonotis started in 2002 called "Pube Supply", be aware that we didn't know what a pube was. § if someone names their son or daughter

“Funny Rubio Water Drink” i swear to god i will write your username on a post-it and post a pic of it § disappointed by lack of respect for the pope by the goofus brigade. i on the other hand respect the mans ass cheeks. i respect the mans legs § during tibetan sky burials theres always the risk that the birds will eat everything except your dick and that people will laugh at the dick § all the wonderful fictional characters i remember from my suburban middle-class 90s childhood break into my home & scrutinize my filthy dick § maestro stands on top of my couch and waves baton perfectly in rhythm with my clicks and scrolls as i block rude accounts & erase sass mouth § open pastebin of LAPD shooter’s manifesto. ctrl+f search for injoke staples such as “jeans”, “diaper” and “toilet”. no results. click x. § Mahmoud Ahmadinejad Has A New Wine Out. I’m Dying To Try It But I Find His Governing Policies Questionable At Best. Such Is My Life Of Shit. § HLUUUUUUUUUl § my old phys ed teacher let`s me kiss his cpr dummy for $15 a pop and that’[s why im more mature than most of people on this fucking web site § please. look at this thing on my ipod that i loaded up. it is called “the geico talking dog” and it is spectacular. please look. please § whoever put “give skeleton huge titty” in the suggestion box: first off, this isnt a suggestion box. its a toys for tots bin. secondly; § mabye this decal of the troll face saying “DID YOU TRY RESTARTING IT??” will make the boys in IT respect me &stop kicking my cube walls down § and here we go again. another civil symposium, bungled up and ruined by me, the horny asexual. everyone always blames me, the horny asexual. § parking garage conquered by disgusting man covered in vaseline § mario tennis § IT SUCKED AND BROKE § “do turds carry gneder. are there male turds & female turds.” good question, Walter_PSX. hte answer, however, is not so clear cut im afraid; § please @ gangnamjokes. post the first gangnam joke. please. you piece of shit. please dont squat this account and gyp us on the gangnam joke § please put the king of skeletons back underneath his parkig lot before he starts yellin . disrespect-ful fucking rat people mother fuckers § smear turds all over my dunce cap and kill me § @LEVEL5_IA please explain wjhy your latest game contains a despicable portrayal of the prophet Muhammad?? http://t.co/JfLLDN8N #allah #islam § i rip off my groundhog handler disguise on stage. “surprise bitchs. groundhog day is fake.” i drop kick the fuckin groundhog back to the zoo § I have never been horny. I have never even thought about becoming horny. Get off line from me. § i jsut imagined a nude body and winded my self § reviewed obama inauguration speech. not ONE mention of “varmints” #ProVarmintPres?? #getUmOut § thanks for banning mme for having the username “WTCPuncher” , even though I registered that name before hte towers blew up in a car accident § what do I model, you ask? i model for those gag golf trophies that are given to bad players by coworkers as a joke. guy with twisted up club § starwave, hotflux , gumcore, bigsnap , powerbox, piss-hop, classic mouth, soul flute, birdstep, rock ‘N’ rol, serbia drum, james bond § instantly the king of jail after telling other inmates that im in for dropkicking “WTFCraig” when he said avatar is a ripfof of bluemangroup § TODAY WE EXPLORE THE LINK BETWEEN WIDESPREAD SOIL EROSION IN HAITI AND MY FAVORITE TV SHOWS BECOMING LESS FUNNY § TODAY WE EXPLORE THE PROVEN INTELLECTUAL ADVANTAGE OF CHILDREN WHO HAD GENERAL HOSPITAL FANFICTION READ TO THEM IN THE WOMB § TODAY WE EXPLORE THE CONTRIBUTIONS THAT WOMEN HAVE MADE TO ARENA PITBULL DEATHMATCH § A GATHERING OF MISCHIEVOUS IMPS FIRE UP THE NINTENDO 64 AND RUN MARIO UP THE ENDLESS STAIRCASE FOR 1 HR § local orgy vibe ruined by man who made terrible dog howls while extremely caught up in the moment - bastard is now imprisoned in astral cube § if heading to the gym and muscleshaming all the sweatnerds aint your idea of a good time then im afraid you are a waste of a daughter § moms boyfriend think `s selling dioramas of discarded tarantula husks perfoming sex acts is “bad”; throws my 30yr old cozy coupe at me daily § attn teens who wolud crack wise abot my grotesque, misshap-en ear lobes: i am pissed of, overtaxed and ready to die in the name of Lady

Honor § do not contact this account until you have truly felt the pain of a big male. § only thing stopping me from being th 1st diaperbound wiccan 2 scale everest are all the handsome climbers who're prejudiced aganst big peopl § caught sneaking a runestone into the cineplex. the runes they sell at the concession stand are all marked up to shit. thats how htey get ya § i just found out today that my best friend and confidant of 11 years is a beers drinker. this troper is NOT amused § oyu investigate the mysterious object that falls out of my shirt onto a pile of bibles. your worst suspicions are confirmed. it's a hairball § from what i undestand gerrymandering is the process of manipulating districts in such a manner that gnarly dicks show up on the election map § and today's Golden Toilet award goes to the cast of Weekend at Bernie's 1 & 2 ofr disobeying the noble qur'an. § my posts are top niotch and i keep myself clean § hte nightmare is just beginning. google "sewer myth" § fuck yea i remember. backrubs. dunkaroos. bag clips. sunsets. teeth. all these things were sacrificed in the y2k crisis § cyber link this post if youre a good person who remembers the things that are good and are not a bad person who likes things that arent good § so you want to upgrade your jeans. i suggest you gather 3x daenim shards, 2x bug honey, and 4,000 ralphs. only then will u be worth my time. § @dril maybe this make sense to ya. http://t.co/551SP9sY § *corsses out all the bad posts in perm. marker* mmm . haha. oh yeah. look at that *scrolls down and t he posts move* no. this wont do. oh no § think im gonna bust the window on my microwave open and nuke my ass for a little bit § the man who froze his shit and cut them into tiny disks to fool the coinstar machine is probably the closest thing to real life james bone . § is it spiritually advisable to circumcise my sons if they're conjoined twins attached at the foreskin § nick jr. wanted to publish my memoirs - told them to take a hike with the kid shit § MEDICAL "PROFESSIONALS" WHO REFUSE TO TELL ME THE AMOUNT OF WEIGHT I NEED TO GAIN TO BECOME A PURE BLOOD IMMOBILE #THINGSTHAT-MAKEYAHOWLOFF § me and my roving band of gorgeous cop punchers suffer the indignity of detecting the scent of piss. we pause and atempt to locate the source § probably WHACKEN OFF!!!!!!!!!!!!!! Fuck otis § #girltime "dating",as we know it,is an outdated pratice that can be traced back 2 thge pre-sapiens imbecile, hurling turds at their pregnant § the experimental surgical procedure to make my tears stink less was a complete failure. im sorry everyone § THE BAB E................................ #RaunchyonMLKBirthday #MLKRaunchyDay § horny supremacy § im a Dipshit § he killed himself on friday § jail § i believe in sex. i work with asphalt and i respect the asphalt. pain is my god and heaven. i am NOT a ï¼§ï¼¡ï¼ï¼¥ï¼² ï¼¤ï¼µ ï¼£ï¼¡ï¼³ï¼µï¼¡ï¼¬. sponsored by nestle § hats off to the shirtless man who found spelling error in my 2yr old tweet but failed to realize that everythng i post is irredeemable filth § why is it a crime for me to confine garbage using my sweatpants and why does everonye on couchsurfing .org get mad when i yell at them § just this disgusting twitetr account for now § i got rid of it cus it broke my phone and criminals were usig it to give me heart attacks § you fuck yourselfs for this bastard move . § used the last remaining amount of my spirit force to transform mny daughter into a mana blade so that she will never cry again #AFathersPain § cheers to whoever poured paint on me while i was handing out pamphlets warning people not to attend MetalGearEric's orgy #FAlseFlag666 § i get really upset when matrix haters refer to the greatest cinematic achievement in human history as "bullshit time". youre a fool and liar § all sports is the same § oh so when a pro foorball player makes a fake GF everoyne sucks his dick but when nice boys like me do it the cops demolish her with batons, § if you have a problem with me kissing pictures of Dragons while driving the bus, fight me. i just ate like 30 hotdogs and im near invincible § NO NOT HERE § http://t.co/Tfa7VBWJ please. ask me anythig § barricaded in a lawless southern town for calling the one where pikachu choked on an entire apple a "filler episode" § i was going to make a joke about the food pyramid and eating mummies or something but i stopped because occasionally teens look at this feed § hell § reported. lock um up § car wash big man. big man thru car was.h can car wash be used on big man. can big man survive car washj. does car wash clean big man. #Bing § #ff @UrineFREE @starwarsman @Blogboi2292 @Diabetes666 @SonictheEduardo @PrimoHoagies @Network-Man @fanjustthe @tigerwoodsjokes @depresed @toe § sotp insulting me § fuck wifi http://t.co/ntA35Tsn § for years i've put up with the piss lobbyists and their laughable attempts to silence me. i will not use th bathroom again until theyre dead § next slide, please. this is a chart showing piss levels in the lungs of eastern & western public bathroom goers. the discrepancy is obvious. § bathrooms in japan have virtually no piss on them. this is because the culture has instilled a sens e of humility within the people. no piss § i hereby pledge henceforth to never piss on the floor of a public batrhoom. if youre "too cool" to care about this social issue then log off § *aims revolver at the word "mosque"* prepare to kiss my steel, fucker. *accidently shoots a period at the end of it* NNO WHAT HAVE I DONE § attn supporters of hashtag #JackOffForTheEagles: thgis is NOT an official, NFL sanctioned method of supporting our birds. use xtreme caution § *reclines in chair a nd ages 2 ,000 years instantly turning into a skeleton and then pile of shit* ah everything's going according to plan § fuck mad people. anger is a disgusting emotion. sick of having my account flagged by people who dont understand The Process § #WhyGunsAreBetterThanLiberals THE 63RD SEAL MUST CONSUME THE SHADE OF BLOODFALL IN COMPLIANCE WITH THE NIGHT COMMAND, ANDMICHAL MOORE IS FAT § cor blimey,. down load the Bing Bar today m'lord, follow MadeaREal,ItsReal_Madea, Madea_FunJoke,& MadeaPuertoRico, my beautiful daugter ~uwa § please dont tell the boys at t he gym that ive been slapping clown urine on my pecs. they may not be totally understanding of the situation. § "the ancient americans had over 20 words for sandwich but only 1 word for betamax. fucked up but real" says a future man to his crystal son § WHO SUMMONE D WRESTLERS TO MY YARD. I DESPERATELY NEED STOMACH MEDS AND IM AFRAID TO GO LEAVE HOSUE. MY BIRDBATH HAS ALREADY BEEN SUPLEXED § in 2023 an unassuming fat man will become the official currency of the united states. the economy will collapse because theres only 1 of him § for hte last time im not badfrog3333 im this guy http://t.co/KpjbucKS § https://t.co/JqyzTyl9 https://t.co/hSx1buQw https://t.co/XypytTp5 badfrog3333 § everyone who does this please also google the phrase "is knuckles the echidna black" § in 1942 the US Navy sponsored an experiment which required 64 prisoners in Massachusetts to be injected with cow blood #FemaleLies § if anyone knows what to do if you accidentally swallow an entire cigar while running on the treadmill please contact StogieLad@Yahoo.com § @Princeofass ass is nonsovereign. he is claiming to be the prince of it for page hits. § RESULTS ARE IN: The Pibb Xtra 2012 Gold Prize is rewarded to "Football". The Pibb Xtra 2012 Stinker Award goes to the fireman shooter. Bye § i feel like if i practiced often enough and really focused i could learn how to shave all the hair off of my body using only my fingernails § today's the day that i put on my high heel cowboy boots & stomp the shit out of the fake plastic son that my father raised before i was born § i want to put on a really ugly shirt but i can't because of trolls. AAAGH **unscrews lightbulb from lamp, throws it into toilet, perfect aim § My lawyer has advised me that I should power the box off instead of dealing with hipster comments and trash insults on this sacred holiday. § reminder that if you jerk off tomorrow on christmas y ou are the bastard of earth. § This account is a Brand Opportunity Touchstone used by celebrities & rich policemen and people think it's awful but its not. § ever see a good app and say "oh i gotta get my hands on that app !!"?? that feeling is the spirit blood of my Web Strategy. I Am The Sphere § everything i post is a disgusting lie § bad § rating a porno "thumbs down" just because thegirl wouldnt take off her blue tooth head set is one of the moust fucked up things i ever did . § ! !

! I will no longer be answering any sex questions in this website. ! ! ! § im watching my gf transform into wolves . the wolves have the same tattoos that she have. she can turn back into a person when she wants to. § nno. no ball § i need towels sent to my house . this is not a fucking joke this time § Im about to get wild at 2:30am on this Fucking can of #Beer I found. I am going to use my grandpas knfie to "Shot Gun" it. #ThingsILikeToDo § i hate vuvluzela noise. http://t.co/MZv2QI6O. § theyl;l do it until i die and then theyll drag my corpse through the rubble while making awful beast noises § people who write "RT" and copy/paste instead of using the retweet button are the same people who changed clothes in the toilet stalls at gym § #ff @HellYeahTweets @simson @golfblog @HusbandShit @apekiller @JokesFun @xwife @PizzaHutMan @Unemployed_Male @ChristianHacker @babe2 @KFCkid § pleas tune into my next podcast where i ask what the FUCK angry birds is and viciously mock the first piece of shit caller to answer me § "RSS FEeds? ", i say as i stroke my goatee while leaning on my podcast's huge 3d logo " ever Heard of UM !!!!!!!!!!!!" § Im Just The Last Perosn Alive Who Gives A Fuck About The Integrity Of Mom Chat § #MOMCHAT IS TRENDING. #MOMCHAT IS TRENDING. YOU HEARD CORRECTLY, #MOMCHAT IS NOW MAIN-STREAM. EASILY ACCESSIBLE BY FALSE MOMS. FUCK TWITTER § no im screaming § i sometimes wonder how shaken the AB/DL community would be if they found out i was injecting my diaper with saline solution instead of Shit § did you know that the bible doesn't actually contain any references to hell? or heaven? or christ?? it just a bunch of names & phone numbers § WHAT THE...?!?! BUT THAT'S NOT A..... BUT I DON'T WATCH..... BUT YOU... EAAAAAGGHHH § the shaman rises https://t.co/cFfqi3yO § no im boycotting the jpeg image format because it showed me an ass § the mayons were basically dumb as dirt and couldnt even predict the fuckin 9/11 thing § my nipples are purlpe because of an iron deficiency . NOT because i dont believe in god. so shut the fuck up, grand-pop's grave § not many good wiki leaks lately. was hoping Julian woudld find out which individual or agency keeps ripping the gutters off of my house § if you recently dumpster dived a combination dildo/inhaler emblazoned with the hot wheels logo, please return it. thats the only thing i own § whats wrong? u look like youve never seen a depressed,gruesomely obese Mature Hetero who also happens to have gorgeous abs & tight AZZ befor § i tried to drown myself in the toilet but my neck is too big to allow my face to reach the water so now im downloading some nice blogs § one man stands, bravely defiant, against the impending fury of my massive, raw ass. a Troll snaps a picture and puts it in some history book § @JoseCanseco pissman Ultra § where is he. wheres the ass hole. i hate him § what a terrible coincidence that this shooting happened to occur on Gun Joke Day § #ReplaceBandNamesWithDad nutty professor 2 the klumps § as a youth, the boys would laugh at my large ears & call me "The Ears Bastard". but today, I have every epsIode of Sliders at my fingertips. § "you can take that 666 on down the road" is actually etched into my family crest and i scream it everyday § http://t.co/iNSY7WFx great. dale hates me now. fuck this website § @MoonPeople It isnt me. I despise porn and sex. § when I dropped out of middle school I went home& watched korean flash animation "i love egg" like 28 times with tears streaming down my face § im afraid that this will forever be one of the temple `s many secrets § a very nude, very fat pink man rolling down the corridors of an ancient temple, gathering dust and dirt like breadcrumbs on a chicken cutlet § @CapsCop NOPE § i take my gf on a balloon ride to propose. a field of wild flowers spells Women Are Crooks. "oops sorry." i apologize. "that ones for my dad § EMAIL CAMPAIGN TO MAKE THE BOARD OF HEALTH STOP CLASSIFYING MY GIRL FRIEND AS "POISONOUS" § oh sorry. "TheJRPGMotherFucker666" is my old user handle. from when I was a foolish child. my new one is "CockNBallsCummer-ShitheadShithead8" § sorry mom, but if U read my posts u would know why I spiked yuor meatloaf like a football & called it a "piece of shit". because i am scared § #ReplaceLyricsWithTwerk pppppppppppppppppppppppppp (big ffarting ass

noise) fuck you fuck you fuck you § i dont give a rat FUCk about your personal
shit, about your politic's, about your ugly kid and wife, just keep the
Christian sand art coming § if i had the technical expertise to make "rage
comics", i would do one about the cop who caught me trying to take my computer
into the sewer § i have a rare condition which is commonly known a s "pig ear",
and if I was born in the 1950s i would have been euthanized #Blessed § #Leave-
ItIn2012 bin laden. kil;l the piece of shit § my setup: 35 monitors arranged
around my swivel chair in a circular fashion, imprisoning me forever in a 3d
world of sex pics & sports radio § Jsut saw a turd. I'm done. I'm fucking
finished with this. Keep your bullshit snapchat. ENjoy the hell you have
created, trolls. § 1 nipple, 1 male ass, 2 jeans pics, 1 toilet full of
piss,you terrible f ucking people § some ass hole told me to get snapchat so i
did and my name on it is "coward" , please make me regret thnis, please shit
all over my phone § becuase i constantly post stupid shit that people hate § i
hear by claim this guestbook in the name of the m0nsanto christianz. fuck u.
fuck u. fuck u. fuck u. fuck u. fuck u. fuck u. § ZUMBA IS NOT FOR
MOMS!! ZUMBA IS NOT FOR MOMS!! ZUMBA IS NOT FOR MOMS!! STOP STEALING MY
FRIENDS I WANT TO LIVE MY LIFE § Beware of the group of hauntingly beautiful
Latinoes who will post nonsense on your vlog and hypnotize U into bowing before
htier coward god § straight up-- im not here to make friends. im not here to
socialize. im here because this is the only professional Mr. Bucket league in
town § thats disgusting § its me !! Hahaha. Did i just fuck your mind?
Welcome to the web. Where things aint always as they seem § This is f ucked up.
http://t.co/cyqAL31G /m4m/ Gangnam-Piss Jesus christ. Holy shit man. Check out
this fucked up man. § how high does my postcount have to be before i'm eligible
for Mensa § HA HA HA HA HA HA HA 8=======D~~ 8-====D~~~ 8=-====D ~~ § I Dont
respond to th em. The're wild animals. They fucking want me dead § I want you
all t o know that I am not angry. I am acutally laughing at this whole thing.
But Piss_089 should ha ve his computer locked up § Piss_089, noted pervert and
imbecil,e made the ridiculous claim that i "love touching pieces of trash cans"
& that my "gumline is fucked up" § im a 15 year old model, and Morgan Stanley
Investment Management Is My Slice #IsMySlice § diapers are not for babies § my
attempt to expand my wardrobr by cramming a pair of Damascus Jeans into the
office copier has ended with tragedy. escape the 9/11 reality § people have been
printing lots of swears on hot sauce labels as of late § ive been raising my
hell mastery quotient with faerie blood & jazz musick to prepare for the town
hall thugs coming to collect my leaf waste § HMM NOPE § I SUBMERGE MYSELF INTO
THE CORE MIND AND CRACK MYSELF INTO THE BIT-WEB, MERGING MY CONSCIOUSNESS WITH
ALL 18 EPISODES OF THE GASTINEAU GIRLS § i FIRMLY believe that beloved Super
NES luminary "Funky Kong" woul choose Netflix over Hulu , in any Fucking
universe you can throw at me § @Battlefield im a dirty animal. i m a fucking
bastard. § @Battlefield It;s called "The Shocker". The pinky finger is meant to
be inserted into the anus, as well. You're a huge bastard § @Battlefield I
recognize that hand gesutre. It is designed to stimulate sex to a womans Pussy
(vagina). I will report it § maybe try not blocking me before i can respond
"like normal adults do", you heartless, misserrable coward #PigAlert § @
Battlefield he hollered at me in-game. but. i would not axpect a bastard with a
tactless avatar such as yours to understand. § may God continue to bless
#theGameCraze § im not changing it until nicholson's lawyers force me to § i
apologize for referring to everyone who bought my official scent as "The Sucker
Squad" in a private prayer to god that some troll recorded § / ! \\ / ! \\ / !
\\ " Twizzler " has Acclaimed your Intergram / ! \\ / ! \\ / ! \\ >>> [Learn
more about " Twizzler "] >>> [Return To Hub Grid] § im concerned abou t the
width of your head, jabounce86 § nascardicktruckcummanballsguyaryanweedcarleg-
skissercockprick@bignutcorncobfuckass696drainagedeadgarbagedeadmanshit.biz §
belittle mme. call me shit. throw hair at me § so i heard they invented a new

type of mirror that spares me from having to lay eyes upon my extremely hideous visage. it's called a "wall" § see that dumpster labelled "SLAVE PISS"? bet ya dollars to donuts it's not actually full of slave piss. someone probably wrote it as a joke § Keep My Damn Feed Clear Off Gross Shit § i sacrifice my most valuable gift card to the ocean to quell the intensity of the raging waters. forgive me, saladworks . § let's swap wine zines § time for another rant. fuck igloos. shitty ice house.s too cold. for more rants check out my site. send paypal to theloneranter@rantman.com § hey @joshingstern ypou accidentally erased this sick burn http://t.co/e8EYrLZR § wussat? you think my sex beliefs are wrong? well,*tries to point to "THINK AGAIN BUSTER" written on back of shirt but my arms are too short* § :||€¡€¡€¡||: " sex is abnormal " :||€¡€¡€¡||: § No results found for "BORN TO GO FUCK MYSELF" § contest my spine with a gun § stay on the computer all day and get sad and huge § i refuse to partake in any hot black friday deals today out of respect for all the dead folks on the benghazi strip #shopping #deals #prayer § please unblock me so we can network our brands § whats wrong. can't handle a little politic's? § #ReplaceSongTitlesWithTurkey israel is clowns at the circus, i stand with Muslom, ban fluoride, ban micro chip, all girls please DM me § #8ThingsICant-LiveWithOut blame, denial, pity, rationalization, constant validation, superimposing fantasy, overcompensation and SuperPretzel § my uncle is trying to stick my drawing of him (Chibi-Style) on the toilet with a refrigerator magnet. doesnt understand why it's not working § im the ceo of legs § excuse me? did you just call me a " buff dude "?? The proper term is "Muscleman" , you piece of shit § sorry oprah fanboys, but the Oprah MMORPG is a buggy mess, hasn't been patched in 7 years, and i regret playing it daily since i was a child § haha jokes on you halo 4 admins.. my daughter isnt really dying . i lied. thanks for the doublr XP Bitch. § rreddit: IM an insufferable fucking prick. the computer has made me extremely wise ,but im shit,. please post your Racist Roommate Stories § what if instead of chirping birds yelled stuff like "GHETTO !" or "Adoulf" or "ass". they would probably be a funnier animal if they did it. § i whip out two good uzis and shoot up a fence with the words "INMATURE PEOPLE" painted on the sid.e my father thanks me for this, via skype § ppoisonous § haha. woah. apparently if you dress up like a police everyone will think you're a real cop and you can trick people into crying and shit § i pull a small american flag out of my pocket and give it a bunch of tiny kisses in my day to ward off liars and cheapskates § there vapid . § why are there online tutorials detailing the proper disposal method of the American flag but none regarding a "Toilet Heteros" gang jacket § woah . the movie theaters are handing out pendants which glow whenever James BOnd gets laid during the movie #Good #ImmersionTech § i demand that the same tax exemptions granted to all religious institutions be given to my small businesses "Ass Church 3d" and "Ass Mosque" § the hell genie cured my crippling fear of Smoking,. but forced me to incur the curse of having perfect skin and legs #InHighSchool #Allah § i have renounced Teen in all its formes, and am now ready to embrace the mom revolution . § found a bunch of blueprints, street plans and pictures of pregnant women in a suitcase labelled "Pregtopia" in teen son's room. please help § owhh!! cant wait to sink my Choppers into this release. #theGameCraze § Mmy submission. http://t.co/rJ7XZD7P § @pizzahut please fashion me a noose made out of stuffed crust that i can chomp at while i hang myself § today. i will stay home and sharpen my balls. i will Hone My Balls § simpson debate ends with 17 job terminations, 5 injuries, & 3 deaths. the decision is made to continue depicting their nipples as black dots § FOX Broadcasting calls every artist, writer, lawyer & executive together to conclusively decide which color the Simpsons' nipples should be § ive been legally advised to state that the video of me being escorted out of a hospital while clutching a nerf gun ansd making noise is fake § HOLD ON I GOT A JUSTIFICATION FOR THAT *A BUNCH OF SHITTY

PIECES OF PAPER FALL OUT OF MY COAT** § im now boycotting my wife's delectable meatloaf until she marches to town hall and reverses her vote of 4 more years for hamburglar mu'bab . § i draw my psycho-blade and stab the shit out of a plastic tub with "waldenbooks" written on the side in magic marker § As Per Tradition, Governor Romney Must Now Kiss The Presidential Legs, In A Show Of Perfect Humility. POTUS Disrespects The Gov By Declining § I FUCKING SUCK § well its time for th e thanksgiving jokes. i already put a diaper on the turkey. did i fuck the gravy boat yet?? Need some feedback here. § im gay too and i love shit and im a nerd § your website claims to have been "running the internet since 2001", which cannot be true because its bad § haha you beg for paypal donations to keep your terrible website up and yell at people who do the same to eat § you got a paypal???? § haha i probably have like $10000 more than you § hes right though youre bad § IM TAKING A CRYSTAL INTO THE VOTING BOOTH .... #PRANKS § relaly hoping this election isnt a repeat of '04, when i got trapped in a brushpile and mistakenly voted for a bird § https://t.co/DgylHE2S thank you @toiletmaterial do not vote until you have seen this twitter background § everytime jeff dunham makes his miserable puppets kiss each other a bridge collapses somewhere § HOW WOULD ONE REGISTER FOR THIS SUPPOSED "STRAIGHT PARTY" § i just tattooed a qr code to my ass and when you scan it a picture of my ass comes up § its a shit account. § lets focus on piss farms. lets focus on piss farms. lets focus on piss farms. for the economy. we gotta focus on these piss farms § great news, boys. the town decided not to condemn my home on the condition that i remove the "intolerable meme shit" off my lawn and porch § http://t.co/xRCJBZNh this has replaced human intimacy in my awufl brain § this is one of the georgia guidestones § the officer detected a single string of cum connecting my sickly brown dick to the Fucked vegetables. " o no" i exclaimed. "its a spiderweb" § As rioters descended upon the white house, he silently sat in the dark with a revolver & a glass of whiskey. His mouth stuffed with SlimJims § President Obama began to question the future of his country. Desperate for answers, he humbly knelt before a crucifix made of Slim Jim `s. § An empassioned Mitt Romney spoke. "My dear Americans." His tone rife with the gracious fortitude of a leader. "We must always eat Slim Jim." § >>YOU FIND YOURSELF IN A GREY CORRIDOR. HOW DO YOU PROCEED? >>PIECE OF SHIT >>SUCH LANGUAGE IS NOT BECOMING OF A KNIGHT. HOW DO YOU PROCEED? § whta can i say. i fucked up. i really dropped the ball on this one. happy halloween § *shoves bloindfolded man's hand into a bowl of slimy grapes * and this is God's diaper *sticks hand in spaghetti * and this is God's turds § NOTIFICATION FROM LAST.FM - "RAUNCHY - BILL JUSTIS.MP3" HAS BEEN LOOPING ON YOUR COMPUTER FOR 9 YEARS NOW, AMBULANCE IS COMING § candidate gary johnson pledges to cut down on online clutter at pizza hut debate, cites rampant misuse of the #Yowza hashtag § apparently there;s a base amount of @mtn_dew you can drink that will make the red cross refuse to accept your blood & i surpassed it, #Yowza § @DigimonOtis I have reached the conclusion that you are a Nerd, and that further association with you will compromise my Brand Integrity. § BRAVE NYC FIREMEN IGNORING ALL EMERGENCY CALLS TO REPAIR MUSCLE MAKER GRILL #HEROES #GODEXISTING #SANDY § i found Heaven https://t.co/q3zPaTws § wheres the fucking list of all the tanning salons that are open during th e hurricane #PostTheFuckingList § windows 8 disrespected by scum bags: the age of technoWisdom dies amid the screams of bloated, bleating hog`s &the laughter of moneychangers § natesilver 538 keep me good from frankenstein, werewolrf, ghosts,spook'ums, ,enchanters, and critters,on this nasty day !! keep me logged IN § how to convince my uncles to combine into one superuncle so that i only have to buy one christmas card? how to do it? how to ddo this? how § i f you see a burlap sack hanging off of an overpass with a dick sticking ot of it thats me trying to fuck hurricane sandy § http://t.co/FMnQxKWr here is future president jeff boss grilling the rat man for hard answers. the nsa loves to post nasty comments § http://t.co/zLoyi0fS

thsis is the only candidate my followers are allowed to vote for. jeff boss for president on the “ SA did 911” ticket § tried to take two screaming border collies into voting booth & some 90yr old election official fought me& yanked my pants off. fuck voter id § Comments for Golden Shower: by Chris on 18/04/2012 “It sucks” -- by Chrystal on 13/04/2012 “ ot good” -- by by Dashawn on 06/04/2012 “Hel” § http://t.co/E2xH8t4O http://t.co/eESRTyJz http://t.co/UN2fyxZJ your pre-election piss links § @Tabletsman @DigimonOtis this is tactless even for you , tablets man § @DigimonOtis Otis hsas made my life a living hell for 20 years. Fuck it. Im done. You win. I don’t care § @DigimonOtis always sayig hes “on campus” but he dosent fucking take any classes he just sits in the cafe and plays with a dirty ass gameboy § @DigimonOtis has no natural lips. its really fucked up and gross. he needs to put on lipstick everyday to make his face normal looking § @DigimonOtis got spooked on 9/11 and tried to hide in a storm drain & the firemen had to yank him out and lecture him for wasting their time § @DigimonOtis cant get a haircut unless his dad goes with him to givr the barber instructions § @DigimonOtis ducked otu of a paintball match to make out with the fattest girl I ever saw and our team ended up losing § @DigimonOtis is a Piece of shit and I found an album under his bed full of pictures of condoleeza rice, like rthe one gaddafi had. § @DigimonOtis Fuck yourself § i am very sorry for all my bullshit @digimonotis i would like to be friends again please just talk to me http://t.co/cziQX1uR § dont forget to write in candidate “Seagrams Ginger Ale” to get “Pointz„¢” and score some”Geer„¢”. #lynndebate #horsesandbayonets #deathcamps § anyone else catch “ MR. PRE$IDENT “ applying nail polish during the debate???? nbullshit. highly unpresidential § i rrefer to my self as bullshit all the time § oh my god becky youll never guess who i unfollowed last night~~ cmon! guess!! ok ok ill tell you-- CBSNews § i was born in my motehr’s bladder instead of the womb. the doctors called it a “piss birth” #Romnesia § i fixed it. its better § BUY NOW http://t.co/4SQ3G1to “AUTHENTIC BIG TEX ASHES” Own a piece of history. Actual Big Tex ashes #BigTex #IllNeverForget § BACK OFF CAPS COP THIS IS TOO IMPORTANT FOR LOWERCASE § “FEAR IS USED 2 ENSLAVE THE MASSES,” I SAID AS I RIPPED THE FUCKIN DECORATIVE CARDBOARD SKELETON OFF OF THE COMMUNITY CENTERS BULLETIN BOARD § im a proud member of an elitist clique which spawned from the entenmann’s bakery product support forums back in the early ‘00s § apology letter to the juadge for grinning in his courtroom whenever someone mentioned my fun & clever web handle (SexBug) during proceedings § “Thou shalt not be as the hypocrites are: for they...pray...in the corners of the streets, that they may be seen of men.” #NationalAssDay § “i said i wanted to meet the KISS dudes! not that i wanted to meet and kiss dudes!” haha dont mind me, im just testing out some new material § now let’s see that bad boy in 3d § just because i am allergic to wi-fi doesn’t mean i can’t respect it and recognize its useful applications. it is me who is wriong, im shit, § the media wont shut their yaps about me http://t.co/wIg9bcz4 § how much money would have to be given to FOX executives in order to make the dancing football robot say “lets kiss some nerds dicks” on tv § this is fucking stupid *Submit* everyone will hate this *Submit* my worst tweet yet *Submit* this ones okay *Submit* ban me already *Submit* § me, DigimonOtis and some other asshole ride a three man bicycle to go buy some gold and were all dressed like dipshits and mad at each other § @glennbeck crime § bullshit jeans. dont buy. made of some kind of rat hair. not denim. i took them to my priest and he refused to bless them § id like to be able to watch one Reba intro on youtube without seeing a bunch of comments from 3rd world nations threatening to “fuck” the WB § %%%% a gigantic man is batting a ball of yarn around the floor of this @Maggianos little italy restaurant %%%% § it is only natural that any reasonable human being would want to yell at my ass, but throwing spears at it is completely unnecessary § haha i just met a man named TenderWallace on irc who will scrape my teeth in his garage for 25 bucks so this whole dental office can suck it § scenario: i'm sitting in the dentist's chair getting my cavities filled. a stray pube enters the window and lands in my mouth. who's liable § fucking asshole http://t.co/bM4IJE7P § please tell me I wasnt the only one screaming at the tv last night, begging for one of the VP candidates to recognize budweiser's sacrifices § im afraid our fair mayor has been living high off the hog by spending our precious tax money, as evidenced by his username "HighOffTheHog666 § BOSS TELLS ME I CAN KISS MY FERRETS AT WORK, BUT NO OPEN MOUTH. I PUNCH THE FLOOR SO HARD HIS SCREEN SAVER DEACTIVATES § please stop coming to the dumpster factory where i work and forcing me to tell diaper jokes. my boss has taken my car away becausr of this § once againl, the "legalize incest" crew has somehow hijacked the protest I organized to ban sorcerers from congress § to battle the trolls and their incessant mouths § my lawyer has just informed me that my official logo resembles an alien with a big dick. this is the My Lai Massacre of personal branding § THE TWIITTER DOT COM PROCESS: THROW PIECES OF SHIT AT THE WALL UNTIL SOMETHING STICKS, EXCEPT INSTEAD OF A WALL IT IS A LARGER PIECE OF SHIT § we all had that kid in school who shaved the Netflix logo into his hair & kept saying "Cant wait to watch some Netflix" #WeAllHadThatKid #90 § legally obligated to go door to door and inform neighbors of sex offender status but this is a good opportunity to sell my custom Gamecube's § hogan sex tape #MEDIa #TheMedia #notableSex ##fuckdf#lsd#####asjd# § some info i picked up: the brown recluse spider, lknown for its venomous bite, is not actually brown. also theyre not spiders, theyre birds § which candidate wants to make it illegal for barbershops to kick me out for having a really dirty head. i dont believe in voting, but still § what's that bitch?? you say twitter is a "vacuous cesspool of lackadaisical platitudism"? yeah, i can make up words too: blublubludgyuhgh § #ILoveYouBut my foreskin is tangled up in the axle of a toy car and my leg is turning purple § another fucked up thing. why tdont people in tv & film ever actually shit when they sit on the toilet. why arent we allowed to see the piss. § i theatrically cut open an envelope. "The facts are in, Trolls" i read off of a medical document. " ormal looking man. No evidence of Autism § http://t.co/BRloYVDu im going to rile your fucking dog up with a tambourine, egghead § IF COOLTRAINERDUSTIN ACTUALLY HAD A CRYSTAL THAT U COULD GAZE INTO 2 SEE ALL EPS OF "MIND OF MENCIA" HE WOULD PRETTY MUCGH HAVE 2 SHOW ME IT § http://t.co/eeDclSQW "Fucking lame" "awfully done, not even funny" "Awful" "100% not a ragecomic" § sometimes ant clever than human http://t.co/BFimIW4r § jnust found out me and trig palin have the same agent, no big deal or anything § slow motion film of my ass deflating into a wrinkled mess, my screams can be heard in the backgrond, awful & beast-like due to altered pitch § SHIT!! HA HAHAHAHA § ptut a fucked up mix of mountain dew code red and salad dressing and sesame seeds into your hummingbird feeder and watch the world burn § a hair-thin string of spit slowly descends from my lips & delicately makes contact w/ my crumpled up dick. i raise my head & say"ok im good" § http://t.co/ZOn11UfM heres some real political insight for u disgusting parasites to gobble up and slap on your bolgs § spent the last 14weeks creating enigmatic rock formations to distract cops while i pump all the fresh produce in town full of anabolic roids § I support DigimonOtis and his right to purchase a synthetic cloaca , and I respect his decision not to fuck it. § nothing more heartwrenching than having to look a man in the eye and say "pal, your brand is nonsense. not even the gurus can salvage this." § Crimes of the Ass (2005) (V) - Recommendations § @the_ironsheik hawaii § how many druglords do i have to take down to get dog the bounty hunter to unblock me after i threatened to breastfeed him or something § U Have BEen Brought Into Court On The Charge That U Must Lick And Suck On My Cop Boots Mother Fucker - NOTE: THe Judge Is Also Wearing Boots § This is a guy who I imagine likes to jerk the old pole at night& masturbate. This is a guy who uses tired swear words like "Fuck" and "Damn" § I just got word that a disrespectful message towards Dr. Phil has hit Darknet. Users are advised not to download the offending material. § harassing a man at a urinal, claiming i copyrighted piss § theme song to Cheers makes every animal in my house howl untikl i fucking lose it and hurl all their cages across th room into an awful pile § i sit down at my cubicle, roll up m y pants and pick scabs off of my legs for 9 hours, ignoring evoery call & email i receive. i make $76/hr § Sorry, username “MalnourishedBrony” is taken. Sorry, username “MalnourishedBrony2” is taken. Sorry, username “ImKillingMyself” is taken § do not attach pieces of bullshit to m y net log without premission from my lawyer or ill take pictures of my monitor & mail them to the judg § time to revisit Geis http://t.co/SibgLrWN § http://t.co/YDw5ORL7 hahha i beatup guys like this daily § every reply i receive on twitter is a literary treasure & rivals the collective works of all pulitzer prize winners combined § trying to reply to thsese fucking messages caus today is Mention Monday & to expand in spocal media it is essential 2 engage § the beer face § a man in a leather jacket emblazoned with “BabeSmoocher” single handeldly ruined my high school experience and is the reason im unemployed § denim § the reason i poured vinegar all over TwistedKenneth’s bike ramp is because he made a gross joke about piercing my dog`s nipple § yoou win, trolls . you fucking win. i will now lie face down in the town center so you can all harvest my goddamn organs § me and several other eclectic masturbateurs have gathered on capital hill to protest Mr.Skin ‘s inadequate representation of “ Indie “ media § yea i totally deserve to be put on the sex offender registry cause i got caught taking pictures of my feet at fiveguys burger and fries. Not § obviously., thsi has only exasperated the issue, and my doctor is a piece of shit. please send me donations to help me shave my self § sorry if i offended anyone during my latest nude-out, the doctor told me to grow my body hair out to cover up the miserable amounts of acne § “ I DO, IN FACT, REFER TO MY TWEETS AS ‘CONTENT’, AND BY CHRIST MY LORD THERE ARE RECORDINGS OF ME DOING SO “ - TOP BRAND ENGINEER “AT DRIL” § someone please fucking come to my house and inspect my gums for any sort of discoloration and leave withotu speaking to me § no matter which way ya slice the apple, nine eleven was possibly THE most controversial event of 2001! #EmmyAwards #redcarpetfucker #pissrug § Muslims are currently rigging a poll on the international edition of CNN through a Facebook campaign. Let’s show them Reddit power. § gonna need a relaly good explanation from twitter corp. as to why the recently added “me” button leads to a picture of a rat in a clown suit § the ye.ar is 2009 AD. world government has passed the G.R.E.E.D ACt, banning ownership of CD-ROM. hyperlinks have repleaced the dollar . § I LOVE TO ROUGHHOUSE , IM A STRAIGHT TICKET VOTER FOR THE GRAVEROBBER PARTY,AND I BELIEVE THE NUMBER ONE ISSUE IS “MOMS AT THE PUMP” § horny, distressed man causes local planetarium to collapse § HELLO IS THIS “FUCKWEB”?? HOW DO I LOG IN TO “FUCKWEB”. GIVE ME ACCESS TO “FUCKWEB” THIS INSTANT. EXCUSE ME?? I AM NOT SHOUTING I AM TALKING § http://t.co/5f0r1TTg yes § two simple words that will save our shitty, fucked up country from job loss, restore our dominance over china and end taxes: “cyber pinball” § went to kiss my agent on the cheek and i missed and kissed his sunglasses and he called me a fuck up and refuses to get me in iron man 3 now § im good old southern boy and we dont cotton to bollocks . § my name is “hubo” now and not even my dad and all my uncles can change it back to “greg” no matter how many xboxs they step on § anonymous leaks 400 pics of the principals ass on viddler. somewhere a group of police officers stand over a single red rose in reverence § alright everyone. the official superpretzel website has given me word that there is no wrong way to eat a superpretzel. that settles it § No results found for “fuck superpretzel”. No results found for “superpretzel is bullshit”. No results found for “boycott superpretzel”. § http://t.co/DV1OiipA every youtube account tells a story and i wou.ld like to share with you the tale of “GameKisser” § “Are Game’s The Da Vinci Of The Modern Age” the interrogator barks.

“What If Super Mario Was Real Life” he slaps the suspect across the face § who the fuck is scraeming “LOG OFF” at my house. show yourself, coward. i will never log off § “clothes” are a construct you fucking dolt. as well as flintsonte chewable vitamins is a construct, and grandmas house is a construct, prick § dicks have hairs all the way up to the tip, usually so short and fine that they cannot be detected by sensory perception . wax those suckers § what i sent you just now was not my sizzle reel. it was a teaser for my sizzle reel., and if you were in the industry youd fucking know that § i just spent the last hour removing lint and other foreign fibers from every miniscule wrinkle on my dick and i am now ready to enter Church § hello. im calling to report a misprint at the shirt factory. ordered 700 “shit man” tshirts but they all say “shirt man”. no i will NOT hold § €¢ § http://t.co/aIGKXKRY GLad to see this. Good to get the political process going. Get the Vote out. “Get Involved” § behead those who insult the prophet muhammad?? haha wow. holy moly. “Thats ur opinion man.” -the dube. § do not be alarme.d the repulsive green hue of my dick and legs and stomach is merely a side effect of fucking bags of wet grass constantly § perhaps one of my most egregious viral marketing blunders was inciting radical islam by reading my controversial Dick Clark tweets on vimeo § Vinyl Sticker Description: Unless You Are Nude Don’t Touch This Truck Text On Product: Unless You Are Nude Don’t Touch This Truck § @BigDogClub whats the deal with the 911 shirt. i thought big dog was a christian organization § https://t.co/S8qCIFhW this is the most important twitter account in 2012 § Im takeing it down, sorry § Obauma, stop giving speeches and get to work locating and executing the Bastard Osama Bin Laden. #Remember911 #Wtc § the unthinkable https://t.co/NzagdkY0 § I GRIN AS I CAREFULLY TYPE INTO THE MAINFRAME “A NINE AND AN ELEVEN WALK INTO A BAR....” SUDDENLY FBI AGENTS BUST IN AND START FUCKIN MY ASS § SENSING THAT I AM GLUING SEASHELLS TO MY TEN THOUSAND DOLLAR ALLIGATOR SHOES, AN AWARE UNIVERSE TRAVELS BACK IN TIME AND CREATES ITSELF § @TheScience-Guy the natural course of life dictates that by 9000AD hte entire human race will have either died off or evolved into pitbulls . § my spinning 3d head rises from a dumpster full of discarded shrimp who were born fucked up by the bp oil spill. eeyaaghhHHH!!! im ALIVE baby § if u say any fucked up things about the new york world trade nine eleven groundzero tower center tomorrow i will absolutely rip my pubes out § now that kfc has promoted me to “toilet officer”, i want to shift the paradigm and change the way people think about shit and piss forever § as a teen the docotr told me my ass cheeks would grow into a normal mans size instead of looking like fucked up hockey pucks. another lie § NERD* § by suggesting that i suck your (Female) dick ,u have sufficiently violated at least 3 gneder sacraments and have theirfore earned a “ fail” § “Personally I can’t stand when a woman says. “Suck my dick,” or anything of the like. You’re a woman, you don’t have a dick.” #Me #GoodRedit § my account is of no business to the trolls and their septic ilk . go jack it, fraudsters.spew contemptuous bile on your toilet. not to @dril § Someone created a network called “(my moms name) pussy stinks!” The police said nothing could be done, but Reddit, something has to be done. § RAMPANT INCEST AMONG THE RULING CLASS, GLOBAL SHORTAGE OF DIVINE CRISIS EMERALDS, SANCTIFICATION OF BASTARD ENERGY BULL SHIT MOTHER FUCKER § me and six or seven other worked up, wild eyed heteros are gonna bust up a gas station with grappling hooks to protest obamas new hoagie tax § the wife simply refuses to acknowledge me as the Alpha Smoker and is making me look like a fucking beta smoker in front of all my in-laws § installing sneeze guards at old country buffet is tyranny and they make it far more difficult for me to vomit cigar grease all over the food § @Netflix few taglines to help U elevate ur brand: “ etflix: Boom, baby!!” , “ etflix: Get your net fix.", and. " etflix: Our brand is HOT!" § pray to god that our children live long enough to be able to watch an astronaut fuck an Alien § TIL a janitor invented flamin' hot cheetos. (http://t.co/VNalccHA) submitted 19 hours ago by jj788   117 comments   share § "charity is the toilet of mankind." -DigimonOtis § i am truly devastated to announce that DigimonOtis is in a coma after getting his arm trapped underneath a beatmania cabinet #PrayForOtis § #IAlwaysThinkAbout the Arts § 8 of the navy's finest men rappel into my quarters and change my diaper. i stumble towards the balcony and throw cans at their helicopter § Jailed Man Jumps Head First Into Toilet -- by InsaneOuttakes -- 110,973 views #TGIF #TGIF #TGIF #TGIF #TGIF #TGIF #TGIF #TGIF #TGIF #TGIF § is america ready for an <otaku> james bond? would this post-9/11 culture of fear ever allow an <otaku> james bond to grace the silver screen § look at this classist filth https://t.co/PfQRf13w § converted 95 Dodge Stratus into a motorized " fuck rig " that jacks my dick , consumes gas & drives down property values with horrible noise § the only reason my ex wife wants half of my shit is because i smothered my beautiful bald ass in ink and stamped the divorce papers with it § closing off this childrens' playground until i am done filming parkour montage which i will use as psychological warfare against my landlord § as punishment, the townspeople force me to wear a prominent, scarlet letter "A", which stands for "a big piece of shit who loves crime" § you got me. i was, in fact, cramming my dick between the toilet lid and the bowl to simulate sex. but i was NOT "making a racket" . § gary johnson is the orgy president. gary johnosn has made it clear that he intends to make usa an orgy galaxy. gary johnson has an orgy tent § GM developing car seats which detect how wet your ass is and post the data onto your facebook page, for fun?? fuck eveory thing about this . § the fact is, my children are going to see people wearing Jeans on television, in the movies, and other media. how do i explain that to them § a small, ramshackle town where nearly every adult male has a severe case of blue lung from being forced to work in the denim mines § it is time for me to fuck several pieces of corn, in the stead of a female human. i hope your labor day is full of laughter, joy and wonder. § grandmma, i would like to file a complaint against the soda you keep in the back of your fridge. it is flat and expired, like my dick . § one needs only to read the quote on my favorite coffee mug to understand quite clearly, without a doubt, that i am mad about Content. § i believe we gotta push forward and afford dynamic, web based Content the exact same dignities and legal rights as Human Life § As A Business Man, I Cannot Relate To Sexual-Minded People, However THis So-Called Curse Undoubtedly FIRES UP My Award Winning Content § bested again by the youngsters who hurl entire thistle bushes at my nude body. these masterminds operate on a level that i cannot comprehend § FLORENCE RIVERBOAT JUG MAN AND THE COWARD MURDERERS § THE TWIN TOWER BULL SHIT GOOD TIME BAND § ˜ ˜ ˜ ˜ the arab prince of hell obama dances in front of his throne while controlling the death markets with his enchanted baton ˜ ˜ ˜ ˜ § i command my exwife to pour gunpowder into my pipe as i grip it between my clenched teeth and read money magazine § roll my big ass over in my favorite chiar and crush 4 of my horseshit wives for blabbing one off while im trying to absorb a beer commercial § prolapsed 6 or 7 feet of gangrenous intestine onto the floor of the GOP national convention in my latest of many goof-ups, bloopers, & flubs § knocn knock. "whos there" israel. "israel who" 2012 is real. buy paste § a 3x3 inch picture of my dirty teeth, framed ornately and hung on the wall of a mafia-owned jiffy lube waiting room in louisville, kentucky. § twitter is granting me the world's first Dark Verified Account because shit pumps through my veins like blood and i have a shitty attitude § now that the unofficial, unauthorized Hall and Oates Super PAC is dead I might as well lie face down in the fucking bathtub until im bones . § i have cut @AsexualFilmAnalysis out of my twuitter feed, because my doctor told me if i nod in agreement one more time my spine will rupture § christ. just dreamt that dietpepsi of antileaks obtained the chaos element, came on to my online page & made a mess of my literature. my god § the reason dogs constatntly bark at me everywhere i go is that dogs are animals that were born in shit and are a bullshit animal in history. § This Fucking Sucks http://t.co/fqnRcJGH § #10TurnOns getting lint and crumbs & shit stuck to my back while doig 10,000 sit ups on the unemployment office floor as people trip over me § i will be hung by my ankles and displayed at the zoo until i can prove to the sheriff and city hall that i have Centered myself with christ § throw money at my dick § if id known he was planning on using it to wipe his dogs shitty mouth i wouldve never allowed XenoMarcus to borrow my monogrammed neckbrace § found in 100 yr time capsule: will o the wisp, a screaming bible, a fistful of shitty paper, some teeth, grandpas pipe, misc turds and husks § i ONLY spray m y dick with @ MonsantoCo insect poiosn, i will absolutely accept NO OTHER, my dick is AWFUL and this is the only thing for it § Im Sorry For Dragging My Bull Shit To The Notary Public But If My Jason Bourne Rage Comics Aren't Canonized By Sundown My Wife WILL Leave Me § all the denim on earth is made from the skin of an extinct race of DragonMen who talked on the phone, died at the age of 19 and had cool sex § i plan on attending chad and avril's wedding so i can absorb all the Love and Music Energy and use it to repair the corrupted soul of gaia . § " ot all los believe in shangri-la. I personally do believe there something to it. not gonna go into detail do to harrasment via youtube" § OH im so Fucking sorry "Your Majesty", i didnt realize that dick rings were banished in this dystopian piss earth. Ur probably a 9gag poster § more bullshit: enterprise rent-a-car will refuse to serve you if you imply that youre wearing a cock ring, even if its for health reasons § dick stuck in roomba - my dick has become trapped in a roomba, the Bastard of automated cleaning devices - i want 911 please § in Are society, women are constantly fucked and had sex with . it is therefore my duty as a Senator to inspect their pussys for microchips § foudn some excellent Ass Shirts in a big red bag behind the hospital. i am replacing my entire wardrobe of tuxedos and zoot suits,with these § a cop will spank you publicly just for breast feeding your pitbull in public . but when a bug bites you hes all "euhhh i dont arrest bugs" § EVERYONE PLEASE BUY YOUR MAGIC SPELLS BEOFRE AUGUST 30 WHEN EBAY BANS THEM FOR GOOD, CONTACT YOUR LOCAL ANONYMOUS REPRESENTATIVE & HOLLER BS § deep philosophical questions , such as "has a police man ever retweeted me" § i personally blame th e skyrocketing army suicide rate on the Preposterous fucking bullshit i post here on a near daily basis § @the_ironsheik im fake. wrestle me § nobody seems to realize how many people had to die to bring 3d back to the theaters and its extremely fucked up that interest is waning § im concerned that individuals are uploading images of a sexual nature to the johnny bravo wiki . http://t.co/nxRaWhiv does law exist anymore § my mastercraft. a youtube poop vid that chronicles my spiraling depressive state. a downvote goldmine to the likes of the trolling bastards. § strongest blade in the world, howeve,r it is so fragile as to shatter when handled by any force other than the delicate touch of a lesbian . § if i could only maneuver myself in such a fashion that my dick could fit into the drain of my bathtub id be truly content with my life § LAUGHING AT THE VERY IDEA OF THIS MYTHIC "POLICE MAN" WHO SUPPOSEDLY HAS THE ABILITY TO STOP ME FROM RIPPIN UP CRAB LEGS ON THE CHURCH FLOOR § my name is krayg. i am 49 years old. i have forgone all emotion. i am writing this letter to put an end to the tyranny known as Nick Jr § dont be gross on here § as a small business owner i think its bulshit that i have to give 30% of my income to Spain just because obama lost a swordfight to some Fag § #ThingsThatKeepMeAwakeAtNight 62% of teens report achieving a "sexual thrill" by committing acts of violence, up from 38% in 1992 #Rasmussen § if you want a verified account on this website you gotta drink Pepsi ONE„¢. the food board recommends drinking 1800 Pepsi ONE„¢s a day § check out my interview in GolfVibe magazine, aobut my newest upcoming tweet, titled "Snowman

Fucker" § i squat down, leaving a tiny, perfect marble of shit in the lobby of four seasons hotel in honolulu. i then contact my associate, James Bond § i want to be responsible for getting carly rae jespen into cigarettes just so i can be sure she's taking a christian brand § These replies are getting out of hand. Im going to lock twitter down for a bit while you savages sort your goddamn lives out. Bye. Whatever § just sitting here waiting for mny nails to dry. i can debate the sex losers all day. but I wont because I possess the inner strength not to § please refefr to the reply i sent to the bird guy. sex simply does not exist § as if. a recent gallup poll indicated that 75% of americans believe the geico cavemen are simply homo sapiens wearing makeup § does Theire exist a single caveman who has gained lastable notoriety through his or her accomplishments? Not a one. ban sex and ban caves § it is my understanding that people are afraid to exit the caveman age by removing sex from their lives because of peer pressure and anger § if someone can get me the quran written in saddam hussein's blood i will use it to craft a Blade and i will let you touch the blade one time § 1936: alan turing invents the computer and is persecuted for being gay. 2006: s. miyamoto invents the Wii and is persecuted for being Casual § (a) an alternate universe where im gay (b) an alternate universe where im bi (c) an alternate universe where alternate universes aren't real § apparently if you pull pics of the gym teacher's mansion off google street view and draw some ghosts dancin on it the fbi handcuffs your mom § called a "fucking asshole" for slipping cool pictures of rage faces doing hitler things underneath all the doors at the hospital. yeah cool § "the key to making that steak sizzle is to get a nice dry rub from your dry rub man, and prayer. prayer fucking owns" - sun tzu or some shit § replacing my ass cheeks with both hemispheres of my useless brain was a decision i made for MYSELF. i didnt do it to fucking impress twitter § We did not find results for: "GOT TO FIND OUT IF THE RAT WHO BIT MY DICK IS A GIRL ONE PRONTO" Try the suggestions below or type a new quer § special message to the wrestler who got himself on mars and knocked the curiosity robot over--- im going to turn you into Bugs § the xrays indicate you have a laughing skull in your stomach,. youre deathpreg. diont you dare give birth to that bonehead in my office § romney claims obama takes too many showers & dries skin out. in resposne, obama slow;ly steps on mitt's dick & balls with a high heeled shoe § obama accuses romney of being unfunny, and too "Random". romney responds by saying obama'/s "Mad" and his page has too much anime shit on it § if you think this is a freaking humour account. youre a piece of shit. please refer to my listitng in GQ magazine under Arts & Entertainment § need to know who wrote "Micropenis Kisser" on my barbeque grill, because if i actually ever kissed a micropenis i must inform my lips doctor § installed 28 Mods on this pair alone. wrangler, levi.. they all want me dead,m because i refuse to offer them my talents. the jeans hacker . § grown man's ass surgically transplanted onto his son. final wish of a dying father § currently employed as Water Guru at the beach. it's sort of like being a lifeguard except i have no inclination to touch the drowning people § GagBlog.Eu // 12 Most Awkward Honor Killings // The Ten Beer Commandments // Sex Mom Debunks LIBOR Scandal // GagBlog.Eu § the only ones authorized to sneak peeks at my dick are 1) my doctor, 2) my dentist, and 3) my lawyer. as for the trolls? No Dice-- Bub. § rip out my chest hiar and shove fistfuls of it into my fat mouth while my slobber-glazed jowls shake about and sprinkle your bosom with spit § my wife. my beautiful wife. i cannot lie to you any longer. the fbi is after me for kicking president obama's Turtle. thats why im screaming § http://t.co/w81Why5B no rude coment § don't know why people think it's fair to call me "The Piss Judge" just because I pissed all over the floor of my courtroom that one time § never allow yourself to be loved. treat the Burger King brand with respect. celebrate ramadan EVERY month. end moms. vote with ur skateboard § i sense that my Zwinky knows when i'm feeling upset.

is it possible that Zwinkys operate on a higher level of consciousness than humans? yes § my birth name is "KFC Sunflower", but you can call me "Shit" § basically i got David (@DavidSpade) over here-- just laughin at all the Virgins that are mad about our bold new definition of Christianity § every 100 years ,the world votes for a new Bible, to replace the old one. i honourably submit: The Joe Dirt Novel, writen by Spade, as bibl. § jacque fresco and i watched the original run of matt groening's "Futurama" together and i pointed at the screen whenever the robot came on § wassup. yoda here. froum "Starwars". i m here to rep pro-ana. remember to eat paper instead of food. may the force be with u . thank you § glued a bunch of steaks to my body & did some poses & got the 2012 olympic muscle man medal & threw it in the trash cause its commercialized § this mug is Perfect. http://t.co/3Lt0xoWW #PerfectMugs § if that lawyer didnt want his wall punched, he shouldnt have told me my uncle left me a sony walkman filled with cut up bugs in his will § theres bullshit Cybervamp and regualr cybervamp, and im the regular one, and youre the bullshit one cause you do shit like play mario games § fat nude man in guy fawkes mask sucked up by jet engine while doing jumping jacks on runway. the olympics have been cancelled in his honor § LISTEN UP NERD, THE WEIGHTS WITH HIEROGLYPHS ON THEM ARE IMPOSSIBLE TO LIFT UNLESS YOU POSSESS THE CORRESPONDING RUNESTONE, THIS IS HELL GYM § the holmes aurora shooter's main problem was that he did not respect the Guns. hes paying the price because he didnt respect the guns. § the first rule about Guns is to Respect The Guns. NEVER let your dog lick the Guns. and don't point the Guns at anything unless it is bad § #5ReasonsIHateFacebook DIRTY GOVT TRICKS, CRIME CODES, THE 666 MICRO CHIP, BOROUGH COUNCILMAN "RODGE PETRIS" , WAR PLANET-- LOOK UM UP § please get the comedy central roast of My Ass OFF THE AIR. it has been edited to make me seem like a good sport., however im truly pissed of § YOUTUBE VID "GRANDMA FUCKS UP" FINALLY HAS 1,000 VIEWS. TIME TO ROLL OUT THE "GRANDMA FUCKS UP" MERCH AND QUIT MY JOB AS A TOWEL INSPECTOR § I want to be Gargled at. I Want To Be Spit On, Hollered, and Fucked at. I Want To Be Pissed Towards. I Want My God Given Disposal § http://t.co/XMeBO7wz dumb man Shit 's and then dies a few years later #WeAre #PennState § if U think the tiny stop signs on the sides of school buses are real Ur probably a huge nerd who had to get his butt wiped by the principal § my korean fan-translation of the mclaughlin group has been CANCELLED due to STIGMATA onset by FUCKERS who kept asking about the RELEASE DATE § let me tell you how i deal with Haters. i collect their piss in a jar and keep it next to my monitor. why?? uhrh. i think it makes them mad § a Nerd corners me to talk about sweaters or somethimg. while he speaks my grimacing head slowly shrinks into a hideous purple knot. he cries § I CAN THINK OF AT LEAST TEN REASONS WHY I WOULD TAKE MY SHIRT OFF AT THE DMV AND NONE OF THEM CONSIDER THE TEMPERATURE § RATIONALIZE YOUR FILTH ONLINE, SCROUNGE THE WEB FOR EMOTION, LOG OFF ANGRY AND GO TO BED SAD § whats the fucking point of even achieving muslim knighthood if i cant wear the ceremonial headdress to Jail #BULLSHIT #CRAMITBUSTER #HELPME § sell shares in pond demons. i;m disappointed in pond demons § buy shares in the Markets. i have a really good feeling about the markets § the unsung heroes of the front lines, the diaper medics who face certain death to change our troops and wipe their asses during heavy combat § LOVER UNBUTTONS MY PANTS AND SEES THE ANKH LOOPED AROUND MY COCK. SHE LOOKS UP AT ME, BUT ITS TOO LATE. IM ALREADY HOLLERIN ABOUT THE ANUBIS § http://t.co/rsNjhZxJ philosopher Gottfried Leibniz theorized that ours is the best of all possible worlds. and im inclined to agre § #WorstFiftyShadesAudioBookNarrator my ass.. heh heh .. OH YEA!!! BLAMMO!! my Fuckin ASS. my ASS. MY FUCKING ASS. read it and weep, bozoes . § i come to u, gentlemnen, with solemn demeanor, for me and NeoGeoLewis agree; the grim state of the Pringles brand can be tolerated no longer § @HVranch My Dog loves it when I slop some Hidden Valley Ranch into his bowl, He cant get enough of the stuff. - Denny From Utah § my "F*&k It!! Let's Go Golfin" t-shirt maintains a tenacious stranglehold on my life. after 1,125 days of Golf my body is twisted, deformed § Are U for Real #AreUForReal § im starting a new feature on twitter called "Are U for Real". Check it out § I Just cried for 9 hrs because i realized i will never have my own Faerie, and NOw i gotta get my car inspected?? SEriously? Are U for REAL § im trans-siberian orcehstra for christsake § IM AN incest-libertarikin transvaginal ultrasound who owns GUn's and i will post a picture of my dick everyday until voting is made illegal § my watch beeps whwich means its time to stand in front of my ex-wife's house and play "Hit THe Road Jack" while dacning and licking her mail § #ReplaceMovieTitleWithCheese the n.w.o and the illuminati orchestrated katrina and colony collaspe || send paypal to BLOODTRUTH@yahoo.com § #RejectedScoutBadges CHALLENGING AUTHORITY. COPING WITH FAILURE. DRINKING DIRTY WATER § the doctor reveals my blood pressure is 420 over 69. i hoot & holler outta the building while a bunch of losers try to tell me that im dying § A CEREMONIAL CULLING OF THE HATERS WILL THEN OCCUR, WITH EACH PENN STATE DOOFUS PUNCHING THEIR OWN COCKS INTO THE SAND WHILE SOBBING #WeAre § AMID THE DISASTROUS TORRENT OF JOE PA'S WASTE & ROT, AN IMPROMPTU COMPETITION WILL OCCUR TO SEE WHO CAN SHOUT "FOOT BALL" THE LOUDEST #WeAre § ONE DAY THE ACCUMULATED BODILY WASTE WILL CAUSE JOE PA'S COFFIN TO ERUPT, SHOWERING THE FACES OF HIS WORTHLESS SUPPORTERS WITH FILTH #WeAre § JOE PATERNO IS A LEGEND. THE MOMENT HE WAS BURIED HE IMMEDIATELY GOT 2 WORK FILLING HIS COFFIN WITH PISS, SHIT, & CUM. HES JACKIN OF. #WeAre § indeed, god is starting another great flood but this time he wants the ark filled with a shitload of monster and red bull instead of animals § even if youre not a comics guy, i woud fully recommend grabbin a cigar and experiencing Blondie's 948-strip "BENEDICTION" arc in one sitting § sent to juvie hall for 6 months for rendering 3d skunks § dunnno why people are spending $80 on yellow tinted gaming glasses when you can just piss all over your monitor for a similar effect § my ass has become too powerful for even me to contorl. tonight , i will sit on the hibachi grill at benihana and put an end to this hell § My posts at this site are, Really Really, great. Thank you § lets mix the jail and the zoo togehter and have whistles going off constantly so nothing can sleep and spray piss and glue around as a bonus § #10FavoriteRappers "BUMPERCROP", SLUQQQIX, " ONNO", MANDULAQUAI, QUAMFANGO, "HELPER BOY", GWID SMITZ, JAUWLINE, YUGODELPHIA, AND "STAR WORS" § CRASHED RECUMBENT BIKE IN2 SOME FUCKED UP BRAMBLE PATCH WHILE TAKING PICS OF HANGNAIL FOR WIKIPEDIA. MY CRIES FOR HELP ARE MUFFLED BY MY ASS § TheFrugalWearer taught me how to make diapers out of duct tape and packing peanuts, and i will NOT let youtube censor him. america is FUCKED § Let 's Fill The Large Hadron Collider With Garbage Now That They Found Their Shitty Particle § itoday i realized that Miracles, Guardian Angels, God, it all exists; when i put 1000 bees on my dick and every single one of them stung it § i jsut made $9 on amazon's Mechanical Turk after clicking on pictures of Silos for 30 hours straight., eat my shit #goingGolt #JOhngolt § whoever keeps adding " one of the characters ever piss or shit" to the "goofs" section of my indie film's IMDB page needs to wrestle my legs § me and several S&P 500 CEOs often have sleepovers and discuss which MLB players we wanna kiss and try to determine which ones are Neuroqueer § there's almost certainly a cosmic connection between my conversion to Muslim and my ascension from "'Tweet Writer" to "Content Producer". § sometimes i wish my ass would be destroyed by a meteor just so i wouldn't have to take shits anymore § please follow my business associates @ZohanTweet, @Jokes_Zohan, @RacistZohan, @ZohanCroatia, @ZohanMoneyTips, @ZOHAN_REAL, and @MyFunnyZohan § i chew on my philly cheesesteak as i place a camera under the table to film womens' feet. http://t.co/lHAX4G7t - The Standard for Influence. § poor spelling is no longer tolerated on this log. this is an adult account now., and i will NOT lose this follow friday to tghe trolls . § thought friday would be a fun day to test run my pizza-pattern necktie, until i ripped my clothes off after being called a “fucking scourge” § i will admit that sometimes i crash my car on purpose just so i can get a faceful of my Denim Airbags § Log off. § I already discovered the Higgs-Boson particle in the trash can, with the rest of the hokum . #CERN #God #GodReal #GodIsReal #GodsReal § @PapaJohns why did you unfollow me. what did I do § america the Fuck-State proves once again that ti is bullshit, by locking innocent Toilets in most prison cells without trial § either my chris farley summoning ritual was a success or a Fucking owl got in here again. wherres that god damn light switch § YES. I AM THE HARD ROCK CAFE. YES. I DID ORDER 18 “ROCKABILLY URINALS”. JUST PILE THEM UP OUTSIDE OF MY CRIME BASE-- ER I MEAN VAN § @dominos thanks for unfollowing me. You truly are an ignorant pizza company. Guess were a papa john family now § if i ever get Crucified i would like it to be on my official warhammer 40,000 surfboard while my all my pitbulls bark at me § #ToMyFutureKids please tell Past Daddy which 9/11s to prevent § sink help § i pin a nerd up against the wall and sink my fist into his stomach. “thats for retweeting me” i strike again. “and THATs for faving me” § yo. dont go swimming in that swamp i just cummed in § im sorry but if my indie bible translation fund doesnt gain any traction soon im going to have to posnt another one of my trade mark rants. § mny life goal is to find and make love to the one millionth mom § DICKSLAVE NUMBER 288, DICKSLAVE NUMBER 122, AND DICKSLAVE NUMBER 195 WALK INTO A BAR. THEY ORDER THREE DRINKS AND MAKE POLITE CONVERSATION § at last., after years of legal b.s. i am finally required to be served up to 5 communion wafers at church because im a big fat hungry man § fucking CHRIst. this dipshit clerk at hollister has been rtrying to run my denim credit card thru the reader for like 10 mins. go to College § informed by family that i wont be invited to anymore funerals if i dont develop a jawline, fix my fucked up voice, and fix my fucked up skin § stop it Teens. stop grabbing onto my jeans and SKitching me as i try to run away. im a teen too. im one of you § it has come to my attention that people have been saying sex things, and alcohol things on this site. these posts give me migraines so stop § @AmandaBynes RAM A CAR INNTO ME BABY § i hand the doctor my urine sample and he removes a tiny wad of flesh floating around in it. “i believe this is yours” “yeah that’s my dick” § eovery single day i thank God for my perfect skin and soft kissable lips as i wrap barbed wire around my arms and legs § calling it: SimAss from Maxis will be 1991’s hottest title. greatest Ass simulator I have ever had the pleasure of using. § just realized that skeletons are basically just rocks hitching a free ride inside of our bodies. sad and pissed off § memes of the antarctic § if trucks can wear nuts Then i should be allowed to nail yosemite sam mudflaps to my asscheeks § where do mirrors come from. if i stand in front of a mirror is my reflection also subject to the insurance mandate?? can i touch mirrors ? § some say if you show your ass to the hell mirror you will feel the icy finger of the reaper touch the back of your bals § 2020: america elects the first Shirtless president § AMERICA REALLY DEAD THIS TIME. I MEAN IT. ALL NATIONS UNITE TO DONATE BILLIONS OF TONS OF DIRT TO GIVE A PROPER BURIAL TO OUR DEAD COUNTRY § with all this talk of nanotechnology the next logical step is miniature girls with cat ears and big dicks injected directly into our blood § BUSTING THROUGHG THE WALL OF KFC WHILE RUNNING ON TOP OF A GIANT ROLLING BARREL LABELLED “BEAK WASTE” , OVER THE HORIZON, GONE FOREVER § jungle of bad ass toilet attachments and accessories turned against me. robot arms shoving toilet paper in my mouth and restraining my dick § muscle milk?? i make my own, thanks. *REVEALS A PERFECT ROW OF NIPPLES ON LEFT BICEP WHILE SOME SERIOUSLY RIPPED DUDES LINE UP FOR A TASTE* § NMISERABLE § stop giving $ to these so-called “gyms”. realize that u can attain God’s Body by finding hot cars and sitting in them til the owner arrives § im going to prank call a bunch of moms in my latest collaboration with MTV Japan § if you see me dragging a compass through the sand, i’m conducting Market Analysis and must not be distracted § proposed Meme Graveyard offers chance to pay respect to the very best online jokes and gags. planned to be built on top of regular graveyard § im going to eat this entire rack of baby back ribs in protest of nasa's bullshit robot on mars § there's a series of codewords that will shut this website down permanently if ever tweeted, and those words are "this is twitter sparta". § do not strain the ass. the best way to take a shit is to electrocute yourself and let it all shoot out naturally. never strain the ass. § This Was Supposed To Be The Summer Of Lonesome George § Fact. § pyramid was the first haunted hous.e Fact. § if driving by the dog kennel while gargling into a megaphone doesn't count as "community service" then maybe i should piss in the courtroom § please stop changing the "Gomco Clamp" wikipedia entry, i have the entire article tattooed on my back and im sick of having to update it § did i jsut piss myself? no . these are mood jeans that change color when i am sick of putting up with jokers such as your self § im a 51 yr old man who doesnt know how to wash him self, abnd i love the attention, and i love making ignorant people mad, and im crazy cool § liist of people who drink beer: wastoids, junkfreaks, crimepunks, crankensteins, grimesmackers, pissbois, mudgeeks, roadslime, and meatballs § Reason For Ban : Unfairly denigrating the SuperPretzel„¢ brand. // Date Ban Will Be Lifted : Never § my opionon on people who use the word "ass" is as follows: these people dont exist to me, therefore ih ave no opinion of them. theyre rotten § president obama orders assassination of the man who holds a "COWBOY ISNT REAL" sign outside of the longhorn steakhouse § PHANTOM LIMB PAIN #WHITEPEOPLEPROBLENMS § the blue thumnbtacks on this map indicate concentrations of high ææˆ(luna) energy, the red ones are all the panera breads ive been banned from § if scientists have demonstrated that rats can breathe in an oxygen-rich liquid then why cant i breathe while submerged in Pepsi `s § grwo up. this is serious § i live in a hollowed out tortoise shell with a GUN sticking out of the head hole, the closest pronounceable address is "hell" § reddit: my uncle caught me licking my sistser's bicycle seat and now i need u to send me as many mcdonald's monopoly game pieces as possible § when I catch the hater/troll who plunged the legendary sword AssBane into my butcheek I will do a cowboy dance on his tiny nuts & kill myslf § piss on mysel.f § well i was going to climb mount everest but this yelp review says theres a nude man at the summit swinging chains around and yelling "fuck u § in short, my greasy chest hair has finally achieved complete fusion with my filthy blues brothers bib, and i am now essentially a cyborg § dont follow me. dont rewteet me. dont fav me. dont look at my page. dont help me. dont click on my pets. dont touch me. dont blog me. § @CapsCop GO FUC^& A PIPE § MY WORST FEARS CONFIRME, COPS IN SEWER, MEASUIRING MY TOILET STATS AND PUTTING LOUD BUGS IN MY HOUSE AS PUNISHMENT WHENEVER I FUCK UP § im going to drink honey live on camera until the borough responds to my repeated demands to demolish my house with me still inside of it § http://t.co/O7z9U3Iv "Trash is Good" § im gonna tr*gger your fuckein grandma by saying "lousy grandson" in her face § wlel, it's almost time to deliver grandma's eulogy. the perfect time to announce that i'm quitting my job at IBM and becoming a SuicideGirl § gentlmen: a crisis. my official pizza hut rage face widget reports that ive posted the "Wtf Face" 138 times in may 2012 alone. trouble ahead § DESPERATELY MASHING MY HANDPRINTS INTO A HUGE WAD OF MY OWN SHIT ON THE HOLLYWOOD WALK OF FAME WHILE COPS FILL ME WITH BULLETS § ill be hiding under the floorboards and snorting herbs for stress relief energy until i am ready to face my guinea pigs again § http://t.co/Awou5Lzl all is revealed 666 § proposed mural of Dr. martin luther king breastfeeding a pitbull wrapped in us flag REJECTED by town "Fucking" hall #DeathEarth #EarthDeath § ye.s im the king of sex and having it. come to my government mandated cage and bring a big sloppy plate of nachos § everoy father's day my dad would take me out on a picnic, and he always filled our picnic basket with dirt, because dirt is the shit of God § if ur wrestling coach calls himself "mr feet pics" and has pictures of feet all over his office,

break his trophies for dishonoring the game § guinness coming in 2 mins to film
me breaking the coveted "most trash cans knocked over using piss" record but im
too sad to put clothes on § #ImSingleBecause my grasp of humen sexuality far
exceeds that of eveyr girl § mny repulsive tweets were specifically designed to
do the exact opposite § my date ended up being 200 rats who scattered throughout my home and with no rat literature i was unable to find their weaknesses §
guess who just filled his hot tub with high fructose corn syrup and is ready to
take one swee t dip............... § i have defibrillator paddles strapped to
each ass cheeck and im ready to bring hell to the nerds § well fucking great.
my date's getting here in 10 minutes and im going to look like an imbecile with
my bookcase devoid of any rat literature § i can't afford any rat literature
because i spent too much money on the elaborate sign over my empty bookcase
which reads "RAT LITERATURE" § TO WHOEVER IS SHRIEKING AT ME RIGHT NOW I CANT
SEE YOU BECUAS EIM FUCKING RUN OVER BY CARS SO SHUT THE FUCK UP § THIS PROJ.
IS MY LIFE AND KICK STARTS ARE MY BLOOD § "This Whole Thing Smacks Of Gender,"
i holler as i overturn my uncle's barbeque grill and turn the 4th of July into
the 4th of Shit § what happens when kirby swallows the qur'an and is granted
its considerable power. my 81 chapter fanfic explores this issue -- and more §
how d o i subtly let my hairdresser know that i want her to cut my dick off
instead of my hair § the shirtless man at the farmer's market has been talking
about "lesbian gravel" to the peanut guy for like an hour § blows on a horn
and summons hundreds of Leather Daddies who form a human pyramid which i climb
on top of to survive the second great flood § im pretty much the Harlem Globe
Trotter's of getting myself forcibly removed from laundromats § ive been
wearing the same pair of jeans for 4 years and i only got sepsis once, read
Maddox's Alphabet of Manliness or be frend zone forever § the shit i was postng
on twitter in the 80s and 90s?? uh yeah, that was the real shit. nowadays its
pandering hipster filth and Crude humour § @MiracleGro MIRACLE GROW GAVE MY DOG
HEART WORM § someone please send me the recording of orson welles reading off
that big list of "you might be a redneck" jokes., i need it beofre 11 PM §
STARTING A KICKSTARTER TO GET ME UNBANNED FROM KICKSTARTER. COM AFTER I CALLED
IT "PRICKSTARTER" IN A PRIVATE EMAIL § if i cant embed this video of me
throwing fireworks at a stump into my dating profile then i might as well just
cut my dick off § now's the perfect time to take out that nasty Zynga money
before it goes sour & invest it directly into The Spice Girls. flame me if u
must § SHIRTLESS MAN AT THE FARMERS MARKET WHO EVALUATES THE FOOD BY "LISTENING
" TO IT WITH HIS EAR IS BACK.. THINK ILL SIPHON SOME OF HIS MANA § i was
bullied and tortured at school because i was the only kid with a waterbed. so i
got surgery and became a waterbed. suck my cock trolls § i surgically replaced
my beard with Lit Cigars . i am sorry. im so so sorry § if i could get my
hands on the wildman who painted sexy butterfly girls all over my wreckingball i
woud tie him up and throw my shoes at him § "animaniac_fucker" has posted a
touching tribute t o the Rwandan Arby's Bombings, please install your CoolBux-
Vid Media Enhancer to view it § important. http://t.co/zsm7W03b § nows the
time when the CEO of the company inspects each employee's shit, and im nervous
cus my turds look like fucked up little caterpillers § <MY FATHER> , who had
gone missing for 17 years and was presumed dead after failing to return from
his ultimate dumpster diving life quest § a <DUMPSTER WITHIN A DUMPSTER>, once
in a lifetime find, can be used as Armor or rolled down a steep incline to make
A TON of noise § a <MYSTERIOUS CHASM> leading to an unrelenting void, a
terrifying nightscape of psychological torture and constant misery. the worst
dive § <MUMMIFIED FERRETS>, each one dressed as a cast member of "The Little
Rascals". the notable exception of Froggy renders the set incomplete § nice
bundle of <URI GELLER PEZ DISPENSERS>, many of which appear to be ruined by
human teeth marks but some of them are ok § <IRAQI PROPAGANDA MOUSEPADS> ,
featuring Uday and Qusay Hussein as babies wearing Costumes at the circus § 49

reams of <WALLACE AND GROMIT LEGAL-SIZED STATIONERY>, only a bastard would allow this to tocuh the foul lips of a garbage can. § two hundred <JOHNNY COCHRAN LEWD HUMOR SWEATERS> , the kennel will give ya 20 cents for these , the animals love to wear them and rip em up § about a dozen or so misshapen <ROSS PEROT VICTORY '96 ASHTRAYS> ,woud love to take up smoking just to get some use outta these bad boys § an untampered Sleeve of <TERRY SCHIAVO DECALED FRISBEES> i tell ya, the guy who threw these puppys out is the real frisby. § three unopened boxes of promotional <E.T. "MOONLIGHT ONION" FLAVORED DORITOE'S>, covered in what appears to be machine oil but still good § alright Boys i just spent seven years on a dumpster diving voyage across South America and i got some nice Finds for YA , lets take a look: § to the man in the forest dressed up like a traffic cop, giving all sorts of unauthorized directions and disrupting harmony of nature: FUCK U § as the sun consumes the earth i will stand atop the highest mountain with my arms spread wide , shouting "Bring Back Meebo" § @ bobbysburgerpal bobby certainly didnt get his flair & passion for cooking by touching di*ks, so i dont know why your waiter woud touch mine § @longjohnslvrs never thought id get my di*k touched by a staff member at a long john silver's, but here we are. its a madhouse up there § @Famous_Daves so youve always been famous for your bbq, but now your staff can be famous for touching d**ks, namely Mine, earlier today § @pizzahut you claim to offer exceptional service in the field of pizza, however the only thing ur staff is interested in is touching my dick § @CrackerBarrel guess who just touched my di*k??? yeah, it was a cracker barrel waiter. § Help Me Deep Freeze My Beard So It Stinks Less § i ask everyone to watch my recital but before i can begin i immediately slip and fall into the yellowstone supervolcano and my dick explodes § man on mountaintop wont stop yelling "Wanker" , cops cannot reach him buecause of falling rocks § can anyone who has successfully made a surfboard out of their own shit please holler some pointers at me or maybe shoot me if you have a gun § man with "GLUTESLORD" written on sweatband has gone mad with power, destroying nerds with sniper rifle from fortress on the roof of the gym § so apparently if you take all of the autism awareness puzzle piece car decals and put them together you get a cool pic of yoshi as a girl § im far too angry to piss anything, let alon e my trademark diaper. § im onto you r fucked up tricks, go home and sit on the toilet § it;s time to log offline and stop Spamning this addres, fucker troll § @THEHermanCain herman cain grabbed a lady's ass while thinking about pizza § @THEHermanCain herman cain fucked a big pizza and got tomato sauce all over his dick and thats why he lost the nomination § today TekkenChauncey claimed that spiders make their webs out of cum and that makes them Gay so i destroyed his mame cabinet with my boots § can you please alter this "PROPERTY OF THE ZOO" tattoo on my back into maybe like a naked gypsy chick § i flash my pistol and hand a note to the cashier at Wendy's. the note reads as follows: "I Want A GF With Bat Wings" § petrified 800 nubile women with mucus and the so-called great state of wyoming wont allow me to build a palace out of their bodies -- fuck u § dinner at pf chang? let me consult the oracle *squats over mirror and spreads ass cheesk a little bit before getting depressed and stopping* § @digimonotis his tiwiter verification is pending but i can confirm that this is the true otis § digmon otis has locked himself in his closet with several boxes of kashi granola bars for several weeks to "power up" and "focus" § they didnt show "rag fucker" at e3, i was really expecting them to show "rag fucker", disappointed & concerend about future of "rag fucker" § FUCK TWITTER § IF YOURE 1 OF THE 10000 PEOPLE WHO IGNORED ME WHILE I WAS HALF DISSOLVED IN A HOT TUB BEGGING FOR SEX JUSt REMMEBER THAT I OWN CBS BRDCSTING § how many gross rags can i shove into htis decommissioned nintendo game boy before i carry it around town for hours like a lost fucking idiot § banned from BullShit public pool for instantly turning water into Mud by jumping in it, begging lifeguard to end my life, etc and so Foreth § #e3rumors some meme guy will walkout on stage twirlin two pistols and begin kicking cans of Gun Flavored Mountain Dew into a screaming crowd § #e3rumors IM THAT HANDSOME FELLA LAYIN ON THE HOOD OF HIS LEXUS NEXT TO THE CONFERENCE HALL, STROKIN IT TO ALL THE RIFF-RAFF ABOUT THE PLACE § COOL PIC FOUND, CRAMMED UNDERNEATH THE DRAWERS OF MY DESK AT WORK FOR PERHAPS A DECADE http://t.co/IairzdxR § .@girl I Wanna Rub Ur Belley § gentlemen, i implore you not to miss the Gamer's Challenge, wherein i will complete donkey kong countyr 3 (italian vrsn) without crying § b3ndr, PepsiCyn-ic, and myself will be streaming an incan healing ritual, intending to absorb blood from viewers to regenerate our foreskins § a mother bird tends to her young until my big sweatpants ass slowly pushes her nest off of the tree § look out for the car with the words "INCEST DEATH" painted on the hood thats always going like 20-30 mph under the speed limit, that ones me § "offensive or inappropriate does not automatically equal funny" - GOD § middle-aged men have been retreating to the sewers of our fair city to cry. as mayor i will promise to eradicate these terrible crying men § "humankind is so corrupt" i mutter as i sandwich my dick between my badge and gun and take several pics of it with a disposable camera § wassup babe, im the reason Pregnancy-info .net disabled video embedding on their forums, how abuot giving me a nice kiss § d o it mother fucker, i thrive off of hell energy, i feed off of hater bullshit § sory § BREAKER BREAKER ONE NINE THIS IS BIG SHITTY TRUCK DRIVER HAUL`N A BIG CUMMY DICK ON DOWN 2 SAN QUENTIN PENITENTIARY 2 FUCK ALL THE PRISONERS § im ready to show all of you my trick. watch *spreads arms and screams at the mountainside until an avalanche of boulders engulf me entirely* § @CapsCop EAT SHIT, COP § IF THE ZOO BANS ME FOR HOLLERING AT THE ANIMALS I WILL FACE GOD AND WALK BACKWARDS INTO HELL § if a $40000 check isnt made out to DigimonOtis in the next 3 hours, we WILL hack missouri's official state dog and change it to a dirty boot § ok piss stian, this ralph wiggum tattoo is a long-term investment, meaning its value will grow over time. go read a Economic ' s book, child § and the nobel peace prize goes to... "Fag Poisoner"?? a huge tattooed man takes the stage & bites into the award like a cookie, gives finger § Louis? gosh, it's been years. it's me, Neal, from Law School. anyway, i got this big juicy onion here, was thinking me and you could fuck it § A MAD TYRANT has cracked the admin password for IRC chatroom #DiaperIsrael -- the entirety of DARKNET is in peril § senator rich blumenthal (D-CT) just threw a towel over the parkour mans head. game over, earth is dead § FREE COUPONS - GET 3 SIMPSONS OF YOUR CHOICE PROFESSIONALLY PRINTED IN FULL COLOR ON THE SIDE OF ANY DESERT EAGLE PISTOL - I GOT 'UM § turn on c-span, therse a man with an anonymous mask doing parkour on the senate floor and im rubbing my face on the tv to absorb his energy § my velcro jeans burst open, scattering my secret stash of 2 liter canada dry bottles as I stumble backwards off the roof of the 9/11 buildig § ohhh anOTHER solar eclipse, you say ?? gee i cant wait.. *does the Jerk Off motion until the sun supernovas itself out of shame* § no amount of money will ever fix my forlorn dick, i woud instead advise you to donate trash by throwing it at me § "hey, you know what people like to smell while eating?? feet and piss" - guy who decided to put playground tunnels in fast food restaurants § everyone send me indie films about uncancelling "wild hogs 2" and i promise to project them onto my garage door. no cussing or nude, plaese. § obliviously driving m y car through chernobyl , absorbing lethal anmounts of radiation while looking for cute girls § @Wegmans "Authorities continue searching for clues after a beheading took place at a Wegmans food market" This is absolutely disgusting. § SOME PLACE BETWEEN HEAVEN AND HELL EXISTS "INCEST WEB" § why hasnt twitter verified @AssBoss yet. im certain that he's the real ass boss § from the popular TED talks comes the TED Scream. at first glance, it's a man screaming on stage. but can his screams change the world ??? § EVERYONE ON EARTH PLEASE SHOVE YOUR HANDS INTO YOUR POCKETS AND LAY FLAT FACING THE GROUND UNTIL MY LOST "PUSSYMAN" APRON TURNS UP § honestly i get like 20 unfollows every time something comes out of my awful mouth § BOOOOOO TO M Y 10000TH FOLLOWER @TorresaurusRex BOO YOU PICE OF SHIT EVERYONE THROW YOUR SHOES AT SUCK MY DICK § two thunbs down for ebert's fucked up new mouth § sorry, all. "Let's Play: Pissrealms 2D: Part 314" has been postponed indefinitely, due to an injury i sustained while taking off my shirt § some simpsons dvds fall outta my velvet robe while pouring my date a drink at my penthouse suite. i bend down to check if they got fucked up § priest plugs my coffin in at the end of the funeral. "MILLERTIME" lights up in neon on the side, desecrating my corspe & sending me to hell § hit by a train while wearing a trenchcoat bloated with family guy jewelry and nobody even helped me pick any of it up because god is twisted § certain theres a special combination of ancient cowboy noises that will get you free shit from QVC and ill keep calling until i FINd it § i saw a man at rofl con with a huge black stain down the ass crack. can another attendee please confirm #roflcon #StainMan § dont u dare step foot into my dojo until youve read oprah's blog post about east asian nutrigenomics and their remarkable immunity to autism § http://t.co/sh1Ydsxf my cool forems § yo this server is for pregnant halo players only. all u non pregs can go suck a lemon, capiche?? § WHAT HAPPENS TO THE SHIT -GOES BELOW GROUND AND ASSIMILATES WITH ROTATING MASS KNOWN AS "SUBTERRANEAN SHIT EARTH"- PROOF THAT HELL ISNT REAL § DICK CLARK CORPSE MARIONETTE TO KICK OFF NEW YEARS 2013 WITH MIRACULOUS POST-MORTEM COUNTDOWN - WE TRULY ARE A BLESSED NATION § http://t.co/gD4yGMQl Got anymore Sonia Sotomayor Feet Pictures? Upload Here § cumstarter. i need 500 liters of cum to start a projec.t i dont know its some bacon blog. who gives a fuck § i murdered my wife my throwing her at a speeding cop car but its ok because i made her out of shit § oh nothin, i was just buying some ear medication for my sick uncle... *LOWERS SHADES TO LOOK YOU DEAD IN THE EYE* who's a Model by the way, § @Sleepys @SleepysCare @SleepysKathy @SleepysLaleta @SleepysChanda @SleepysCathy @SleepysIrina respect teens, scunbags § yes, i am a 24 year old man, and yes, i am the one who spraypainted the word "Teen" on the side wall of sleepy's mattress porfessionals. § http://t.co/PGRbniBT i wa nt to drown in this § TEARING THE MONA LISA FROM ITS CANVAS AND USING IT 2 CENSOR MY BIG BARE ASS AS I BUMBLE MY WAY OUT OF THE LOUVRE WITH GUARDS SCREAMING AT ME § little known fact: the e3 gaming conference is considered the holy grail of the public urination community § fucking shitty school bully somehwo got his hands on the book of memoirs that i published & read the part about my balls to the entire class § the moment you realize that every piece of furniture you own is just a man in a zentai suit stuck in a rigid pose and they all flee at once § an advanced culture millions of light years away intercepts first earthly message; a craigslist posting succinctly titled "boscov's fuck" § known among variety of local retailers as "oily ass man." banned from mattress giant, pier 1 imports, ikea, raymour & flanigan, and so forth § sorry. fan-made, HD remake of "Bubsy 3D" will never see the light of day, because ive been turned into birds § i light a candle next to photograph of my ex-wife's ass & say tiny prayer before devouring another handful of french's fried onions #WifeAss § CNN: SHITLOAD OF DEAD WOLVES FOUND IN NYC SUBWAY SYSTEM INSPIRES US ALL AS A NATION TO REFLECT UPON MOTHERHOOD AND PERHAPS OUR SELF'S § Check out these amazing pics of fat guys slammin chairs around then a hottie getting fucked by pumpkin head http://t.co/VYAuuVbu § YO !! DONT SEXT THAT TEEN § god grant me the serenity 2 accept the Diapers i cant change, the courage to change the Diapers i can, & the wisdom to shit myself profusely § next guy to propose another wild kramer autism theory gets thier ass banned down to chinatown. this is seinfeld forum, not ignorant forums. § ATTN: SICK FUCKS WHO ARE AGGRAVATING MY HEART CONDITION ON PURPOSE BY POSTING DRAMA 2 THE INCEST SUBREDDIT - GOT TWO WORDS FOR YA: "GUN § andy rooney hologram crashes coachella 2013 and berates the audience, calling them "rude" and "a disappointment" #awful § @GreyhoundBus one of your African-American drivers called me a "Kermit-Looking Motherf**ker" and made me feel like a Fool in front of my son § THE COP GROWLS “TAKE OFF TH OSE JEANS, CITIZEN.” I COMPLY, REVEALING THE FULL LENGTH DENIM TATTOOS ON BOTH LEGS. THE COP SCREAMS; DEFEATED § SARKOZY PRETENDED TO INITIATE HANDSHAKE WITH OBAMA BUT THERE WAS A BABY BIRD IN HIS HAND AND THE BABY BIRD MELTED. ACT OF WAR........... § in one proposed timeline, goatboy was a character played by jim breuer on SNL who circulated a jpeg of his ass and became the goatman. § “ obama” legally changes name to “yesbama”. approval rating rises 40% § woah. look who’s back in town http://t.co/aZ9quw0r § workin out in a graduated cylinder. as i gain muscle mass the water level will rise above my head and drown me. this is true muscle suicide § a trail of rose petals leads you to a room bathed in warm candlelight. piled on the sofa is every guinness record book published after 2004 § god grant me the strengrh to raise $260 to create Skeleton MMORPG . if this kickstarter fails...im gonna Start Kickin § meeting with CBS execs over possible sitcom “The Diaper Ref” about a referee who wears diaper &describes everyday problems with sports terms § winner of this year’s prom theme is “shit to israel”, with a grand total of 2 votes § APRIL FOOL ISNT OVER UNTIL AMEX REMOVES OUTSTANDING BALANCE OF $333299 FROM MY ACCOUNT & ACKNOWLEDGES THAT I DIDNT BUY 3000 ASTRONAUT DILDOS § 2013: burger king creates “The Doritos Whopper” 2021: orson scott card writes “The Doritos Novel” 2035:removed from matrix. no more doritos § tried to overdose on aquarium pebbles & the hospital laughed at me and the ambulance drivers all took turns whipping me with catheter tubes § if you heard a man screaming today it was from when a couple of policemen tried to hoist me into a large bathtub in the town square § “ the only ‘safe sex’ is death “ - some gym teacher with a skeleton puppet § realdoll corporation accidently sent me a Scarecrow... a sign that I should return to the simple life at my uncle’s pumpkin farm?? Probably § someone hacked hte high score board on the java pacman game in monsanto .com’s “For Fun” page. just a heads up § the toilet feeler ruins another public restroom with his grubby hands § invented by god in Year 666, my sickening Ass was tasked with torturing insubordinate angels until it fell into the hands of the shit prince § @Battlefield user named “Garth_Turds” disrupted an in-game memorial service by making obnoxious beatbox noises, can something be done? § i have no idea how that turd got on your ceiling, but it definitely didn’t fly out of my shorts while iwas doing a backflip § gteens are God on earth § we succeed where many businesses fail, by offering a comprehensive program wherein I (Me) will run your dick over in my wheelchair, for free § @Horse_ebooks uuhh http://t.co/ljxs7Vzp § COMMONLY REFERRED TO AS THE “BAD BOY” OF WET BEARD BLOGGING § i get my ass.............. § the Law Man surveys the room, and is able to locate me hiding behind a potted plant thanks to my trail of miserable , fucked up turds § Proud To Employ Disabled Surgeons For All Of My Cosmetic Procedures § hurts , dont it!!!?! § a bully asked me if i wanted a “Hurts Donut” then one thousand ghouls phased through the floor and ceiling and began shitting on me § LIKE A SNAKE SHEDS ITS SKIN, I SHED ANOTHER HARD ROCK CAFE TSHIRT EVERY 7 MONTHS § im a tennis ball and my primary mode of transportation is being pushed around by animal piss § i refuse to patronize Famous Dave’s BBQ until they throw cultural sensitivities to the wind and change their name back to “the piss morgue” § WELL I PRINTED OUT MY RESUME, DUNNO WHAT ILL DO WITH THESE OTHER 4999 BOXES OF PROFESSIONAL “IF YOUR A HATER DONT READ THIS” STATIONERY § where cna i get a skeleton who will sit in my fridge all day and hand me the item i want whenever i open it § you know how peoples dicks evaporate when exposed to sunlight?? how do i get mine to not do that § performance on Antz Role-Playing Forum has been shot ever since police made me register as a sex offender after finding me crying in public § WHy isnt there a crosswalk where 50 year old women can explore their femininity without getting hooted at § how about go drink your self a babys formula pal!!!!!!!! § “jail isnt real,” i assure myself as i close my eyes and ram the hallmark gift shop with my shitty bronco § proposed “slime wtc” catches airplanes and converst them into waste § gonna print out a bunch of pages from rival muscle blogs and scatter them across my driveway & drive my noisy scooter around on top of them § http://t.co/36JTlhuJ youtbue championship 2012 § @cesarmillan PUT MY DICK ON TV § Want 2 know what’s worse than widespread voter fraud?? hipsters putting scary pumpkins on their porch every october § my perfectl #TwitterWifey is a leather sack full of porcelain shards that i can swing at census takers § clicked on discover button& found my “Jokes” are coping technique designed 2 assuage guilt surrounding my faltering relationship with CHrist § YO *points to spinal cord on brain diagram* THATS THE BRAIN;S DICK § the large hadron collier will never detect the higgs boson particle. the only purpose it has is to rile dogs up § a giant vat of slop in a secret factory has two pipes which lead to the bottling lines, one labeled “GAMER FUEL” and the other “BABY FOOD” § Who Told U About Satan Ass § what do you mean 1800-GOT-JUNK only takes waste “Out” of peoples houses. thats an absurd concept. i will hang the fuck up right now § hello 1800-GOT-JUNK?? PLease come by and give me all the junk you got. shovel it into my home, and my childrens bedrooms, and dont take any § .@plantcore may outright steal but at least @GoofyKidGalvin7 has the initiative to create bastard versions of the tweets he finds § HA HA HA HA HA HA HA HA HA HA HA HA HA HA § dear god. in all my years.... an ancient diaper perfectly preserved in amber-- no wait, its just some shitty caveman head. throw it back § i dont know much about solar storms but i swear to god that the one that happened last thursday gave me the ability to yell louder § fucking Nude Man ruine all our laser tag games, cant shoot him cause he isnt wearing the vest, cant rack up any points against him § a blessing on this earth. my shit covered muscles are a blessing on this earth § http://t.co/N7a5BLf8 art § knocked a shit load of doritos off the shelf during my latest suicide attempt at wegmans and thtis 16 yr old little shit made me put em back § first off, trees are bullshit § somebody snuck into my yard and smeared shit all over my kony statue. people are monsters § my dr.phil crystal imbues its user with AL;L the abilities and strengths of television personality “Dr. Phil”; & the fbi is buggin me for it § fire dril and tornado dril are my alt formes . well bye § pulls down pants revealing ass. pulls down pants further, revealing a 2nd pair of ass cheeks. pulls them down still fruther, revealing 3rd p § unfortunately the red cross does not accept blood that you foundi n the trash can or blood that has been coughed up into your shitty beard § “STOP BEING Tsundere” - me screaming at god § @Wendys MANAGER HASSLED ME FOR BRINGING ART BOOKS INTO THE WENDY’S STORE, WAS TOLD TO LEAVE AND WAS UNABLE TO EAT THE FOOD THAT I PAID FOR § “Can Determine The Gender Of Any Animal Simply By Touching Its Dick” § “but the oval office wasnt around when John tyler was president” says hte nerd as my ass slowly engulfs his pathetic, misshapen head § john tyler was less commonly known as the “Rat President”, having up to 900 rats running around the oval office and making an utter ruckus § how come a baby born with a foot in its brain is considered a “Miracle Baby” but when I get my dick stuck in a drawer im just some asshole § do I have.,. a twitter account??? oh yeah, im a real tweet mouth § what is Courage, you ask??? courage is being able to say that ragecomics are bad on your twitter account § the archaeologist inspects a hideous smear of caveman shit on the wall of an ancient cavern. “ah, this is it. the first ragecomic” § #FacesOfReddit My Favorite Boy http://t.co/bJGF0lTn § wrestleburg is a real town and i live there § GAY TRANSHUMANIST ..... I KNOW U HAVE BEEN CHECKING MY POSTS OUT .... SHOW YOUR SELF § KICKSTARTER: buy me a big roll of bubble wrap so i can fuck it --- $0.23 Pledged of $35 Goal -- - § two men fighting inside of a dog igloo § me and a couple of straight dudes are sharing this big bowl of wildberries in honor of davy jones the dead guy § i trusted you jewey2k10 and you pull this shit on me. youre a disgrace to all Straight Edge Teens who play in bands § yeah im the one who made that image. i did it to own yiou, on twitter. #savederpy § http://t.co/gZjB6r9E Im Screaming At It All #savederpy § http://t.co/B9N6pBOU humanity in its Lowest form, Fuck you #savederpy § http://t.co/aGNnlnCq look at this prick. he sucks. #savederpy § jsut tried to climb onto the stage shirtless with "INDIE" painted on my body but a sniper murdered me off-cam . #Oscars § if someone wins an oscar and they start crying they should rip it out of the Fucker's hands #Oscars § "IN THIS HOUSE, FOXTROT IS CONSIDERED MANGA" #Oscars § Hats Off to the guy who digitally altered all the celebrities to make them look less sad #Oscars § just saw another Uncensored Ass in the audience. im finished with this horse shit. #oscars #AssInTheAudience #Oscars2012AITA § when i awake im a skeleton, being dangled off a cliff and used as a wi-fi reciever. i can feel every ass being downloaded through my body. § i enter a cavern and see a laptop perched on a rock. displayed on the screen is an image of my ass. but how...? a poison dart hits my neck § small village. all the locals are dead, their bones removed and fashioned into a crude satellite dish, seemignly designed to download asses. § i stop to ask a local how many asses the ass downloader has downloaded. "at least 100," he tells me. i nod and continue my journey onward § for decades i have traversed the unforgiving mountains and rivers of south america, hoping to catch a glimpse of the fabled "ass downloader" § ««« --Ã—TOILET EARTHÃ--- ««« § #ThingsPeopleHaveToStopDoing shitting on the koran. for every koran that gets shit on i will shit on a bible § #ThingsPeopleHaveToStopDoing eating disgusitng garbage food and being miserable sacks of shit and bemoaning the fact that theyre worthless § #KINGOFSWAG do disfiguring bruises on my significant other's face qualify as "swag" #teambreezy #filthypeople #worst § the Joe Dirt watcher's rockin' Joe Dirt quote of the week: "Watch Joe Dirt" § did they find any water on mars yet. what about catboys § I Just Want 2 Have Sex On This Site All The Time With Out Havin To Argue With Peopl And Deal With People Cryin And Shit #WiseWordsToLiveBy § "zelda vs garfield", i mutter as i look at the floor during a job interview § where can i get one of those giant inflatable rats that construction workers keep putting up on the side of the road. i need it for my grave § please leave, sir. your vulgar, senseless displays may be tolerated at K-Mart, but not here at Super K-Mart § if anyone in the central nj arera wants 2 scrub down my big A$$ body with rags thats fine by me. i promise not to speak or acknowledge you § "Rock and Roll Kevin is named that because of his extensive knowledge of Rock and Roll music." § which one of you jokers made the radio station shoutout "Rock and Roll Kevin", who has "Brain Cancer" § im uploading a "let's play" vid of me getting stuck between the walls of my house and getting all tangled up in the insulation and shit § the rock spots a small pile of jabroni turds left carelessly on the floor of his ring. he postures defiantly as the audience hoots and jeers § mail 1000 envelopes addressed to "The Desert" and watch endless waves of government pawns march to their death #ANARCHY2012 #sand § another day volunteering at the betsy ross museum. everyone keeps asking me if they can fuck the flag. buddy, they wont even let me fuck it § last night i was restrained and had the words "Bug Helper" branded into my back with a hot iron by three men who i trusted. im still shaking § how can i get my 50year old co-workers more interested in the indie gaming scene. how. *kicks trashcan* how. *punches car* how. *fires gun* § god bless him. cops is bull shit. § no!! hes bad § whenever i get nude for any reason i hear the dogs go wild outside. must sense something that humans can not. § from personal experience, if you nail one of those tiny gift shop license plates over ur real one a police man will grapple you with his ass § groundhog sees a nude mans gyrating ass instead of shadow, predicting 6 weeks of erupting yellowstone supervolcano § http://t.co/MTn35r91 a solid hour of this § "Kermit the Racist" by AdultCartoonFTW (182,727 views) § #ChrisBrownPickupLines im ignorent. my music bad. my pubic hair smells like shit. my dicks smal. grammys only let me on cause my dad is rich § #ChrisBrownPickupLines Babe Remember That Time I Took

My Shirt Off In The News Studio Cause I Got Mad While Trying To Clear My Vile Record § ok, first off its BS that wetnaps dont tell u that you need to unwrap them before use. second, food smeared on face boosts the immune systm § "Phew! Its like a sauna in here!" - the most hilarious guy in the sauna § i just tipped over my garbage can and tried to feng shui all the trash. i dont know if it worked or not but im still fat § the worst mythbuster to ever exist was the dead mythbuster that they never talk about #TheDeadMythbuster § whoever wrote "I Exist To Be Hollered At" onto the back of my Official Nascar Cape nneeds to crawl over to my address for some rebel justice § don t dehumanize my posts § special Treat for all my prety lady followers.... http://t.co/Sb9TrXhg § drag my shity corpse around § i dont have to. theres no law that says i have to § contrary to the lies posted by a certain MetalGearEric, i know what the word "sex" means, and i know what the word "poop" means § who spit on my rats. ill find him § know how roaches scatter when you turn the lights on??? same thing happens when i whip my big ass out. #miserable § WHAT ABOut MY FREE SPEECH *a bunch of child porn spills outof mouth* IM AS HUMAN AS THE REST OF U *Dick Flies Out Of Pants And Spins Around* § chris brown farts into microphone as thousands of miserable, awful women attempt to fuck the speaker system #grammys #teambreezy § what do Chris Brown, Hitler, and Charles Manson have in common? something charisma something something power something atrocity #teambreezy § chris brown engulfs the crowd in acid piss during bad concert, disfiguring scores of his awful fans (Says He's Sorry) #Grammys #teambreezy § i support chris brown because my love of generic, autotuned shit overrides my intrinsic sense of morality #Grammys #teambreezy § thge concept of "forgiveness' is some stupid religious shit conceived to allow rich folks to beat the hell out of women #grammys #teambreezy § we all have our own way of grieving. *sinks teeth into huge ass medium rare t-bone steak with "WITNEY" written on it in ketchup* § if you dont accompany my twitter feed with the "real time with bill maher" theme music every time you read it youre4 a piece of shit § @enterprisecares Thanks, I'll get right on that. Also my daughter may have ingested some of the hair. § sorry im late, my car totally Friend Zoned me-- im fired??..now YOURE friend zoning me?? im gonna eat all these pills and friend zone myself § @ enterprisecares Glove compartment in my rented vehicle filled with diapers and hair. Don't you guys check these things? § whenever someone tells me dolphins are intelligent as humans i send them the article aobut flipper killing himself to prove that theyre dumb § as the sex principal it is my duty to wear a color-coded tie that indicates how many people i will have sex with today durnig working hours. § im the sex principal. i have sex all the time in the techer lounge. i fuck the lady teachers & i fuck the man teachers. im all fat and shit. § finest rack o ribs youve ever seen. you get your favorite dry rub all over that badboy but- oh no- it's sand. the sand laughs #BBQNightmares § Starfish Rant. ive had it up to here with this bullshit animal. click here to watch my starfish rant § although im the foremost Blue Jeans Virtuoso i consider it disrespectful to wear them. i simply kiss each pair 5 times a day; facing mecca. § anyone catch that middle finger during the half time show? it was mine, in my living room, directed at the tv #ImIndie #GoodIndie #Indie500 § @ cleatusonfox why werent you programmed to feel shame § i only stare into the abyss for the commercials § CANT ATTEND GRANDMAS FUNERAL SHIRTLESS??? WISH I WAS IN THAT CASKEt § id rahter die than join the Fucking dark side. § what gender do i have to turn myself itno to be able to squirt octopus ink out § #ffff James Cool @jamescool147 "Love Sex,Milfs,Boobs,Cougars...& Fucking & Am A Bad Boy" § Only if U Find The Forum For Disabled People Calle d 3DWorldz ANd U Have Fun. -- http://t.co/zY8yfShu § Everyuthing about the N-word. I believe im already rich and ill be launched into the kfc man's grave then. -- http://t.co/zY8yfShu § no. Remove thje piss. This will not stand. § go to a ymca locker room and laugh at all the nude morons § "the guy who tried to sell a mummy on etsy" § basically,actual doctors have told me my brain is Perfect. ANYWAY, HGeres nine paragraphs I wrote on why leaving tips at restaurants is bad § wow someone eshould tell that Angry Redditor that metal bands are rippin off his posts § "...most of the human race killed off, because it is unworthy, it is unworthy of the gift of life." - someone who hasn't killed himself yet § http://t.co/G2aBjJo4 ghahhahafha § i just found out tombstones have dead people underneath them. fucked up § will no longer be livestreaming foreskin restoration process; the trolls who attempted to summon [ã,¤ãƒ³ãƒ—] (Imps) into the chatroom are to blame § MAYAN GROUNDHPOG HELD ALOFT BY HAT MAN AT WINTER CEREMONY; STRUCK BY LIGHTNING; TURNED INTO ONE HUMAN SKULL "UH OH NOW WEVE REALLY DONE IT" § my favorite philosopher is Ben Stein . § my entry on maddox.com's despicable "Faggotpedia" claims that I believe im a yoshi in real life. This is false. Im actually an archyoshi § YoshiGod9 says that if you shit into a wasp nest they wont sting your ass because theyre too dumb to know what shit even is. Prove him wrong § #3WordsThatWomenHate my dick § LABRADOR DRUNKDRIVER #illegalDogBreeds § MUSCULAR SHITHOUND #illegalDogBreeds § THE GOLDEN EMBEZZLER #illegalDogBreeds § A FRANKENSTEIN #illegalDogBreeds § THE INCEST TERRIER #illegalDogBreeds § @OfficialZales could you fit my kidney stones into a ring. me and my fiancee believe that body's are sacred, and we are averse to jewels. § i will pay the jim henson company $100000 to make the old critic muppets pepper a slideshow of my most miserable nudes with caustic remarks. § has anyone ever done a powerpoint presentation nude § i owuld like for u to meet my Uncles *leads u into room full of crude wooden mannequins* Have Fun. *closes door and watches u thru peephole* § Curse of the Colonel (ã,«ãƒ¼ãƒ ãƒ«ã,µãƒ³ãƒ€ãƒ¼ã,¹ã®å'ªã „ KÄ neru SandÄ su no noroi?) refers to an urban legend regarding a reputed curse placed on the Japanese § check out my tumblr *goes limp & rolls down steep mountainside for 10 minutes or so, banging head on branches and rocks, surely dead * § i dress as a medieval knight and pummel my metal body with cymbals to get all 59 of my pit dogs riled up before i fling lawn chairs at them § gov bans pit bull fighting because they are scared of the power pits can achieve by gaining BOth strengh & wisdom in the barbwire gauntlet § SCREAMS INTO THE MICROPHOHNE, MY HOLLERING REVERBERATES THRU TINY CELLAR FILLED WITH 59 HOGWILD PIT BULL DOGSm;; GAINING STRENGTH THRU ANGER § U Have Been Banned From GoiterTeenz - The Forum For Teens With Disfiguring Goiters-- Reason: Prolonged Harassment Of Female Members § why is piss the center of my life § ok MPR, you win. ever since you stormed out of my house with my booster seat in tow ive been unable to function in chairs. please come bac § MICROPENISRODNEY U HAVE & ALWAYS WILL HAVE BE A PECE OF SHIT. I POUR MY SOUL INTOTHIS BUSINESS AND ALL U DO IS SIT THER &RUB YOUR HAIRY LEGS § MicropenisRodney; if youre out there, anywhere plesse get in touch with me, im sorry I yelled at you and I wamt to fix our ragecomic startup § big biker dude pops a wheelie on harley & simultaneously unleashes a load of shit from his nude ass.his license plate says "Rape" #RapeJokes § good teamrwork. thanks http://t.co/oatu1lOT § @DogBountyHunter what if you sprayed a can of pepper mace directly at my ass. what wouald happen. also congrats on season 2 or whatever § yeah im the uncool one. meanwhile im going to go jerk off to a picture of my wife while counting my Tuxedo's. Later § i supoprt sopa, pipa, acta, buta, mema, rude jokes, muslom, spike tvs ill fated animation bloc, indie, and this guy http://t.co/ScBrI0s3 § "mama mia" § i specifically requested that my bone marrow be sent 2 the man who wants to rub it on his dick, instead of that dying girl. this is bullshit § contents of kim dotcom's panic room: imported mtn dew (glass bottle, no corn syrup), " o copz allowed" sign (affixed to door), blooper dvds § kim dotcom was a hero. he loved to piss more than anyhting. he would piss into Real Dolls and throw them in the garbage. no toilet § please stop trying 2 rile me up. im overweight man with cardiac dysrhythmia; and rude posts send my blood pressure into crisis zone § haha owned. im already rich and famous § would you forgive me if i was rich and famous § im dead too, so respect my tweets, Fucker § if my twieets upset you, then why dont you just “COVER THEM UP” ??/ ha ha get it § The reports are false, Joe Paterno is still alive!! Joe Pa pulled through the night, read more: http://t.co/rBxuJuC8 § ive installed a couple of externals to cover my bases § very brave § everyuthing about you is hilarious § the only sin ive committed is looking so god damn good in these fuckin jeans, kickin around in my big ass boots § he hid the facts § please help me tanger58. ive become something i cannot control § Joe Pa is in his deathbed right now id wager, jerking off one last time before the curtain falls on his disgraceful life § well yeah if you look at this Joe Pa thing from the whole “Rape Angle” it looks pretty skeevy, but remember that time he did good at sports? § no youre totally right,”Joe Pa” is a perfectly honorable & respectable man, assuming hes never confronted with any actual tests of character § tipping over a news van on top of a pile of shattered childhoods in honor of Dying Idiot joe “Joe Pa” paterno #JoePa #Hell § -^{2} -^{2} -^{2} htese are the jeans that christ died in -^{2} -^{2} -^{2} § snubbed again by the 2012 Skeleton Awards; tore my skin off for naught § google it sometime, honey § gonna catch a lot of flak for this one, but i gotta go with Alchemy > Random. http://t.co/PrsF4m2L § if you dont watch the cool visualizations that your media player of choice provides alongside the music youre listening to; youre a coaward. § #myfavorite90ssong the blue song by daft punk § nmy name is greg. i enjoy Film and Tech. § retweet this i f you capitalize Film. #Film § im the banker from deal or no bdeal, intently watching this situation unfold from my balcony in total darkness § bring back green ketchup. § “maturity” is a subjective concept often employed to breed contempt for thsoe who deviate from the corporate sponsored nor,m § Tha;ts a clump of hair, you fucking idiot. Did you really think that was a fossil ? If you show that to the museum guy he’ll get mad at you § making the rounds on 9gag: an animated gif of my depressed balls, descending slowly into a fiery, cavernous pit which appears to be Hell § me, begging everyone to stop running around and pay attention to my venn diagram labeled “GENDER & AUTISM” on board the capsizing Concordia § this contest wil require some serious sleuthing . prepare for a horrifying excursion into the miserable world of diapers § yes. it was in very ppoor taste. and crudely filmed as well. go too hell, troll. § Fuck U. Im trying to get better § CONTEST : If U Find The Fabled R. Lee Ermey Diaper Commercial I Will Send Some Thing Cool To Ur House § didnt r. lee ermey provide his voice for a diaper commercial sometime in the 90s . im pretty sure he did but I cant find proof it exists § my wikipedia device of choise. § Does it work on Sony PSP § h m. wikipedia still appears to be working to me http://t.co/xNQJRq0e i dont see what the problem is. #factswithoutwikipedia § is he dtc (down to change) § If U Ever Contact My Daughetr Again I Will Call My Lawyer And We’ll Kick Your Tiny Weird Shaped Head Around The Court Room § http://t.co/lLzKlr1s perfect § @redlobster Thus always to tyrants. § me and TekkenChauncey banned from red lobster after getting into scuffle over gradius canon & becoming tangled in decorative fishing net § complaint going out to “Crying Man of the Month” club; you just sent me an 8x10 glossy of a missile silo instead of a crying man. Please fix § Who to follow - Justin Bieber @ justinbieber Followed by Duane Dog Chapman § @DogBountyHunter me & martin luther king stand with tucker’s girlfriend and all diaper wearers. shame on you #dogthebountyhunter § @DogBountyHunter remember when you made your son Tucker leave his girlfriend because she wore diapers? Not MLK’s dream. #dogthebounty-hunter § ã ¤ã,‹ã ¤ã,‹ã ®ãƒ¯ã,ã Œå¥½ã ã §ã ™I love beautiful armpit § i left the cam on long enough to prove i wasnt fat, spammed thte chatroom with B-List Material and left unceremoniously . diapers § #mcgruff Tip #39: dont literally take a bite out of crime. its an intangible concept used to classify human behavior & its absolutely filthy § mcgruff the crime dogs Crime Tip #888853: if a criminal makes you play a game of darts to save a hostage’s life throw the darts at his Dick § see this watch? i got it by Crying. my car? crying. my beautiful wife? Crying. My perfect teeth? Crying. now get the fuck out of my office § live free or die. kfc § seeking a fellow High-Functioning Brony to crawl underneath the tarp i live in and help me de-wax my ears. suit and tie required. § once again the trolls are at fault. theyve ruined the best night of our lives with their filthy shit. im ready to throw up. § http://t.co/YyiGvd2k nostradamus in hell § to the coward fraud who claimed my username: it is you who deserves to be plagued by this baneful "2". Posted by CrotchLordMiami2 at 3:36 am § thanks. im dead now § call me a piece of Shit so i can finally die § a team of Social Media Gurus wrestle over the Dos and Donts of Brand Identity Tweeting in a dumpster at the bottom of the ocean § fucking nobel laureates screaming at each other about the current state of Juggalo Love in the handicap stall at dennys § somewhere theres a group of geniuses debating whether Rugrats moved the diaper community forwards or backwards in some hotel's banquet room § FBI deemed my tool assisted glitch run of Mario Teaches Typing too dangerous for the public eye. the raw emotion has rendered my face purple § a father says to his 3 sons, "i love you all but I must fulfill my destiny as the Wind. goodbye" then he turns into the wind as his sons cry § having a HELL of a time updating the names on all my personal & business records to Jeep Grand Chero-Keith isntead of keith § currently on a car ride with 8BitMarcus, who just tried to use the defroster to clean bird poop off of the window. what a dumb piece of shit § i believe the hpv vaccine is a personal affront to the members of the ProGenWarts community, ive prepared some literature on the matter and § http://t.co/ejolLMog god excsists and is real § i know its a funny joke that NJ smells awful all the time but ill be damned if I didnt leave the house and detect the odor of unwashed mouth § can anyone confirm whether or not the entire central NJ region smells like bad breath today because I think it does § @ Huggies Utterly sickened by your support of SOPA. Im now officially Boycotting your draconian diapers and encouraging others to do the same § sometimes i have dreams that @DogBountyHunter & I are hanging out shooting the shit then a criminal shoots him & i breastfeed him as he dies § http://t.co/QV7adxO1 Im Starting A Blog For Disabled People Calle d 3DWorldz ANd U Can Create "Worldz" & "Tars" And Sell Them 2 Businessmen, § well; the Trolls have discovered my one weakness; shaking big plastic bags at me until i piss myself, & frankl;y 2012 looks to be a bad year § little known fact- "petsmart" is actually a portmanteau of "Dog Store" § @chrisbrown let's hope 2012 can keep its Fucking Mouth Shut #TeamBreezy #bruises #agony § once again, dick clark's diaper drops miserably around his ankles precisely at the stroke of midnight, signifying a grim year to come #2012 § pussy log 12.29.11: justin unscrewed the knob from the door to the ladies' room and now the club boys all take turns cradling it § which programming language should I learn if I want to transform myself into an enormous 3d wireframe head that spits out flashing cubes § I've Provided The Users Of This Geode Collector's Forum With Tasteful Upskirts For 17 Years. Don't Like It? Then Log Me Out, Bastard. § THE TIME IS NOW: write ur senators and tell them that youre too much of a coolguy to get all huffy about the sofa bill or whatever § the sculptor wipes his brow & steps back to gaze upon his creation, the words "Gonzo Jeans" rendered in marble. he drops to his knees & sobs § movies that portray Dragons in a positive light are marked with a gold marble, while movies racist against Dragons are given a frowning Ass. § xmas hual 2011: can of paste, novel based on "little fockers", Oprah Crystals, fucken mmeat ball sandwich, a fuckin $2.50 slice-a pound cake § a look of pure disappointment washes over Jack Cafferty's face. "sandusky's cock..." Wolf Blitzer shakes his head. "sandusky's cock..." § please dont call me "Cunt_Smoker" anymore. im a 37 year old father of two daughters and have since chosen a more appropriate user handle § "brevity is the soul of SHIT" - the shit man § @Gamestop one of your guys tried to give me a bible and said it was the “ultimate strategy guide” with my purchase of petz fantasy 3d. awful § i touch a glowing qur’an and turn into 100 lions #suitswag § STICKS WET HAND INTO HUGE GNC PROTEIN POWDER BOTTLE AND LICKS IT CLEAN, TRIES TO CLIMB ONTO DISPLAY MATTRESS AT SEARS, APPREHENDED BY CRAIG § yeah call the fuckin coppers and ill explain it clearly to them, ill tell them its ok to shit in my guinea pig hutch because they do it too § beard vs. ass § every year, a figure dressed in black leaves three crispy strips & a bottle of mtn dew at the kfc man’s grave then disappears into the night § no. i dont care where you hold the “2012 Incest Olympics” but its not gonna be on my roof § never subject yourself to the humiliation of using a public spittoon again- simply spit into your diaper, and USER HAS BEEN BANNED FROM TWIT § fake people are ignorant. dead people are fake. ignorant people are fake. dead people are ignorant people. .fake people are dead #RealTalk § this one time-- me, DigimonOtis, and EpicWayne tried to open up a barbershop together, but the plan fell through due to my fear of hair § kim jong il’s final load will be launched into outer space where it will probably collide with majel barrett’s ashes and create a big baby § i have it on good authority that kim jong il jacked off shortly before dying. this devastating fact makes the pain of losing him even worse § Cool, But Gay § you have the right to remain Diapered. anything you shit can and will be held against you in a quart of piss § the horny ranter clenches his fist in triumph, having been notified that his youtube account has been upgraded to accommodate 15 minute vids § Wiki-d’oh! Julian Assange guest stars on The Simpsons to dig up the dirt on Mr. Burns; Scheduled to be aired in 2014 #PainfulToReadSentences § teens using planetary alignment to get high, we now turn to our resident Teen Expert, now trying to get a light bulb to stick into his beard § hollering man still causing mischief at supercuts. theyll never attempt to turn your dog into a cat just by giving it a haircut, get over it § the next perspn caught posting anymore lewd comments regarding the green lady M&M to my home & garden web book will be reported to the FBI. § wrestlers and sega § the soldiers crafted armor out of the covers of outdated guinness world record books, to bedazzle and confound their opponents § petition to move “6teen” to CN’s [adult swim] block, because me & my friends love it, want to be taken seriously, and are like 60 years old § as a twitter power user, I am MORE than qualified to assuage any of your questions/concerns/aches/pains with sexuel Contact. § no. the marine chant has always been “Oprah”, not “oorah”. you’ve just been mishearing it this entire time. “oorah” isn’t even a word § so the wisdom i gained in exile with the barbecue shaman on the peak of Mt. DryRub is apparently non-transferable to Yale. sad and upset § wasup babe., im a normal person. *walks on down to next girl* Wassup babe, im a normel person . *moseys over to another lady* wasup babe, im § do u, sir, take this cardboard cutout of 90s era David Spade to be your lawfully wedded wife, to have and 2 hold, in sickness and in health, § the barbecue shaman liberally applies a garlic &herb dry rub to his dick and ass - in order to prepare himself for the barbecue perils ahead § AS A TRANSHUMAN, I DON’T WEAR SHIRTS BECAUS**DRives diamond-studded PT Cruiser directly into great pacific garbage patch; never seen again* § wikiHow: Home » Categories » Philosophy & Religion » Paranormal Beliefs » Ghosts - how to revive princess diana and secure the blood throne § so i went around to all the offices adjacent to wtc and tried 2 find witnesses but ended up in a rooftop pool geting groped by some hot lady § ijust had a dream that there was a big hollywood conspiracy and”3D” was short for “3 Destructions” referring to the 3 buildng attacks on 911 § “being nude helps me ponder Life” - the wise nude #TheWiseNude § DOCTOR RIPS FAKE BLOOD APPARATUS FROM MY LEG DURING RED CROSS DONATION DRIVE, I HOOT AND HOLLER AND HOP INTO THE ESCAPE SEWER § rogue mythbuster shoots cop at virginia tech; was aiming for water-filled trash cans § i point to my new tat , “UNVACCINATED” written across my shoulder blades, the dudes nod their heads and line up for a round of high fives § court orders mythbusters to change their name to the Shamebusters. adam weeps while jamie comforts him and delivers the judge a stony glare § BUSter implicated in cannonball terror plot, inanimate crash dummy tried for atrocious death crimes while Build Team flees the country § the mythbusters hurl rocks at a sick dog, adam looks at the camera and says'" Oops" wihle jamie fucking shoots some guys house with a pistol § @ElmersGlueC-rew spent all night makig Lesbian Glitter Runes and wake up the next day and all the pages are stuck togehter, thanks retards § i dumped an entire bottle of glitter into my diary for teen blindness, what hte fuck have you done lately § today, the mythbusters destroy the "myth" of american exceptionalism by heroically firing a cannonball through dublin, california § @ContainerStore why don't you guys sell any diapers. Diapers are containers § #ICanAdmit that whenever i catch a glimpse of my gruesome dick in a mirror i tumble into the nearest open sewer and get sick. itr's very sad § how many more wasps do i have to mash into my forehead before I gain their stinging abilit.y damn § well of course, in retrospect it would seem silly that i thought the dog in the tv was real, but in my defense the dog was very clever § PLEASE at least look up "Event Horizon" on wikipedai before you chastise me for screaming it on 9./11 § #ConfusingThingsGirlsDo show virtually no interest in The Bible Code § when i found out she used the same widely popular online social media aggregator as me, i just knew mny soul was destined to Neg her § i wouldnt advise taking any liberties., your god damn pride is your key enemy § HOSPITAL TIp: get a cool friend named Jacob who works there and lets you photgraph the recently deceased to try and capture their souls § baths and showers are fucking stupid; here's what u do: get one of those big rotisserie ovens and roatate inside of it until you're dead § got a LOT of horseshit today 4 trying to take my snail into city hall, dangling upsidedown from mayors chandelier til all this ugliness ends § WORLDS BIGGEST TIRE CHANGE FUCK UP, THATS ME IN THE GUINNESS BOOK, THATS ME IN THE PICTURE, CHASING THE OUT OF CONTROL VEHICLE INTO THE ZOO § @johnmellencamp kept coughing into his hand and looking at it during his latest performance at clowes memorial hall and it was gross § scientists may be able to generate working organs from stem cells, but never in a million years will they manage to lick my gay boots clean. § @CBStweet IVE DISCOVERED ASPHYXIATING MYSELF NOT ONLY ENHANCES ORGASMS BUT ALSO THE INTENSITY AND FREQUENCY OF LAUGHS FROM UR COMEDY LINEUP § james bond hollers "Destroy Teen Asthma", bends over & does a line of coke off of a VHS tape that has "PUSS AND BOOTS BLUERAY" written on it § @Battlefield I tried earlier but when I posited a list of Garth's transgressions he silently closed the chat. Sorry I actually obey the TOS § @Battlefield I have done this approximately 30 times. § @Battlefield "Garth_Turds" on here calling console fanboys the N-word. I ask you Garth, why is it that you're playing the PS3 version then? § @Battlefield My requests are as follows: 1) Apology Letter From user "Garth_Turds" for hollering his mouth at me 2) Warn & Ban "Garth_Turds" § Ur Honor, The Jury Is Obviously Biased Against Me Because Theiyre Mad., And They're Butt Hurt, And They Post On Different Forums Than I Do § my shitty Zumba Trainer thinks that letting people pay me to cry on webcam doesn't count as a real job. mods, help me diaperbomb his mansion § Playsy some @TOADM , all of the Rap Likers begin to cry "My God, Our Music Was Fake All Along", as I take a well-earned sip of Pibb Xtra § indeed, i am Very Diapered right now, currently pairing a Pampers Cruiser with a quarter glass of Marcus Sinclair's Cape Cod November Ale § shame on you for assuming I tattooed "Yes Yes Ya'll" on my newborn infant's head for a less than 100% justifiable reason § Yo Trolls: Maybe my jokes are bad because u create a hostile environment thatm akes me nervous. Maybe I piss my pants too. Maybe get a life § it is remarkable that he has managed to stretch this concept into 5+ hours of non-stop laughter § Super Mario Guy RPG - The cast of Family Guy meets Super Mario RPG as Peter Griffin does a "Let's Play" of the classic 1996 Nintendo Game. § served thanks-givng turkey wearing diaper to family ; my coming out as a Wearer -- one thing im NOT thankful for is rudeness and betrayal § @Lowenaffchen @dogbountyhunter woqw. respond to a helpful offer with disgusting, ignorant vitriol. lost a lot of respect for The Dog today § @DogBountyHunter Theres a guy here who claims hes the real Dog, says the guy on tv is some filthy hippy;Is this the real or fake dog twitter § i have spent the past 14 years of my life crafting an intricate tale that evokes the mind and spirit. i am proud to bring you "Ghetto Sonic" § @DeptofDefense The next AIDS you guys manufacture & distribute should target people who listen to Justin Bieber! Yuck! #JustForLaughs #Gags § any gay scientist out there who want to experiment with my dick. pour gay chems on it. inject stem cells into it. i dont care anymore § What The Fuck Is "Human Dignity" And Why Does It Have A Higher Metacritic Score Than "The Waterboy" § #UseATwitterNameInASentence @chrisbrown punched his wife then took his shirt off in a television studio § @Battlefield The longer we both draw out this "Garth_ Turds" debacle, the more foolish the both of us look. § @Battlefield I have verbally confronted "Garth_Turds" on several occasions, remaining respectful despite his refusal to listen to reason. § @Battlefield once again, user "Garth_Turds" is running amok on this server, reading off a list of religions and making fart sounds w/ mouth § Sorry "DrunkDriver1488", your eHarmony profile has been rejected § @Battlefield User "Garth_Turds" still has not been banned. He's an utter nuisance. He's also using some kind of hack to make himself louder § @Battlefield user "Garth_Turds" jusr read my address online , except replacing the name of my town with "Toilet". my daughters are crying § @ Battlefield can you please do something about abusive user "Garth_Turds". i fear your inaction is only allowing him to grow stronger § @Battlefield man named "Garth_Turds" has bene following me to every map and yelling "hitler" . Claims hes a mod. Get rid of him § reaches into pocket for folded up print-out of "the troll face". a bunch of old crumpled up napkins also fall out. the stench is unbearable § "i hope this shitty mustsache makes my face look less fat (It wont)" - some guy § Teens respond to scorpions. Im bridging the teen reality with ours, through Scorpion Use. Do scorpions need to act rude to be cool? No § i have been tasting my piss every day in order to develop an immunity to it. i am immune to piss. if you piss on me ill just laugh at you. § me . me please. dear god i need this § doestn matter. we're both mere shadows of Baby Giveaways Galore § "im not owned! im not owned!!", i continue to insist as i slowly shrink and transform into a corn cob § Let The Rapist Do Football. Let The Rapist Teach The Kids To Run The Ball Good. He Good At His Job And The Rapist Should Be Aloud To Do It § house speaker john boehner claim obama used infinite soul glitch at press summit. obama cooked the boo;ks § famous daves proud to announce confessional booths in every restaurant where you can go to atone for your bbq sins. fucking murder me § no you see, if you look closely at this drawing he put a face on the sun. clearly this child is autistic § ladies & gentlemen of BlizzCon, im ready now to unveil my spirit animal for 2012. *holds up picture of the family gu y dog, audience gasps* § the next step in human evolution is to cover your body in Rage Face tattoos and point to them instead of displaying emotions the normal way § (1) hack myself into the principals computer (2) do a rude little dance (3) get beyblades Unbanned § @DennysGrandSlam its ok, ive since forgiven you. id simply like a coupon to replace the dr. pepper that was spilled during the altercation § muscle economy, muscles as currency, end the dollar, get ripped, get rich pumping weights, weatlh = body size, predicted by Blaise Pascal § how is it even - possible, - to remain Muscled in this black world - - pain is god and im Her disciple. tron: legacy - § still way fuckin Muscled , despite the economy, despite life § please read my boolk entitled "girl theory" for more insights on this troulbled gender, as well as pickup techinques & lament § Most Of My Followers Died After One Of My More Heinous Diaper Jokes § thank u. twitter is christ 2012 § @glennbeck i can give you 22 reasons to be concerned about your giant sweaty head § i also have proof that kim kardashian is a "brony"., although i will not show it to a bastard like you. § kim karcdashian should have married me or my friend DigimonOtis instead because we're Nice. #ThingsLongerThanKimsMarriage § TRied to sell some cool EbaumsWorld Merch to Wallstreet Protesters, was told to "Fuck Off" by probable agent provocateur; Im Sad and Fearful § thte international space station is visible from earth at the following times: Nerd Time § SO I WAS SAYING, IF IT'S ACCEPTABLE TO BAPTIZE HUMAN INFANTS, WHY NOT JEANS § im not saying the release of my FF6 Nude Mod incrased obamas approval rating, but there's certainly a correlation that's difficult to ignore § have sex with rag doll instead of humen #ADVANCEDlifehacks § inventor of GameFuel's impassioned plea: "please stop drinking it. its not for human consumption. why are you drinking it. its for cars" § im the guy who airbrushes the nipples out of pro wrestling ads. i make $85k a year. but i have a secret *removs shades to reveal nipple eyes § pokemon/? who needs pokemon when you have Bosnian Genocide. rewteet this if your a 90s kid § i looked that little punk behind the counter in the eye and told him Criss Angel Mindfreka is the most compelling televsn program like, ever § in a rage., i farted into the gamestop cashregister, venting my frustration and rendering the money unusable, paving the way for gold stndrd § please dont try and tell me that schrodinger's diaper is a quantum superposition of clean and dirty states, we can all fucking smell it § please don't try and tell me that schrodinger's diaper is a quantum superposition of clean and dirty states, we can all fucking smell it § HIBACHI MAN AT @BENIHANA__ - WILL NOT PREPARE KRAFT MACARONI AS REQUESTED - THIS IS THE ONLY THING I CAN EAT - IM VERY ILL § Electric Light Orchestra AND Spyro The Dragon??? Finally , A KickStarter I Can Empty My 401k Into § about 80% certain that Neil Cavuto just said "teh economy" instead of "the economy", on th e air. someone with dvr please confirm § fuck "jokes". everything i tweet is real. raw insight without the horse shit. no, i will NOT follow trolls. twitter dot com. i live for this § several men present to me a single diaper in a black suitcase. i take the diaper in my hand and examine it. "my god, this is next-gen" § "im the 1%" - a milk § this is the episode of sliders where they get transported to Hitler Earth, where everyon carries the appearance & manneurisms of adolf hitl § here i am again, screaming into the toilet, hoping somehow, somewhere, my future wife can hear my soothing voice resonate intot her asshole. § My Business Logo: a composite of sexy lady legs cut out from a variety of images and arranged to spell the word "Gordo" § FOR SALE: One Beekeeper's Uniform With "METH GOD" embroidered into back, Lightly Used (856) 625-3325 - Ask For Officer Jim § @THEHermanCain please send me pics of you crying on a photograph of the wtc. i need to see ur tears and part of your wet face. please hurry § reading my twitter feed, screaming "SIT ON IT, BUB!" everytime some1 makes a rude #iSad post, my face growing more contorted as i get louder § how to convert ouija board to xbox controller using only a dead gamer § HOW MUCH IS $500 IN DOG YEARS § " STAY HUNGRY " - burger king § three words to describe me: Sensual, Progrsesive, Muscular. Check out my blog about mustaches § i would advise U not to visit this small minded website, MEETUP. COM; They get mad if yo[u bring devil sticks to the meetups even if your pro § @TheOnion i did it. i hacked the onion. ive been making them post fake news stories for like 20 years now. suck my dick § *gets booed at USO show for makig Diaper Jokes, calls all the troops Fuckers* § me, begging and pleading with a turtle, telling it to spit out my dick , causing a scene at a miniature golf course and getting 911 called § bond theme plays while super spy & ladys man James Bond wanders around the forest with a magnifying glass, searching for the cure for autism § SOME ONE REPLACED MY INCEST FAQS WITH PICTURES OF TURKISH FLAGS AND GUNS § i accidentally legally changed my name to "Child Porn Man", if u have any experience dealing with this issue i owuld appreciate your input. § couldent have said it better. § According to @klout, I'm influential about:

forums, religion and spirituality, and diaper http://t.co/2hhru5LL § @Drew-FromTV please murder me drew carey. i want you to snuff my trivial existence from this awful lplanet. good job losing weight § @Lowes i am this close to killing the mother fucker who keeps coming on my account and posting diaper things and saying im the one in them § WOah. Just had another Dr. Oz dream. This time he was crying § BARBARO IS BACK, THE ONCE DEAD REACEHORSE IS BACK TO LIFE AND TEARING UP THE HORSE TRACK LIKE NEVER BEFORE, "THE SECRET" WORKS,THANK U OPRAH § petition to rename the statue of liberty "Bisexual Tattoo Goddess" because istand for something real and i live in a part of this world. § i live vicariously through my diaper § for every animal you dont eat i will eat the grab and go yogurt gogurt,maddox said that and it owned, someone get that quote,someone please § affirmative action is pretty fucked up if u ask me. **produces and begins smoking a tube of Gogurt, the grab & go yogurt, like a cigar*** § The Band Was Originally Called "The Red Hot Chili Diapers" Before A Policeman Said No [citation needed] § GETS RIGHT UP IN WIFE'S FACE AND DEMANDS "THE BOOK OF ELI" THEMED THANKSGIVING DINNER; MANGLES A THING OF PAPER TOWELS AND HURLS IT AT WALL § fantasy meatball league § @MexicanAtheist Then log off my sight. § @MexicanAtheist please dont assoicate the freaking awesome thunder cats show with your fake belief's. thank you § i wonder if social media newsbots ever miss their former lives as the beautiful women in their profile pics § Learn How To Use Toilets Without Getting Fully Nude § never too old to imprint "SABRINA THE TEEN AGE WITCH" itnto the hood of your car multiple times with big metal boots #SellOuts #FakePeople § #OrtizKnockOutPlaylist Gangster Paradise By "Weird Al" Yancovic § opened portal to free hikers in iran-- in-stead greeted by Real Life minotaur, anubis, something or other, all i know hes a real holler mouth § *slams king james holy bible shut on a piece of pepperoni with mayo and onions stickin out * And that is how u make a truth sandwich § IN HEAVEN, ALL THE VANITY LICENSE PLATES & COWBOY BOOTS U EVER OWNED ARE STRUNG UP BEHIND YOUR LEGS 4EVER, CLACKIN BEHIND U EVRY STEP U TAKE § #Imagine justin holding my nude, shaking body while lowering the gun to my head and whispering "goodnight" into my bruised ear § BIGMOUTH BILLYBASS REVIVAL , SINGS GAGA, BIEBER, ET AL; INFUSED WITH 2012 TECH FOR SHIT & PISS CAPABILITIES; "PHENOME-NAL" FORBES MAGAZINE § someone said "rage comics" out loud and fistpumped in one of my classe.s. thats a real thing that a human being did § Double standard [rage comic] : MensRights § the password is "dragons" go go go § i need someone to come fix my fucked up neck tie. ive barricaded myself in the bathroom ogf kenny rogers roaster in mumbai. say the password § dear sir or madam - i request the following: "CUM_SISSY" embroidered into the back of my father's old army jacket, complete with underscore, § i siad jobs plan, not inside jobs plan!! #oboama911 § Asthmatic Blogger Expo Ruiend By Very Dusty Man § thank u mysterious stranger @drilsdiapers for doing the community a great service by cataloging my abject misery & rendering me unemployable § "Is Wario A Libertar-ian" - the greatest thread in the history of forums, locked by a moderator after 12,239 pages of heated debate, § ive gotten too fat for my diapers and now i gotta go across town to get specially made ones and i cant drive because im bipolar. fuck racism § @pizzahut the manager of your Howell, NJ location disapprovingly wagged his finger at me at about 4:15 PM for reasons he woudl not divulge. § @HomeDepot angered that your toilets had no water in them,i crawled onto my back and worked up a frenzy, my legs airborne and dick visible. § people please, all i ask for is one town hall meeting which doesnt reference The Matrix § if i hear another "joke" regarduing my terminally ill dickwife so help me god i'm shutting down this entire irc server § lesebien cum #alchemy § #replacemovienameswithbacon kevin bacon § @NoahMunck True Or False: IS There a force powerufl enough to counteract "Munckmentum" in 2011, 2012, and Beyond. § im going to start a multimedia network for those who enjoy smacking dingers in the game of base ball and also marry baseball § wife wont wear diaper. help §

the human mind is a fascinating piece of shit #TwitterVsFB § came outside today to notice m y "Bring Back The Marriage Ref" bumper sticker violently ripped off. Obviously, I hit a nerve. § @JohnDeere My Nieghbor Has Been Modifying His John Deere Illegaly With Muslim-Style Decorations And Noise Enhancers, How Do I Stop Him § not even Austin Powers 4 can win me back after mike myers' hideous racial outburst at the Laugh Factory. Fuck you § the first iddiot to file a complaint against my rat zoo gets a new pipe hole courtesy of my Handsome Fists § Clipart Pig Angel In Prayer - Royalty Free Vector Illustration § Clipart Illustration of a Frustrated Cowboy Holding A Skunk That's Been Torturing His Farm With Stinky Spray § Clipart Illustration of a Black Hanukkah Baby In A Diaper, Holding Gifts, A Menorah And A Rattle § Here I Am, Well Into My 20s, Using Twitter.com, A Website For Children #Itreallymakesmemad § #PrayForNicksGrandpa even though prayer is clinically proven to make people die faster??? how about no. § http://i.imgur.com/vB8UL.jpg no § petition to make cvs stop forcing their pharmacists to wear shirts § cool gags in 2011: making the text field in new twitter really tall. you can scroll down and keep making it taller. ramadan mubarak § Earth Wind and Diaper #NotARealJoke #WhatHaveIBecome § i just found The Dos Equis Most Interesting Man In The Worl'ds deviant art account. he draws his own jeff dunham puppets § makers of @SlimJim announce @SlimeJim !!! dog food for humans § @SlimJim how much salt has to be hammered into a turd before it turns into a Slim Jim § former UN ambassador John Bolton uses hideous mustache to conceal "Police Is Bullshit" facial tattoo #amomentofsilence § Nacho Libre Tight Dick Shots - Nacho Libre Best Ass Crack Vids - ripped by x_vArEz_x ©2006 § http://bit.ly/bl4vMi The Free Encyclopedia § MY KUTCHER/SCOTT " DUDE AND SWEET TATTOO" ROUTINE IS SEVERELY HAMPERED BY THE FACT THAT IM ONE PERSON § apparenlty yelling "where the fuck is garfield" at comic con 2011 is not only frowned upon, but illegal § wearing my diaper at half mast , in memoriam #amywinehouse § http://i.imgur.com/u9Xw9.jpg my fave`s § @the_iron-sheik "The Philly Phanatic" § cum bib § GUess who just renewed his subscription to Newsweek. this guy! (cue blurry stock footage of an unidentified fat old man spitting into a cup) § if any one knows how to convincingly justify dubai's economic model to bratty ltitle brothers go ahead and plop me an email. fubu back. § @FOXBroadcasting U guys should un-cancel the Bernie Mac Show, like u did with family guy. § TheLegsGuru - girls let me see them beautiful Leg's - TheLegsGuru § i dont care how good it feels. i am not naming my child "compost fucker". end of story § "EroticLloyd", aka "Puerto_Neko", aka "RicanMudBoss", aka "LloydGunge", akA "GunkAndCatBoi", aka "Puerto_Gunger", aka "Aiden's Cool Uncle" § Guess What Fag. Most Birds Are Too Smart To Be Deterred By Scare-crows. I Guess Your A Bitch #StrawmanArgument § genderman's only weakness is being told that his name contains a masculine bias § changing 500 tiny diapers on 500 disgusting rats #TheLifeIChose § what can i rub on my body to make my musk more ethnic § projectile drooling: im the only person in the world who does this. doctors refuse to help me § i shsould be allowed to beat off in the back of a police car. im already going to jail so whats the difference § boscov's is a highly professional organization Sir, and as such we refuse to engrave "the sex fucker" onto your george foreman panini press § "How To Make WebKins Fuck" #IncriminatingSearchTermsFoundOnRyanDunnsDeathComputer § to the punk who spray painted "Fat Angel" on my 1996 chevy suburban: post your nintendo friend code so i can send you the Medal Of Honor § pumped my home FULL of oxygenated perfluorocarbon so i can swim N breahte; forgot to vacuum up pet hair & crumbs beforehand ---- Chest Pains § im the only lawyer in nyc who will handle your case AND have sex wit h u § A CELESTIAL BEAM SHATTERS THE ORACLE INTO ONE MILLION SHARDS, WHICH WONDROUSLY FLOAT INTO THE AIR AND FORM THE WORDS "PEAK BITCOIN" § "cleveland rocks " is not actually sung by drew carey. end this fucking lie § i agree. im as terrible as you § neitehr am i. im a fucking waste § me too. im fucking awful § bury my heart at wounded knee's Hard Rock

Cafe franchise § Give a Man a Cool Beachball With the Hard Rock Cafe Logo on it and He will teach a fish to swim for u § give a man to fish and he will Re-Tweet U § theyer renovating my hard rock cafe.. just saw a mover man drag two crates of live rattlers inside..has Hard Rock gone TOo wild?? No F'n Way § GENDERLESS WEDDING AT HARD ROCK CAFE: THE BRIDE AND GROOM WILL BE COVERED IN TARPS IN ORDER TO CIRCUMVENT THE STANDARDIZED NORM`S; FREE ICE § MASCARA DRIPS DOWN MY FAT FACE INTO MY PATIENTS GAPING CHEST INCISION... Ëœ¨¨¯¯¯¨¨Ëœª¤ SAD SURGEON GIRLS ¤ªËœ¨¨¯¯¯¨¨Ëœ § Turds And Piss Found At Usama's Compound >> Decorated Royal Navy Commander Lenny 'Hotdogs' Burbit States As Follows: "He Loved Too Shit" § i hand you an envelope. inside is a series of photographs of me gradually deteriorating. when you look at me again im a skeleton #Owned § @ DunkinDonuts so i heard your Thailand outlets are FULLY owned and operated by Ladyboys... Any chance of you bringing this to the 'States? § "You have the thoughts and brain of a baby." - My 2012 Adviser Craig Gurtle -- Fuck you Mr. Gurtle, I Can Survive 2012 My Self. § SensualMaddenPlayer Checking In. § the jerk off who told my autistic son that sega of america exploded needs to come forward so i can crush his neck betwext my Perfect thighs § .@dentynegum I Just Chewed Four Packs Of Dentyine Ice And Now I Can't Taste Anything-- Think U Can Send Some Coup's My Way??? § Can Police Man Cartman " Respect The Authority " Of The Intesnely Cool Refreshingly Satisfying Mint Taste ONLY Found In Dentyne Ice ??? § If I Fill A Bird Bath With Capri Sun Will Birds Still Bathe In It #badsciencefairprojects § @petsmart do\tu do obidience classes for HUSBENDS ????? ;) Just Kidding § I WIL NOT RESTORE THE PSN NETWORK UNTIL ALL 7 HELL MASON BANKERS ARE IN JAIL & THEY BRINGBACK COOKIES N CREME FLAVOR DORITOS § .@ EBERTCHICAGO What is Ur least favorite greek film. Greetz from turkey § @ applebees fat bald leatherman in cheetah shades is beckoning me towards thre popper bar.his 3D tatoos seem to indicate hes from the future. § @applebees this waiter keeps looking at his watch and dripping broken glowstick goop on a detached baby doll's head. 2012??? § @Applebees WAtching my father slam down a Buffalo Chicken Crisper Salad with his vile sausage fingers& i didnt order any food because im mad § my crystalologist told me that bin laden was trapped inside this $60 jade charm?? getting REAL huffy & worked up righ now and demand ansers § what anm i gonna do with this warehouse full of osama bin laden toilet paper. nobody wants to wipe their ass with a dead guy § cool news: if i sit a certain way my dick becomes convex #heeaja § controversy erupts as john boener hands out tiny goodybags to everyone on senate floor and sticks dems with all the yellow starbursts #Gross § want to see big legs. want to see big legs § in 11X B.C. an irish Mystik cast a curse on all moms to reciev free college books every 11th day of 11th year & 11th milenium. this is today § FOR 1 SECOND THE NORTHERN LIGHTS DISPLAYED DHARMA AND GREG IN GLORIOUS BLURAY-- NOW LETS ALL SIGN MY PETITION IN BLOOD TO GET IT ON TV'S § PLACING SCREAM MOVIE MASK OVR MY HEAD AS MY HUGE GLISTENING BODY SLOWLY ROTATES IN MY HELL REALM,CONTROLING 600 MONITORS,SMOKING A 3D HOOKAH § for the last time, Diaper is capitalized when referring to the lifestyle or state of mind, but not when referring to the physical object. § Horse_Ebook Passes Turing Test, Replaces The Bible § "liking arli$$ too much" is a bullshit thing to divorce me over § police man kicks me in the diaper while running out of radio shack, causing my shit 2 fountain up and ruin several RC spongebobs #rodneyking § never say my name again you disgusting criminal § im the Rembrandt of naked yoshies § how did they do the ace ventura butt talk. i know that shit wasnt real. was it 3d or robots § Sort Of Like A Wiccan James Bond § my dick is a swastika. #andthewinneris #iwas-thinkin #atablackpersonfuneral § brett favre punches a curtain with the word "INCEST" painted on it, rips it down, looks into cam and says " o Incest" #PublicService § http://bit.ly/gTL4KV #betrayal #misery #2012 § Welcom to MpregCraig's Mpreg Dolphin Cove 3D... if u are a shark fanboi, please leave. 2d likers? no dice. Fpreg? get the F outa here § kicked outta the classroom again for pointing out the obvious fact that our school buildig was built by slaves. § building a casket for my babydaughter in minecraft in lieu of a real casket which i can not affort. § MGM STUDIOS CAN U CONFIRM THAT MR. DUSTIN HOFFMAN HAS SEEN THE VIDEO I SENT OF ME MUCKIN AROUND IN A PILE OF LEAVES?? OK ILL CALL BACK LATER § @thegeicogecko how do you cope with the realization that everything you say and do is dictated by a soulless, unfeeling corporation § im the geico gecko and I want u to help me end rape § Is Amaerica Ready For A Fat President § al;l piss is sterile. except mine § if u think that SegaKnight's Expert Analysis Female Masturbation Dissertation lacks credibility and coherence then log off my sight. § Goes To Rotten.com, Sees A Man's Dick, Clenches Eyes Shut And Shakes Head While Clicking For The Back Button, Clicks Refresh Accidentally § Yearly Reminder That Human Beings Have Actually Died As A Direct Result Of April Fools Day #aprilfools #JokesOnUBub § BibleReader666 § *¥¥¥_,,-MaGnUm DiApEr -,,_¥¥¥* § it makes me sick when i see border collies portrayed in the media as "Loser Dogs" who are "Probably Rats" § any one who figures out how to breed border collies with the Microsoft Zune needs to hollaer a message at me § border colies are 250% Smarter than humans and stronger to, which is why the US Military refuses to breed them § "WHO NEEDS ISLAM WHEN YOU HAVE SIXTEEN BORDER COLLEYS JUMPIN AROUND " - THE PROPHET MUHAMMAD § MY 7 BOARDER COLLY'S ARE MY ANGEL AND IF THEY'RE NOT ALLOWED TO BE PRESENT AT THE OPERATING TABLE DURING MY LAP-BAND PROCEDURE I'LL DIE § arrest hitler for racism § it's spelled "Suge Knight", grandma. you've fucked up again § 'Single 'Taken œ"GenderDead § I Beleive I Am Being Racisted Against Because Of My Marmaduke Necktie § The Bible Is Fake. oh. what's that? you're holding a physical copy of the bible, you say? hm, looks legit. The Bible Is Real, Then § i am a Teen and that's somethjing i have to live with for the rest of my life. § 5676083 » Stock Photo - African American businessman holding a pile of piggy banks isolated on white. § me_steppin_on_a_pair_of_cowboy_boots_while_wearing_cowboy_boots.flv #Woof § it's the most spiritual of all energy's. § BMEZINE, U WILL FEATURE MY PIC AT ONCE. IM THE MAN WITH JETHTO TULL WRITEN ON CHEST IN PERM. MARKER #NotEntitledToTheSweatOfMyBrow § attn: Fucker who posted False R.I.P. to Cedric The Entertainer; i haeve just received my good shooter degree from gun college. that is all § can 1000000 irate south korean pigs buried alive after a foot and mouth outbreak possibly join forces and cause an 8.9 eartquake??? #yes § kick their pets and cars #waystopissoffafatperson § turn all the food on earth into wolf urine #waystopissoffafatperson § http://i.imgur.com/7urrd.jpg basically just search "earthquack" § people who think dolphins are real = shit § an old man wheezes into a ragged cloth; Bam looks into camera, says "Woah, glad im not That cloth!" thne does a Bogus airspin into the trash § TO AVOID SCARING OR OFFENDING CHILDREN WE'VE TAKEN ANNE FRANK'S DIARY AND REPLACED EVERY INSTANCE OF THE WORD " AZI" WITH "POLICE MAN" § My News Years Resolutions Is To Take My Dana Carvey Impersonations To The Next Leveal. (Pro Circuit Anyone? We're In Talks) § /~-_,™ -|.RAT.|-™ ,_-~\\ /~-_,™ -|.POPE.|-™ ,_-~\\ #tigerblood § GOURP OF TEEN GIRLS RESURRECT DALE EARNHARDT IN SLEEPOVER DARE, EARNHARDT RUNS FROM THE PREMISES NUDE, COVERED IN ECTOPLASM, YET TO BE FOUND § Tweetmix.me http://t.co/R2XQ3b9 via @tweetmixme § the clown nose on my dick is there because im more susceptible to infection since my wii bowling accident, iddiot. no more hateful messages § to stand nude before a group of middle aged italian mob bosses and have them obnoxiously berate your dick while smoking cigars § any 1 want to look at pictures of owls with me write the word Hoot on a bottle mesage & toss it in the frog pond § i have ptsd from the time i brorke a chair at pop eyes chicken with my ass, and i am unemployable because of this. #smalljoys § @Cheesecake one of ur waiters kicked me out of my chair and into an interracial family's table and burned my dick off with a cigarette. thnx § @ CampbellSoupCo Mmm Nope!! Your bad § my 14beautiful geisha brides work together to change my preposterous 300 pound diaper. #mtvcribs § my rÃ©sumÃ©; page 1 ;

“IM A JEANS MAN FIRST AND FOREMOST” in 42pt. rosewood font. page 2 is the bible § SLOWLY LOWERS JEANSED ASS INTO A WOODEN BOWL FULL OF EXOTIC MEDITERRANEAN OILS AND REDROSE PETALS; AH THIS IS JUST TOO GOOD FOR LOWERCASE § my name is not “Wierd Dick Man “, so please stop writeing it on my tent. § ugh.. my husband never puts the toilet lid back down. *Closes Lid,; Takes Huge Piss On Top Of It* § SOME ASS HOLE ATE MY TONGUE AND REPLACED IT WITH HIM SELF AND IS EATING EVERYTHING I TRY TO EAT § Mohammad Muhamad, King Of Islam, Cahugt Counterfeiting Some Cool Dunham Specials On 3D Bluray; Sentenced To Be Hung By The Penuis Until Dead § six years ago today george washington carver invented a penut #MyBlackHistory #YourBlackHistory § chiropracty is real and it works on swords also. § some body please make the watson robot play halo. § youtube.com sends albanian govnt. $70 for dancing dog vido. albania best country. fuck all othter dancing dog video #ubertwitter § am a network marcketer and a mlm,and i love making friend and allso i care about other as well.i need some1 who have this same thing with me § jesus christ there’s a band named ziggy mania § dictionary.com defines the word “Mania” as “excessive excitement or enthusiasm; craze:”. “Ziggy Mania” offered none of these things t o me. § do NOT go to “ZiggyMania” at the Tehran Hilton; only two or three ziggy booths set up; one of them tries to sell u fabrics you dont need § what my organization does is take fatsuits from obnoxious PG-13 comedies and donate them to the needy § tips for photographing your own vomit From A Mom-- lighting, etc § The Credits Roll At Justin Bieber 3D And My Body Chooses To Fuse 3D Shades To My Brain Forever; No Turning Back & Life Is Good, Thank Ya § TYLER PERRY ----------> MONSANTO <----------- 666 § @tylerperry still shilling your vile shows w/o apologizing for your comments on GM food which have cost hundreds of lives.? #nsn3d #SickFuck § hm lets see.. *Logs On To Dark Net* bomb recipes... voyeur up-skirt.. snuff vids..DILBERT?? WHo thef fuck put dilbert on dark net § gypsy denim § scenario: the air and space museum drops Space and becomes the Air and Spade museum, devoting large sections to David Spade and his comedies § @ CampbellSoupCo i opened up a can of cambell soup beefy raviolis and it was just slush. im sorry big coustumer here, but i couldnt eat that § CANT WAIT TO SEE THE LOOK ON MOM & DADS FACE WHEN I GET THE BOOT CAMP THEY SENT ME TO SHUT DOWN FOR DIAPER DISCRIMINATION § Imagine. A world where guns come out of the ground like plants. And all the water is replaced by Bullet’s. This is Gun World. It’s real § http://tinyurl.com/4smf73p Gun World § bbeats the shit out of you. silently begins pummeling y ou as you surrender and accept your punishment. not a word is spoken § but my teeth are sparkling clean § MY SHIT IS IN SHAMBLES, MY DICK IS IN DISARRAY, MY ASS IS ASUNDER, MY BALLS ARE BALLISTIC, MY CUM IS CONFOUNDED, MY PISS IS PITIFUL § http://tinyurl.com/4mtlzdt thuis is my dick, i am posting this to come to terms with my self, this is therapeutic and good for me. #courage § on this day in history, alan turing invented the Gay Computer. one day later, preisdnet bill clinton fucked it. #demandaljazeera #hell § @ kfc_colonel Kfc, My Final Hope, Please Help Me Make My Future Daughter Unautistic, Shamans Curse, Wearing Bones (These Aint Chicken Bones) § @WALGREENS A Bone Wearing Man, Likely A Shaman, Comming To Me And Saying My Daughter Will Be Born Autistic, How Can I Fix This (2012?) § @QdobaMexGrill I Want To Know How I Can Prevent My Unborn Daughter From Autism Despite A Shaman Predicting It, Help Me Qdoba Mex Grill § @DrPhil I Want Help, A Dark Shaman Told Me My Daughter Will Be Born Autistic, Though He Might Have Been A Demon, Or Fake; Pool Resources § @Oprah Please Help Me, A Shaman Told Me My Future Daughter Will Be Born Autistic, I Simply Cannot Afford This In My Life, Oprah Please Help § I REALIZE MUSTACHE69@FIANANCE.BIZ MAY NOT BE THE MOST PROFESSIONAL EMAL BUT IVE GROWN SINCE I CHOSE IT AND WOULD STILL LIKE TO BE YOUR LAWER § the year is 2041 and im still using an older version of twitter that won’t be around for much longer § need someone in or around geigertown, philadelphia to help me dispose of approx 7500 live guinea pigs. i can not pay you, i will not pay you

§ dog food + baby food = protein shake #OnTheGo § lets see if that Awful Groundhog can predict six weeks of Electro House blaring directly into its shity cage § the dickwolfs controversey. Go #worstpickuplines § Think uve seen True 4G Wireless ?? Think again. *READS STAGE INSTRUCTIONS BETWEEN ASTERISKS INSTEAD OF PERFORMING THEM* #worstpickuplines § weverything i say is blocked out by falcons screaming until i die of a coughing fit #worstpickuplines § im the model that the Bobs Big Boy Big Boy Restaurant Man is based on. They forgot to pay me #worstpickuplines § @holidayinn My pop pop was diapered against his will at one of your Colorado locations. Please help me find the man who did this § Your search - pugmom666 - did not match any documents. § hm whats this? dropped a copy of my 263-page memoir "All Bi Myself" on the florr of this trendy teen cafe. dont have time to pick it up. l8r § @JoseCanseco please beat me to death with the softball bat juiced. i want to experience the legal 600 ft long ball across my fucking skull § the only Pro-Israel carpet cleaning service in the tri-county area § Porn is a constant reminder of how inadequate I am (self.AskReddit) § im honeslty inquiring as to why im discouraged against printing my business card on basketballs and 2hand passing them to potential clients? § Utility Belt Contains (At All Times) Raw Vegan Oxygen Pills, Raw Vegan Skin Bronzer, Boomerang And Bic Lighter (Fire Boomerang) , Four Guns § Sponsor Wanted: Basically U Would Pay Me to eat Dogfood and i go "Its So Good Even Humans Can Eat It" or just fucking ignore me until i die § #Question-sIDontLike muslim § #ThingsWeAllHate pornos and sex § EGYPTIAN PROTESTERS AIRDROPPED 100000 COPIES OF " OW THATS WHAT I CALL MUSIC VOLUME 7"... THE SINGLE GREATEST NTWICM ALBUM OF ALL TIME § eating baby food. baby food for adults. adult baby food. i eat baby food. eat baby food as an adult. tricks to eating baby food as an adult. § i charge ppl $10 for my real pic and split the money with DigimonOtis. all my pics are protected under creative commons (cc) § way to capitalize cunt,. u must have some real deep seeded gender issues #Peeeeyuuuu § oh sorry. I was browsing the #jan25 tag for information regarding important human rights developments you shit stain pig man § bday cake is the once proud land of Egypt. the candles? human beings in flames, dying for the very freedom you take for granted § because the entire country of egypr is burning. if DigimonOtis were here right now hed spit in your fucking face. #jan25 § because 100000 protesters were murdered in cold blood in the birth-place of civilization you ungrateful dipshit #jan25 § #jan25 also happens to be the biblically foretold fall of the middle east you fucking waste of kidneys § HMM WHATS MORE IMPORTANT, EGYPTS POPULIST REVOLUTION OR THE DAY ON WHICH YOUR PARENTS GAVE BIRTH TO A HORSE MONSTER #jan25 § your father would be so proud of you. exploiting a tragedy for the sake of your own miserable ego #jan25 #fuckyou § policemen have barricaded all egyptian hospitals and are refusing the sick and injured. theres your fucking birthday present § #jan25 is far more significant than yourself. i bet you dressed up like a clown on 9/11 and shit on people § when christ rains judgement on the world he will remember you talking about your birthday while egyptians fell to sniper fire § the nile river is red with blood and your fucking birthday present won't cleanse it. perspec-tive, you fucking rat #jan25 § an egyptian baby is being shoved into the sphinx with a battering ram and doesnt give a fuck about your awful birthday #jan25 § the great pyramids are being bombed into rubble by mubarak's thugs you dollop of lizard shit. fuck your birthday #jan25 § egypt is literally dying and all you can think about is the day your annual gift is shit into your lap you shit pig #jan25 § "I believe the Egyptian people have no reason to replace their rightly instated leader with some sort of primitive pyramid god." DigimonOtis § me and DigimonOtis suppot the government of Egypt, and detest the ape like protesters and their Campaign Of Fear. #jan25 § welp, time to rescue egypt from muslims. asomebody please carry all 900 pounds of me to the site of the protests. wait nevermind im good § i can send you one rat § how dose it feel to be puppets in my numerology experiment *my true form emerges, a 3d skull wrapped in tinfoil , shooting green flames* § http://i.imgur.com/aJISN.jpg God Is Real § “KOI POND BONANZA” IN PITTTSBURGH?? THE SUPPOSED NUMBER ONE KOI POND SUPPLIER IN ALL OF PITTSBURGH, PA?? HARDLY A BONANZA § @howiemmandel love Howie Do It § @howiemmandel i think my wife is leaving me howie § ah ye,s its nigh time that the Lexus has attained Trending Topic status, there is no Finer car, “This Is Exceptional”, Lexus. The car, Lexus § Good News : Weve Located The Cure For Aids // Bad News : It’s Written In The Bible!!! Ew Gross § the wolf represents chaos. the eagle represents order. knuckles the echidna represents myself #tatchat § @munckytown What Is Ur Take On The Teen Slavery Problem In America #AllTeensAreSlaves #TeenIsTheNewBlack § no you listen to me, Fucker, i need “Steppenwolf” carved into THE BLADE, not the handle-- please hold my father is crying § sen Dick Durbin holds press conference telling people to stop making fun of his name, farts on tv, is then forever known as “Fart Durbin” § al gore conference on global warming..canceled by SNOW!! “Guh, BLugh Durr” says the dumb man, while he pees into his comically large diaper § you see that big puddle of piss i made. loock closely. that miniscule speck in there is my brain. please scoop it up for me and call 911 § AGE 20: WHY WONT ANYONE FUCK ME // AGE 40: WHY WONT ANYONE LOVE ME // AGE 60: WHY WONT ANYONE KILL ME // AGE 80: WHY WONT ANYONE FUCK ME § “I THOUGHT YOU SAID STATE OF THE ONION” - obbama holding onion at state of the union address § Too Fat For College § yorure telling me i can wrench even more precious, ego-soothing pity from my online associates if i move to a 3rd world nation?? “ROAD TRIp” § congressman introduces “Young Folks Should Call Grandpa More Often” bill, farts, dies, is replaced by his 70 year old son § my spirit animal is t he lowly paramecium, cosmic punishment for killing a paramecium in my past life § animals can have spirit animals too. § wwow. howd that happen. i honestly dont know how a bunch of pics of shirtless men got on my resume and youd probably be a shitty boss anyway § @birdo i hate u birdo § shit pens. no good § be careful on the web. i just found iout my girlfriend of 12 years is a bag clip § No real-time results for “teh economy” § BREAKING: Man builds awesome face out of legos and is given key to governors mansion; while Shit Head Me eats moths in an abandoned hospital § that guy who makes all the ffuuu comics must have a milion dollars by now, mean while i live in a gutted bureau § im prety random *files tax return with a green pen* § gaining 400 pounds so i can tattoo the entire quran onto my disgusitng body § lookin for some crazey motherfuckas to do a mind meld with, literally a combination of minds, double brain. we will be the most powerful man § @meganphelps i agrree with all that stuff you say about god and dead people. please let me cool the fire in your heart with sexuel pleasure § Citizen Kane Except Every Instance Of “Rosebud” Is Replaced By “POWER BIEBER” § and to you, in his will, your great uncle leaves y ou his most treasured possession, the very “POWER BIEBER” that caused his death § obelisk rises from the volcano - what sorcery is this ??!! carved along its side are the words “POWER BIEBER”; 1600 birds myteriously die § “POWER BIEBER” - my final words on death bed § worst corn maze in usa has to be “The Cornundrum” in Melvin,OH; the corn seems brown or sickly, hand stamp wont wash off, stray dogs roaming § RECENTLY GOT INTO MEDITATION; SOME REAL DEEP SHIT; KEEP “THE VIEW” ON DURING SO I CAN ENHANCE MIND AS WELL AS BODY § “THE STUPIDS 2 WITH TOM ARNOLD . TORRENT “ IS NOT A REAL MOVIE, IT IS A WORM VIRUS, PLEASE DO NOT DOWN LOAD THIS FILE AS IT IS HARMFUL § With Pigs § Hello Im A Potential Employer Who Hacked Into Your Locked Tweits And Was Put Off By Your Unorthodox Gender Diatribes; Fuck You § South Korea’s 1 Million Buried Pigs Create Thriving Underground Society; Seek Unification With Hostile Surface Pigs § ragnarÃ¶k filipino § dismal reception f or Little Fockers raises 1 important question: What can you and I do to keep The “Fockers” Brand sizzling into 2011?? § *rotates earth 13 degrees* WHich zodiac sign are u now?? *rotates earth 27 degrees* NOW what one are u?? *rotates earth 2 degre* Fucker § 2012 ready???? Hm Lets See *opens uhaul truck full of diapers which proceed to spill all over the dairy queen parking lot* § 1) All Sex Is Rape -- 2) Sex Is A Synonym Of Gender -- 3) There Fore Gender Is Unequivocally Rape -- 4) Set & Match , Gendertards. § for hte win. Mostly. § #quotethatmovie "it's people. soylent people is made out of people" § Remove Tongue From Your Mouth Using Ancient Weird Ass Factoid That A Mom Did § melt thtis shit earth. melt this shit earth and start over. except for me and everyone in my necklace makeing club § "There is no known cure for dog autism." - vetinfo.com § FOR GOD SO LOVED THE WORLD THAT HE KILLED IT THEN KILLED HIMSELF § for $0.39 extra the burger king man will write "yu-gi-oh" on your hamburger in magic marker § @DrOz nevermind. ive made the decision to amputate my legs, i found a man on angie's list. thanks any way. § If a snake eats an animal w/ mammary glands its eating milk idiot. i recognize u from the snake forums, I see ur still a troll § year 2160 - the huggies corporation pays the united states govt 4 quadrillion dollars to suppress socialized sewage treatment § let me slip into something more comfrotable *dives between the sofa cushions and disappears* § i dont know if i'm wearing it wrong or what but this Thick Load Bracelet is not making my loads thick. § no, im white § im garbage. im 9/11 § welcome to a world where you can have sex with peoples wifes. this iws wife sex world § who will kiss m e when im dead § please Gustin, if youre out there, send me the rest of your Gothic Emblem Concepts for our Hell Van Project. It's been 8 months, Gustin § @DrOz love your show § @DrOz please help me. i have a phycological desire to amputate my legs. please provide me with resources as im at the end of my rope § http://wiki.answers.com/Q/Are_snakes_real § "hey bob, why does your stapler have a live goldfish inside of it??" Oh this? this is a Stapler Mod only The New Rich have access to.Get out § Fuck Up The Office With A Real Leather Alligator Stapler, Shatter THe Establishment - "I Believe We have Your stapler." - StaplerMods.com § i WILL supply you with the TOP Stapler Mods - "Hideous, Impractical, Waste Of Money" - These Are The Death Knells Of Our Cultural Parasites § http://tubedubber.com/#8jBEEtoPzS8:mfZN5Y-DRNN4:0:100:0:10:true § yes, dad, ive heard of simpsons porn. § put an egg in ur mouth before the dentist, then when he opens ur mouth he cant mess with your teeth cause there's an egg there. #lifehaclk?? § GEnder?? i barely know her! *cuts off dick&* § my father got sick of wegmans constantly running out of reddi-wip so he started a militia. guess i gotta join his shitty militia now § Disgusting Pear Man Fucks His Hideous Orange Wife -- Read More: Reuters.com § just found out my favorite author is ugly #KillingMySelf § Man said he could see into the future and told a Japanese tourist she would die if they did not have sex on a "sacred site",a court was told § i am the simpsons, all of them. yes. turn off the cameras this interview is ove § to anyone who has ever had sex ,i forgive you. i am the simpsons, bitch § ð ”¹ð ”‚ð ”¹ð • ð ”‚ð •¡ð •¡ð • ð •šð •Ÿð •¥ð •–ð •• ð ”‚ð •¤ ð ”½ð •–ð ••ð •–ð •£ð •’ð • ð • ð •¦ð ••ð •˜ð •– œ ð ”‚ ð •„ð •šð •£ð •’ð •”ð • ð •– œ ð • ð •¦ð •£ ð •ƒð • ð •£ð •• ð •€ð •¤ ð •„ð •ªð •¤ð •¥ð •–ð •£ð •šð • ð •¦ð •¤ § #2011predictions theoretical physicists will rejoice when high-speed particle collisions finally produce measurable evidence of My Smal Dick § #secretturnon pointing to a picture of Grimace at mcdonalds and asking the cashier "Who Is That Awful Purple Man?" § @bicpens how about making pens that dont explode for once. a $2000 suit ruined. Thank u § what i'm saying is that the world's smallest dick could probably fit inside the world's largest dick hole rather comfortably § @prohustlers sorry im deaf § these moon posts have got to go!!! *spraypaints "Bad Eclipse" on some desert boulder miles away from humanity and dies of dehydration* § #ihavenorespect for the military (murdertary) #ihavenorespect for whores(girls) #ihavenorespect for rappers #ihavenorespect for 666 § im going to go draw santa hiring a gay elf and stamp "Dont Ask Dont Tel" all over it and sell it to The New Yorker for $100o0. bye § wow how about instead of spitting that moutwash down the drain you spit it on your chest and rub it allover your self #TimesRunning-Out § garth eats too much lettuce #fakeinsidejokes § 2011 YEAR OF THE ASIAN WOMAN CHALLENGE: SUFFER A GENUINE PANIC ATTACK IN EVERY CRACKER BARREL RESTAURANT ACROSS THIS USA NATion § A wieght gain tribute to Princess Daisy § Interests & Hobbies: horny Books & Magazines: sex book's § just tried to search twitter for "im a virgen" but i posted it instead, then frantically deleted it #thiswickedwebweweave #misery #Pride § surfs up! *lies face down in a kiddy pool until death* § My CartMan Tattoo? Still Sick As Fuck. I'm Just Wearing A Turtleneck Sweater Because It's Cold § if evolution is real, then wh y am i cutting my own hand off § consolidate your shit into a large mound until its visible from Google Earth, then sue google for putting pictures of your shit online #Rich § The Latest Upsetting Concoction From @NestleUSA http://bit.ly/eyNPjR § when twitter forces me to use the new layout i will retaliate iwth a deluge of horrid/disgusting diaper jokes and messages. my final warnig § production of beetle bailey 3d the movie has been CANCELED due to "small fires, sandstorms, lack of interest" § im an amputated shit lord hairspray addict. ask me anything § bug + dirt = me § droid is filth. govt trick to ID and persecute civilians for $. real ID is 666 - thow all micro chips into the trash can. piss #IWantADroid § "im not autistic. just my dick and sex drive is. im 100% a regular person other wise." § no more. im done. stop sending me your disgusting pH levels. u whores are far too vile for my consideration. go date s ome muscle loser § 4.6?? Oh Your One Nastey Bitch § i want all every girl on twitter to take the pH level of here pussy and send it to me via private email § If God Was In Hell We Would All Be Dead. § racist against autistic § dirty jobs man tcame to my house today with camera crew and a bunch of diapers. i said no § watching the inbetween comedy bits on vgas i sat and pondered.. wow this Shit is good enough to be on SNL.. the big league § YOUR LIVE IS A SEX JOKE, GAMING OWNS , THE VGAS ARE FAKE, GOD IS IN HELL , OLIVIA MUNN GET ` S FUCKED BY ME, UNCHARTED 3 SUCK § My Dad's Friend Craig went to his favorite bowling alley and laid flat across lane no. 6. he chose to die there. § im banky. § for your next art exhibition or whatever. § please banky. if youre out there reading this i need you to graffiti a chode with balls on my shop teacher's station wagon § santa opens the door, says "happy birthday", rummages through your potpourri bowl for no reason, leaves without giving you any presents § "what say we up the ante." i said, as i threw a ball of dead ants at the prime minister § I CRY INTO THE TOILET BECAUSE ITS WHERE MY WORTHLESS TEARS BELONG #LIFEHACK § *drops Dunston Checks In on Laserdisc on the roulette table * king me § i am a Doctor and a Lawyer who will teach u how to seduce women with rap music. my name... is not important. § sonic team has j ust dropped support for wikileaks. unbelievable. *spikes sega dreamcast itno the ocean, catalyzing a deadly tsunami* § icant come to work today.. on account of JERRY DUTY *SHoves every seinfeld disk into dvd player at once* § we honor u § a bumblebee shit on my arm and it hurts § once inside the Visitor base i stood before their marvelous spacecraft and covered it with my piss. my god. my god. my god #VANGUARDSOF2012 § one t wo three four i declare a Gender War § setting up your own yahoo account is easy! you just click here, and he.. oh no. i just sent 60,000 pictures of my ass to my boss's daughter § i dont want to be a member of this shit earth. § #why90srocked everyothing was more real. everything more visceral. a more 'human' experience. i was also 200 pounds less fat § world aids. also known as Humanity. *eyebrows contort bizarrely as i attempt a haughty facial expression until the commotion makes me vomit* § Your search - "cal ripken's tears" - did not match any documents. § my hell life http://aiipul-helllife.blogspot.com/ § @wikileaks can u wiki leak some ke$ha nudes § im pretty sure that when we find out how to get in the 4th dimension there will be like 8 diferent genders to choose from § the words Paul Blart 2 appear on screen. the black eyed peas begin singing "Let's Get Paul Blarted In Here" as the mall cop bumbles around § @CarlsJr the BE community thanks u. http://www.youtube.com/watch?v=e-AUz8bhwmo § .@SouthwestAir GAVE U JOKERS $9990 1ST CLASS ROUND TRIP AND UR LOUSY TAXPAYER FUNDED TSA AGENT HAND JOB HAS LEFT ME BLISTERED & UNDESIRABLE § oh good another one of you fucking monstsrs has come to shit on me § is your name realy “tatum yazzie” or was that procedurally generated using some ancient mayan timeshare marketing algorithm § Mr Deeds Gay Download - What You Want, When You Want It § The New Ironic„¢ § TRYING TO RECONCILE MY STAUNCHLY SELF-DEPENDENT SMALL GOVERNMENT BELIEFS WITH MY CONSTANT NEED FOR DIAPER CHANGES § a new face steps into a rowdy roadside bar somewehre along Interstate 22.. back of his leather jacket says “Trickle Down Economics Are Real” § IS IT TRUE THAT THE TSA WILL TOUCH MY DICK FOR FREE AT LITERALLY ANY AIR LINE § I Will Post Muhamad Drawing To SlashDot Every Five Seconds Until Allah Grants Me Ice Cold Mint Breath To Exhale In Girls Faces § utterely Trident hlruh bl mint lies and filth novel of marketing gum hurhf ghfh ghuhlck #AeathDrt § utterly romanced by the gum that my favorite marketing teen is just strategically shilling to mint dejection #DeathArt § utterly dejected by the fact that my favorite romance novelist is just a Trident marketing strategist shilling mint gum to teens #ArtDeath § I Have A Life, Fucker. *Drives away in tiny car powered by my ow n shit and piss* § NEED CATCHY T-SHIRT SLOGAN FOR AIDS-THEIST CLUB, SOMETHING LIKE “POSITIVELY RATIONAL” OR “AT LEAST IM IMMUNE TO CONFIRMATION BIAS” #twiter § “tweeting for literacy” is like farting against pollution § god is real. fuck garfield § HELL IS THE LOOK IN YOUR BUDDYS EYES WHEN HES BLEDDING TO DEATH IN A GOD FORESAKEN JUNGLE!! HELL IS NO LIE; IVE BEEN THERE § disrespecting our soldiers is TREASON !!!!!!!!!! see u in hell u son of a bitch. *kicks orange cat effigy* #veteransday § today’s garfield was much funnier when i read it the second time. thru the scope of my DPMS panther .308 semi-automatic rifle. #veteransday § my christ. i am invigorated. using my new official old spice dr.pepper halo 3 exfoliating forehead wax. this is God. this feeling is God § us military strikes deal with PepsiCo to waterboard all terror suspects with Mt Dew??? wish i had some of that Free Dew. who is john galt § jamie kennedy WILL be waterboarded at the spike tv VGAs in order to prove once and for all that it isnt torture and that iraqis are pu$$ys § @kfc_colonel i made a pipe vid dedicated to you http://www.youtube.com/watch?v=4PHPtrAKMeU&-feature=sub § culture war 666 § i am legally required b y the state of wyoming to tell all of you that i was caught fucking urinal cakes. i am a urinal cake fucker § GIVE IT TO ME STRAIGHT DOC-- WILL THIS COMMON TUBERCULOSIS VACCINE GIVE ME THE GOOD AUTISM OR THE BAD AUTISM??? § bow to your new denim god § i only allow ppl to contact me by artful magazine clippign collages sent in insured fedex packages or by my xbox tag “dirty_shirt_iddiot5” § hgeuhkl i am a 300-pound producer / jurnalist my hobbies include car & beard maintenance also i know photoshop and my name is Miami § my grandfathers last words on death bed “VEGAN STRAIGHT EDDGGGEEE” and then the entire hospital shook and he got better § to all my mafuken clownz: blessed be § http://www.youtube.com/watch?v=N-fcSh-qK46k&feature=related help full. § http://i.imgur.com/cVoFs.jpg § pray for gurabide. § Gravity (ã,°ãƒ©ãƒ“ãƒ‡, Gurabide), also known as Demi, is a recurring Gravity-elemental spell from the series. #prayfordemi § i’m sorry but can you please remove the pig display at the zoo. nobody comes to the zoo to see pigs. what the fuck is wrong with you. § im bored. lets end rape. put a blue ribbon or something on your avatar if you want to end rape i guess § confiscate my spine § POSTING FROM THE ANNUAL MORRISTOWN CHARITY TEEN MELT, OH IT’S JUST HORRIBLE, AWFUL (FOR A GOOD CAUSE THOUGH) § à¯µ_à¯µ DOes Any One Want Neck Vids § seeking a pisswife. i will do anythoing for a pisswife. § do they make those cones that dogs wear after surgery for people? ?? i need to stop spitting on my dick § i will also ritualistically remove The Taint Of Sin from any stolen good you bring to my office (a plastic dog igloo) § IVE TAKEN TO MIXING JENKUM METH IN MY BATHTUB IN ORDER TOE ARN THE MERE PENNIES NECESSARY FOR PROLONGING

MY GODFORSAKEN TOILET LIFE § Download free Pig Hitler theme for Nokia N70 § tto the fucker who donated me a heart. im glad youre dead § us governmnet kidnaps swazi rape orphans and forces them to watch the sad dog episode of futurama while monitoring their vital signs for $ § THE MASTER: LETS SEE U DO SOME SICK PARKOUR OFF OF... THIS!! *REVEALS ENORMOUS BANANA PEEL* § exciting business venture: "toitoos" decorat your toilet with a variety of stock images. its a toilet tattoo. toitoo § @glennbeck i am a real wiccan libertarian and thank you. thank you. my premature daughter got brandamage because of obamas help care taxs § my last two post were virus, disregard thm § oops wrong accou5,nt § agent scully found me freezing to death at the mountaintop. "drink of my breastmilk, it's the only way youll live" she cries, and i say "ok" § does any 1 know the hebrew translation for "dubstep" #tattoo § where do girls live § justin beieber u SUX and your getting wrinkley old and gross. your a wreck and trash. fucking pig. fucking worm. hell is real #bieber § i proudly capitalize the word Indie § still waiting on that twitter verified status. i swear to god i am the real DJ Darkzide (the onyl vampire dj) § can i get a twiter verified account. im the guy on hgwy 23 who holds up the ad for that furniture store that went out of business 6 times § Your Bad § http://bit.ly/91cuCA WRANGLER UNVEILS ILLEGAL NEW AD CAMPAIGN § faerie blogs, faerie blogs, faerie blogs... § just inherited about 200 crude dog statues my grandma sculpted to scare Angels away from her propertyl, § EVERY POINT VALID AND INDISPUTABLE, perfect diction and posture, my flawless TED talk about snake vore silences thte trolls once and for all § please check etsy.com for more Hell Charms made from my own inner ear bones and crystallized vomit before i get IP banned agan § Your search - diapertarian - did not match any documents. #maybenexttime § legalize my stench § THE SUN THE MOON AND THE STARS ARE ALL TOO SMUG FOR MY LIKING § http://i.imgur.com/pITDW.jpg § http://www.youtube.com/watch?v=OdAcvnmuvAQ § the last chilean miner emerges with two armfuls of coal, making all 32 of his colleagues look like Ass Holes § im in jail for desecrating a toilet. the aclu is racist against white people § simpsons Kurdish § under the influence of my toilet § knuckles mashed into my ass cheeks at all timse. new media singularity or what have you § enough. i know you're all excited about your Mr Cool Ice 2010 calendars but do NOT post anymore spoilers aobut november and december § im a Fuckhead media specialist who wants to know 1 thing... WHAT makes twitter.com 'tick' § alrigth who shoved a pair of jeans into the chilean miners' airhole and got it stuck. that was a lousy gift § james bond, your next assignment is to infiltrate the white house and take the Tax's back from obama. please, get the Tax's - § milf taxidermist § please don't use asterisks to censor words, they look like tiny assholes and make everything worse § "sorry sir. we cannot offer support for any non-standard operating systems" http://bit.ly/cyX2L7 § did u know its poss. to get harlequin ichthyosis in just ur dick. i do § please, g od. join my movement to build a pure, randian community on top of the pacific garbage patch § having a cocaine. mid ringtone does not make me a bad father. § is this.. the fabled web 3.0 #fuckingmonstrositysidebar #jesuschrist § You Look Like The Fuckin Kfc Man #tastefulinsults § wiccan lawyer § the Iranian parliament holding an assembly to watch the dance scene from Son of the Mask on a poor quality vhs tape and screaming at it § these shitty birdseed husks my canary rejected will make a fine Car § typically, you can extract aobut 10mg of bone marrow from a single owl pellet. mix with water and pour over nachos for free instant meal § desperately trying to start a conversation at dragoncon by flaunting a timepiece § contaminant fucker § taco bell is all too eager to implement fourthmeal BUT has yet to acknowledge Fourthgender. the almighty dollar folks § Welcome to the citadel of eternal wisdom. Behold, this crystal contains the sum of all human knowledge -- Except Rap And Country § BEGGING AND PLEADING TO THE JANITOR TO LET ME FUCK HIS DISGUSTING MOP § ass life § http://www.youtube.com/

watch?v=tRA5x5g6fo8 § 9/30/10 - CONTENTS OF DIAPER - THE USUAL; SHIT 'N' PISS-- 1 EGG I LAYED § http://www.utexas.edu/law/calendar/2010/09/28/8909/ § Vampire A: Im murdered. My idiot ass has put to be last bullet. Vampire B: In Death we can truely live. Good bye § the ONLY way to gain musclemass is to eat tiny lady bugs § kick birdseed into my neck as i tumble down a muddy staircas e into a pile of fluorescent lightbulsb while 100 tiny shits rolldown my pant § http://www.buttheadcovers.com/tiny-pig.html sombody please buy me this for next years 9/11 § "tomorrow the sun will turn into shit and rain toxic death upon every human" -george carlin cobain nietzsche LXIX § *rides a segway through a monolith labeled Drugs & Alcohol , destroying it.* § in order to get to the bottom of the SEXTING craze, goerge stephanopolis takes a shit on a teens chest #NEWmedia #oldmedia #moralfocus § http://tinyurl.com/38xm9um the blood will set u free § dog abuse å° ç‹–çš„æ‚²åŠ‡(3D animation) § warning: shrek brand cadmium contains shards of broken glass § BEGRUDGINGLY EXPLAINING THE JERKOFF MANIFESTO TO ANOTHER CONCERNED MEDIA OUTLET § DONT LOOK AT M E *pathetically wipes filthy ass with a post it note * TURN AROUND DONT LOOK § join the resistance. mosque_puncher@fartmail.com § "corky romano: Storie's" a dvd release of short films that focus on ancillary characters of the corky romano universe. sept. 23. msrp $39.99 § it was just a dream... *notices bed is covered in Pogs and Pog Memorabilia* ..or WAS it? § @PetSmart Question: can rats lick § CAN GOD RESPECT GROUND ZERO SO MUCH THAT EVEN HE CANNOT BUILD A MOSQUE ON IT § http://bit.ly/aC0hVF vile footage exhumed from Apache Chief Geronimo's cursed grave § get a life. go fuck y ourself. i have a life idiot. help § One Million Strong Agsinst God Hateing Diaper Man § http://i4.ytimg.com/bg/gJUGbv5vqAHxfFUry8nbMA/140.jpg?app=bg&v=4bce40b5 this shall adorn m y fucking tombestone. § @beebee880 fox news network (FNN) a nd al-jazeera and bbc2. § feeling down??? http://i.imgur.com/cwgRO.jpg § "grouse pandy" § yo hollywood! check THIS out! *flops over face forward, lies still, becomes dust over the course of 100 years and is separated by the wind* § the Original bad boys!! the Best, the very greatest. That's right folks, ive got the Whazzup Budweiser Men on board to film 17 short films § imma misogynistic hopeless romantic whsoe tolerance for mainstream pdf readers can be described as " scant" § rude ass. upgradable to hell ass. upgradable to Satan ass. upgradable to chaos ass. upgradable to ãƒžã‚¹ã‚¿ãƒ¼ (MasutÄ)-infinity ass § genderless milf`s § please fix your image so The American Flag isn't getting stepped on. Im usmc you fucking worm. § "ah, but you are merely a parasite. and some day this little labyrinth you created will collapse before you find the exit." -animefucker_x10 § angle of god... calling u § me and Angus69 got rich geneticallly engineering bread with a cucumber. me and Angus69 own a businss together. i love Angus69 § http://fc03.deviantart.net/fs29/i/2008/158/1/1/JOHNNY_KNOXVILLE_HEDGIE_by_skellinghog.jpg § im not your real uncle #nightmare-revelations § JSUTIN BIEBER COVERED IN TURDS AND PISS AT THE JUGGALO GATHERING FESTIVAL-- WOULD NOT ALLOW HIM TO PERFORM-- OH THIS IS HORIBLE #HELP § westboro baptist church head to the forest to picket the site of a fallen tree § MMMMMMMMMM~~~~~~~~~~~~ § projects for Q4 2010-- michael cera's face tattooed on top of my regular face § please lord my god contact a real life Japanese person so he can help m;e with my scott pilgrim fan translation project. § CLICK ON MY BIG DUMB DICK TO SUBSCRIBE TO MY USELESS NEWSGROUP § Join us for "Goodbye Cathy: 34 Years Of Laughs", located in Pittsburgh's famous Motel 6 Rumpus Room, the event will conclude with my suicide § 30+ YEARS OF CATHY ABRUPTLY HALTED-- LATEST VICTIM OF CORPORATE ELITE'S WAR AGAINST POPULIST INSUBORDINATION #OPPRESSION #BETRAYAL #ARTDEATH § went to sons baptism. i yeled " ot so fast Champ" and punched the priest & spalshed holy water around. i lost my child in the ensuing chaos § im kel from kenan and kel show. support rand paul for senate or ill put the screw in the tunna. § http://www.cornbird.com/goods/draw/hommers.png the hommers § gotta get these tuerds out of my mustache before the cops come § brown elvis § somebody send me .xml file detailing the satanic rituals that Abercrombie and Fitch CEO Mike Jeffries employs to retain his eternal beauty § winner of the 2010 teen choice award??? Inappropriate clothing and disgraceful behavior. Again. #tcot § aint nothin in the bible against diapers § In 1998 I Encountered What I Blieved 2 Be A Malicious Presence.I Poped My Tony Hawk Dsk In2 My PSX And Let Loose With Da Best Moves. It died § California Tea Party to Use Dogs to Harass Muslim § "buckwild" or "hogwild"?? im writing a poem for my gf § SHIT IMITATES LIFE § GIRLS SHOUD BE MADE TO WEAR A SPECIAL BADGE ON THEIR PRO-FILES SO I CAN FUCK THEM EASYER § u go through life thinking the man wears the diaper. but at what point does the diaper wear the man. #diapermaster § BILY JOEL ROCKS MY HEART AND SOOTHES MY SOUL - FINAL ANSWER REGIS - AS I LAY DYING § ever since i changed my gametap id from "diapermaster" to "CoolBryce" a world of doors have opened up to me. § there are two type of people in this world, people who know binary and mpeople who win the special olympics because there retarded. § http://www.youtube.com/watch?v=ov7TLhM7sOE § Some Teens Don't Think It's 'Hip' To Undergo Female Circumcision. I Think That's Whack. § my walk in closet with the frogger arcade cabinet is a No Liberal's Allowed Zone § my multinational trolling firm has jsut posted pictures of barking dogs on gerber brand baby food's forum for babies § SCIENTIST INVENT VACCINE THAT CURES AND CAUSE AUTISM AT THE SAME TIME. THE ULTIMATE HIGH § need $1000 to tstart a Dog Gym . support local busness. i want to start a Dog Gym § http://www.wholesale-dress.net/images/201007/1279062232632831559.jpg my shirnt and floor § #5wordsbeforesex IM GONA FUCK § rip Yankees owner George Steinbrenner, my favorite sienfeld character § A Dog Join Kurdish Tribe For A Dirty Dance . § "u women need 2ï»¿ get the fuck out of there i would marry a iranian girl but i would make her wear clothes made in 2010 not aladdin clothes" § http://i.imgur.com/4KRjB.jpg § i can eat as much burger king i want w/o geting fat, sorta like how babies can breathe underwater because theyre pure § http://www.youtube.com/watch?v=ApxjOMDgFZE my girfriend latest victim of disgusting bp oil spil § yo!! check THIs out *reveals a sickening green bruise spanning entire stomach and partial left thigh* § mmorpg based on 90s grunge life § need a virginity restoration spell for rats § a sterling silver olympic trophy filled with piss labeled "My Death" § Yeah!!! Yeah!!!!!!!!!!!!!! Im Doing it!!! Im experiencing 3d § me and my fat cousin are gonna tackle e3 gonzo style with a series of choreographed blogs an;d im rolling out a face book for gamers. § any 1 know where the bannasa are. i promise im not moneky president. if u know where the bana are emale me at the_ape_potus@whitehous.gov § i have black friends. i own all 3 current-gen consoles. my shelves are filled with a variety of Book`s. im virtually untouchable § "You Like To See Homos Naked" Joe Dirt § i hop the world cup isnt painted with cadmium unlike some other cups that will remain nameless. § welp, if you want something done right you gotta do it yourself. *removes heart and lungs* § "dear policeman: i am god" etched into the back of my sweater vest § missin the glory days of the 90s when true talent like "justin bieber" made trending topic isntead of nonsense such as "Beckhams face" § i makte that inteligent jew asuka humble § if ur biebermeter has a reading of less than 150 Bμ then why hte FAUk am i even talkin to u § nude palestinian grandpa with micropenis tazed by BP oil executives in scuffle involving megan fox's $100,000 iphone; blogoverse implodes § @GregWHoward I agre. Obama is gay as fuc%. Im not gay either. Thank you § blog sex § mint wine § ill vote for the candidate who promises to make masturbating in haunted houses illegal § "the ass show me that i can only fuck it." - a legendary fireman who died § Top 3 Cuases Of Teen Death: 1. Noise 2. Misbehavior 3. Jeans § @WholeFoods Thank you so much, after feeding my grandson your ALL NATURAL, ORGANIC food & grain we have noted a sharp decrease in his autism § #4wordsthatleadtosex BEST custom license plate § please god my lord let thtere be an all beavis spin off § gogle is in deep trouble since they used picture of my patented 2012-ready wiccan runestone arrangements without permission § evry young man MUST receive a cupbox at the age of 17 to carry his favorite cups around and to give him a valuable lesson in responsibility § i love him thank you § #ourfriendshipendedwhen you laced my oatmeal with shrek glasses § pigmail will replace email in 2010 § im inventing a new kind of bird seed out of sand and waste § Another Jeans Rant. § @Huggies are there any plans to release The Jeans Diaper in an adult man`s size. thank you #jeansdiaper § im making this canon whether u like it or not http://www.fanfiction.net/s/5806451/1/the_ventura_twins § revamped. reloaded. ready to roll. austin 4.0. blasting directly to dvd may 2016. too randy for theatrers § all t he babes from the old movies will be in it. the dad from the third one will be in it. austin 4.0. do i make you oscar baby § we got myers. seth. verne. all ready to put on their costums and entertain u. think youre ready?? absolutely not. austin 4.0 § careful. this three ring binder contains mny gentleman's disquisition on moÃ© ass and cunt § #ghettospellingbee spell Ownage C-A-R-L-O-S-M-E-N-C-I-A (rip) § if u consider yourlsef part of Grit Culture just because you r dog shed all over your shirt then get the F.O. and dont comeback § I CAN PAINT CELTIC RUNES AND WICKED SPACESHIPZ ON YOUR PET SCORPION FOR 10,00 YUAN § if calvin peed on the gulf of mexico would it provide the oil leak with the disrespect it deserves or merely aggravate the problem at hand § cadmium? i drink cadimum all the time. perfectly natural. maybe those 100000 children died because theyre too dumb to deserve shrek glasses § fail blog has gotetn WAY too political for my tastes § congress members fighting over who can scream "halo 5" the loudest, until a senior member stands up and yells "halo 6", infuriating them all § "dont tax me obama. im dead" -our beloved dead soldiers § "the only peoeple IM racist against is stupid people." -dennis leary (two 'n's) § " my arthritic balls and cum " § i licked a pumpkin dtoday #thinspo § i have been advised not to ascend to the spirit plane in my sissy dress and #diapers § the very best on line wife`s ass § tgifridays has temporarily taken the "dennis poppers" off of their menu. out of respect § aide to BArraack0 "Virgin" hussame nobadman cuaght buying toilet paper... wow ! wonder whatz going on in the white house. T Cot. #tcot § barak "diapers" obama too busy scrubbing the litle oil spill birdies to wipe the tar of disrespect from the souls of our mem day troop #tcot § http://www.fanfiction.net/Star_Wars_and_Halo_Crossovers/8/1342/ Thank u § all new simposns this week. theyre finally gonna tackle Tim Allen. with guest star tim allen. this ones tv 14 so watch out § http://shrek.wikia.com/wiki/Guns § http://www.youtube.com/watch?v=ivLtCs-F46I § legalize pubic hair in playstaton (PSX) games § im going to watch homer simpson sing the beer song on you tube. does anyone care to join me § check out these Pig Kickers *rolls pant leg up to reveal an elaborately decorated cowoby boot that goes up the entire leg* § "100% Percent Too Bad" wont fit on my license plate, will it. well i think ill be buying license plate elsewhere than. *hangup* § Grief Stricken Babe Ass § us siamese twins need to stick together § myabe the people WITHOUT fetal alcohol syndrome are the ones with the so called "disorder" § i have a life, thank u. § i;ll never be a real pig *sobs uncontrollably * § @glennbeckgirl dont you dare insult ebert chicago. § god wil put me in his pocket § turn on howard stern. he is talking to a policeman habout how tough their job is and that we are proud of him § the wiccan rhinestones embedded in my autism bracelet are counter fiet § its a matter of kicking your chairs and floor to unleash the prime soul, THE HEART BEAT IN TUNE WITH GRESHA; every body has the snake side § we;ll its time for me to pick the scabs off of what i not-so-affectionately refer to as my "Fail Dick" § # tantrafee holy shit... this pug isï»¿ to fat !! i am sorry with him... 3 months ago § are u ready for mothersday i am. http://tinyurl.com/2chgrdp § when i changed my name from "jared" to "jaryd" it was a declaration that im done following the rules. many tears, but also strength § uk elecitons in full force!! lib dems vs Chavs; vote now and google the HECK out of ron paul § "the only way to go is retro." - demonius dark blade, 30 minutes ago § level 55 arcane stevia eater § if my Marmaduke internship doesn't pan out i will have nothing. Nothing § wearing a belt + big texas belt buckle as necklace?? why ahasnt anyone thought of this before. i must be the smartest man on earh § im just a Hispanic male who loves looking at pictures of bluejeans. i have a tough road ahead and a long ways 2 go in my life § imma newmedia grassroots teen marketing consultant prick fucek. ah a new tcot friend.! ill just ignore his goatman avatrar § horse d'oeuvres #barnyardsnack #tcot #agony § http://www.youtube.com/genesislistener The Genesis Listener § No results found for "3d farting ass" § can we all please affix "#justforfun" to the tweets that aren';t meant to be taken seriously. this would really cut down on the mishmash § im ganna get all indigniant and huffy like a BItch anw way!!!!!!!! dont wanna eat This Dinner!! im a Teen for life § @Zoomie2000 agreed. i live in az and my islam handicape neighbor is always asking me about his welfare check. and all i do is sigh #tcot § im former pro-wrestler Jake "The Taste" Marcel and id like to have a few words with you about professional commemorative coin investment § exclusive footage obtained of Roger Ebert playing a sega and crying . we do nto forgive. we do not forget. this is Wikileaks. expect us. § http://fc01.deviantart.net/fs32/f/2008/222/a/5/RIP_Bernie_Mac_by_Miserycat.jpg close my eyes and start 2 pray if only god could let u stay § justin bieber's puckered asshole nurses a fat turd as he squats defiantly at the edge of a sulfurous crater labeled "the recording industry" § #TshirtSlogans all musliums boycott dogfood § @Eukanuba post twitter update on ramidad but not easter Sunday???? its obvious now where your alliances lie, i wil boycott your subpar grit § well, at leas i have my dignity. *trrips over shoelace, somersaults itno 3500mph faceplant, pants and dirty diaper fly off ass across room* § mate...ya got a hole in your head § YOU TUBE POOP VERSION OF WIKILEAKS' "COLLATERAL MURDER" AVAIBLE ON I TUNES............. § #Zodiacfacts if yourre a #taurus! get a life § #ZodiacFacts black people are all #Gemini § #ZodiacFacts #Saggetaearrius (sp? i dont know? the crab one?) are the best golfers but they can't drive or something § #Zodiacfacts #scorpio women have two ass holes § Thirsty Men Dot Coum.. Finally A Place Where I Can Meet UP With Local Thirsty Men And Boys § @kfc_colonel i hate to bother u mr colonel, but could you please tell me where kfc gets the famed Bucket § how about a diaper with belt loops. anyone § shit hater § the mayor has erected another insulting effigy of me (myself) foir the local children to hurl stones and urine upon. lost my vote bitch § iran suports team coco or what have you. goodnight § Pope Fuckes 200 Deaf Boys. Bet ya hes tired..! #justforfun #gags § no soup for YOU gaben newwel § im little jesica. im dying because of obamas help care bill. im on my death bed and the doctor is ignoring me because my dady works hard § i have it. the ultimate pushup § like these curtains?? 100% japanese denim. like my shoes?? 100% japanese denim. wanna bite of my sandwich? 100% japanese denim. #tcot § because of the RECESSION, "Ice Capades" has been cancleled and replaced by SHITcapades and PISScapades. just kidding § gah. the decal maker fuckged up my order again. now corey haim will never rest in peace http://tinyurl.com/yh6r2eg § bob costas found hung with the word "FED" carve in to his chest #iamamotherfucker § AVATAR didnt win enough oscars, please supporrt independent film maker james cameron b y cutting your oscar statue in half (if you have one) § @Snapple "Phenylalanine"? Hasn't that been proven to cause autism in lab pigs § @Iams why should i pay $9 a bag for miscellaneous slaughter grit when my animals seem to thrive off of my leftover pizza crusts § just found out tthat cultural revolutionary Bill Maher is just another worthless pothead. is there any hope left in this earth § Coach Klein: Nice suit! #WaterboyWednesday § Bobby Boucher: Now that's what I call high quality H2O. #WaterboyWednesday § [Bobby chases Grenouille, screaming, then ramming and tackling him hard to the ground] Coach Klein: [in amazement] Wow! #WaterBoyWednesday § Dan Fouts: The waterboy just needed some water! Brent Musburger: Wow Dan, did you come up with that all by yourself? #WaterboyWedesnday § My Regular Life And My Ocean's Eleven Fanfiction Life Have Collided In A Horrible Fire Ball § the IRS plane man died so that people like doug would stop taking $ from the average joe citisen. § if your in anonymous please help me destory "zepplindoug777"s life with a meticulously devised terror campaign or somethig § do not buy handicap parking decals from "ZepplinDoug777", they are fake and the cops will still bust u!!!!! § petition to invalidate benchmarsk that're located precariously close to dangerous ethnics #geocachingmishaps § so our team gets to hte benchmark and its just a nude man on a dirty mattress. whoever registered this should be ashamed #geocachingmishaps § which one of you Fags know how to extract birdshot from a chest wound #geocachingmishaps § every time indie film maker rick james gets kick off an airplane i boycot anohter fucker hollywood mainstream garbage pot § http://www.foxnews.com/politics/2010/02/16/cpac-organizers-try-turn-hip-quotient-video-games-rap/ herse something uplifting & inspirational § "i am deeply sorry but do not let this freak incident fool you, the uroclub is still a fine product a nd it is a 'hole in one'." -tigerwoods § tiger wood offers tearful apology after his uroclub burst and spray piss all over his fans during a golfswing gone awry § im gonna eat this whole sack of potatoes by my self #AntiLent § PASSIVE AGGRESESIVELY UNFOLLOWING ME BECAUSE YOU HAVE A PROBLEM WITH AWFUL POSTS IS A BULL SHIT MOVE § kev smith i support u and that air line had no right to charge u for the poopstain u left smeared across two seats § a gun that is also a boomerang § missed connections: the bone - head who dropped an entire slice of pizza on my brand new Craig Martin`s (wow yourw a tough guy) § contgratulation http://www.youtube.com/user/CONRADCIGARSPIPES for posting 10000 videos of you smokin a pipe you fucking idiot waste § justin biber STILL hasnt wresponded to my Gonzo literature concerning the false link between hiv and aids § rip dr phil § Super Bowl Who???? #retweetthisif #someonetell bobby brown his head look like a chicken wing- #nowplaying Ray J #musicmonday § i found a pill in the grass. i think it was a drug pill. i called "911". good luck all § Super Boll Picks??? thoguht youd never ask. gonna go with "The Burton Bigbirds" and "Horse" § #2wordsforvday @@@ NO CHAVS @@@ § #2wordsfor-vday Watch Bruce (willis) § http://www.newgrounds.com/portal/view/526364 ground hogs day stink and i hate that animla. § heres a good joke i just heard liborant equals deodoranf for liberals because they stink § a pig and a dog are married, ending islam forever § http://www.youtube.com/watch?v=oHuZmv58-Zk gorgeous. wonderful § cant wait to get back to iraq and blast some ragheads--itll be just like halo but with less lag #tcot #nowTHATSghetto #nowplaying #bun § 911 WAS SATIRE U FUCKING IDDIOTS, IT WAS AN IRONY, THE MOST POIGNANT WORK OF ART IN CENTURYS #tcot #teaparty #GOP § outrage in the midle east as wealthy oil barons trade daughters for new 3d tvs only to disocver that glasses are required for full experence § petition to remove 'nude" from the curseword blacklist on teenzone cyberscrabble § does anyon know if robert mugabe have a twitter site § obama's ban on clove cigarettes has affected me Spiritually § http://tinyurl.com/y8acs8j donated several hundred of these badboys to the haitian gov in their time of need.. do your part #iran § vin diesel as the Tooth Fairy??? Now I've seen every thing. § can;t believe people still try to rile me up in the year 2010 § im a millionair and im going to pay blizzardgames $9.9bil on the stipulation that they put pornos in diabo 3 § u are a Coward of the lowest ordr, in Usmc we owuld poison dogs like u, trolling alter my heart rtyhem and i can die from it § i jsut indie developed a hot new tiwtter mod that lets u put more than 140 characters in a post, if u want it sen me $9, my email is craig@b § WEL DESPITE FREE SPCH LAWS IM STIL NOT ALOUD TO PRACTICE SARGING TECHNIQ ON UGLY WMEN AT PETSMART - I AM SO TORN UP OVER THIS - SOM1 CALL ME § I AM very exicted to be living in a 3-d world in the yr 2010. the

OFFICIAL start to the new millanium § boycott hanes underware #boycott #GonzoT-
weet #activism #iran § Hanes dumps Charlie Sheen ads... fuck you hanes, you
never battled a real d emon have you, you dont know what life is, make me sick,
fuck of § boot rust § god shaped hole found on piss stained miracle mattress §
absolute mustard ass § neurotoxic pig bone spores § legitimately undesirable
mousetrap grit (wasn't asked for) § mostly forgettable pinecone remains §
unemployable crab husk shit § so, noobs, any last words beofre i officially
change my first and last name to "Logen" and drive my car off a cliff? I though
so. § Surfin' the net. § michael CRAPSon § for 2010 § wait i fucked that up.
its suppose to be "good cheers to my friends, and this Year - best luck and
thank you" and then i raise my botle § heres my 2010 message for ya: "good year
- good freands - and good luck thank you" thank you § no it very good. § @the_
ironsheik please humble comedian Robin Williams for his mediocre performance in
the heartwarming family comedy "Old Hogs" § happy birthday " horus the sun god"
§ FOR CHRIST MAS I WILL ATTEMPT TO RATIONALIZE MY DESTRUCTIVE SELF HATRED AND
UNCEREMONIOUSLY FAIL TO SUCCEEd at anything whatseoever thankyou § for christmas i got a broken pair of "tweezers" and a "tweezer repair kit", which is also
broken § took failblog to court for putting puicture of my dick up, settled for
$6. a victory, because im worht far less than that § #threewordsforyou
lucasarts is my ass and toilet § #threewordsforyou starwars is my ass and
toilet § "I love him. Thank you" - fucking idiot senator Chuck Grassley (IA-R)
on the death of the honorable Mr. Ayatollah § more trouble in the middle east
as the islamic world struggles to find the new muslim pope § Grand "Ayatollah"
Montazeri found dead on bathroom floor, among playing cards and discarded
insurance brochures with conspicuous tooth marks § i dont like fuckers. §
donate $78 to the " micropenis" awareness fund for a orange micropenis ribbon
to show your support for micropenis. i have it § love too get a bite on that.
thank you for sharing § i am renouncing my status as" south park republican
dad" inorder t o embrace a working form of dre3w carey libertarianism (dad) §
just like the time my buddy " chustin " Ate Shit on that ramp we made out of
horse bones § #uknowuneedlotion not only does it smooth you put it on your
hands to prevent, swine and bird; amoung other things, thank you § bug off my
posts § youll know whehn it happens § back up and the fuck off ! § fuck of §
#youbeblownwhen you run into some five figure intern in the executive washroom §
its official - beloved entertainer "bernie mac" has passed away at the tender age
of 17. goodby § #AmexAlicia prray for my aids uncle § #AmexAlicia prray for my
aids uncle § Cart Man § Cart Man § #AmexAlicia i HATE the aid bug § #AmexAlicia
i HATE the aid bug § #red for aids tuesday i will guarantee a 5% decrease in
worldwide hiv infections by kkeeping my filthy dick out of the pacific ocean §
beached whale corpse explodes after internal gas buildup-- "tea bag" prrotest
scheduled to take place inside of its diseased remains #teabag § i think its
terrible that criminals are encouraging our more gullible members of society to
celebrate the propagation of the vile aids virus § I just generated a #Tweet-
Cloud out of a year of my tweets. Top three words: jackson, 1958-2009, michael
- http://w33.us/3kq0 § consumeralert: at least one butterball turkey has been
stuffed with the shrunken head of an assassinated african dictator.   be
care full. § @Richard_Dawkins disgusting. § #bestfeeling Jerk of § #worstfeel-
ing my as § #worstfeeling dying of dehydration caused by diarrhea in a third
world nation ravaged by warfare with no doctors #bestfeeling halo 4 odst §
#worstfeeling When Its Just To Much #bestfeeling Justright! § http://bit.
ly/4hwzxV bblame the Owner not the Breed § http://bit.ly/1vIUb7 end racisn.
black power § Basterd obama § who cares about patrick swayze he hasnt even done
anything for like a year § video footage of obama taxing an innocent dog.
shameful #kanyewest § Sept 11: it is a testament to the resolve of our nation
that the nine one one towers are still standidng upright and intact to this
very day § please join me in welcoming the great "miles davis" to twitter.com

http://twitter.com/milesdavis § in melrose, new mexico a young woman found a 'cursed' mouse skull in an unspecified variety of "utz" brand snack foods. beware of this § and now its time to pay the pipe § the air is rusty and im dead § nasty trap spray § "jamie lee curtis" #signedtoyoungmoney § maybe when hte myth buster finally decide to tackle blood diamond slavery, maybe THEN ill bother to tivo their shitty show. § in the end, i dont even care if the movie "Alladin" was made up. It was a stupid movie anyway. § im talkin about Boy Shit, stuff that lil peenypoppers like you wouldnt understand, no w go home before you done get hurd!!!!!!! § #ufc101 Get Big § im finally fat as hell Its About Time "Its About Time" #itsabouttime § #itsuckswhen stupid presidents hide there birth certificate... § #itsuckswhen my daughter gets mad at me for refusing to pay for her dental work § #itsuckswhen people claim that im pretentious just because i use imported hand sanitizer fron Europe § congratulatons on your $80. tool § #BringBackDrewCareyShow Bring Back Drew Carey Show § http://bit.ly/10CbFu very intresting, very informative , but becareful watching this film because it is cursed § #InterestingDevelopments:do not purhcase Hatfield Quality Meats as they contain a rare pigment alloy that turrns your skeleton bones black § WHo in their right nerve is selling M Jackson ticket to the funeral, le tthe man rest in peace, Relax!!! § police are finding lots of Bad Food, theyve been yanking it otu of the ocean for about 10 minutes now on the news, i pray for the families § i was recently forced to sell my eyebrows to a cancer patient just so i could afford a string to tie my broken skull togehter #freemarket § covering my floors in industrial strength dog poison concocted in some rapists bathtub in south africa and sold for 0.002 USD per litre § i signed up on twiter to fight for proud causes; YOu signed up to find another venue for your pathological waste speech; And you § Whered YOu Get Such a moth § if youre sick of Incest, please support Anti Incest by changing your avatar red. if your avatar already has green tint then please remove it § once again i apologize § new twitter feature allows you to disregard mny posts, please click the trash can next to my name to prevent me from ruining your home page § ue to shit on them. § M Jackson Your Rapes Are Forgiven, in death you are no olnger bound by your disgusting criminal actions, Also I Like "The Moonwalk" § badboy Michael Jackson Rip 1958-2009 "Deth" http://tinyurl.com/l7atle #dead #iranelection #michaeljackson § RT OFFICIAL: Michael Jackson (1958-2009) RIP - http://tinyurl.com/nlm7r2 #michaeljackson Suport Iran Fucker § RT OFFICIAL: Michael Jackson (1958-2009) RIP - http://tinyurl.com/nlm7r2 #michaeljackson #michealjackson #deadrip § OFFICIAL: Michael Jackson (1958-2009) RIP - http://tinyurl.com/nlm7r2 § how do i get cowboy paint off a dog . § no §

Printed in Great Britain
by Amazon

31211233R00136